CURRENT ISSUES OF
ECONOMIC POLICY

CURRENT ISSUES OF
ECONOMIC POLICY

Edited by

LLOYD G. REYNOLDS
Sterling Professor of Economics
Yale University

GEORGE D. GREEN
Associate Professor of History and Economics
University of Minnesota

DARRELL R. LEWIS
Professor of Economic Education
University of Minnesota

 1973

RICHARD D. IRWIN, INC. *Homewood, Illinois 60430*
IRWIN-DORSEY LIMITED *Georgetown, Ontario*

© Richard D. Irwin, Inc., 1973

First printing, January 1973

ISBN 0-256-01441-8
Library of Congress Catalog Card No. 72–90535
Printed in the United States of America

PREFACE

Economics shares with other social sciences a commitment to the pursuit of truth through the scientific method. The complexity of the economic "real world" is simplified, explained, and analyzed with models or theories, and the theories or hypotheses are tested and modified by comparing their implications with "real world" factual evidence (usually quantitative data). On the other hand, economics is also a policy science, which may be useful to businessmen and consumers, political leaders and voters. Where scientific objectivity is the goal of the economist as social scientist, the economist as policy adviser must also consider (and may seek to influence) more subjective matters—the preferences, goals, and values of his clients or of the larger society. Policy issues will also draw the economist beyond his own scientific expertise, into matters of politics, law, social structure, or philosophy.

We believe that these problems of subjective values and broad interdisciplinary perspective make economic policy questions especially exciting and challenging for economists and their students. Where a principles textbook must necessarily emphasize the basic scientific theory and analysis, we have focused this book of readings on current economic policy issues. Virtually ignoring the policy problems of individual businessmen or consumers, we have concentrated on issues of *political* economy—questions with broad social impact which have aroused public debate and proposals for political action.

We hope that the focus on economic policy will enable the student to apply his economic learning to the troubled, changing world. We have deliberately selected readings to represent different interests—business and labor—and different political perspectives—conservative, liberal, and radical. This atmosphere of debate and conflicting values should help the student to read his text and other current writings by economists more critically, and to know and apply his own personal values more self-consciously. It should also encourage livelier discussion of economic and social issues, in the classroom and elsewhere.

Beyond the desire for diversity and debate our selection criteria included an aversion to brief newspaper clippings and polemical statements lacking in economic analysis and a preference for well-written, longer articles which more coherently display the author's economic analysis, his policy position, and his personal style and values. Wherever we have abridged the original version, we have tried to preserve the author's meaning and his main line of argument. A footnote to each article indicates any abridgment and gives the source publication and the author's professional affiliation.

Our special thanks go to Ms. Delma Burns, Ms. Grace Wilson, and to the staff of Richard D. Irwin, Inc., for their capable help in preparing the manuscript for publication.

December 1972

L. G. R.
G. D. G.
D. R. L.

CONTENTS

PART IV. THE INTERNATIONAL ECONOMY

Part I
MACROECONOMICS

A. The unemployment-inflation dilemma

One of the most puzzling and frustrating characteristics of the modern industrial economy is the simultaneous coexistence of unemployment and price inflation. According to the classical theory, a competitive economy should normally remain at full employment, and (given a stable money supply) with stable prices; any temporary departure from this norm was explained by "frictions" or "rigidities" in the market's automatic adjustment processes. In 1936, John Maynard Keynes attacked this classical theory, arguing that the economy might remain at equilibrium away from full employment—either in depression with too little aggregate spending, or in inflation with too much spending. But in the early Keynesian theory, both problems could not exist at once. Moreover, the government could control aggregate spending through fiscal and monetary policies to keep it balanced at precisely the (noninflationary) full employment level.

As our first reading illustrates, the effort to explain the unemployment-inflation dilemma requires both macroeconomics (the study of aggregate spending, income, output, and prices) and microeconomics (the study of individual markets and prices).

To see why even the best Keynesian macroeconomic policies cannot achieve noninflationary full employment, we reexamine the classical market "frictions" and "rigidities": the technical immobility of specialized labor or capital, the consumer's lack of information, and, above all, the market power of large corporations and labor unions to manipulate prices and wages. Where inflation has become chronic, the expectations (by producers, workers, and consumers) of future inflation may aggravate the wage-price spiral; but these inflationary expectations both reflect the market power of business and labor (as well as expansionary monetary policy) and require it for their fulfillment.

The testimony by Madden and Woodcock illustrates the views of business and labor organizations on the unemployment-inflation dilemma. Not surprisingly, business blames "wage push" and labor blames "profit push" and "administered prices." Madden argues that labor contributes to inflation by limiting labor supply (entry to skilled crafts), by slowing produc-

3

tivity gains ("featherbedding" work rules), and by imitative wage demands where each union seeks the highest wage level negotiated in other industries. Woodcock questions the acceptability of a 4 percent unemployment level as a policy goal, and argues that even wage increases in excess of productivity gains are not causing inflation, because they have not permitted workers to "catch up" with past inflation in their cost of living.

All three readings propose a variety of policy changes which might alleviate the dilemma, moving the "U-I curve" (often called a "Phillips curve") downward toward a more favorable trade-off (compromise) between the two goals. The reader should compare these various proposals with the actions of the Nixon administration, including the Phase I wage-price freeze and the Phase II creation of price board, pay board, and other administrative controls over wage and price determinations by labor and business. How far along are we towards designing a satisfactory "incomes policy" for the 1970s?

1 The unemployment-inflation problem*

CABINET COMMITTEE ON PRICE STABILITY

. . . . .

THE NATURE OF THE PROBLEM

Figure 1–1 registers the relationship between the percentage change in the Consumer Price Index (CPI) and the rate of unemployment for each year since 1960; it also shows the relationship between the percentage change in the industrial component of the Wholesale Price Index (WPI) and the rate of unemployment over the same period. Using the CPI and WPI as alternate measures of inflation, two curves are depicted; one relates percentage changes in CPI to the unemployment rate and the other similarly relates the WPI to unemployment.

Many observers have seen in this relationship the existence of an unemployment-inflation trade-off problem: Can we simultaneously achieve high employment and price stability or must we trade off higher rates of inflation for lower levels of unemployment? The fact, however, that price stability has not been achieved in the past with low unemployment rates does not imply the existence of an immutable relationship.

Unemployment and the price level are each influenced by a great many factors. The relationship between unemployment and the price level is neither simple nor direct. Because a low level of unemployment has been an important public objective, analytical attention has often focused on the overall unemployment rate as the proxy for a wide range of economic forces, e.g., general prosperity, the rate of utilization of economic resources, trends in wage rates and profits. The separate impact on the price level of these other economic characteristics has only recently begun to receive detailed study. The following analysis suggests a variety of public policies

* From "The Unemployment-Inflation Problem," *Study Paper Number 4*, Studies by the Staff of the Cabinet Committee on Price Stability, January 1969, pp. 125–48.

FIGURE 1-1. Price level changes and unemployment rates: 1960–1968

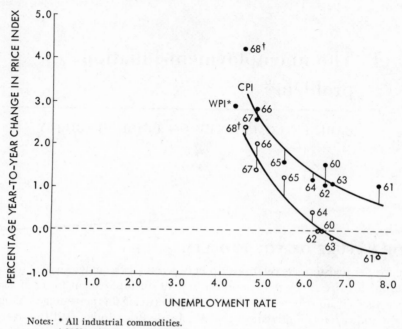

Notes: * All industrial commodities.
       † 1968 estimate.
Source: Department of Labor (Bureau of Labor Statistics).

and private actions that can be expected not only to reduce the inflation problem without incurring higher unemployment rates, but also to lessen the uneven burden of unemployment among subgroups of the labor force without undue inflationary pressures.

This apparent inverse relationship between unemployment and inflation, associated with growth and high employment, has been variously called the unemployment-inflation dilemma and the Phillips curve. Technically, the Phillips curve refers to the relationship between the unemployment rate and the change in wages, a relationship in which unemployment is considered to be a major determinant of wage changes. Popular usage has also tagged the unemployment-inflation relationship as the Phillips curve, but we shall refer to it as the unemployment-inflation or U-I relationship.

Two important measures of a problem are a widespread recognition of its existence and the persistence and variety of attempts to solve it. By these measures, the unemployment-inflation relationship is a problem of the first magnitude. Every major free industrial nation has recognized the problem and has experimented with policies and institutions in attempts to cope with the problem.

Free societies, of course, pursue other economic goals besides high employment and price stability. These include an acceptable rate of economic growth, a balance of payments equilibrium, an equitable distribution of income, and free institutions.

．　．　．　．　．

Macroeconomic factors

Macroeconomic factors include such *broad* or *aggregative* phenomena as aggregate demand, employment, growth, and the general level of prices. Monetary and fiscal policies—our principal demand-related policies—are frequently called macro policies because they are attempts to influence these aggregate factors. For example, monetary policy, by easing credit and increasing the supply of money, and fiscal policy, by lowering taxes and increasing government expenditures, increase aggregate demand and decrease unemployment. These macro policies can differ in a wide array; for example, they can differ as to pace, purpose, timing, and chosen instrument.

Type and mix of policies. In addition to the usual distinction between monetary and fiscal policies, it is convenient to differentiate countercyclical, expansion, and growth policies. Countercyclical policies are essentially defensive or reactive; they are less concerned with sustaining growth or closing the GNP gap than that growth not get out of hand. Their drama is provided mainly by reactive and restrictive measures.

Expansion policies, on the other hand, attempt to expand actual GNP up to potential GNP, i.e., to close the GNP gap. In the same context, growth policies aim to stimulate the growth of potential GNP; consequently, expansion policies tend to be more demand oriented and growth policies more capacity oriented. Both, however, represent an affirmation to impart a direction to our economic development, reaching for higher utilization of men and equipment and for greater output. Their drama is provided mainly by stimulative measures.

There is no unique countercyclical, expansion, or growth policy. Each of these policies can be implemented by highly diversified mixes of policy instruments and timing. It is significant to the development of our U-I performance, for example, whether fiscal policy stresses taxes or expenditures, investment or consumption. And shifts in policy or changes in policy mix can cause a change in the composition of demand; this change, as we note later, can contribute to "sectoral" or "demand-shift" inflation. Macro policies can also be used to increase unemployment and decrease the rate of inflation. In fact, when designed to achieve price stability, such policies rely heavily on increasing unemployment and have an adverse effect on the rate of growth.

．　．　．　．　．

Microeconomic factors

Macro policies are essentially demand-related influences. They are, however, only a part of the U-I story; they are one blade of the scissors. Individual prices change because of demand-related and supply-related influences in their respective markets. The aggregate price level rises because price increases on individual items are not offset by decreases on other items. Macro policy affects demand in individual markets because of its impact generally on the evolution of aggregate demand and directly, through specific programs or expenditures, on the development of demand in particular markets. *Microeconomic* factors include both supply-related and demand-related characteristics of *individual* product and labor markets. In the present context we emphasize those micro factors that operate essentially from the supply side; they influence reaction, in terms of price and output response, to changes in demand. These supply-related influences provide the second blade of the scissors.

If individual markets were perfect, they would adjust smoothly to changes in demand. Labor, material, and capital equipment would move readily to small changes in prices: labor would quickly acquire new skills; information generated by product and labor markets would be accurate and timely; buyers and sellers would be well informed; and markets would be competitive. If these conditions were characteristic of individual markets, macro policy could expand output and lower unemployment, maintaining stable prices, until the economy reached some hypothetical level of full employment. Expansion would encounter no resistance or assertive action from the supply side. At full employment, attempts to utilize additional, non-existent labor and equipment would dissipate in inflation [Figure 1–2 (a) depicts a relevant U-I curve]. Under these circumstances, the only impediment to the simultaneous achievement of full employment and price stability would be faulty macro policies. There would be no U-I problem.

Market conditions, however, are not perfect; they do not always effect smooth adjustments. Generally speaking, market imperfections are of three types: those associated with immobilities, inadequate information available to buyers and sellers, and discretionary power in product and labor markets. Before proceeding to a discussion of these imperfections, however, we shall try to conceptualize their significance.

Given a policy goal, we assume an optimum macro policy for any given set of micro conditions. These micro conditions will be limited to (1) the structures of particular markets and (2) the observed pattern of conduct by private decision-makers. Market structure consists of the mobility, information, and competitive characteristics of individual markets. Both structure and observed conduct reflect a given set of micro policies, as enforced. The given set of supply-related influences will change, therefore, if any of these four factors change: market structure, observed conduct, micro policies, or their enforcement.

These given micro factors provide resistance to or assert themselves against macro policy as it directs or conditions the private decision-making sector. As the optimum macro policy reduces unemployment, these supply-related and demand-related forces interact. As a result, a U-I curve unfolds that represents the best U-I performance that macro policy, given the micro conditions, can achieve. We shall call this curve the U-I limit or the macro boundary; macro policy, given the structure and conduct characteristics of individual markets, cannot penetrate the line and achieve U-I combinations which lie below it [See Figure 1–2 (b)].

FIGURE 1–2.

(a) U-I Curve: Perfect market conditions   **(b) U-I Curve: Imperfect market conditions**

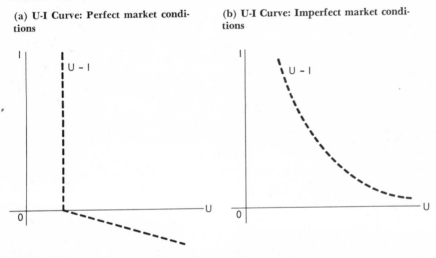

The inflation represented by the macro boundary is what has usually been called supply inflation. It can be the result of involuntary and defensive response or of aggressive and assertive behavior in the private sector. This type of inflation or variants of it have been called: nondemand, seller's, cost-push, cost, premature, administered, etc.

Any U-I combination above the limit is possible. Given the micro set, such combinations would result from inappropriate or faulty macro policy. For example, macro policy that pushed too rapidly against supply resistance would record U-I combinations above the boundary. Such inflation would be both supply and demand inflation; demand inflation would be measured up from the U-I limit. This has also been called demand-pull inflation.

The macro boundary can be shifted up or down by private or public decisions. Increased militance by labor or management in their reach for income gains greater than productivity increases will shift the boundary up.

On the other hand, behavior that conformed to the wage-price guideposts would shift the limit down. Changes or innovations in government micro policies that affected structure or conduct would also change the U-I limit.

In short, our quest for a suitable U-I performance must involve not only an appropriate macro policy but also micro policies that can effectively alter market structure and conduct. These micro policies are attempts to make market conditions more nearly perfect: to enable labor and capital to be more mobile, to improve information, and to reduce or influence discretionary power in product and labor markets.

Immobilities. The distribution of labor and output shifts among industries in response to changes in relative wages and prices. If supplies of labor, material, and capital equipment do not react to small changes in price, then larger price increases are necessary to overcome immobilities or to increase supplies. Alternatively, materials and equipment whose supplies are sluggishly adapted to change or labor that is slow to acquire new skills can cause significant levels of excess capacity or unemployment to persist at relatively high rates of inflation. Furthermore, the impact of these market imperfections on prices is aggravated when demand surges against such immobilities and rigidities; a more deliberate expansion of demand would generate less upward pressure on prices.

The more obvious immobilities tend to be rather persistent by nature or artificial in origin. Persistent immobilities are frequently found in the skill composition of the labor force; shortages develop in highly skilled occupations as demand increases more rapidly than additional manpower can be trained. At the other extreme are those individuals, lacking even basic skills or characterized by geographic or cultural inertia, who cannot be adopted by the labor market. Artificial immobilities are usually institutional or legal in origin and are frequently the result of some market power. Example would include some construction codes and work rules.

．　．　．　．　．

Information. Markets operate less efficiently when buyers and sellers are ignorant of alternatives. Improving the flow of information to buyers and sellers can raise or lower prices, depending upon the nature of the improvements and who experiences them. Regardless of the effect on the price level, however, improved information should generate prices that are desirable for the effect on allocation. Furthermore, if employers and employees have inadequate information relative to prospective employees and employers, unemployment declines more slowly and greater wage movements are probably required to overcome the lack of information.

The goals of the recent consumer movement include the creation of greater consumer intelligence and the improvement of consumer information. It is believed that more rational consumers could increase the discipline buyers wield over sellers of consumer goods. Consumers, for example, could contribute to price stability if, being able to evaluate quality with greater accuracy, they consistently chose the cheaper of several items with equivalent quality. It is generally recognized that producers buy more rationally than consumers and that, consequently, producers exercise more discipline over their suppliers than the consumers exercise over the sellers of consumer goods.

. . . . .

Discretionary power in product markets. In monopolies and oligopolies, private decision-makers possess discretionary power. This power is evident in the ability of firms in such protected industries to enjoy a markup that generates persistent monopoly profits as well as in their ability to maintain their prices despite excess capacity.

DISCRETIONARY MARKUP. Firms in a truly competitive market have no discretionary power; the market determines a price that allows no persistent profits above the competitive level. Monopolistic and oligopolistic industries, on the other hand, are less constrained by their structural characteristics. These characteristics—including concentration, barriers to entry, product differentiation—determine for each industry the maximum price above the competitive level than can be charged: i.e., the maximum markup protected by structure. This maximum markup will, of course, vary from industry to industry and explains why some industries earn persistently higher returns on investment than others. Within this range, bounded by the competitive price and the maximum markup, firms in an industry can exercise discretion; within this range a price is then established that reflects, in great measure, the attitudes and goals of significant firms in an industry. This discretion may, but need not, result in a profit maximizing price.

. . . . .

Both guidepost policy and competition policy can be employed to lower price, minimize an increase, or postpone undesirable action; the former by introducing a new goal into the private decision-making process and the latter by narrowing the range of discretion. Either technique would reduce price in a one-shot manner but the total impact need not be that limited. To the extent either technique contributed to the undoing of a wage-price spiral, the impact of the one-shot adjustment would become cumulative. These influences of competition and guidepost policies on price need have no adverse effects upon the allocative efficiency of markets, because the price being lowered was not competitive in the first place. And, finally, in our concern with U-I performance it should not be forgotten that the possession and exercise of discretionary power in product markets impairs the efficiency of the economy and has a disturbing effect on the distribution of income.

PRICE RIGIDITY.   The ability to maintain price against excess capacity has particular relevance to the question of inflation. This type of discretionary power differs among industries just as does the power to exploit a discretionary markup; and the latter need not always be associated to the same degree with the former. Uncertainty which results from an oligopolist's recognition of mutual interdependence with other large firms in the industry, causes him to be hesitant toward changing prices in the face of changed demand and supply conditions. Prices become particularly sticky on the downward side. The discretionary ability to maintain prices contributes to inflation by enabling firms to prevent prices from falling despite the existence of excess capacity necessary to effect deflation. Such power gives rise to what has been called "demand-shift" or "sectoral" inflation and is an important element in the ratchet mechanism by which our economy resists downward pressure on prices and wages.

·　·　·　·　·

The resistance of prices and wages to downward pressures constitutes one the toughest problems confronting achievement of an effective stabilization policy. One of the difficulties is the simple matter of identification. Rising prices can be seen; prices that should have fallen are not as obvious. If the competitive forces of individual markets cannot effect warranted price reductions, other sanctions must be used if inflation is to be avoided.

·　·　·　·　·

Discretionary power in labor market.   Although corporations hire individual workers, labor is not sold by unions. Unions negotiate jointly with management to establish the rules within which individuals are hired, rewarded, and disciplined. This joint negotiation is collective bargaining. Collective bargaining is not a simple, impersonal exchange relationship; it is essentially a political relationship designed to achieve certain economic consequencees.

·　·　·　·　·

Considerations germane to collective bargaining on economic issues would undoubtedly include: acceptable standard of living, living cost changes, wage comparability, ability to pay, productivity, and effect of settlement on inflation and employment. There seems to be some agreement that the three considerations of greatest significance in the outcome of a negotiation are: living cost changes, wage comparability, and ability to pay. It is noteworthy that two of these three significant considerations—changes in living costs and wage comparability—are reactions to events outside the scope of the industry directly involved. In this sense, they represent a defensive reaction to events beyond the control of the unions or of the particular bargaining relationships. They also provide a mechanism by which inflationary pressures can be diffused and thereby become cumulative.

The ability to pay can be measured by the ability and willingness of management to resist demands based on living cost changes and comparability. This resistance tends to be low where management possesses appreciable discretionary power; the unusually large profits allowed such firms by the market attract and enlarge labor's demands, and the power to pass through cost increases reduces resistance. Productivity is given short shrift. In brief, discretionary power to *demand* and to *grant* wage increases in excess of average productivity gains can give an upward thrust to the price level. The ability to pay can also be easily pushed over into an attempt to effect an income shift. Unfortunately, attempts to shift income by demanding wage increases in excess of productivity increases, without effective constraints on product price increases, are also inflationary.

Discretionary power possessed by union leaders at the bargaining table is influenced not only by forces derived from the relevant product and labor markets but also by pressures generated by political relationships internal to the union. Pressures from the rank-and-file, implemented by internal union democracy, are in many instances a powerful constraint upon leadership; they are, however, unfortunately a constraint that rarely induces leadership to make a more "responsible" settlement. Given the relevant laws and the nature of the organizations, union leaders must be more responsive to their membership than corporate management must be to stockholders. And union members, witnesses to obvious asset inflation, fearful of an adverse income shift, and suspicious of their tax burden, seek theirs at the bargaining table.

Expectations and discretionary power. The role of expectations gives an additional dynamic quality to the interaction of discretionary power as exercised by labor and management representatives. The result is what might be called a consensual explanation of the wage-price spiral, although it also depends upon the possession of discretionary power by both labor and management.

According to this view, collective bargaining contains a conventional element: a consensus of expectations that parties bring to the table. This consensus is shaped by such events as a conspicuous settlement, recent price movements (including increases in the competitive sector), implicit or explicit action by the government, statements by influential private parties, etc. These events, of course, are not a grin without a cat; they reflect the accelerating realities of the imperfect market conditions that underlie the U-I curve. As E. H. Phelps Brown observed:

Once formed, it (consensus on a wage and price rise) tends to realize itself. Any one party to a negotiation feels himself no longer a free agent but impelled by all around him. No one is conscious of pushing out in front; the union is only struggling to overtake arrears, the employer cannot afford to be left behind. To resist a claim for the expected amount will be costly and ultimately futile, to grant it will prove harmless because the others will be granting it too. The same spontaneous collusion permits the subsequent price rises that enable higher costs to be borne without squeezing profit margins. A tacit combination thus develops the capacity for self-propulsion.

Such "tacit" combinations of labor and management, reflecting a change in the shared consensus of expectations, change the micro conditions that determine the macro boundary. The boundary shifts up and, unless macro policies are changed, a less desirable U-I performance results.

· · · · ·

GOALS IN CONFLICT

Implicit in the unemployment-inflation dilemma is the proposition that full employment and price stability, as goals, are in conflict.

· · · · ·

There is sometimes a temptation to resolve the difficulties of the relationship between high employment and price stability by defining the former in terms of the latter; if a 6 percent level of unemployment were necessary to stabilize prices, under this definition 6 percent would be an acceptable employment goal. In this instance, price stability dominates the employment goal. The employment goal, however, can also become a constraint when the employment goal becomes associated with levels of unemployment greater than those which provoke some critical degree of political resistance.

Such an employment goal involves no constraint as long as those suffering the unfavorable rates have only limited access to the political process and do not express themselves outside it. Militant objections, however, within or without the political process, can convert the employment goal into a constraint. The United States may well have experienced such a conversion; it is probable that the disadvantaged will no longer accept passively their previous burden of an aggregate unemployment level in excess of 5 percent.

Economic growth is another major goal of policy. Growth is desirable because it raises per capita income and reduces the burden of meeting our great national problems—for example, the rebuilding of our central cities and the employment of presently marginal members of the labor force. It would appear obvious, for example, that a necessary condition for a satisfactory achievement of rates of unemployment nearer to 3 percent and price stability is an industrial plant capacity that can employ that many workers without strain. In addition, an adequate growth policy should reduce the tension in the struggle to effect or defend against income shifts and thus reduce inflationary pressures. Growth policy may hold the long-run key to the simultaneous realization of high employment and price stability.

Such a growth policy, however, operates under conditions characterized by a small or non-existent GNP gap. Actual output pushes against potential output, relieved by occasional and temporary accumulations of excess capacity. Under these circumstances, inflationary pressures can be anticipated. Similar consequences occur as expansion policy successfully exerts pressure on potential GNP. What is needed and what most industrial countries are struggling to develop are micro stabilization policies that will reduce inflationary pressures as we simultaneously pursue high employment and acceptable growth rates.

Expansion policies are basically demand oriented. Growth policies are essentially supply or capacity oriented. Both are macro policies in that, relying on monetary and fiscal policies, they affect broad or aggregate phenomena. Micro stabilization policies operate on both the demand and supply sides of particular markets and units. Because these stabilization policies are micro policies, it is possible for a conflict to arise between them and free economic institutions. It must be remembered, however, that private as well as public decision-makers must be controlled by some means if society's purposes and any type of stability are to be achieved. The preservation of free institutions as a goal implies a preference for impersonal controls such as those of a competitive market or for self-imposed controls such as those essential to democracy; free institutions should not be construed as representing a preference for ineffective or no social controls. Adequate social controls of some sort—impersonal, self-imposed, or governmental—will be imposed if existing sanctions or inducements fail to achieve society's valued goals.

POLICY CONSIDERATIONS

Relevant policies derive from the identification of the problem. In our view, U-I performance is strongly influenced by aggregate demand as it is distributed over particular supply conditions. Observed U-I relationships that evolve as aggregate demand changes depend, therefore, upon the macro policies and forces that affect aggregate demand as well as upon the structure of individual product and labor markets and the attitudes and goals of private decision-makers. In short, the U-I performance is the result of the interaction of demand-related and supply-related factors. In order to achieve a more desirable U-I performance, government policy should, consequently, be designed to affect both demand-related and supply-related factors.

The U-I performance is also strongly influenced by the pace of productivity improvements. For example, increases in productivity can be expected to reduce upward pressure on prices resulting from a wage increase.

To the extent, therefore, that wages rise with decreases in the unemployment rate, we should expect productivity increases to reduce the rate of inflation at given rates of unemployment.

Productivity is an extraordinarily complex measure of performance. Simplistically, we can distinguish between changes in productivity that result from changes in the rate at which capital equipment is utilized and from longer run improvements in the capital plant itself. As the economy expands—actual GNP approaching potential GNP—productivity increases up to some point principally because fixed costs are being spread over a larger output. Such productivity increases can reduce the inflationary impact of wage increases during the period of expansion. However, as the gap closes, increases in productivity from this source may tend to level off or decrease significantly; consequently, at this time wage increases begin to press more directly upon profits and prices. Accordingly, productivity changes that are a function of the rate at which existing capital equipment is utilized cannot be relied upon to reduce inflationary pressures as the rate of unemployment declines aand industry capacity becomes fully utilized.

Productivity can also increase because of the introduction of improved capital equipment. This is a long-run source of productivity improvement and can be expected to moderate inflationary pressures at low rates of unemployment. Other sources of long-run productivity improvement include improvements in the quality of the labor force, shifts of labor and capital from less productive use to more productive use in response to enduring shifts of demand, and increases in the stock of capital. As the GNP gap closes and we shift from expansion to growth, we must rely on these long-run types of productivity improvements if stability is to accompany growth. The stimulation and support of such improvements should be an object of government policy. Such policies can be both macro (e.g., investment tax credits) and micro (e.g., research in the construction industry).

. . . . .

Macro policies

The first step in pursuit of a better U-I performance is the adoption of appropriate monetary and fiscal policies. Even an optimum mix of such policies, however, cannot assure an acceptable U-I relationship because of the resistance and assertive action of those product and labor markets that are relatively inefficient and imperfect. The second step, therefore, is the development and application of micro stabilization policies that are designed to make markets function more efficiently and less imperfectly.

Micro stabilization policies

Micro stabilization policies are complementary to macro policies. In general, they are attempts to increase mobility, to improve information, and to reduce or influence the exercise of discretionary power and, thereby, to improve the U-I performance. The general outline of such policies can be observed in existing legislation and governmental action. They can affect both demand and supply conditions of individual markets. Manpwer programs, for example, function as both demand-related and supply-related policies. Manpower employment programs—in contrast to supply-related training programs—are demand-related; work experience and public service employment programs reduce unemployment among selected subgroups of the labor force experiencing comparatively high unemployment rates. The Nation has not yet developed an efficient and effective set of micro stabilization policies. Much innovation, experimentation, and coordination remain to be done.

At present, four basic micro stabilization policies are operative in the United States. Manpower policies, competition and international trade policies, a guidepost or incomes policy, and the consumer information program. Although in their present form these policies and programs do not constitute an adequate and coordinated micro policy set, they provide a foundation upon which effective micro stabilization policies can be built.

Competition and wage-price guidepost policies are complementary in product markets characterized by discretionary power. Competition policy, through antitrust action on the structure and conduct of industry, attempts to narrow the range of prices within which private parties exercise their discretion. Guidepost policy, in seeking to influence the exercise of discretion, introduces the national interest as an important criterion in labor and management decisions. These policies are complementary in product markets because each seeks to influence the exercise of discretionary power; competition policy by reducing it and voluntary restraint policies by influencing its exercise.

· · · · ·

The manifold activities of the Federal Government have significant impact on many individual prices. Some prices are directly regulated by the Government; others are indirectly regulated. For many goods and services the Government is the only or, at least, the dominant buyer. In other cases it provides the funds to finance purchases by others. To the extent possible, efforts by the Government to minimize the inflationary impact of these many direct and indirect purchases as well as the inflationary impact of price changes for which the Government has singular responsibility (e.g., regulated industries and relevant agricultural programs) would aid in our pursuit of a better U-I performance.

2 Construction wages: The great consumer robbery*

CARL H. MADDEN

Soaring wage rates in the Nation's giant construction industry are approaching a national scandal. President Nixon has labeled the construction situation a "crisis" and invoked his powers in an "emergency" to suspend the Davis-Bacon Act. The fantastic climb of construction wage rates is a growing social and economic menace, called the most important obstacle in the way of subduing inflation by a national magazine.

The reason is that unless the United States finds a way to stop the wage explosion in construction, the pattern will spread into many other industries, sever the tie between productivity and income gains, and undermine the credibility of market-determined incentives and rewards. One result, seen in Britain, of such labor anarchy is chronic inflation with high unemployment, called "stagflation." Another result, threatened in Sweden where pay for workers is climbing above salary levels of organized professionals, is growing class animosity that may shake the stability of that welfare state.

THE GREAT CONSUMER ROBBERY

The wage push in building amounts to an unabashed and unique giant consumer robbery. Recently, one State building trades president said, "There is no reason why a union man should not be earning $30,000 a year." In fact, many electricians in New York City now earn, according to some contractors, more than $35,000 per year. If Ralph Nader and his coworkers and imitators really want to protect consumers from exploitation, they could do no better than train their big guns on the wage monopoly in our Nation's biggest industry.

---

* From "Construction Wages: The Great Consumer Robbery," *The 1971 Economic Report of the President,* hearings before the Joint Economic Committee, 92nd Congress, First Session, 1971, pp. 670–77. Abridged and reprinted with permission of the author. Carl H. Madden is Chief Economist, Chamber of Commerce of the United States.

The building trades have got a stranglehold on the huge $90 billion construction industry, which usually accounts for 10 percent or more of the Nation's annual output (GNP) and is bigger than the auto and steel industries put together. It is a case of the tail wagging the dog. The 17 AFL–CIO construction trades unions and their nearly 3 million workers in 10,000 locals threaten to dominate the U.S. work force of more than 80 million by setting the pace for wage negotiations, accelerating price increases, and fueling the inflation.

Construction is not only the nation's biggest industry, but it has a pervasive effect on nearly every other industry. When the price of roads, schools, hospitals, factories, and housing rises faster than the productivity of the men who build them, vast pressure is put on Government to pass the bill on to consumers and taxpayers through inflation. Construction costs have risen almost twice as fast as general U.S. prices. Building costs, to be sure, are pushed up also by recent interest charge rises now abating and by soaring land prices in urban areas which may double again in the next 10 years. But without doubt it is mainly wage cost inflation that is pushing up the cost of new homes beyond the reach of more and more middle-income families and forcing middle-income as well as low-income families to seek out Government-subsidized rental apartments.

Some people cite the cost of living to explain construction settlements, but their contention is not supported by the facts. During 1969, the consumer price index rose 6.1 percent while the median first year construction cost settlements was 14 percent, with many settlements much higher. Other people cite the seasonality of construction work. But today building goes on in summer and winter in the North and the South with relatively few interruptions. The surveys of income actually received by construction workers already cited belie the seasonality argument.

Unions occasionally cite profits of corporations to justify higher wage rates. But from 1966 to 1970, corporate profits have shrunk as a share of GNP while investment spending rose from around $65 billion to more than $80 billion. While inflation in recent years has lifted replacement costs of buildings and equipment, corporate profits in dollar terms have fallen since 1969. There is very little in the record of corporate profits in recent years to justify higher and higher wage increases. Meanwhile, the credit restraint from 1969 to early 1970 sharply cut the demand for housing and caused increased bankruptcies and losses among builders.

WHAT LABOR POWER HAS DONE

President Nixon last December in a speech before businessmen said that "when construction wage settlements are more than double the national average for all manufacturing, at a time when construction workers are out of work, then something is basically wrong with that industry's bargaining process." The plain fact is that craft unions have been able to bully outsize increases from contractors because they control most of the labor supply.

Most Americans don't seem to realize or be concerned that this is true. Ever since New Deal days, public opinion has sentimentally sided with the political and legal climate so favorable to the building trades as to produce an irresponsible labor monopoly strong enough politically and economically to remain beyond the reach of legislative reform. Although the American public does not appear to care, in construction the real conflict of interest is not between management and labor. It is between labor and consumers, with the contractors merely serving as a medium to pass on labor's exactions to the public at large.

The reason is that while building trades unions have been traditionally strong, contractors have been in a notoriously weak bargaining position. Of an estimated 870,000 contractors in the United States, only 1,200 have 100 or more employees and most are quite small. Only about one-tenth of 1 percent of contractors hire 100 or more people. No one contractor does even 1 percent of the total industry volume. According to Census Bureau figures, the operative builder employs 5.6 people per firm. In 1967, the average for all contract construction was 9.7 employees per firm. The building industry operates as a multiple of builders representing management, subcontractors who are responsible for certain portions of the work, and supplier-distributors who provide materials for construction. Because the market for building in the United States is discretionary, cyclic, and local, there is no single market for a relatively few standardized models as in the auto industry.

Taking advantage of the industry's fragmentation, the craft unions have been able to dominate management. In the construction industry, the union, not the employer, decides who gets which job, supplies foremen as well as craftsmen, has a decisive voice in the management of pensions, insurance, vacations, and other employee benefits, and so largely controls both manpower and production.

TROUBLE WITH OUTPUT AND SUPPLY

Labor power in construction has led to productivity trouble and artificial shortages of labor supply. When local unions do their own bargaining city by city and craft by craft, it is no wonder that one-third of construction negotiations end in strikes. Featherbedding and work preservation practices echoing a depression philosophy are notorious. So we have plumbers who cut off threads already on pipes and rethread the pipe on the job; carpenters who refuse to install prehung doors or sash; painters who won't use spray techniques and limit the sizes of brushes; bricklayers who will lay only 400 bricks a day compared with 800 bricks normal for open shop work; electricians who require skilled craftsmen to install a light bulb. According to Roger Blough's congressional testimony, these practices exist on a widespread scale. The result is that productivity, as best measured, is lagging if not trending downward in construction.

Labor unions limit membership to create artificial labor shortages through restricting apprenticeship training. An artificially created shortage is the main reason for higher than normal wage increases in some trades and among laborers. It takes only 18 months to train an airport controller, but unions insist that plumbers helpers spend 3 to 5 years learning the craft. There are far too few apprentices trained. In 1968 there were only some 125,000 building trade apprentices in the entire industry, less than 4 percent of the construction labor force. That year, only 37,300 apprentices "graduated" while attrition by death or retirement was 70,000.

In fact it seems that Government itself has participated in fostering excessive pay and restrictive practices in building unions. The Davis-Bacon Act, recently suspended by President Nixon in the present emergency, is one example of Government policies that lend support to excessive union wages. The law, passed in 1931 in the midst of the Great Depression, requires that not less than "prevailing" wages, as determined in a locality by the Department of Labor, be paid on all work contracted for or assisted by the Federal Government. In practice, the prevailing wage seems often to be the union scale in the city or metropolitan area nearest to the local site and to be actually higher than the local scale. The President's action, which makes it possible for merit shop contractors to compete for jobs with union contractors, was condemned by President George Meany of the AFL–CIO as "antiunion," even though suspension in no way affects union arrangements.

THE SPREAD OF WAGE-PUSH

Government recently has increased its concern about labor union power and its use to shortchange the consumer, not so much because the power is new but because its abuse is now so obvious. Arthur F. Burns, Chairman of the Federal Reserve Board, last December declared, "Monetary and fiscal tools are inadequate for dealing with sources of price inflation such as are plaguing us now—that is, pressures on costs arising from excessive wage increases." Burns called for market-oriented incomes policies covering a wide spectrum of measures. Included were suspension of the Davis-Bacon Act, a teenage minimum wage law to improve job opportunities for youngsters, establishment of national building codes, compulsory arbitration of labor disputes in industries vital to the public interest, and the like. Burns also proposed a high level Price and Wage Review Board that, "while lacking enforcement power, would have broad authority to investigate, advise, and recommend on price and wage changes."

Other leading Government policymakers such as George P. Schultz, Director of the President's Office of Management and Budget, have opposed incomes policies because they believe that only monetary policy—that is, the power to increase the money supply—can create inflation. They are, of course, technically correct. They have lost the argument because of a certain overly simple view of how changes get made in the political process and because they fail to appreciate the political environment in which monetary policymakers must necessarily carry out their responsibilities.

Vice chairman Larry of U.S. Steel, has argued it is not enough merely to recognize that ours is now a wage-push inflation; rather, what we need to see is that "something is clearly out of balance in the bargaining processes as presently structured." It is easy enough for some to dismiss the concerns of businessmen, but the steel industry is rightly concerned. Currently it is caught in the middle, facing contract negotiations with a powerful, industry-wide million-member industrial union, and beset by increasing competition from suppliers abroad with modern technology and lower wage rates. The steel industry has to face up realistically to the national and international implications of the wage spiral.

WHAT TO DO?

Here we are brought back full circle to the great consumer robbery in construction. The fact is that agriculture and manufacturing have been the source of the largest productivity gains which lie at the base of rising real incomes for Americans. But these sectors are employing a smaller and smaller portion of our work force. Today only about one-fourth of our work force is in manufacturing. Two-thirds of it is in what are broadly called the service industries, and the trend is upward for the future.

One central problem in the 1970's is to improve productivity in the service industries, including construction. The really big wage increases did not start in manufacturing but in construction, followed by transportation, other service industries, and public employment. The rapid rise of unions in public employment spreads union gains in construction or manufacturing—whichever public unions think they can get—into sectors of public employment such as education, where we don't even know how to define productivity but wonder whether, however defined, it is not falling rather than rising.

One necessary answer to the trend to service employment is to keep productivity gains high in manufacturing. The Nixon administration suspended the investment tax credit early in 1969, ostensibly to shift from private to social investment. Subsequent events seem to show things are not that simple. Private investment has lagged during the recent readjustment but social investment does not yield the same measurable productivity gains. The President's National Commission on Productivity has argued for more investment incentives for business, and the President's recent changes in depreciation schedules may be followed by other measures soon.

But improved productivity is not enough. Despite many improvements in productivity in building and reductions of costs, the results are obscured by rising prices for land, materials, more supplements, and above all, wage costs. There is no denying that conventional housing is better engineered, employs more power tools, better fastening equipment, and better management of the process of building than ever before. Indeed, widespread industrial construction of housing is not necessarily the boon to productivity which common mythology believes, as is made clear by Michael Sumichrast, NAHB economist in the survey earlier mentioned.

One answer, offered by J. K. Galbraith of Harvard, is a wage-price freeze to precede institution of a comprehensive, permanent, and enforced system of wage and price controls. Galbraith has managed to convince himself that the market doesn't work to our benefit anyway, and so he would make short shrift of what he now considers a competitive charade that exists in the "mega-economy" of large firms. Galbraith believes that the entrenched power of giant firms and giant unions is bad, so he wishes to substitute the entrenched power of central government, which is standard socialist mega-psychology. One does not have to agree with Galbraith in order to acknowledge that he is not a proponent of halfway measures. His views about the market power of giant firms, however, entirely overlook interindustry and international competition. Galbraith is most correct about his own political allies, the labor unions.

The plain fact is that some new form of bargaining structure is needed in unions, particularly construction. Reform of labor unions is surely less Draconian than Galbraith's abandonment of the market process. A call for union reform is inevitably interpreted by unions as a threat to their existence and therefore antiunion. This is the conditioned reflex of leadership that is oriented to the era of depression in the United States and is still haunted by past struggles for recognition. It is a cultural hangover, though, in an effluent society in which the problem is equitable sharing of rising affluence. During the depressed 1930's, Henry Simons noted that "questioning the virtues of the organized labor movement is like attacking religion, monogamy, motherhood, or the home." Surely we are living today in an era when, in our effort to improve and renew our institutions, valid criticism of labor practices need not be viewed as smashing idols, but should be considered on its merits. There is no escaping it; it is clearly in the interest of labor to recognize that, as Larry points out, "a continuation of the wage trends of the past is a luxury this Nation simply cannot afford."

3 Workers are the victims, not the cause of inflation*

LEONARD WOODCOCK

CAPACITY UTILIZATION AND UNEMPLOYMENT

When the Nixon Administration took office two years ago its immediate diagnosis of the nation's ailment was "excessive demand." The cure for excessive demand was to be monetary and fiscal restraint. The economy was "overheated" and needed "cooling off."

While American society and the American economy are afflicted with many ills, "excessive demand" is not numbered among them. "Effective demand," that is, demand supported by purchasing power and so translated into production and jobs, has not in any recent year come close to touching the dimensions of our needs or our capabilities. There has been no *general* excess of demand nor was there when the Administration took office.

True, demand has pushed against the limits of capacity in some sectors of the economy, most notably the capital goods sector where demand in recent years has soared to unsustainable highs. And there have been troublesome supply bottlenecks in other sectors, a notorious example being our shameful performance in failing to supply adequate health care to our people. We probably pay more per capita and get less value per dollar in the health care field than any other nation. These special situations and others have indeed put pressure on some prices.

But overall monetary and fiscal restraint are hardly appropriate measures for relieving these kinds of strain, and in fact are more likely to aggravate than to alleviate them.

The general case for "excessive demand" can be made only if the economy as a whole is straining the bounds of the human and physical resources that are available to produce goods and provide services. By these yard-

* From "Report on Economic Prospects and Policies," *Economic Prospects and Policies,* hearings before the Joint Economic Committee, 92nd Congress, First Session, 1971, pp. 143–70. Abridged and reprinted with permission of the author. Leonard Woodcock is President, International Union, United Auto Workers.

24

sticks—employment and capacity utilization—we have been afflicted with too little rather than too much demand.

There have at times been shortages of labor in certain occupations and certain areas, but there has been no general shortage of labor. The lowest unemployment rates we have achieved in recent years would seem shockingly high, for example, in any of the industrial democracies of Western Europe.

Our record in reducing unemployment has been a disgrace compared to the accomplishments of other modern industrial societies. The table which follows compares U.S. unemployment rates of the 1960s with those of five European countries and Japan. In each case the rates have been adjusted to U.S. definitions:

Unemployment rates adjusted to U.S. definitions

Year	United States	France	Great Britain	Italy	Japan	Sweden	West Germany
1960	5.5	2.5	2.0	4.3	1.7	(1)	0.8
1961	6.7	1.9	1.9	3.7	1.5	1.5	.5
1962	5.5	1.8	2.8	3.2	1.3	1.5	.4
1963	5.7	2.1	3.5	2.7	1.3	1.7	.5
1964	5.2	1.6	2.5	3.0	1.2	1.5	.3
1965	4.5	[2]2.0	2.2	4.0	1.2	1.2	.3
1966	3.8	[2]2.1	2.4	4.3	1.4	1.6	.3
1967	3.8	[2]2.7	3.8	3.8	1.3	2.1	1.0
1968	3.6	[2]3.2	3.7	3.8	1.2	2.2	1.2
1969	3.5	[2]2.8	3.7	3.7	1.1	1.9	[2] .7

[1] Not available.
[2] Preliminary.
Source: Bureau of Labor Statistics.

Of the six countries, only Italy had unemployment rates even remotely as high as ours during the 1960s. Rates in France were held below three percent in nine of the ten years. Great Britain's worst unemployment experience was about equal to our best. Unemployment rates in Japan never reached two percent at any time during the decade and in the latter half were reduced almost to one percent. Rates in Sweden were generally below two percent. Rates in West Germany were held below one percent in eight of the ten years.

By no stretch of the imagination could it be said either that there have been excessive demands on our physical capacity to produce. Capacity utilization rates in manufacturing had, in fact, been trending downward for more than two years at the time the Nixon Administration took office, from about 90.5 percent in 1966 to 85.3 percent in 1967 and 84.6 percent in 1968.

The real pressure on prices came first from the "administered price" sector of the economy—more specifically, from the hundred or so major corporations which so dominate the industries in which they are established, and are so well equipped with internally generated sources of funds for continued growth, that within relatively wide limits they are independent either of the competitive forces of the market place or of governmental attempts to influence their decisions through the operation of fiscal or monetary constraints. This pressure has, admittedly, been reinforced more recently by the perfectly justifiable efforts of working people to gain wage increases which would at least enable them to maintain a stable standard of living in the face of a growing inflation which they had not initiated and did not desire. To this theme we shall return.

PRICES

The recession was brought on deliberately, in blind adherence to an economic dogma which says that plentiful jobs and price stability are incompatible. According to this brand of economics, to slow down the rate of price increase, the pace of the economy must be slowed. In plain English this means that people have to be thrown out of work to stop inflation.

The trade-off of unemployment for price stability would be morally reprehensible even if it were economically sound. Inflation is not the cruelest tax of all. Joblessness is a far crueler tax.

However, the trade-off is not even sound economics, and predictably has been a dismal failure. While more than two million jobs have been wiped out in the name of "what is best for all of the American people," the claimed deceleration of the inflationary spiral has not yet been established. And those same Administration economists to whom so many Americans owe their joblessness would be sorely pressed if they were required to demonstrate that the game plan was at all a factor in any price relief which may have occurred.

Fifteen months ago President Nixon said: "Let me be careful not to mislead anyone: Prices are still going up. They may continue to do so for a while—a 5 year momentum is not easy to stop. But now prices are no longer increasing faster and faster. The increases not only have slackened but the rates of increase are actually down. Without shock treatment, we are curing the causes of the rising cost of living."

If the game plan had any validity, surely those who were advising the President would have had some grasp of the outlook for prices. But they obviously did not and, consequently, the President's words *were* misleading. The pace of inflation was not slowing down when he made the speech, but continued to accelerate for many, many months.

Recently, we have again been hearing that inflation is finally on the wane. In his recent televised press conference the President flatly claimed: "We are beginning to make real progress in fighting inflation."

While I would like to hope that he has been correctly advised this time, the evidence seems less than convincing. It has just been revealed that the GNP deflator, which is the most comprehensive price index available, rose at a 5.7 percent annual rate in the final quarter of 1970, up sharply from the third quarter rate of 4.6 percent and from the fourth quarter 1969 rate of 4.9 percent.

WORKERS ARE THE VICTIMS, NOT THE CAUSE OF INFLATION

It is fashionable to date the beginnings of the present inflation in the year 1966. However, its roots are to be found in the years 1960–1965. It is equally fashionable to attribute the inflation to wage increases but again its real roots are elsewhere. In an illuminating analysis of the causes of inflation the *Wall Street Journal* of August 5, 1968 stated:

Any attempt to fix the blame for today's inflation, however, shouldn't be limited simply to a consideration of labor costs. The blame, it can be argued, belongs in many places.

A major culprit may be corporate profits. A glance at the economic history of the post-World War II era certainly suggests that inflation often has been just as much "profit-push" inflation as "wage-push." Consider a few facts of the postwar era: "In the past 20 years, there have been three distinct periods in which factory prices climbed substantially over a prolonged interval. In each instance, labor costs per unit of factory output were *declining* when the price climb began and these costs continued to decline for a considerable period after the price rise was under way. In each case, corporate profits began to increase sharply well *before* the price climb started."

Such facts, at least to some economists, bear an obvious message. "The pattern is clear enough," says Peter L. Bernstein, president of Bernstein-Macaulay Inc., a New York investment counseling service. "Instead of labor costs pushing prices up, what we see instead is a sort of profit-push. Profits are already well on their way up before prices begin to rise, and prices are well on their way up before wages begin to rise faster than output."

Indeed, some analysts say that the postwar economic record suggests a chain of events that runs something like this: Profits begin to climb, first through the impact of better machinery and work methods on unit labor costs, and then through higher prices; the rising profits finally prompt labor to attempt to "catch up" by seeking sharply higher pay; ultimately, unit labor costs begin to rise, too, giving inflation a further push. (Emphasis in original.)

As the *Wall Street Journal* points out, and as I documented in great detail before the House Banking and Currency Committee last June, labor costs were falling when wholesale prices began to rise sharply at the end of 1964. There were no pressures of labor costs to justify the price increases which started the upward spiral on its way. Moreover, unit profits were rising even before prices were increased; there were no nonlabor cost pressures either which would justify any increase in prices. On the contrary, with unit labor costs falling and unit profits rising, clearly it was a period when price *decreases* were in order.

Nor was there an excess of demand relative to supply to cause a "bidding up" (the economist's euphemism for price-gouging in a rapidly rising market) of prices by consumers during this period when the inflationary spiral started. Unemployment, while declining, remained excessively high throughout the period. Capacity utilization, while on the increase throughout much of the period, remained far below optimum rates. The most obvious explanation for the price increases which launched the inflationary spiral is that the business community saw an opportunity to increase profit still further and seized it—with no concern for the inflationary consequences of its actions.

As a result, the economy had gotten badly out of joint by the end of 1965, with income imbalances that sorely needed correcting. Boosted by unwarranted and excessive price increases, corporate profits had increased by 56.5 percent during the preceding 5 years. Dividend payments to stockholders had increased by 47.8 percent. Personal interest income had increased by 65.3 percent. Wages and salaries, on the other hand, had increased by only 32.5 percent.

The upward pull of prices on unit labor costs has been apparent since 1966 as workers have been forced to seek increases in money wages at rates in excess of productivity gains to protect their living standards against further erosion by inflation and to attempt to correct the distortion in the distribution of national income that was made at their expense. They have met with indifferent success.

SHOULD WE ADOPT AN "INCOMES POLICY"?

The question has been raised as to whether or not we should have an "incomes policy" for the United States. The only answers I can give to that question are that no one has yet provided what I could consider a satisfactory definition or description of an incomes policy, and that, to the best of my knowledge, wherever anything called an "incomes policy" has been attempted, it has failed.

In the first place, what *is* an "incomes policy"? Is it a policy by which the government attempts to regulate the income of every individual in the nation? If we agree to that definition, then we have to admit that such a policy would be universally unacceptable, and impossible to carry out except in the most totalitarian of societies.

Unfortunately, most of those who say they believe in an "incomes policy," but who would certainly repudiate one such as I have just described, turn out to have defined "incomes policy" in their own minds as a policy of regulation of the incomes of wage-earners, and particularly of wage increases negotiated by organized labor.

The gross inequity and total impracticality of such a policy should be immediately obvious. Are workers alone to be asked to bear the entire cost and burden of stabilizing the economy and maintaining its stability, while others are permitted to make unlimited profits at their expense? In Great Britain, even a Labor government which attempted an "incomes policy" which turned out to be primarily one of restrictions on wage increases quickly lost the support of its own followers, and was ignominiously turned out of office at the first opportunity.

That was also essentially the nature of the "guideposts" policy adopted in the early 1960s by the Council of Economic Advisers, which also turned out to be a failure. Again, the main reason was that the "guideposts" covering price policy were nebulous in the extreme, and even then were departed from whenever any individual business chose to do so, and the Council lacked the necessary powers to get at the facts which would enable it in most cases to determine whether or not firms were adhering to the guideposts.

The "guideposts" for labor, on the other hand, were expressed in terms of a single figure for percentage wage increases, and although a number of exceptions were formally admitted, they never made any impression on the public mind, and the wage guideposts revolved around the "magic figure" of 3.2 percent which was used to hit labor over the head with in every round of negotiations until it became obvious that an annual 3.2 percent increase in money wages would not even be sufficient to maintain the standard of living of workers and their families in a period of inflation initiated primarily by the refusal of business to follow the price guideposts.

So far did business stray from the guideposts, that the Council found it necessary to say in its 1964 Report:

"It is appropriate to focus special attention this year on price *reductions*. The guideposts call for reductions in those industries whose trend productivity gains exceed the national trend. *It is fair to say that large industrial enterprises thus far have not widely heeded this advice. And yet, as noted earlier, there will be ample room for such reductions in 1964. If they are not forthcoming, over-all price stability will be rendered more difficult.*" (Underlined emphasis in the original.)

There, in a nutshell, you have the reason why the guideposts failed, and why the present spiral of inflation started later in 1964.

Another question to be considered is whether business and labor could be expected to cooperate in a voluntary incomes policy. Again, I am afraid the answer is no, and my opinion is based on my own immediate experience and that of my Union, the UAW. Time after time, in negotiations going back at least to 1958, the UAW has proposed to the major automobile producers, and in particular to General Motors which acts as their leader, that if the companies would announce a reasonable reduction in car prices, we would be prepared to negotiate within the framework of the financial situation in which they found themselves as a result of that price cut.

That was a genuine effort on our part to establish a cooperative, voluntary incomes policy. But every time the answer we received was a blunt, un-shakable "No."

A further possibility is that of mandatory controls. One of the most in-teresting comments on that subject recently was that of Stewart S. Cort, chairman and chief executive of Bethlehem Steel Corporation, who was re-ported in the *Wall Street Journal* of January 11 last as having "remarked approvingly" on a suggestion that Congress ban for two years any wage and fringe-benefit increases exceeding 3 percent per year. (Incidentally, if such a ban had been in effect during the past two years, the result for every full-time worker and his family would have been a reduction in living standards of 5 percent.)

According to the *Journal* Mr. Cort went on to say, however, that no form of price control was necessary, because prices would "follow unit costs" and thus would be restrained by any limit on wage increases as well as by com-petition.

The very next day, Bethlehem Steel Corporation announced price in-creases of as much as 12.5 percent on plates, structural shapes and other of its products—with no indication of a wage increase for its workers.

The corporation at the same time revoked its former guarantees that it would impose no more than one price increase in any year.

If I were asked my opinion about the respective merits of mandatory price and wage controls respectively, my opinion would be the exact op-posite of Mr. Cort's. I am confident that mandatory price controls would effectively control wages also, because after many years in the front line of collective bargaining I know only too well that you just can't get the wage increase you might like if the money isn't there.

In fact, however, I am opposed to either mandatory price or wage con-trols, because I believe they would require a monstrous bureaucracy to administer, and I am sure that except in a time of large-scale war that threatened our country's existence they would be totally unacceptable to the public and for that reason just as impossible to administer as Prohi-bition was in the 1920s.

In short, if by an "incomes policy" we mean any program, either volun-tary or mandatory, which would attempt to regulate the incomes of one group in the population only, I would consider it grossly inequitable; and if we mean a program that would attempt to regulate all incomes, or even to regulate all prices and wages, I believe it would be totally unworkable.

The best we can do in the direct area of incomes, I believe, is first to put a genuine and adequate floor under all incomes, so that no person and no family shall be forced to live in poverty; and second, to proceed with the tax reforms which have already been started, so as to share the burden of taxation more fairly, lessening it upon those with relatively low or mod-erate incomes, and closing the loopholes which still permit wealthy in-dividuals, families and some corporations to escape paying their fair share.

AN ALTERNATIVE COURSE

In the area of prices and wages, however, I believe there is a course to be followed which would require no great bureaucracy to administer, would be both welcomed by and informative to the public, and could have the effect not only of restraining unjustifiable price and/or wage increases, but also of rolling back present unjustifiably high prices. I refer, of course, to the adoption of a Price-Wage Review Board, which has long been endorsed by me and my colleagues in the UAW, but has recently received support also from some of the country's leading economists, including some in the Administration itself. Thus, for example, on November 19 last, the Hon. Murray L. Weidenbaum, assistant secretary of the Treasury for economic policy, called for:

". . . the conscious effort to create a new climate in which more reasonable and sensible wage-cost-price decisions are made and particularly in those areas of the economy where substantial concentrations of private power exist. Until this climate is achieved, or unless these substantial concentrations of private economic power are reduced, I find it hard to see how we can soon arrive at those two highly desirable and interrelated objectives—the return of full employment and the substantial and sustained reduction in inflation. That is the challenge of economic policy that now faces us all."

A short time later, on December 7, Chairman Arthur F. Burns of the Federal Reserve Board, in an address on "The Basis for Lasting Prosperity" was still more specific. He said:

"We might bring under an incomes policy also, the establishment of a high-level Price and Wage Review Board which, while lacking enforcement power, would have broad authority to investigate, advise, and recommend on price and wage changes." (Emphasis in original.)

Finally, on December 16 last the *Washington Post* reviewed a book soon to be published by John M. Blair, who was chief economist for the Kefauver Committee, which made many studies of economic concentration and its effect on prices. The review, written by Hobart Rowen, is worth quoting at length. It says:

"The seeming paradox of persistent inflation at a time of rising unemployment troubles many thoughtful people; somehow, the idea of rising prices seems inconsistent with recession. This is the specter of 'the worst of both worlds' that the Nixon administration had desperately hoped to avoid."

PRICES ARE THE MAIN ISSUE

As all of the above comments indicate, and as we in the UAW have made clear many times, it is necessary to provide a mechanism that would, when required, expose attempts at wage-gouging by big trade unions. . . . We believe that when any union tries to abuse its economic power it should be subject to public scrutiny in just the same way as any big corporation.

We also believe, however, that the major activity of such a Board will of necessity be directed toward the area of prices, primarily for the following reason.

Wage decisions are not made unilaterally by unions. Except in unorganized shops, where wage decisions are made primarily by the employer, they are the result of collective bargaining between the two parties concerned. And major bargaining, between large corporations and large unions, normally takes place under the close scrutiny of all the media— television, radio, newspapers and magazines, all are at hand to listen, to observe, to report and to comment. Even when the parties, at a crucial stage of bargaining, may agree to a news blackout, it will have been preceded by weeks of bargaining in which both parties explain and justify the decisions that have been made.

Those major price decisions which most seriously affect the whole economy, on the contrary, are made in the privacy of executive boardrooms, and the data as to costs, productivity and profit goals on which they are based are among the most closely guarded of corporate secrets. Repeatedly in the past such data have been refused even to Congressional investigating committees. Yet such information is vital to the public, especially in an inflationary period such as we are now experiencing, because without it there is no way in which the people can decide whether price increases are justified, or, if they are not, where the responsibility for them lies. Informed decisions on those matters could be made if the necessary information were made available through a Price-Wage Review Board.

B. How much does money matter?

In the following readings Professors Friedman and Samuelson offer differing views of the proper role for monetary policy and of the contribution it can make to achieving such macroeconomic goals as full employment and price stability. Both authors recognize that many early Keynesian economists (if not Keynes himself) believed that "money does not matter" as a stabilization tool. Monetarists and (post-) Keynesians seem to agree today that "money does matter." But how much? And for what purposes?

Friedman believes that the money supply is the most important determinant of aggregate spending. In other writing he has sharply questioned the effectiveness of fiscal policy, where the shifts in government spending or taxes involve no changes in this money supply. He argues here that, contrary to modern Keynesian opinion, monetary policy cannot maintain a target level of interest rates or of unemployment (except by renewing inflation or deflation, a policy which nearly everyone would reject). In the short run (which may last months or even years!) increased money may temporarily lower interest rates or unemployment, but in the long run both will return to their "natural" levels. Because of these limits on the power of monetary (or fiscal) policy, and also because of our ignorance on the exact timing or channels of monetary impacts, Friedman advocates a strict regimen for Federal Reserve policymakers: They should renounce "fine tuning" manipulations of money or interest rates, steering a steady course of 3 to 5 percent monetary expansion per year. Part of Friedman's preference for this policy rests on his faith in the natural adjusting powers of the market system, and part also on his consistent desire for minimum government intervention in the economy.

Samuelson questions the direct connection between money and spending, asserting that it depends on how the money creation affects private liquidity and wealth (bond holdings), or interest rates.

Most Keynesian economists would question Friedman's emphasis on long-run equilibrium analysis. Keynes himself commented that "in the long run we are all dead." (Note Samuelson's argument on bondholder mortality and its affect on his wealth calculations.) If money can even temporarily lower interest rates and unemployment, these more interventionist

33

Keynesians would favor using it actively as a stabilization tool, along with a similarly activist fiscal policy (see the following reading by Arthur Okun). Whether this will result in accelerating inflation, as Friedman predicts, depends on shifts in private expectations, effects of interest rates upon monetary velocity, the shape and movement of Phillips curves (see Reading 1), and other complex issues. These readings provide only a glimpse of that larger discussion.

4 The role of monetary policy*

MILTON FRIEDMAN

There is wide agreement about the major goals of economic policy: high employment, stable prices, and rapid growth. There is less agreement that these goals are mutually compatible or, among those who regard them as incompatible, about the terms at which they can and should be substituted for one another. There is least agreement about the role that various instruments of policy can and should play in achieving the several goals.

My topic for tonight is the role of one such instrument—monetary policy. What can it contribute? And how should it be conducted to contribute the most? Opinion on these questions has fluctuated widely. In the first flush of enthusiasm about the newly created Federal Reserve System, many observers attributed the relative stability of the 1920s to the System's capacity for fine tuning—to apply an apt modern term. It came to be widely believed that a new era had arrived in which business cycles had been rendered obsolete by advances in monetary technology. This opinion was shared by economist and layman alike, though, of course, there were some dissonant voices. The Great Contraction destroyed this naive attitude. Opinion swung to the other extreme. Monetary policy was a string. You could pull on it to stop inflation but you could not push on it to halt recession. You could lead a horse to water but you could not make him drink. Such theory by aphorism was soon replaced by Keynes' rigorous and sophisticated analysis.

Keynes offered simultaneously an explanation for the presumed impotence of monetary policy to stem the depression, a nonmonetary interpretation of the depression, and an alternative to monetary policy for meeting the depression and his offering was avidly accepted. If liquidity preference is absolute or nearly so—as Keynes believed likely in times of heavy unemployment—interest rates cannot be lowered by monetary measures. If

* From "The Role of Monetary Policy," *American Economic Review,* 58 (March 1968), pp. 1–17. Copyright American Economic Association, 1971. Reprinted with permission of author and publisher. Milton Friedman is Professor of Economics at The University of Chicago, Chicago, Ill.

investment and consumption are little affected by interest rates—as Hansen and many of Keynes' other American disciples came to believe—lower interest rates, even if they could be achieved, would do little good. Monetary policy is twice damned. The contraction, set in train, on this view, by a collapse of investment or by a shortage of investment opportunities or by stubborn thriftiness, could not, it was argued, have been stopped by monetary measures. But there was available an alternative—fiscal policy. Government spending could make up for insufficient private investment. Tax reductions could undermine stubborn thriftiness.

The wide acceptance of these views in the economics profession meant that for some two decades monetary policy was believed by all but a few reactionary souls to have been rendered obsolete by new economic knowledge. Money did not matter. Its only role was the minor one of keeping interest rates low, in order to hold down interest payments in the government budget, contribute to the "euthanasia of the rentier," and maybe, stimulate investment a bit to assist government spending in maintaining a high level of aggregate demand.

These views produced a widespread adoption of cheap money policies after the war. And they received a rude shock when these policies failed in country after country, when central bank after central bank was forced to give up the pretense that it could indefinitely keep "the" rate of interest at a low level. In this country, the public denouement came with the Federal Reserve-Treasury Accord in 1951, although the policy of pegging government bond prices was not formally abandoned until 1953. Inflation, stimulated by cheap money policies, not the widely heralded postwar depression, turned out to be the order of the day. The result was the beginning of a revival of belief in the potency of monetary policy.

This revival was strongly fostered among economists by the theoretical developments initiated by Haberler but named for Pigou that pointed out a channel—namely, changes in wealth—whereby changes in the real quantity of money can affect aggregate demand even if they do not alter interest rates. These theoretical developments did not undermine Keynes' argument against the potency of orthodox monetary measures when liquidity preference is absolute since under such circumstances the usual monetary operations involve simply substituting money for other assets without changing total wealth. But they did show how changes in the quantity of money produced in other ways could affect total spending even under such circumstances. And, more fundamentally, they did undermine Keynes' key theoretical proposition, namely, that even in a world of flexible prices, a position of equilibrium at full employment might not exist. Henceforth, unemployment had again to be explained by rigidities or imperfections, not as the natural outcome of a fully operative market process.

The revival of belief in the potency of monetary policy was fostered also by a re-evaluation of the role money played from 1929 to 1933. Keynes and most other economists of the time believed that the Great Contraction in the United States occurred despite aggressive expansionary policies by the monetary authorities—that they did their best but their best was not good enough. Recent studies have demonstrated that the facts are precisely the reverse: the U.S. monetary authorities followed highly deflationary policies. The quantity of money in the United States fell by one-third in the course of the contraction. And it fell not because there were no willing borrowers—not because the horse would not drink. It fell because the Federal Reserve System forced or permitted a sharp reduction in the monetary base, because it failed to exercise the responsibilities assigned to it in the Federal Reserve Act to provide liquidity to the banking system. The Great Contraction is tragic testimony to the power of monetary policy —not, as Keynes and so many of his contemporaries believed, evidence of its impotence.

In the United States the revival of belief in the potency of monetary policy was strengthened also by increasing disillusionment with fiscal policy, not so much with its potential to affect aggregate demand as with the practical and political feasibility of so using it. Expenditures turned out to respond sluggishly and with long lags to attempts to adjust them to the course of economic activity, so emphasis shifted to taxes. But here political factors entered with a vengeance to prevent prompt adjustment to presumed need, as has been so graphically illustrated in the months since I wrote the first draft of this talk. "Fine tuning" is a marvelously evocative phrase in this electronic age, but it has little resemblance to what is possible in practice—not, I might add, an unmixed evil.

It is hard to realize how radical has been the change in professional opinion on the role of money. Hardly an economist today accepts views that were the common coin some two decades ago. Let me cite a few examples.

In a talk published in 1945, E. A. Goldenweiser, then Director of the Research Division of the Federal Reserve Board, described the primary objective of monetary policy as being to "maintain the value of Government bonds. . . . This country" he wrote, "will have to adjust to a 2½ percent interest rate as the return on safe, long-time money, because the time has come when returns on pioneering capital can no longer be unlimited as they were in the past."

In a book on *Financing American Prosperity*, edited by Paul Homan and Fritz Machlup and published in 1945, Alvin Hansen devotes nine pages of text to the "savings-investment problem" without finding any need to use the words "interest rate" or any close facsimile thereto. In his contribution to this volume, Fritz Machlup wrote, "Questions regarding the rate of interest, in particular regarding its variation or its stability, may not be among the most vital problems of the postwar economy, but they are certainly among the perplexing ones." In his contribution, John

H. Williams—not only professor at Harvard but also a long-time adviser to the New York Federal Reserve Bank—wrote, "I can see no prospect of revival of a general monetary control in the postwar period."

Another of the volumes dealing with postwar policy that appeared at this time, *Planning and Paying for Full Employment,* was edited by Abba P. Lerner and Frank D. Graham and had contributors of all shades of professional opinion—from Henry Simons and Frank Graham to Abba Lerner and Hans Neisser. Yet Albert Halasi, in his excellent summary of the papers, was able to say, "Our contributors do not discuss the question of money supply. . . . The contributors make no special mention of credit policy to remedy actual depressions. . . . Inflation . . . might be fought more effectively by raising interest rates. . . . But . . . other anti-inflationary measures . . . are preferable." *A Survey of Contemporary Economics,* edited by Howard Ellis and published in 1948, was an "official" attempt to codify the state of economic thought of the time. In his contribution, Arthur Smithies wrote, "In the field of compensatory action, I believe fiscal policy must shoulder most of the load. Its chief rival, monetary policy, seems to be disqualified on institutional grounds. This country appears to be committed to something like the present low level of interest rates on a long-term basis."

These quotations suggest the flavor of professional thought some two decades ago. If you wish to go further in this humbling inquiry, I recommend that you compare the sections on money—when you can find them—in the Principles texts of the early postwar years with the lengthy sections in the current crop even, or especially, when the early and recent Principles are different editions of the same work.

The pendulum has swung far since then, if not all the way to the position of the late 1920s, at least much closer to that position than to the position of 1945. There are of course many differences between then and now, less in the potency attributed to monetary policy than in the roles assigned to it and the criteria by which the profession believes monetary policy should be guided. Then, the chief roles assigned monetary policy were to promote price stability and to preserve the gold standard; the chief criteria of monetary policy were the state of the "money market," the extent of "speculation" and the movement of gold. Today, primacy is assigned to the promotion of full employment, with the prevention of inflation a continuing but definitely secondary objective. And there is major disagreement about criteria of policy, varying from emphasis on money market conditions, interest rates, and the quantity of money to the belief that the state of employment itself should be the proximate criterion of policy.

I stress nonetheless the similarity between the views that prevailed in the late 'twenties and those that prevail today because I fear that, now as then, the pendulum may well have swung too far, that, now as then, we are in danger of assigning to monetary policy a larger role than it can perform, in danger of asking it to accomplish tasks that it cannot achieve, and, as a result, in danger of preventing it from making the contribution that it is capable of making.

Unaccustomed as I am to denigrating the importance of money, I therefore shall, as my first task, stress what monetary policy cannot do. I shall then try to outline what it can do and how it can best make its contribution, in the present state of our knowledge—or ignorance.

I. WHAT MONETARY POLICY CANNOT DO

From the infinite world of negation, I have selected two limitations of monetary policy to discuss: (1) It cannot peg interest rates for more than very limited periods; (2) It cannot peg the rate of unemployment for more than very limited periods. I select these because the contrary has been or is widely believed, because they correspond to the two main unattainable tasks that are at all likely to be assigned to monetary policy, and because essentially the same theoretical analysis covers both.

Pegging of interest rates

History has already persuaded many of you about the first limitation. As noted earlier, the failure of cheap money policies was a major source of the reaction against simple-minded Keynesianism. In the United States, this reaction involved widespread recognition that the wartime and postwar pegging of bond prices was a mistake, that the abandonment of this policy was a desirable and inevitable step, and that it had none of the disturbing and disastrous consequences that were so freely predicted at the time.

The limitation derives from a much misunderstood feature of the relation between money and interest rates. Let the Fed set out to keep interest rates down. How will it try to do so? By buying securities. This raises their prices and lowers their yields. In the process, it also increases the quantity of reserves available to banks, hence the amount of bank credit, and, ultimately the total quantity of money. That is why central bankers in particular, and the financial community more broadly, generally believe that an increase in the quantity of money tends to lower interest rates. Academic economists accept the same conclusion, but for different reasons. They see, in their mind's eye, a negatively sloping liquidity preference schedule. How can people be induced to hold a larger quantity of money? Only by bidding down interest rates.

Both are right, up to a point. The *initial* impact of increasing the quantity of money at a faster rate than it has been increasing is to make interest rates lower for a time than they would otherwise have been. But this is only the beginning of the process not the end. The more rapid rate of monetary growth will stimulate spending, both through the impact on investment of lower market interest rates and through the impact on other spending and thereby relative prices of higher cash balances than are desired. But one man's spending is another man's income. Rising income will raise the liquidity preference schedule and the demand for loans; it may also raise prices, which would reduce the real quantity of money. These three effects will reverse the initial downward pressure on interest rates fairly promptly, say, in something less than a year. Together they will tend, after a somewhat longer interval, say, a year or two, to return interest rates to the level they would otherwise have had. Indeed, given the tendency for the economy to overreact, they are highly likely to raise interest rates temporarily beyond that level, setting in motion a cyclical adjustment process.

A fourth effect, when and if it becomes operative, will go even farther, and definitely mean that a higher rate of monetary expansion will correspond to a higher, not lower, level of interest rates than would otherwise have prevailed. Let the higher rate of monetary growth produce rising prices, and let the public come to expect that prices will continue to rise. Borrowers will then be willing to pay and lenders will then demand higher interest rates—as Irving Fisher pointed out decades ago. This price expectation effect is slow to develop and also slow to disappear. Fisher estimated that it took several decades for a full adjustment and more recent work is consistent with his estimates.

These subsequent effects explain why every attempt to keep interest rates at a low level has forced the monetary authority to engage in successively larger and larger open market purchases. They explain why, historically, high and rising nominal interest rates have been associated with rapid growth in the quantity of money, as in Brazil or Chile or in the United States in recent years, and why low and falling interest rates have been associated with slow growth in the quantity of money, as in Switzerland now or in the United States from 1929 to 1933. As an empirical matter, low interest rates are a sign that monetary policy *has been* tight—in the sense that the quantity of money has grown slowly; high interest rates are a sign that monetary policy *has been* easy—in the sense that the quantity of money has grown rapidly. The broadest facts of experience run in precisely the opposite direction from that which the financial community and academic economists have all generally taken for granted.

Paradoxically, the monetary authority could assure low nominal rates of interest—but to do so it would have to start out in what seems like the opposite direction, by engaging in a deflationary monetary policy. Similarly, it could assure high nominal interest rates by engaging in an inflationary policy and accepting a temporary movement in interest rates in the opposite direction.

These considerations not only explain why monetary policy cannot peg interest rates; they also explain why interest rates are such a misleading indicator of whether monetary policy is "tight" or "easy." For that, it is far better to look at the rate of change of the quantity of money.

Employment as a criterion of policy

The second limitation I wish to discuss goes more against the grain of current thinking. Monetary growth, it is widely held, will tend to stimulate employment; monetary contraction, to retard employment. Why, then, cannot the monetary authority adopt a target for employment or unemployment—say, 3 percent unemployment; be tight when unemployment is less than the target; be easy when unemployment is higher than the target; and in this way peg unemployment at, say, 3 percent? The reason it cannot is precisely the same as for interest rates—the difference between the immediate and the delayed consequences of such a policy.

Thanks to Wicksell, we are all acquainted with the concept of a "natural" rate of interest and the possibility of a discrepancy between the "natural" and the "market" rate. The preceding analysis of interest rates can be translated fairly directly into Wicksellian terms. The monetary authority can make the market rate less than the natural rate only by inflation. It can make the market rate higher than the natural rate only by deflation. We have added only one wrinkle to Wicksell— the Irving Fisher distinction between the nominal and the real rate of interest. Let the monetary authority keep the nominal market rate for a time below the natural rate by inflation. That in turn will raise the nominal natural rate itself, once anticipations of inflation become widespread, thus requiring still more rapid inflation to hold down the market rate. Similarly, because of the Fisher effect, it will require not merely deflation but more and more rapid deflation to hold the market rate above the initial "natural" rate.

This analysis has its close counterpart in the employment market. At any moment of time, there is some level of unemployment which has the property that it is consistent with equilibrium in the structure of *real* wage rates. At that level of unemployment, real wage rates are tending on the average to rise at a "normal" secular rate, i.e., at a rate that can be indefinitely maintained so long as capital formation, technological improvements, etc., remain on their long-run trends. A lower level of unemployment is an indication that there is an excess demand for labor that will produce upward pressure on real wage rates. A higher level of unemployment is an indication that there is an excess supply of labor that will produce downward pressure on real wage rates. The "natural rate of unemployment," in other words, is the level that would be ground out by the Walrasian system of general equilibrium equations, provided there is imbedded in them the actual structural characteristics of the labor and commodity markets, including market imperfections, stochastic variability in demands and supplies, the cost of gathering information about job vacancies and labor availabilities, the costs of mobility, and so on.

You will recognize the close similarity between this statement and the celebrated Phillips Curve. The similarity is not coincidental. Phillips' analysis of the relation between unemployment and wage change is deservedly celebrated as an important and original contribution. But, unfortunately, it contains a basic defect—the failure to distinguish between *nominal* wages and *real* wages—just as Wicksell's analysis failed to distinguish between *nominal* interest rates and *real* interest rates. Implicitly, Phillips wrote his article for a world in which everyone anticipated that nominal prices would be stable and in which that anticipation remained unshaken and immutable whatever happened to actual prices and wages. Suppose, by contrast, that everyone anticipates that prices will rise at a rate of more than 75 percent a year—as, for example, Brazilians did a few years ago. Then wages must rise at that rate simply to keep real wages unchanged. An excess supply of labor will be reflected in a less rapid rise in nominal wages than in anticipated prices, not in an absolute decline in wages. When Brazil embarked on a policy to bring down the rate of price rise, and succeeded in bringing the price rise down to about 45 percent a year, there was a sharp initial rise in unemployment because under the influence of earlier anticipations, wages kept rising at a pace that was higher than the new rate of price rise, though lower than earlier. This is the result experienced, and to be expected, of all attempts to reduce the rate of inflation below that widely anticipated.

To avoid misunderstanding, let me emphasize that by using the term "natural" rate of unemployment, I do not mean to suggest that it is immutable and unchangeable. On the contrary, many of the market characteristics that determine its level are man-made and policy-made. In the United States, for example, legal minimum wage rates, the Walsh-Healy and Davis-Bacon Acts, and the strength of labor unions all make the natural rate of unemployment higher than it would otherwise be. Improvements in employment exchanges, in availability of information about job vacancies and labor supply, and so on, would tend to lower the natural rate of unemployment. I use the term "natural" for the same reason Wicksell did—to try to separate the real forces from monetary forces.

Let us assume that the monetary authority tries to peg the "market" rate of unemployment at a level below the "natural" rate. For definiteness, suppose that it takes 3 percent as the target rate and that the "natural" rate is higher than 3 percent. Suppose also that we start out at a time when prices have been stable and when unemployment is higher than 3 percent. Accordingly, the authority increases the rate of monetary growth. This will be expansionary. By making nominal cash balances higher than people desire, it will tend initially to lower interest rates and in this and other ways to stimulate spending. Income and spending will start to rise.

To begin with, much or most of the rise in income will take the form of an increase in output and employment rather than in prices. People have been expecting prices to be stable, and prices and wages have been set for some time in the future on that basis. It takes time for people to adjust to a new state of demand. Producers will tend to react to the initial expansion in aggregate demand by increasing output, employees by working longer hours, and the unemployed, by taking jobs now offered at former nominal wages. This much is pretty standard doctrine.

But it describes only the initial effects. Because selling prices of products typically respond to an unanticipated rise in nominal demand faster than prices of factors of production, real wages received have gone down—though real wages anticipated by employees went up, since employees implicitly evaluated the wages offered at the earlier price level. Indeed, the simultaneous fall *ex post* in real wages to employers and rise *ex ante* in real wages to employees is what enabled employment to increase. But the decline *ex post* in real wages will soon come to affect anticipations. Employees will start to reckon on rising prices of the things they buy and to demand higher nominal wages for the future. "Market" unemployment is below the "natural" level. There is an excess demand for labor so real wages will tend to rise toward their initial level.

Even though the higher rate of monetary growth continues, the rise in real wages will reverse the decline in unemployment, and then lead to a rise, which will tend to return unemployment to its former level. In order to keep unemployment at its target level of 3 percent, the monetary authority would have to raise monetary growth still more. As in the interest rate case, the "market" rate can be kept below the "natural" rate only by inflation. And, as in the interest rate case, too, only by accelerating inflation. Conversely, let the monetary authority choose a target rate of unemployment that is above the natural rate, and they will be led to produce a deflation, and an accelerating deflation at that.

What if the monetary authority chose the "natural" rate—either of interest or unemployment—as its target? One problem is that it cannot know what the "natural" rate is. Unfortunately, we have as yet devised no method to estimate accurately and readily the natural rate of either interest or unemployment. And the "natural" rate will itself change from time to time. But the basic problem is that even if the monetary authority knew the "natural" rate, and attempted to peg the market rate at that level, it would not be led to a determinate policy. The "market" rate will vary from the natural rate for all sorts of reasons other than monetary policy. If the monetary authority responds to these variations, it will set in train longer term effects that will make any monetary growth path it follows ultimately consistent with the rule of policy. The actual course of monetary growth will be analogous to a random walk, buffeted this way and that by the forces that produce temporary departures of the market rate from the natural rate.

To state this conclusion differently, there is always a temporary trade-off between inflation and unemployment; there is no permanent trade-off. The temporary trade-off comes not from inflation per se, but from unanticipated inflation, which generally means, from a rising rate of inflation. The wide-spread belief that there is a permanent trade-off is a sophisticated version of the confusion between "high" and "rising" that we all recognize in simpler forms. A rising rate of inflation may reduce unemployment, a high rate will not.

But how long, you will say, is "temporary"? For interest rates, we have some systematic evidence on how long each of the several effects takes to work itself out. For unemployment, we do not. I can at most venture a personal judgment, based on some examination of the historical evidence, that the initial effects of a higher and unanticipated rate of inflation last for something like two to five years; that this initial effect then begins to be reversed; and that a full adjustment to the new rate of inflation takes about as long for employment as for interest rates, say, a couple of decades. For both interest rates and employment, let me add a qualification. These estimates are for changes in the rate of inflation of the order of magnitude that has been experienced in the United States. For much more sizable changes, such as those experienced in South American countries, the whole adjustment process is greatly speeded up.

To state the general conclusion still differently, the monetary authority controls nominal quantities—directly, the quantity of its own liabilities. In principle, it can use this control to peg a nominal quantity—an exchange rate, the price level, the nominal level of national income, the quantity of money by one or another definition—or to peg the rate of change in a nominal quantity—the rate of inflation or deflation, the rate of growth or decline in nominal national income, the rate of growth of the quantity of money. It cannot use its control over nominal quantities to peg a real quantity—the real rate of interest, the rate of unemployment, the level of real national income, the real quantity of money, the rate of growth of real national income, or the rate of growth of the real quantity of money.

II. WHAT MONETARY POLICY CAN DO

Monetary policy cannot peg these real magnitudes at predetermined levels. But monetary policy can and does have important effects on these real magnitudes. The one is in no way inconsistent with the other.

My own studies of monetary history have made me extremely sympathetic to the oft-quoted, much reviled, and as widely misunderstood, comment by John Stuart Mill. "There cannot . . . ," he wrote, "be intrinsically a more insignificant thing, in the economy of society, than money; except in the character of a contrivance for sparing time and labour. It is a machine for doing quickly and commodiously, what would be done, though less quickly and commodiously, without it: and like many other kinds of machinery, it only exerts a distinct and independent influence of its own when it gets out of order."

True, money is only a machine, but it is an extraordinarily efficient machine. Without it, we could not have begun to attain the astounding growth in output and level of living we have experienced in the past two centuries—any more than we could have done so without those other marvelous machines that dot our countryside and enable us, for the most part, simply to do more efficiently what could be done without them at much greater cost in labor.

But money has one feature that these other machines do not share. Because it is so pervasive, when it gets out of order, it throws a monkey wrench into the operation of all the other machines. The Great Contraction is the most dramatic example but not the only one. Every other major contraction in this country has been either produced by monetary disorder or greatly exacerbated by monetary disorder. Every major inflation has been produced by monetary expansion—mostly to meet the overriding demands of war which have forced the creation of money to supplement explicit taxation.

The first and most important lesson that history teaches about what monetary policy can do—and it is a lesson of the most profound importance—is that monetary policy can prevent money itself from being a major source of economic disturbance. This sounds like a negative proposition: avoid major mistakes. In part it is. The Great Contraction might not have occurred at all, and if it had, it would have been far less severe, if the monetary authority had avoided mistakes, or if the monetary arrangements had been those of an earlier time when there was no central authority with the power to make the kinds of mistakes that the Federal Reserve System made. The past few years, to come closer to home, would have been steadier and more productive of economic well-being if the Federal Reserve had avoided drastic and erratic changes of direction, first expanding the money supply at an unduly rapid pace, then, in early 1966, stepping on the brake too hard, then, at the end of 1966, reversing itself and resuming expansion until at least November, 1967, at a more rapid pace than can long be maintained without appreciable inflation.

Even if the proposition that monetary policy can prevent money itself from being a major source of economic disturbance were a wholly negative proposition, it would be none the less important for that. As it happens, however, it is not a wholly negative proposition. The monetary machine has gotten out of order even when there has been no central authority with anything like the power now possessed by the Fed. In the United States, the 1907 episode and earlier banking panics are examples of how the monetary machine can get out of order largely on its own. There is therefore a positive and important task for the monetary authority—to suggest improvements in the machine that will reduce the chances that it will get out of order, and to use its own powers so as to keep the machine in good working order.

A second thing monetary policy can do is provide a stable background for the economy—keep the machine well oiled, to continue Mill's analogy. Accomplishing the first task will contribute to this objective, but there is more to it than that. Our economic system will work best when producers and consumers, employers and employees, can proceed with full confidence that the average level of prices will behave in a known way in the future—preferably that it will be highly stable. Under any conceivable institutional arrangements, and certainly under those that now prevail in the United States, there is only a limited amount of flexibility in prices and wages. We need to conserve this flexibility to achieve changes in relative prices and wages that are required to adjust to dynamic changes in tastes and technology. We should not dissipate it simply to achieve changes in the absolute level of prices that serve no economic function.

In an earlier era, the gold standard was relied on to provide confidence in future monetary stability. In its heyday it served that function reasonably well. It clearly no longer does, since there is scarce a country in the world that is prepared to let the gold standard reign unchecked—and there are persuasive reasons why countries should not do so. The monetary authority could operate as a surrogate for the gold standard, if it pegged exchange rates and did so exclusively by altering the quantity of money in response to balance of payment flows without "sterilizing" surpluses or deficits and without resorting to open or concealed exchange control or to changes in tariffs and quotas. But again, though many central bankers talk this way, few are in fact willing to follow this course—and again there are persuasive reasons why they should not do so. Such a policy would submit each country to the vagaries not of an impersonal and automatic gold standard but of the policies—deliberate or accidental—of other monetary authorities.

In today's world, if monetary policy is to provide a stable background for the economy it must do so by deliberately employing its powers to that end. I shall come later to how it can do so.

Finally, monetary policy can contribute to offsetting major disturbances in the economic system arising from other sources. If there is an independent secular exhilaration—as the postwar expansion was described by the proponents of secular stagnation—monetary policy can in principle help to hold it in check by a slower rate of monetary growth than would otherwise be desirable. If, as now, an explosive federal budget threatens unprecedented deficits, monetary policy can hold any inflationary dangers in check by a slower rate of monetary growth than would otherwise be desirable. This will temporarily mean higher interest rates than would otherwise prevail—to enable the government to borrow the sums needed to finance the deficit—but by preventing the speeding up of inflation, it may well mean both lower prices and lower nominal interest rates for the long pull. If the end of a substantial war offers the country an opportunity to shift resources from wartime to peacetime production, monetary policy can ease the transition by a higher rate of monetary growth than would otherwise be desirable—though experience is not very encouraging that it can do so without going too far.

I have put this point last, and stated it in qualified terms—as referring to major disturbances—because I believe that the potentiality of monetary policy in offsetting other forces making for instability is far more limited than is commonly believed. We simply do not know enough to be able to recognize minor disturbances when they occur or to be able to predict either what their effects will be with any precision or what monetary policy is required to offset their effects. We do not know enough to be able to achieve stated objectives by delicate, or even fairly coarse, changes in the mix of monetary and fiscal policy. In this area particularly the best is likely to be the enemy of the good. Experience suggests that the path of wisdom is to use monetary policy explicitly to offset other disturbances only when they offer a "clear and present danger."

III. HOW SHOULD MONETARY POLICY BE CONDUCTED?

How should monetary policy be conducted to make the contribution to our goals that it is capable of making? This is clearly not the occasion for presenting a detailed "Program for Monetary Stability"—to use the title of a book in which I tried to do so. I shall restrict myself here to two major requirements for monetary policy that follow fairly directly from the preceding discussion.

The first requirement is that the monetary authority should guide itself by magnitudes that it can control, not by ones that it cannot control. If, as the authority has often done, it takes interest rates or the current unemployment percentage as the immediate criterion of policy, it will be like a space vehicle that has taken a fix on the wrong star. No matter how sensitive and sophisticated its guiding apparatus, the space vehicle will go astray. And so will the monetary authority. Of the various alternative magnitudes that it can control, the most appealing guides for policy are exchange rates, the price level as defined by some index, and the quantity of a monetary total— currency plus adjusted demand deposits, or this total plus commercial bank time deposits, or a still broader total.

For the United States in particular, exchange rates are an undesirable guide. It might be worth requiring the bulk of the economy to adjust to the tiny percentage consisting of foreign trade if that would guarantee freedom from monetary irresponsibility—as it might under a real gold standard. But it is hardly worth doing so simply to adapt to the average of whatever policies monetary authorities in the rest of the world adopt. Far better to let the market, through floating exchange rates, adjust to world conditions the 5 percent or so of our resources devoted to international trade while reserving monetary policy to promote the effective use of the 95 percent.

Of the three guides listed, the price level is clearly the most important in its own right. Other things the same, it would be much the best of the alternatives—as so many distinguished economists have urged in the past. But other things are not the same. The link between the policy actions of the monetary authority and the price level, while unquestionably present, is more indirect than the link between the policy actions of the authority and any of the several monetary totals. Moreover, monetary action takes a longer time to affect the price level than to affect the monetary totals and both the time lag and the magnitude of effect vary with circumstances. As a result, we cannot predict at all accurately just what effect a particular monetary action will have on the price level and, equally important, just when it will have that effect. Attempting to control directly the price level is therefore likely to make monetary policy itself a source of economic disturbance because of false stops and starts. Perhaps, as our understanding of monetary phenomena advances, the situation will change. But at the present stage of our understanding, the long way around seems the surer way to our objective. Accordingly, I believe that a monetary total is the best currently available immediate guide or criterion for monetary policy—and I believe that it matters much less which particular total is chosen than that one be chosen.

A second requirement for monetary policy is that the monetary authority avoid sharp swings in policy. In the past, monetary authorities have on occasion moved in the wrong direction—as in the episode of the Great Contraction that I have stressed. More frequently, they have moved in the right direction, albeit often too late, but have erred by moving too far. Too late and too much has been the general practice. For example, in early 1966, it was the right policy for the Federal Reserve to move in a less expansionary direction—though it should have done so at least a year earlier. But when it moved, it went too far, producing the sharpest change in the rate of monetary growth of the postwar era. Again, having gone too far, it was the right policy for the Fed to reverse course at the end of 1966. But again it went too far, not only restoring but exceeding the earlier excessive rate of monetary growth. And this episode is no exception. Time and again this has been the course followed—as in 1919 and 1920, in 1937 and 1938, in 1953 and 1954, in 1959 and 1960.

The reason for the propensity to overreact seems clear: the failure of monetary authorities to allow for the delay between their actions and the subsequent effects on the economy. They tend to determine their actions by today's conditions—but their actions will affect the economy only six or nine or twelve or fifteen months later. Hence they feel impelled to step on the brake, or the accelerator, as the case may be, too hard.

My own prescription is still that the monetary authority go all the way in avoiding such swings by adopting publicly the policy of achieving a steady rate of growth in a specified monetary total. The precise rate of growth, like the precise monetary total, is less important than the adoption of some stated and known rate. I myself have argued for a rate that would on the average achieve rough stability in the level of prices of final products, which I have estimated would call for something like a 3 to 5 percent per year rate of growth in currency plus all commercial bank deposits or a slightly lower rate of growth in currency plus demand deposits only. But it would be better to have a fixed rate that would on the average produce moderate inflation or moderate deflation, provided it was steady, than to suffer the wide and erratic perturbations we have experienced.

Short of the adoption of such a publicly stated policy of a steady rate of monetary growth, it would constitute a major improvement if the monetary authority followed the self-denying ordinance of avoiding wide swings. It is a matter of record that periods of relative stability in the rate of monetary growth have also been periods of relative stability in economic activity, both in the United States and other countries. Periods of wide swings in the rate of monetary growth have also been periods of wide swings in economic activity.

By setting itself a steady course and keeping to it, the monetary authority could make a major contribution to promoting economic stability. By making that course one of steady but moderate growth in the quantity of money, it would make a major contribution to avoidance of either inflation or deflation of prices. Other forces would still affect the economy, require change and adjustment, and disturb the even tenor of our ways. But steady monetary growth would provide a monetary climate favorable to the effective operation of those basic forces of enterprise, ingenuity, invention, hard work, and thrift that are the true springs of economic growth. That is the most that we can ask from monetary policy at our present stage of knowledge. But that much—and it is a great deal—is clearly within our reach.

5 Monetarism re-evaluated*

PAUL A. SAMUELSON

There are fashions within science. Nowhere is the oscillating pendulum of opinion more marked in the field of economics than in the area of money. By the end of the 1930s, after the so-called Keynesian revolution, courses and textbooks continued to be devoted to money. But in fact money had almost completely dropped out of them and the emphasis had shifted to analysis of income determination in terms of such Keynesian concepts as the multiplier and the propensity to consume.

If the market quotation for monetary theory sagged in the decade after 1936, by the early 1950s there were unmistakable signs of a comeback. It was Professor Howard S. Ellis of the University of California who coined in those years the expression, "the rediscovery of money." And the famous Accord of 1951, which gave back to the Federal Reserve its freedom to pursue an autonomous monetary policy independently of the needs and desires of President Truman's Treasury, was the objective counterpart of the reappearance of money in the theoretical models of academic scholars.

FRIEDMAN AND THE CHICAGO SCHOOL

Undoubtedly the popularity of monetarism can be traced in large part to one man, namely Professor Milton Friedman of the University of Chicago. His monumental *Monetary History of the United States, 1867–1960*, written with Mrs. Anna Schwartz, is the bible of the movement; and let me say as an infidel that it is a classic source of data and analysis to which all scholars will turn for years to come. In addition to this scholarly work, Professor Friedman has published numerous statistical studies in learned economic journals. He has testified before Congress and lectured before lay groups. His influential columns in *Newsweek* and writings for the financial press have hammered away at one simple message:

---

* From "Monetarism Re-evaluated," *Monetarism No.* Copyright Paul A. Samuelson, 1971. Reprinted with permission of author. Paul A. Samuelson is Professor of Economics at Massachusetts Institute of Technology, Cambridge, Mass.

It is the rate of growth of the money supply that is the prime determinant of the state of aggregate dollar demand. If the Federal Reserve will keep the money supply growing at a steady rate—say 4 to 5 percent by one or another definition of the money supply, but the fact of steadiness being more important than the rate agreed upon—then it will be doing all a central bank can usefully do to cope with the problems of inflation, unemployment, and business instability.

Fiscal policy as such has no independent, systematic effect upon aggregate dollar demand. Increasing tax rates, but with the understanding that money growth remains unchanged, *will have no effect* in lessening the degree of inflation; it will have no *independent effect* in increasing the level of unemployment in a period of deflation; changes in public expenditure out of the budget (it being understood that the rate of growth of the money supply is held unchanged) will also have *no lasting effects on inflationary or deflationary gaps.*

In the past, budgetary deficits and budgetary surpluses have often been accompanied by central bank creation of new money or deceleration of growth of new money. Therefore, many people have wrongly inferred that fiscal deficits and surpluses have *predictable* expansionary and contracting effects upon the total of aggregate spending. But this is a complete confusion. *It is the changes in the rate of growth of the money supply which alone have substantive effects.* After we have controlled or allowed for monetary changes, fiscal policy has negligible independent potency.[1]

This is my summary of the Friedman-type monetarism. No doubt he would word things somewhat differently. And I should like to emphasize that there are many qualifications in his scientific writing which do not logically entail the *simpliste* version of monetarism outlined above. Indeed it is one of the purposes of this article to demonstrate and emphasize the point that the weight of the evidence on money, theoretical and empirical, does not imply the correctness of crude monetarism.

Among the central bankers of the world, financial journalists, statesmen and politicians, business and academic economists, and men of affairs generally, monetarism seems almost paradoxically simple and perverse. Can President Nixon really suppose that it makes no difference for the control of the 1969–70 American inflation, whether or not he proposes to extend into 1970 the tax surcharge? Professor Friedman is but one of his advisers, and it is evident that Paul McCracken, Chairman of the Council of Economic Advisers, and Arthur F. Burns, the new chairman of the Federal

---

[1] Professor Friedman is careful to specify that fiscal policy does have important effects upon the *composition* of any given total of gross national product. Thus increases in government expenditures will pull resources out of the private sector into the public. John Kenneth Galbraith might like this but Milton Friedman does not. Also, increasing taxation relative to public expenditure, although having no independent effect on aggregate demand, will tend to lower consumption and reduce interest rates. This contrived increase in thriftiness will move the mix of full-employment output in the direction of more rapid capital formation; it will speed up the rate of growth of productivity and real output, and will increase the rate of growth of real wages. If the trend of the money supply remains unchanged, this will tend toward a lower price level in the future or a less rapidly rising one.

Reserve Board named by Nixon, do *not* see eye to eye with Friedman in this matter.

Yet Professor Friedman does not stand alone. His mountains of data, cogency of reasoning, and formidable powers of patient persuasion have raised unto him a host of followers. Graduates of the Chicago workshops in monetary theory carry to new universities the message. A number of other scholars, such as Professors Allan Meltzer at Carnegie-Mellon University in Pittsburgh and Karl Brunner of Ohio State University, have also produced research in support of monetarism. Professor Harry Johnson leads the campaign to export monetarism to the British Isles. One of our twelve regional Federal Reserve Banks, that of St. Louis, has carried the torch for monetarism, providing up-to-date numerical information on the vagaries of the money supply, and promoting quantitative research on the lagged potency of money. Distinguished graduates of the University of Chicago, such as Dr. Beryl Sprinkel of the Harris Trust Company Bank in Chicago, and Dr. James Meigs, of the First National City Bank of New York, profess to be monetarists who improve the accuracy of their business forecasts by concentrating primarily on money. At one time or another the editorial pages of the influential *Washington Post* and *New York Times* have become permeated by monetarism. Finally, the Joint Economic Committee of Congress, when it was under the chairmanship of Senator William Proxmire, reacted strongly against the use of fiscal policy as a stabilization device, and recommended to the Federal Reserve Board that it never permit the money supply to grow at rates widely different from some agreed-upon constant.

KEYNESIAN ECONOMICS

Thus monetarism is a movement to reckon with. I believe monetarism could be deemed fruitful, to the degree that it has pushed economists away from a *simpliste* Keynesian model, popular in the United States during the Great Depression and still lingering on in Britain, and made economists more willing to recognize that monetary policy is an important stabilization weapon, fully coordinate with fiscal policy as a macroeconomic control instrument. However, my reading of the development of modern economic doctrine does not suggest to me that the post-Keynesian position that I myself hold, and of which Professor James Tobin of Yale and Franco Modigliani of M.I.T. are leading exponents, has been materially influenced by monetarism. Indeed, speaking for myself, the excessive claims for money as an exclusive determinant of aggregate demand would, if anything, have slowed down and delayed my appreciation of money's true quantitative and qualitative role.

Although the neglect of money is often said to be a characteristic of Keynesian economists and a heritage of the analysis in Keynes' 1936 classic

General Theory of Employment, Interest and Money, it is doubtful that Keynes himself can be properly described as ever having believed that "money does not matter." If one writes down in the form of equations or graphs the bony structure of the *General Theory,* he sees that money enters into the liquidity-preference function in such a way that an increase in the money supply lowers interest rates, thereby inducing an increase in investment, and through multiplier mechanism causes a rise in employment and production, or, if employment is already full and output at capacity levels, causes upward pressure on the price level.

How is it that some Keynesians should ever have become identified with the doctrine that money does not matter? Most converts to Keynesianism became converts during the slump years of the late 1930s. Then the deep-depression polar case did seem to be the realistic case. It is a sad fact about many scholars that they learn and unlearn nothing after the age of 29, so that there exist in chairs of economics around the world many economists who still live mentally in the year 1938. For 1938, when the interest rate on Treasury Bills was often a fraction of a fraction of a percent, even a monetarist might despair of the potency of central bank monetary policy.

HOW IT WORKS

By the 1950s and 1960s a body of analysis and data had been accumulated which led to a positive, strong belief that open-market and discount operations by the central bank could have *pronounced macroeconomic effects upon investment and consumption spending in the succeeding several months and quarters.* One of the principal preoccupations of the post-Keynesian economists, which is to say of the ruling orthodoxy of American establishment economics, has been to trace out the *causal* mechanisms whereby monetary and fiscal variables produce their effects upon the total of spending and its composition.

Thus, an open-market purchase of Treasury bills by the Fed first bids up bond prices and lowers their yields; this spreads to *a reduction* in *yields* on competing securities, such as longer-term government bonds or corporate bonds or home mortgages. The lowering of interest costs will typically be accompanied by *a relaxation in the degree of credit rationing,* and this can be expected to *stimulate investment spending* that would otherwise not have taken place. The lowering of interest rates generally also brings about an *upward capitalization of the value of existing assets,* and this increase in the money value of wealth can be expected to have a certain *expansionary influence on consumer spending,* and in a degree on business spending for investment. As a limit upon the stimulus stemming from money creation by orthodox open-market operations, must be reckoned the fact that as the central bank pumps new money into the system, it is in return taking from the system *an almost equal quantum of money substitutes* in the form of government securities. In a sense the Federal Reserve or the Bank of England is merely a dealer in second-hand assets, contriving transfer exchanges of one type of asset for another, and in the process affecting the interest rate structure that constitutes the terms of trade among them.

What needs to be stressed is the fact that one cannot expect money created by this process of central-bank open-market operations *alone,* with say the fiscal budget held always in balance, to have at all the same functional relationship to the level of the GNP and of the price index that could be the case for money created by gold mining or money created by the printing press of national governments or the Fed and used to finance public expenditures in excess of tax receipts. Not only would the creation of these last kinds of money involve a flow of production and spendable income in their very *act of being born,* but in addition the community would be *left permanently richer* in its ownership of monetary wealth. In money terms the community *feels* richer, in money terms the community *is* richer. And this can be expected to reflect itself in a higher price level or a lower rate of unemployment or both.

By contrast, money created through conventional central-bank operations quite divorced from the financing of fiscal deficits or the production of mining output does not entail an equivalent permanent increase in net wealth as viewed by people in the community. Post-Keynesians emphasize that extinguishing the outstanding interest-bearing public debt, whether by a capital levy or by open-market purchase of it, does rationally make the community *feel poorer* than would be the case if the same amount of money existed and the public debt had been unreduced. All men are mortal. Most men do not concern themselves with the wellbeing of their remote posterity. Hence, government bonds as an asset are not completely offset in their minds by the recognition of the liability of paying in perpetuity taxes to carry the interest on those bonds. Only if people live forever, foreseeing correctly the tax payments they (or the posterity as dear to them in the most remote future as is their own lifetime wellbeing) must make on account of the perpetual future interest payments on government bonds— only then would it be true to say that retirement of public debt would have no substantive effects upon the reckoning of wealth, the levels of spending, and the level of prices generally. Rejecting such a perpetual-life model as extreme and unrealistic, we must debit against an increase in money through open-market operations a partial offset in the form of retirement of some of the outstanding public debt.

Finally, to clarify the significant difference between the post-Keynesian analysis which most modern economists believe to be plausible as against the tenets of monetarism, I must point out that even when the money supply is held constant:

1. Any significant changes in thriftiness and the propensity to consume can be expected to have systematic independent effects on the money value

of current output, affecting average prices or aggregate production or both.

2. Likewise an exogenous burst of investment opportunities or animal spirits on the part of business can be expected to have systematic effects on total GNP.

3. Increases in public expenditure, or reductions in tax rates—and even increases in public expenditure balanced by increases in taxation—can be expected to have systematic effects upon aggregate GNP.

All these tenets of the modern eclectic position are quite incompatible with monetarism. (Indeed that is the differentiating definition by which we distinguish the Chicago School monetarism from the post-Keynesian positions with which it has so much overlap.) The eclectic position is incompatible with monetarism, but it is not incompatible with a *sophisticated* version of the Quantity Theory of Money. For as soon as one follows the logic of neoclassical analysis (expecting that less of any kind of inventory will be held if, other things equal, the cost of holding it has gone up) and postulates that the *velocity of circulation of money is a rising function of the interest rate,* the post-Keynesian (and even the simple Keynesian) model becomes compatible with the Quantity Theory. One way of looking at Keynesian liquidity preference is as *a theory of the velocity of circulation.*

FAULTY LOGIC

When post-Keynesians study recent economic history, they find that interest rates and money do enter into their estimating equations and with the theoretically expected algebraic signs. Case studies bear out the importance for investment decisions of the cost and availability of credit. Properly phrased questionnaires to business elicit answers that point in the same direction. And plausible theories to explain how businessmen make their investment decisions and how they ought to also bear out the fact that monetary policy does matter. So there is simply no excuse for living in a 1938 dream world in which money does not matter.

The bearing of all this on monetarism is well illustrated by an incident a few years ago at an American Bankers Association symposium where leading academic economists were commenting upon Professor Friedman's writings. Professor James Tobin went to the blackboard and wrote down three sentences:

1. Money does not matter.
2. Money matters.
3. Money alone matters.

He went on to say: "Professor Friedman produces evidence to prove that the first proposition, Money doesn't matter, is false: he purports to have demonstrated from this that the third proposition, Money alone matters, is true; whereas the correct logical conclusion is that the second proposition,

Money does matter, is all that follows. And on that there is no quarrel among leading modern macroeconomic economists."

I think there is much wisdom in this. When Professor Friedman defends monetarism, as for example in a late-1968 debate at New York University with new economist Walter Heller, he refers to a mountain of evidence that supports monetarism. But how many members of the thousands in the overflow crowd attending that debate were able to appraise that evidence to see whether it supports the proposition 2, that money matters, rather than the central tenet of monetarism, that (when it comes to predictable systematic effects on aggregate demand and on inflationary or deflationary gaps) money alone matters? Sir Ronald Fisher, the greatest statistician of our age, pointed out that replication a thousandfold of an inconclusive experiment does nothing to add to its value. In terms of the language of statistics, most of the evidence compiled about money has little or no power to differentiate between propositions 2 and 3.

What does a monetarist do when confronted with the fact that his causal factor, money, does not empirically lead his response factor, general business? One desperate artifice is to change his focus from the *stock* of money to its *time derivative*, its *rate of growth*. It is a mathematical fact that any periodic fluctuation that behaves a bit like a sine curve will have its derivative turndown a quarter cycle before itself; so if money itself does not lag business by as much as one quarter, one cannot help but get some lead at turning points by using the rate of change of money. But by that kind of frivolous action, one could use the derivative of production, its rate of change, to predict the turning points of the stock of money: or, with recognition of noise in the data, use production's own rate of change to predict its turning points.

Dimensional traps.   Obviously, we have to find the reason for using dM/dt, the rate of change of money, rather than M, the stock of money, as our causal variable. One ridiculous argument for using the former is dimensional: both the level of GNP and the rate of growth of the money supply are measured in terms of dollars *per year*. Therefore, relate GNP and dM/dt, not GNP and M. This argument is ridiculous because the whole basis of the quantity theory of money is that V, the velocity of circulation of money or its reciprocal, is the dimensional constant that exists to relate the stock of money and the flow of national product. Professor Friedman, more than any other modern economist, has sloshed through the mountains of Yugoslavia to demonstrate that every peasant holds seventeen-weeks purchasing power in his pockets. The whole demand-for-money concept is for the purpose of making hypotheses about how that number 17 will change when interest rates, branch banking, or price expectations change. Moreover, there is involved a profound misunderstanding of how dimensional analysis is to be used in any science. The behavioral equation of a simple pendulum has for its very purpose the relating of two dimensionally different magnitudes—the position of the pendulum as measured in centimeters or dimensionless angular degrees and its acceleration as measured in centimeters per time squared. Nor is this a special example: Newton's universal law of gravitation, the greatest system of the world produced by man's thoughts, relates dimensionally different magnitudes in precisely the way that Dr. Friedman criticizes.

CRUCIAL TESTS IN 1966–1967 AND 1968–1969

Personally, as a scientist, I would cheerfully accept *any hypothesis that would deliver the goods and explain the facts.* As a fallible human being, I do not relish having to change my mind but if economists had to hang from the ceiling in order to do their job, then there would be nothing for it than to do so. But monetarism does not deliver the goods. I could make a fortune giving good predictions to large corporations and banks based on monetarism if it would work. But I have tried every version of it. And none do.

To this there are two standard answers. The first is that nothing works well. Fine tuning is an illusion. There is much "noise" in the data. No one can claim that monetarism would enable the Federal Reserve to iron out all the variation in the economy. All we can say for it is that stabilizing the growth rate of money is the best policy that the ingenuity of man can ever arrive at. All this involves what I call the chipmunk syndrome. The nimble monetarist sticks his neck out in an occasional prediction: that prediction is not always free of ambiguity, but it does seem to point qualitatively in one direction, often a direction counter to the conventional wisdom of the moment: then if subsequent events do seem to go in the indicated direction, the prediction is trumpeted to be a feather in the cap of monetarism. If, as is happening all the time, events do not particularly go in that direction—or if as happens often, events go somewhat in a direction that neither competing theory has been subjected to a test of any resolving power—the chipmunk pulls in his head, saying that there is no way of fine tuning the economy or making completely accurate predictions.

The other argument against the view that monetarism simply does not work is the assertion, "Monetarism does work. So and so at the Blank bank uses it and he beats the crowd in batting average." I believe this to be a serious and important subject for investigation. Let me therefore, because of space limitations, confine myself to a few observations based upon preliminary investigations of the matter.

1. Those analysts who use their monetarism *neat* really do *not* perform well.

2. A number of bank economists, who give great weight to the money factor but who *also* pay attention to what is happening to defense spending and inventories and a host of other factors, seem to me to have compiled

an excellent record at forecasting. Not a perfect record. Who has a perfect record? And not, as far as quantitative studies known to me suggest, a better record than the best macroeconomic forecasters who do not consciously put special stress on the money factor (but who do not neglect it either!). In short, it is impossible to separate "flair" in forecasting from success attributable primarily to use of money-supply variables.

3. The years 1966–67 are often referred to as years of a crucial test in which monetarism defeated Keynesianism. I have gone over all the main forecasts used by both schools during that period and I must report that this is a misapprehension. There was *wide range* of forecasts by practitioners of both schools: there was a *wide overlap* between these two ranges. On the whole, the monetarists averaged better and *earlier* in their perception of the slowdown beginning to be seen in late 1966 in consequence of the money crunch of 1966. And one would expect this to be the case from an eclectic viewpoint since the independent variable of money received the biggest alteration in *that* period. But many of the monetarists went overboard in predicting a recession in 1967 of the National Bureau type: indeed some of the more astute monetarists warned their brethren against following the logic of the method, lest it discredit the method! And some of the largest squared errors of estimate for 1967 that I have in my files came from dogmatic monetarists who did not heed the warning from inside their own camp.

4. Again, the year 1969 is thought by some to provide a test of some power between the two theories. Yet I, who am an eclectic, have my own GNP forecast for the year nicely bracketed by the two banks that have been most successful in the past in using monetarism in their projections. And though I must admit that the last part of 1968 was stronger than those who believe in the potency of fiscal policy and the mid-1969 tax surcharge to be, I do not interpret that extra strength as being a negation of any such potency or as due solely or primarily to the behavior of money during the last 12 months. Without the tax surcharge, I believe the GNP would have surprised us by soaring even faster above predictions. Since history cannot be rerun to perform controlled experiments, I cannot prove this. But the weight of all the evidence known to me does point in this direction. In a soft science like economics, that is all even the best practitioner can say.

CONCLUSION

The bulk of my remarks have been critical of an overly simple doctrine of monetarism. But they must not be interpreted as supporting the view that money does not matter. There are parts of the world, particularly in Britain and the Commonwealth, where it might be better to believe in overly simply monetarism than in overly simple denial of the role of money.

In the *Sunday Telegraph* (London, December 15, 1968) I was able to invert the Tobin syllogisms to isolate the fatal flaw in the reasoning of the Radcliffe Report. The Radcliffe Committee heard much convincing testimony to show that there existed no invariable velocity of circulation of money to enable one to predict GNP accurately from the money supply alone. In effect then, Radcliffe established the falsity of Tobin's third proposition, Money alone matters. And, in a *nonsequitur*, they concluded the truth of his first proposition, that Money does not matter. For all their talking around the subject of liquidity as a substitute concept for money alone, they and the fossil-Keynesians who hailed their report should have recognized the fact that both theory and experience give to money (along with fiscal and other variables) an important role in the macroeconomic scenario of modern times.

C. New dimensions of fiscal policy

The "eclectic post-Keynesian" policies, to which Samuelson alluded in his criticism of Friedman's monetarism, are neatly outlined in Okun's essay. Notice that his recommended rules for monetary policy are almost diametrically opposed to Friedman's. He would use "middle of the road" monetary policy to stabilize interest rates rather than the money supply. Frequent and active monetary "fine tuning" would compensate for more sluggish fiscal decision making. He would give the major burden for offsetting major disruptions to fiscal policy actions whereas Friedman would reserve monetary action for that purpose. Okun prefers "activist" policies and sees little evidence to support Friedman's fear of destabilizing over-reactions.

Okun rejects cyclical shifts in public works and other government spending or transfer programs as a major budgetary stabilizer, believing that the adjustment lags are too great and that such programs ought to be shaped by long-run social priorities rather than short-run cyclical responses. He relies mainly on quick and frequent shifts in income tax rates for his fiscal action. Monetarists and other critics have emphasized the political uncertainties for such tax changes, and have also questioned whether consumers would adjust their spending in response to frequent small and temporary tax shifts.

Okun praises President Nixon for using the full employment budget, rather than the current budget, as a measure of fiscal impact on GNP; but he objects to Nixon's efforts to sanctify a full employment budget surplus as a criterion of "sound" fiscal policy. He also sharply criticizes Nixon and his Federal Reserve cohorts for "underreacting" to the recession of 1970.

Okun's assessment of the Nixon program should provide the reader with one bit of evidence to judge Ulmer's contention that Democrats and Republicans have adopted the same basic stabilization programs. His assertion that these bipartisan Keynesian policies have resulted only in an ineffective "seesaw of instability," oscillating between excess unemployment and inflation, should be compared with the "Phillips curve" analysis of Reading 1. Note also that Ulmer's proposed solution—a large program of public works and government job creation differs sharply with Okun's recommendations for fiscal stabilization. Try to identify the differing social and political goals, as well as the differing economic analyses which underlie these alternative strategies.

6 Rules and roles for fiscal and monetary policy*

ARTHUR M. OKUN

When economists write textbooks or teach introductory students or lecture to laymen, they happily extol the virtues of two lovely handmaidens of aggregate economic stabilization—fiscal policy and monetary policy. But when they write for learned journals or assemble for professional meetings, they often insist on staging a beauty contest between the two. And each judge feels somehow obliged to decide that one of the two entries is just an ugly beast. My remarks tonight are in the spirit of bigamous devotion rather than invidious comparison. Fiscal policy and monetary policy are both beautiful; we need them both and we should treat them both lovingly.

THE GENERAL ECLECTIC CASE

In particular, both fiscal and monetary policy are capable of providing some extra push upward or downward on GNP. In fact, if aggregate stimulus or restraint were all that mattered, either one of the two tools could generally do the job, and the second—whichever one chose to be second—would be redundant. The basic general eclectic principle that ought to guide us, as a first approximation, is that either fiscal or monetary policy can administer a required sedative or stimulus to economic activity. As every introductory student knows, however, fiscal and monetary tools operate in very different ways. Monetary policy initially makes people more liquid without adding directly to their incomes or wealth; fiscal policy enhances their incomes and wealth without increasing their liquidity.

In a stimulative monetary action, the people who initially acquire money are not simply given the money; they must part with government securities to get it. But once their portfolios become more liquid, they pre-

* From "Rules and Roles for Fiscal and Monetary Policy," *Issues in Fiscal and Monetary Policy*, Chicago: DePaul Press, 1971, pp. 51–71. Reprinted with permission of author and publisher. Arthur M. Okun is Senior Fellow at the Brookings Institution, Washington, D.C.

sumably use the cash proceeds to acquire alternative earning assets, and in so doing they bid up the prices of those assets, or equivalently, reduce the yields. Thus prospective borrowers find it easier and less expensive to issue securities and to get loans; and investors who would otherwise be acquiring securities may be induced instead to purchase real assets such as capital goods. Also, because market values of securities are raised, people become wealthier, if in an indirect way, and may hence increase their purchases of goods and services. Thus many channels run from the easing of financial markets to the quickening of real economic activity.

A stimulative fiscal action is appropriately undertaken when resources are unemployed; in that situation, an action such as expanded government purchases, whether for good things like hospitals or less good things like military weapons, puts resources to work and rewards them with income. The additional cash received by some people is matched by reduced cash holdings of those who bought government securities to finance the outlay. But the securities buyers have no income loss to make them tighten their belts; they voluntarily traded money for near money. In contrast, the income recipients become willing to spend more, and thus trigger a multiplier process on production and income. So, while fiscal and monetary routes differ, the ultimate destination—the effect on national product—is the same, in principle.

Indeed, the conditions under which either fiscal tools or monetary tools, taken separately, have zero effect on GNP are merely textbook curiosities rather than meaningful possibilities in the modern U.S. economic environment. For stimulative monetary policy to be nothing more than a push on a string, either interest rates would have to be just as low as they could possibly go, or investment and consumption would have to show zero response to any further reduction in interest rates. The former possibility is the famous Keynesian liquidity trap, which made lots of sense in describing 1936, but has no relevance to 1971. With prime corporations paying 8 percent on long-term bonds, interest rates are still higher than at any time in my lifetime prior to 1969. There is plenty of room for them to decline, and, in turn, for states and localities, homebuyers and consumer installment credit users, as well as business investors, to be encouraged to spend more by lower costs of credit.

The opposite extreme, impotent fiscal policy, is equally remote. Fiscal policy must exert some stimulative effect on economic activity (even when the monetary policy makers do not accommodate the fiscal action at all) unless the velocity of money is completely inflexible so that no economizing on cash balances occurs. Though the money supply does not rise in a pure fiscal action, spending will tend to rise unless people are totally unable or unwilling to speed up the turnover of cash. And money holders do economize on cash to a varying degree—they do so seasonally and cyclically, and they do so dependably in response to changes in the opportunity cost of holding money. The holder of zero-yielding cash is sacrificing the opportunity to receive the going interest rates of earning assets. The higher interest rates are, the more he sacrifices; and hence, economic theory tells us, the more he will economize on his holdings of cash.

And the facts confirm the theory. The negative relationship between the demand for money and the rate of interest is one of the most firmly established empirical propositions in macroeconomics. So a pure fiscal stimulus produces a speedup in the turnover of money and higher interest rates, and more GNP.

The fact that people do economize on cash balances in response to rises in interest rates demonstrates the efficacy of fiscal policy. Anybody who reports that he can't find a trace of fiscal impact in the aggregate data is unreasonably claiming an absolutely inflexible velocity of money—a vertical liquidity preference function—or else he is revealing the limitations of his research techniques rather than those of fiscal policy.

A few other artful dodges, I submit, make even less sense. Try to defend fiscal impotence on grounds of a horizontal marginal efficiency schedule— that means investment is so sensitive to return that even the slightest interest variation will unleash unlimited changes in investment demand. Or make the case that people subjectively assume the public debt as personal debt and feel commensurately worse off whenever the budget is in deficit. Or contend that businessmen are so frightened by fiscal stimulation that their increased demand for cash and reduced investment spoils its influence. Or use the argument that Say's law operates even when the unemployment rate is 6 percent. It's a battle between ingenuity and credulity!

The eclectic principle is terribly important, not because it answers any questions, but because it rules out nonsense questions and points to sensible ones. It warns us not to get bogged down in such metaphysical issues as whether it is really the Fed that creates inflation during wartime. Every wartime period has been marked by enormous fiscal stimulus, and yet that fiscal fuel-injection could have been neutralized by some huge amount of pressure on the monetary brakes. In that sense, the Fed could have been sufficiently restrictive to offset the stimulus of military expenditures. Anyone who chooses to blame the resulting inflation on not slamming on the monetary brakes, rather than on pumping the fiscal accelerator, can feel free to exercise that curious preference. Take another example: Did the expansion following the tax cut in 1964–65 result from monetary policy? Of course it did, the eclectic principle tells us. If the Fed had wished to nullify the expansionary influence of the tax cut, surely some monetary policy would have been sufficiently restrictive to do so. There is no unique way of allocating credit or blame in a world where both tools can do the stabilization job.

SIDE EFFECTS AS THE CENTRAL ISSUE

So long as both tools are capable of speeding up or slowing down demand, the decisions on how to use them and how to combine them must be made on the basis of criteria other than their simple ability to stimulate or restrain. Nor do we typically get any help by considering *how much* work monetary or fiscal tools do, because usually the right answer is, "as much as needed," providing the shift in policy is large enough. In more formal terms, two instruments and one target produce an indeterminate system.

Of course, there are two basic targets of stabilization policy: price stability and maximum production. But the two tools will not serve to implement those two goals simultaneously. A pen and a pencil are one more tool than is needed to write a letter, but the second tool can't be used to mow the lawn. In the same way, fiscal and monetary policy can both push up aggregate demand or push down aggregate demand, but neither can solve the Phillips curve problem. Subject to minor qualifications, the fiscal route to a given unemployment rate is neither less nor more inflationary than the monetary route to that same unemployment rate.

We can have the GNP path we want equally well with a tight fiscal policy and an easier monetary policy, or the reverse, within fairly broad limits. The real basis for choice lies in the many subsidiary economic targets, beside real GNP and inflation, that are differentially affected by fiscal and monetary policies. Sometimes these are labeled "side effects." I submit that they are the main issue in determining the fiscal-monetary mix, and they belong in the center ring.

Composition of output. One of the subsidiary targets involves the composition of output among sectors. General monetary policy tools, as they are actually employed, bear down very unevenly on the various sectors of the economy. Homebuilding and state and local capital projects are principal victims of monetary restraint. Although the evidence isn't entirely conclusive, it suggests that monetary restraint discriminates particularly against small business. In the field of taxation, we agonize about incidence and equity. The same intense concern is appropriate in the case of monetary restraint and, in fact, increasing concern is being registered in the political arena. In the 1969–70 period of tight money, many efforts (such as Home Loan Bank and Fannie Mae operations) were made to insulate housing from the brunt of the attack. But the impact on homebuilding was still heavy. Moreover, there is considerable basis for suspicion that these actions defused—as well as diffused—the impact of monetary restraint. A more restrictive monetary policy, as measured in terms of either monetary aggregates or interest rates, is required to accomplish the same dampening effect on GNP if the sectors most vulnerable to credit restraint are shielded from its blows.

The concern about uneven impact may be accentuated because, in 1966 and again in 1969–70, monetary restraint hit sectors that rated particularly high social priorities. But that is not the whole story. Any unusual departure of monetary policy from a "middle-of-the-road" position may lead to allocations that do not accord with the nation's sense of equity and efficiency. For example, in the early sixties, it was feared that a very easy monetary policy might encourage speculative excesses in building because some financial institutions would be pressured to find mortgage loans in order to earn a return on their assets.

In the last few years, some economists—most notably, Franco Modigliani —have argued that monetary policy may have a significant impact on consumption through its influence on the market value of equity securities and bonds in addition to its more direct impact through the cost and availability of installment credit. In my view, the jury is still out on this issue. On the one hand, it's easy to believe that a huge change, say, $100 billion, in the net worth of the American public, such as stock market fluctuations can generate, could alter consumer spending in relation to income by a significant amount like $3 billion, even though that change in wealth is concentrated in a small group at the very top of the income and wealth distribution. On the other hand, previous empirical work on this issue came up with a nearly unanimous negative verdict. In 1966 and 1969, however, the timing of stock market declines and the sluggishness in consumer demand seemed to fit fairly well with the hypothesis. One would like to believe the wealth hypothesis because it would suggest that monetary policy has broad and sizable effects on consumption, especially on that of high-income consumers; monetary restraint would then be revealed as less uneven and less inequitable. But before embracing that judgment, one should wait for more decisive evidence.

Interest rates and asset values.   Another major consideration in monetary policy is its effects on interest rates and balance sheets. Some economists may argue that the only function of interest rates is to clear the market and the only sense in which rates can be too high or too low is in failing to establish that equilibrium. Every Congressman knows better! Interest rates are a social target. That is the revealed preference of the American public, reflected in the letters it writes to Washington and the answers it gives to opinion polls. And this is no optical illusion on the part of the citizenry. They have the same good reasons to dislike rising interest rates that apply to rising prices—the haphazard, redistributive effects. And they are concerned about *nominal* interest rates just as they are concerned about prices. It is not clear that such major groups as businessmen or workers are particularly hurt or particularly helped by tight money (or by inflation), but the impacts are quite haphazard in both cases. The resulting lottery in real incomes strikes most Americans as unjust.

The largest redistributive effect of tight money, like that of inflation, falls on balance sheets rather than income statements. People care about their paper wealth and feel worse off when bond and equity prices nose dive. Even though society is not deprived of real resources when security prices drop, it is hard to find gainers to match the losers. Although Alvin Hansen stressed the social costs of distorted, fluctuating balance sheets in the 1950's, this issue gets little attention from economists. But it never escapes the broader and keener vision of the American public.

Financial dislocation. A restrictive monetary policy may also have important, dislocating effects on the financial system. The key function of a financial system is to offer people opportunities to invest without saving and to save without investing. If people want risky assets, they can acquire them beyond the extent of their net worth; if they wish to avoid risk, they can earn a moderate return and stay liquid. The trade of funds between lovers of liquidity and lovers of real assets produces gains to all. "Crunch" and "liquidity crisis" are names for a breakdown in the functioning of the financial system. Such a breakdown deprives people of important options and may permanently impair their willingness to take risks and to hold certain types of assets. To the extent that very tight money curbs an inflationary boom by putting boulders in the financial stream, a considerable price is paid. And to the extent that extremely easy money stimulates a weak economy by opening the flood gates of speculation, that too may be costly.

Balance of payments. The pursuit of a monetary policy focused single-mindedly on stabilization goals would have further "side effects" on the balance of payments, to the extent that it changes international interest rate differentials and hence influences capital flows. There are strong arguments for fundamental reforms of the international monetary system—especially more flexible exchange rates—that would greatly reduce this concern. But those reforms are not on the immediate horizon; nor is the United States prepared to be consistently passive about international payments. Meanwhile, the external deficit casts a shadow that cannot be ignored in the formulation of fiscal-monetary policies.

Growth. A final consideration in the mix of stabilization tools is the long-run influence of monetary policy on the rate of growth of our supply capabilities. An average posture of relatively easy money (and low interest rates) combined with tight fiscal policy (designed especially to put a damper on private consumption) is most likely to produce high investment and rapid growth of potential. That becomes relevant in the short-run because the long-run posture of monetary policy is an average of its short-run swings. If, for example, the nation relies most heavily on monetary policy for restraint and on fiscal policy for stimulus, it will unintentionally slip to a lower growth path. The contribution of extra investment to growth and the value of the extra growth to a society that is already affluent in the aggregate are further vital issues. Recently, enthusiasm for growth-oriented policies has been dampened by the concern about the social fallout of rapid growth and by the shame of poverty, which calls for higher current consumption at the low end of the income scale. Nonetheless, the growth implications of decisions about the fiscal-monetary mix should be recognized.

In the light of these considerations, there are good reasons to avoid extreme tightness or extreme ease in monetary policy—even if it produces an ideal path of real output. Tight money can be bad medicine for a boom even if it cures the disease, just as amputation of the hand is a bad remedy for eczema. The experience of 1966 provides an object lesson. Judged by its performance in getting GNP on track, the Federal Reserve in 1966 put on *the* virtuoso performance in the history of stabilization policy. It was the greatest tight-rope walking and balancing act ever performed by either fiscal or monetary policy. Single-handedly the Fed curbed a boom generated by a vastly stimulative fiscal policy that was paralyzed by politics and distorted by war. And, in stopping the boom, it avoided a recession. To be sure, real GNP dipped for a single quarter, but the unemployment rate did not rise significantly above 4 percent; the 1967 pause was as different from the five postwar recessions, including 1970, as a cold is different from pneumonia. Moreover, inflation slowed markedly in the closing months of 1966 and the first half of 1967. What more could anyone want? Yet, you won't find the 1966 Fed team in the hall of fame for stabilization policy. In the view of most Americans, the collapse of homebuilding, the disruption of financial markets, and the escalation of interest rates were evils that outweighed the benefits of the nonrecessionary halting of inflation. The Fed itself reacted by refusing to give an encore in 1967–68, accepting renewed inflation as a lesser evil than renewed tight money.

All of this leads up to my first rule for stabilization policy: *Keep monetary conditions close to the middle of the road.* Let me explain that, no matter how monetary policy affects GNP, the rule must be interpreted in terms of interest rates and credit conditions, and not in terms of monetary aggregates. Suppose, for a moment, that the monetary impact on GNP is so powerful and the growth rate of the money supply is so critical that a growth rate of money only a little bit below normal will offset the aggregate demand impact of a huge fiscal stimulus (just for example, a $25 billion Vietnam expenditure add-on). The results would still be very tight money in terms of credit conditions, interest rates, and the impact on the composition of output. The shift in financial conditions required to "crowd out" $25 billion of private expenditures can hardly be trivial—even if the needed shift in monetary growth were trivial.

The "middle of the road" is deliberately a vague concept, relying on the existence of some general long-run notion of appropriate and normal interest rates and liquidity ratios. To be sure, it is hard to tell when we are in the middle of the road, but it is easy to tell when we are far away from it.

THE IMPLICATIONS FOR FISCAL POLICY

My second rule follows immediately from the first: *Operate fiscal policy to avoid forcing monetary policy off the middle of the road.* If fiscal policy is inappropriately stimulative or restrictive, a conscientious and (at least somewhat) independent monetary authority will be obliged to shoulder most of the burden for stabilizing the economy. In historical perspective, it is important to recognize that this sense of responsibility has not always prevailed. In World War II and again in the initial stages of the Korean War, the Federal Reserve reacted to an inflationary fiscal policy simply by pegging interest rates and creating all the liquidity demanded in an inflationary boom. Through these actions, the Federal Reserve not only passed the buck right back to fiscal policy but became an active accomplice in the inflation, intensifying excess demand by holding nominal interest rates constant as prices accelerated. It was technically feasible for the Federal Reserve to behave similarly during the Vietnam war. The fact that it picked up the ball after the fiscal fumble of 1966 demonstrated a new and greater sense of responsibility by the central bank for overall stabilization. So long as both fiscal and monetary policy makers feel that responsibility, as they appropriately should, an inappropriate fiscal policy is bound to push monetary policy off the middle of the road. Obviously, fiscal buck passing can also occur in a situation when stimulus is in order. In 1971, a rather neutral fiscal program accompanied by ambitious targets for recovery threatens to overburden the Federal Reserve with the responsibility for stimulus.

FISCAL TOOLS AND COMPOSITION

To avoid pushing monetary policy off the middle of the road, fiscal policy must itself depart from the middle of the road—turning markedly more stimulative or more restrictive than its normal long-run posture—when private demand is especially weak or especially strong. But such swings in fiscal policy must also be made in light of compositional constraints that apply to federal expenditures, and especially to federal purchases of goods and services. Our preferences about the composition of output imply some notion of appropriate levels of civilian public programs. No one would wish to double or halve the size of the Census Bureau or the Forest Service in order to accord with the cyclical position of the economy.

Moreover, these limitations based on principle are reinforced by limitations of a practical character. First, federal civilian expenditures on goods and services involve a mere 2½ percent of GNP and thus afford very little leverage for stabilization. Second, most federal programs involving purchases of goods and services have long start-up and shut-off periods that make it extremely difficult to vary timing greatly without impairing efficiency.

Popular discussions of fiscal stabilization tend to stress expenditure variation despite these clear constraints. Why are the lessons ignored? Could any informed person have seriously regarded a curb on civilian public programs during the Vietnam build-up period as a meaningful antidote to the stimulus of increasing military expenditures? Could anybody familiar with the history of the lags in public spending support a public works program as a way to create jobs and strengthen recovery in 1971 or 1972? The evidence suggests that people with strong views on the desirable size of the public sector tend to invoke the cause of stabilization as a rationalization for their social preferences. To an advocate of additional government spending, a recession provides a useful additional talking point; to a crusader for cutbacks in government spending, excess demand inflation offers an excellent excuse.

Federal "transfer" programs, such as social security, unemployment compensation, and veterans' benefits, are not subject to serious implementation lags, but their room for maneuver is limited by the principle of intertemporal equity. The aged, the poor, or the unemployed cannot justifiably be treated better in a recession than in prosperity or in a boom. The unfortunate people who are jobless when the unemployment rate is low deserve no less generous benefits than those who are unemployed when the rate is high; indeed, if misery loves company, those unemployed in prosperity may suffer psychically because they have less of it.

Some significant elbow room nevertheless appears for varying such transfer programs. Society's agenda always contains some new initiative or additional step to strengthen transfer programs in a growing economy with growing overall income; and the next step can be timed to come a little sooner or a little later, depending on the economy's cyclical position. In the present context, the administration's family assistance program provides a good example. The proposed initial date for benefits is July 1, 1972, but the program could be made effective six months earlier. Similarly, there is some opportunity for varying the timing of benefit liberalization and of payroll tax increases with respect to the social security program. Congress displayed wisdom early in 1971 by deferring for a year the proposed increase in the maximum earnings base of the payroll tax.

While this pure timing flexibility is important, it may not provide enough leeway for a flexible fiscal policy to respond to the needs of a very slack or very taut economy. Beyond it, the most attractive fiscal tool is variation in personal income tax rates. In principle, significant and indeed frequent changes in these rates are acceptable. Because they affect the huge consumption sector most directly and because their impact is spread over Americans throughout the middle- and upper-income groups, personal taxes are an ideal instrument for flexibility. While the income tax is specifically aimed to redistribute income in a more egalitarian way, the basic function of taxation is simply to restrain demand, given the socially desired level of public expenditures. A prima facie case exists for suspending or repealing any tax (or tax rate) that is not essential for the purpose of restraining demand sufficiently to avoid both inflation and monetary restraint. Moreover, according to compelling historical evidence, changes in personal tax rates—upward or downward, permanent or temporary—have reasonably reliable effects on consumer spending and hence on GNP.

Political implementation is the one troublesome problem with changes in personal tax rates. Obviously, unlike shifts in monetary policy, any change in tax rates requires legislative action. And the record of congressional response to presidential requests for such changes has left much to be desired. Many constructive proposals have been made to improve that story. In 1961, the Commission on Money and Credit asked Congress to delegate authority for tax changes to the President subject to congressional veto; others have urged Congress to enact rules that would commit it to fast action—favorable or unfavorable—in response to a presidential request. Presidents Kennedy and Johnson made proposals for speeding the legislative process in their Economic Reports of 1962 and 1969, respectively. Herbert Stein presented a constructive proposal along similar lines in 1968. Even the Joint Economic Committee of the Congress expressed its concern in its 1966 report, "Tax Changes for Shortrun Stabilization." But the Congress has generally ignored these proposals, jealously guarding its prerogatives over taxation, and refusing to bind its own hands with respect to procedures.

Under the present rules of the game, the President must ask Congress to do what seems best for the country and must count on presenting the case persuasively. The discussion and debates of recent years have put Congress on its mettle to respond promptly and pragmatically to any presidential request for tax changes designed for short-run stabilization purposes. Moreover, the 1963 and 1967 stalemates reflected special factors that seem obsolete—budget orthodoxy in the earlier case and Vietnam strategy in the later one. Our traditional procedures deserve another try.

These thoughts on the uses of alternative fiscal tools can be summarized as my third rule: *When additional fiscal stimulus or restraint is needed, opportunities for varying the timing of new initiatives in federal spending or tax programs should be the first line of attack: if these are inadequate to achieve the desired swing in fiscal policy, a change in personal tax rates should be sought.* We must keep urging and prodding the Congress to respond more promptly when tax changes are proposed. And we must not give up, for it will heed this message eventually.

FULL EMPLOYMENT SURPLUS

The problems of executive-legislative coordination apply to expenditures as well as taxes. The fractionated process by which appropriations are made on Capitol Hill leads to frightful difficulties in the overall control of federal spending. As I have suggested elsewhere, one path to improvement might involve the following procedures: The President would make explicit the fiscal decision underlying his budget; and the Congress would then focus on that decision, approving or modifying it; and it would then commit itself to undertake an iterative review of appropriations and tax legislation during the course of the year to assure that the budget stayed within the bounds.

I believe that the concept of the full employment surplus can be extremely useful as the focus of the fiscal plan and review. It is a simple enough summary number of the budget's impact on the economy to be understood by the participants, and it is a good enough summary to serve the purpose. It permits the stimulus or restraint in the budget to be compared with that of the previous year and other relevant previous periods. While administration officials cannot hope to provide a scientific demonstration that the budget has the proper amount of stimulus or restraint, they can generate an informed discussion and enlightened decision process by explaining their forecast of the strength of private demand, the proper role for monetary policy, and the likely response of the economy to proposed fiscal changes.

The main function of the full employment surplus in policy discussion is to correct the misleading impression generated by the actual budget surplus or deficit when the economy is off course. In a weak economy, revenues automatically fall far below their full employment level and the budget is hence pushed into deficit. That automatic or passive deficit may be misread as evidence that the budget is strongly stimulating the economy and hence that further expansionary action is inappropriate. By the same token, a boom resulting from a surge in private demand or an easing of monetary policy would automatically swell federal revenues, thereby tending to produce a surplus in the budget. These automatic shifts in federal revenues are important and significant; such built-in stabilizers help to cushion cumulative declines and dampen cumulative upsurges, but they should be properly recognized as shock absorbers rather than either accelerators or brakes.

I believe the focus on the full employment budget by the administration this year has helped to raise the level of fiscal debate. It reveals that the big deficits of fiscal years 1971 and 1972 are symptoms of a weak economy, rather than of a strong budget.

Guide versus rule. The full employment budget shows where the fiscal dials are set; but it cannot say where the dials *ought* to be set. It is an aid to safe driving much like a speedometer, but it cannot prescribe the optimum speed. That depends on road conditions. A maintained target for the full employment surplus represents a decision to drive by the dashboard and to stop watching the road. Road conditons do change significantly from time to time in our dynamic economy. The evidence of the postwar era suggests that zero is too low a full employment surplus for a period of prosperity and too high a full employment surplus for a period of slack and slump. From long-term saving-investment patterns, one might guess that a full employment surplus of one-half of one percent of GNP would be about right on the average to accompany a middle-of-the-road monetary policy. But even that judgment would be highly speculative; and it would not tell us how to identify the rare case of an average year or how to quantify the departure of any particular year from the average. Economists have no right to be presumptuous about their ability to forecast in either the short-run or the long-run; and it is far more presumptuous to claim that the proper size of the full employment surplus can be determined for the long-run than to believe that it can be nudged in the correct direction in any particular year on the basis of the evidence then at hand.

Adoption of a fixed full employment surplus implies a firm determination by fiscal policy makers to counteract any major surprises that arise *within* the federal budget. If Congress rejects the President's proposals for major expenditure programs such as revenue sharing or family assistance, the advocate of a fixed full employment surplus is committed to propose alternatives for those stimulative actions. Similarly, if uncontrollable expenditures spurt, some compensatory action is required to keep the overall full employment budget close to its original position.

At the same time, however, the advocate of the fixed full employment surplus is determined *not* to act in response to surprises in private demand or monetary policy, no matter how large or how definite these may be. The resulting decision rule is illogical and indefensible. Once it is recognized that some surprises within the federal budget are large enough to call for offsetting fiscal action, it must be conceded that some surprises in consumer spending, plant and equipment outlays, or Federal Reserve decisions might also point to shifts in the fiscal course.

In fact, the Nixon administration has not adopted a fixed full employment surplus, but rather a rule that the full employment budget shall be *at least* in balance on the unified basis of budget accounting. The doctrine of balancing the full employment budget has obvious antecedents in the less sophisticated orthodoxy of balancing the actual budget. The new rule is

far less harmful than its predecessor, but it is equally arbitrary. Its arbi-
trariness is perhaps illustrated by the fact that zero on the unified basis for
the 1972 fiscal year turns out to be $7 billion on the national income ac-
counts basis, which is the way Herbert Stein first unveiled the concept and
the way every economics student has learned full employment budgeting
for a generation.

Statics versus dynamics. The rule really reflects the administration's
concern about overdoing fiscal stimulus, and that concern has a valid basis.
There is genuine danger that stimulative fiscal action appropriate to today's slack and sluggish economy could commit the nation to stimulative
budgets in future years when they would be markedly inappropriate. We
might then be obliged to offset that stimulus by relying on monetary restraint or by seeking tax increases or cutbacks in expenditure programs once
the economy approached full employment. Reliance on monetary restraint
as an antidote to excessive budgetary stimulus violates rules one and two
above. And to count on subsequent neutralizing measures of fiscal restraint
is to ignore the serious doubts about the political feasibility of such legislative action. Congress is particularly unlikely to raise tax rates for the
purpose of bailing out an overly enthusiastic anti-slump program that
added mightily to federal spending. It would see such action as an open
invitation to continued upward ratcheting of federal expenditures through
time—with major expenditure initiatives in slumps and offsetting tax increases in booms. Whatever, one's views on the appropriate size of the
public sector, a cyclical ratchet is not a proper tool for decision making in
the democratic process.

All of this argues for making stimulative fiscal policy with one eye on
preserving our fiscal fitness for the next period of full employment. And
that does require a rule, or at least some form of discipline that guards
against excessive long-term commitments of revenue or expenditure.
Hence, my fourth rule: *Stimulative fiscal programs should be temporary and self-terminating so that they don't jeopardize our future budgetary position.* The rule reminds us that the key issue is not whether full
employment balance is maintained when the economy needs fiscal stimulus,
but whether the budget remains in a flexible position from which it can be
moved back readily into full employment surplus when restraint once
again becomes appropriate. It cautions against permanent changes in the
levels of taxation or expenditure programs for stabilization purposes; it
puts a time-dimension on the third rule, which identifies the types of
fiscal variation consistent with compositional objectives. Both rules argue
against public works as a tool for stabilization. They also cast doubt on
the recent liberalization of depreciation allowances as a stabilization device; that measure sacrificed $4 billion of revenue annually on a permanent
basis in order to get $2 billion into the economy in 1971.

THE DEPENDENCE ON FORECASTING

The rule for relying on quick-starting and self-terminating fiscal measures is designed to ensure flexibility and thus to limit the time horizon over which the forecasting of aggregate demand is essential to policy decisions. But that time period remains substantial and the success of policy remains dependent on the accuracy of economic forecasting. Tax cuts, for example, add cumulatively to aggregate demand for a considerable period after enactment. Thus, while they deliver some prompt stimulus to aggregate demand, they also involve a package of future add-ons to demand. The only way to lift the economy this quarter is through a tie-in sale that lifts the economy further for several subsequent quarters.

If any fiscal or monetary tool exerted its full impact instantaneously, stabilization policy making would be a different ball game. Indeed, this difference has been highlighted by the Laffer model, which finds that the effects of a shift in the money supply on aggregate demand are concentrated in the very quarter of the policy action. While GNP is determined by the money supply in the Laffer model, the implication for policy strategy is diametrically opposite to that of previous monetarist views. Because of its instantaneous total effects, the Laffer model issues an unequivocal mandate in favor of monetary fine tuning. Monetary policy makers are encouraged to take all the action appropriate to hit their economic targets today; and they should then wait for tomorrow and correct any errors by twisting the dials again. Unlike more traditional views about the timing impact of economic policies, the Laffer model finds no tie-in sale or longer-term commitment that would caution against large and abrupt changes in policy.

Because Keynesians and most monetarists agree that the time stream of economic impact following a policy action begins virtually at once but continues into the more distant future, they seat the forecaster at the right hand of the policy maker. When policy decisions necessarily affect the future, they must be made in light of uncertain forecasts of the future and not solely on the basis of the facts of the present. To act otherwise is to adopt implicitly the naive forecast that the future is going to be merely a continuation of the present. The historical record of economic forecasting in the past two decades demonstrates that professional forecasting, despite its limitations, is more accurate than such naive models. Moreover, even the naive model that tomorrow will be like today is far more accurate than the super-naive or agnostic model that tomorrow's aggregate demand is just as likely to be below the social target as above it regardless of where today's aggregate demand stands. That agnostic model is the extreme point in the decision analysis set forth by Milton Friedman and William Brainard. If forecasts could not beat the agnostic model, it would be important to do nothing. The stabilization policy maker should simply stay home, for action by him would be just as likely to push the economy in the wrong direction as in the right direction and it could push the economy off the proper course when it would otherwise be there.

In fact, the professional forecaster can beat the agnostic model by a wide margin. I can think of only two years in the past twenty—1955 and 1965—when the January consensus prediction of economic forecasters would have led policy makers to administer stimulants when they were inappropriate and no cases when the consensus forecast would have pointed toward sedatives when stimulants were really appropriate.

A PROPENSITY TO OVERREACT?

Nonetheless, the fact that forecasters can guide policy makers to the right choice as between sedatives and stimulants is not necessarily decisive. Even if some sedative medicine would help a patient, he may be better off with nothing than with a massive overdose of sedation. And it is sometimes claimed that policy makers tend to prescribe overdoses. According to this claim, because their medicines operate only with a lag and because neither the time shape of that lag nor the total impact of the policy is readily determined in advance, the policy makers become impatient; hence they continue to take more and more action until they have done too much of a good thing, which may be worse than nothing.

This intuitive argument has a certain appeal as a description of a human foible. We have probably all behaved in much this way in taking a shower. When the water is too cold, we turn up the hot faucet; and, if we are still cold ten seconds later, we may turn up the faucet some more, assuming that the first twist was inadequate. As a result of our first impatience, we may find ourselves scalded. And even after one or two experiences of this sort, we repeat that behavior and indeed find it difficult to discipline ourselves completely. If, indeed, fiscal-monetary policy makers have the same proclivities as the man in the shower, rules or discipline may help them to resist their impulses to overreact. But whether the Federal Reserve Open Market Committee or the Troika overtwist the faucets in their respective showers is an empirical issue, a proposition about their behavior that ought to be supportable or refutable by evidence. And I have yet to see evidence to support the proposition.

In the case of fiscal policy, I believe the record shows that policy makers generally have not behaved like the man in the shower. Below is a list of the major changes in fiscal policy during the past fifteen years, as defined by shifts in the full employment surplus, and a capsule evaluation based on hindsight.

1. During 1958, the full employment surplus was reduced from more than 1 percent of GNP to near zero.

   Stimulative direction proper; inadequate size, and timing delayed.

2. In 1959–60, fiscal policy was sharply reversed toward restraint with the full employment surplus reaching 2½ percent of GNP in 1960.

   Inappropriate restraint.

3. During 1961–62, that surplus was gradually trimmed.

   Stimulative direction proper; inadequate size and timing delayed.

4. After backsliding during 1963, fiscal policy became considerably more stimulative with the enactment of the tax cut at the beginning of 1964.

   Appropriate stimulus.

5. From the second half of 1965 to the end of 1968, the full employment budget was in deficit, reflecting the buildup of Vietnam expenditures.

   Inappropriate stimulus.

6. In 1969, as the result of the tax surcharge and expenditure cutbacks, a full employment surplus of 1 percent of GNP was restored.

   Appropriate restraint; much delayed timing.

7. In 1970 and the first half of 1971, fiscal policy was relaxed a bit with the full employment surplus roughly cut in half.

   Relaxation proper; inadequate size.

Items 1, 3, 6, and 7 all depart from the ideal in the direction of too little and too late rather than too much and too soon. In each of these cases moves that were larger or earlier or both would have produced better stabilization results. Item 5—the inappropriate fiscal stimulus of the Vietnam period—was not the overreaction of the man in the shower. The hot water was turned up, but not because anyone believed that the economy needed warming.

Item 2—the shift to restraint in 1959—can be viewed, in a sense, as a premature and excessive cooling of economic expansion. But that policy simply was not keyed to the general economic diagnosis or forecast, which saw the temperature as remaining extremely mild, but rather to a noneconomic budgetary orthodoxy. The full employment surplus was jacked up enough to balance the actual budget, as an end in itself rather than as a means to curb any present or prospective boom.

By any standard, the preponderant balance of mistakes in fiscal policy is revealed as errors of omission rather than commission—errors of doing too little too late, rather than too much too soon. Our fiscal man in the shower, in fact, tends to wait too long to ascertain that the water is really staying cold before he decides to turn it up. When he finally does turn the faucet, he acts timidly and hesitantly. When the water is hot, he also hesitates too long and moves indecisively. To shift metaphors, he is not trigger happy, but, rather, slow on the draw. And so I come to my fifth rule: *Face the fact that policies must be made on the basis of a forecast, and don't be slow on the draw!*

My rules for fiscal discretionary judgment will work well only if stabilization policy is guided by the professional expertise of economists. Obviously, that has not always been the case; and when politics vetoed economics, serious fiscal destabilization resulted. Indeed, in the past generation, the economy has been more severely disrupted by government actions obviously inconsistent with the objective of economic stabilization than by autonomous shifts in private demand. The 1950–51 Korean inflation, the 1953–54 post-Korean recession, the 1960–61 recession, and the Vietnam inflation were all government-induced fluctuations, in which the budget departed from any and all professional prescriptions for stabilization. In three of the four cases, swings in military expenditures created the problem; in the remaining case, it was caused by attachment to a taboo of budgetary balance. In light of these instances, one might well find that a fixed, moderate full employment surplus in peace and war, even years and odd years, would have yielded better overall results than those obtained from the actual fiscal process. But this is no argument for fixed parameters! The proposal to control political officials with a nondiscretionary rule reminds me of the suggestion to catch birds by pouring salt on their tails. Neither the political officials nor the birds will cooperate. If every economist in the nation had sworn (falsely) to Lyndon Johnson and Wilbur Mills that any deviation of the full employment surplus from 0.5 percent of GNP was a mortal sin, that wouldn't have changed fiscal policy in 1965–68. Why not tell our statesmen the truth and try to convince them to heed professional advice on fiscal policy? As unpalatable as that message might be, it has more chance of convincing elected public officials than the rule of maintaining a fixed and rigid full employment surplus for all time. And so I offer my sixth rule: *Presidents should listen to the advice of their economists on fiscal policy and so should the Congress.*

SIGNALS FOR THE MONETARY AUTHORITIES

Under the circumstances I envision, the tasks of the Federal Reserve would depend upon how well the fiscal rules operate. If the budget no longer generates disruptive shifts in aggregate demand and if it offsets, to some degree, any major autonomous shift in private demand, then the monetary policy makers may be able to hold money and credit conditions close to the middle of the road without much difficulty. Under those best of all possible circumstances, economists might begin to wonder what all the shouting was about in the debate on the relative importance of aggregate quantities and interest rates as guides to monetary policy. In 1962–65, a monetary policy that was oriented toward interest rate targets did not produce large or abrupt shifts in the growth of the money stock, simply because the demand for money did not undergo enormous fluctuation. Presumably, if monetary policy had been pursued with respect to quantity rather than rate targets, those quantity guides would have left interest rates reasonably stable. If the demand for goods and the demand for money stay on course, then it makes little difference whether the directives to the trading desk are couched in terms of maintaining a given set of interest rates in the money markets or a given growth of the money supply.

It is not safe, however, to count on the world becoming that tranquil. Surprises will occur, and the policy markers will be forced to decide on the emphasis they wish to give to interest rates and aggregate quantities relative to one another. And it is a matter of degree—of relative emphasis. Anyone interested in diagnosing or influencing financial markets would obviously pay attention to both prices and quantities, just as he would in looking at any other market. Nobody has ever improved on Paul Samuelson's summary that Federal Reserve governors were given two eyes so that they could watch both yields and quantities. In a more serious vein, James Duesenberry has recently sketched how the monetary authorities might appropriately be guided by both quantities and interest rates. At a theoretical level, William Poole has shown the conditions for preferring rate-oriented, quantity-oriented, or mixed monetary strategies.

Quite apart from the issue of appropriate guides, the chief problem facing the monetary authority is likely to be when and how much to depart from a "normal" or average posture in order to provide additional stimulus or restraint to economic activity. Monetary policy can and should find some elbow room without major deviations from the middle of the road. For one thing, monetary policy is light on its feet; the short implementation lag in Federal Reserve decisions provides an enviable contrast with the long lags in the legislative process for altering fiscal policy. In nudging economic activity to offset modest surprises, the speed of implementation makes monetary policy particularly useful.

Second, there is a case for a belt and suspenders strategy of making fiscal and monetary changes in the same direction when stimulus or restraint is desired. The quantitative effect of specific fiscal and monetary changes on GNP is uncertain. Errors in the estimates of these effects are likely to be negatively related or at worst unrelated—if the economy's response to monetary changes is larger than expected, the response to fiscal swings seems likely to be less than our estimates. How extensive the monetary swings should be and at what point the benefits in aggregate stabilization are outweighed by the costs of the side effects discussed above, are issues that require careful judgment and the best use of discretion.

Any recommendation for discretionary monetary policy runs into the contention that the Federal Reserve also shares a propensity to overreact; I find it more difficult to interpret that contention than the one regarding fiscal policy; but, as I read the evidence, it is also untrue. Whether judged in terms of interest rates or of aggregate quantities, I cannot see that the Federal Reserve has behaved like the man in the shower. It was not overly expansionary during most recessions and early recoveries. If the monetary policies of 1957–58, 1960–62, or 1970 could be replayed with the aid of perfect hindsight, monetary policy would surely be more expansionary than it was in fact. The only example of such a period that might stand on the opposite side is late 1954, when in retrospect the Fed seems to have been excessively generous.

Nor in periods of strong economic advance has the Fed generally applied the brakes too strongly or too soon. It may have done so in the case of 1959, but it clearly stayed off the brakes too long in 1965 and probably in 1955. Most clearly, the Federal Reserve has revealed the propensity to underreact to economic chill in late expansions and early stages of recession: with perfect hindsight, it is clear, restriction was maintained too long in 1953 and again in 1957. In my judgment, the error in the 1969 performance should also be interpreted as unduly prolonged restraint—staying on the brakes too long and too hard late in the year—although others might argue that the restraint was applied too vigorously early in the year. There have been other mistakes in monetary policy, like the misdiagnosis of 1968, but they have little to do with either overreaction or underreaction, so far as I can see. Nor does the basic decision of 1967, which gave side effects priority over aggregate stabilization targets, reveal a propensity to overreact.

Thus I come to my final rule: *The makers of monetary policy should be guided by both aggregate quantities and interest rates and by the present and prospective state of aggregate demand; they will serve the nation best by using fully their capability to make small and prompt adjustments in light of the best current evidence and analysis.*

7 The non-answer to Nixonomics*

MELVILLE J. ULMER

Economics, so they say, will be the dominant issue of the coming presidential campaign, overshadowing war, and law and order. If so, President Nixon's new economic program, wobbly and rickety though it may be, looks sturdy enough as of now to carry him to victory. All the polls show the President outdistancing every potential Democratic rival, as well as getting a solid vote of endorsement on his economic policies. Even his wage and price controls, despite the wariness of labor and the uncertainties confronting business, have won clear majority support. Such popularity cannot be attributed to the merits of President Nixon's program, which are in fact highly questionable, or to his past record in the economic sphere, which is one of conspicuous failure; rather the source must be found in the quality of the alternatives as presented by the opposition—Muskie, Humphrey, Kennedy, McGovern, Jackson, Lindsay and others who have had or could have presidential ambitions. All have whooped and hollered about small details of the President's policies, and have had as much impact on public opinion as a position paper by the vice president of the freshman class of a junior high school. Not one of the Democratic frontrunners has challenged Nixon's basic economic ideas, for the excellent but unfortunate reason that they share them.

The President's approach to the nation's central problem of economic instability is grounded in the conventional wisdom of orthodox economic doctrine, and his past or present advisers in this area—Herbert Stein, Paul McCracken, Ezra Solomon, Hendrik Houthakker, and Arthur Burns—are acknowledged authorities. The economic advisers to Muskie, Humphrey, Kennedy, *et. al,* are similarly well versed in the traditional doctrine, adept masters of the identical textbooks. But those who say "Me too, only better!" do not make dramatically attractive alternatives to those who are already running things. They do not offer the nation the imaginative alternate

* From "Democrat's Default: The Non-Answer to Nixonomics," *The New Republic* (December 1971), pp. 19–21. Reprinted by permission of *The New Republic,* © 1971, Harrison-Blaine of New Jersey, Inc. Melville J. Ulmer is Professor of Economics at the University of Maryland, College Park, Md., and contributing editor to *The New Republic.*

route, the prospect for real improvement over a dismal past, that it ought to have.

The key difficulty is that the traditional tools of economic stabilization —the best that conventional economic advisers, both Democratic and Republican, now offer—have been tried for more than 20 years and been found wanting. President Nixon's present cure for unemployment, a proposed reduction in taxes, is the same technique used with considerable fanfare in the Kennedy-Johnson administrations. True, there is a typical and predictable Republican bias favoring reductions for business as against the remainder of the population. But to attack the bias, as virtually every Democratic leader has, is not to challenge the basic technique but only a serious imperfection in its form. In any case the flaw has been corrected at least in part by Congress in the new revenue bill, and the President has offered little opposition to the revisions, except for the hot issue of the checkoff for election campaign financing and, to a lesser extent, the magnitude of overall reduction in taxes.

In invoking mandatory wage and price controls President Nixon actually went farther to the left than the proposals of most Democracts, whose economic experts such as Walter Heller and Arthur Okun had generally asked for no more than jawboning. Of course, with direct controls, the President also moved to the left of his own economic advisers. The important point though, is that Democrats cannot logically or convincingly challenge this seminal component of the President's economic program, nor have they tried. At most, they may complain as has *The New Republic* ("What Prices?," Oct. 30, and "Where the Shoe Pinches," Nov. 20, 1971), that the administration's wage and price regulations are poorly conceived, ineffectively enforced, inadequately planned, and biased in their impact. Although framed in colorful and sometimes dramatic rhetoric, the typical Democratic critique of Republican economics is best characterized as quibbling. The speakers themselves, whether "centrists" Muskie and Humphrey or "leftists" McGovern and Kennedy, must be excellent actors, as they are, to get excited about it. At worst, their self-righteous carping seems petulant. Thus, all leading Democrats and their most faithful journalistic interpreters, such as Hobart Rowen of *The Washington Post,* have deplored the persistent sluggishness of economic activity and continuing high unemployment. Nixon's New Economic Policy is failing, they complain, and more vigorous measures must be taken to push production and sales ahead. Yet every newspaper reader must know that President Nixon has proposed stimulative measures—the tax reductions mentioned above— and that the resulting Revenue Act of 1971 has since been debated for more than three months in the Democratically controlled Congress and is only at present writing being readied for executive approval and implementation. No doubt the President's proposals have been strengthened and liberalized through this legislative process. But it will take some time, after the revenue bill's provisions have been put into effect, before they can have much impact on the pace of business.

Ironically, though you wouldn't know it from the Democratic rebuttal, the Nixon economic program is highly vulnerable. The use of traditional Keynesian fiscal policy to reduce unemployment on the one hand, or to check inflation on the other, has repeatedly been proven ineffective, even though it has been tested again and again, under both conservative and liberal auspices, ever since the end of World War II. Each time the economy is pumped up with tax reductions or additional government spending, unemployment recedes but inflation accelerates. Each time, then, that government "corrects" inflation with higher taxes and/or reduced public spending, it succeeds in slowing prices but produces unemployment. In this way the orthodox fiscal measures, which the Nixon administration persists in using, have kept the nation on a seesaw of instability. Nor have direct price controls, though of some temporary help in emergencies, ever checked inflation for long when pressures were intensified, either at home during World War II or Korea, or during the several tests applied in peacetime in most of the countries of Western Europe. Almost constantly over the past 25 years the U.S. economy has operated with seriously excessive unemployment, sometimes more, sometimes less, the chief exceptions being war periods. Yet over that 25-year span the price level more than doubled. In seeking stability, with the orthodox tools, we have found unemployment and inflation too. This is the economic dilemma that President Nixon has studiously neglected to confront, and that his Democratic critics have either failed to understand or have timidly avoided.

President Nixon's present plan, apparently, is to elude the next showdown, the next crisis in economic policy, until after Election Day. The immediate strategy, which the President has announced, is to permit a slow expansion in business activity through next year, stimulated mainly by the proposed tax reductions. According to the most popular administration estimates, unemployment may be down to around 5.2 percent of the labor force by election time, a distinct improvement over recent experience but still a substantial distance—a good 2 percentage points—short of full employment. With such sluggish, though improving, performance, following 12 months of stagnant recession, inflation should be held reasonably in check, particularly if a modicum of help is obtained from wage and price controls. But not long after the election, should the President win, he will have to confront the dilemma he has thus far been avoiding. If business activity continues to move ahead, inflation will surely gather force and break through even a vigorous and comprehensive system of price controls, not to mention the flimsy and incomplete system the administration has erected. The only way to stop it, with the conventional Keynesian tools, is to "dampen" the economy by inducing recession, as government did in 1949,

1954, 1958, 1960, and under Nixon in 1969. Thus, the nation would be returned once again, perhaps in early 1973, to the dismal downside of the economic seesaw, with the weakest segment of society—the first to be fired —required to sacrifice their welfare for the benefit of a stable price index for us all.

To expose and exploit this vulnerability in the Republican economic position, the Democrats need a position of their own that is different and better. It is primarily their inability to develop one, thus far, that has given the President the initiative and the advantage as reflected in the polls. A more constructive and effective approach to economic stability is available. It involves turning over to the public sector a larger portion of the nation's economic activity than is customary in peacetime. For a growing proportion of the population I think this characteristic may appear as an advantage—especially for those who value purer air and water, better schools and medical care, more attractive cities, recreational areas and countryside, safer streets, more generous concern for the aged, mass transportation, adult education, vocational training, day care centers and other services that can best be offered, or can only be offered, by government. Democratic leaders who give lip service to these needs but in legislative practice cling to the middle of the road may be hit by the traffic of history, in this instance a fourth party movement.

At the bottom of the problem of instability is a marked disparity between the structure of the demand for labor and the structure of the available supply. Increasingly, modern technology has required well educated, skilled personnel in industry. Hence a progressively larger proportion of the nation's unskilled workers, who now account for at least 80 percent of the unemployed, have been converted to economic discards. This autumn, unemployment rates were only 2 percent or less for professional employees, technical workers, and administrators, but from 8 to 12 percent for the unskilled and semiskilled. Of course, the jobless always include a significant number of those who have been disadvantaged by special circumstances (such as space engineers and physicists in 1970 and 1971) or by technological change and skill obsolescence. But these, too, are in a sense economic discards, pending retraining or a more productive redirection of their talents. What history teaches is that it is not possible to put the economic discards of either type into jobs simply by pumping up business activity. For when the nation's aggregate demand is vigorously expanded, the scarcity of skilled workers in relation to the needs of industry is intensified, bringing reinforced pressure on wages and salaries and the price level.

At best, during such business expansions, only a relatively small portion of the unskilled and the technologically displaced are absorbed, temporarily, into jobs. Meanwhile, mounting inflation ultimately forces a turnabout in policy, with restraints on the pace of business activity and then deepening unemployment. The year 1969 is a case in point. The overall level of unemployment was pressed down to 3.5 percent of the labor force, and for the highly skilled such as technicians, professionals, or supervisors, the jobless rate was just one percent or less. But for the unskilled the improvement was modest. Even in ebullient 1969, with the still spreading Vietnam War implacably spurring business activity, 7 percent of all non-farm laborers were out of jobs, a rate that if extended to the entire labor force would have spelled depression. Yet market pressures in general were severe enough to boost the consumer price index by more than 6 percent, and in the middle of the year President Nixon turned on his "game plan" to fight inflation and transform boom into recession.

One important part of the answer to this basic problem is to alter the *structure of the demand* for labor so that the jobless can be put to work without generating inflation. In other words, instead of futilely trying to place square pegs in round holes, we need to shape the holes to fit the pegs. A large number of those who are commonly unemployed—the hard core—cannot be absorbed into jobs in business, except under the most inflationary circumstances, because their aptitudes, whatever they may be, do not fit commercial business needs. But such men and women can make worthwhile contributions to the noncommercial needs of the public sector, and it is with this in mind that the structure of labor demand can be favorably altered. For the public sector—that is, government—is in the unique position of being able to calculate the *social* costs and the *social* benefits of its projects, rather than adhering to purely pecuniary directives. The unemployed remain a cost to society, like the rest of us; even though we are shamefully ungenerous, we do not let them die of hunger or cold.

Hence the cost of employing the jobless in government may be calculated as their salaries *minus* the welfare allowances, unemployment insurance or other benefits that would otherwise maintain them. For government, they represent very low cost labor, and it would pay to put them to work on sorely needed public projects, even in some instances on jobs that in private industry might be performed by machines. As every engineer and efficiency expert knows, there is more than one way to produce practically any good or service. For society, represented by government, it will pay to suit the method to the resources at hand—to the particular skills, aptitudes and training capacity of the unemployed.

My estimate is that if 2½ million of the jobless were employed by government in this way—producing useful public services that are now inadequately supplied, if at all—full employment could be maintained in the United States steadily, and without inflation. Stability in the price level, under these conditions, could be further assured by meeting all the extra expenses of public employment through taxation, so that inflation-inducing excess demand would become a thing of the past. By "extra" expenses, I mean the payroll and material costs of the public employment less the welfare allowances or other public payments the new employees would otherwise have received. I would estimate that net cost—that is, the net tax bill—at probably not more than $6 billion, or about 25 percent less than the Defense Department now spends on research. In return, the nation could look for true economic stability, with no need for recurrent recessions and inflations; a faster rate of long-term growth, since all resources would be used; and a reordering of national priorities that in the past has won the solid sentimental support of the country's orators, but very little money.

This is the heart of the plan that I think Democrats, who have the nation's future as well as their own in mind, ought to be pushing.

D. The great automation question

Technological change has played a heroic role in American economic development, while the potential adverse social "side effects" of new technology—unemployment, ecological damage, and income distribution—have aroused fear and controversy. Yet both Solow and Heilbroner point out that economists have offered only minimum facts and the simplest theories to enlighten the discussion of the impact of technological change. Within the past few years, however, research and publication has accelerated sharply.

Some social prophets have been predicting for the past decade or more that industrial society faces massive unemployment as a result of automation and the "cybernetic revolution." Heilbroner seems worried about the decade ahead. Anticipating rapid expansion in the supply of labor (especially youth and women), he sees little chance of meeting this through shorter working weeks or working lifetimes (prolonged education or early retirement), or through job expansion in private industry. He therefore urges a program quite similar to Ulmer's (see Reading 7) for massive government employment programs aimed to meet America's priority social needs. Solow sharply rejects these pessimistic predictions, pointing out that labor productivity for the whole economy has accelerated slightly, but is still rising at only 3.4 percent annually. More important, he argues that we have ample fiscal and monetary policies to sustain any desired level (or growth) of aggregate demand to offset any technological unemployment which might arise.

Both authors emphasize that technological unemployment is not only a macroeconomic problem, but that it hits some industries, regions, and labor skills hard and others almost not at all. The severity of this localized, microeconomic impact depends on the industry's "elasticity of demand" (see Heilbroner), its price/wage/profit structure, and other factors. The authors might have emphasized more strongly that at this microeconomic level we also see the adverse effects of new technology on income distribution and "human capital" as incomes and accumulated skills are destroyed by machines. Even while recognizing the inequitable damage to individuals and communities, economists seek to preserve the efficiency benefits which technological change offers to the larger society; thus Solow favors government policies to "speed and cushion the necessary transitions," rather than to slow or prevent the changes as some of the victims would naturally prefer.

8   Technology and unemployment*

ROBERT M. SOLOW

Whenever there is both rapid technological change and high unemployment the two will inevitably be connected in people's minds. So it is not surprising that technological unemployment was a live subject during the depression of the 1930's, nor that the debate has now revived. The discussion of thirty years ago was inconclusive, partly because there were more urgent things to worry about and partly because economists did not then have a workable theory of income and employment as a whole. They have now. Curiously, the current discussion seems to take place mainly outside of professional economics. That may be because economists feel there are no longer any very important intellectual issues at stake. If that is so, it may be worth stating what the agreed position is.

First, however, one should have an idea of the orders of magnitude involved: how fast is technology changing? After all, an analysis that will perfectly well cover moderate rates of technological progress and moderate increases in the rate may not apply nearly so well if there are catastrophic changes in the role of labor in production. Fortunately this is a fairly straightforward question. Its answer does not depend on what fraction of all the scientists who have ever lived are now alive, or on the number of computers produced and installed last year, or on the existence of an oil refinery with nobody in it, or on any such exotic facts. Any major change in the quantitative relation between output and employment must show up in the conventional productivity statistics. Here productivity means nothing but the value of output per manhour, corrected for price changes. It goes up whenever labor requirements for a unit of final output go down, and by the same percentage. There are productivity statistics for certain industries, for manufacturing as a whole, and for even broader aggregates. It doesn't matter much which aggregate is selected. What such figures show is easily summarized.

* From "Technology and Unemployment," *The Public Interest*, 1 (Fall 1965), pp. 17–26. Copyright © National Affairs Inc., 1965. Reprinted with permission of author and publisher. Robert M. Solow is Professor of Economics at Massachusetts Institute of Technology, Cambridge, Mass.

For the private economy as a whole, the average annual increase in output per manhour between 1909 and 1964 was 2.4 percent. But if we divide that long period at the end of World War II, it turns out that the increase was faster after 1947 than before. From 1909 to 1947 productivity rose by 2 percent a year on the average, while from 1947 to 1964 it rose by 3.2 percent a year. Moreover, from 1961 to 1964, productivity rose by 3.4 percent a year.

I said that this was a fairly straightforward question: only *fairly* straightforward because it is not easy to interpret changes in productivity extending over just a few years. Recessions and recoveries have their own productivity patterns and there are erratic fluctuations besides. The 1961–1964 rise, part of a long upswing, is especially suspicious. Still, it is hard to mistake what the figures are trying to say. There was a definite acceleration of the productivity trend about the time of the war. (The biggest year-to-year increase came in 1949–50 for reasons not hard to understand.) There may even have been a slight further acceleration after 1961. It is too early to say, and in any case the amount involved is small.

This rough statistical indication is enough. It does not suggest the immediate disappearance of the job as an institution. But what does it say about the possibility of slower, less dramatic technological unemployment, if only a million or so at a time? Popular writing suggests that there are two schools of thought. One claims point-blank that automation necessarily—or at least in fact—"creates more jobs than it destroys." From this it would seem to follow that, if technological progress went at any slower pace than it now does, there would necessarily be more unemployment than there now is. The other school claims that automation necessarily—or at least in fact—destroys more jobs than it creates. So that if technological progress went at any faster pace than it now does, or only just as fast, severe unemployment would be inevitable.

Which school is right? I think the economist's answer has to be that both are wrong or, to be more precise, both are irrelevant. They have simply missed the point. Perhaps the question "Does automation create or destroy more jobs?" is answerable *in principle;* perhaps it is not. What is perfectly clear is that the question is simply unanswerable *in fact.* I doubt that anyone could make a good estimate of the net number of jobs created or destroyed merely by the invention of the zipper or of sliced bread. It would be a fantastically more complicated job to discover the net effect of *all* technological progress in any single year on employment. No one can possibly know; so no one has the right to speak confidently.

The Great Automation Question, as I have phrased it, is not only unanswerable, it is the wrong question. The important point is that, to a pretty good first approximation, *the total volume of employment in the United States today is simply not determined by the rate of technological progress.* Both theory and common observation tell us that a modern mixed economy can, by proper and active use of fiscal and monetary policy weapons, have full employment for *any* plausible rate of technological change within a range that is easily wide enough to cover the American experience.

THE EUROPEAN EXPERIENCE

Consider, for example, the West German economy. Output per manhour has been increasing considerably faster there than in the United States— about 6 percent a year since 1950, and 5 percent a year since 1955. While the American *level* of productivity is unsurpassed anywhere, the economy of West Germany has certainly been no less technologically dynamic than our own in the past 15 years. Yet for some time the German unemployment rate has been below 1 percent of the labor force (compared with 5–7 percent here) and there have been 7 to 10 unfilled vacant jobs for every unemployed person. What is even more striking is that this technologically advanced and advancing economy seems to have an insatiable appetite for unskilled labor. Having exhausted the domestic supply, it goes to Italy, Spain, Portugal, Greece and Turkey to recruit workers who have only minimal education and can surely neither read, write, nor even speak German. One has the impression that even an American teenager could find employment in a German factory. Of course there are many special things that might be said about the recent history of the German economy, from the need for postwar reconstruction to the now-ended flow of refugees from the East. But they do not affect the point at issue.

Or take an example on the other side, Great Britain. Their productivity has grown a bit more slowly than ours. The conventional belief is that the British economy offers more resistance to technological progress than most others. The British economy has also had all sorts of other troubles— but the maintenance of high employment has not been one of them. The unemployment rate in Britain is now about 1½ percent. There is even some discussion as to whether the economy might not function a bit more efficiently and smoothly with a slightly higher unemployment rate, say 2 percent.

Polar examples like these give a strong hint that no simple yea-saying or nay-saying can be the right answer to the question about the likelihood of technological unemployment. The right answer is more complicated and goes something like this: At any one time, we can hope to identify something we can call the capacity output of the economy as a whole. (Sometimes it is called "potential" or "full employment" output; the idea is the same.) This is at best a rough and ready concept. Under stress an economy can produce more than its capacity for quite a while, so capacity output is not a rigid upper limit. Moreover, a modern economy can produce a wide variety of "mixes" of goods and services, heavily weighted with military hardware, or automobiles, or machinery, or food and fiber, or personal services, according to circumstances. When the economy as a whole is operating at or near its capacity, there may be some industries straining their plant and equipment to the limit while others have quite a bit of slack. Nevertheless, under normal circumstances the output-mix changes slowly. We can know what we mean by capacity output and, subject to some error, we can measure it. (In the first quarter of 1965, the country produced a Gross National Product of about $649 billion, annual rate; the Council of Economic Advisers estimated that capacity output was about $25 billion higher.)

The productive capacity of an economy grows fairly smoothly—not with perfect regularity, of course, but fairly smoothly. The growth of productive capacity is determined by an array of basic underlying factors: the growth of the labor force in numbers; changes in the health, education, training, and other qualities of those who work and manage; changes in the number of hours they wish to work; the exhaustion and discovery of natural resources; the accumulation of capital in the form of buildings, machinery, and inventories; and the advance of scientific, engineering and technological knowledge and its application to production. This is one of the important ways in which the level of technology enters our problem. If the rate of technological progress accelerates or decelerates, then the growth of capacity is likely to speed up or slow down with it. The different factors are not entirely independent of one another: new knowledge may require better-trained or differently-trained people or wholly new plant and equipment for its successful application. It is also possible for changes in one of the underlying trends to be offset by changes in another, coincidentally or consciously engineered. In any case, they are likely to move with some smoothness, and their net resultant—capacity output—even more so.

The actual output produced by the economy fluctuates more raggedly around the trend of capacity, sometimes above it, sometimes—more often, in the case of the U.S.—below it. When production presses hard against capacity, it is capacity limitations that keep it from going higher. In all other cases, what governs the current level of output is the *demand* for goods and services. Demand is exercised by the interlocked spending decisions of all the final purchasers in the economy: consumers, business firms, all levels of government, and the foreigners who buy our exports. Technological developments play a part here too, among many other determinants of spending decisions. Changes in military technology may cause governments to spend more—or less; the invention of new commodities and new ways to produce old ones may induce industry to invest in new facilities and consumers to shift their purchases (and perhaps to change the total amount). Of course there are other reasons why the flow of consumption, investment, and government expenditures may vary. So long as capacity pressure is not too strong, bottlenecks not too pervasive, when total demand rises, total output will rise to match it; when total demand falls, total output will fall with it. This doesn't happen instantaneously; inventories provide one buffer. But it happens.

The picture, then, is of a fairly smoothly rising trend of capacity, propelled by some rather deep-seated forces. Moving around it is a much more volatile, unsteady curve of current output, driven by whatever governs aggregate expenditures, including economic policy decisions. Current output cannot be far above capacity for long, but it can drag along below for years at a time. During the first half of this century, the trend of capacity output in the United States seems to have risen on the average at about 3 percent a year. From the end of the Korean War until very recently the rate of growth of capacity was more like 3½ percent a year; and the best evidence seems to be that the current and immediately prospective growth rate of capacity will be in the neighborhood of 4 percent a year, possibly a bit lower now, possibly a bit higher later. The postwar acceleration was mainly a result of the speedup in productivity already mentioned. The current acceleration may draw a little something from further speedup in productivity, but its main source is the arrival at working age of the first postwar babies.

THE TRIUMPH OF ECONOMICS OVER FABLE

Now the crucial fact is that when output is rising faster than capacity the unemployment rate tends to fall; when output is rising more slowly the capacity—even though it is rising, mind you—the unemployment rate tends to get bigger; and if output rises at about the same rate as capacity, so that the percentage gap between them stays constant, then the unemployment rate stays pretty nearly constant. It is a fairly safe generalization about the past ten years that when aggregate output has risen at about 3½ percent a year between any two points in time, just about enough new jobs have appeared to occupy the increment to the labor force, with nothing left over to reduce unemployment. The tax cut of 1964 is a kind of landmark in American economic policy, the triumph of Economics over Fable. I like to think that it was helped along by the sheer cogency of the arguments for it. But any realist has to give a lot of credit to the fact that, from the middle of 1962 to the middle of 1963, with the economy rising and setting "new records" every quarter, the unemployment rate stuck at about 5.6 percent of the labor force and stubbornly refused to go anywhere, especially not down. Be thankful for small favors; but note also that during that time the GNP corrected for price changes rose only by a little more than 3 percent. The gap between output and capacity was not narrowing; unemployment was not reduced. If it turns out to be right that the growth of capacity during the next few years will be nearer 4 percent annually, then it will take a 4 percent increase in demand every year to hold the unemployment rate constant; what was good enough to keep unemployment level in 1963 may by 1967 not be adequate to stem slowly rising unemployment.

Closer study of the facts suggests a more powerful generalization. On the average, an extra 1 percent growth of real (i.e. price-corrected) GNP in any year has been associated with a reduction in the unemployment rate of roughly one-third of a percentage point. Or, what is the same thing, to get the unemployment rate to fall by one full point from one year to the next requires that real output (real demand) increase by about 3 percent *over and above the increase in capacity.* To see how this works, consider the behavior of the economy since the tax cut.

From the middle of 1963 to the middle of 1964, real GNP gained 5 percent. "Capacity GNP" probably went up by something less than 4 percent. The rule of thumb I have mentioned (which sometimes goes under the name of Okun's Law) would predict a drop in the unemployment rate of something like 4/10 of a percentage point. In fact, the unemployment rate did go down, by 5/10 of a point, from 5.7 percent to 5.2 percent. In the half-year from the third quarter of 1964 to the first quarter of 1965 real GNP gained almost 2½ percent; this is more than one-half of 1 percent over and above the rise in capacity. It should, therefore, have reduced the unemployment rate by some 2/10 of one point. The unemployment rate actually fell from 5.1 percent to 4.8 percent.

In all honesty I cannot leave the impression that the national economy ticks over like a bit of clockwork, predictable from a few simple rules of thumb. I have picked out a few instances in which the pat relation between output, growth, and unemployment worked just fine. It is not always so. The relation itself is compounded of the effects of changes in demand on hours worked, on the number of people seeking employment, on the short-run ups and downs of productivity itself. Each of these connections has some slippage; none is precise; there are lags sometimes before the expected response occurs. Moreover, something must depend on what mix of goods and services happens to be demanded. A billion dollars of services probably provides more employment than a billion dollars of goods, a billion dollars of missiles perhaps less than a billion dollars of aircraft. And yet, it's not at all a bad rule of thumb. If I had to predict what would happen to unemployment during the next year I would certainly begin by trying to estimate what is going to happen to the gap between capacity output and aggregate demand.

What does all this have to do with the question of technological unemployment?

Suppose that a surge of technological progress takes place, whether you call it automation or something less ominous-sounding. Productivity will begin to rise at a faster pace than it used to. So will the trend-line of capacity output. If the demand for goods and services continues to grow only at its old rate, the gap between demand and capacity will get wider. In other words, if the increase in capacity is not matched by an increase in demand, the result will be an increase in unemployment. (All this, mind you, while new records are being set regularly and columnists assure us that the economy is "booming.") You can call this unemployment technological, if you like, but it is not different from ordinary unemployment. The way to get rid of it is to make sure that demand rises in step with the economy's capacity to produce.

I have already mentioned that changes in technology also have an effect on demand. New commodities, new materials, major cost reductions cannot fail to leave a mark on the way in which the public spends its income. (The "public" here includes businesses and governments as well as individual families.) It is possible that any particular burst of technological progress will carry along with it the extra demand necessary to keep extra unemployment from appearing. It is also possible that it will not. It is even possible that a series of innovations should generate a bigger increment to demand than to capacity, and therefore a net reduction in unemployment. The trouble is that nobody can say in advance which will actually be the case. Indeed, as I have suggested, nobody may be able to tell after the fact which has been the case. One can, of course, say whether unemployment has gone up or gone down. But there are many other influences on employment. Faster growth of the labor force, for example, can also push up the capacity trend; it can also have effects on demand. Except under the best of circumstances, it may prove impossible to identify the particular effects of technical progress and separate them from the effects of other forces.

The moral of this analysis is that such an identification doesn't much matter. Unemployment above the "frictional" level occurs, usually, because total dollar demand fails to keep pace with productive capacity. Whether or not an acceleration of technological progress happens to be among the causes is not all-important. The remedy in any case is to keep total demand moving in step with capacity. And this, governments in the mixed economy do have the fiscal and monetary policies to ensure—if they will use these powers.

So, as the examples of Germany and Britain confirm, it is possible to have full employment with slow technical progress and full employment with fast technical progress. *But it does not happen automatically.* It requires conscious policy to manage the volume of demand and keep it going at approximately the right pace. (Do not be misled, in this connection, by the case of Germany. The Federal Republic talks the best game of *laissez-faire* in the world. At the same time it does dozens of things each one of which would be instantly denounced in the United States as creeping socialism.)

In the modern mixed economy, there is no shortage of instrumentalities for operating on aggregate demand: monetary and credit policy, changes in taxation, adjustments in transfer payments—such as unemployment compensation, family allowances, and social security benefits—and, finally, the direct purchases of goods and services by the government. Since each of these instruments must serve other purposes as well, it may not always be clear exactly what is the best policy. That is what the discussion ought to be about, rather than mere anecdote about the wonders and horrors of modern technology.

THE FINE STRUCTURE OF UNEMPLOYMENT

This analysis of the interrelations among technological progress, output, and employment is, as I have said, a first approximation, though a usable one. A second approximation would have to take account of the fact that each of these global concepts has a fine structure. The main new implication is that a period of rapid change is likely to be accompanied by much displacement of labor. Even if the total volume of unemployment is held unchanged, its composition may shift noticeably. This calls for additional policy measures designed to speed and cushion the necessary transitions.

Technological progress, whether it takes the form of new products or "automation," can be more or less labor-saving in its effects. And, however labor-saving it is, it can fall more or less heavily on the availability of skilled jobs or unskilled jobs, manual or white-collar jobs, manufacturing or service jobs, jobs for uneducated or jobs for highly-educated workers. Any innovation has direct and indirect effects on employment, some of them very complicated. New products and new methods of production require new machinery, new materials, new locations, and perhaps still other changes in economic activity. It is well to realize that *almost nothing is known about the full labor-saving effects of major innovations,* nor even whether "automation" is more or less labor-saving than earlier changes in technology, nor even whether it causes any consistent change in the general level of skill needed in production. There is always a small supply of anecdotes, but anecdote is a poor sort of evidence, given the universal tendency to tell the same anecdote more than once.

The second of our global quantities—output—also has a structure. I have already mentioned that shifts in demand between goods and services, and among various kinds of goods, may change the basic relations connecting total output and total employment. This is because the different things that families, firms, and governments buy contain different amounts of labor, and especially different amounts of labor of different types and from different places. The shift in defense procurement from aircraft to missiles may well have meant less employment per dollar of spending; it has certainly meant more employment for the sort of people who are at work in the electronics industry in the places where the electronics industry has settled, and less work for the occupations more at home in the making of airframes and engines in the places where that industry has been most concentrated. A similar story could be told about the replacement of natural by synthetic fibers and, above all, about the shift from agriculture to industry.

I remember that in 1961 one often heard the opinion that the shift from goods to services was accelerating, and that the demand for durable goods, in particular, was essentially saturated. The burden of the argument was that the blue-collar occupations and the traditional industrial cities— Detroit especially—were finished, would not respond to general economic expansion. The prescription was for salvage operations rather than fiscal and monetary stimulation. Well as it happens, the expansion that began early in 1961 has been to an unusual extent concentrated in the goods-producing industries, especially in the durable-goods industries, most especially in the automobile industry. One result has been that employment has risen (and unemployment has fallen) relatively more rapidly in blue-collar than in white-collar occupations, more in manufacturing than in the service industries, and more among the unskilled and semi-skilled than among others. I do not conclude from this experience that white-collar occupations and service industries have had it; I conclude only that people ought to stifle the tendency, in matters they do not understand, to project the last six months into an irreversible trend.

As this discussion indicates, and as everyone must realize anyhow, there is also a fine structure to unemployment. Everyone in the labor force does not have the same probability of becoming or staying unemployed. Unemployment rates differ according to age, sex, color, education, skill, occupation, place, and industry of attachment. The differences are far from trivial: in the first quarter of this year less than 3 percent of white men 20 years old and older were unemployed, but more than 30 percent of Negro girls between 14 and 19 years old were unemployed. The character of unemployment as a social problem depends critically on the composition of the unemployed. It is one kind of situation when unemployment is concentrated, as it now is, among the young; it would be a different, but perhaps even more serious, situation if the same amount of unemployment were concentrated among heads of families with long-standing attachment to the labor force. An economist will wish to separate the two questions: How much unemployment is there? Who has to bear it? I myself would not want to push the difference between these questions too far; but it is important to push the difference far enough. Otherwise confusion arises.

If, in fact, we are in for a period of comparatively rapid productivity increase in white-collar and service jobs, then some of the traditional unemployment *differentials* may shift. Whether they do so will depend on the speed with which the supply of different categories of labor adjusts to the demand. One cannot draw any simple conclusions about *total* employment in this way.

THE ARIZONA FALLACY

I have argued that the main determinant of the total amount of unemployment is the size of the gap between the economy's aggregate capacity to produce things and the aggregate purchasing power the economy is willing to devote to buying them. When it comes to the composition of unemployment, the important things to talk about are the particular nature of technological progress, the fine structure of demand, the path by which the present situation has been reached (I shall mention why in a moment), and perhaps the forces that govern the relative wages of different categories of labor.

That is a subject to itself. I want to make only a negative point, directly related to the Great Automation Question. It is all too easy to fall into a fallacy which goes like this. Many of the unemployed are uneducated and unskilled, and many of the uneducated and unskilled are unemployed. It must follow that the source of our high unemployment has to be something which strikes particularly at the unskilled and uneducated. What can that be but the tendency for automation to render the unskilled and uneducated unemployable? It is not often realized that the logic of this argument is about on a par with the logic that observes a relatively high incidence of deaths from tuberculosis in Arizona and concludes that the Arizona climate must be a powerful cause of tuberculosis.

It does seem true that, with the present state of the arts and the present wage structure, the skilled, the educated, the middle-aged and the permanently established are, generally speaking, more "desirable" employees than others. This suggests that in any substantial period of tranquility employers may succeed in exchanging their undesirable workers for more desirable ones. It does not at all deny that a sustained increase in output would induce them to absorb the "undesirable" workers. You do not have to be a high school graduate to sell soap in a department store. But so long as high school graduates can be had, they will be hired first; the drop-outs will go to the end of the line, and remain unemployed. This sort of explanation is especially plausible in the circumstances we now face.

The American economy has sidled along with excessive but not catastrophic unemployment for almost ten years. There has been no deep recession, so there have not been extensive layoffs. With labor markets slack and new jobs hard to find, the number of voluntary quits and job-changes has also stayed fairly low. When unemployment is generated by inadequate growth rates rather than by recession, labor turnover may thus be relatively slow. The natural result is that unemployment is disproportionately heavy among newcomers to the labor force, both young people just out of school and older women seeking work after raising children. This mechanism, together with the relative "desirability" of the better educated and with discrimination against Negroes, seems capable of explaining the observed distribution of unemployment. It gets a little more confirmation with each month that the current upswing lasts. The "imminent" skill shortages fail to appear; the hard core slowly melts; nearly all categories of unemployment dwindle; employment increases most rapidly among those groups with the highest unemployment rates. And if, as many observers fear, by the end of the year the growth of aggregate output slows down to about the growth of capacity and the unemployment rate stops falling, I shall take that as further confirmation, the hard way.

9 Men and machines in perspective*

ROBERT L. HEILBRONER

It is curious that technological unemployment has always been the intellectual stepchild of capitalism. One would think that nothing would have so interested economists as the economic impact—and above all, the impact on labor—of machines that suddenly alter the speed, the technical requirements, the human relationships, not to mention the end products, of the economic process. Instead, a consideration of technology in any guise has always made economists uncomfortable, and the thought of technology as a labor-affecting force has simply been too much for most of them. There was Marx, of course, who put technology and its labor-displacing effects into the very center of his diagnosis of capitalism, but no one paid any attention to him. Alfred Marshall and John Maynard Keynes, the two greatest economists of mature capitalism, managed to conduct their inquiries without admitting the subject of technology at all. Only in the underworld of economic thought, in the intellectual descendants of the Luddites, do we find a persisting concern with machines as things that do man's work and thereby lessen the need for his labor. But to the great majority of recognized economists these rude doubts remained as inadmissible as they were unexamined.

In itself, this is no doubt a subject for fruitful investigation—the problems society avoids are usually significant. But the long neglect of technology as a labor-displacing force also has an immediate relevance for our subject. It helps explain why automation catches us so intellectually unprepared. The necessary empirical data concerning technology, the essential statistical indicators of its impact on employment, simply do not exist, or are only now being hurriedly assembled. More important, in regard to the most elementary problems of theory—which is to say, in regard to the question of how to think about the question of technological unemployment—we find the same fuzzy notions, or the same dogmatic assertions

* From "Men and Machines in Perspective," *The Public Interest*, 1 (Fall 1965), pp. 27–36. Copyright © National Affairs Inc., 1965. Reprinted with permission of author and publisher. Robert L. Heilbroner is Professor of Economics at the New School for Social Research Graduate Faculty, New York, N.Y.

100

masquerading as thought, that thirty-five years ago characterized our first attempts to explain the Great Depression.

So it is not surprising that the debate on automation is something less than a model of clarity. On the one hand we have the bland assurances of the Establishment that technological unemployment has never been more than a "frictional" problem for the economy; on the other hand, organizations with chilling names like "cyberculture" schedule the arrival of Total Unemployment for the day after tomorrow. In this fruitless exchange, two things are essentially missing. First, we lack some very important knowledge, the nature of which I will have a chance to point out as we go along. Second, we lack some kind of framework, compounded of history and theory, into which to put the current debate. It is the latter that I shall try to present in this article.

I

I wish to begin with a very simple proposition, although in our present state of unknowledge, it must be offered in a tentative rather than an assertive tone. It is that inventions and innovations have not entered society at random, shedding their advantages or disadvantages indifferently over all industries or individuals. On the contrary, I believe that technology enters our kind of society in a systematic fashion, and that there is a discoverable pattern behind its appearance, now in this area of social effort, and now in that particular area.

Very simply, the pattern is due to the enormous magnetic pull exerted by an existing economic structure on the minds of men who are concerned with making and applying inventions and innovations. There is, of course, a large element of freedom, of chance, of individual adventure, in the advance of scientific understanding. But when it comes to the incorporation of the existing body of scientific knowledge into daily work in a society activated by private gain, I suspect that attention and effort will naturally be concentrated on those tasks and challenges that predominate at a given time. To put it as concretely as possible, I imagine that in a largely agricultural society, the focus of technical inventiveness would naturally fall on agricultural processes, that in a society turning toward industrialism, the focus would be spontaneously directed toward machines having to do with manufacture, etc. Needless to say, the pace and direction of technological change will be powerfully influenced by other factors, such as the relative dearness of labor or capital; but, other things equal, as the economist says, I would think that the changing nature of the social task itself will serve as a major guide.

Is this proposition empirically demonstrable? Here our woeful lack of systematic knowledge begins to get in our way. Yet I think one can discern a grand sequence of inventive endeavor in the United States, with, needless to say, many overlaps and anachronisms. The sequence begins, chronologically as well as in terms of concentration of effort, with agriculture. For all the early improvements in textile machinery, or the introduction of railroads and steamships, I think it is fair to say that the sector of the economy that initially experienced the grand impulse of technology was basic farming. First the epochal cotton gin, then the iron plow, the harrow and the seed drill, then the mechanical reaper, and all along the way the gradual substitution of horsepower for manpower—taken in its entirety, this was nothing less than a technological revolution which was in full force by the 1860's. It was not only the quality, but the quantity of capital, that worked its dynamic effect. By 1900 more money was invested in the reaper than in any other machine in the world save only the steam engine, and by 1960 the average worker in agriculture employed more capital ($21,300) than the average worker in manufacturing ($15,900).

The table below gives us some idea of the enormous increase in the productivity of farm labor that resulted from this revolution:

Man-hour requirements per acre

	1800	1840	1880	1920	1960
Corn	86	69	46	33	10
Wheat	56	35	20	12	4
Cotton	185	135	119	96	66

Source: W. D. Rasmussen, "The Impact of Technological Change on American Agriculture," *Journal of Economic History*, December 1962.

The statistics clearly bespeak the long history of agricultural improvement. By contrast, in the field of manufacturing—or rather, in that congeries of tasks associated with handling, shaping, assembling, processing and transporting goods—the main entrance of technology begins rather later, around the time of the Civil War. As late as 1869, for instance, nearly half of the mechanical power in manufacturing still came from water wheels rather than steam engines. Although immensely important inventions and improvements begin to revolutionize some aspects of manufacturing early in the 19th century, the great transformation of industrial production does not gain momentum until the latter half of the 19th century, reaching its climax in the mass production techniques of the 20th century.

There is an important consequence to this wave-like succession of technological salients of advance. It is that the productivity of all workers in all sectors and echelons does not rise straight across the board, like a well-drilled parade of soldiers, but changes in uneven fashion as different areas of work are successively affected by technology.

We have already seen the improvement in agricultural man-hour productivity which we could trace back to the beginning of the 19th century.

The statistics of manufacturing are less satisfactory, partly of course because many of the manufacturing processes do not extend as far back in time as do basic agricultural tasks. Hence in following the general trend of manufacturing productivity somewhat more impressionistic estimates have to suffice. We know, for instance, that a man in a pulp and paper plant in the late 1950's produced about three times as much output in an hour as did his predecessor after World War I; that a worker in a steel plant over the same period quadrupled his hourly output of steel; that a worker in a cigarette factory increased his or her production by six times. Taking "manufactures" generally, it is usually estimated that an average worker today produces about five or six times as much, per unit of time, as did his great-great grandfather at the time of the Civil War.

II

To these essentially familiar statistics we must now add a third set of figures having to do with the impact of technology on productivity—or rather, in the absence of reliable statistics, we must add our impressions as to what the figures would be if they existed. These concern a group of occupations distinct from those of farm and "factory," that we will label "office" and "service" work, meaning by this a wide variety of jobs that administer, supervise, service, instruct and cater to society.

Some of these employments, and the roughly-estimated numbers of people who are engaged in them can be seen below:

Office and service occupations, 1962

Teachers, including college	1,900,000
Salesmen and salesclerks	3,700,000
Nonfarm managers and proprietors	5,400,000
Bookkeepers	900,000
Waiters, waitresses, kitchen help (not private household)	1,100,000
Cooks (not private household)	600,000
Protective service workers	700,000
Clergymen	200,000
Lawyers	200,000
Doctors and dentists	300,000
Hospital attendants	400,000
Cashiers	500,000
Secretaries, stenos, typists	2,300,000
Nurses	600,000

This is of course only a sampling of the various kinds of activities I have in mind. I have omitted 100,000 editors and reporters, 300,000 musicians, 100,000 social workers, 350,000 insurance agents, 200,000 newsboys, and so on. In all, perhaps 35 million people have some kind of nonfarm, nonfactory public or private job.

Whatever shortages of data troubled us before vex us to an even higher degree here. By and large there are no estimates of the increased productivity of clerks and barbers, administrators and janitors over the years. Hence we are perforce reduced to very uncertain evidence when we try to measure the impact of technology on this last group of occupations. But the overwhelming—and I think trustworthy—impression one gets is that the manhour productivity of these jobs has not risen to anything like the extent of improvement in farm and "factory" work.

There are, to be sure, technological changes that have appreciably—even very greatly—raised the level of particular office employments. One thinks of the plane and the automobile that have added cubits to the stature of the traveling salesman, the telephone that has vastly extended the productivity of all supervisory tasks, the office adding machine that has helped the bookkeeper, and the indispensable typewriter. These improvements notwithstanding, one cannot easily establish a steady upward march of productivity in the office as one does in the factory. Manhour productivity indices for "distribution," for instance, shows a rise of only one-sixth that of manufacturing between 1900 and 1929. Many occupations—waiters, for instance—are virtually the same today as a hundred years ago, not to say worse. And as every businessman will testify, what eats up costs these days is not so much production as "overhead." What this means, of course, is that technology has not yet entered the "office" to nearly the degree that it has overrun farm and factory.

III

We will return shortly to the significance of this laggard area of technological advance. First, however, we must add an important economic generalization to our general historic schema. It is that the impact of technology on output, when it is introduced into a new industry or sector, is not alone determined by the new physical capabilities of production stemming from the new techniques. Rather, it is determined by the interplay of these new capabilities with the stern economic realities of demand.

An illustration may make this clearer. Suppose we have an industry producing, let us say, clothespins. Presumably it is already producing as many clothespins with its existing techniques as consumers will buy at going prices. Now suppose that a technological improvement doubles the productivity of each man, thereby halving the cost of clothespins (we will forget about the cost of the new machines). Clearly, unless sales increase we will not be able to employ the former labor force. But will sales increase? That hinges entirely on the response—or "elasticity"—of demand when clothespin prices are now cut. If clothespin prices are cut in half, and as a result consumers buy three times as many pins as before, employment in the industry will rise. But if they only buy 50 percent more than before the price cut, employment will fall.

This little excursion into elementary economics is necessary if we are now to proceed from our general discussion of technological entry to its effect on employment. For everything, it must now be clear, depends on the responsiveness of demand for the various kinds of goods that technology makes available. In the case of farm products, for instance, demand has always been notoriously *inelastic*—that is, very unresponsive to price cuts. Hence as agricultural output steadily expanded throughout the 19th century, it met a wall of consumer indifference. The desire to buy wheat and corn at prevailing prices did not by any matter of means keep pace with the enlarged capacity to produce them, with the result that employment on the farm fell precipitously. At the beginning of the 19th century perhaps 75 or 80 percent of the labor force was engaged in farm tasks. By the end of the century this had been cut to 30 percent. By mid-20th century it was down to 8 percent.

Thus the entry of technology into a sector where demand was relatively unresponsive forced an exodus of labor into other areas—which is to say, into the city and its "factory" jobs. And fortunately, at least in the beginning and middle of the 19th century, the demand for factory products was much more elastic than that for farm goods. Even though individual productivity was steadily rising in "factory" work throughout the 19th century, particularly after the Civil War, the demand for manufactured and processed goods was sufficiently buoyant so that employment could also steadily expand. In the year 1800 "factory" occupations accounted for perhaps only 5 to 10 percent of the nation's labor distribution, but by 1900 they constituted a full 37 percent.

Thereafter, a somewhat different constellation of forces seems to have prevailed. Perhaps the elasticity of consumer demand for further manufactures began to fall; perhaps the productivity of "factory" work rose at an accelerated rate. Whatever the cause, the percentage of the nation's work force engaged in "factory" jobs remained fairly constant. By 1960 only 39 percent of the labor force was in manufacturing, mining, transportation, utilities, construction, etc., compared with the 37 percent at the turn of the century. And this much more sluggish rate of growth is given further significance when we recall that weekly hours of work had been reduced from 60 in 1900 to 40 in 1960. Were it not for this fall in hours of work per week—in other words, had we combined the new technology with workmen who labored the long week of the 1900s—the volume of employment needed to satisfy the demands for "factory" goods would have fallen sharply. Indeed, from 1957 to 1962, despite rising output, there *was* a steady gradual shrinkage of 100,000 jobs in manufacturing, and whereas this trend has recently been reversed, there continues to be a fall in employment in mining and utilities.

Meanwhile, what of the labor that was inexorably being pushed off the farm all through the 20th century? Since the growth of "factory" occupations was slowing down, clearly employment had to be provided on some

other front. And so it was, by the wide range of "office" and "service" jobs
we have already noticed. Here, not only was demand elastic for the services
they performed but—and this is the crucial point of the whole analysis—
the productivity of these occupations had not risen greatly: As a result, the
rising demand for the output of "office work" resulted in a very large rise
in the number of people hired to perform this work. In 1900 only a quarter
of the labor force was in the spectrum of the service, administrative and
other functions embraced by this last sector of employment. By 1965 over
50 percent of the labor force had entered these jobs, thanks mainly to the
fact that technology had not yet duplicated their tasks as it had in farm
and factory labor.

IV

So much by way of background. I move now to a suggestion that may
put the problem of automation into the perspective of theory and history
that we have sought. It is that technology is belatedly gathering momentum
in the direction of "office" and "service" tasks, thereby invading those sheltered precincts of the economy in which labor has not yet been exposed to
the full competition of machinery.

My suggestion—it cannot be more than that until we know more about
the nature of contemporary technology and its points of application
throughout the economy—puts the concern about "automation" into a
somewhat different focus than is customary. Ben Seligman, for example, in
Dissent (Winter, 1965) lists an impressive number of instances where the
new technology of computers, feedback systems, sensory equipment, etc.,
has displaced labor, much of it "factory" labor. I do not question the validity of his instances, but I do question whether dollar for dollar this
new factory equipment is any more labor-displacing than "old-fashioned"
equipment such as fork-lift trucks, overhead conveyors, high-speed machinery, and so on. I must confess that I can neither see any reason *a priori*
why a dollar's worth of "automation" equipment should replace any more
labor than a dollar's worth of less fancy mechanical equipment, nor can
I, as yet, find any statistical evidence that manufacturing productivity is
rising faster today than over a number of periods in the past—for instance,
from 1920 to 1924.

In other words, I do not see the threat of automation in any unusual
characteristics possessed by modern day "factory" technology. What I *do*
suspect, on the other hand, is that the new technology is threatening a
whole new group of skills—the sorting, filing, checking, calculating, re-
membering, comparing, okaying skills—that are the special preserve of
the office worker. Moreover, it is not just complicated computers that are
threatening to take over functions in this hitherto sheltered area of work,
although no doubt the new technology is conducive to more complex ad-

ministrative tasks. Very simple machines may also invade the field—vending machines, or organizational innovations such as discount houses, or zip code numbers that speed mail sorting. To put it differently, it seems to me that office and service work is now the area that cries out to be rationalized, simplified, and abridged by machinery, just as did farm work in the early 1800's and factory work later in the 19th century. In an economy where effort usually follows incentive, it would be unusual if technology did not turn in this beckoning direction.

V

How severe a challenge does this pose to the economic system? The answer, if we assume that technology is in fact moving in the direction I suggest, is not a simple one. It will depend on the conjunctions of many forces which buffer or aggravate the displacement effect of technology alone.

One aggravating factor will be the growth in the labor supply itself. Each year sees a small but significant increase in the number of married women looking for work, whether lured by the prospect of a two-income household, by the lessened chores of housework, or by "The Feminine Mystique." Even more important will be the coming-of-age of the bumper crops of war babies, now about to graduate from high school and college. All in all, the number of jobseekers is slated to rise alarmingly over the coming years. From 1947 to 1957 the number of people within the "working-age" brackets of 15 to 65 increased by 8.3 million. In the six years between 1964 and 1970 it will rise by nearly *fifteen* million. Thus the changing composition of the labor force will crowd the labor markets and intensify the struggle for jobs (and the failure-rate in finding jobs) for reasons having nothing to do with automation.

A second factor bearing on unemployment is our over-all rate of economic expansion. In *The Price of Prosperity*, Peter Bernstein has reminded us that our current rate of economic growth of about 4 percent a year is a third higher than our long-run "secular" rate of growth. He points out that even if the workweek is cut to 37.5 hours, and if technological improvements come no faster than in the recent past, our unemployment could reach 10 million people by 1970, should our rate of growth fall back to the "norm" of 3 percent. It might even touch 15 millions, if the rate reverted to the 2.5 percent growth figure of the 1957–1960 era.

The remedy, says Bernstein and most other economists, is to use every device to make sure that our growth does not slacken, but rather increases. But the matter is not quite so simple as that. For if our rate of growth is accelerated by a burst of labor-saving technology, we could experience both a higher rate of output *and* a higher rate of unemployment. There is, of course, always the chance and the hope that our growth could be hastened by the emergence of a great new employment-generating industry, comparable to the auto industry in the 1910's and 1920's. All one can say, when this possibility is raised, is that such an industry is not now visible, and that expansion in private output since World War II—impressive both in volume and in new kinds of goods—has not been very conducive to an expansion of employment. According to no less an authority than Secretary of Labor Willard Wirtz, of the 4 million new full-time jobs created between 1947 and 1963, *only 5 percent* originated in the private sector.

There remains another general solution, largely advocated by the labor movement—the contraction of the workweek. The rationale is simple and incontestable. By shortening the workweek (through the imposition of overtime rates after, say, 30 hours of work), employers are induced to spread the existing volume of work among more people. Or they may simply throttle back their output to 30 hours, thereby making it more attractive for a new plant to be built to cater to the market.

There can be no doubt that the shortening of the workweek has been a principal method of absorbing the "surplus productivity" of machines, and there can be no doubt that it will continue to constitute a main avenue of social adjustment. After all, the whole purpose of the introduction of technology is to enable men to work less hard, or at least to enable them to transfer their labor from unpleasant to pleasant tasks. The trouble with adjustments in hours is that they require the cooperation of labor as regards the cost of the new shorter workweek. If we suppose that the work-week were suddenly reduced to 20 hours, we can easily see that employers would be willing to hire twice as many workers as they now have—provided that the men who did the first twenty hours of work did not demand as much pay as they formerly got for 40 hours.

The adjustment of the workweek, in other words, depends on how much of a cut in wages (if any) labor is willing to take, and on how a rise in labor costs will affect employers' willingness to expand their work forces (or intensify their search for labor-saving machinery). It is impossible to make firm predictions about any side of this problem, other than that the issue itself is not likely to be rapidly resolved. Ten or twenty years from now we may have eased ourselves into a "normal" workweek of 30 or even fewer hours, but during the next crucial decade it seems fruitless to look to this source for a major alleviation of the unemployment issue.

This seems to leave, as the main buffering force during those years, and indeed for many years thereafter, the deliberate use of public employment-generating or spreading policies. There are a number of possibilities that might be tried. For instance, the government could try to reduce the number of people looking for work by subsidizing young people to remain in school and college. Another policy along similar lines would encourage earlier voluntary retirement by lowering the Social Security retirement age and raising benefits. A much more drastic course would be the use of discriminatory taxation against two-income families to hold back the growth of the female labor force, although this would be harder to defend on social grounds. Turning the coin over, it should also be possible for government to create employment in the private sector—for instance, by giving tax benefits to employers who expand their labor forces, or in certain carefully controlled situations by permitting a reduction of the minimum wage, paying the lost income differential directly to the employees concerned.

But I suspect that the main line of defense against unemployment, whether caused by the incursion of technology or by the burgeoning of the labor force, will have to come from a different direction. What is needed above all is a new expansive group of employments to offer the same absorptive cushion once given by office and service jobs. And if this is the objective, it is not difficult to know where to look to find such employments. We have merely to ask ourselves: what tasks in society are clearly and admittedly undermanned? The answer is provided by every city, in its shortage of adequate housing, its unbeautified and ill-maintained streets and parks, its under-protected citizens, under-educated children, under-cared-for young and old and sick. The trouble is, of course, that all these employments, the need for which seems incontestable, require for their realization vast new funds for the public or private philanthropic agencies if they are to be tomorrow's employers of today's unemployed. If those funds are to be sufficient to rebuild the warrens of our cities, and to offer good work to the five to ten million who seem the minimal number of the otherwise unemployed, what is needed is nothing less than a whole new attitude toward the appropriate public-private mix for the peace-time economy.

There will be difficulty enough in creating such a new attitude in time to meet the inrush of technology and the pressure of the growing labor force. Yet in this essay that covers so much ground, albeit so casually, it must be admitted that even this necessary redirection of social effort is only a palliative. In the end, as machines continue to invade society, duplicating greater and greater numbers of social tasks, it is human labor itself—at least, as we now think of "labor"—that is gradually rendered redundant. The underworld of economic thought, where wish and fantasy often take the place of thought and fact, is nonetheless right in its basic premonitions. The machine does challenge man, mechanical energies do replace human energies, the harnessing of nature does imply the releasing of humanity. The question is—and it is not too early to ask it, even though the answers be only visions for the future—for what is it to be released?

E. Does economic growth conflict with America's goals?

In 1960 John F. Kennedy campaigned for the presidency with a promise to "get this country moving again," which meant, among other things, increasing the growth rate of GNP (gross national product) from about 3 percent to 5 percent per year. America's economic growth did accelerate during the 1960s. For the economists and others who guided the growing economy, it was axiomatic that economic growth would help to "form a more perfect union, establish justice, insure domestic tranquility, provide for the common defense, promote the general welfare, and secure the blessings of liberty to ourselves and our posterity." But by 1970 this success had soured, as critics increasingly questioned the desirability of economic growth and the value and distribution of its promised benefits.

All three authors in the following readings remind us that GNP is not a true measure of economic success or welfare, since it includes such social "bads" as pollution, commuting costs, or militarism; excludes the production of housewives (male chauvinist arithmetic!), and ignores income distribution, leisure, and other indicators of the 'quality of life'."

Boulding emphasizes the conflict between economic growth and environmental survival. We live on "spaceship earth," a closed economic and ecological system in which garbage is the final output and consumption a necessary evil. Because of the finite limitations on resources, energy, and waste disposal capacity we must accept a fully recycling economy which aims at constant output for some constant world population.

Weisskopf raises broader questions, from the perspective of a Marxian economic analysis, about the rationality of capitalist economic growth. With their penchant for profits and proliferating investment opportunities, capitalists must invent new sources of aggregate demand to absorb the ever-increasing potential GNP or "surplus." We resort to wasteful consumerism, subsidized highways or government projects, and, above all, to military spending. Capitalists oppose directing the surplus toward larger incomes and consumption for the poor (American or worldwide), or toward more voluntary leisure, because these changes would threaten the work ethic, capitalist profits, and social control.

Heller's essay is mainly directed to answering Boulding's ecological attack on the virtues of economic growth. He doubts the pessimistic forecasts of insufficient energy and materials, emphasizing the possibilities of new technology, plus substitution and conservation for the scarcer resources. He urges new environmental policies to redirect growth into ecologically less harmful directions (see Readings 17–19). But most of all he emphasizes the benefits of economic growth to society, for financing a cleaner environment and solving other social problems. Heller's reform program, and his affirmation of the necessity of growth to prevent "unbearable social and political tensions," return us to Weisskopf's basic question: If economic growth must continue under capitalism, how are we going to use it?

10 Fun and games with the gross national product—The role of misleading indicators in social policy*

KENNETH E. BOULDING

The Gross National Product is one of the great inventions of the twentieth century, probably almost as significant as the automobile and not quite so significant as TV. The effect of *physical* inventions is obvious, but social inventions like the GNP change the world almost as much.

The idea of the total product of society is fairly old, certainly dating back to Adam Smith, but the product's measurement is very much a matter of the second half of the 1900s, which I suppose we can call the fortieth half-century. Before 1929 we did not really have any adequate measure of the Gross National Product, although its measurement was pioneered by Simon Kuznets and others at the National Bureau of Economic Research from 1919 on. We began to get theories which used it in the '30s, and the cumulative effect has been substantial.

Every science must develop its own Tycho Brahe, the sixteenth century Danish gentleman who painstakingly plotted the planets' positions and thus paved the way for Johannes Kepler and Isaac Newton. In a way, Wesley Mitchell was the Tycho Brahe of economics. He painstakingly collected time series of economic quantities, although (like Tycho Brahe) he was operating with a largely erroneous theory. However, the studies at Mitchell's National Bureau of Economic Research led to the invention of the Gross National Product as a measure, and this has had an enormous effect on economic policy.

* From "Fun and Games with the Gross National Product—The Role of Misleading Indicators in Social Policy," *The Environmental Crisis*, edited by Harold W. Helfrich, Jr., New Haven: Yale University Press, 1970, pp. 157–70. Copyright © 1970 by Yale University. Reprinted with permission of the publisher. Kenneth E. Boulding is Professor of Economics at the University of Colorado, Boulder, Colo.

It is hard to underestimate the impact of economic measures on the world. A good example of a rather deplorable measure was the parity index, which had a tremendous impact on our agricultural policy—especially in the 1930s and '40s. The Bureau of Agricultural Economics in the Department of Agriculture developed indexes for the prices paid by farmers and for the prices received by farmers; then some enthusiast divided one by the other and came up with the parity index, which is a measure of the terms of trade of agriculture. This then became an ideal.

The danger of measures is precisely that they become ideals. You see it even in the thermostat. If we had no Fahrenheit, we would not be stabilizing our room temperature too high. There is a magic about the number 70, and we tend to stabilize the temperature at it, when for the sake of health it might be better at 64 degrees. Certainly, one should never underestimate the power of magic numbers. We are really all Pythagoreans. Once we get a number, we sit down and worship it.

The parity ideal was a mistake, but it proved to be astonishingly successful. I do not want to get into this because it is another subject, but one of these days after I retire I want to write a history of the United States on the principle that we always have done the right thing for the wrong reasons. Our agricultural policy for the last 30 years is a prize example of this. Parity was sold to the people and to Congress under the name of social justice. The measure of social justice was the parity index, which was an index of terms of trade of agriculture with 1909–14 as a base.

Well, how stupid can we get? There is nothing sacred about terms of trade if the differential rates of productivity change, and they have changed. You do not establish social justice at all by stabilizing terms of trade. Terms of trade of progressive industries often worsen, as in agriculture; the terms of trade of stagnant industries like education ought to get better, as they have done. Educators today are richer, not because *they* are more productive (which they are not) but because *other people* are more productive. As education's terms of trade have improved substantially, the unit cost of education has correspondingly risen.

Incidentally, when we tried to establish social justice with "parity," which meant, of course, that we raised agricultural prices, we subsidized the rich farmers and penalized the poor. If you try to establish social justice through the price system, you always benefit the rich because the rich have more to start with. Agricultural poverty is always the result of people having not very much to buy and sell. If you do not have anything to buy and sell, it does not matter what prices you do not buy and sell it at. So manipulation of prices—whether of agricultural policy or of cheap education—always succeeds in subsidizing the rich in the same way that state universities subsidize the rich.

All of this may seem to be a long way from the GNP. Actually, I am trying to illustrate this: when you measure something, you inevitably affect people's behavior; and as a measure of the total gross output of the economy, the GNP has had an enormous impact on behavior.

A fascinating book, *The Fiscal Revolution in America* (University of Chicago Press, 1969), has been written by Herbert Stein. He is a member of the Council of Economic Advisers who are the Three Wise Men in our society, the bishops of the modern world, Congress having established an economic episcopate. Stein has done an extremely interesting study, an intellectual history explaining the great change in economic policy from the administration of Herbert Hoover to that of John F. Kennedy.

In the depths of the depression, Hoover engineered a tax increase which exacerbated the depression. That dark hour in the global economy contributed to the rise of Adolf Hitler who precipitated World War II. Had it not been for all those developments we might not have had today's Russian problem; we might not even have had Vietnam. Hoover never knew what hit him because he did not have a Council of Economic Advisers. We did not know much economics in those days. We did not know about the GNP.

Kennedy, in a much milder situation, fostered a tax cut which was an enormous success. As a result, we have had the bloated '60s, the decade without a depression. That should go down in the history books as something spectacular. It is the longest boom ever enjoyed in the United States. Economics has had something to do with it. So has the GNP.

These days, if the GNP starts to go down, an economic adviser will go to the President and say, "Oh, look, Mr. Nixon. The GNP dropped half a point. We have to do something about this." This is the beauty of having social cybernetics, an information system that we can use to our advantage.

I suspect that without economics we might have had a Great Depression in the 1950s and '60s. The rate of return on investment in economics may be at least 10,000 percent per annum, because we have not put much into it and we have gotten a lot out of it. On the other hand, this very success worries me. I have revised some folk wisdom lately; one of my edited proverbs is "Nothing fails like success," because you do not learn anything from it. The only thing we ever learn from is failure. Success only confirms our superstitions.

For some strange reason which I do not understand at all a small subculture arose in western Europe which legitimated failure. Science is the only subculture in which failure is legitimate. When astronomers Albert A. Michelson and Edward W. Morley did an experiment which proved to be a dud (in some eyes), they did not just bury it the way the State Department does. Instead, they shouted the results from the housetops, and revised the whole image of the universe. In political life—and to a certain extent in family life—when we make an Edsel, we bury it. We do not learn from our mistakes. Only in the scientific community is failure legitimated. The very success of the GNP and the success of economics should therefore constitute a solemn warning.

I am something of an ecologist at heart, mainly because I am really a preacher, and we know that all ecologists are really preachers under the skin. They are great viewers with alarm. Is there any more single-minded, simple pleasure than viewing with alarm? At times it is even better than sex.

I propose, then, to view the GNP with alarm.

The Gross National Product is supposed to be a measure of economic success, or economic welfare, or something like that. Of course, it is not. So we have to modify it.

In the first place, the Gross National Product is too gross. It includes a number of things which should be netted out. If we are going to get the net benefit of our economic activity, we have to net the national product, and the real question is how net can we make it? We get first what we call the Net National Product, which technically is the Gross National Product minus depreciation.

The GNP is like the Red Queen in *Alice Through the Looking Glass:* it runs as fast as it can to stay where it is. It includes all the depreciation of capital, so we net that out.

We really ought to net out all sorts of other things such as the military, which is also in the GNP and does not produce much. The world war industry is really a self-contained exercise in mutual masochism. The war industry of each country depends on the other's war industry, and it is a largely self-contained system. It has little to do with defense. It is extremely expensive and very dangerous, and we certainly ought to net it out of the product. That takes out about 10 percent.

Things like commuting and pollution also should be netted out. When somebody pollutes something and somebody else cleans it up, the cleanup is added to the national product and the pollution is not subtracted; that, of course, is ridiculous. In fact, I have been conducting a mild campaign to call the GNP the Gross National Cost rather than the product. It really represents what we have to produce, first to stay where we are and second to get a little further along.

I have been arguing for years (and nobody has paid the slightest attention) that the real measure of economic welfare is not income at all. It is the state or condition of the person, or of the society. Income is just the unfortunate price that we have to pay because the state is corruptible. We have breakfast, and breakfast depreciates; so we must have lunch. The sole reason for lunch is metabolism, and metabolism is decay. Most change is truly decay. Consumption is decay—your automobile wearing out, your clothes becoming threadbare. It is burning up the gasoline. It is eating up the food. Consumption is a bad, not a good thing; production is what we must undergo because of consumption. Things will not stay as they are because of a reality which I sometimes call the Law of Moth and Rust. What causes our illusion that welfare is measured by the Gross National Product or anything else related to income (that is, any flow variable)? The more there is, the more is consumed; therefore, the more we must produce to replace what has been consumed. The bigger the capital stock, the more it will be consumed; hence, the more you have to produce to replace it and, of course, add to it if you want to increase it. In this sense the GNP has a kind of rough relationship with the stock or state, but I think it should always be regarded as a cost rather than a product.

Another minor item, perhaps just a technical point: as we measure it, the GNP neglects household production and only includes items in the market. If a man marries his housekeeper, the GNP falls; I argue that if he was a moral man the GNP ought to rise because he is enjoying all he had before and then some. Obviously, there is a small technical defect. However, household production probably is not much more than 5 percent, certainly not more than 10 percent, of the GNP, and thus it is a minor issue.

Much more fundamental is that all of economics, the whole GNP mentality, assumes that economic activity is a throughput, a linear process from the mine to the garbage dump.

The ultimate physical product of economic life is garbage. The system takes ores and fossil fuels (and in a boom the unemployed) out of the earth, chews them up in the process of production, and eventually spews them out into sewers and garbage dumps. We manage to have a state or condition in the middle of the throughput in which we are well fed and well clothed, in which we can travel, in which we have buildings in which we are protected from the atrocious climate and enabled to live in the temperate zone. Just imagine how the GNP would fall and welfare would rise if man abandoned the temperate zone and moved into the tropics. An enormous amount of the GNP is heating this building because the plain truth is that nature is very disagreeable. It is cold, damp, and miserable, and the main effort of human activity is to get away from it. As a matter of fact, we do not even like pure air. Otherwise we would not smoke. All of this indicates that a great deal of man's activity is directed toward what we might call desired pollution.

The throughput is going to come to an end. We are approaching the end of an era. People have been saying it for a long time, but nobody has ever believed them. Very often they were wrong in their forecasts, but this time I suspect they are right. We really are approaching the end of the era of expanding man.

Up to now, man has psychologically lived on a flat earth—a great plain, in fact a "darkling plain" where "ignorant armies clash by night," as Matthew Arnold says. Man has always had somewhere to go. There has always been a Kansas somewhere to beckon him as a virgin land of promise. There is no longer any Kansas. The photographs of the earth by astronauts in lunar orbit symbolize the end of this era. Clearly the earth is a beautiful little spaceship, all blue and green and white, with baroque cloud patterns on it, and its destination unknown. It is getting pretty crowded and its resources rather limited.

The problem of the present age is that of the transition from the Great Plains into the spaceship or into what Barbara Ward and I have been calling spaceship earth. We do not have any mines and we do not have any sewers in a spaceship. The water has to go through the algae to the kidneys to the algae to the kidneys, and so on, and around and around and around. If the earth is to become a spaceship, we must develop a cyclical economy within which man can maintain an agreeable state.

Under such circumstances the idea of the GNP simply falls apart. We need a completely different set of concepts for that eventuality, and we are still a long way from it technologically because we never had to worry about it. We always have had an unlimited Schmoo, Al Capp's delightful cartoon creature that everlastingly gets its kicks from being the main course for gluttonous man. We could just rip the earth apart and sock it away. We used to think Lake Erie was a great lake; now it smells like the Great Society. We used to think the oceans were pretty big, but events like the oil leakage in California have spotlighted that fallacy. Suddenly, it is becoming obvious that the Great Plain has come to an end and that we are in a very crowded spaceship. This is a fundamental change in human consciousness, and it will require an adjustment of our ethical, religious, and national systems which may be quite traumatic.

On the whole, human society has evolved in response to a fairly unlimited environment. That is not true of all societies, of course. It is not so true of the Indian village, but the societies that are mainly cyclical are almost uniformly disagreeable. Even the societies which are cyclical (where you return the night soil to the farms) are not really circular. They rely on water and solar energy coming down from somewhere and going out to somewhere. There is some sort of an input-output.

Up to now we have not even begun to solve the problem of a high-level circular economy. In fact, we have not even been interested in it. We did not have to be, because it was so far off in the future. Now it is still a fair way off. Resources for the Future says, "We're all right, Jack. We've got a hundred years." Its report points to our fossil fuels and our ores, and reassures us that they will be adequate for a century. After that, the deluge. I would not be a bit surprised if we run out of pollutable reservoirs before our mines and ores are exhausted. There are some signs of this happening in the atmosphere, in the rivers, and in the oceans.

The nitrogen cycle, the extraction of nitrogen from the air, exemplifies the development of what looks like the beginning of a spaceship technology. Surely, when man looks back on the twentieth century, he will regard the development of the Haber process in 1913 as its most important event, even though it did permit World War I. If it had not been for Fritz Haber, the Germans would not have been able to fight that war because they were cut off from Chilean nitrates. Historically, there was a famous viewer-with-alarm about 1899, the English chemist Sir William Crookes, who predicted the exhaustion of Chile's nitrates and consequent global starvation by 1930. His prophecy did not pan out, thanks to the Haber process.

That process was the beginning of an anti-entropic process of production, entropic in the sense of material entropy. We need a word for this, and it does not exist. Ordinary economic processes diffuse the concentrated. We start off with concentrations of ores and fuels, and we spread them over the earth into dumps or into oceans. This is entropic in the sense of returning to chaos. The Haber process concentrated the diffuse; it showed that if you put energy into the system, you could reverse the material entropy.

That is an old trick. It is called life, and it was invented a long time ago. However, Haber's process marked the first time that any living organism had invented a new formula for it. Without Haber we would certainly be in much worse shape than we are today. We would have had mass famine in this century, without question. Barry Commoner, Professor of Plant Physiology at Washington University, says that in the Middle West, for instance, we are now dumping into the cycle about twice the amount of nitrogen we used in the days before artificial fertilizers were developed. This means that nearly all the rivers in Illinois are now eutrophic, and where will it all lead?

Can we overload the nitrogen cycle without creating extremely alarming ecological consequences? That is something we shall have to answer. My IBM spies tell me that a fundamental doctrine applied to computers is called the Gigo Principle, standing for "garbage in, garbage out." It is a basic law that what you put in you have to take out. This is throughput. Otherwise, we have to recycle everything, and we have not begun to consider the problems of a high-level, recycled economy. I am pretty sure there is no nonexistence theorem about it. I am certain that a recycling technology is possible which, of course, must have an input of energy. Nobody is going to repeal the second law of thermodynamics, not even the Democrats. This means that if we are to avoid the increase of material entropy, we must have an input of energy into the system. The present system has an enormous input of energy in fossil fuels which cannot last very long unless we go to nuclear fusion. In that case there is an awful lot of water around, and it would last a long time.

Fission is not any good; it is just messy. I understand that if we began using uranium to produce all our power requirements in this country, we would run out of it in ten years. So actually nuclear energy is not a great source of energy; this planet's coal probably has more. Nuclear energy is not a great new field opened up. I suspect it could turn out to be rather dangerous nonsense.

What does this leave us with? The good old sun. At the most pessimistic, you might say we have to devise a basic economy which relies on the input of solar energy for all its energy requirements. As we know, there is a lot of solar energy.

On the other hand, what we do not know is how many people this spaceship earth will support at a high level. We do not know this even to order of magnitude. I suggest that this is one of the major research projects for the next generation, because the whole future of man depends on it. If the optimum population figure is 100 million, we are in for a rough time. It could be as low as that if we are to have a really high-level economy in which everything is recycled. Or it could be up to 10 billion. If it is up to 10 billion, we are okay, Jack—at least for the time being. A figure somewhere between 100 million and 10 billion is a pretty large area of ignorance. I have a very uneasy feeling that it may be towards the lower level, but we do not really know that.

We do not really know the limiting factor. I think we can demonstrate, for instance, that in all probability the presently underdeveloped countries are not going to develop. There is not enough of anything. There is not enough copper. There is not enough of an enormous number of elements which are essential to the developed economy. If the whole world developed to American standards overnight, we would run out of everything in less than 100 years.

Economic development is the process by which the evil day is brought closer when everything will be gone. It will result in final catastrophe unless we treat this interval in the history of man as an opportunity to make the transition to the spaceship earth.

Now that I have been rude to the Gross National Product, let me show how it *can* be used and the things it suggests. In an interesting little empirical trick (it is not much more than that) I have plotted the *GNP per capita,* which is a very rough measure of how rich a country is already, against the logarithm of the *rate of growth* of GNP per capita for all the countries where information was available. Despite the measure's defects, I think that the data are meaningful.

The GNP per capita varies from about $50 for Haiti to more than $3000 for the United States; when the range is that much it must mean something—even if you do not know what. The yearly rate of growth per capita ranges from about 10 percent in Japan to minus 2 percent for Uruguay in the first half of the 1960s.

The countries of the world then divide clearly into two groups. One, which I call the A countries, includes Japan, the USSR, Yugoslavia, Hungary, Belgium, Italy, Denmark, and, indeed, most of the countries of the temperate zone; they lie along a downward-sloping straight line, with Japan at the top and the United States at the bottom. In this group the richer you are, the slower you grow. This is a fundamental law of growth and, so far as I know, all natural growth systems obey such a rule. Certainly, exponential growth of anything never goes on for very long. If it ever did, it would be the only thing in the universe. Obviously, there is a nonexistence theorem about exponential growth. The A countries exhibit logistic growth, or at least the appearance of it.

The other group, the B countries, are all in the tropics with some exceptions, mainly in Latin America. They occupy a circular area in the bottom left-hand corner of the figure. They do not seem to be going anywhere, but they have sort of a Brownian movement. Their rates of growth are far below countries of equal poverty in the A group. This suggests that the developmental process has a "main line." If you are on this line, you will go on getting richer; but as you get richer, you get rich more slowly—which is not surprising. If this goes on for a century, all the A countries will begin to slide down the line to the bottom, and will be equally rich and equally slow. In the meantime, unless some of the B countries get on the main line they are not going anywhere.

This is the most significant example I have found to illustrate the use of the GNP as a measure of some kind of process. Consequently, I am not prepared to ditch the GNP altogether. It is a measure of some process in the United States that took us from about $100 per capita at the time of the Revolution to $3000 today. It is a real process, and the difference between Haiti and the United States is very real. We are rich and they are poor; no question about it. This is mainly a result of the development process, not of exploitation. The one thing it suggests is that exploitation is a minor element in explaining the differences of wealth in the world. If some countries are rich and some are poor, it is because the rich countries are on the main line of development, or have been on it longer, and the poor countries are not. The reason for the United States' wealth today is that we have had fairly consistent economic growth for well over 150 years.

The American Revolution cost a generation of growth, as all revolutions do, whether they are one-generation revolutions like ours or two-generation revolutions like that of the Soviet Union. Revolutions always set nations back, although they may start off the process of growth. We recovered from the Boston Tea Party by about 1815, and then we took off. From that point on, we approximately doubled the per capita income every generation. If you do that, you go 100, 200, 400, 800, 1600, 3200. It takes six generations that way. On the whole, this has been the rate of development before World War II.

Now the Japanese GNP is growing at 8 to 10 percent per capita per annum, which is absurd. This means that in Japan the children are six times as rich as their parents, which I think is greedy. I am quite happy with a 4 percent rise, which makes the children twice as rich as the parents, as in the United States. In the same 150 years India (or Haiti even worse) has gone 100, 100, 100, 100, 100. Or perhaps 100, 110, 120, 90, or something like that. It is the difference in the rate of development which explains the difference in per capita GNP.

On the other hand, this kind of process does not at all answer the question that I raised in the first half of this discussion. When we get to $10,000 per capita, what does it really mean? Does it simply mean that we are exhausting the resources of the earth at a much more rapid rate? Of course, we have a process here of increased efficiency in exploitation of the earth, not exploitation of man. We go on, we become terribly rich, and suddenly it is all gone. We may have a process of this sort.

What may happen is that we are going to have to face something of this sort in the next 500 years. Unquestionably, we will have to aim for much lower levels of growth, because the cyclical process costs more than the throughput does. However, if we devote our knowledge industries to solution of the problem of the cyclical economy, maybe it will turn out all right.

The idea that we are moving into a world of absolutely secure and effortless abundance is nonsense. This is an illusion of the young who are supported by their parents. Once they have children of their own, they realize that abundance is an illusion. It is a plausible illusion, because we have had an extraordinary two centuries. We have had an extraordinary period of economic growth and of the discovery of new resources.

But this is not a process that can go on forever, and we do not know how abundant this spaceship is going to be. Nobody here now is going to live to see the spaceship, because it is certainly 100 years—perhaps 500 years—off. I am sure it will be no longer than 500 years off, and that is not a tremendously long period of historic time.

An extraordinary conference was held last December [1968] on the Ecological Consequences of International Development. It was an antidevelopment gathering of ecologists, who presented 60 developmental horror stories, among them predictions that the Aswan Dam is going to ruin Egypt, the Kariba Dam will ruin central Africa, DDT will ruin us all, insecticides will ruin the cotton crops, thallium will ruin Israel, and so on all down the line. Some of these forecasts I take with a little grain of ecological salt. The cumulative effect, however, is significant, and suggests that no engineer should be allowed into the world without an ecologist in attendance as a priest. The most dangerous thing in the world is the completely untrammeled engineer. A friend of mine was at the Aswan Dam talking to the Russian engineer in charge. He asked him about all the awful ecological consequences: snails, erosion, evaporation, and such. The engineer replied, "Well, that is not my business. My job is just to build the dam."

We are all like that, really. I have recently discovered the real name of the devil, which is something terribly important to know. The real name of the devil is *suboptimization,* finding out the best way to do something which should not be done at all. The engineers, the military, the governments, and the corporations are all quite busy at this. Even professors try to find the best way of giving a Ph.D. degree, which to my mind should not be done at all. We are all suboptimizers.

The problem of how to prevent suboptimization is, I think, the great problem of social organization. The only people who have thought about it are the economists, and they have the wrong answer, which was perfect competition. Nobody else has any answer at all. Obviously, the deep, crucial problem of social organization is how to prevent people from doing their best when the best in the particular, in the small, is not the best in the large.

The answer to this problem lies mainly in the ecological point of view, which is perhaps the most fundamental thing we can teach anybody. I am quite sure that it has to become the basis of our educational system.

I have added a verse to a long poem I wrote at that ecological conference. There are some who may still shrug off its somber tone, but the wise man—and nation—will take heed.

> With development extended to the whole of planet earth
> What started with abundance may conclude in dismal dearth.
> And it really will not matter then who started it or ran it
> If development results in an entirely plundered planet.

11 The problem of surplus absorption in a capitalistic society*

THOMAS E. WEISSKOPF

In the last century, the advanced capitalist economies of the world have witnessed a tremendous expansion of productive capacity. There can be little doubt that—whatever its implications for the quality of life—the capitalist system has enabled the richest countries of the world to multiply steadily their riches. Even the periodic crises of output and employment that afflicted capitalist economies in earlier times, culminating in the Great Depression of the 1930s, seem to have yielded to the control of Keynesian macroeconomic policy measures since the Second World War. The evidence is that rates of growth in developed capitalist countries have increased substantially in the postwar period.

Yet the expansion of productive capacity, which has become both more regular and more rapid in recent years, is not an unmixed blessing for the capitalist system. Behind the superficially impressive rates of growth lies a major problem which poses a continual threat to the stability of a capitalist economy: the problem of "surplus absorption." In order to understand the nature of this problem, it is necessary first to define the concept of the surplus and then to discuss the process of its absorption in a capitalist society.

THE CONCEPT OF THE SURPLUS

The surplus of an economy in any given year represents the excess of potential total production over socially essential production in that year. Potential total production is a measure of the maximum that the economy

* From "The Problem of Surplus Absorption in a Capitalistic Society," *The Capitalist System: A Radical Analysis of American Society,* written and edited by Richard C. Edwards, Michael Reich, and Thomas E. Weisskopf, © 1972, pp. 365–71. Abridged and reprinted by permission of Prentice-Hall, Inc., Englewood Cliffs, N.J. Thomas E. Weisskopf is Associate Professor of Economics at the University of Michigan, Ann Arbor, Mich.

could produce, given its natural and technological environment and its employable productive resources. Socially essential production is the minimum amount of production required to maintain the (growing) population at a standard of living necessary to its survival. It includes both production contributing directly to the essential consumption of the population and production required to replace whatever capital stock and/or natural resources are used up in the process of that production.

The key to the definition of the surplus is the concept of socially essential production. Socially essential production will vary not only with the population of a society but also with such factors as the climate, the degree of urbanization, the nature of conventional social customs, and so on. More clothing and stronger shelter is required to survive in a cold than in a hot climate; more elaborate health, sanitation, and transportation facilities are required in urban than in rural areas. Although socially essential production is extremely difficult to measure precisely, it is not difficult to conceptualize. What basically distinguishes socially essential production from the surplus is that the former represents a first and largely unavoidable charge on the output of a society—without which it would begin to decay—whereas the latter is that part of its productive capacity that a society has some potential freedom to allocate among competing alternatives.

In a very significant sense, the nature of a society is revealed by the manner in which it disposes of its surplus. Societies are different to the extent that they make different choices about how to use the natural and human resources they have available. But there is little choice to make about the provision of essential consumption such as food, clothing, and shelter; these are necessary for the subsistence of the people and the survival of the society. There is a real choice to make only about the use of the surplus. The surplus could be used to provide additional (nonessential) consumption for some or all the people; it could be used to invest in expanding the productive capacity of the economy; it could be used in fighting wars, in building palaces or churches; it could go unused if leisure were substituted voluntarily or involuntarily for the full use of productive capacity. In various parts of the world, and in various historical periods, different societies have been characterized by the different ways in which they have used their surplus.

It is characteristic of a capitalist society to devote a significant part of its surplus to investment that expands the productive capacity of the economy. Increases in productive capacity can be generated both by increasing the supply of resource inputs into the production process (labor power and capital) and by increasing the productivity of the production process through improved organization and technology. The economic growth of the advanced capitalist countries has been due in considerable part to the increases in the quantity and the quality of both labor power and capital made possible by investment in education and new plant and equipment.

The growth of total output in the advanced capitalist countries has been sufficiently rapid to allow for a substantial growth of per capita output in spite of unprecedented increases in population. Even allowing for occasional shortfalls of total output below productive capacity, it is clear that potential output per person has been increasing steadily and is likely to continue doing so. At the same time, to be sure, the increasing urbanization and the mounting complexity of industrial life under capitalism are causing a gradual increase in socially essential production per person. Yet it can hardly be doubted that the rate of growth of potential output per person in advanced capitalist societies is faster than that of socially essential production. As a result, the surplus tends to rise more or less steadily both as an absolute amount and as a proportion of potential output. It is this steady rise of the surplus that raises the problem of surplus absorption: how can a capitalist society absorb (utilize) the surplus that it causes to rise continuously?

THE ABSORPTION OF THE SURPLUS

The problem of absorbing the surplus can be viewed as the problem of finding enough buyers to purchase all the goods and services that the capitalist economy can produce. In economic terms, the problem is to maintain a sufficiently high level of total or "aggregate" demand so as to provide a market for the potential output of the economy. To the extent that aggregate demand falls short of potential output, producers will not be able to sell all that they can produce, and they will fail to realize maximum profits from their productive activity. If aggregate demand remains below potential output, either goods and services will go unsold or producers will have to curtail their output. Since producers only have an interest in producing what they can sell, the capitalist economy as a whole will tend toward an equilibrium at which actual output is equal to aggregate demand.

The consequences of a failure to maintain sufficient aggregate demand to absorb the surplus are several. First, the shortfall in actual output below potential output results in a corresponding loss of goods and services and a decline in the profits realized by producers. Second—and far more important from a human point of view—it also results in a loss of employment opportunities and a rise in unemployment. In a society in which both one's income and one's self respect depend on regular full-time employment, the loss of one's job is catastrophic. High levels of unemployment due to a failure to asborb the surplus can prove to be very unstabilizing for a capitalist society.

The problem of surplus absorption in a capitalist society is not insoluble. In recent decades the surplus has in fact largely been absorbed in most of the advanced capitalist nations: there has been varying degrees of unemployment, but not on a scale approaching that of the 1930s. Yet it remains critical to examine *how* the surplus is absorbed, for this has profound implications for the nature of a society. It will be argued below that the capitalist system sets important constraints on the manner in which aggregate demand is maintained sufficiently high to absorb the surplus.

There are three principal sources of aggregate demand in a capitalist economy: private consumption, private investment, and government expenditure. In the following sections of this paper, the private and public sources of demand are considered in turn.

THE PRIVATE SECTOR

The pronounced inequality of income distribution under capitalism implies that while people with low incomes will have to spend most or all their income on essential consumption, people with high incomes will have much more than they need to spend to maintain even a high standard of living. Thus, there will always be more total income than total private consumption demand; and the more unequal the distribution of income, the greater the gap is likely to be. Since total income in an economy is necessarily equal to the total value of actual production from which the income derives, private consumption demand will remain well below actual output and *a fortiori* below potential output.

A second principal source of private demand in a capitalist economy that can help to raise the level of aggregate demand is investment demand. Businesses desiring to expand their productive capacity will devote part of their profits to increasing the capital stock of the enterprise, and they may also borrow some of the income saved by private consumers in order to undertake further investment. The rate at which businesses want to expand through investment clearly depends on their expectations about the prospects of selling additional output in the future. Whether or not such investment demand will be sufficient to make up for the deficit between total consumption demand and potential output remains a key question.

In dealing with this question, it should first be observed that, to the extent that investment demand fills the gap in any given year, it exacerbates the problem in the following year. For the more output that goes into investment this year, the greater will be the increase in capital stock, and the greater will therefore be the potential output and the potential surplus of the economy in the following year.

There is no general agreement as to whether private demand can remain sufficiently buoyant in the long run to absorb the surplus in a capitalist economy. The early orthodox Keynesian economists were very pessimistic on this score and believed that stagnation was inevitable—that the growth of private consumption and investment demand would be insufficient to match the growing productive capacity of the capitalist economy. More recently, bourgeois economists have tended to assume optimistically that the appetites of consumers and investors will be continuously and sufficiently stimulated by new products and new techniques of production. However, in an increasingly affluent as well as unequal society, it is no trivial matter to ensure the steady growth of private demand.

One would ordinarily expect the urgency of consumption for an individual to diminish as his level of consumption increased beyond the minimum necessary for survival. It is true that even in a country as rich as the United States there are many people who have less to spend on consumption than what would be considered a socially essential minimum, for example, all those families whose income is below the "poverty line." Yet the majority of the population clearly have more to spend, and the rich have very much more. What is to induce the more affluent to raise their demand for goods and services continually over time?

The answer lies in one of the most deeply rooted characteristics of capitalist society—the ethos of consumerism. Consumerism derives from a fundamental tenet of capitalist ideology: the assertion that the primary requirement for individual self-fulfillment and happiness is the possession and consumption of material goods. Like all aspects of capitalist ideology, this consumerist assertion is grounded in the basic capitalist relations of production. A society based on alienated labor allows most people little opportunity for individual expression in production; the main outlet for expression is in one's life as a consumer. Relations among people in capitalist production assume the form of relations among commodities. The resulting commodity fetishism reinforces consumerism, for it emphasizes the importance of material goods—rather than social relations—as the primary source of individual welfare.

Within this ideological framework, there are also more direct mechanisms that operate to stimulate consumption. No person in the United States, nor in other advanced capitalist nations, can escape the effort of producers to induce consumers to buy their wares. Massive advertising is only the most obvious manifestation of the pervasive sales effort that characterizes the capitalist system. Frequent model changes, fancy packaging, planned obsolescence, contrived fads, and so on, all serve to increase private consumption demand at a considerable cost in wasted sources. Irrational as it is, such stimulation of private expenditure plays a functional role in helping to absorb the surplus of a capitalist economy.

THE PUBLIC SECTOR

Yet even the widespread propagation of the consumptionist ethic has not enabled the growth of private demand to keep pace with the growth of productive capacity under capitalism. The historical evidence for most advanced capitalist countries—and notably so for the United States—is that, in order for aggregate demand to match potential output, it has become increasingly necessary to rely on *government* expenditure, the third major component of demand. The share of government expenditure (G) in total output (GNP) has been rising over time in almost every capitalist country. In the United States, the ratio of G to GNP has risen from 10.8 percent in 1929 to 16.4 percent in 1949 and to 20.6 percent in 1969.

Increases in government expenditure do not necessarily imply equal increases in aggregate demand. To the extent that the government finances its expenditure by taxing the private sector, private consumers and businesses sacrifice income and presumably cut back on private consumption and investment. But economists are in general agreement that the net effect of raising government expenditure and taxation by an equal amount is to raise aggregate demand. This is because private individuals would have used only *part* of their taxed income for consumption purposes, saving the rest of it, while the government typically spends *all* the money it receives.

Thus higher levels of government expenditure do lead to higher levels of aggregate demand. Had the share of government expenditure not been increasing in most of the advanced capitalist countries, they might well have had much greater difficulty absorbing the surplus. In fact, it is precisely because the governments of these countries have learned to use their budgets to bolster aggregate demand that the production and employment crises of earlier years have been more successfully avoided in the postwar period.

The mere fact of a rise in government expenditure does not carry any negative implications for the quality of life in a capitalist society. In order to evaluate the social consequences of the growth of government expenditure, it is clearly necessary to examine its nature as well as its size.

To some extent, the increasing importance of government expenditure in advanced capitalist countries reflects a growing supply of essential public services that meet genuine social needs. This is certainly true of at least part of the public provision of health care, educational facilities, housing, and so on. Yet many of the activities undertaken or supported by the capitalist state serve primarily to socialize the costs of private production. Public programs of highway construction, vocational schooling, job training, and pollution control, often have the effect of shifting some of the costs of private production on to the taxpaying public. Finally, an important share of government expenditure serves neither of the above two functions but represents simply a wasteful way of absorbing the surplus. Such waste is most evident in military spending, but it permeates other government programs as well.

There are significant constraints on the ability of any capitalist government to undertake public programs that serve genuine social needs. As a result, growing levels of government expenditure are likely to involve increasing socialization of private production costs and/or increasing waste.

In the United States, the historical record suggests that for the past forty years the government has had to rely largely on military spending to absorb the surplus. In general, the growth of government expenditure in a capitalist society is likely to be no more rational than the growth of private consumption.

THE EXCLUDED ALTERNATIVES

The irrationality of the process of surplus absorption under capitalism can be fully appreciated only when one considers the more rational alternatives excluded by the capitalist mode of production. In a rational society, productive capacity would be expanded and utilized only insofar as it contributes to the satisfaction of genuine individual and social needs. Rather than attempt to create new wants among those people who have more income than is required to satisfy their existing wants, a rational society would use its productive capacity to meet the needs of people whose current income does not allow them to satisfy even their most basic needs. Rather than spend enormous sums of money on military weapons, space exploration, and other expensive pursuits of dubious social value, a rational state would devote itself to the provision of adequate health care, cultural and recreational facilities, and many other essential collective services.

Such a reorientation of production priorities would require major changes in basic capitalist institutions. In effect, it would require that claims to the output of the economy be distributed according to need rather than according to productive "ability." The distribution of real income, as well as the distribution of power to influence the state, would have to be greatly equalized. But inequalities of income, wealth, and power are inherent in the capitalist mode of production.

A rational society would not only reorient its production priorities; it it would also determine the overall scale of production in a rational manner. If actual output falls below potential output in a capitalist society, many people lose their jobs while others remain fully employed. To avoid the inequalities of a high rate of unemployment, it is therefore essential to maintain a level of actual output close to potential output. Since the logic of capitalist expansion leads to continual growth in potential output, it calls for continual growth in actual output as well.

But ever increasing levels of actual output may not be necessary and may in fact be undesirable in an affluent society. The uninhibited growth of material production leads to a growing ecological imbalance between people and their environment and to a growing psychological imbalance within people themselves. Thus it becomes increasingly rational for a wealthy society to limit the growth of production and for individuals to substitute leisure for work.

To do this equitably, it would be necessary to reduce working hours across the board rather than to lay off a fraction of the labor force. Individual workers would need to have the option of reducing their working hours rather than being forced to choose between full-time work or no work at all. Yet in a society in which private firms compete with one another to maximize their profits, and in which capitalists and their managers retain firm control of workers and the work process, a general reduction of working hours is bound to proceed very slowly, and individual options on working hours are unlikely to be granted at all.

In conclusion, the surplus generated by a capitalist society is necessarily absorbed—if indeed it is successfully absorbed—in a very irrational manner. The rational alternatives of limiting the scale of production and devoting all productive activity to socially useful ends are excluded by the capitalist mode of production.

12 Economic growth and ecology— An economist's view*

WALTER W. HELLER

Let me set the framework for my discussion in terms of the apparent differences in perception between ecologists and economists. These have to be narrowed or reconciled if we are to make a productive joint attack on the growth-energy-environment problem.

In starkest terms, the ecologist confronts us with an environmental imperative that requires an end to economic growth—or a sharp curtailment of it—as the price of biological survival. In contrast, the economist counters with a socioeconomic imperative that requires the continuation of growth as the price of social survival. Some ecologists see the arresting of growth as a necessary, though not sufficient, condition for saving the ecosystem. The economist sees growth as a necessary, though not sufficient, condition for social progress and stability. To focus differences even more sharply, the economist tends to regard growth not as the root of environmental evil but one of the prerequisites to success in restoring the environment.

Second, the ecologist counters that the Great God Growth has feet of clay. If the full costs of water, air, land, visual, and noise pollution—that is, the drawing down of our environmental capital—were counted, the advance of Gross National Product in the past 25 years might well turn out to be an illusion. In responding, the economist is at pains to make clear that he is under no illusion that GNP is an index of social welfare. But he does believe that a careful reading of economic and social data yields persuasive evidence that (1) real GNP per capita has advanced even after adjusting for increases in population, prices, and pollution, and (2) a rise in social welfare has accompanied the rise in output of goods and services.

* From "Coming to Terms With Growth and the Environment," *Energy, Economic Growth, and the Environment,* edited by Samuel Schurr, Baltimore: Johns Hopkins University Press for Resources for the Future, Inc. Reprinted with permission of publisher and author; as abridged in *Monthly Labor Review* (November 1971), pp. 14–21. Walter W. Heller is Regents Professor of Economics at the University of Minnesota, Minneapolis, Minn.

Third, in a very real sense, the most vexing differences between ecologists and economists may not be in their conflicting interpretation of the evidence but in their divergent modes of thinking. At the risk of exaggerating a bit, I perceive the dedicated environmentalist as thinking in terms of exponential rates of deterioration, thresholds, flash points, and of absolute limits to be dealt with by absolute bans. (And I confess to a bit of absolutism myself when it comes to roads in the North Cascades, oil exploration in Puget Sound, and 70,000 tons a day of taconite tailings dumped into Lake Superior.)

In basic approach, the economist could hardly disagree more. He thinks in terms of marginalism, trade-offs, and a careful cost-benefit calculus. He urges that in striking a balance between nature and man, between environment and growth, and between technology and ecology, the right solution would be the one that pushes depollution to, but not beyond, the point where the costs—the foregone satisfactions of a greater supply of additional goods and services—just equal the benefits—the gained satisfactions of clear air, water, landscape, and sound waves. What the economist regards as rational is to seek, not total or *maximum,* cleansing of the environment but an *optimum* arising out of a careful matching of the "bads" that we overcome and the "goods" that we forego in the process.

Fourth, when economists and ecologists turn to the search for solutions, they readily agree that many environmental problems can be handled only by government prohibitions and regulations (mercury and DDT come to mind) and by public expenditures for collective sewage disposal, land reclamation, and environmental clean-up. They can also join hands in identifying the essentially costless changes that serve growth and the environment simultaneously, thus requiring no trade-offs. One thinks, for example, of technological advances that have substituted coal and oil for wood as energy sources (indeed, the per capita consumption of timber is no higher today than 30 years ago), have enabled us to reduce both costs and diesel engine pollution by transporting oil by pipeline rather than rail. And one looks forward to the day when thermal byproducts of energy production can be converted from pollutants to a productive source of space heating and cooling for industrial, commercial, and apartment buildings.

But where hard choices will have to be made, the economist wants to put as much of the load on the price system as it can efficiently carry. His main device would be to put price tags—for example, in the form of effluent fees or pollution permits or refundable materials fees—on the now-largely-free use of air, water, and land areas for dumping industrial and commercial wastes. The environmentalist's instinct is to recoil against this "license to pollute." By the same reasoning, perhaps, he feels way down deep that to let mineral resources and fossil fuels be managed through the pricing system constitutes a "license to exploit" the biosphere, a license that should be revoked or subject to tighter regulation.

As we examine these issues in greater detail, we will need to remember that the contest between economic growth and environmental quality is in one sense a mismatch: growth is a means, an instrumental goal, while quality of the environment is an end in itself or at least an important component of the quality of existence. I do not mean to beg the central question—does the process of economic growth, the rising level of economic activity and energy use, inexorably lead to degradation of the environment? But let me start with the role of growth as an instrument, as a means to social ends, as a bestower of benefits.

COULD GROWTH BE STOPPED?

To discuss the benefits of growth in the context of environmental quality implies, first, that we have a realistic option—one that is conceptually and institutionally possible—of stopping growth or slowing it to a crawl and, second, that there is a trade-off or inverse relation between the rate of economic growth and the quality of the natural environment. We can't settle these questions here, but we can't ignore them either.

Whether a no-growth policy is a conceivable alternative depends first on the sources of growth and the nature of the growth process. Growth of our economy, that is, growth of output per capita, is anchored in (1) increases in the stock of human capital through investments in education, training, and experience; (2) increases in the stock of nonhuman capital through investment in equipment, machinery, and plant; and (3) improvements in the state of our scientific and managerial technology through investments in research and development, better management and organization, and more efficient production techniques. The deepest wellspring of modern economic growth is the advance of technology in its broadest economic sense, that is, the advance of knowledge.

Since it is inconceivable that we could quench man's thirst for understanding through better education and throttle his quest for increased knowledge and easier ways of doing things—through research and development, large-scale experimentation and small-scale tinkering—it follows that we can't stop growth in output per man-hour.

Conceivably we could hold total output in check by highly restrictive taxes and tight monetary policy or by direct controls. Since output per man-hour would continue to rise, it would require a rapid decline in the average workweek—one calculation puts it at 26 hours by 1980—and a corresponding increase in leisure and nonmarket activity. (My secretary asks: "What's so bad about that?") This appraisal recognizes also that the labor force would continue to grow. Even with a zero-population growth policy, it would take several decades to stabilize the population.

Since the point of a no-growth policy would be to check and reverse the erosion of the environment, one also has to posit active and costly steps in this direction. This would involve an absolute reduction in material living standards in exchange for a more livable natural environment.

Just to sketch this picture is to raise serious questions of its social, political, and economic feasibility. Short of a believable threat of extinction, it is hard to believe that the public would accept the tight controls, lowered material living standards, and large income transfers required to create and manage a stationary state. Whether the necessary shifts could be accomplished without vast unemployment and economic dislocation is another question. It may be that the shift to a no-growth state would throw the fragile ecology of our economic system so out of kilter as to threaten its breakdown.

Like it or not, economic growth seems destined to continue. To cope with growing contamination of the environment, we are thus driven to a redirection of growth and to a reordering of priorities in the uses of growth.

But this still does not resolve the question of whether we should continue to stimulate growth or consciously act to retard it. That depends not just on the benefits we will look at in a moment, but on the environmental costs, on the growth-ecology trade-off. To the question of how much growth we have to give up to protect the natural environment and maintain a habitable planet, we find a wide range of answers among both ecologists and economists.

AN ECONOMIC ASSESSMENT

Among those who focus on global environmental problems, the spectrum runs from those who are persuaded that global pollution puts life on this planet in jeopardy to those who conclude that we don't know enough to answer the question.

Among economists there are those who accept the "Spaceship Earth" concept of finite limits to the assimilative capacity of the environment and believe that growth will test those limits within a historically relevant period and must therefore be retarded. But a majority of the economics profession would lean toward the findings of the recent econometric probe of this problem by William Nordhaus and James Tobin:

With respect to appropriable resources like minerals and fossil fuels which the market already treats as economic goods, their estimates show "little reason to worry about the exhaustion of resources." As in the past, rising prices of fossil fuels are expected to provide strong incentives for conserving supplies and developing substitute materials and processes.

For nonappropriate resources, "public goods" like air and water, they see the problem of abuse as much more serious. But the environmental disturbances and misdirection of resources that result from treating public natural resources as if they were free goods could, they believe, be corrected by charging for them. "The misdirection is due to a defect in the pricing system—a serious but by no means irreparable defect and one which would in any case be present in a stationary economy."

With respect to global ecological collapse, they conclude that "there is probably very little that economists can say."

The issue is far from resolved. But the evidence to date supports the view that it is less the *fact* of growth than the *way* we grow and the *uses* we make of our growth that lie at the bottom of our environmental troubles. Elusive as a consensus on the growth-environment trade-off may be, a consensus on the urgency of changing the forms and uses of growth is already materializing. It is already confronting us with hard choices and the need for painful institutional changes. I submit that both the hard choices and painful changes required to restore the environment will come much easier in an atmosphere of growth than of stagnation.

BENEFITS OF GROWTH

In turning to the benefits side of the picture, we are well advised to take growth out of the one-dimensional context of abuse of the natural environment. In a broader context, the environmental claims for a share of growth's proceeds include funds for cleansing (1) the physical environment of air, water, and land pollution and of urban congestion and sprawl; (2) the social environment of poverty, ignorance, malnutrition, and disease; (3) the human environment of the urban ghetto and rural slum that blight territory and lives; and (4) our personal environment of crime and violence.

Even with the aid of a rise of 55 percent in GNP and 34 percent in real per capita personal income from 1959 to 1969 (in 1969 dollars), we have found that our inroads on these problems have not kept pace with our rising aspirations and expectations. Imagine the tensions between rich and poor, between black and white, between blue-collar and white-collar and other workers, between old and young, if we had been forced to finance even the minimal demands of the disadvantaged out of a stationary national income instead of a one-third increase in income.

Let's take a specific example. Between 1959 and 1969, the number of persons below the poverty line (less than $3,700 income for a family of 4) fell from 39 million to 24 million, from 22.4 percent to 12.2 percent of our rising population. The improvement came from a 3 percent increase in productivity per year, a drop in unemployment from 6 to 4 percent, shifts of the poor from lower to higher income occupations and regions, and an extraordinary growth in government cash transfers, from $26 billion in 1960 to over $50 billion in 1970. Every one of these factors is in some way the direct outgrowth of, associated with, or facilitated by, per capita economic growth.

Looking ahead, the Council of Economic Advisers projects a rise in GNP (in 1969 dollars) of roughly $325 billion, or 35 percent, from 1970 to 1976. In the face of claims on these increases that are already staked out or clearly in the making, it will be hard enough to finance the wars on poverty, discrimination, and pollution even with vigorous economic growth.

Consider the problem in a no-growth setting: to wrench resources from one use to another, to wrest incomes from one group for transfer to another, to redeploy Federal revenues from current to new channels (even assuming that a substantial part of the $70 billion of military expenditures could be made available)—and to do so on a sufficient scale to meet the urgent social problems that face us—might well involve us in unbearable social and political tensions. In this context, one rightly views growth as a necessary condition for social advance and for improving the quality of the total environment.

Apart from the tangible bounties that growth can bestow, we should remember that change, innovation, and risk thrive in an atmosphere of growth, which fosters social mobility and opens up options that no stationary state can provide. This is not to deny that a no-growth economy, with its large rations of leisure, would appeal to those who lay less store by the work ethic and material goods. But if they associate this with domestic tranquility—in the face of the intensified struggle for shares of a fixed income on the part of their more numerous and more competitive contemporaries—they are mistaken.

COST OF GROWTH

Let me return now to the context of the natural environment, to the growing consensus that we have to stop and reverse the ugly and destructive waste disposal practices of our modern society. To accomplish this, we will (1) have to call on the taxpayer to foot huge bills to overcome our past neglect as well as finance future collective waste treatment and preserve open space and wilderness; and (2) have to ask producers and consumers to bear the brunt of outright bans on ecologically dangerous materials and to pay rent for the use of the environment's waste assimilation services that they have been enjoying largely free of charge.

A common estimate of the demands on the federal budget for an adequate environmental program would raise the present outlay of $5 billion a year to $14 billion, an increase of about $50 billion for the next 5 years. Without growth, and given limits to the congressional will to tax, how could we hope to raise the required revenues?

Or take the case of agricultural and industrial pollution. Imagine the resistance of producers to the internalizing of external costs in a fixed-profit society. Or picture the resistance of consumers to price increases in a world of fixed incomes. If the only alternative, if the ultimate cost, were biological self-destruction, the answers would be different. But in the absence of that fate or its extreme remoteness, growth enters as a vital social lubricant, our best bet for getting people to give up private "goods" to overcome public "bads."

What I have just said in defense of GNP growth should not be misunderstood. Many people seem to feel that economists worship at the shrine of GNP, that growth is our Holy Grail. True, GNP is indispensable as a measure of the economy's productive potential and of its performance in utilizing that potential. But we labor under no illusion that GNP is a measure of welfare or that it can, as such, be turned into one.

Granting that GNP is not an index of human betterment is not to deny that one is generally associated with the other. It should require no lengthy demonstration to show that while a significant part of GNP is illusory in a welfare sense, wide differences and large advances in per capita GNP are associated with significant differences and advances in well-being. It will be hard to persuade a $3,000 per year family that it's not worse off than a $6,000 a year one.

In a careful appraisal of the growth-welfare correlation, Robert Lampman found a 37 percent gain in real per capita consumption between 1947 and 1962, a distinct improvement in income security, and a significant reduction in poverty. He concluded, "All things considered, the pattern of growth in the United States in the post-war years yielded benefits to individuals far in excess of the costs it required of them. To that extent, our material progress has had humane content."

ECONOMISTS AND ECOLOGISTS

It may well be that the nub of the problem in achieving a meeting of the minds between economists and ecologists is that the economist tends to seek optimality by selecting the right procedures—for example, creating incentives to eliminate or curb pollution by forcing the producer to bear the cost and the consumer to pay the price for waste-disposal access to the environment—rather than prescribing the right outcome, namely, ending or drastically reducing pollution. He is dedicated to that outcome, but wants the market system, rather than a government regulator, to do as much of the work for him as possible. Whether a meeting of minds evolves remains to be seen. Moderates in both camps are moving toward a middle ground, but given existing attitudes, I doubt that full accommodation will be easy.

On one hand, the ecologist will have to overcome his natural impatience with concepts of fine balancing of costs and benefits, an impatience that probably grows out of his feelings that cost-benefit analyses lack ethical content and moral inputs and that the more or less infinite benefits of environmental preservation make refined cost calculations more or less irrelevant. And he rightly stresses the nonlinearity of the cost curves of waste disposal as output rises: no-cost or low-cost in the early stages when discharges stay well within the absorptive capacity of the environment, then rising fairly sharply when accumulation and concentration begin to exceed that capacity, and exponentially when they saturate it.

On the other hand, the economist will have to break out of the web of marginal cost-benefit balance in cases where the relevant costs and benefits can't be captured in that web. And he needs to beware of forcing onto the pricing mechanism jobs that it will almost surely do badly. But he rightly insists that, despite these limitations, the cost-benefit principle is applicable to a very broad range of pollution problems where measurements or reasonable approximations are possible.

The question of nonlinearity is a tougher one in application if not in concept. Few would dispute that there is an initial zone where discharges are not pollutants because they are well within the regenerative ability of land and water ecosystems that eliminate waste by cycling it through plants and animals and decomposers. Nor is it difficult to agree that at the opposite end, costs can rise exponentially and ecocycles can be destroyed by overloading waters with nutrients, the atmosphere with noxious gases and particulate matter, and so on.

It is in the middle zone that things get sticky. An economist tends to believe that the zone of gradual and roughly linear rise in environmental damage is broad and that it widens—that the cost curve moves to the right—especially when the impetus of full-cost pricing moves science and technology to devise and put in place new techniques of waste disposal and recycling. Where the zone of tolerance or reasonable cost is very limited, as in the case of mercury or DDT, marginalism obviously won't do. The total or near-total ban is the only remedy. Whether mercury and DDT are proxies for just a handful of cases or the forerunner of an exponential rise in contamination of the earth, land surface, air mass, and waterways, will determine in good part our relative reliance on total versus marginal approaches to environmental action.

The economist is inclined to doubt that such cases will multiply rapidly. Past demonstrations of the capacity of our economy, our technology, and our institutions to adapt and adjust to changing circumstances and shocks are impressive. We are still in the early stages of identifying, quantifying, and reacting to the multiple threats to our environment. It may be that we are too quick in accepting the concept of finite limits and closing physical frontiers implicit in the concept of Spaceship Earth (dramatized by Kenneth Boulding, the ecologist)! At least two previous episodes in our history come to mind to suggest that we may yet escape (or push into the remote future) the ultimate biophysical limits, may yet be able to turn the ecological dials back from the "self-destruct" position by redirecting rather than giving up growth in output, energy, and technology.

The first was the closing of America's geographical frontiers, which allegedly robbed this country of much of its mobility and dynamism. But other frontiers—scientific, technological, economic—soon opened up new vistas and opportunities, new frontiers which far surpassed any physical frontiers.

The second episode is much more recent. Our memories need not be stretched very far to recall the great furor about "running out of resources" about 20–25 years ago, especially energy, minerals, and other natural resources. As we now know, intensive scientific research and technological development—responding partly to the alarms that were sounded, but mostly to the signals sent out by the pricing system—resulted in the upgrading of old resources, the discovery of new ones, the development of substitutes and the application of more efficient ways of utilizing available resources and adjusting to changes in relative availabilities.

Now, of course, our problem is less one of limited resource availability and more one of growing threats to environmental quality and to the metabolism of the biosphere. Concentrations of toxic and nondegradable wastes pose a mounting problem. But it seems far too soon to conclude that mounting problems are insurmountable. If scientific and technological discoveries enable us to import solar energy, at least for purposes of photosynthesis, and enable us to build a proxy for the sun in the form of fusion power sometime in the next half century or so, we may well find the key to unlock the doors that the ecologist tells us are closing all around us. One gallon of water would give us the energy we now get from seven gallons of crude oil. Electricity would be penny cheap but no longer pound foolish. Recycling of wastes would be routine. Reconstituting of natural resources would come into the realm of the possible. I do not assert that this will happen, only that it may.

PRICES AND PROHIBITIONS

Side by side with rigorous pricing efforts should be a very careful delineation of the cases which cannot be handled by full-cost pricing, which instead call for direct prohibitions, regulation, public expenditure, tax reform, changes in our agricultural subsidy programs (to end the idling of good land with consequent chemical "overkill" to force more output from other land), changes in transport regulation, and so on.

In all this, we should not underestimate the possibility that there may be more complementarities than our limited experience leads us to think. Once we end the free rides in waste disposal and put the appropriate price tags on access to the environment, we will create a sharp spur to pollution-abatement technology. Once such abatement is made mandatory or non-abatement painfully costly by some system of waste disposal charges, the relevant technology will no longer be treated as a corrective band-aid, an approach that is likely to be inefficient and costly. Instead, it will be done on a preventive and planned basis. It will be built in. As economic growth leads to replacement of old with new processes, equipment, and plants, it will hasten the change to cleaner and healthier methods of production.

In the past, under the spur of the price system we have successfully substituted technology for resources. This allayed the fears that we were exhausting our natural resources like coal, iron, and oil. But we did not reduce the pressure on the environmental ecosystem as a whole. The things on which we put a price were conserved. But the things that we ordinarily left out of the pricing mechanism suffered—air, water, and landscape.

Is it unreasonable to assume that just as the market mechanism (with some assistance from government inducements, incentives, and R&D investments) altered the technical coefficients for traditional natural resources in response to the signals sent out by the pricing mechanism, so the internalizing of external costs of air, water, quiet, and landscape will cause new shifts leading us to conserve these resources and postpone the days of local and global reckoning?

Finally, as we work to terminate the subsidies that are implicit in our failure to charge for fouling the environment with liquid, solid, gaseous, and thermal wastes, we should not overlook the huge explicit subsidies in our tax system that have the same effects, namely, overproduction of many products and over-exploitation of natural resources. To continue stimulating the over-exploitation of oil, coal, timber, and every mineral from iron to vermiculite and spodumene by big tax subsidies in the form of excessive depletion allowances, capital gains shelter, and special deductions becomes every more anomalous. Here is another case where the believers in the market pricing system ought to live by it. The public is subsidizing these industries at least twice—once by rich tax bounties and once by cost-free or below-cost discharge of wastes and heat. Far from stimulating conservation and rational exploitation of fossil fuels, both the form and the price impact of our tax preferences work the wrong way.

DISTRIBUTIONAL EFFECTS

As we increasingly inject the costs of waste disposal into the prices of our products, GNP will not suffer in quantity, but will change in quality, containing more environmental amenities and less material output. The intuitive reaction of most readers of this article will be inwardly to smile with satisfaction.

But how will the poor and the black ghetto dweller view the matter? What do environmental attraction, aesthetics, and amenities mean to them? Perhaps somewhat cleaner air and water, but more pertinently,

—higher prices of the goods that will now bear the cost of producing those three A's;

—little help with what the congressman from Harlem said "ecology" means to his constituents: "Who's gonna collect the damn garbage?"

So before we take much solace in the improved mix of the national output *as we see it,* we had better be sure (a) that the ghetto dweller (as a proxy for "the poor") is cut in on the environmental dividends as *he* sees them, and (b) also that as we end industry's free ride on public air and water and land and thereby raise the price of goods bought by the poor, we simultaneously compensate them through more effective measures to redistribute income and opportunity.

CONCLUSION

In the complex and often baffling field of environmental control, no one —least of all the economist—has all the answers. What the economist believes he can contribute is a better understanding of how the market pricing system and economic growth can be made to work for us, rather than against us, in the battle to protect our natural environment and improve the quality of existence. The economist readily recognizes, however,

—that environmental quality is a highly subjective "good" on which it will be difficult to put price tags;

—that where environmental damage is irreparable, as it may well in the Alaskan tundra, or where a substance or a process threatens irreparable damage to health, to life, or to the biosphere;

—that is, where costs are infinite—the pricing system has neither the capacity nor the speed to deal with the problem.

But recognizing such limits, the economist rightly asserts that across a large part of the pollution spectrum the pricing system is applicable. By charging the producer—and ultimately the consumer—for the full cost of waste disposal we will put their self-interest to work in slowing or even reversing the march toward a degraded or exhausted environment.

It won't be easy. Even after ecologists identify the source of the trouble, engineers identify solutions and develop monitoring devices, and economists identify appropriate taxing and pricing schemes, there remain crucial tests of public will and political skill. To get producers and consumers to pay the full cost of using the environment for waste disposal, and to get the public to accept the reordered priorities and pay the higher taxes that will be needed to redirect growth and clean up past environmental mistakes, will require great acts of both will and skill.

Part II
MICROECONOMICS

A. Healthy competition or a corporate oligarchy?

One of the most persistent issues of economic theory and policy in 20th-century America has been the relationship between "big business" and "competition." The classical theory of perfect competition—with its assumption of many small firms selling identical products at competitive, market-determined prices—still implies that all big business is at least somewhat "monopolistic," or "imperfectly competitive." This classical theory has provided both the normative and objective rationale for America's "antitrust" policies, traditionally the main governmental instrument for sustaining competition in the market economy.

For the past 25 years Galbraith has written some of the most literate funeral sermons over the death of classic market competition. His 1947 book *(American Capitalism)* pointed to the emergence of "countervailing power" between Big Business, Big Labor, and Big Government as a hopeful alternative to the market mechanism. In 1967 *(The New Industrial State)* he saw corporate planning in the industrial state as the inevitable new dominant economic form. He has consistently emphasized the technological pressures (economies of scale) which have given birth to the corporate giants, but also the political and social forces which helped to create them and now assure their survival. Rather than nostalgically attempting to dismantle big business, we should accept it and seek political or other ways to use it to greater social advantage.

Reponding to Galbraith's earlier work, *Fortune* magazine argues that big business has not killed competition, but transformed it. Instead of, or in addition to, the classic price competition, the oligopoly firms compete through product differentiation and new product innovation, new technology, customer services, and advertising. Other writers question *Fortune's* optimistic conclusion that these forms of "workable competition" serve consumers or society as well as strict price competition (see Readings 15 and 16 on consumer sovereignty).

In a 1967 "seminar" sponsored by the Senate Committee on Small Business, Adams, Mueller, and Turner replied to Galbraith's "corporate planning" theory. Adams basically agrees with Galbraith that giant corporations have acquired great market power, but he denies that this reflects their greater efficiency in production or in technological innovation through research and development (as *Fortune* claimed). Mueller and Turner, on the other hand, believe that competition remains stronger than Galbraith admits, even in the oligopoly industries; they suggest that large and growing markets can accommodate many big efficient firms (instead of a few inefficiently gigantic firms), and they emphasize the potential for innovations in products or technologies to erode existing market concentrations.

All commentators agree that antitrust policies have not in the past prevented the triumph of giant and largely uncompetitive corporations. The *Fortune* essay suggests dropping the attacks on big business (Galbraith's view also) and using "performance" criteria to regulate corporate behavior. Adams and Turner clearly favor new antitrust programs to dismantle existing corporate concentrations of market power. But Galbraith argues that this is a technologically and politically impossible goal (note Turner's pessimistic comment). Adams broadens the framework to advocate other shifts in government policy (patents, tariffs, "friendly" regulatory agencies) to promote a more competitive economy. The reader must ask himself: How likely are such major reforms? And, in their absence, how useful are present antitrust efforts to "preserve" the existing forms (and ideology) of competition?

13   The new competition*

EDITORS OF *FORTUNE*

Here is a nation that is the home and sanctuary of free competitive enterprise, distinguished from all other nations for such determined adherence to the principles of competition that it has written them into the law of the land with constitutional force. Virtually every American businessman, manager or owner, big or small, producer or distributor, uses the word "competition" habitually and usually sincerely in describing American capitalism. So do his employees, and so do editors, journalists, and even labor leaders.

But here also is a nation about whose competitiveness many "objective" and professional observers are very dubious. Certainly the country's economists, the men whose job it is to describe, analyze, and interpret the economy, do not talk of competition as businessmen do. Many seem to deny that the word competition has much relevance in the twentieth-century U.S.A.

In his new *American Capitalism,* Harvard's J. K. Galbraith makes what is perhaps the most sweeping statement so far. He says in effect that there is no competition in the classic sense, and hasn't been for years. Real competition has all but disappeared and oligopoly, or a few big sellers—the "Big Three," "Big Four," and so forth—dominate American markets. The economy is workable because big concentrations of industrial power almost automatically beget "countervailing power"—other concentrations of power organized against one another—which tends to prevent abuse. But the time has come, says Dr. Galbraith, to call an economic fact an economic fact, and to cast out "this preoccupation with competition."

The paradoxes of modern American capitalism are not lost on "realistic" Europeans. Probably few things amuse the sophisticated French businessmen and the cynical German industrialist more than the "romantic" American attempts to demonopolize the Continent. The British, too, are amused. Only last December 15, the London *Economist* chaffed the "evan-

---

* From "The New Competition," *Fortune,* June 1952. Copyright *Fortune,* 1952. Reprinted with permission of the publisher.

gelical" American businessmen for preaching competition and practicing something else. The Kremlin, of course, harps endlessly on its old, well-worn theme that *all* American business is monopolistic.

If the concept of competition has no relevance today, why does the American businessman stubbornly insist that competition is the heart of the enterprise system? Is he hypocritical or merely naive? Is it possible, on the other hand, that he is right? For the good of the national psyche, for the honor of the national reputation—and last but not least for intelligent administration of the antitrust law—it is time to try to resolve this great paradox of the new American capitalism.

The paradox arises in the fact that American capitalism in the past fifty or sixty years has experienced a profound transformation. It *is* a new capitalism, and the period of change coincides with the rise of the big modern corporation with large aggregations of capital and nationwide markets. This corporation changed the pattern of the critical producing areas of the economy from one of many sellers to one of few sellers and more recently to few buyers. The corporation, moreover, is usually run by paid managers who, in the long-term interest of their company, are forced to be responsible not only to stockholders but also to employees and to consumers.

One result of this change is that the word competition no longer means what it once did. American business today, and particularly Big Business, is practicing a new kind of competition. This competition is not *Fortune*'s invention. It has been developing for more than fifty years, and although it is belittled by many economists, a growing number of respected ones have espoused it. And most businessmen have a very good idea indeed of what it is.

They know for one thing that the "new competition" has been a stunning success, especially when measured in terms of delivering a standard of living to the consumer. Could "classic" competition have done any better? As businessmen see it, that's a fair question, the only question. They ask to be judged by results, not by theory. If they tend to grow apoplectic when they are discussed in learned papers as "monopolists" or "oligopolists," it is because they *know* the U.S. is competitive.

As buyers and sellers, businessmen recognize this new competition in terms of such things as prices that respond to market pressures, products that are constantly being improved, and choice for the buyers. They apply such standards pragmatically, not only because they are unfamiliar with formal economic thought but because they know all too well how markets change with industries, products, companies, regions, and from year to year or even month to month. This approach is more or less what the new competition amounts to. It is also more or less what modern economists think of when they talk about "workable" competition. M. A. Adelman of M.I.T., for instance, suggests that workable competition exists when non-collusive rivalry occurs with a sufficient number of alternates open to both buyer and seller.

What causes the great paradox is that most of the economists and experts who have until recently shaped the accepted notions of competition do not describe it that way. Competition to them is a way of life that can be defined fairly rigidly. They conceive of competition in terms of the grand old original or classic model of Adam Smith and his followers.

THE GRAND OLD MODEL

Now this model is based on a great and wise principle, verified by the experience of man through the ages and back into the abyss of time—the principle that the peoples of the earth, if they know what's good for them, should never trust their welfare to the discretion of a powerful few. Thus competition is free society's main safeguard against economic injustice. It drives people to produce more rather than less because it enables them to make more money by producing more to sell for less. It tends to make the best use of resources. It is both a regulator and a spur, and its ultimate benefactors are people as consumers.

On these general truths the early British economists reared an ideal superstructure. Its chief characteristic was a market with many sellers turning out practically the same product, and with no seller large enough to have any power to control prices. Competition was assumed to occur by price alone; supply and demand, the impersonal forces of the market, "the hidden hand," automatically regulated the price of everything, including the price of labor. Everybody got no more or less than he deserved, and resources were used with maximum efficiency.

The model was natural and just. It was infinitely superior to socialism in that it recognized the validity of individual incentive. Because it was so comprehensive and fundamental, it became the academic model. When pedagogues expounded capitalism to their pupils, they expounded it in terms of the classic model.

But like many great concepts it was a model of perfection rather than of reality, even in its time. It was set up when no one wielded great economic power. Although the concept of the market and the law of supply and demand retained their validity, the notion that competition was effective only when many sellers competed by price alone gradually lost relevance.

Even in the U.S., the only nation that continued to take the model seriously in the twentieth century, the ideal of many sellers went by the board. Large companies grew up swiftly, both by internal growth and by acquisition and merger. The U.S. antitrust laws, of course, were inspired by and partly based on the classic model. But they at first punished only clear conspiracies and accomplished monopolies. And although the Clayton and its subsidiary acts were passed to *prevent* monopoly by catching it in its "incipiency," confusion and irresolution prevented the new law from being effective until the middle 1930s, and even then it did not reform the economy in its image. It could do nothing about the prorationing of the state commissions, which in effect decides the level of the world's oil prices. It could do relatively little about the price "leadership" of big companies—the judgment of the leader, who posts prices in response to his "feeling" about the market, replaces the impersonal forces of the classic market.

The law, finally, could do nothing about the rise of Big Little Business, Big Agriculture, and Big Labor, which proceeded to use political means to gain what Big Business had gained by political and economic means. They not only emulated but outdid Big Business. All three carried their war to the citadel itself, amending the antitrust laws to exempt themselves from many if not most of the effects of price competition.

The classic economists realized that their model was not working well; the last of the great classicists, Alfred Marshall, made due allowances for the fact that competition in practice was bound to be imperfect. The classicists nevertheless went on preaching and teaching orthodox theory because they believed and still believe it provides them with valid principles for measuring a free, competitive society. Let the U.S. strive for perfect competition, they say in effect, and it will be likely to remain tolerably competitive.

THE PRAGMATIC STANDARD

The new competition is an approach, not a model: it cannot be, or certainly hasn't been, rigidly defined. It does not cast aside the classic model. It simply retains the basic principles and discards as much of the model as is necessary to make it consistent with reality. It has no use for collusion, monopoly, or deliberate restraints of trade. But it puts the consumer's interest ahead of theory, and shuns perfect competition for the sake of perfect competition. It makes allowance for the fact that the American economy has delivered to people the benefits that perfect competition was calculated to give.

Therefore, it does not hold that business, to bring maximum benefit to consumers, must necessarily consist of many small sellers competing by price alone. It does not hold that the rivalry of a few large sellers necessarily means economic injustice. And it does not necessarily think of competition as the impersonal, pervasive force of the classic model, but grants it can be, in the words of Michigan's Clare Griffin, "conscious and personal." It corresponds roughly to the businessman's pragmatic description of competition. And in terms of such a concept, the businessman who talks sincerely of our competitive way of life is right. Just look at our economy today.

To begin with, that economy is too complex to encompass with a few generalizations. It is a matter of considerable doubt, for example, whether a relatively few large companies—"the oligopolists"—do "rule" the nation's prices and markets. Professor George Stigler is an outstanding classicist, and certainly cannot be accused of partiality to Big Business. But even he estimates that only 20 percent of the industries he was able to classify with inadequate data were, in 1939, represented by what he defines as unregulated monopoly or oligopoly. It is his thesis that competition, even judged by the classic model, has been increasing, not decreasing, over the years.

Professor Clair Wilcox of Swarthmore also challenges easy assumptions about oligopoly, but from the standpoint that most figures on concentration are irrelevant. "Meaningful conclusions as to the structure of markets," he insists with considerable plausibility, "are not to be obtained until someone devises a product classification that groups goods according to the readiness with which one can be substituted for another."

Therefore he denounces the habit of judging the whole economy in terms of manufacturing, which after all accounts for less than two-fifths of unregulated, nonbanking private enterprise. Breaking down the consumer's expenditures, by categories, he finds strong evidence that "oligopoly" does not dominate the market.

Clair Wilcox's emphasis on the consumer is much to the point. The consumer has an immense choice of goods and prices; even in the wilderness he has the mail-order catalogue. American retailing is often highly competitive by almost any standard, sometimes almost by that of the classic model.

Not only do retailers compete briskly, they force manufacturers that supply them to price their products competitively. This is an example of what Mr. Galbraith terms "countervailing power"—the idea that big sellers cannot control markets if buyers are strong enough, nor buyers if sellers are strong enough. Sears, Roebuck and the A & P can buy almost anything at the lowest market prices because they buy so much—just as the motor industry is able to buy steel at a competitive price because it is a big buyer, and labor unions can sell their members' services at good prices because they are so well organized.

Countervailing power, however, is plainly not a substitute for competition, as Mr. Galbraith seems to imply it is. Without a concept of competition translated into public policy, this power can be a monopolistic force—as it is in Europe, and indeed as it is for the American labor unions that wield power *as* power because they are exempt from antitrust. But countervailing power, plus the competitive principle, does result in delivering to the consumer the benefits that classic competition was presumed to bring.

NOT CLASSIC BUT EFFECTIVE

Many manufacturers, of course, need no direct pressure to be competitive. Certainly most makers of new consumer products don't. The frozen-orange-juice industry is compelled by circumstances beyond its control to be so competitive it hurts badly. And, of course, garment manufacturers must compete incessantly or go out of business. They do not gang up to fix production or prices. None dominates the market. Their marginal costs often equal—and sometimes exceed—their prices. What keeps them from being an example of classic competition is David Dubinsky and his I.L.G.W.U., which has insulated garmentworkers from the wage market.

And the consumer today certainly enjoys a wonderfully competitive market in appliances, radios, and television sets. Most are made by a fair number of manufacturers, none of whom can control the market, at least not for very long. These durables are today easy to get into (and to fail in, too). Prices are flexible at the retail level, which is where price counts. And they are flexible at the retail level because manufacturers allow for price competition when they set the markup.

Only two years ago, remember, manufacturers were assuring people that they would never again be able to buy a first-line, eight-foot refrigerator for less than $250 or a sixteen-inch television set for less than $350. Today they are both selling at about $150. It is certainly hard to describe as monopolistic and therefore antisocial an economy whose refrigerator industry has sold the astonishing number of 48 million units since 1940; whose radio industry has sold the even more astonishing number of 188 million units since 1922; whose television industry has sold some 18 million units in five years. The competition that made this possible may not have been classically perfect, but who will deny that it has been effective?

This kind of competition, moreover, does not seem destined to wither away but to increase as the nation's productivity increases and the nation's selling apparatus is pressed to get rid of the goods. Buying or countervailing power will surely come into greater play. Retailers will press manufacturers for better buys; manufacturers will press suppliers for cheaper raw materials and components.

Thus the chances are good, unless retailers gang up and legislate sweeping fair-trade laws, that the consumer will continue to buy most of his soft and durable goods, accounting for perhaps 25 percent of his expenditures, as cheaply as he could were they made and sold under the classic model. (At least no one can demonstrate otherwise.) And although many farm prices are exempt from market forces, the competition of the food chains will doubtless continue to give the consumer a good break on the 30 percent or so of his income that he spends on food.

THE "OLIGOPOLISTS"

Now what about Big Business itself—the "oligopolistic" unregulated industries like autos, steel, chemicals, cigarettes, rubber, oil, tin cans, and so forth—wherein a few big sellers are said to rule the markets? To begin with, none is describable as a true monopoly. Their prices usually respond to the market; prices may be "sticky" at times but they do move. These industries offer a choice to the buyer (and seller), and they are constantly improving the quality of their products. Many are subject to countervailing power. And all are subject to the pressure of public opinion.

By classic theory, of course, they are presumed to get a higher price for goods than "perfect" competitors. Prices no longer "rule" them; they "rule" prices. But thanks to the American preoccupation with competition, this phenomenon is often inconsequential even when it is true.

Price leadership occasionally takes the form of "dominant firm" leadership—i.e., one or two firms hold the price umbrella steady, regardless of market conditions. Such instances can be—and are—dealt with by antitrust law. But price leadership often is evidence of competition of the new kind. It can be observed as the "barometric" leadership practiced in the oil and rayon industries. "The leader bears the onus of formally recognizing market conditions," an oil-industry spokesman describes it. Eugene Holman, president of the Jersey Co., explains it further: "You paste your price on a wall, but you can't be sure it'll stick." Sometimes the leader's prices don't stick. In 1947, after President Truman's plea to keep prices steady, Esso Standard tried to hold the line as smart public relations. But it could not hold the line, at least for very long.

Another demonstration of big business' ability to "rule" prices was offered by the motor and steel industries, which after the war held prices considerably below the point where market forces alone would have carried them. The classic argument is that prices should be left to find their own level, not only to encourage more production but to ration what is available "by the purse." But letting prices find their own level, with the restrictions then prevailing, probably would not have resulted in an appreciably greater production. And rationing by the purse, which is theoretically the best way to ration anything, would have created a storm of angry protests from consumers (as the auto dealers' practice of rationing by the purse in fact did).

RISE AND FALL

The motor industry, indeed, could argue without double talk that genuine *competitive* considerations dictated that prices be held. The fundamental purpose of competition after all is not to throw the economy into a tailspin, but to make it function naturally, to dispense economic justice to the consumer. Classic price competition in motorcars after the war might have meant a precipitous rise followed by an equally precipitous drop, and then perhaps by serious economic disruptions and certainly by economic injustice. The restraint of the motor industry thus seems justified from the short-term view of a competitor seeking public approval and the long-term view of an industry cast in a workably competitive mold.

Whether big business is bigger than it needs to be for efficiency and technical progress is a proposition that can be argued endlessly, but there is little doubt that without modern "oligopoly" much of our immense technical progress would not have occurred. Modern research and development not only demand a lot of money which big companies have; the prospect of making unusually good or "monopoly" profits from research and development before competitors get in the field is what drives big companies to do the research and development.

Thus it can be argued that this incentive, which results from product or "quality" competition, brings society more benefits than classic price competition would have. If the chemical industry, for example, had cut prices to the bone as soon as costs declined, it today might be charging more for its products than it is.

Certainly "quality" and service competition indulged in by big companies cannot be summarily dismissed, as it is in strict classic theory, as a wasteful if cheap substitute for price competition. The plain fact, verified by anyone who compares consumer goods of thirty years ago with those of today, is that quality competition has given him more for his money.

THE UTILITY OF LUXURY

And the plain fact, verified every day by anyone who travels anywhere, eats or drinks in any save the meanest places, or buys anything at retail, is that much service competition is not wasteful unless anything remotely "luxurious" is defined as wasteful. Free delivery and other amenities may add nothing to the national stock of goods. But in a nation whose rising standard of living is measured in terms of rising services, they are an important part of life.

Even in capital-goods industries, anything but an example of classic competition, much real competition is evident as service competition. A small specialty steel company, for example, may quote the same prices as the big companies. But it goes to considerable trouble and expense in tailoring shapes and preparing metal content to the special needs of its customers.

And what about big-business advertising and selling? Many economists say they are economically wasteful methods of bolstering monopoly position and thus excluding potential competitors by differentiating between goods that in fact have little difference. "We may assume," writes Arthur Burns in his *Decline of Competition,* "that sales pressure by one or more firms in an industry has no effect on total demand—it merely shifts demand from one seller to another. . . ."

This might be true in a threadbare society hardly managing to keep body and soul together. It might also be true in a model society inhabited by clairvoyant manufacturers who always make the right things and by consumers who promptly buy up everything as soon as it is produced. But in this realm of comparative plenty, most people have more money than they need for subsistence, and are "optional" and therefore arbitrary and erratic spenders. Advertising and selling provide the only means of persuading them. And as *Fortune* suggested last April, advertising and selling may provide an important means of keeping over-all consumption up to production, thus helping to prevent oversaving and the consequent deflation.

POWER AND SELF-RESTRAINT

Modern American capitalism, finally, exhibits a kind of long-term drive to behave as if it were competitive even when it is not driven by countervailing power or the impersonal forces of classic competition. It is a fact that businesses often tend to go on expanding sales whether profits are immediately maximized or not. As M. Adelman says of the A & P, it tries not for the largest possible profit over a planned period but for the best possible position at the end of it. "They recognize," says economist J. M. Clark, "that it is bad business to sacrifice future growth to an exorbitant rate of present profit, even if the curves on paper would permit it."

One reason it does so is that it understands the advantages of adjusting itself to public opinion and the moral climate of the times. Big business is more and more run by professional men whose primary aim is to keep their companies strong, and who therefore cannot exploit the rest of the country. As *Fortune* has put it, the American manager "is part of a group that enjoys power only so long as it does not abuse it—in other words, precisely so long as it does not exercise power the way men and groups of men used to [exercise it]."

THE "CREATIVE DESTRUCTION"

Another reason companies take the long view is that they sense or understand that in the U.S. economy no one's place is secure. Research and a free-money market have seen to that. Well-heeled companies, no longer beholden to Wall Street, plow back their earnings and constantly look for new things to get into. No company is safe in a field that is too green, uncrowded, or technically backward. General Motors is not only the largest auto maker; it is the largest refrigerator maker; and because the locomotive industry fell behind the times, G. M.'s Electro-Motive Division is now the largest locomotive maker. Crosley is not only a large refrigerator maker but a large television maker. "Anybody today can make anything," one manufacturer puts it, and it's not much of an exaggeration.

Industrial research, furthermore, is providing hundreds of new products that can substitute for older ones—nylon for silk, aluminum for steel and copper, plastics for leather, wood, metals, etc. The laboratory, today, is the great creator of competition.

No one's place is secure, finally, because the consumer has a great many choices and enough money to indulge the luxury of making them. Thus autos compete with fur coats, television sets with furniture, food with gasoline, and so on all down the line. Any manufacturer who wants to achieve volume must sell at a price that overcomes the competitive pressure of the other dissimilar goods.

On such facts the late Joseph Schumpeter based his notion of the "creative destruction" of capitalism. He argued that actual competition is perhaps less important than the threatened competition of the new technology, the new market, the new product. In the long run, he said, this threat "may enforce behavior very similar to the competitive pattern. It disciplines before it attacks. The businessman feels himself to be in a competitive situation even if he is alone in the field." In the short run Schumpeter noted what we already have digressed upon: precisely because corporations can look forward to good profits for a while, they risk big money for research and technological progress.

Such analysis has been attacked as a plea for letting well enough alone and giving up the fight for a competitive economy—and it is probably true that the country will not stay competitive by itself. But this argument would be valid only if the antitrust laws were not very effective.

"THE BROODING OMNIPRESENCE"

Taking everything together, one of the most important reasons why the U.S. economy is competitive is the "contradictory," "impotent," and yet on the whole profoundly effective body of antitrust laws. They were inspired by and based on the classic model, and their contradictions and failures are those of the model itself. They have won comparatively few victories, and some of these, like the basing-point, Alcoa, and Morton Salt decisions, raise as many difficult questions as they answer.

But the law's greatest achievement is not what it has done, but what its "brooding omnipresence" has induced business to do voluntarily. As the saying goes, it has made the ghost of Senator Sherman an ex officio member of every board of directors in the land. No businessman of consequence makes price, employment, advertising, acquisition, or expansion policies without considering whether or not they will violate the law. "I can't even write to a friend in a competing company," laments one company economist, "and ask him any information pertaining to the business, even if it has appeared in print."

THE ECONOMIC APPROACH

A good case can be made for tightening up some parts of antitrust law and enforcing it more vigorously. But an even better case can be made for the proposition that the law applies the classic model too literally. In general, it lacks an economic approach to what are essentially economic problems. In its preoccupation with "maintaining" competition, as ordained in the various amendments to the Clayton Act, it has tended to produce an opposite result, i.e., to protect competitors from the effects of competition. The recent Alcoa decision has laid it down in effect that business can violate the law merely by growing up to bigness and achieving the *power* to violate the law. And the Federal Trade Commission's stand that identical pricing and "conscious parallelism" are the same as collusion if their consequence is substantially to lessen competition has set a legal basis for prosecuting bona fide competitors.

The concept of the New Competition—"workable" competition—provides not a hard-and-fast definition but an approach to the problem of keeping competition effective. The job of formulating new policies is not easy. But it is not impossible.

Dr. Galbraith, for example, suggests a plausible rule of thumb: let the government encourage countervailing power when that power opposes existing market power, let it even create countervailing power where it is needed; and let it attack market power that is opposed by no countervailing power. As Michael Hoffman of the New York *Times* remarks, that is pretty much what antitrust does now. But Dr. Galbraith's suggestion has merit, and might well be studied by lawyers, prosecutors, judges, and analysts of antitrust policy.

Another and more carefully worked out guide is offered by Clare Griffin in his *"An Economic Approach to Antitrust Problems,"* recently published by the American Enterprise Association. He details five economic performance tests that he thinks should be used in deciding when to prosecute, how to determine penalties, what to legislate, and how to judge. The tests: (1) Is the company or industry efficient? (2) Is it progressive? (3) Does it show a reasonable and socially useful profit pattern—i.e., are its profits the reward of efficiency and progress rather than the result of artificial advantages? (4) Does it allow as much freedom of entry as is consistent with the business? (5) Is it well suited for defense?

Such tests place a heavy responsibility on the discretionary powers of the authorities, and may assume more intelligence and all-around judgment than the authorities possess. But the tests are apt and carefully thought out, and should not be overlooked. They or similar economic tests will have to be applied if antitrust law is to shape competition to benefit the people whom the creators of the classic model themselves intended it to benefit: the consumers.

14 Planning, regulation, and competition*

JOHN KENNETH GALBRAITH,
WILLARD F. MUELLER, WALTER ADAMS,
and DONALD TURNER

STATEMENT OF JOHN KENNETH GALBRAITH

In the lectures that precipitated this discussion and the book I have just published, I took it for granted that American business has become very big.

The element of surprise in this conclusion is very small; I doubt that this conclusion will be much disputed. There are still a large number of small firms and small farms in the United States. They are, however, no longer characteristic of the American economy. In 1962, the five largest industrial corporations in the United States, with combined assets in excess of $36 billion, possessed over 12 percent of all assets used in manufacturing. The 50 largest corporations had over a third of all manufacturing assets. The 500 largest corporations had well over two-thirds. Corporations with assets in excess of $10 million, some 2,000 in all, accounted for about 80 percent of all the resources used in manufacturing in the United States.

In the mid-1950s, 28 corporations provided approximately 10 percent of all employment in manufacturing, mining, and retail and wholesale

* From "Planning, Regulation and Competition," hearings before Select Committee on Small Business, 90th Congress, First Session, 1967, pp. 4–30. Abridged and reprinted with the permission of the authors. John Kenneth Galbraith is Paul M. Warburg Professor of Economics at Harvard University, Cambridge, Mass.; Walter Adams is Distinguished University Professor of Economics at Michigan State Universilty, East Lansing, Mich.; Willard F. Mueller is Vilas Research Professor at the University of Wisconsin, Madison, Wis., and was Chief Economist and Director, Bureau of Economics, Federal Trade Commission, Washington, D.C., at the time of these hearings; and Donald F. Turner is Professor at the Harvard School of Law, Harvard University, Cambridge, Mass., and was Assistant Attorney General, Antitrust Division, Department of Justice, Washington, D.C., at the time of these hearings.

trade. Twenty-three corporations provided 15 percent of all the employment in manufacturing. In the first half of that decade—June 1950–June 1956—a hundred firms received two-thirds by value of all defense contracts; 10 firms received one-third. In 1960 four corporations accounted for an estimated 22 percent of all industrial research and development expenditure. Three hundred and eighty-four corporations employing 5,000 or more workers accounted for 85 percent of these research and development expenditures; 260,000 firms employing fewer than 1,000 accounted for only 7 percent.

If I might continue this somewhat exaggerated dose of statistics for just a minute, in 1965, three industrial corporations, General Motors, Standard Oil of New Jersey, and Ford Motor Co., had more gross income than all of the farms in the country. This is relevant to my statement that these are the typical, characteristic parts of the economy. The income of General Motors, of $20.7 billion, about equalled that of the 3 million smallest farms in the country—around 90 percent of all farms. The gross revenues of each of the three corporations just mentioned far exceed those of any single state. The revenues of General Motors in 1963 were 50 times those of Nevada, 8 times those of New York, and slightly less than one-fifth those of the Federal Government.

These figures, like all statistics, are subject to minor query on matters of detail. As orders of magnitude they are not, I believe, subject to any serious question. Nor are the consequences.

The large firms that dominate the nonservice and nonagricultural sector of the economy have extensive power over their prices. They have large influence over the prices that they pay—at least those costs that are important to their operations. And also the wages they pay. They supply themselves with capital; some three-quarters of all savings now come from the retained earnings of corporations, which is to say that the latter have largely exempted themselves from dependence on the capital market. And, with varying degrees of success, firms with the resources to do so go beyond the prices that they set to persuade their customers as to what they should buy. This is a persuasion that, in various and subtle ways, extends to the state. There is great room for difference of opinion, and accordingly for debate, on how decisive are these several manifestations of power. But nearly all will agree that "There is a large correlation between the concentration of output in the hands of a small number of large producers and the existence of firms with significant degrees of market power." The observation just cited is that of Mr. Carl Kaysen and Mr. Donald F. Turner in their authoritative volume, "A Policy for Antitrust Law."

They add, as would I, that a policy that deals with "the existence and significance of market power is not aimed at *merely marginal or special phenomena, but at phenomena spread widely through the economy.*" Still quoting Professor Kaysen and Mr. Turner.

In my own volume I have gone on, at no slight length, to argue that this trend to the large corporation and this resulting exercise of substantial power over the prices, costs, wages, capital sources, and consumers is part of the broad sweep of economic development. Technology; the extensive use of capital; affluent and hence malleable customers; the imperatives of organization; the role of the union; the requirements imposed by public tasks, including arms development and space exploration, have all weakened the authority of the market. At the same time, these developments have both enabled and required firms to substitute planning with its management of markets for a simple response to the market. Bigness and market power, in other words, are but one part of a much larger current of change. To see them in isolation from other change is artificial. In part it is what results when a social discipline passes however partially from the custody of scholars to that of specialists and mechanics.

I have also been concerned in this book with the problem of how we are to survive, and in civilized fashion, in a world of great organizations which, not surprisingly, impose both their values and their needs on the society they are assumed to serve. But these further matters are not directly at issue this morning. In any case they do not directly involve the question of the antitrust laws.

The issue of the antitrust laws arises in response to a prior question. That question is whether we can escape the concentration and the attendant market control and planning which I have outlined and whether the antitrust laws, as now used, are an effective instrument for this escape. The present hearings materialized when I urged the contrary—when I said that the trend to great size and associated control was immutable, given our desire for economic development, and that the present antitrust efforts to deal with size and market power were a charade. I noted that the antitrust laws legitimatize the real exercise of market power on the part of the large firms by a rather diligent harassment of those who have less of it. Thus, they serve to reassure us on the condition they are assumed to correct.

The facts which lead to the foregoing conclusions are not at all obscure. Nor are they matters of great subtlety. They are accepted by most competent economists and lawyers including the very distinguished men here this morning. Only the rather obvious conclusions to be drawn from these facts encounter a measure of resistance. This, no doubt, is purely temporary, but while it persists it does cause a measure of confusion.

The most effective manifestation of economic power, all must agree, is simply the big firm. To be big in general and big in an industry is by far the best way of influencing prices and costs, commanding capital, having access to advertising, and selling resources, and possessing the other requisites of market power. And, as we have seen, by common agreement the heartland of the industrial economy is now dominated by large firms. The great bulk of American business is transacted by very large corporations.

And here enters the element of charade in the antitrust laws. If a firm is already large it is substantially immune under the antitrust laws. If you already have the basic requisite of market power, you are safe. The Assistant Attorney General in Charge of the Antitrust Laws in the distinguished book to which I have already adverted argues that the market power of the large firm should now be made subject to the antitrust laws. This indeed is the main thrust of Mr. Turner's and Mr. Kaysen's book. If something needs to be done, he would not, of course, argue that it has been done. And in responding to the questions of this committee on May 2 of this year he affirmed the point, if in slightly more cautious language:

> It is more difficult under present law to bring a case attacking *existing* concentration in an industry than to prevent further concentrations which firms attempt to realize through merger.

But this we see is no minor qualification. If firms are already large—if concentration is already great—if the resulting power to use Mr. Turner's own words, is not "merely marginal" but is "spread widely through the economy" as he says, then it means that all so favored have won immunity or virtual immunity from the antitrust laws. And this, of course, is the case.

Meanwhile, the antitrust laws are effective in two instances where the firms do not have market power but are seeking to achieve it. Where firms are few and large they can, without overt collusion, establish and maintain a price that is generally satisfactory to all participants. Nor is this an especially difficult calculation, this exercise of power. This is what we economists with our genius for the neat phrase have come to call oligopolistic rationality. And this market power is legally immune or very nearly so. It is everyday practice in autos, steel, rubber, and virtually every other industry shared or dominated by, relatively, a few large firms. But if there are 20 or 30 or more significant firms in the industry, this kind of tacit price-making—this calculation as to what is mutually advantageous but without overt communication—becomes more difficult, maybe very difficult. The same result can only be achieved by having a meeting or by exchanging information on prices and costs and price intentions. But this is illegal. It is also legally vulnerable. And it is, in fact, an everyday object of prosecution as the Department of Justice will confirm. What the big firm in the concentrated industry can accomplish legally and effortlessly because of its size, the small firm in the unconcentrated industry does at the pain of civil and even criminal prosecution. Moreover, with this my colleagues will, I believe, agree.

The second manifestation of the charade has to do with mergers. If a firm is already large, it has as a practical matter nothing to fear under antimerger provisions of the Clayton Act. It will not be demerged. It can continue to grow from its own earnings; if discreet, it can even, from time to time, pick up a small and impecunious competitor, for it can reasonably claim that this does little to alter the pattern of competition in the industry. But if two medium-sized firms unite in order to deal more effectively with this giant, the law will be on them like a tiger. Again if large, you are exempt. If you seek to become as large, or even if you seek to become somewhat larger, although still much smaller, you are in trouble. And again I doubt that the committee will encounter a great deal of dissent.

Here we have the nature of modern antitrust activity. It conducts a fairly effective war on small firms which seek the same market power that the big firms already, by their nature, possess. Behind this impressive facade the big participants who have the most power bask in nearly total immunity. And since the competitive market, like God and a sound family life, is something that no sound businessman can actively oppose, even the smaller entrepreneurs who are the natural victims of this arrangement do not actively protest. It is possible that they do not know how they are being used.

As I say all of this is agreed—or at least is supported by the past writings and speeches of participants in this discussion. All I have done—I wish I could lay claim to greater novelty—is to state the rather disagreeable conclusion flowing from this agreement. The antitrust laws give the impression of protecting the market and competition by attacking those who exercise it most effectively. I wonder if the committee thinks that charade is an unjust word?

Now let me clear up two or three secondary matters which may seem to affect this discussion but really do not. The first requires me, I think for the first time—in substance as distinct from terminology—to quit company with Attorney General Turner. Mr. Turner, while conceding that the law is largely helpless in attacking achieved as distinct from aspired-to power, holds that it is important to act preventatively to keep smaller firms from getting larger. This he has emphasized in his responses to this committee. It will surely have occurred to the committee, as it must have occurred to Mr. Turner, that this does not meet the issue of gross discrimination as between those who already have and those who aspire to market power. Nor, one imagines, can a major law officer of the Government be entirely happy about such discrimination. It condones professional and accomplished wrongdoing, as it were, but stresses the importance of cracking down on amateur wickedness. Surely this is bad law. Also, given the size and market power that has already been achieved, and given its immunity, it will be evident that this justification amounts to locking the stable door not alone after the horse has been stolen but after the entire stud has been galloped away.

Next, I must correct a misapprehension of Attorney General Turner. His responses to the committee and his extremely interesting lecture attacking my general position in London convey the impression that I am concerned with making the economic case for the large corporation. I am, he suggests, especially concerned to defend its efficiency and technical virtuosity. To this he responds by arguing that, while the big corporation is more efficient than the small firm, there is no great difference between the big corporation and the giant corporation. He doesn't make altogether clear, incidentally, how big a big as distinct from a giant corporation is. All would, I imagine, be among the five hundred or thousand firms that dominate industrial activity. But I have a more fundamental objection. He attacks me on a point that concerns me little and which is of no importance for my case.

I am not concerned with making the case for big business. Nor am I especially concerned about its efficiency or inefficiency. Doubtless efficiency is worth having. But, like truth, regular bathing and better traffic regulation, it has an adequate number of exponents. I have always thought it unwise to compete with the commonplace. Mr. Turner may be correct in his conclusions about the giants. I am content to argue that we have big business, and that the antitrust laws notwithstanding we will continue to have it, and that they give an impression of alternative possibilities that do not exist.

I conclude also that while big business and giant business may not be more efficient, their market power as manifested only on what they sell and what they buy and over buyers does give them advantages in planning their own future and insuring their own survival. Since big business is inevitable and will not be affected by the antitrust laws, I naturally go on to consider how we may come to terms with it. Much of my book is concerned with that. If my colleagues this morning disagree, as is their right, they must tell you how the antitrust laws are to be brought effectively to bear on the large corporation. Otherwise—and here let me interpolate an important point—there is no escape from the conclusion that the antitrust laws, so far from being a threat to big business are a facade behind which it operates with yet greater impunity. They create the impression, the antitrust laws, that the market is a viable control. Then, if a drug firm has exorbitant profits, it can say this is what the market allows. Or if an automobile firm does not want to install safety appliances, it can say that the market does not demand it. Or if there is resistance to Government price guideposts to prevent inflation, it can be said that these interfere with the market.

In each case, the antitrust laws effectively protect the large business from social pressure or regulation by maintaining the myth that the market does the regulating instead.

Finally, I agree that the antitrust laws have purposes other than those related to the structure of industry and the resulting power and planning. I agree in particular they are a code of what is deemed fair and decent as between seller and buyers. They exclude the resort to activities—naked aggression, as in the case of the old Standard Oil Co. in the last century—based on superior economic resources, favoritism, surreptitious and unfair discounts, numerous other practices which the civilized commercial community holds in disesteem. I have no complaint about these aspects of the antitrust laws. On the contrary, I consider them serviceable. But only in the most marginal fashion do they thus affect the structure of industry. They are, in large part, a separate matter and do not affect the discussion here.

To what then does this all lead? It is possible that my distinguished colleagues here this morning will call for an all-out attack on achieved market power along the lines which Attorney General Turner has adumbrated in his book, which Prof. Walter Adams has long favored, and which I have just said would be necessary if they disagree with my conclusions on the inevitability of market power. This means action, including enabling legislation leading to all-out dissolution proceedings against General Motors, Ford, the oil majors, United States Steel, General Electric, IBM, Western Electric, Du Pont, Swift, Bethlehem, International Harvester, North American Aviation, Goodyear, Boeing, National Dairy Products, Procter & Gamble, Eastman Kodak, and all of comparable size and scope. For there can be no doubt: All are giants. All have market power. All enjoy an immunity not accorded to those who merely aspire to their power. Such an onslaught, tantamount, given the role of the big firms in the economy as I described it, to declaring the heartland of the modern economy illegal, would go far to make legitimate the objections to my position. It would mean that achieved market power was subject to the same legal attack as that which is only a matter of aspiration.

But I will be a trifle surprised if my distinguished colleagues from the Government are willing to proclaim such a crusade. I am frank to say I would not favor it myself; as I indicated at the outset, I do not think that the growth of the modern corporation can be isolated from other and intricately related changes in modern economic development. I doubt that one can operate on one part of this fabric. The political problems in proclaiming much of the modern economy illegal will also strike many as impressive.

If this crusade is not to be launched, then my good friends have no alternative but to agree with me. They are good men; they cannot acquiesce in a policy which by their own admission attacks the small man for seeking what the big firm enjoys with impunity. I readily concede that it would be quixotic to ask the repeal of the antitrust laws although other industrial countries function quite competently without them. But the antitrust laws are part of the American folklore. They receive strong support from the legal profession and vice versa. They have a reserve value for dealing with extreme and sanguinary abuse of power as occasionally occurs. I would be content were we simply to withdraw our faith from the antitrust laws—

were we to cease to imagine that there is any chance that they will affect the structure of American industry or its market power and, having in mind the present discrimination in their application, were we then to allow them quietly to atrophy. Then we would face the real problem, which is how to live with the vast organizations—and the values they impose—that we have and will continue to have. This being so, nostalgia will no longer be a disguise for that necessity.

STATEMENT OF WILLARD F. MUELLER

At the outset, let there be no mistake about it: Although Galbraith has articulated a provocative thesis concerning the causes and implications of "the new industrial state," he has not borne the burden of mustering the evidence to validate this thesis.

Time permits joining issues on only his key points. I shall challenge three of his major contentions:

1. Technological imperatives dictate vast industrial concerns and high levels of market concentration and, hence, the death of the market.

2. Public policy aimed at maintaining a market economy has failed in the past and is doomed to fail in the future.

3. The necessity for state planning in certain areas further diminishes the need for reliance on the market as a regulating and planning agent.

THE TECHNOLOGICAL IMPERATIVES

Most fundamental to Galbraith's thesis are the so-called technological imperatives which he views as the root causes of modern industrial organization. He asserts that we must have very large industrial complexes and high market concentration because of the requirements of large-scale production, invention, and innovation. As he puts it, "The enemy of the market is not ideology but technology." But what are the facts on this point?

Recent studies of this subject are almost unanimous in concluding that productive efficiency dictates high concentration in only a small and declining share of all manufacturing industries. On this point, there seems to be little disagreement.

There is a growing body of research into the extent to which economies of large scale dictate large business enterprise and high market concentration. The evidence is sharpest in the area of productive efficiency. This is an especially crucial area because of the public policy dilemma posed by industries with increasing returns to large scale. In clear-cut cases where large-scale production dictates monopoly, as with telephone and electric power, the American answer has been either regulation or Government ownership. But, if such industries prove the rule rather than the exception, this raises a basic question as to the compatibility of productive efficiency and a competitively structured economy. It is, therefore, extremely significant that recent studies are unanimous in concluding that productive efficiency dictates high concentration in only a small—and declining—share of all manufacturing industries.

But Galbraith does not rest his case on the requirement of large-scale production. He further argues that economies of scale in research and innovation make high concentration and near monopoly an inevitable outcome of modern capitalism. Since Joseph Schumpeter first set forth this doctrine in 1942 and Galbraith expanded upon it in 1952, it has been subjected to extensive empirical testing. There has been a virtual flood of studies in recent years. All students of the subject are not in complete agreement. But as a minimum, a careful reading of the evidence shows that the theory has no general validity in explaining inventive and innovative activity in American experience. Indeed, recent studies indicate that the thesis is on the verge of collapse. One of Schumpeter's disciples recently discovered no systematic relationship between the degree of market power and inventive success. He concluded:

These findings among other things raise doubts whether the big, monopolistic conglomerate corporation is as efficient an engine of technological change as disciples of Schumpeter (including myself) have supposed it to be. Perhaps a bevy of fact-mechanics can still rescue the Schumpeter engine from disgrace, but at present the outlook seems pessimistic.

Students of the problem owe a debt of gratitude to the Senate Subcommittee on Antitrust and Monopoly, chaired by Senator Philip A. Hart, for the exhaustive hearings it has held on the subject of the role of technology and industrial organization. Over the past 3 years these hearings have reviewed systematically nearly all of the recent authoritative work on this subject. I shall not review this evidence here, but it is must reading for anyone genuinely interested in getting at the facts in this area. Regrettably, Professor Galbraith apparently has failed to explore this and other authoritative work on the subject. Until he, or others, can come up with contrary evidence, the chief pillar of his thesis lacks an empirical foundation.

I think his use of illustration betrays his case. He illustrates, as you will recall from his Reith lectures and also his books, the matchless capability of the vast enterprise in planning inventive and innovative activity by a hypothetical example of how General Electric would go about the conception and birth of a new popup toaster. But insight into this process is better revealed by experience than by hypothetical example. What support in experience is there for predicting that vast size is prerequisite to the development and introduction of new products and processes? Let's consider the electrical home appliances sold by General Electric. Perhaps the past is prolog to the future.

To begin, the electric toaster was not invented or introduced by a great corporation such as General Electric, which would fit so nicely Galbraith's invention-innovation-planning framework. On the contrary, according to the late T. K. Quinn, former vice president of General Electric, it was developed and brought into the market by a relatively small firm, the McGraw Co. And, according to Mr. Quinn, "for many years none of the giant companies were able to come near to matching [McGraw's] toaster." This is no exception. Mr. Quinn credited small companies with discovery and initial production of electric ranges, electric refrigerators, electric dryers, electric dishwashers, the hermetically sealed compressor, vacuum cleaners, clothes-washing machines, deep freezers, electric hot irons, and electric steam irons. Indeed, Mr. Quinn summarized his own experience with GE in this way:

I know of no original product invention, not even electric shavers or hearing aids, made by any of the giant laboratories or corporations, with the possible exception of the household garbage grinder, developed not by the research laboratory but by the engineering department of General Electric. But the basic idea of this machine came from a smaller concern producing commercial grinders.[1]

He concluded:

The record of the giants is one of moving in, buying out, and absorbing the smaller concerns.

Nor is this record unique to household appliances. In many other industries smaller companies generate at least their proportionate share of inventions and innovations, and frequently they do a good deal better than the industrial giants.

Perhaps Galbraith's "technological imperatives" assumption has greater validity in areas where invention and innovation costs are higher and the planning horizons are more distinct than they are in consumer goods products. But here, too, Galbraith's premises are based more on sands of fancy than rocks of evidence.

IS THE MARKET DEAD?

As a corollary of his assumptions concerning technology, Galbraith argues that we can no longer rely on market forces to allocate resources. Because of this, he continues, the struggle to maintain competition alive "has obviously been a losing one. Indeed, it has been lost." These assertions go to the heart of Galbraith's thesis, for it is because the market has perished that we must be saved by extensive extra market planning. Should this premise prove faulty, Galbraith's thesis comes tumbling down.

We have already seen that the evidence does not support his thesis that as a general rule technological imperatives require high levels of industrial

---

[1] T. K. Quinn, *Giant Business,* 1953, p. 117.

concentration. It should therefore come as no surprise that in many industries competitive forces are considerably stronger than Galbraith suggests and that in many industries where concentration is highest, the market
position of industry leaders is being eroded. I recently presented to this
committee a rather comprehensive summary of postwar concentration
trends. Very briefly, during the postwar years—between 1947 and 1963—
market concentration tended to decline across a broad front in the producer
goods sector of manufacturing. While this is in direct conflict with the
predictions of Galbraith's thesis, it is entirely consistent with the empirical
evidence referred to earlier and which Professor Adams has mentioned.
While in some industries technology may make it impossible for very small
companies to operate efficiently, it does not dictate mammoth size and high
levels of market concentration. Most American markets have become so
large that they can sustain a rather considerable number of efficient-size
enterprises.

Surprisingly, it is in consumer goods manufacturing industries where
concentration has been on the rise in the postwar years. Surprisingly, I say,
because the technological requirements in these industries demand relatively smaller enterprises than in producer goods manufacturing. Of course,
the reasons for increasing concentration in consumer goods manufacturing
are to be found in the requirements of product differentiation (especially
the costs of large-scale promotion) and distribution, not in the technological imperatives that Galbraith assumes to be the kingpins of market power.

When postwar concentration trends are viewed together with the recent
findings concerning the relationship between technology and industrial
organization, we have a valuable insight into the future viability of the
market as a regulator and planner of economic activity. Modern technology
has not made obsolete our competitive, market-oriented economy. For it is
precisely in the producer goods manufacturing industries where economies
of large-scale invention, innovation, and production are most pronounced.
Yet these industries have experienced a significant drop in market concentration. This has occurred because many industrial markets have grown
more rapidly than have the requirements of large-scale business organization.

These trends in market concentration may yet be irrelevant if Galbraith's concept of market power is correct. Throughout his discussion he
implies that, "characteristically," American industries are concentrated
"oligopolies," and that the firms operating in them have great discretionary
pricing power independent of the market. But like Gertrude Stein, Galbraith has difficulties with shades of difference. Fortunately, however, all
oligopolies are not alike and there are important differences in the degree
of market power conferred by varying market structures. The accumulating
evidence of the relationship between an industry's structure and its performance leaves little room for agnosticism concerning the powerful role

played by the market in limiting discretionary pricing power. And, importantly, there is now persuasive evidence demonstrating that in the larger part of American manufacturing industry market forces limit quite severely the discretionary pricing power of firms. But, again, Galbraith has ignored the mounting evidence which runs counter to one of his central premises.

This isn't to imply that there are no strong positions of entrenched power in our economy—there are. Again, however, Galbraith greatly overstates his case. But, importantly, whereas he pays tribute to the firms with substantial market power—indeed, he believes such power is essential—the evidence indicates that firms with great power perform less admirably than he assumes. Hence, the facts support a precisely opposite public policy than that advocated by Galbraith—we need more competition, not less. (We shall consider shortly whether or not this is feasible.)

The rising concentration in consumer goods industries at first blush seems to bear out Galbraith's thesis of managing consumer wants to suit the needs of the business enterprise. But the causes of developments here are not rooted in Galbraith's technological imperatives. As noted earlier, the requirements of large-scale production, invention, and innovation are less demanding in the manufacture of consumer goods than in other areas of manufacturing. It is true that many sellers try to manage consumer wants. But this is because of the form which competition takes where opportunities for product differentiation exist. True, the market operates less perfectly as a result—though I suspect it operates better than Galbraith assumes. If Americans really are strongly dissatisfied, however, they can do something about this problem; though they probably won't. Nor will Galbraith's "new industrial state" change things on this score.

Despite its shortcomings, particularly in the area of some consumer goods, the market clearly has not disappeared as the key coordinating and integrating force in allocating resources in most of the economy. The picture that emerges when one studies the entire industrial landscape is not that painted by Galbraith. Whereas he concedes his thesis does not encompass the entire economy, close inspection shows it captures only a small part of the real world.

IS ANTITRUST A CHARADE?

But the mere absence of factors requiring high market concentration does not guarantee that excessive concentration will not arise or that it will decline in industries where it already is too high. Simply put, effective competition is not a flower that thrives unattended. Powerful firms may engage in competitive strategies which counteract the forces working toward deconcentration. Specifically, until the passage of the Celler-Kefauver Act in 1950, horizontal and vertical mergers often had the effect of offsetting these forces, with the result that in many industries concentration remained unchanged or even increased.

Again, I feel that Professor Galbraith has neglected his homework. He has not kept abreast of contemporary antitrust policy or its effects. He asserts that it is a "charade" acted out, "not to prevent exploitation of the public," but, "to persuade people in general and British Socialists and American liberals in particular, that the market is still extant," He sums up his views of current antitrust policy as follows (he has already mentioned them this morning):

> A great corporation wielding vast power over its markets is substantially immune. . . . But if two small firms seek to unite, this corporate matrimony will be meticulously scrutinized. And, very possibly, it will be forbidden.

These assertions simply do not square with the facts. Antimerger effort has been directed almost exclusively against the largest industrial concerns. It has not, as he suggested, been an attack on industrial midgets. Over 60 percent of the largest, those with over a billion dollars, and merely a third of the top 200 have been subjects of antimerger complaints. Practically all of these complaints have not involved the challenging of miniscule mergers, but rather have involved an attack upon mergers by large concerns. I have discussed this at greater length elsewhere. My major conclusion, however, is that there has been an enormous effort. Perhaps Professor Galbraith would say that my intellectual outlook has been affected somewhat by the technostructure within which I now operate. But even if I were back at the University of Wisconsin—or even at Harvard—I would still come to the same conclusion, as I am sure he will when he reads my other statement. In my opinion, this enforcement effort represents a great victory for competition, as well as a clear demonstration that antitrust policy can be an effective instrument of public policy in the last half of the 20th century.

It is true that antitrust policy cannot easily—and certainly not quickly —solve problems of deeply entrenched power. Fifty years of ineffective public policy toward mergers resulted in unnecessarily high concentration in many industries. But recent developments show that much can be accomplished. I say categorically: Whether or not the market survives in the greater part of our economy, or is destroyed by vast aggregations of market power, will not be determined by technological imperatives but by public policy toward the achievement and retention of power. The market may well be destroyed in the next generation as Galbraith predicts, but not for his reasons. It will be a matter of public will or neglect, not technology.

PLANNING AND THE STATE

In the "new industrial state" the Government plays a central role in economic planning with a concomitant diminution in reliance upon the market. Specifically, it stabilizes aggregate demand, underwrites expensive technology, restrains wages and prices in limiting inflation, provides technical and educational manpower, and buys upwards of a fifth of our economic output.

It is true that the Government does these things, and more. But Galbraith exaggerates the role of the state (as opposed to the market) in the planning process. He points out correctly that one of the main responsibilities of the modern state is to sustain aggregate demand and stimulate economic growth. He fails to perceive, however, that the state's planning in this respect is neither in competition with, nor a substitute for, planning by business enterprise, and it certainly does not require abandonment of the market. On the contrary, the basic philosophy of the Employment Act of 1946 is that the state create a general economic environment within which private enterprise can generate economic growth. Within this environment the basic "planning" decisions of what and how much of each product to produce are left to private enterprise responding to aggregate demand.

Experience increasingly demonstrates the heavy role played by the market in implementing or frustrating monetary and fiscal policy aimed at full employment. Only if competition is effective are extensive price controls not a necessary adjunct to planning for rapid economic growth without inflation.

STATEMENT OF WALTER ADAMS

In the *New Industrial State,* Galbraith once again examines the reality of corporate giantism and corporate power, and outlines the implications for public policy. He finds that the giant corporation has achieved such dominance of American industry, that it can control its environment and immunize itself from the discipline of all exogenous control mechanisms— especially the competitive market. Through separation of ownership from management it has emancipated itself from the control of stockholders. By reinvestment of profits (internal financing), it has eliminated the influence of the financier and the capital market. By brainwashing its clientele, it has insulated itself from consumer sovereignty. By possession of market power, it has come to dominate both suppliers and customers. By judicious identification with, and manipulation of the state, it has achieved autonomy from government control. Whatever it cannot do for itself to assure survival and growth, a compliant government does on its behalf—assuring the maintenance of full employment; eliminating the risk of, and subsidizing the investment in, research and development; and assuring the supply of scientific and technical skills required by the modern technostructure.

In return for this privileged autonomy, the industrial giant performs society's planning function. And this, according to Galbraith, is not only inevitable (because technological imperatives dictate it); it is also good.

The market is dead, we are told; and there is no need to regret its passing. The only remaining task, it seems, is to recognize the trend, to accept it as inexorable necessity, and, presumably, not to stand in its way.

Mr. Chairman, here is a blueprint for technocracy, private socialism, and the corporate state. The keystone of the new power structure is the giant corporation, freed from all traditional checks and balances, and subject only to the countervailing power of the intellectual in politics—those Platonic philosopher-kings who stand guard over the interests of the Republic. Happily, this blueprint need not cause undue alarm: first, because Galbraith's analysis rests on an empirically unsubstantiated premise; and second, even if this analysis were correct, there would be more attractive public policy alternatives than Galbraith suggests.

Galbraith's contention that corporate giantism dominates American industry requires no adumbration. On that there is consensus. But Galbraith fails to prove that this dominance is the inevitable response to technological imperatives, and hence beyond our control. Specifically, he offers little evidence to demonstrate that Brobdingnagian size is the prerequisite for, and the guarantor of—

(1) operational efficiency;

(2) invention, innovation, and technological progress; and

(3) effective planning in the public interest.

Let me comment briefly on each of these points, and in so doing indicate that the competitive market need not be condemned to the euthanasia which Galbraith thinks is inexorable, and perhaps even desirable.

Efficiency. In the mass-production industries, firms must undoubtedly be large, but do they need to assume the dinosaur proportions of some present-day giants? The unit of technological efficiency is the plant, not the firm. This means that there are undisputed advantages to large-scale integrated operations at a single steel plant, for example, but there is little technological justification for combining these functionally separate plants into a single administrative unit. United States Steel is nothing more than several Inland Steels strewn about the country, and no one has yet suggested that Inland is not big enough to be efficient. A firm producing such divergent lines as rubber boots, chain saws, motorboats, and chicken feed may be seeking conglomerate size and power; it is certainly not responding to technological necessity. In short, one can favor technological bigness and oppose administrative bigness without inconsistency.

Two major empirical studies document this generalization. The first, by Dr. John M. Blair, indicates a significant divergence between plant and company concentration in major industries dominated by oligopoly. It indicates, moreover, that between 1947 and 1958, there was a general tendency for plant concentration to decline, which means that in many industries technology may actually militate toward optimal efficiency in plants of "smaller" size.

The second study, by Prof. Joe Bain, presents engineering estimates of scale economies and capital requirements in 20 industries of above-average concentration. Bain finds that—

... Concentration by firms is in every case but one greater than required by single-plant economies, and in more than half of the cases very substantially greater.

In less precise language, many multiplant industrial giants have gone beyond the optimal size required for efficiency. Galbraith acknowledges the validity of Bain's findings, but dismisses them by saying:

The size of General Motors is in the service not of monopoly or the economies of scale, but of planning. And for this planning . . . there is no clear upper limit to the desirable size. It could be that the bigger the better.

If size is to be justified, then, this must be done on grounds other than efficiency. I shall return to this point in a moment.

Technological progress. As in the case of efficiency, there is no strict correlation between giantism and progressiveness. In a study of the 60 most important inventions of recent years, it was found that more than half came from independent inventors, less than half from corporate research, and even less from the research done by large concerns. Moreover, while some highly concentrated industries spend a large share of their income on research, others do not; within the same industry, some smaller firms spend as high a *percentage* as their larger rivals. As Wilcox points out:

The big concern has the ability to finance innovation; it does not necessarily do so. There is no clear relationship between size and investment in research.

Finally, as this committee well knows, roughly two-thirds of the research done in the United States is financed by the Federal Government, and in many cases the research contractor gets the patent rights on inventions paid for with public funds. The inventive genius which ostensibly goes with size would seem to involve socialization of risk and privatization of profit and power.

The U.S. steel industry, which ranks among the largest, most basic, and most concentrated of American industries, certainly part of the industrial state that Professor Galbraith speaks of, affords a dramatic case in point. It spends only 0.7 percent of its revenues on research and, in technological progressiveness, the giants which dominate this industry lag behind their smaller domestic rivals as well as their smaller foreign competitors. Thus, the basic oxygen furnace—considered the "only major breakthrough at the ingot level since before the turn of the century" was invented in 1950 by a miniscule Austrian *firm* which was less than one-third the size of a single *plant* of the United States Steel Corp. The innovation was introduced in the United States in 1954 by McLouth Steel which at the time had about 1 percent of domestic steel capacity—to be followed some 10 years later by the steel giants: United States Steel in December 1963, Bethlehem in 1964, and Republic in 1965. Despite the fact that this revolutionary invention involved an average operating cost saving of $5 per ton and an investment cost saving of $20 per ton of installed capacity, the steel giants during the 1950s according to Business Week, "brought 40 million tons of the wrong capacity—the open-hearth furnace" which was obsolete almost the moment it was put in place.

Only after they were subjected to actual and threatened competition from domestic and foreign steelmakers in the 1960s did the steel giants decide to accommodate themselves to the oxygen revolution. Thus, it was the cold wind of competition, and not the catatonia induced by industrial concentration, which proved conducive to innovation and technological progress.

Planning in the public interest.   Modern technology, says Galbraith, makes planning essential, and the giant corporation is its chosen instrument. This planning, in turn, requires the corporation to eliminate risk and uncertainty, to create for itself an environment of stability and security, and to free itself from all outside interference with its planning function. Thus, it must have enough size and power not only to produce a "mauve and cerise, air-conditioned, power-steered, and power-braked automobile" —unsafe at any speed—but also enough power to brainwash customers to buy it. In the interest of planning, producers must be able to sell what they make—be it automobiles or missiles—and at prices which the technostructure deems remunerative.

Aside from the unproved premise—and I keep coming back to this: technological necessity—on which this argument rests, it raises crucial questions of responsibility and accountability. By what standards do the industrial giants plan, and is there an automatic convergence between private and public advantage? Must we, as a matter of inexorable inevitability, accept the proposition that what is good for General Motors is good for the country? What are the safeguards—other than the intellectual in politics—against arbitrary abuse of power, capricious or faulty decisionmaking? Must society legitimatize a self-sustaining, self-serving, self-justifying, and self-perpetuating industrial oligarchy as the price for industrial efficiency and progress?

In conclusion, I would note that industrial giantism in America is not the product of spontaneous generation, natural selection, or technological inevitability. In this era of "Big Government," it is often the end result of unwise, manmade, discriminatory, privilege-creating governmental action. Defense contracts, R & D support, patent policy, tax privileges, stockpiling arrangements, tariffs, subsidies, etc., have far from a neutral effect on our industrial structure. Especially in the regulated industries—in air and surface transportation, in broadcasting and communications—the writ of the state is decisive. In controlling these variables the policymaker has greater freedom and flexibility than is commonly supposed; the potential for promoting competition and dispersing industrial power is both real and practicable.

It seems to me that Professor Galbraith keeps coming back to the charade of antitrust, but a competitive society is the product not simply of negative enforcement of the antitrust laws; it is the product of a total integrated approach on all levels of government—legislative, administrative, and regulatory. An integrated national policy of promoting competition—and this means more than mere enforcement of the antitrust laws—is not only feasible but desirable. No economy can function without built-in checks and balances which tend to break down the bureaucratic preference for letting well enough alone—forces which erode, subvert, or render obsolete the conservative bias inherent in any organization devoid of competition. Be it the dictates of the competitive market, the pressure from imports or substitutes, or the discipline of yardstick competition, it is these forces which the policymaker must try to reinforce where they exist and to *build into* the economic system where they are lacking or moribund. The policy objective throughout must be to promote market *structures* which will *compel* the conduct and performance which is in the public interest.

The disciplining force of competition is superior to industrial planning —by the private or public monopolist, the benevolent or authoritarian bureaucrat. It alone provides the incentives and compulsions to pioneer untried trails, to explore paths which may lead to dead ends, to take risks which may not pay off, and to try to make tomorrow better than the best.

STATEMENT OF DONALD TURNER

On the impact of antitrust law, I think it is undeniable that it has been more vigorous and more effective in attacking price fixing, other restrictive agreements and mergers than in dealing directly with existing market power. I suppose that may even be characterized as a massive understatement. But, on the failure of antitrust law to deal adequately with undue existing market power, I do have a few comments.

The first is that to some extent this failure to deal with existing market power makes sense. I think it clearly makes sense to the extent that size and whatever market power that happen to go with it truly reflects economies of scale. I think it may also make some sense, although in my opinion perhaps less, where market power was acquired by initial competitive superiority and has been maintained without exclusionary behavior of any kind.

We have here, at least arguably, a problem of incentive. The fundamental purpose of the antitrust laws is to encourage competitive striving. It would be a little paradoxical, to say the least, to turn on the winner when he wins. If that were regular practice, one might anticipate some disincentive problems which may reach serious proportions.

I do now know the answer to that argument, but I just suggest, as I said, that it may make some sense to permit some conditions of market power which may be acquired and maintained in unexceptionable ways. Beyond this, I agree it would be desirable to increase the effectiveness of antitrust in dealing directly with existing market power. Of course, in saying so, I am proceeding on the premise that my friends Mueller and Adams more accurately access the current validity of the competition than Professor Galbraith has. There may be some ways of expanding the scope of antitrust within the confines of existing legislation. That is worth probing, and it is being probed.

I would also add that I still subscribe to the views Professor Kaysen and I set forth, now some 8 years ago, in which we urged additional legislation which would make it easier to deal with monopoly and oligopoly problems. However, I suppose it is highly likely that if I sent such a proposal forward to the administration, it would not be rushed over to the Hill the following morning.

Even assuming, however—and I will make that assumption for the purposes of the balance of my remarks—that our present relative inactivity in dealing with existing undue market power shall continue for the indefinite future, I do not agree that it is bad public policy or bad law or bad anything to continue to attack price fixing and other restrictive agreements and mergers likely to increase market power in those areas where we still have hope.

To put it somewhat differently, the fact that for historical reasons of one sort or another we have had to accept a measure of unfortunate development in one or more areas of our economy does not mean, it seems to me, that we are compelled to make things worse by permitting more.

It seems to me that to describe the kind of policy we have been carrying on as "discrimination" is to apply a most inappropriate term. In antitrust or in any other area of public policy it has always been true that even though we cannot undo the past we can try to do better for the future, and we cannot rationally measure prospective public policy by past mistakes. Past mistakes by no means compel repetition.

In this regard, while monopoly and oligopoly are, indeed, a problem, I think we should be careful not to overstate it, as I believe Mr. Galbraith has. To quote from his book, "Oligopoly is not a special but a general case. It is the market structure of the industrial system."

Now, unaccustomed as I am to calling attention to the nonoligopolistic sector of our economy, I do feel compelled to put Professor Galbraith's remarks in perspective. Taking mining and manufacturing together with transportation and public utilities, Professor Kaysen, a man whom we both view with high regard, estimates that the oligopolistic sectors produce around 20 percent or probably 25 percent of national income. Concededly, this is not a trivial figure. But neither does it amount to the domination that Professor Galbraith's remarks suggest.

That being so, we have wide areas of the economy which have not been afflicted or badly afflicted, and it seems clear to me that it makes good public policy sense to endeavor to preserve competition where it can be preserved in those areas. I see no reason why we should not continue to attack outright price-fixing agreements, even though, in some industries, concentration is so high and the nature of the product is such that the sellers, as Mr. Galbraith indicates, can achieve close to the kind of price determination that an outright agreement would.

I have already given some general reasons for this. I would add a particular one. That is that price-fixing agreements involving a rather large number of firms in a way is the worst of all possible worlds. You get all of the disadvantages of price fixing and the kind of interference with competition and allocation of resources that that gives you without any of the economies of size that come from growth of firms—except, I should say, perhaps some planning advantage. But I doubt very much the episodic kind of price fixing that we have seen really makes any significant contribution to this.

Now, turning to mergers, where industries are currently relatively unconcentrated, why permit further concentration by merger? There may, indeed, be some economic changes taking place in some industries which tend to indicate that the current size of firms is below that which would be necessary for the achievement of economies. But typically, substantial economies will be developed by internal growth, and without having any figures, I would guess that internal growth has been the means by which most economies of scale have been achieved in the past.

Where there is already a fair degree of concentration in an industry, even where there may be one or two or three dominant firms, the problem posed by merger involving firms other than the largest is indeed a somewhat more difficult problem than it appears to be in the unconcentrated industry. But it is also, I suggest, much more complicated than Professor Galbraith suggests by using the term "discrimination."

Let me give you a specific example: In the steel industry, several years ago, Bethlehem, the No. 2 firm, and Youngstown—I forget which, No. 5 or No. 6—proposed to merge. Both were substantially smaller than the United States Steel Corp. and the merged company was still considerably smaller. Indeed, the argument was made that we should have permitted those two companies to merge in order that they could more adequately deal with United States Steel. It seems perfectly plain to me that apart from any moral reason, which I reject, there was no persuasive economic reason to permit this merger and, the decision was eminently correct. I will only give a couple of reasons.

Even assuming that the merger would have increased the competitive ability of the merged firms, which was disputable, there was no reason to suppose that the merger would have made the industry in fact any more competitive than it was or, to put it somewhat differently, that a merged

Bethlehem-Youngstown would have embarked upon a competitive pricing spree or any kind of other competitive spree as a consequence of the merger. Moreover, to have permitted the merger would have made it much less likely that future technological changes, if they came, that would have lowered the size of firm necessary for economies of scale, would have led to an appropriate deconcentration of that industry.

Now, in all of these activities, as in attacks on patent licensing restrictions and the like, the purpose of the antitrust laws, even assuming that we can do nothing about existing concentration, is to preserve the opportunity for declining concentration in the future as new developments take place—new entry, new products, and the like. And I would cite in this connection, lest there be doubt that any such happy developments will ever take place, that Dr. Mueller's figures over the past 15 years show more often than not, many more oftentimes than not, there has been declining concentration in the producer-goods industries.

To sum up, even if we did nothing more than we now do in directly attacking undue market power, I am firmly convinced that a strong antitrust preventive policy makes economic sense and, on the basis of evidence now available to us, would still appear to promote longrun benefits for the economy.

B. The consumer: Strong and sovereign or weak and unprotected?

One of the fundamental assumptions behind the economist's theory of a perfectly competitive market economy is the sovereignty of the independent, rational consumer. The cumulative dollar votes of individual consumers, and the competitive rivalry of the business suppliers, dictate what goods and services shall be produced and assure the consumer a low price based on low-cost, efficient methods of production. According to this theory of perfect competition the sovereign consumer gets what he wants and at bargain prices.

But of course the real world marketplace is not perfectly competitive; there is heated debate over how much sovereignty, or power, the consumer actually has in the marketplace. Galbraith (see Reading 14) has argued that businessmen have almost completely subverted consumer power, by using advertising to create and manipulate consumer tastes and demands for the products they want to sell. Ralph Nader has acquired national fame (or notoriety, depending on your viewpoint) through his efforts to expose and publicize cases of business abuses of the consumer. In the following reading Nader indicts business for dishonest packaging, for price fixing, and for producing unsafe, unhealthy, or unreliable consumer products. While identifying past instances of governmental weakness or collusion with business interest, Nader advocates new government programs for consumer protection. His proposals for fuller corporate disclosure of product safety and performance qualities, and more accurate packaging and other consumer information, would make the present market structures perform more efficiently. He has also strongly advocated a more vigorous antitrust program and other "corporate reforms" which would more basically alter the existing market structures.

The Dutch economist Jan Pen offers a more optimistic view of the consumer's position. He has more faith than Galbraith in the consumer's "hardheaded" ability to detect the seductive appeals of romanticized advertising and poor product quality. He suspects that much of business advertising and product differentiation offer the consumer more attractive choice and variety, and that some of the criticism of advertising slogans or

179

appeals represents a moral or aesthetic criticism of the whole culture, of which advertising and business are only an interdependent part. On the other hand, he sharply attacks deceptive advertising and government inhibitions of price competition through resale-price maintenance laws, and he advocates aggressive consumer associations and unions.

Questions: Does Nader share Galbraith's pessimism on the consumer's ability to fulfill his own independent rational desires? How closely is the consumer's weakness related to the concentration of business power in oligopoly industries? What are the economic justifications for government interventions in the consumer marketplace?

15 A case for more consumer protection*

RALPH NADER

The rhetoric of consumer protection in recent years has been as impressive as the reality of the consumer interest's expendability. The thunderous acclaim for such legislation or pending legislation as the truth-in-lending bill, the cigarette-labeling law, the truth-in-packaging bill is not measured commensurately by the forcefulness of the legislation in fact. I sometimes think that industry is perfectly willing to trade off a particular name with a particular legislation, such as truth-in-lending, in return for very effectively gutting its adequate provisions. The threat is very often not so much whether we have consumer-protection legislation but whether or not we have a law or a no-law law—a no-law law which simply deludes the consumer, deludes the public into thinking it receives a protection when in fact it is the industry which receives the protection by a bizarre, ironic twist.

The cigarette-labeling act is a perfect case study here. This act effectively excluded any action for five years by the states and cigarette-protection legislation. It effectively excluded the Federal Trade Commission from any action. It effectively excluded any attendance to the problem of advertising in cigarettes. And it effectively provided a convenient defense in civil liability suits for the cigarette industry by requiring a warning on the package that [smoking] may be hazardous to health. This was a bill which the tobacco industry simply could not do without. And yet it was touted as . . . consumer-protection legislation.

I think that it is important to recognize that, even when laws are passed that are adequately drafted, the administration of these laws can effectively render them impotent. A good example here, in terms of abundant au-

---

* From "Ralph Nader Faces the Nation's Business," address to the National Consumer Assembly, Washington, D.C., November 1967. Abridged and reprinted with permission of the author. Ralph Nader is associated with the Center for the Study of Responsive Law, Washington, D.C.

thority and not so abundant administration and enforcement, affects the Federal Trade Commission, which I think can be called the government's better business bureau with all that implies.

A MYTH PERPETUATED

One of the sad by-products of the Federal Trade Commission's pronouncements and activities, with some outstanding exceptions, is that the Commission has perpetuated a myth over the years that deceiving the consumer or harming the consumer is primarily a fly-by-night phenomenon in terms of the fringe participants of American business that really isn't the mainstream of solid, upstanding businessmen—it is those near-bankrupt firms that are besmirching the reputation of American business in general.

I find this rather difficult to appreciate in the light of the facts. I don't think the packaging problem in this country just affects a few fringe marketeers. I don't think the credit practices in this country just affect a few corner pawn shops. I don't believe that the electric price-fixing conspiracy which bilked the consumers to the tune of hundreds of millions of dollars over the three decades of the conspiracy, ending in 1961, simply was a result of a few fly-by-night electric firms. I don't think the lack of safety in automobiles is due to a few small garages who hand-make some hazardous automobiles. I don't think the adverse effects of drugs and lack of adequate disclosure is due to makeshift pharmaceutical houses in the back of a large pharmacy or two. I think in effect that the problem of consumer protection is very much the problem of American business in general, very much the problem of the largest industry and the largest company, very much the problem of those who should be able to perform far better and far more responsibly than those fringe businesses who might be up against the wall in terms of their sheer economic survival.

A recent example is the Greyhound Bus Company, which has been routinely using, until very recently, bald regrooved tires, regrooving them again and again, leading to accidents in which people were killed and injured—leading to accidents whose investigations remain secret within our Department of Transportation, because the motor carrier industry wrote that secrecy into legislation years ago—the kind of practices by Greyhound which have never received enforcement. . . . The first enforcement process is now underway in New Jersey for a Greyhound fatal accident involving regrooved tires. The maximum penalty on conviction is $500.

Now, are we dealing with a company—a small bus company—whose back is against the wall, and for sheer survival is trying to cut costs on tires? No. We are dealing with the largest bus company in the world—a bus company whose liquid capital is so embarrassingly ample that it owns outright 27 Boeing 707/727 planes, which it leases to the airlines.

INADEQUATE FULFILLMENT

I think another problem of the Federal Trade Commission as an example of the inadequate fulfillment of its authority comes in areas where there is absolutely no doubt, where there are absolutely no shades of judgment possible in terms of the course of action that should be pursued. For years the odometers have been overregistered—that is, they have been designed in a way to make you think . . . you are traveling more than you are. Now there is . . . far more than a mere psychological consequence to this rigging of a basic measurement device. When an odometer is rigged to the plus side, you tend in the aggregate to trade in your car faster. You think your car is a little older. Your warranty runs out in terms of mileage. You tend to pay more to a rent-car-company which, of course, collects on the mile. You also tend to think you are getting better gas mileage, which is something the auto companies want desperately to convey to their buying public. And yet this problem of odometer deception, which has been going on for years with the knowledge of the Federal Trade Commission, did not achieve attention until about 1964 when the National Bureau of Standards decided to rewrite the standard. Now, even though the standard was rewritten, odometers are still capable of being overregistered and still capable of meeting the new standard. But the important point in the history of the odometer is the statement finally conveyed by an old hand at the Federal Trade Commission, who when confronted with the suggestion that it was the National Bureau of Standards who took the initiative, not the Federal Trade Commission, blurted out, "That is utter nonsense. Why, we have been concerned with odometer problems since the Hoover Administration."

MEAT INSPECTION

Another problem dealing with laws, their adequacy in drafting and their administration and the responsibility of a consumer protection agency or department in government deals with the recent meat inspection controversy. Here we have the Department of Agri-Business, misnamed the Department of Agriculture, which . . . has had the responsibility—since Upton Sinclair wrote the book, *The Jungle*—for roughly sixty-one years to inspect meat packaging, meat processing, slaughter houses that trade in interstate commerce. Unfortunately, over the years, there has been a substantial traffic in intrastate meat shipment, and at present 25 percent of all processed meat in this country does not cross state boundaries and herefore escapes the Federal inspection service. This is eight billion pounds a year.

The surveys of the Department of Agriculture in 1962 on a state-by-state basis revealed what everybody in the industry knew all along, but revealed it authoritatively—that there were three basic and endemic problems affecting the intrastate meat industry. The first was a kind of Gresham's law: believe it or not, bad meat is good business. And bad meat drives out good meat in some of these local markets. Bad meat, meaning the 4-D animals: trafficking in dead, dying, diseased or disabled animals, where, for example, the cancerous portions of the cow are simply cut out and the rest of the carcass sent to market.

The second problem: unsanitary, grossly unsanitary, conditions in the meat-processing plant. The reports here are so nauseating—and they are not made by laymen, they are made by veterinarians or inspectors—the reports here are so nauseating on a state-by-state basis that nobody could ever read them through at one sitting and remain with his equanimity. These descriptions reveal, for example, the prevalence of roaches, flies and rodents having free play of the meat-processing plant and willingly or unwillingly finding their way off into the meat vats, the paint flakings from the ceilings dripping and dropping onto exposed food. There was some indication that some of these inspectors couldn't get close to the plants because of the overwhelming potency of the odor, and sometimes they did get close enough, but they couldn't talk clearly with the manager because of the flies that screened out visibility.

The third problem deals with what do you do to make this product—this 4-D product—presentable to the consumer. Of course, here the ingenious misuse of modern chemistry comes into play. Seasoning agents, preservatives and coloring agents do the job, and the basic natural detection processes of the consumers are masked. He is no longer able to taste, smell or see diseased or contaminated meat. And he pays out his money accordingly. This problem was documented in 1962, and our friendly Department of Agriculture felt it was more important to protect the meat-packing industry than to protect the consumer. So for five years they have sat on these reports—for five years they did nothing until there were hearings at the congressional level and new reports were forthcoming to confirm the 1962 reports.

With all of these problems, with all of these disclosures, the House of Representatives by a vote of 140 to 98 passed a weak and meaningless meat inspection act, as far as the control of intrastate plants is concerned. The alternative bill, called the Smith-Foley Amendment, would have brought roughly 98.5 percent of all the meat processing in the country under Federal inspection. That bill was defeated.

LOBBY SEEKS MONEY

The interesting aspect of the situation is the immediate disclosure after the passage of the legislation that a large meat-packing trade association had recommended in a letter to its members . . . that they make contributions to the political campaigns of friendly congressmen (mind you, at the same time, these congressmen were considering the meat inspection bill and its alternative); the recommendation was that the contributions be from $25 to $99—$99 so that the individual contributors need not be disclosed. Now this situation was brought to the attention of the chairman of the House Agriculture Committee, who favored the weak bill. He immediately replied to the director of this trade association that it was a terrible thing to have done—it placed the meat industry in a potentially untenable situation, . . . it jeopardized the meat bill which the meat industry favored. In other words, all his concern was directed towards the welfare of the meat industry and being able to escape Federal inspection of its intrastate activity.

Not a word in these letters, mind you, as to the welfare of the consumer. Not a word [of] the need to publicize this impropriety the moment it was located. In effect, the entire effort of some of these friendly congressmen at the House Agriculture Committee was to sweep it under the rug, to squash it, to keep it from being disclosed so that nobody learned exactly what [was] going on.

I think it's time to look into this situation with a far greater degree of thoroughness. A congressman who is not known to make very flippant and unsubstantiated remarks has said that he has never seen a bill where so much money was involved in the negotiation. I would think a congressional investigation particularly in the context of the campaign-financing reform that is now pending in Congress would be well advised.

There are other aspects of the meat bill which I think give us good lessons to ponder. These are the kinds of lessons, incidentally, which are similar to the battles over . . . water pollution, soil contamination, chemical and radiation hazards, inadequately tested and prescribed drugs and so forth. At first, it is a [mistake] to think that the meat problem is one of tiny, filthy meat-packing plants. Swift and Armour are involved here—they have plants which operate exclusively within state boundaries. Surveys of these plants have shown very substandard conditions and it's quite clear that Swift and Armour as well as their smaller colleagues have been engaging in marketing of meat which has no place in being sold to the American consumer.

NOT ONLY LIP SERVICE

The role of the Administration is interesting here as well. At the last hour the Administration finally neutralized the Department of Agriculture, with no small achievement, and came out basically through its consumer office and Miss Furness with a stronger version of legislation. That is very encouraging, but obviously that is only the first step in the position which I think the Administration should reflect. The Administration should not only be on the record for consumer protection; it should be on the ramparts. It should not only give lip service. It should give muscle service. It often intrigues me why the administration is so successful[ly] and so powerfully lobbying for the supersonic transport, that great sensational mass alarm clock that is on the horizon, and so ineffective, so reticent and so inhibited when it is asked or expected to lobby for meat inspection laws and for auto safety appropriations, to give just two recent examples. I think it is encouraging that next year will be the first year that the Federal Government will spend more money on traffic safety than the safety of migratory birds. But I don't think it says much for our allocation of our resources in this land. Not when we can spend some $45 million next year for a problem that is killing 53,000 Americans and injuring over 4.5 million at the same time that a nuclear submarine is costing $110 million. That's just one nuclear submarine.

I think, in other words, that it is time not just to give a serious look at the Administration policy on consumer protection but to [ask to] what extent it is going to really begin to effectively advocate it beyond rhetoric and to effectively reallocate some of our resources to this area. The legislation doesn't mean much if you don't have money to administer it with. I think, for example, it is a reflection of a distorted sense of values when we can spend last year $150 million on highway beautification and about $10 million on highway safety. The presumption here against that kind of allocation of resources is that the best way to get more money for traffic safety is to see that the blood gets on the daisies. . . .

It is necessary to stop concentrating exclusively on the syndromes of the consumer protection phenomena, and penetrate through to the more basic preconditions which give rise to the syndrome. I think, to be more specific, that one side of the coin may be consumer protection but the other side of the coin is, inescapably, corporate reform. I think it's important to go to the roots of the problem so we don't place ourselves in the situation of running around trying to plug the holes in the dike before it overflows. And in this sense, in the sense of the controllability of catching these problems before they arise, that focus on corporate reform is a must. For example, corporations now should be required to meet much stiffer disclosure requirements. They should be required to tell specifically the safety performance of their products so that the marketplace can be put to work in a way which they will not perhaps fail.

I think that it is an important distinction to make, that however much lip service corporations give to the free market, they are really more inerested in the control market. If they were interested in the free market they would tell you the safety performance of their products, such as automobiles, so that the consumer [could] go to the marketplace and compare make and model and make his choice on the basis of quality and in this way generate the feedback mechanism of the marketplace by rewarding good workmanship and penalizing shoddy workmanship. This is the kind of disclosure requirement that really puts the market to work to a higher degree of efficiency.

PENALTIES NEEDED

Another requirement, I think, is to beef up our sanction for corporate violations. We are reaching a point in this country where it is no longer possible to sweep under the rug the tremendously wide double standard operating between the penalties imposed on individual behavior and the penalties imposed on corporate behavior. Corporate behavior, more and more, is being immunized from legal accountability. You see the decline in criminal penalties in safety legislation for knowing and willful violation. And look at the disparity. A driver negligently driving down the highway kills an individual. He can be subjected to manslaughter charges and put in jail for negligence. But a manufacturer can willfully and knowingly leave a defective product on the market . . . in such a way that it can take human life, under the new auto safety legislation, and there is no criminal penalty whatsoever. Only civil penalties—the kinds of penalties that don't penetrate the corporate framework[—exist]. A perfect and recent example here is the Lake Central Airlines crash in March [1966] with thirty-eight people killed in a crash directly attributed to a soft piston problem, with the propeller coming off and ripping into the fuselage. It so happens that Allison, the division of General Motors that builds the engine and propeller, had known about this defect some time before the crash, and instead of advising all operators to immediately ground this plane and disassemble it, which is the only conclusion that could be reached once a defect of that seriousness is located—instead of doing this, they sent a vague advisory saying why don't you have an oil check to see if the oil's contaminated by metal filings. And the doomed plane was given an oil check and the result was negative. And thirty-eight people died because the Allison Division was worried about its corporate image and was worried about facing up to this problem. The fine by the Federal Aviation Agency was $8,000—about $200 a head. Perhaps one must not be too harsh with the FAA; they resisted General Motors pressure to reduce the fine to $4,000.

RESEARCH A NECESSITY

Another area deals with research and development, which is no longer a luxury on the part of the large corporations, it is an absolute necessity, because simple inaction can bestow on the public welfare and safety immense cruelty. Simple inaction [in] researching ways to clean up the internal combustion engine, or find an alternative, has resulted in a critical air pollution problem in our cities, inaction stemming back many, many years by industry leaders. And so, the problem of research and development, the problem of requiring them to shoulder a responsible portion of this innovative input is one that is on the first agenda, in my judgment.

STANDARDS MOST IMPORTANT

And a final area deals with standards, and I think this is probably the most important one; [I urge] that when safety bills are passed, when standards are set for products, that these standards be set by government, that they not be set by private standards groups, who have succeeded in insinuating into legislation their particular standards and codes. That is, government must make these standards, allowing democratic access to the administrative process on the part of both industry and public groups. This is an extremely critical problem. It is one which will be more critical the next year, as the United States Standards Institute of America begins its campaign to receive a congressional charter, take on the aura of a quasi-governmental agency and in effect begin to determine the level of standards of safety in product after product. . . .

PROTECTION REQUIRED

I think a stake here in the whole consumer movement is not just the quality of the goods, not just honest pricing, which of course improves our allocation of resources, but also in my judgment the most critical area of all—an area which might be termed as the area of bodily rights. The right of one's physiological integrity from being invaded, assaulted or destroyed by the harmful by-products of industrial products and processing.

Now against this threat we have something to be encouraged by. Unlike prior [eras] in history we now have a technological period where we can actually program innovation in human welfare and safety. We can invent the technological future if we will to do so. And no better was this stated than by the vice president of Ford Motor Company, Donald Frey, who said of his industry that basically our engineers can do anything we want them to do; they "can invent practically on demand." Now with an increased capability like this the ethical imperatives to act become all the more insistent because I think it is fair to say that to a substantial degree . . . what we should do proceeds from what we can do. And as the capability increases . . . so does our ethical requirement to follow through.

It is a serious disservice to consumerism, if I may use a recent term coined in a deprecatory manner by one of our large business executives last year[—it] is disservice to consumerism to view this as a threat to the private enterprise economy or to big business. It is just the opposite. . . . Of course, the upshot of consumer protection, when it succeeds, is simply to hold industry to higher standards of excellence, and I can't see why they should object to that kind of incentive. And hopefully, as it gains momentum, the consumer movement will begin to narrow the gap between the performance of American industry and commerce and its bright promise.

16 Business against the consumer*

JAN PEN

According to an old Dutch saying, the customer is king. But many of these kings are of the opinion that constitutional monarchy has gravely undermined their royal prerogatives; others firmly believe that they are living under a republic. People do not feel that they can make the producers dance to their tune. And yet that is what the optimum theorem would have us believe: businessmen can best serve their own interest by doing exactly what the consumer dictates via the price system. That is also the philosophy propagated by many large companies: we want to serve the public. Must we reject this idea? Is the consumer in a weak position? Is he misled, pushed about? Is the dictum "the passenger is a nuisance" applicable to customers in a general sense? It will become clear that I share the opinion of those who, despite advertising, hidden persuaders, price manipulation and inflation, believe that a clash between producers and consumers occurs only occasionally, in spite of the fact many sellers are powerful oligopolists—but that is why I also believe that the exceptions are all the more important.

Perhaps this issue can best be discussed in terms of the typical textbook distinctions of the market forms. Under perfect competition the producer can in fact do nothing else but follow "the market," and harmony reigns. Under product differentiation and oligopoly he can try to have his own way. This applies *a fortiori* under monopoly.

The situation with product differentiation is somewhat complex. On the one hand, this form of market strengthens the harmony between seller and customer. The manufacturer tries to create a market of his own by offering a more attractive product than his competitor. The consumers profit from the wider assortment; this quality competition is to their advantage. On the other hand, this process has its limits and its counterforces.

* From "Business against the Consumer," *Harmony and Conflict in Modern Society*. Copyright © 1966, McGraw-Hill Publishing Company Limited, pp. 130–47. Abridged and reprinted with permission of publisher. Jan Pen is Professor of Economics at the University of Groningen, The Netherlands.

An increasingly progressive refinement of the nature of the products evokes new wants again and again without it being certain that these can always and everywhere be satisfied. The abstract philosophy of the optimum theorem takes the wants "as given"; a blindfold which economics has itself donned. In fact the demands made by the consumers are in part a consequence of the manufacturers' pursuit of a market of their own and of new products and new refinements.

It may happen that the producer can no longer satisfy the preferences which he himself has created, since the costs of this extra service seem too high to him. This leaves the customer dissatisfied. There is also a serious danger that a number of consumers want to splurge and that their uncritical tastes are satisfied by shoddy products. If this happens on a wide scale, manufacturing standards are lowered and those members of the public who demand a better product quality may have reason for complaint: their wishes may not be met. This is conceivable, and it certainly happens; but it seems to me that this clash of interests is not very important, as long as the expansive urge displayed by business stays lively enough. Although the customer does not immediately get his wishes granted, in the long run the producers do satisfy his steadily increasing wants. Fords have long been available in every conceivable colour. In so far as the question of poor products arises, the issue is of a cultural nature. Business may prod consumers in objectionable directions: the record companies promote rock and roll or worse, and the yellow press competes by coarsening public taste. However, this could never happen against the will of the public. If the consumer takes a firm stand, his preferences are respected.

It is in that light, too, that we must regard the worries about the "hidden persuaders," which have so greatly attracted attention since Vance Packard's book of that name was published in 1957. I do not deny their importance to the whole cultural pattern. It may be that society is being led by advertising in the direction of a more extensive and childish consumption. It also may be that many people do not know what they want before the advertisements tell them. Greed is certainly an important factor in present society, and it is increased by advertising. But it would be an exaggeration to derive from this a general conflict between individual businessmen and consumers. Packard leaves this impression with the reader. The typical consumer emerges from his sensational book as a poor fool abused by diabolical producers, smart admen, depth psychologists and black magicians. That is misleading, in two ways. Firstly, advertising and the formation of consumers' preferences are not necessarily in opposition to each other; they are both part of a common culture. Secondly, the power of advertising to influence the sales of a given product is limited by the quality of that product. Soap manufacturers can turn as much depth psychology loose on the housewife as they like, but if a detergent does not do its work or is relatively too expensive, it will only be able to conquer a temporary market. The huge advertising campaigns for shirts and whisky are perhaps an unattractive phenomenon—opinions may differ on that—but at most they succeed in shifting buying habits a fraction from one brand to another—and so what? And the psychoanalytical nonsense which Packard and others volunteer about the relations between the driver and his car can spread a pall of gloom over only the most melancholy: the majority of readers of *The Hidden Persuaders* will doubtless have taken the passages in question with a pinch of salt. The hidden persuaders do not form a serious threat to the consumers' interests; they do contribute to daydreaming and to the trivialization of society, but that is something else again.

A sober look at advertising must make a distinction between three things: constructive information, emotional influence and deception.

The first category obviously fits into the harmony between producers and consumers. Technical development leads to so many new products that the consumer threatens to lose his bearings. Objective information is not only in his interests, but also in the interests of the firm that has something to offer—and many firms have something to offer; that is a fact. Should they make their offers sound somewhat better than they are; that is not serious, as long as the consumer knows what is going on and can discount the advertising element. Harmony calls for a clear head.

Emotional influence does not create an obvious conflict, but a number of cultural problems. The anti-rational rigmarole of advertising copy may stimulate greed, restlessness and dissatisfaction, in the same spirit as some newspapers, books and films do. These are not typical consumers' problems in the narrow sense. Consumption of material goods cannot remedy the human condition; nor can advertising create it. The consumer buys specific goods, and advertising tries to influence his choice. It does this by building up an "image" of a product. Most of these images are quite innocuous. What is less innocuous is the image of man, which is beyond the advertising business: a being that will achieve bliss by buying, possessing and using things. This implies a promise that will not be fulfilled. In this sense advertising may lead to frustration, but this is the frustration of modern culture.

Of course we should be concerned about downright deception, but I have sufficient confidence in the hard-headedness of the consumer not to set this possibility very high. However, this probability is increased by the fact that a peculiar aspect has entered price policy—resale price maintenance—to which I shall return presently, and, as it happens, the danger of misleading information does not so much come from Madison Avenue as from the retailer. The sheer lie and the factual half-truth are not characteristic of the big campaign (the unfulfilled promise is). Also, the consumers are in no way powerless against false advertising. They can in association find the means to inform themselves about the properties and qualities of products. This information is extremely useful. Technology advances too quickly for the buyer himself to be able to assess what is good for him. The old way of evaluating a product—hearsay from other people who used it—operates too slowly and is too costly in terms of wrong choices. Comparative testing of products on a more or less scientific basis is a good thing. It is done by consumers' associations, which have attained a great vogue in many countries. Examples: which ballpoint writes the longest? Which washing machine washes best, is easiest on clothes, is least likely to break down? What is the comparative covering power and lifetime of various brands of paint? The sober style of *Which?* may neutralize the romantic nonsense of the advertisers.

A good deal more could be done in this way. Besides the consumer organizations the press has a task which it is not yet adequately fulfilling. We are used to reading in the papers a criticism, often in no uncertain terms, of the performance of a pianist or a football team. Why should the press abstain from writing about the quality of new products? This is occasionally done with cars: a special correspondent has driven the new model and recounts his experiences; the car accelerates and corners well, but there is not much legroom. Why not do the same thing with houses? The architectural correspondent has seen the new block of flats built by the XYZ Company, and it has struck him that they are anything but soundproof, the walls are already cracking and there is not enough cupboard room. Other products also qualify: the paper has performed the three-bite blindfold test on so-and-so's cooking fat and found that it in no way differs from the existing brands A and B, which are cheaper. If this testing were to catch on in a big way, both the consumers and the better producers would profit from it in mutual harmony. It would of course lead to difficulties with some advertisers; even now certain cinemas ring up the editorial staff to have a talk about the film reviews. A decent newspaper rejects intimidation. Business would have to get used to the independent press informing the public in the way it thinks fit. (It is true that the word "independent" in the last sentence conceals a number of serious complications.)

The opponents of advertising have another string to their bow. Advertising appropriates factors of production, and these can perhaps be employed more usefully. Total expenditures are estimated at about 2 per cent of the national income. From the side of business it is sometimes argued that advertising increases sales, as a result of which the production costs per unit product are lowered. This counterargument is sometimes true, and sometimees not. If it is considered for business as a whole the argument is not a particularly strong one. At a given national income an increased turnover can be achieved only by a reduction of savings, and so far not a single advertiser has been prepared to adduce that in his favour. Macroeconomically there is something to this defence of advertising only if it could be proved that it leads to an increase in the turnover of precisely those products whose production costs are considerably reduced as a result of large-scale output (e.g. cars), this being at the expense of those products of which the costs are not much higher despite the lower turnover. This is possible, but it cannot be proved. Nor is it very probable.

However, the simple fact that advertising demands factors of production may not lead us to decide that we have here a conflict between business-men and customers. This is true only if too much advertising is done. What is too much? An unambiguous answer to this question cannot be given, especially because, when all is said and done, advertising also has a positive effect. But as soon as the advertising budget is at the expense of investments, or of the furtherance of productivity, or of research, there is every reason to speak of too much. For some firms it is a temptation to increase the advertising budget above what is desirable in the long run. Sometimes this effort is backed by a pressure group inside the firm—for instance, the pub-licity or the marketing department, which hopes in this way to improve its position. This may lead to a battle for the limited financial means, in which advertising comes off best. To the extent that the latter happens, it is as much in conflict with the interests of the firm as with those of society.

But I repeat that I do not think that we may speak of a general conflict. Advertising as such is not bad; in so far as it is, the customer is not at all powerless. We shall have to put up with it and make the best of it, which means that the consumer should be educated. He has to resist the New Greed and the romanticism of the "unique selling proposition." The circu-lation of *Which?*—300,000—is an encouraging sign. Advertising is part of our culture, for better or for worse; the whole business is, after all, not un-amusing. And what would Piccadilly Circus and Times Square be without their light signs?

Things are probably more unfavourable with regard to another method of encouraging sales: consumer credit and hire purchase. This is praised as a means of making consumption immediately possible in cases where income follows later, and so bringing about a uniform distribution of ex-penditure over a period of time. This does in fact apply in some cases, in particular with young families who can count on a quickly rising income over the years. But in the majority of cases hire purchase could better have been avoided. It keeps people's noses to the grindstone and contributes to the general atmosphere of disappointment, instead of leading to the fuller and richer life. First save, then spend, is as a rule better than the other way round. This is quite clear in the cases in which the original harmony between seller and buyer changes into an open conflict: the buyer has be-come overburdened by debts which exceed his means. For society as a whole, too, this form of credit is questionable, since it stimulates excep-tional boom times (if all is going well people are more easily inclined to get into debt) and, worse still, intensifies recessions. Instability is furthered. There is no doubt that these forms of credit have assumed greater propor-tions than they should.

Of course most consumers will not describe the conflict with their suppliers in the first place by pointing to consumer credit (any more than to advertising, come to that). Instead, they believe that they are often overcharged. This brings us to the clash of interests which, next to that on wages, is perhaps the strongest in contemporary folklore: the businessman is frequently regarded as the consumers' natural enemy, if not as a swindler. In another terminology and from a somewhat different standpoint this is also a matter of concern for many economists. They have sought the injurious effect of oligopoly, not so much in advertising as in the distortion of the price structure which imperfect competition may bring about.

For, according to the Great Harmony, prices are the signals which control production. This presupposes that they come about without being subject to anyone's influence. In imperfect competition that is no longer the case. Branded lines, for instance, obviously have a price fixed by the producer. As a result it is no longer certain that this price reflects the scarcity of the product. This has been a considerable worry to economists, above all since E. H. Chamberlin; under product differentiation the price and the marginal costs are no longer equal. The outsider is inclined to consider this inequality no great disaster, but a good deal of learned criticism of the market mechanism has been derived from it. A. P. Lerner has based the "degree of monopoly," a criterion of the operation of competition, on the difference between price and marginal costs. This magnitude is defined as price minus marginal costs divided by price; it is approximately equal to the marginal gross profit margin. As long as this magnitude is positive, competition is imperfect and the price is not a good signal for controlling production.

The economists' worries prove upon further examination to be in no way those of the average consumer. The latter considers his purchases too expensive. The economist fears an incorrect pattern of production; he has the Paretian optimum in mind, and sees that some prices work out too high. Well then, other prices are too low. (An idea which does not enter the minds of most consumers!) Less is produced of some goods than the consumer wants; of other goods the production is therefore too great. This is quite different from a general swindle. It is not the extra profit that is criticized but an incorrect allocation of productive forces. This is the burden on society.

Now this burden proves to be more uncertain than it looks at first sight, when one studies the neat diagrams of the equilibrium of the firm. In 1952 T. Scitovzky proved that the injurious effect of manipulated prices on production is more or less neutralized if the differences between prices and marginal costs balance each other in the various industries. The conflict which is born of the presence of a powerful oligopolist in one industry is alleviated if another strong firm appears in another industry! That brings the Paretian optimum somewhat closer again. It is not, of course, exactly achieved; a departure from harmony remains.

Whether we take this conflict seriously or not depends, among other things, on whether the goods for which the demand has been choked off by the high prices are important to welfare or not. Economists usually do not ask this question because they are neutral with regard to consumers' preferences. It is all the same to them whether the demand for medicine or that for hand-chased silver is harmed; but this is an attitude I do not recommend.

Now it is not improbable that the big profit margins are to be found above all on luxury goods. One reason for this is that some shoppers tend to judge quality by price. They see in a high price a sure sign of a superior product. This leads to high profits but the disharmony which proceeds from this need not be taken seriously. If cosmetics and fancy cars are too expensive no great harm is done; it restricts demand, but that will just have to be accepted. Labour and raw materials are left for more important things. Real conflicts are to be expected when disproportionate profit margins exist on goods and services which people simply have to buy or which they should buy.

From recent discussions in a number of European countries one might get the impression that an instance of this is the case of resale price maintenance. This means that manufacturers fix the price that retailers ask for their product. It may occur with branded lines, which form some 60–70 percent of the retail trade's turnover. The shopkeeper may give no discount. Thus price competition between retailers is curbed. They cannot pass on the benefits of a possible lead in efficiency to the consumers. Now, apart from the effect on the whole level of prices, of which more later, this can cause a certain distortion of the price structure. Large profit margins are possible and the situation is analogous to that discussed above. Here, too, the effect of high prices on the demand for various goods may be neutralized, and the aberration from Paretian optimality is important only in the case of goods of high social value. As a rule, the conflict is not very sharp.

True, the practice presents another source of trouble. It becomes in the interests of the manufacturers to increase the profit margin which is available for the retailer so as to make sure that the shopkeeper will recommend their special product to the customer. This is called margin competition. The faults of this are not only the increasing of profit margins but also the untruthful element which enters into the shopkeeper's work. He is supposed to be the customer's confidant and to give proper advice. The chance of this is reduced by margin competition. The retailer is induced to recommend the product with the highest margin. So this kind of competition encourages a conflict between supplier and buyer; it comes close to deceptive advertising and it may even seem a little worse. It could be alleviated if fixed prices were made illegal. This has happened in most countries, although only recently and after a good deal of debate. The general objective of the indictment is to activate competition.

Meanwhile, many a person will be inclined to seek the threat offered to the consumer by high prices and imperfect products in the direction of large, powerful firms, in a network of mysterious agreements, in astute managers who scratch each other's backs. That is not only a popular fear but also a typically theoretical construction which applies in some cases (patent medicines) but which is certainly not a rule. A matter-of-fact look at daily life suggests the opposite conclusion: the modern consumer is having more and more trouble with the weak industries. Not the small number of powerful concerns, but the large number of inefficient producers pushes up prices. Typical examples: the retail trade in France and undertakers in some parts of the United States. European agriculture is another case in point (but a complicated one, because of agricultural protection). Each firm has a small turnover; because its owner tries to wring a living out of it, prices are too high. Yet much capital is gradually lost, efficiency is low, and business mortality is high. Newcomers keep entering the industry, spurred by false hopes. They are, economically speaking, their own enemies as much as the enemies of their customers. The conflict is of a rather perverse nature: both producers and consumers are hurt.

. . . . .

So far we have considered the clash of interests between suppliers and their customers against the background of the optimum theorem. That is to say, our suspicions were directed towards the pattern of production, or, in other words, towards prices which do not form good signals and consequently, in connection with advertising, margin competition and inelastic supply, may misdirect production. But there is quite a different side to price determination. One might suppose—in company with celebrated economists—that all prices can work out too high, so that all sellers are favoured and all buyers harmed. In other words, price inflation brought about by businessmen who do well out of it. If I see it aright, this is the fear which tends to be rather strongly felt by the salaried middle classes who are not themselves in commerce. They regard their own group as weak, and business as an aggressive bloc against whom they come off second-best.

The economists who see this in more or less the same way are above all G. C. Means and J. K. Galbraith. They believe that in some sectors of business—steel, automobiles and the chemical industry—the concentration of power has advanced far enough to increase prices in an inflationary sense. And they expect other sectors to follow; the latter increase prices in the footsteps of the strong leading industries. The mechanism of supply and demand has been replaced by a system of administered prices. The consumer is no longer helped by the competition in business; he is the victim of a lack of competition all along the line. He has to help himself and reinforce his position by bloc-forming: the consumers' association. Galbraith regards this fortification of the groups of interests as one of the characteristics of modern society. Everywhere where there is power countervailing power comes into being. In this way unions, cartels, cooperatives, consumers' organizations have been born. However, this does not mean that the blocs necessarily keep each other in equilibrium. So far the consumer bloc has come off second-best; that can be seen from the gradual rise in the level of prices in recent decades.

That sounds plausible. Yet Galbraith's theory has been attacked on various grounds. Firstly, it presents the danger of an underestimation of competition. Competition is not dead; it is restricted, transformed, but only rarely eliminated. Oligopolists also compete, if only for the consumer's general purchasing power. Elimination of competition is the exception rather than the rule. Consequently, Galbraith overestimates the possibility of the independent fixing of prices by sellers. His evocative choice of words makes us easily forget that the price of a Chevrolet cannot be fixed at will. General Motors can do so, but then the company loses its market to its competitors. Secondly, Galbraith does not make enough allowance for the expansive urge of concerns. (Elsewhere, especially in his celebrated *The Affluent Society*, he does precisely that.) The pursuit of more sales and greater market shares spurs on many large concerns and makes it unattractive to demand high prices. This expansive urge brings the interests of producers and consumers closer together; it gives the customer a helping hand. Thirdly, the figures do not always bear out the Galbraithian view. The most concentrated sectors of business do not display the biggest profits. O. Eckstein in particular has shown that American profit margins did not obviously grow in the course of the price increases of the 1950s. The latter evidence is, however, not quite convincing. If a firm does well, and profit margins widen on account of a strong market position, part of the profit is often transformed into costs. These may be research expenditures, which is all to the good, but also high advertising budgets. Moreover, organizational slack may develop in the form of high overhead costs: executives are provided with roomy offices, generous expense accounts and luxurious transport facilities; multiplication of administrative work is no longer resisted. These forms of inefficiency escape the profit figures. They may form a factor in the conflict between business and the consumer, though this is slightly different from the Galbraith-Means theory of high prices.

And there is something else. The opinion that the whole level of prices is governed by powerful firms is an appealing one, but it is in contradiction to another well-known view, viz. that the level of prices depends on the quantity of money in circulation. If the latter is true, and the monetary inflation theory is correct, the entrepreneurs have absolutely no say in the level of prices. The guilty party when prices rise is—yes, who is it really? The Exchequer, the banknote press, the bankers, the velocity of circulation of money, or even more ethereal things such as the multiplier and the inflationary gap; but not the business blocs designated by Galbraith.

It cannot be denied: the oppressed consumers' bloc is a less tangible phenomenon than the simple theory of countervailing power would have us believe. It is in fact probable that limited competition is connected in some way—if only by organizational slack—with price increases, but the place of this phenomenon in the midst of other forms of inflation is not at all clear.

Indeed, different opinions are possible on this. For the sake of brevity I shall only give the opinion which I share, but which is just one of many. It is known as the theory of ratchet effects, and runs as follows. Owing to the limited competition prices hardly ever go down. The reason is to be found in a potential clash between the oligopolists; they dislike price wars, and avoid price cuts which might start an avalanche. In the first instance the prices are not driven up; it is just that they go down again with difficulty. But now productivity rises; that is a process that goes on year in, year out. It leads to lower costs, especially in efficient concerns. These cost reductions are not passed on sufficiently to the consumer. As a result of this profit margins rise. However, the statistician does not record this, partly because of organizational slack and partly because the increased profits create a possibility of increased wages of which the unions gladly avail themselves. In itself this does not lead to higher prices. But in the less efficient firms, where productivity lags behind, the higher wages lead to higher wage costs; if the total extent of demand, i.e. the economic situation, in any way permits, these increased costs are passed on to the consumer. As the producers know that wage demands will be regularly made, they are even less inclined to make price cuts where this could be done. Their price policy is asymmetrical. Through the combination of limited competition, wage policy and uneven increase in productivity, we thus see the possibility of a gradual rise in the level of prices looming up.

The interplay of oligopolistic sellers and unions may be called a conflict between organized business and the consumer. But before this contrast is dramatized it should be borne in mind that the recipients of profits and workers are also consumers. (That is one of those drawbacks which make almost every clash of interests slippery and hard to grasp, and which fill this essay.) Even organizational slack is a form of income, though here real waste may be involved: factors of production are used for less productive goals. Rising prices mean rising incomes, since every price is built up from incomes. This simple truth is often forgotten, which is more or less natural; rising prices lead to a reduction of someone's real income if his money income remains the same. But what holds good for an individual need not hold good for society as a whole, and it is wrong to think that a rising level of prices leads to a reduction of the real national income. For we now have the paradoxical phenomenon that high prices are less conflictive according as there are more of them and the higher prices and incomes are more widely distributed.

Take for instance aluminium, which in the United States is produced by a number of unusually strong sellers. Let us suppose—I do not know whether it is true or not—that this product is unreasonably expensive. The gains benefit many workers, many shareholders and a small number of managers. The burdens are borne by you and me and all of us, since aluminium is used directly and indirectly by everybody; but rich people consume relatively more than poor ones (for instance, they travel by plane). Now who is exactly in conflict with whom here? And the general conflict between producers and consumers vanishes even more quickly into thin air when we again consider all products together. The clash is then passed on to the group whose incomes do not rise. These are not the middle classes, the teachers or the public works engineers; their incomes now usually keep pace with the rise in prices quite nicely. Those who suffer from inflation are the real forgotten groups.

Personally I should therefore prefer to regard a *general* rise in prices not as a conflict between businessmen and consumers, but rather as a clash between recipients of income: the bulk of the profits and, to a lesser extent, wages and salaries against small pensions, interest incomes and low wages and small profits which have not risen along with the rest. Such a conflict can be bad enough: it brings us back to the inequality of the distribution of incomes, but it is rather different from a consumer being swindled at every turn.

I *would* be prepared to speak of a conflict between businessmen and consumers in those cases in which production is not in accordance with the consumer's wishes, in which he is not given enough information or is even misled, in which he is incited to buy too much on credit or in which the prices of socially desirable products are too high. The consumer must watch out for these special cases in the first place. In my opinion one of the important functions of the consumers' associations lies here: they, and also the authorities, must exert counterpressure on these phenomena.

We may not speak of a general collision between businessmen and consumers. Conflicts between sellers and buyers do occur in various situations, but they are scattered and incidental; they pop up now here, now there. It is not always big business which is the consumer's enemy; small and very small business may be worse, nor do the professions always escape criticism. A general theory glances off these conflicts; it is better to keep the special cases in mind, like the building and medical sectors. Apart from these there is a good deal of harmony, which is brought about by the market, though it hardly ever occurs in a pure form. It seems to me worth while holding on to the conclusion which in my opinion typifies the situation of a modern society: conflicts do not so much exist between clear-cut groups and blocs; they are mostly fragmentary, diffuse. Where they are sharp and concentrated, governments can mollify the situation. We may derive a certain optimism from that. . . .

C. Prices, external effects, and the environment

Adam Smith hoped that the "hidden hand" of the market would orchestrate the selfish behavior of individuals into an efficient harmony. But now we discover that the perfectly competitive economy often encourages pollution of the environment! When producers and consumers dump their wastes into air or water (or along highways) at no cost to themselves, their market decisions will ignore the damages and costs which they impose on those who share their environment. We can sometimes hope that the injured parties could equalize private and social costs through civil lawsuits or private bargains (bribes or contracts between victim and polluter). But the prerequisites for such private compensation (accurate estimates of costs and benefits to all affected parties, and clearly defined property rights) usually do not exist, so that market failure becomes a case for government intervention.

Ruff tells us how far the government should go in reducing pollution: as far as the marginal benefits (of cleaning it). Admittedly, these benefits and costs are hard to evaluate in dollar terms. Ruff considers several alternative forms of government action—direct regulation, fixed tolerance levels, subsidies, or taxes. He favors a pollution tax or waste disposal charge as the most efficient method.

Despite the market-oriented, businesslike flavor of Ruff's proposal to "put a price on pollution," Lumb's testimony shows that at least some businessmen oppose it. His main objections seem to be the fear of reduced profits (because of the higher taxes and costly investments for pollution control equipment) and political objections to further government controls over business. He also stresses that a pollution tax might close some plants entirely, bringing unemployment and dislocation to their communities.

If government must intervene, instead of awaiting the large investments which businesses are already making, Lumb prefers direct regulation (with fullest rights to appeal in the courts) and a tax credit or rapid depreciation allowance for the investment in pollution control. He argues that spreading the cost through such a tax subsidy is "fair," since society at large reaps the environmental benefits. The reader should ask himself why Lumb would object to Ruff's method of spreading the clean-up cost to society through higher consumer prices.

For those environment-lovers who have learned enough economics to shout "put a price on pollution," Dolan turns the same economic analysis around to shout "put a price on the wilderness." It cuts both ways! If the price-market mechanism is good enough for pollution, why not for national parks? If we should not give a free ride to polluters, why should we subsidize middle-class nature lovers? Dolan's analysis emphasizes the distributional or "equity" aspects of environmental economics, where Ruff concentrated more on the "efficiency" aspects. Both aspects must be considered in the formulation of public policy.

17 The economic common sense of pollution*

LARRY E. RUFF

We are going to make very little real progress in solving the problem of pollution until we recognize it for what, primarily, it is: an economic problem, which must be understood in economic terms. Of course, there are *noneconomic* aspects of pollution, as there are with all economic problems, but all too often, such secondary matters dominate discussion. Engineers, for example, are certain that pollution will vanish once they find the magic gadget or power source. Politicians keep trying to find the right kind of bureaucracy; and bureaucrats maintain an unending search for the correct set of rules and regulations. Those who are above such vulgar pursuits pin their hopes on a moral regeneration or social revolution, apparently in the belief that saints and socialists have no garbage to dispose of. But as important as technology, politics, law, and ethics are to the pollution question, all such approaches are bound to have disappointing results, for they ignore the primary fact that pollution is an economic problem.

Before developing an economic analysis of pollution, however, it is necessary to dispose of some popular myths.

First, pollution is not new. Spanish explorers landing in the 16th century noted that smoke from Indian campfires hung in the air of the Los Angeles basin, trapped by what is now called the inversion layer. Before the first century B.C., the drinking waters of Rome were becoming polluted.

Second, most pollution is not due to affluence, despite the current popularity of this notion. In India, the pollution runs in the streets, and advice against drinking the water in exotic lands is often well taken. Nor can pollution be blamed on the self-seeking activities of greedy capitalists.

* From "The Economic Common Sense of Pollution," *The Public Interest*, 19 (Spring 1970), pp. 69–85. Copyright © National Affairs Inc., 1970. Reprinted with permission of author and publisher. Larry E. Ruff is with the Environmental Protection Agency, Washington, D.C.

Once-beautiful rivers and lakes which are now open sewers and cesspools can be found in the Soviet Union as well as in the United States, and some of the world's dirtiest air hangs over cities in Eastern Europe, which are neither capitalist nor affluent. In many ways, indeed, it is much more difficult to do anything about pollution in noncapitalist societies. In the Soviet Union, there is no way for the public to become outraged or to exert any pressure, and the polluters and the courts there work for the same people, who often decide that clean air and water, like good clothing, are low on their list of social priorities.

In fact, it seems probable that affluence, technology, and slow-moving, inefficient democracy will turn out to be the cure more than the cause of pollution. After all, only an affluent, technological society can afford such luxuries as moon trips, three-day weekends, and clean water, although even our society may not be able to afford them all; and only in a democracy can the people hope to have any real influence on the choice among such alternatives.

What *is* new about pollution is what might be called the *problem* of pollution. Many unpleasant phenomena—poverty, genetic defects, hurricanes—have existed forever without being considered problems; they are, or were, considered to be facts of life, like gravity and death, and a mature person simply adjusted to them. Such phenomena become problems only when it begins to appear that something can and should be done about them. It is evident that pollution has advanced to the problem stage. Now the question is what can and should be done?

Most discussions of the pollution problem begin with some startling facts: Did you know that 15,000 tons of filth are dumped into the air of Los Angeles County every day? But by themselves, such facts are meaningless, if only because there is no way to know whether 15,000 tons is a lot or a little. It is much more important for clear thinking about the pollution problem to understand a few economic concepts than to learn a lot of sensational-sounding numbers.

MARGINALISM

One of the most fundamental economic ideas is that of *marginalism,* which entered economic theory when economists became aware of the differential calculus in the 19th century and used it to formulate economic problems as problems of "maximization." The standard economic problem came to be viewed as that of finding a level of operation of some activity which would maximize the net gain from that activity, where the net gain is the difference between the benefits and the costs of the activity. As the level of activity increases, both benefits and costs will increase; but because of diminishing returns, costs will increase faster than benefits. When a certain level of the activity is reached, any further expansion increases costs more than benefits. At this "optimal" level, "marginal cost"—or the cost of expanding the activity—equals "marginal benefit," or the benefit from expanding the activity. Further expansion would cost more than it is worth, and reduction in the activity would reduce benefits more than it would save costs. The net gain from the activity is said to be maximized at this point.

This principle is so simple that it is almost embarrassing to admit it is the cornerstone of economics. Yet intelligent men often ignore it in discussion of public issues. Educators, for example, often suggest that, if it is better to be literate than illiterate, there is no logical stopping point in supporting education. Or scientists have pointed out that the benefits derived from "science" obviously exceed the costs and then have proceeded to infer that their particular project should be supported. The correct comparison, of course, is between *additional* benefits created by the proposed activity and the *additional* costs incurred.

The application of marginalism to questions of pollution is simple enough conceptually. The difficult part lies in estimating the cost and benefits functions, a question to which I shall return. But several important qualitative points can be made immediately. The first is that the choice facing a rational society is *not* between clean air and dirty air, or between clear water and polluted water, but rather between various *levels* of dirt and pollution. The aim must be to find that level of pollution abatement where the costs of further abatement begin to exceed the benefits.

The second point is that the optimal combination of pollution control methods is going to be a very complex affair. Such steps as demanding a 10 percent reduction in pollution from all sources, without considering the relative difficulties and costs of the reduction, will certainly be an inefficient approach. Where it is less costly to reduce pollution, we want a greater reduction, to a point where an additional dollar spent on control anywhere yields the same reduction in pollution levels.

MARKETS, EFFICIENCY, AND EQUITY

A second basic economic concept is the idea—or the ideal—of the self-regulating economic system. Adam Smith illustrated this ideal with the example of bread in London: the uncoordinated, selfish actions of many people—farmer, miller, shipper, baker, grocer—provide bread for the city dweller, without any central control and at the lowest possible cost. Pure self-interest, guided only by the famous "invisible hand" of competition, organizes the economy efficiently.

The logical basis of this rather startling result is that, under certain conditions, competitive prices convey all the information necessary for making the optimal decision. A builder trying to decide whether to use brick or concrete will weigh his requirements and tastes against the prices of the materials. Other users will do the same, with the result that those whose needs and preferences for brick are relatively the strongest will get brick. Further, profit-maximizing producers will weigh relative production costs, reflecting society's productive capabilities, against relative prices, reflecting society's tastes and desires, when deciding how much of each good to produce. The end result is that users get brick and cement in quantities and proportions that reflect their individual tastes and society's production opportunities. No other solution would be better from the standpoint of all the individuals concerned.

This suggests what it is that makes pollution different. The efficiency of competitive markets depends on the identity of *private* costs and *social* costs. As long as the brick-cement producer must compensate somebody for every cost imposed by his production, his profit-maximizing decisions about how much to produce, and how, will also be socially efficient decisions. Thus, if a producer dumps wastes into the air, river, or ocean; if he pays nothing for such dumping; and if the disposed wastes have no noticeable effect on anyone else, living or still unborn; then the private and social costs of disposal are identical and nil, and the producer's private decisions are socially efficient. *But if these wastes do affect others, then the social costs of waste disposal are not zero. Private and social costs diverge, and private profit-maximizing decisions are not socially efficient.* Suppose, for example, that cement production dumps large quantities of dust into the air, which damages neighbors, and that the brick-cement producer pays these neighbors nothing. In the social sense, cement will be over-produced relative to brick and other products because users of the products will make decisions based on market prices which do not reflect true social costs. They will use cement when they should use brick, or when they should not build at all.

This divergence between private and social costs is the fundamental cause of pollution of all types, and it arises in any society where decisions are at all decentralized—which is to say, in any economy of any size which hopes to function at all. Even the socialist manager of the brick-cement plant, told to maximize output given the resources at his disposal, will use the People's Air to dispose of the People's Wastes; to do otherwise would be to violate his instructions. And if instructed to avoid pollution "when possible," he does not know what to do: how can he decide whether more brick or cleaner air is more important for building socialism? The capitalist manager is in exactly the same situation. Without prices to convey the needed information, he does not know what action is in the public interest, and certainly would have no incentive to act correctly even if he did know.

Although markets fail to perform efficiently when private and social costs diverge, this does not imply that there is some inherent flaw in the idea of acting on self-interest in response to market prices. Decisions based on private cost calculations are typically correct from a social point of view; and even when they are not quite correct, it often is better to accept this inefficiency than to turn to some alternative decision mechanism, which may be worse. Even the modern economic theory of socialism is based on the high correlation between managerial self-interest and public good. There is no point in trying to find something—some omniscient and omnipotent *deus ex machina*—to replace markets and self-interest. Usually it is preferable to modify existing institutions, where necessary, to make private and social interest coincide.

And there is a third relevant economic concept: the fundamental distinction between questions of efficiency and questions of equity or fairness. A situation is said to be efficient if it is not possible to rearrange things so as to benefit one person without harming any others. That is the *economic equation for efficiency. Politically,* this equation can be solved in various ways; though most reasonable men will agree that efficiency is a good thing, they will rarely agree about which of the many possible efficient states, each with a different distribution of "welfare" among individuals, is the best one. Economics itself has nothing to say about which efficient state is the best. That decision is a matter of personal and philosophical values, and ultimately must be decided by some political process. Economics can suggest ways of achieving efficient states, and can try to describe the equity considerations involved in any suggested social policy; but the final decisions about matters of "fairness" or "justice" cannot be decided on economic grounds.

ESTIMATING THE COSTS OF POLLUTION

Both in theory and practice, the most difficult part of an economic approach to pollution is the measurement of the cost and benefits of its abatement. Only a small fraction of the costs of pollution can be estimated straightforwardly. If, for example, smog reduces the life of automobile tires by 10 percent, one component of the cost of smog is 10 percent of tire expenditures. It has been estimated that, in a moderately polluted area of New York City, filthy air imposes extra costs for painting, washing, laundry, etc., of $200 per person per year. Such costs must be included in any calculation of the benefits of pollution abatement, and yet they are only a part of the relevant costs—and often a small part. Accordingly it rarely is possible to justify a measure like river pollution control solely on the basis of costs to individuals or firms of treating water because it usually is cheaper to process only the water that is actually used for industrial or municipal purposes, and to ignore the river itself.

The costs of pollution that cannot be measured so easily are often called "intangible" or "noneconomic," although neither term is particularly appropriate. Many of these costs are as tangible as burning eyes or a dead fish, and all such costs are relevant to a valid economic analysis. Let us therefore call these costs "nonpecuniary."

The only real difference between nonpecuniary costs and the other

...lies in the difficulty of estimating them. If pollution in Los Angeles ..arbor is reducing marine life, this imposes costs on society. The cost of reducing commercial fishing could be estimated directly: it would be the fixed cost of converting men and equipment from fishing to an alternative occupation, plus the difference between what they earned in fishing and what they earn in the new occupation, plus the loss to consumers who must eat chicken instead of fish. But there are other, less straightforward costs: the loss of recreation opportunities for children and sportsfishermen and of research facilities for marine biologists, etc. Such costs are obviously difficult to measure and may be very large indeed; but just as surely as they are not zero, so too are they not infinite. Those who call for immediate action and damn the most, merely because the spiny starfish and furry crab populations are shrinking, are putting an infinite marginal value on these creatures. This strikes a disinterested observer as an overestimate.

The above comments may seem crass and insensitive to those who, like one angry letter-writer to the Los Angeles *Times,* want to ask: "If conservation is not for its own sake, then what in the world *is* it for?" Well, what *is* the purpose of pollution control? Is it for its own sake? Of course not. If we answer that it is to make the air and water clean and quiet, then the question arises: what is the purpose of clean air and water? If the answer is, to please the nature gods, then it must be conceded that all pollution must cease immediately because the cost of angering the gods is presumably infinite. But if the answer is that the purpose of clean air and water is to further human enjoyment of life on this planet, then we are faced with the economists' basic question: given the limited alternatives that a niggardly nature allows, how can we best further human enjoyment of life? And the answer is, by making intelligent marginal decisions on the basis of costs and benefits. Pollution control is for lots of things: breathing comfortably, enjoying mountains, swimming in water, for health, beauty, and the general delectation. But so are many other things, like good food and wine, comfortable housing and fast transportation. The question is not which of these desirable things we should have, but rather what combination is most desirable. To determine such a combination, we must know the rate at which individuals are willing to substitute more of one desirable thing for less of another desirable thing. Prices are one way of determining those rates.

But if we cannot directly observe market prices for many of the costs of pollution, we must find another way to proceed. One possibility is to infer the costs from other prices, just as we infer the value of an ocean view from real estate prices. In principle, one could estimate the value people put on clean air and beaches by observing how much more they are willing to pay for property in nonpolluted areas. Such information could be obtained; but there is little of it available at present.

Another possible way of estimating the costs of pollution is to ask people how much they would be willing to pay to have pollution reduced. A resident of Pasadena might be willing to pay $100 a year to have smog reduced 10 or 20 percent. In Barstow, where the marginal cost of smog is much less, a resident might not pay $10 a year to have smog reduced 10 percent. If we knew how much it was worth to everybody, we could add up these amounts and obtain an estimate of the cost of a marginal amount of pollution. The difficulty, of course, is that there is no way of guaranteeing truthful responses. Your response to the question, how much is pollution costing *you,* obviously will depend on what you think will be done with this information. If you think you will be compensated for these costs, you will make a generous estimate; if you think that you will be charged for the control in proportion to these costs, you will make a small estimate.

In such cases it becomes very important how the questions are asked. For example, the voters could be asked a question of the form: Would you like to see pollution reduced *x* percent if the result is a *y* percent increase in the cost of living? Presumably a set of questions of this form could be used to estimate the costs of pollution, including the so-called "unmeasurable" costs. But great care must be taken in formulating the questions. For one thing, if the voters will benefit differentially from the activity, the questions should be asked in a way which reflects this fact. If, for example, the issue is cleaning up a river, residents near the river will be willing to pay more for the cleanup and should have a means of expressing this. Ultimately, some such political procedure probably will be necessary, at least until our more direct measurement techniques are greatly improved.

Let us assume that, somehow, we have made an estimate of the social cost function for pollution, including the marginal cost associated with various pollution levels. We now need an estimate of the benefits of pollution—or, if you prefer, of the costs of pollution abatement. So we set the Pollution Control Board (PCB) to work on this task.

The PCB has a staff of engineers and technicians, and they begin working on the obvious question: for each pollution source, how much would it cost to reduce pollution by 10 percent, 20 percent, and so on. If the PCB has some economists, they will know that the cost of reducing total pollution by 10 percent is *not* the total cost of reducing each pollution source by 10 percent. Rather, they will use the equimarginal principle and find the pattern of control such that an additional dollar spent on control of any pollution source yields the same reduction. This will minimize the cost of achieving any given level of abatement. In this way the PCB can generate a "cost of abatement" function, and the corresponding marginal cost function.

While this procedure seems straightforward enough, the practical difficulties are tremendous. The amount of information needed by the PCB is staggering; to do this job right, the PCB would have to know as much about each plant as the operators of the plant themselves. The cost of gathering these data is obviously prohibitive, and, since marginal principles apply to data collection too, the PCB would have to stop short of complete information, trading off the resulting loss in efficient control against the cost of better information. Of course, just as fast as the PCB obtained the data, a technological change would make it obsolete.

The PCB would have to face a further complication. It would not be correct simply to determine how to control existing pollution sources given their existing locations and production methods. Although this is almost certainly what the PCB would do, the resulting cost functions will overstate the true social cost of control. Muzzling existing plants is only one method of control. Plants can move, or switch to a new process, or even to a new product. Consumers can switch to a less-polluting substitute. There are any number of alternatives, and the poor PCB engineers can never know them all. This could lead to some costly mistakes. For example, the PCB may correctly conclude that the cost of installing effective dust control at the cement plant is very high and hence may allow the pollution to continue, when the best solution is for the cement plant to switch to brick production while a plant in the desert switches from brick to cement. The PCB can never have all this information and therefore is doomed to inefficiency, sometimes an inefficiency of large proportions.

Once cost and benefit functions are known, the PCB should choose a level of abatement that maximizes net gain. This occurs where the marginal cost of further abatement just equals the marginal benefit. If, for example, we could reduce pollution damages by $2 million at a cost of $1 million, we should obviously impose that $1 million cost. But if the damage reduction is only $1/2 million, we should not and in fact should reduce control efforts.

This principle is obvious enough but is often overlooked. One author, for example, has written that the national cost of air pollution is $11 billion a year but that we are spending less than $50 million a year on control; he infers from this that "we could justify a tremendous strengthening of control efforts on purely economic grounds." That *sounds* reasonable, if all you care about are sounds. But what is the logical content of the statement? Does it imply we should spend $11 billion on control just to make things even? Suppose we were spending $11 billion on control and thereby succeeded in reducing pollution costs to $50 million. Would this imply we were spending too *much* on control? Of course not. We must compare the *marginal* decrease in pollution costs to the *marginal* increase in abatement costs.

DIFFICULT DECISIONS

Once the optimal pollution level is determined, all that is necessary is for the PCB to enforce the pattern of controls which it has determined to be optimal. (Of course, this pattern will not really be the best one, because the PCB will not have all the information it should have.) But now a new problem arises: how should the controls be enforced?

The most direct and widely used method is in many ways the least efficient: direct regulation. The PCB can decide what each polluter must do to reduce pollution and then simply require that action under penalty of law. But this approach has many shortcomings. The polluters have little incentive to install the required devices or to keep them operating properly. Constant inspection is therefore necessary. Once the polluter has complied with the letter of the law, he has no incentive to find better methods of pollution reduction. Direct control of this sort has a long history of inadequacy; the necessary bureaucracies rarely manifest much vigor, imagination, or devotion to the public interest. Still, in some situations there may be no alternative.

A slightly better method of control is for the PCB to set an acceptable level of pollution for each source and let the polluters find the cheapest means of achieving this level. This reduces the amount of information the PCB needs, but not by much. The setting of the acceptable levels becomes a matter for negotiation, political pull, or even graft. As new plants are built and new control methods invented, the limits should be changed; but if they are, the incentive to find new designs and new techniques is reduced.

A third possibility is to subsidize the reduction of pollution, either by subsidizing control equipment or by paying for the reduction of pollution below standard levels. This alternative has all the problems of the above methods, plus the classic shortcoming which plagues agricultural subsidies: the old joke about getting into the not-growing-cotton business is not always so funny.

The PCB will also have to face the related problem of deciding *who* is going to pay the costs of abatement. Ultimately, this is a question of equity or fairness which economics cannot answer; but economics can suggest ways of achieving equity without causing inefficiency. In general, the economist will say: if you think polluter A is deserving of more income at polluter B's expense, then by all means give A some of B's income; but do *not* try to help A by allowing him to pollute freely. For example, suppose A and B each operate plants which produce identical amounts of pollution. Because of different technologies, however, A can reduce his pollution 10 percent for $100, while B can reduce his pollution 10 percent for $1,000. Suppose your goal is to reduce total pollution 5 percent. Surely it is obvious that the best (most efficient) way to do this is for A to reduce his pollution 10 percent while B does nothing. But suppose B is rich and A is poor. Then many would demand that B reduce his pollution 10 percent while A does nothing because B has a greater "ability to pay." Well, perhaps B does have greater ability to pay, and perhaps it is "fairer" that he pay the costs of pollution control; but if so, B should pay the $100 necessary to reduce A's pollution. To force B to reduce his own pollution 10 percent is equivalent to taxing B $1,000 and then blowing the $1,000 on an extremely inefficient pollution control method. Put this way, it is obviously a stupid thing to do; but put in terms of B's greater ability to pay, it will get considerable support though it is no less stupid. The more efficient alternative is not always available, in which case it may be acceptable to use the inefficient method. Still, it should not be the responsibility of the pollution authorities to change the distribution of welfare in society; this is the responsibility of higher authorities. The PCB should concentrate on achieving economic efficiency without being grossly unfair in its allocation of costs.

Clearly, the PCB has a big job which it will never be able to handle with any degree of efficiency. Some sort of self-regulating system, like a market is needed, which will automatically adapt to changes in conditions, provide incentives for development and adoption of improved control methods, reduce the amount of information the PCB must gather and the amount of detailed control it must exercise, and so on. This, by any standard, is a tall order.

PUTTING A PRICE ON POLLUTION

And yet there is a very simple way to accomplish all this. *Put a price on pollution.* A price-based control mechanism would differ from an ordinary market transaction system only in that the PCB would set the prices, instead of their being set by demand-supply forces, and that the state would force payment. Under such a system, anyone could emit any amount of pollution so long as he pays the price which the PCB sets to approximate the marginal social cost of pollution. Under this circumstance, private decisions based on self-interest are efficient. If pollution consists of many components, each with its own social cost, there should be different prices for each component. Thus, extremely dangerous materials must have an extremely high price, perhaps stated in terms of "years in jail" rather than "dollars," although a sufficiently high dollar price is essentially the same thing. In principle, the prices should vary with geographical location, season of the year, direction of the wind, and even day of the week, although the cost of too many variations may preclude such fine distinctions.

Once the prices are set, polluters can adjust to them any way they choose. Because they act on self-interest they will reduce their pollution by every means possible up to the point where further reduction would cost more than the price. Because all face the same price for the same type of pollution, the marginal cost of abatement is the same everywhere. If there are economies of scale in pollution control, as in some types of liquid waste treatment, plants can cooperate in establishing joint treatment facilities. In fact, some enterprising individual could buy these wastes from various plants (at negative prices—i.e., they would get paid for carting them off), treat them, and then sell them at a higher price, making a profit in the process. (After all, this is what rubbish removal firms do now.) If economies of scale are so substantial that the provider of such a service becomes a monopolist, then the PCB can operate the facilities itself.

Obviously, such a scheme does not eliminate the need for the PCB. The board must measure the output of pollution from all sources, collect the fees, and so on. But it does not need to know anything about any plant except its total emission of pollution. It does not control, negotiate, threaten, or grant favors. It does not destroy incentive because development of new control methods will reduce pollution payments.

As a test of this price system of control, let us consider how well it would work when applied to automobile pollution, a problem for which direct control is usually considered the only feasible approach. If the price system can work here, it can work anywhere.

Suppose, then, that a price is put on the emissions of automobiles. Obviously, continuous metering of such emissions is impossible. But it should be easy to determine the average output of pollution for cars of different makes, models, and years, having different types of control devices and using different types of fuel. Through graduated registration fees and fuel taxes, each car owner would be assessed roughly the social cost of his car's pollution, adjusted for whatever control devices he has chosen to install and for his driving habits. If the cost of installing a device, driving a different car, or finding alternative means of transportation is less than the price he must pay to continue his pollution, he will presumably take the necessary steps. But each individual remains free to find the best adjustment to his particular situation. It would be remarkable if everyone decided to install the same devices which some states currently require; and yet that is the effective assumption of such requirements.

Even in the difficult case of auto pollution, the price system has a number of advantages. Why should a person living in the Mojave desert, where pollution has little social cost, take the same pains to reduce air pollution as a person living in Pasadena? Present California law, for example, makes no distinction between such areas; the price system would. And what incentive is there for auto manufacturers to design a less polluting engine? The law says only that they must install a certain device in every car. If GM develops a more efficient engine, the law will eventually be change to require this engine on all cars, raising costs and reducing sales. But will such development take place? No collusion is needed for manufacturers to decide unanimously that it would be foolish to devote funds to such development. But with a pollution fee paid by the consumer, there is a real advantage for any firm to be first with a better engine, and even a collusive agreement wouldn't last long in the face of such an incentive. The same is true of fuel manufacturers, who now have no real incentive to look for better fuels. Perhaps most important of all, the present situation provides no real way of determining whether it is cheaper to reduce pollution by muzzling cars or industrial plants. The experts say that most smog comes from cars; but *even if true, this does not imply that it is more efficient to control autos rather than other pollution sources.* How can we decide which is more efficient without mountains of information? The answer is, by making drivers and plants pay the same price for the same pollution, and letting self-interest do the job.

In situations where pollution outputs can be measured more or less directly (unlike the automobile pollution case), the price system is clearly superior to direct control. A study of possible control methods in the Delaware estuary, for example, estimated that, compared to a direct control scheme requiring each polluter to reduce his pollution by a fixed percentage, an effluent charge which would achieve the same level of pollution abatement would be only half as costly—a saving of about $150 million. Such a price system would also provide incentive for further inmprovements, a simple method of handling new plants, and revenue for the control authority.

In general, the price system allocates costs in a manner which is at least superficially fair: those who produce and consume goods which cause polluion, pay the costs. But the superior efficiency in control and apparent fairness are not the only advantages of the price mechanism. Equally important is the ease with which it can be put into operation. It is not necessary to have detailed information about all the techniques of pollution reduction, or estimates of all costs and benefits. Nor is it necessary to determine whom to blame or who should pay. All that is needed is a mechanism for estimating, if only roughly at first, the pollution output of all polluters, together with a means of collecting fees. Then we can simply pick a price—any price—for each category of pollution, and we are in business. The initial price should be chosen on the basis of some estimate of its effects but need not be the optimal one. If the resulting reduction in pollution is not "enough," the price can be raised until there is sufficient reduction. A change in technology, number of plants, or whatever, can be accommodated by a change in the price, even without detailed knowledge of all the technological and economic data. Further, once the idea is explained, the price system is much more likely to be politically acceptable than some method of direct control. Paying for a service, such as garbage disposal, is a well-established tradition, and is much less objectionable than having a bureaucrat nosing around and giving arbitrary orders. When businessmen, consumers, and politicians understand the alternatives, the price system will seem very attractive indeed.

WHO SETS THE PRICES?

An important part of this method of control obviously is the mechanism that sets and changes the pollution price. Ideally, the PCB could choose this price on the basis of an estimate of the benefits and costs involved, in effect imitating the impersonal workings of ordinary market forces. But because many of the costs and benefits cannot be measured, a less "objective," more political procedure is needed. This political procedure could take the form of a referendum, in which the PCB would present to the voters alternative schedules of pollution prices, together with the estimated effects of each. There would be a massive propaganda campaign waged by the interested parties, of course. Slogans such as "Vote NO on 12 and Save Your Job," or "Proposition 12 Means Higher Prices," might be overstatements but would contain some truth, as the individual voter would realize when he considered the suggested increase in gasoline taxes and auto registration fees. But the other side, in true American fashion, would respond by overstating *their* case: "Smog Kills, Yes on 12," or "Stop *Them* From Ruining *Your* Water." It would be up to the PCB to inform the public about the true effects of the alternatives; but ultimately, the voters would make the decision.

It is fashionable in intellectual circles to object to such democratic procedures on the ground that the uncultured masses will not make correct decisions. If this view is based on the fact that the technical and economic arguments are likely to be too complex to be decided by direct referendum, it is certainly a reasonable position; one obvious solution is to set up an elective or appointive board to make the detailed decisions, with the expert board members being ultimately responsible to the voters. But often there is another aspect to the antidemocratic position—a feeling that it is impossible to convince the people of the desirability of some social policy, not because the issues are too complex but purely because their values are "different" and inferior. To put it bluntly: many ardent foes of pollution are not so certain that popular opinion is really behind them, and they therefore prefer a more bureaucratic and less political solution.

The question of who should make decisions for whom, or whose desires should count in a society, is essentially a noneconomic question that an economist cannot answer with authority, whatever his personal views on the matter. The political structures outlined here, when combined with the economic suggestions, can lead to a reasonably efficient solution of the pollution problem in a society where the tastes and values of all men are given some consideration. In such a society, when any nonrepresentative group is in a position to impose its particular evaluation of the costs and benefits, an inefficient situation will result. The swimmer or tidepool enthusiast who wants Los Angeles Harbor converted into a crystal-clear swimming pool, at the expense of all the workers, consumers, and businessmen who use the harbor for commerce and industry, is indistinguishable from the stockholder in Union Oil who wants maximum output from off-shore wells, at the expense of everyone in the Santa Barbara area. Both are urging an inefficient use of society's resources; both are trying to get others to subsidize their particular thing—a perfectly normal, if not especially noble, endeavor.

If the democratic principle upon which the above political suggestions are based is rejected, the economist cannot object. He will still suggest the price system as a tool for controlling pollution. With any method of decision—whether popular vote, representative democracy, consultation with the nature gods, or a dictate of the intellectual elite—the price system can simplify control and reduce the amount of information needed for decisions. It provides an efficient, comprehensive, easily understood, adaptable, and reasonably fair way of handling the problem. It is ultimately the only way the problem will be solved. Arbitrary, piecemeal, stop-and-go programs of direct control have not and will not accomplish the job.

SOME OBJECTIONS AREN'T AN ANSWER

There are some objections that can be raised against the price system as a tool of pollution policy. Most are either illogical or apply with much greater force to any other method of control.

For example, one could object that what has been suggested here ignores the difficulties caused by fragmented political jurisdictions; but this is true for any method of control. The relevant question is: what method of control makes interjurisdictional cooperation easier and more likely? And the answer is: a price system, for several reasons. First, it is probably easier to get agreement on a simple schedule of pollution prices than on a complex set of detailed regulations. Second, a uniform price schedule would make it more difficult for any member of the "cooperative" group to attract industry from the other areas by promising a more lenient attitude toward pollution. Third, and most important, a price system generates revenues for the control board, which can be distributed to the various political entities. While the allocation of these revenues would involve some vigorous discussion, any alternative methods of control would require the various governments to raise taxes to pay the costs, a much less appealing prospect; in fact, there would be a danger that the pollution prices might be considered a device to generate revenue rather than to reduce pollution, which could lead to an overly-clean, inefficient situation.

Another objection is that the Pollution Control Board might be captured by those it is supposed to control. This danger can be countered by having the board members subject to election or by having the pollution prices set by referendum. With any other control method, the danger of the captive regulator is much greater. A uniform price is easy for the public to understand, unlike obscure technical arguments about boiler temperatures and the costs of electrostatic collectors versus low-sulfur oil from Indonesia; if pollution is too high, the public can demand higher prices, pure and simple. And the price is the same for all plants, with no excuses. With direct control, acceptable pollution levels are negotiated with each plant separately and in private, with approved delays and special permits and other nonsense. The opportunities for using political influence and simple graft are clearly much larger with direct control.

A different type of objection occasionally has been raised against the price system, based essentially on the fear that it will solve the problem. Pollution, after all, is a hot issue with which to assault The Establishment, Capitalism, Human Nature, and Them; any attempt to remove the issue by some minor change in institutions, well within The System, must be resisted by The Movement. From some points of view, of course, this is a perfectly valid objection. But one is hopeful that there still exists a majority more concerned with finding solutions than with creating issues.

There are other objections which could be raised and answered in a similar way. But the strongest argument for the price system is not found in idle speculation but in the real world, and in particular, in Germany. The Rhine River in Germany is a dirty stream, recently made notorious when an insecticide spilled into the river and killed millions of fish. One tributary of the Rhine, a river called the Ruhr, is the sewer for one of the world's most concentrated industrial areas. The Ruhr River valley contains 40 percent of German industry, including 80 percent of coal, iron, steel and heavy chemical capacity. The Ruhr is a small river, with a low flow of less than half the flow on the Potomac near Washington. The volume of wastes is extremely large—actually exceeding the flow of the river itself in the dry season! *Yet people and fish swim in the Ruhr River.*

This amazing situation is the result of over forty years of control of the Ruhr and its tributaries by a hierarchy of regional authorities. These authorities have as their goal the maintenance of the quality of the water in the area at minimum cost, and they have explicitly applied the equi-marginal principle to accomplish this. Water quality is formally defined in a technological rather than an economic way; the objective is to "not kill the fish." Laboratory tests are conducted to determine what levels of various types of pollution are lethal to fish, and from these figures an index is constructed which measures the "amount of pollution" from each source in terms of its fish-killing capacity. This index is different for each source, because of differences in amount and composition of the waste, and geographical locale. Although this physical index is not really a very precise measure of the real economic *cost* of the waste, it has the advantage of being easily measured and widely understood. Attempts are made on an *ad hoc* basis to correct the index if necessary—if, for example, a non-lethal pollutant gives fish an unpleasant taste.

Once the index of pollution is constructed, a price is put on the pollution, and each source is free to adjust its operation any way it chooses.

Geographical variation in prices, together with some direct advice from the authorities, encourage new plants to locate where pollution is less damaging. For example, one tributary of the Ruhr has been converted to an open sewer; it has been lined with concrete and landscaped, but otherwise no attempt is made to reduce pollution in the river itself. A treatment plant at the mouth of the river processes all these wastes at low cost. Therefore, the price of pollution on this river is set low. This arrangement, by the way, is a rational, if perhaps unconscious, recognition of marginal principles. The loss caused by destruction of *one* tributary is rather small, if the nearby rivers are maintained, while the benefit from having this inexpensive means of waste disposal is very large. However, if *another* river were lost, the cost would be higher and the benefits lower; one open sewer may be the optimal number.

The revenues from the pollution charges are used by the authorities to measure pollution, conduct tests and research, operate dams to regulate stream flow, and operate waste treatment facilities where economies of scale make this desirable. These facilities are located at the mouths of some tributaries, and at several dams in the Ruhr. If the authorities find pollution levels are getting too high, they simply raise the price, which causes polluters to try to reduce their wastes, and provides increased revenues to use on further treatment. Local governments influence the authorities, which helps to maintain recreation values, at least in certain stretches of the river.

This classic example of water management is obviously not exactly the price system method discussed earlier. There is considerable direct control, and the pollution authorities take a very active role. Price regulation is not used as much as it could be; for example, no attempt is made to vary the price over the season, even though high flow on the Ruhr is more than ten times larger than low flow. If the price of pollution were reduced during high flow periods, plants would have an incentive to regulate their production and/or store their wastes for release during periods when the river can more easily handle them. The difficulty of continuously monitoring wastes means this is not done; as automatic, continuous measurement techniques improve and are made less expensive, the use of variable prices will increase. Though this system is not entirely regulated by the price mechanism, prices are used more here than anywhere else, and the system is much more successful than any other. So, both in theory and in practice, the price system is attractive, and ultimately must be the solution to pollution problems.

"IF WE CAN GO TO THE MOON, WHY . . . ETC?

"If we can go to the moon, why can't we eliminate pollution?" This new, and already trite, rhetorical question invites a rhetorical response: "If physical scientists and engineers approached their tasks with the same kind of wishful thinking and fuzzy moralizing which characterizes much of the pollution discussion, we would never have gotten off the ground." Solving the pollution problem is no easier than going to the moon, and therefore requires a comparable effort in terms of men and resources and the same sort of logical hard-headedness that made Apollo a success. Social scientists, politicians, and journalists who spend their time trying to find someone to blame, searching for a magic device or regulation, or complaining about human nature, will be as helpful in solving the pollution problem as they were in getting us to the moon. The price system outlined here is no magic formula, but it attacks the problem at its roots, and has a real chance of providing a long-term solution.

18 Economic incentives to control pollution*

H. C. LUMB

A POLLUTION TAX WON'T HELP CONTROL POLLUTION

American industry is not interested in a license to pollute. Let me make that absolutely clear. This year, United States industry is spending $3.6 billion on new pollution control facilities in addition to hundreds of millions of dollars it will spend every year in operation of billions of dollars worth of pollution control facilities already in place.

The principal obstacle to even greater pollution control expenditures by industry is the generation of enough cash to pay for these non-productive facilities. Taking money away from industrial companies in the name of a tax on pollution would not help—it would harm the cause of pollution control.

Proponents of a pollution tax claim that it would provide an incentive for research and development in the pollution control field. One witness at this hearing suggested that such a tax should be applied in circumstances where there is no current technology available to solve the particular problem. Industry plans to spend $926 million this year on pollution control research and development. It is impossible to understand how industry could spend even more if it had money siphoned away by an additional tax on its operations.

The proponents of a pollution tax appear to favor it on the basis of disappointment with the results of the regulatory approach. What they overlook is that pollution resulting from manufacturing operations is only one segment of the total pollution problem. Government figures indicate

* From "Economic Incentives to Control Pollution," hearings before the Joint Economic Committee, 92nd Congress, First Session, 1971, pp. 1261–68. Abridged and reprinted with permission of the author. H. C. Lumb is Vice President, Corporate Relations and Public Affairs, Republic Steel Corporation, Cleveland, Ohio, and a member of the Board of Directors and Chairman of a Task Force of the Environmental Quality Committee of the National Association of Manufacturers.

that manufacturing activities contribute less than 20 percent of total air pollution. Industrial water pollution is but one fraction of a total which includes pollution from municipal, recreational, agricultural and natural resources, with some of the biggest problems coming from drainage, erosion and siltation. A pollution tax would be even less effective in getting at these non-industrial sources than direct regulation.

We recognize statutory regulation of certain aspects of private enterprise as an essential function of the federal government, and as being in the public interest. Where such regulation is proper and advisable, it should be prescribed in advance by specific statutes, and should embody provisions which will, without overlapping or duplication, assure uniform application and interpretation, and deal impartially with all. The authority to issue rules should be limited strictly to those required for the purposes of administering the law within the limitations and standards fixed by the Congress. Administrative orders or decisions should be based upon the preponderance of the credible evidence produced in accordance with the rules of evidence applicable in courts, and should be subject to adequate judicial review of the law and the facts by the judicial branch of government.

We believe that the use of the tax system to achieve regulation by indirection is highly undesirable, and that the concept of a pollution tax is completely incompatible with the concept of impartial regulation.

One witness at these hearings said that such a tax would exert "a steady pressure to eliminate the last of the pollutant, instead of leaving the amounts permitted by clean-air standards to go untouched." We submit that it is unjust and inequitable to impose a so-called pollution tax on companies which are complying with standards established by government as being protective of the public health and welfare. The complete inconsistency of a pollution tax with government by impartial regulation is obvious.

One witness stated that the goal is to have no money coming into the Treasury. On the other hand, one wonders whether a pollution tax might not give the U.S. Treasury an entrenched interest in the continuation of pollution. The history of so-called "temporary" taxes in this country indicates that all taxes tend to become permanent revenue measures. The concept of a tax as a revenue-raising measure is contradictory to the objective of pollution control. The taxing power should be used primarily for fiscal purposes. The power granted to the Congress under the Constitution to raise revenues should be exercised in the light of that fundamental purpose.

HISTORY OF EFFLUENT CHARGE PROPOSALS

At this point, let us go back into some of the history of proposals for effluent charges. In 1966, the chairman of President Johnson's Council of

Economic Advisers set up a working committee to evaluate several proposals for creating economic incentives for industrial pollution abatement. The committee was asked to rank each proposal on the basis of those incentives which it considered most efficient, effective and equitable.

The committee report, dated August 31, 1966, was later altered by a larger committee and captioned "Cost Sharing with Industry?" (November 20, 1967). This in turn was edited and later released as a report to Congress.

The proposal strongly favored by the committee and endorsed by the later reviewing group was one of effluent fees. These reasons were cited:

"Effluent fees encourage *the total least cost combination of methods* to reduce waste discharges within the plant;

"Effluent fees encourage *least cost* methods to reduce pollution flows among a number of plants in a river basin;

"Effluent fees can provide a source of revenue for water control purposes external to the plant and containing economics of large scale facilities;

"Effluent fees can be implemented quickly;

"Effluent fees are used to control waste treatment and finance water quality programs in many places throughout the world."

That the arguments are fallacious—either as direct misrepresentations or as limited presentation which distort a true appraisal—can be illustrated.

For example, contrary to the assertion in the report, effluent fees are not in use anywhere to control waste treatment. Rather, the truth is that there is in wide practice user-service charges whereby a waste discharger pays for having wastes treated. The sewer service charge which a homeowner pays is an example.

Another is the service charge paid by industries in the Ruhr Valley for treatment of waste waters. In the Ruhr, contrary to popular reporting, there is no penalty tax on effluents. There is a treatment service charge for waste waters unable to be returned to the Ruhr. Such waste waters are diverted to the Emscher River which is maintained as an open sewer for transmission to in-stream treatment facilities. The Emscher is lined with concrete and shrubbery conceals it from the eyes of the public. Most American cities have the same fee service but no river basin in the United States has available a second river for use as an open sewer.

Again, the assertion that effluent fees can be quickly implemented is totally inaccurate, even if there are some drastic assumptions, such as, that all industries utilize the same volume of air and water per unit of production, that all industries produce exactly the same weight of waste to air and water per unit of production, that the unit rate of tax would be equal for all discharges on the assumption that it would represent the impact cost on the environment—because such implementation would demand that the existing tax collecting machinery absorb this additional burden without difficulty. It has not been made clear as to whether a pollution tax would be administered by the Environmental Protection Agency as a pollution control measure or by the Internal Revenue Service as a revenue measure. In either event, the organizational and administrative problems would be of major proportions.

The argument that effluent fees encourage the "total least cost combinations of methods to reduce waste discharges within a plant" is not supported in the operating controls in industrial plants in the Ruhr basin, yet the Ruhr is erroneously reported as the leading example of control via effluent fees.

Ruhr plants vary widely in plant processes and equipment and differ little from comparable plants in the United States. Factors other than waste treatment costs control their in-plant changes just as they do here, and will continue to do so here unless the costs of an effluent tax are raised to such extremes as to force a cessation of discharge. It might be possible that a process modification might be available to meet the situation at some cost level, but the decision could just as easily be to cease operation. The committee report ignored this possibility and also ignored the possible consequences of such cessation of production on corporate and local area economies.

The same error lies in the assumption that effluent fees encourage least cost methods to reduce pollution flows from a number of plants in a river basin. The committee believed that since cost of reduction varies from plant to plant, an effluent fee would encourage a greater than average reduction in those which could do so at least cost and, thus, they felt this would reduce the net total cost to all plants from what it would be if all plants had to provide the same degree of reduction. Unmentioned in the report is the residual penalty to be sustained by the company which had to continue the higher effluent tax because it couldn't easily reduce the load. Also unmentioned was the point that such plants are usually the older ones and more likely the marginal plants which would then face one more hurdle for survival. Nor does the report discuss the economic impact on an area when such plants are closed. Thus the underlying fallacies are the assumptions that the environmental concern is limited to one of reduction of waste loads and that any program directed towards waste reduction will have no possible adverse consequent effect. Obviously, this is not the case.

The committee's fifth point is possibly true. The effluent tax could be a source of revenue for controls outside a plant, such as in-stream treatment of flow augmentation as suggested in the report, but this is true only if the effluent fee is a direct charge for services rendered, such as where in-stream treatment is actually provided as is the case in the Ruhr. But when an effluent tax is collected at the federal level, the argument is fallacious.

In brief, the fallacies in the proposal to tax effluents are these:

"There is no guarantee the tax will accelerate industrial cleanup and it will definitely not cure municipal agricultural or recreational sources of pollution.

There are many unknowns in implementing such a proposal and it is not in practice anywhere at the present time. The Ruhr program is comparable to that of such cities as Philadelphia which charge for services rendered in the treatment of industrial wastes, but no American river basin has a situation comparable to the Ruhr.

The tax requires an administrator with such broad discretionary authority that he can control industrial expansion and operation.

The tax will definitely have an adverse impact on marginal industries and thus on the economy of areas which can be of much more significance than the present pollution. In effect, it will transform physical environment blights to social, cultural and economic environment blights.

The tax disrupts the present ongoing pollution abatement program and institutes a hiatus while new ground rules are developed.

To be self-sustaining, the rate tax must be increased as the pollution decreases so there is no real incentive to clean up.

Minimizing or avoiding a tax on discharges to water, for example, will promote discharges to air or land. The cost of the tax, not the effect on the environment, will control."

There are three areas of interest in the pollution tax proposal which merit attention:

The *first* is that the idea has been advocated for a number of years by Allen Kneese of Resources for the Future. His publications on the subject are numerous and highly theoretical, but simplified to two quality parameters, BOD and chlorides. Of fundamental importance is the fact that in his proposal, all water users, not just industry, should pay for use of the water, and that discharge of a waste should be permitted (even encouraged) if the cost of treatment to the discharger exceeds the cost to handle the polluted waste water downstream. Moreover, Mr. Kneese uses as his illustration the Ruhr, Germany, river authority but fails to accurately report on what is being done there. There is no tax on pollution discharges to the Ruhr. If the company exceeds defined limits, the company can treat the water or it can discharge it to a parallel river system which acts as an open sewer to convey the wastes to point of treatment. The cost of this treatment is assessed to the sources.

The *second* point meriting attention is that the researching and drafting of the bill introduced by Chairman Proxmire in the last session, S. 3181, obviously relied heavily on Mr. Kneese's theory. The bill added a provision for using the funds to finance municipal construction and policing. The proposal for taxing effluents developed in the Johnson Administration was based on the concept that a properly scheduled tax would force marginal and obsolete production facilities out of action and thus encourage higher efficiency and lower cost production without polluting effects. The Nixon Administration has been somewhat divided and was more against taxing discharges until the deficit in the budget suggested additional revenue. But what has not been worked up in detail are the mechanics of collection, how much will be collected, the impact on the marginal plants, the impact of closing marginal plants on local economies, the net effect on the federal tax structure by payments which will be operating costs and, therefore, deductible, but assigned to specific federal accounts and, therefore, truly reducing the net general federal income. Nor have there been any estimates of the costs of collection, the means of monitoring or the records involved.

The *third* area of concern relates to where this is leading. Suppose for a moment the taxing proposal is adopted. In many instances a quarter of a cent per pound can make or break a market potential. Costs are measured to tenths of a cent and the process was installed with such margins anticipated. The additional costs of pollution control facilities—and the operating costs are often more critical than the capital costs—are for many industries something that was not anticipated. In addition, other unanticipated costs of doing business have been added but most of these are uniformly applied.

But with the uncertainties in measuring discharges there is a fertile field for negotiation and compromise. Also, with the conversion to an effluent tax the stream and air standards will no longer be controlling. The issue resolves itself to one of a negotiated agreement with the taxing authority.

The potential for making higher assessments on one stream than another provides opportunity to define areas of economic development. The potential to measure discharges differently provides opportunity to curtail production.

But this taxing potential can also set the rates so that a company is forced to convert from coal to gas or to low sulfur oil. What this will do to these energy industries is obvious. The relative availability of fuels in various regions can have a tremendous impact on economic development. Some aspects of this are now within the authority of the Federal Power Commission.

There is also the effect on the tax structure, which at present is under terrific strain. With a population which has changed from primarily one of manufacturing to one of services and government and with a continually increasing demand for higher cost services, the objective has become one of a new tax base which would not fall on the majority—the services-oriented and government personnel. Agriculture has little promise, so industry is the best bet.

Nor is the concept of pollution taxes limited in application to those industries not connected to municipal treatment plants. The Administration is presently considering the policy of excluding from eligibility for federal grants that portion of the capacity of a municipal treatment plant used or expected to be used by industry. Part of the reasoning is to require separate monitoring of industrial discharges so the pollution tax could be applied to all industry. Otherwise, there would be a claim of discriminatory taxation. But again, the objective is revenue, not effective pollution control, for there are major environmental protection benefits from joint treatment with third person control.

Other programs are underway in the United States which will provide prerequisites to a pollution tax. A number of government agencies are insisting effluent standards must be adopted as essential to federal enforcement but, in reality, enforcement could proceed now if there is violation of quality standards. The objective is one of attaining effluent standards, essential for a taxing program.

Another essential is public reporting of waste load discharges in pounds-per-day and this is being promoted via applications for Corps of Engineers permits on discharges, by recommendations of the General Accounting Office, by legislation pending before the Senate Public Works Committee, and by reports and hearings of the House Government Operations Subcommittee.

Still another essential is the authority of the federal government to have right of entry and subpoena records of finances and operation. This, too, is in proposed legislation and so is the authority to actually define the kind of controls to be installed, as well as the control over the actual site location of sources of discharges, so there can be a definition or calculation of possible adverse impact which will influence the charges.

Lastly, there must be punitive controls to enforce compliance and these are manifested in criminal and civil penalties of large magnitude in all recently proposed legislation.

To sum up, the National Association of Manufacturers believes that taxes on effluents and emissions represent an unmanageable, uneconomic and negative approach and in principle would allow polluters to continue to adversely use our environment by payment of a tax.

THE TAX CREDIT APPROACH

On the other hand, a positive approach would involve establishment of a system of accelerated amortization and tax credits.

But, first, let us examine the dimensions of American industry's pollution control efforts. The $3.6 billion figure previously referred to for capital expenditures for industrial air and water pollution control facilities during 1971 was established by a survey conducted by McGraw-Hill Publications Company and released on May 14. This survey showed that industry plans to spend nearly $2.1 billion on new air pollution control facilities and about $1.6 billion on new water pollution control facilities. In manufacturing, 7.6% of total capital expenditures will be allocated to control of air and water pollution. Spending on research and development devoted to solving pollution control problems is expected to total $926 million, some of which will be federally financed. Where technologically and economically feasible solutions are not yet available, the survey report stated that some companies said they were now closing down many of their polluting facilities rather than attempting to upgrade them.

No very good figure is available as to American industry's total capital expenditures for pollution control over the past decade. The only good benchmark we have is a survey by the National Association of Manufacturers, in cooperation with other industrial organizations, which showed that, at the beginning of the past decade, the replacement value of *water* pollution control facilities being operated was over $1 billion. Annual additions to this benchmark figure have undoubtedly trended upward at an increasingly accelerated pace. It could be concluded that the present replacement value of air and water pollution control facilities now operating is in the neighborhood of $10 billion.

It should be carefully noted that the figures referred to are all capital expenditures, and do not include annual operating and maintenance expenses involved in connection with pollution control facilities. These additional expenses amount to hundreds of millions of dollars annually. A very rough rule of thumb is that such additional annual expenses approximate 10 percent of the total capital expenditures.

As standards become more stringent, it may be that industry will be called upon to spend much more per year for new pollution control facilities than the $3.6 billion it will spend this year.

This raises some fundamental questions as to how big a financial load we should place upon our economic system in this regard and how this load should be distributed. The cost of controlling pollution enters into our national accounts, affects our competitive position in world trade, and consequently affects our balance of payments. A delegation from the National Association of Manufacturers met in Brussels early this year with delegations from the manufacturers associations of the six Common Market countries. These associations are banded together in an organization known as U.N.I.C.E. A major subject of the conference was pollution control. The impression gained by the NAM delegation was that these countries were at least 5 to 7 years behind the United States in terms of pollution control.

This is why it has been urged that, at least for the period that American industry is going through what appears to be a "pollution control crunch," and until other countries catch up to the United States in this regard, industry should be granted a tax credit for some portion of the cost of new pollution control facilities. The concept of special tax treatment of such costs has already been recognized twice by the Congress. The first time was during the suspension of the 7% investment credit. Pollution control equipment was exempted from the suspension. The second time was on the occasion of the repeal of the 7% investment tax credit by the Tax Reform Act of 1969. This Act included a provision for accelerated amortization of pollution control equipment. However, this provision contains so many restrictions that it is generally regarded as meaningless and ineffective. Many people in industry believe that this provision should be replaced by legislation such as is proposed by H.R. 3565, introduced on February 4, 1971 by Representative Charles S. Gubser of California. This bill carries the title of "Pollution Control Incentive Act of 1971," and would provide for a 20 percent tax credit and a 1 to 5 year amortization period of costs for air and water pollution control facilities. These are defined to include the cost of land, buildings, improvements, machinery, and equipment used to control pollution, whereas present law is limited to equipment and buildings used exclusively to house such equipment.

H.R. 3565 calls for certification of the facility by the appropriate State agency, whereas present law requires dual certification by both the State agency and the Federal government. A 3 year carryback and 5 year carry-over of unused credits would be provided.

One rationale for such legislation rests upon the widespread public benefit conferred by pollution control efforts and the generally non-productive and uneconomic character of pollution control facilities. Operation of these facilities usually does not yield a salable production to offset some of the capital and operating costs, let alone make any profit. In addition, these costs divert capital away from investments in productive facilities which could yield profits. It is on this basis that the official policy of the National Association of Manufacturers calls for recognition of the public interest nature of these expenditures, and their uneconomic aspects, through accelerated amortization up to and including immediate write-off at the option of the taxpayer and through tax credits to enterprises which expend private capital for such facilities.

It is sometimes said that the cost of controlling pollution should be considered as an ordinary cost of doing business and should be included in the price of the product. I suggest that controlling pollution is in the process of becoming an *extraordinary* cost of doing business, and I question whether it is wise, in light of foreign competition, the drain on our gold, our balance of payments problem, and the recent battering of the American dollar in foreign money markets, to build all of this extraordinary cost into our price structure.

It might also be noted that raising the prices of products to cover increased costs is all right if the government will not raise objections to your price increases and if customers will not turn to your domestic and foreign competitors. If the public insists on an ultra-high quality physical environment in highly industrialized areas, and insists upon achieving this type of environment within an extremely tight time schedule, a tax credit not only seems equitable, it seems to be the only available economic avenue to diffuse this cost increment among the entire public which benefits.

Having considered some of the reasoning supporting a tax credit for pollution control let us turn to the question, what is the prevailing climate of opinion toward such a proposal? A July 1970 report by Opinion Research Corporation of Princeton, New Jersey gives the results of a survey of the latest public attitudes toward air and water pollution. The results in the report were based upon a nationwide survey of the United States public 18 years of age and older. Personal interviews were conducted with 2,168 respondents in their homes from May 18 to June 18, 1970. One of the questions asked was "Would you be for or against companies being given a tax reduction to help them cover the cost of installing pollution control equipment?" Of the total public, 58 percent were for, and 34 percent were against. The survey report commented as follows: "The public continues to be willing to support tax credits to help companies cover the cost of installing pollution control equipment."

This solid majority support for pollution control tax credits among the general public reflects the same viewpoint prevailing among top-level industrial executives. As reported in the February 1970 issue of *Fortune*, some 270 chief executives of companies listed in *Fortune's* annual 500 Directory were personally interviewed at length to ascertain their opinion about various aspects of the environment problem, as it affects them both as citizens and as leaders of business. In response to the question "What do you think would be the single most effective—least effective—incentives to business to do something more about pollution?", 59 percent considered tax credits for pollution control costs as most effective while 2 percent considered tax credits least effective. "Passing on costs to consumers" was considered most effective by 4 percent and least effective by 47 percent.

Perhaps the best way to conclude a discussion of a tax credit proposal is to quote the President of the United States. The following statement is made on page 133 of the publication, "Nixon on the Issues":

"Tax incentives are a different *kind* of Federal investment from direct expenditures. Both affect the federal funds available for other purposes; but they are very different in their effect. I think my audience understands why I favor incentives. They use and strengthen private institutions, rather than replacing them with public bureaucracies. They disperse administrative responsibilities to lower and more local levels rather than overcentralizing them. They allow for some more variety, flexibility and experimentation rather than perpetuating over-rigid federal directives.

They bring out private investment funds to help get the job done. I like the mix of incentives and direct expenditures, but the balance must be corrected in favor of more incentives."

CONCLUSION

In conclusion, we submit that the Joint Economic Committee should reject the concept of a pollution tax for the following reasons:

1. Taking money away from industrial companies will not help the cause of pollution control and will not facilitate the installation of pollution control facilities or the conduct of pollution control research and development.

2. A pollution tax is inconsistent with the concept of government by sound and impartial regulation.

3. A pollution tax would involve major administrative problems related to setting of the tax rates, monitoring of emissions and effluents, and enforcement.

4. Contrary to repeated assertions, there is no precedent for a pollution tax.

5. A pollution tax could cause unfortunate and unforeseen economic dislocations.

6. A pollution tax could be used to achieve governmental control of industrial expansion and operation.

We further submit that a positive approach which would facilitate even greater expenditures for pollution control facilities and pollution control research and development should be based on the fact that there are broad social benefits which accrue to all the people of the nation through environmental quality control efforts. Because of this and because in most instances money invested for abatement facilities does not bring an economic return, the Association believes there should be some recognition of the cost of installing environmental quality control facilities in relation to the general public interest and the uneconomic portion of the investment. This recognition should take the form of accelerated amortization up to and including the immediate write-off of the facility at the option of the taxpayer, and tax credits to enterprises which expend private capital for such facilities.

We greatly appreciate this opportunity to present our views.

19 Preserving the wilderness—
Public interest or special interest?*

EDWIN G. DOLAN

ON GOOD ECONOMICS AND GOOD GOVERNMENT

The use of general tax revenue to finance projects offering special benefits to a fraction of the population is both bad economics and bad government. It is bad economics since, except in the limiting case where all political decisions are made under the rule of unanimity, each such project will generally be funded beyond the point where the marginal cost of the project equals its marginal benefit. The necessary conditions for efficiency are violated and misallocation of resources results. The use of public funds for such projects is also bad government, because the nonbeneficiary taxpayers are forced to invest a part of their earnings in a way which at best yields them no returns and, more often, causes them positive harm.

Get any good conservationist into a discussion on the subject of the Army Corps of Engineers or the Department of Highways and you will find an ardent supporter of this idea. He will curse the incredible waste and corruption involved in the history of massive federal giveaways to lumbering, mining, grazing, hydroelectric, and construction interests, and then curse them again because he as a taxpayer has been forced not only to suffer from the results of these criminal actions but actually to finance his own suffering!

If you really want to see some fireworks, ask this same conservationist if these same principles of government and economics apply to such projects as national parks and wilderness preservation programs. Ask him why it is that if justice requires motorists to pay for their own roads, hydroelectric firms to pay for their own dams, golfers to pay for their own golf

* From "Preserving the Wilderness—Public Interest or Special Interest?" *TAN-STAAFL* The Economic Strategy for Environmental Crisis. Copyright © 1971 by Holt, Rinehart and Winston, Inc., pp. 85–99. Reprinted with minor deletions by permission of Holt, Rinehart and Winston, Inc. Edwin G. Dolan is Professor of Economics at Dartmouth College, Hanover, N.H.

courses, and gourmets to pay for their own escargots, lovers of the wilderness should not pay for their own wilderness and campers for their own campsites? Why should the special interests of conservationists be subsidized by the taxes of nonconservationists?

You would be well-advised to wear a verbal flak vest while asking this question, because your conservationist interlocutor is armed with quite an arsenal of replies. Let's devote a few pages to an examination of these replies.

I, too, am a wilderness lover, a member of the beneficiary group of conservation legislation, and you may be sure that I have asked these hard questions of myself a good many times and that I am really going to make sure that we sift these replies for any possible shred of a valid argument. I will also suggest some guidelines for a much more effective wilderness preservation program than the National Park system, one which is within the bounds of both good economics and good government.

CONSERVATION AND THE PUBLIC INTEREST

The first gambit of the conservationist in defending public financing of his favorite projects is to argue that conservation and wilderness preservation is not a special interest at all, but, instead, the common interest of the whole population. This contention is without basis in fact. In the absence of strong evidence to the contrary, it seems safe to assume that the distribution of the populace with respect to their degree of interest in wilderness preservation looks something like the curve shown in Figure 19–1. The horizontal scale represents the degree of an individual's interest in wilderness preservation. Toward the right are located the real hard core enthusiasts. These include the 12,000 rugged devotees who visited Rain-

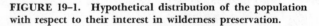

FIGURE 19–1. Hypothetical distribution of the population with respect to their interest in wilderness preservation.

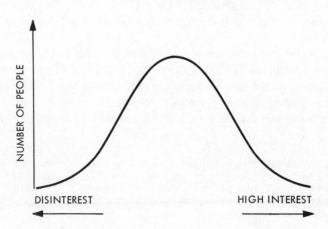

bow Bridge in the first fifty years after its discovery, making the difficult trip up or down river or twenty-eight miles overland by horseback. Somewhat to the left of them come the average backpacker whom one meets along sections of trail more, let us say, than five miles from the nearest road. Further toward the middle are the hundreds of thousands who make a visit to some of our more developed and accessible parks for a weekend or two out of the year, those who appreciate the wilderness through the window of a car, or who are content to patronize a modest state park near their home. At the extreme left of the scale are those who not only get no benefit from the wilderness but view it with positive displeasure, those who look at a tree and think what a waste that it has not yet been turned into a lovely residence or a page of their favorite magazine.

I will make no pretense at putting numbers on the vertical scale or dollar values along the horizontal, but we may be certain that this is a reality: a *few* people who benefit enormously from our national parks, a *great many* who derive a moderate benefit, and a *few* who are positively upset at the thought of a tree looking at a tree.

If the tax burden is assumed to be distributed over the members of this group without respect for the position of individuals on the scale, then it is clear that for any given wilderness preservation project the individual share of the costs will outweigh the individual share of the benefits for all those to the left of a certain point. Government financing of such a project serves only the interests of those to the right of this point.

The conservationists are hardly willing to give up their fight simply because the benefits of the projects which they propose are not distributed with exact mathematical equality among the entire population. Even conceding *this* point, they are able to return to the attack with a number of other reasons for including wilderness preservation among the items receiving government subsidies.

One of the most frequently heard of these is the argument from irreversibility. Suppose, it is said, that you cut down a stand of virgin redwood forest to make lumber, or dam a beautiful canyon to generate electricity. In a few years the housing may have less value than you thought, or atomic power may make the dam obsolete, but no matter how much you regret your decision the trees or canyon are gone forever. But if you mistakenly reserve an area for a park and if, in a few years, you find that interest in this particular park is less than you had thought, or if a really pressing need for timber or power develops, you can easily reverse your decision. Therefore, the argument goes, if there is any doubt in the marginal cases of commercial development versus wilderness preservation, it is best to play safe and decide in favor of the latter.

I think the irreversibility argument contains a grain of truth, but that as an argument for government spending on wilderness preservation its importance has been greatly exaggerated. It is simply not true that the destruction of wilderness areas is irreversible, except in the narrow case where the value of an area lies in its virginity per se. Pure virgin wilderness, although important and extremely valuable, is only a part of the total land available for recreational use.

To anyone who has been to Vermont during the October foliage season or visited the Smoky Mountains, an area which is in much better condition today than when it first became a park, certain Western conservationists, with their haughty contempt for second-growth woodland, must seem a bit narrowminded.

Many conservationists are extremely suspicious of the concept of wilderness restoration because the idea has often been misused in support of the erroneous contention that our remaining virgin areas need not be handled with care. But by refusing even to consider restoration where it is possible, I think they are doing themselves a disservice in the long run.

For those areas like the largest virgin redwoods and sequoias, where restoration is impossible, there is some validity to the irreversibility argument. Consider Figure 19–2. This little graph shows the value, for each

FIGURE 19–2.   Best land use over time

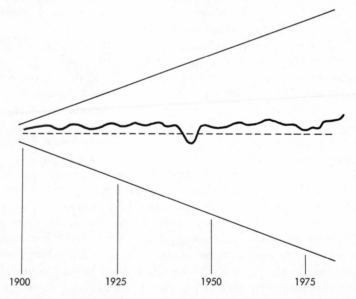

year in the 20th century, of a certain site in its alternative uses as a park and for commercial exploitation. To read the graph for any year you measure the commercial value down from the top straight line to the wavy line; and to measure its value as a park you read up from the bottom. The dashed line in the middle shows the breakeven point. The figure has a wedge shape because, as population and GNP grow, the value of the site in both alternative uses increases. As you can see, although there are some year-to-year fluctuations, the wavy line stays above the breakeven point most of the time, indicating that the best use of the land is as a park, despite the fact that for a few years during the Second World War its current commercial value momentarily exceeded its recreational value. If this land had been logged over or flooded in those years and lost forever to recreation, would this have been a wise use of resources? Without going into technical details, it is possible that because of lack of foresight or temporary emergency conditions this particular wilderness area might have been destroyed and thus lost forever to its best use.

Stated in this form, the irreversibility argument does not indicate that federal ownership and control of our national parks is a necessity for shielding the legitimate interests of conservationists for irreversible damage caused by wars, abnormally high interest rates, or other temporary crises. To the extent that the argument is valid, it does argue for a maximum of procedural barriers and delays to be placed in the way of transferring certain sites from recreational to commercial use. The worst situation would be the one which now prevails for vast tracts of the most valuable federal land where some administrator, at the stroke of a pen, can at any moment make the irreversible decision in question. Conservationists have realized this, and have lobbied for legislation like the Wilderness Bill, which in effect requires that the stroke of the pen be made by Congress, not an administrative agency. This clearly is a help, since as we all know, Congressional decision making is slow and replete with procedural delays. But Congressional decision making is also subject to strong pressures from commercial interests, and in time of war from military interests as well. Wouldn't it be safer if the *conservationists themselves* had control over these irreversible decisions, rather than relying on the whim of a bureaucrat or the treachery of a politician? If, let us say, the Sierra Club *owned* the site in question, they would sell it to be logged only if they were pretty sure that the decision was a wise one, only if, for example, the price were high enough to purchase or improve a superior site elsewhere. If conservationists *really* wanted to lock this site into use as a park, they could not only buy it but write a covenant into the deed which would prevent its sale for commercial use even by future administrators of the Club itself.

In sum, the irreversibility argument turns out to work not in favor of extending our national park system as it now exists but of turning it into a system of private parks to provide surer protection for the future!

As soon as the subject of selling the national parks to the Sierra Club is raised, conservationists come up with another set of arguments in favor of government action, which I will call the organizational arguments. Commercial interests, it is said, are concentrated and well-organized, while conservation interests are badly organized and diffuse. Thus, commercial interests would be able to raise the money to outbid the conservationists, even if the latter might actually be able to make better use of the land. This argument can take several forms. Let's see what truth there is in any of them.

It is sometimes alleged that there is a free rider problem with the national parks. This arises not because a few irresponsible recreationists might sneak past the turnstile at the entrance to the park, using it without paying, but because the parks provide benefits, in the form of externalities or spillover effects, to those who never visit them. National parks should be considered as a public good, albeit an imperfect one, which like education provides major values to the direct beneficiary, but also furnishes significant external benefits to others in society.

Is this all so? Do you get any external benefits from Yosemite National Park, which you have never visited and which, for purposes of the argument, let's say you never will? If so, just what are these benefits?

For a start we might try to measure the extent of these benefits by the strength of the sense of outrage which you would feel if you read one morning that the park had been converted into a test range for new defoliants for use in Vietnam. That might cause you sufficient pain to mail a check to the Save Yosemite Committee, but you also might not bother, hoping that others would do so and make you a free rider. Perhaps the externality takes the form of the increased range of choice among parks, even though you don't choose to visit Yosemite itself. Or perhaps it is that you can benefit from pictures which Ansel Adams takes there, although you may never see the place with your own eyes. Or perhaps the parks which you do use are less crowded and the entrance fees are lower because Yosemite takes the pressure off.

This is an impressive list. It must be admitted by even the most skeptical that we would be less well off were Yosemite to be despoiled. But does this list of "external effects" justify subsidizing the national park system? If it does, I submit, then subsidy of almost any good or service imaginable would also be so justified, since effects like the above are present almost everywhere in the economy.

Let's look at automobiles, for example. When, a few years ago, a change in federal safety standards took the old Morgan off the market, I felt a definite sense of loss. I would even have sent money to a Save the Morgan fund but for the free rider problem. Do you think that sports car lovers were any less indignant about the Morgan than conservationists would be about Yosemite? Can you prove it? I could claim to be benefited by the fact that the availability of Fords increases my range of choice in cars, even though I have never owned one and probably never will. It certainly is true that production of Fords means the demand for Chevrolets is less than it otherwise would be, hence GM showrooms are less crowded and their prices are lower. I certainly benefit from the production of Ferraris and Maseratis

—don't remember ever seeing one on the street around here, but I have enjoyed looking at some really beautiful photographs. Do all these "external effects" mean that the federal government should subsidize automobile production?

Maybe the external benefits of national parks are quantitatively greater than those that arise from automobile production, organized baseball, or the production of women's clothing. Maybe the external damages of national parks to those who want cheap electricity or cheap lumber, those who enjoy watching movies of lumberjacks and reading stories about miners, and so forth are quantitatively very small. But the burden of quantitative proof lies with the conservationists, and in the absence of such proof no subsidies are justified.

Another form of the organizational argument in favor of national parks is more quickly dealt with. It is sometimes said that conservation groups would be unable to buy the parks because of the sheer organizational difficulty of collecting the money. This objection, I think, is based on the misconception that money would have to be collected door to door in advance of purchase, like American Cancer Society contributions. That is not the case. A group which wanted to buy land for a park would be able to borrow the money from a bank, issue stock or float bonds, guaranteeing repayment out of the fees paid by future visitors. What if this stream of future fees were insufficient to pay back the loan? What would be the justification for the park in the first place if only a few would be willing to pay to use it?

I will concede a point to the organizational argument—that at the moment commercial interests do have more ready cash. If all the parks went up for auction tomorrow, the conservationists would be able to bid on very few of them. Consequently, I recommend that the auctioning be done gradually over a period of years, with some of the smaller, less-valuable pieces sold first, to give conservation groups a fair chance to learn the principles of business organization in which commercial interests are already well versed.

Although the public good, irreversibility, and organizational arguments are the conservationists' big guns, there are a number of subsidiary arguments. I will try to deal with these as quickly as possible.

The intergenerational argument states that the wilderness we have now is all we will ever have, so we must pass it on to our children. One generation cannot bind another. We do not have the moral right to deprive our descendants of that which the earth has in limited supply.

This argument would seem to add nothing to the ones already listed. It is in part a variant of the irreversibility doctrine, although that doctrine is even less valid with respect to future generations than to the present. Our sufficiently remote descendants could have, say, all the magnificent groves of four hundred-foot redwoods which we could wish for them, if we just take the trouble to set out the seedlings today. If the wilderness we pass on to our children will be as important to them as to us or even *more* important (something which certainly seems reasonable, given the high income elasticity of demand for outdoor recreation), then they will flock to the parks in more than sufficient numbers with admission fees which will pay the interest on the bonds floated today to reserve those areas for them tomorrow.

Perhaps the most disingenuous argument of all made in favor of our current system of subsidizing national parks out of tax revenue is that this system benefits the poor, who would be excluded by the high fees necessary to cover full costs. The cogency of this argument is seriously weakened by studies which show low-income families to be strongly underrepresented among users of the parks. Far from benefiting the poor, the subsidy to these parks takes taxes collected from the poor, competes in the federal budgetary process with other programs designed to aid the poor directly, and uses the money to pay for playgrounds primarily for the well-to-do! As a poverty program the national parks are about on a par with the notorious agricultural subsidies.

. . . If you want to help the poor give them spendable cash grants through a negative income tax, or guaranteed annual income, or whatever you want to call it. Then, if these disadvantaged individuals consider that their first priority is to enjoy the great out-of-doors, they will spend their grants on park admission tickets. If, on the other hand, they consider it more important to buy shoes, good food, a decent apartment—or for that matter, beer, cigarettes, or a new color TV—why should anyone else impose other values on them?

A similar argument dispatches the conservationist defense based on the value of wilderness to science. Not that this value isn't real enough, but if science is to be subsidized, the scientists also should be given unrestricted cash grants. They will spend some of this money on leasing special tracts from private park systems, some more on cyclotrons, test tubes, and secretarial help. Earmarked grants to science violate the equimarginal principle just as do earmarked grants to the poor. If your aim is to help science, why dictate to science the way in which the subsidy must be spent?

Last but not least let's deal with the old line about the spiritual and esthetic values of the wilderness on which you allegedly can't put a price tag. True, the wilderness does have spiritual value for a great many people. In the words of John Muir, founder of the Sierra Club and great prophet of the wilderness:

Climb the mountains and get their good tidings. Nature's peace will flow into you as sunshine flows into trees. The winds will blow their own freshness into you and the storms their energy, while the cares will drop off like autumn leaves.

But who says that spiritual values must be subsidized by the state; and who says they can't be valued in money? This country has, among its great founding principles, the separation of church and state, based on the belief that nothing is more destructive of spiritual values than putting them in the pay of politicians. Do our churches languish because they are financially on their own? No! Men and women everywhere, knowing the importance of spiritual values in their lives, translate these values into cash gifts. No compulsory fees are assessed, yet the free rider problem, so bothersome elsewhere, turns out to be a negligible barrier to the financing of religious organizations. Inspirational literature, books on philosophy and ethics, and spiritual music enjoy brisk sales and generate profits for their producers.

Anyone who claims he has spiritual and esthetic values and won't put his money where his mouth is is putting you on. Anyone who puts his hand in someone else's pocket—someone else who may prefer to get his spiritual experience from Bach or Michelangelo or Elijah Muhammad—to finance his spiritual uplift is so short on ethics and morality that I would be willing to subsidize a journey for him to a very remote part of the wilderness indeed!

A POSITIVE PROGRAM FOR PRESERVING THE WILDERNESS

At the beginning of this chapter I said that I place a very high value on the wilderness experience. This, plus a few simple principles of economics and demography, make me optimistic about the possibilities for preserving the wilderness, provided conservationists develop the will to stand on their own two feet on this issue instead of kneeling in the halls of Congress with their hands out. Here is my four-point program:

1. Absolute top priority goes to the task of getting the government out of the business of *destroying* the wilderness. The government and its administrative alter egos are wilderness enemy number one—the highway departments, which openly refuse to include scenic values in their cost benefit calculations, but add ridiculously high estimates for equally "intangible" benefits such as the increased comfort of motorists; the Army Corps of Engineers, with their absurd idea of cost-benefit analysis which counts both costs and benefits as benefits;[1] the Department of Agriculture, which promotes the use of deadly and persistent pesticides and fertilizers to line the pockets of the already oversubsidized farm interests; the AEC, which builds, at the

---

1 Read the literature on the Alaska Ramparts Dam. It will cost a billion and a quarter dollars. The promoters list this as the first benefit, that is, a billion dollars worth of jobs and payroll for the state. Then they add to this the output of electricity as a second benefit! On top of that, they refuse to deduct as a cost the value of the wildlife destroyed, and they make their calculations on the basis of a phony below-market rate of interest [see Paul Brooks, "The Plot to Drown Alaska," *The Atlantic Monthly,* May 1965].

taxpayers' expense, commercially unwarranted "experimental" power stations that release deadly isotopes into the air and pollute our rivers with thermal energy, and which even threatens such horrors as lowering the passes through the Sierras with atom blasts! Then how about the role of government in putting tariffs and quotas on oil, wood products, leather products, meat products, and so forth, thus insuring that the destruction engendered by the production of these items will occur within our own borders rather than abroad? Or how about all the assorted legislators, administrators, and bureaucrats who are in the pocket of offshore drillers, strip miners, sawlog foresters, grazers, prospectors, and dam builders? Next to this incredible list of destructive activities—all of which are financed through the taxes of the same conservationists whose interests they trample upon—the ruination which could be wreaked by private industry unaided pales in comparison. Fortunately, conservation groups are already hard at work on this first-priority assignment.

2. The next part of the plan is of almost equal priority—get the government out of the business of *protecting* the wilderness. As was already emphasized in the discussion of irreversibility, when the last shreds of the most beautiful scenery in the world are at stake, conservationists should want the decision-making powers firmly in their own grip and not in the fickle hands of any committee or agency in Washington. Only when the wilderness belongs to the conservationists will it be safe.

3. In order to be ready to take over when objectives 1 and 2 have been accomplished, the third high-priority task is to begin a crash program to convert the wilderness passion which spills forth so freely as a stream of words into an equally abundant stream of dollars. Money talks, and conservationists, unless they are just play acting when they say how much they value their parks, have tremendous potential resources to tap. I am not a specialist in these matters, but I can offer some common-sense suggestions as illustrations of what is possible.

Most important, put an immediate end to queuing as a means of rationing space in recreational facilities which are already overcrowded. When a definite level of capacity can be defined—and this applies to most campsites, for example—charge admission fees high enough to limit applications to available space. This means varying the rate over the course of the season. I can imagine certain key spots where a campground might be filled on Labor Day or the Fourth of July with each camper gladly putting up $100.00. (After all, people already pay prices like this for scalped tickets to the World Series or the Superbowl.) The less wealthy or enthusiastic, and those fortunates who have a more flexible work schedule, will be able to gain admission to the sites for much lower fees on week-days and in off-peak seasons. Waiting in line represents the least efficient, least just, and most easily corrupted form of rationing ever devised. It could be eliminated even while the parks are still government-owned, if conservationists would only have the honesty to tell the park administrators that they are ready to pay their own way and stop trying to take a free ride.

A second useful financial mechanism is the practice of "excess taking," frequently used in New England to finance such establishments as ski slopes. If you want 1000 acres to build a ski run, you buy that 1000 acres *and* the adjoining 1000 acres. As soon as the facility is built, the surrounding land is sold off at several times its purchase price as homesites and commercial properties to those who are attracted to the area by the available recreation. Conservationists have spent much time fulminating against speculators and developers, yet isn't it obvious that wherever a park is built, land values will inevitably go up and speculative profits will be made? So why not get a piece of the action and put these profits to work in a good cause?

The prospects for raising money by both of these methods are greatly enhanced by what might be called Udall's laws after the former Secretary of the Interior who attached great importance to them. Udall's first law: The available open land per capita decreases more than in proportion to the increase in population. (Take 4000 open acres, 1000 people, 1000 residential and commercial acres, 4 open acres per person. Double the population, develop another 1000 acres for commercial and residential use, and you are left with 2000 people and 3000 open acres, 1½ acres per person.) Udall's second law: The demand for outdoor recreation increases faster than in proportion to the increase of GNP per capita.

Take these two laws together and it may be true, for example, that a doubling of the population of an area could increase the demand for outdoor recreation by a factor of nine or ten! Translated into dollars and cents, Udall's laws mean that you are never going to have to worry about demand for your product or how to pay off those wilderness development bonds.

There is also much money to be raised by such methods as conservation window stickers and private philanthropy. By the time the parks go up for auction, the money could be there to buy them, *if* plans are laid now.

4. The fourth point of the program is to get the conservationists down out of the rarefied air of the high Sierras and develop in them a realistic attitude toward outdoor recreation areas of the nonvirgin, nonwilderness variety. As a Secretary of the Interior once put it, the whole question of recreation is analogous to a flood control project. If you let all the masses of people flow into the parks in an uncontrolled fashion, then a great deal of damage will be done. But if upstream, along the watersheds of the cities and highways, you install control works, diversions, overflow areas, holding reservoirs, and so forth, then the flood can be controlled when it reaches true wilderness areas.

Such a program means buying low-grade, unspectacular, logged-over, or cropped-over areas, especially in the Eastern and Midwestern sections of the country, and restoring them to provide maximum recreational potential. Low-grade wilderness surrogates like these, if properly located and properly developed and managed, can protect the remaining virgin wilderness in two ways, both by the flood control function already mentioned and by producing revenue which can be used to maintain the low-use, high-grade havens of the purists elsewhere.

D. Economics of income distribution and poverty

Are the rich becoming richer and the poor poorer in the United States? Is income inequality a necessary condition for American style capitalism to operate? Who are the poor and why are they poor? What has happened to the distribution of income in recent years, and how has the tax system modified it? What policy alternatives do we have for resolving income inequalities?

The following three readings address themselves to these issues from differing perspectives. From a Marxist's perspective, Weisskopf argues that inequality under capitalism is no mere historical accident; rather, "a significant degree of income inequality is functionally essential to the capitalist mode of production." Furthermore, he argues that there are "dynamic forces at work in a capitalist system that tend to perpetuate if not to exacerbate the degree of income inequality over time."

Lampman, on the other hand, argues that significant income equalization has taken place in the United States during the past 40 years. Nevertheless, poverty still exists in our country. Three basic causal categories of poverty are described along with alternative approaches for their reduction —social barriers of caste, class, and custom; limited ability or motivations; and events external to individuals such as age, death, disability, and family dissolution.

In the third paper, Pechman reviews the most recent data concerning income distribution in the United States and examines how the current tax system affects it. He concludes that many features of our federal, state, and local tax structures are surprisingly regressive, imposing a heavier effective tax rate on the poor than on higher income groups. A number of recommendations are offered toward "reforming the national tax system" to correct these regressive features.

20 Capitalism and inequality*

THOMAS E. WEISSKOPF

The rise of capitalism has engendered a tremendous increase in the productive capacity of the capitalist economies of North America, Western Europe, Japan, Australia, and New Zealand. Yet this tremendous growth in the forces of production has been accompanied by vast inequalities in the distribution of the fruits of that production. The disparity in income and wealth between the industrialized nations at the center of the world capitalist system and the underdeveloped areas on the periphery has been increasing continuously since the early days of colonial plunder. Moreover, *within* each capitalist nation tremendous fortunes coexist with indescribable poverty in spite of the growth of the modern "welfare state."

Capitalism has historically always been characterized by great inequalities in the distribution of income and wealth. I shall argue in this essay that inequality under capitalism is no mere historical accident; rather, a significant degree of income inequality is functionally essential to the capitalist mode of production. Furthermore, I shall argue that there are dynamic forces at work in a capitalist system that tend to perpetuate if not to exacerbate the degree of income inequality over time.

Income *inequality* must be distinguished conceptually from income *immobility*. The existence of a hierarchy of income levels at any one point in time need not imply that the same families continue to occupy the same position in the hierarchy from one generation to the next. In principle, a high degree of income inequality in a society could be accompanied by a high degree of intergenerational income mobility, such that opportunities to receive income were equalized for all children irrespective of family background. However, I shall argue that a capitalist society is necessarily characterized not only by a substantial degree of income inequality but

* From "Capitalism and Inequality," *The Capitalist System: A Radical Analysis of American Society,* written and edited by Richard C. Edwards, Michael Reich, and Thomas E. Weisskopf, © 1972, pp. 125–33. Reprinted by permission of Prentice-Hall, Inc., Englewood Cliffs, N.J. Thomas E. Weisskopf is Associate Professor of Economics at the University of Michigan, Ann Arbor, Mich.

also by considerable income immobility, for much of the income inequality in one generation is passed directly on to the next generation.

I will discuss the fundamental characteristics of the process of income distribution under capitalism and argue that income inequality is functionally essential to the capitalist mode of porduction. The argument abstracts from historical and political forces in order to concentrate on the *institutional* contraints on income distribution imposed by the capitalist system. Then I will turn to the dynamics of income distribution and argue that there are strong forces inherent in a capitalist system that tend to prevent the reduction of income inequality over time from any initial historically determined level. Some of these same forces in turn limit mobility between income classes and thereby perpetuate income inequality from one generation to the next. Finally I provide a brief summary of the conclusions to be drawn from the analysis of the proceding sections.

THE NECESSITY OF INCOME INEQUALITY

The most fundamental characteristic of the distribution of income under capitalism is that it is tied directly to the production process. The ethical principle used to justify the capitalist method of distributing income is "to each according to what he and the instruments he owns produces." Thus under the capitalist mode of production the only legitimate claim to income arises from the possession of one's own labor-power and from the ownership of physical means of production.

Each individual receives income in the form of payments for the use of his "factors of production"—the labor-power and the physical means of production that he owns. The amount of these payments depends upon how "valuable" his factors are in the production process, i.e., how much they contribute to the market value of production. The income received by any individual thus depends both on the quantity of the factors of production he owns and on the price which these factors command in the market. Inequalities in income can result either from unequal ownership of factors of production or from unequal prices paid for those factors.

For the purposes of this analysis, I shall distinguish only the two basic factors of production: labor-power and capital. Labor-power includes all of the productive attributes of individuals, from the most elementary manual capacity to the most highly valued personality characteristics and managerial and technical skills. Capital includes all physical means of production: land, natural resources, buildings, plant, and equipment. Capital is thus defined to include all forms of productive property, but to exclude such possessions as residential housing, automobiles, etc., insofar as they are owned only for personal use.

Income from labor-power and income from capital together account for the overall income of any individual. I shall show that income from each of these sources is necessarily unequally distributed in a capitalist society in such a way as to result in overall income inequality.

In the advanced capitalist nations, labor income typically accounts for about three-quarters and property (capital) income for about one-quarter of total national income. The distribution of capital ownership in a capitalist society is necessarily unequal, for if every individual shared equally in the ownership of capital, the fundamental distinction between capitalist and worker would vanish. Each individual would be equally capable of controlling the production process, and no individual would be compelled to relinquish control over his or her labor-power to someone else. But the operation of a capitalist economy is predicated upon the existence of a labor market in which workers are obliged to exchange control over their labor-power in return for wages and salaries. If this obligation were removed, there would no longer be any basis for control of the production process by a limited class of capitalists. Hence equality of capital ownership is incompatible with some of the basic institutions of the capitalist mode of production itself.

If *income* from capital could be separated from *ownership* of capital, the inequality in the latter would not necessarily imply inequality in the former. But to divorce the two would be contrary to the basic capitalist principle that an individual is entitled to income from property as well as from labor. Thus the necessity of unequal income from capital in a capitalist society follows directly from the functional necessity of unequal capital ownership.

The capitalist mode of production likewise requires that the possession of labor-power and the earnings from labor income be distributed highly unequally among workers. For if the labor market is to operate efficiently in developing and allocating labor throughout an economy, there must be a significant degree of inequality in labor earnings. Since workers under capitalism relinquish most control over the process or product of their work, they are not likely to acquire and develop productive attributes for their own sake nor to be motivated to work by intrinsic aspects of the work process. So long as work itself is perceived as a burden to be endured rather than a creative endeavor, workers must be motivated to increase their labor-power and to work hard by extrinsic rewards such as income with which they can purchase material goods and services.

In principle, nonmonetary status rewards could substitute for income rewards and provide an extrinsic psychic rather than material motivation for work. But the *homo economicus* of capitalist society is socialized to value quantitative and "objective" monetary success much more highly than qualitative and "subjective" status achievement. Hence status rewards unrelated to monetary success cannot be expected to play a significant motivational role under capitalism. Instead, material gain incentives are generally necessary to encourage the development of productive attributes and to call forth the energies of workers who do not control the work process.

The productivity of a worker depends on certain relevant personality characteristics, on manual skills, and on certain cognitive skills; the required mix of these types of productive attributes depends upon the nature of the job. The development of these attributes depends to a significant degree on family background and socialization, but later education and job training can also have an impact, especially on the acquisition of cognitive skills. Under the circumstances described above, individuals will be motivated to acquire needed skills through education and job training mainly insofar as this leads to the prospect of higher incomes. Similarly, workers are likely to apply themselves more productively and energetically on the job only insofar as this qualifies them for bonus pay or for promotions to higher-paying positions. In order for this incentive system to operate effectively, it is essential to maintain a hierarchy based upon the differential possession of labor-power and the corresponding differential receipt of labor earnings.

The argument of the preceding paragraphs is not intended to suggest that *no* work would be done in a capitalist society in the absence of significant income differentials. The point is rather that the capitalist mode of production is characterized by a serious conflict between income equality on the one hand and economic efficiency and growth on the other. A high degree of income equality could be attained in a capitalist society only at a very high cost in productive efficiency. In order to remain economically viable, the capitalist mode of production therefore requires significant inequalities in the distribution of labor income.

The inequalities in income from capital and income from labor-power combine to generate an unequal distribution of overall income. In order for the labor market to function effectively, most workers must have little or no capital and correspondingly low capital incomes. The necessary differentials in the labor incomes of workers will therefore be reflected in corresponding inequalities in overall incomes. On the other hand, the necessary concentration of capital ownership will result in inequalities of capital income that are not offset by any contrary inequalities in labor income. Thus it can be concluded that overall income inequality is indeed functionally essential to the capitalist mode of production. No amount of political intervention short of a complete transformation of the mode of production could eliminate income inequality under capitalism.

THE DYNAMICS OF INCOME INEQUALITY

I have argued that a certain degree of income inequality is inherent in any capitalist society. But the actual extent of this income inequality may well be greater than would be strictly essential to the capitalist mode

of production. Current inequality in capitalist societies is in part the result of a historical legacy, but it is also attributable to dynamic forces
operating within the process of capitalist growth itself. To analyze the
impact of capitalist growth on income distribution, it is useful to examine first how the supply of factors of production owned by an individual is determined and how that supply can be increased over time.
This requires a study of the *inheritance* and the *accumulation* of factors of
production. Such a study in turn will shed light on the question of income
mobility under capitalism, for income mobility depends upon the extent
of intergenerational transmission of income-earning opportunities through
the process of inheritance.

The amount of capital that a person owns depends on how much he
inherits from his parents and how much he accumulates himself. Since
there is no limit to the amount of capital one person can own, capital can
be amassed into vast fortunes. The ownership of capital in all capitalist
societies is in fact highly unequal. I shall argue in this section that the
process of capital accumulation within a generation tends to increase the
concentration of capital ownership, while the process of capital inheritance
from one generation to the next fails to arrest this tendency.

Capital is accumulated by an individual when he saves—refrains from
consuming—a part of his income and invests these savings in the purchase
of new capital to add to his existing stock. The ability to increase one's
capital ownership thus depends upon how much surplus income one receives in excess of basic consumption needs. The higher one's overall income, the greater is the surplus available for investment and hence the
greater is the opportunity for capital accumulation. Since basic consumption needs do not vary as greatly as overall income, the distribution of
surplus income among households is necessarily far more unequal than the
distribution of overall incomes. Large owners of capital are clearly favored
over small owners because they receive correspondingly greater incomes
from their capital. Their advantage is due both to the greater size of their
holdings and to the fact that they tend to get higher rates of profit on
their capital because of better access to relevant information and to profitable opportunities. As a result, large holders tend to save and invest much
more than small holders of capital, and inequalities in capital ownership
are thus likely to increase over time.

Since capital consists of material objects (or titles thereto), the inequalities of capital ownership that exist in one generation can be passed directly
on to the next. Whether the process of inheritance tends to increase or
decrease the dispersion of property ownership depends upon the extent of
selective mating and on the relative reproduction rates of the rich and the
poor. So long as the wealthy marry among themselves and the poor do
likewise, the existing degree of inequality in property ownership is perpetuated. To the extent that the wealthy tend to have fewer heirs than the

poor, the inequality is actually increased. On the other hand, anything short of a perfect match of wealth between husband and wife tends to reduce the disparities of ownership in the next generation. On balance, it appears that the process of inheritance in a capitalist society is unlikely to increase or decrease significantly the degree of inequality of capital ownership over time.

It emerges quite clearly from the preceding discussion, however, that inheritance contributes heavily to intergenerational immobility in capital ownership. Perfect mobility would require that each individual have an equal opportunity to accumulate capital. Obviously, differential inheritance of capital transmits much of the inequality of capital ownership from one generation to the next. So long as property can be transferred readily from parents to children through family inheritance, the children of large holders will enjoy great privileges relative to the children of small holders. Only a drastic curtailment or abolition of the rights of inheritance could prevent the transmission of inequalities in capital ownership from one generation to the next. Yet to interfere seriously with inheritance rights would be incompatible with the capitalist mode of production because it would undermine the fundamental capitalist institutions of private property and the legal relations of ownership. As Milton Friedman has appropriately pointed out, "it seems illogical to say that a man is entitled . . . to the produce of the wealth he has accumulated, but that he is not entitled to pass any wealth on to his children."

Like capital, the amount of labor-power that an individual possesses depends both on how much he inherits from his parents and on how much he accumulates himself. But the processes of inheritance and accumulation take on rather different forms in the case of labor-power. As noted earlier, marketable labor-power involves several kinds of productive attributes of an individual: personality characteristics, manual skills and cognitive skills. These attributes are acquired in part at birth (through biological inheritance), in part during early childhood (through family socialization), in part during school age (through the educational system), and in part on the job (through job training, experience, etc.). Labor-power can be inherited —directly or indirectly—at birth and in the process of family socialization; and it can be accumulated—to some extent—through education and job training.

The accumulation of labor-power during an individual's lifetime through investment in education and training is in many respects similar to the accumulation of capital through investment in productive property. The process whereby labor-power is accumulated is also likely to be disequalizing because those individuals with the greatest initial advantages— e.g., personality characteristics or cognitive abilities inherited at birth or developed through the family socialization process—are likely to be the best able to acquire even more. Tracking systems in high schools, competitive admissions procedures in colleges and universities, and the overall emphasis on promoting the "highest achievers" in educational institutions contribute to highly unequal educational opportunities. Such inequalities are further reinforced by the interaction of the possession of labor-power with monetary wealth. Parents who earn substantial labor incomes can use some of their money to invest in a longer and better education for their children than the children of the poor, thereby contributing further to the differential acquisition of productive attributes by the next generation.

There is only one major constraint on the accumulation of labor-power that does not apply to capital. This constraint is due to the embodiment of productive attributes in individual human beings and the fact that every individual life is finite. In order for the accumulation of labor-power to "pay off," an individual must work during part of his life. This means that the time during which he can profitably acquire productive attributes is limited, and hence the extent to which labor-power will be accumulated by any one individual is also limited. Because of this constraint, inequalities of labor-power are unlikely to become as vast as inequalities of capital ownership, and the forces tending toward an increase in the degree of inequality over time are less powerful in the case of labor-power than capital ownership.

The extent to which the inheritance of labor-power accentuates and/or perpetuates inequalities over time depends primarily on the degree of selective mating in a society and to a lesser extent on differential rates of reproduction. Unlike property, which is precisely defined in quantity and must be divided among heirs, personality characteristics and cognitive skills are diffused in a more general way through biological inheritance and the family environment. The greater the tendency of men and women of the same social class to intermarry, the more disequalizing is the inheritance of labor-power. There are clearly very powerful social forces that favor marriage among relative equals in social and educational background, most notably educational channeling and class segregation of neighborhoods. Whether or not this effect is strong enough actually to exacerbate the degree of inequality over time, it is clearly a powerful force working to perpetuate the existing hierarchy of labor-power from one generation to the next.

Having considered separately the patterns of accumulation of the two basic factors of production within and between generations, it remains to examine their interaction to determine their overall impact on the time trend of income inequality and the extent of income immobility under capitalism. Whether increasing inequality in the distribution of labor-power and of capital leads also to increasing inequality in overall income depends upon (1) the extent to which the ownership of labor-power is correlated among individuals with the ownership of capital, and (2) the extent to which the relative shares of labor and capital in overall incomes change over time. Finally, it is important also to examine the impact of technological change on the overall distribution of income in a capitalist society.

The more highly correlated is the ownership of labor-power and capital, the more surely does the perpetuation of inequality in each contribute to the perpetuation of inequality in overall income. In fact, the ownership of and earnings from each of the two sources tend naturally to be associated with one another. People with high incomes from their labor-power are better able to save and to acquire income-yielding capital than are people with low labor incomes. And people with high incomes from their capital ownership are better able to purchase the educational services that can help to increase their marketable labor-power than are people with little capital income. Thus there is a significant degree of correlation of ownership of labor-power and capital that contributes to the existence and perpetuation of an unequal distribution of total incomes among individuals or family units.

Even if the degree of inequality in both labor and capital incomes were increasing over time, and if the two were perfectly correlated among individuals, there still *might not* be an increase in the degree of overall income inequality. This would be the case if the percentage share of total income represented by income from the more unequally distributed factor were diminishing over time. Income from capital is typically much more unequally distributed than income from labor. If the inequality in both types of income is increasing, but if an ever larger share of income represents returns to labor rather than to capital, then the increasing significance of labor incomes could result in a decline in the degree of inequality in overall income. There is, in fact, some evidence of a long-run increase in the share of labor income in the rich capitalist nations. This increase probably reflects the decline in importance of independent proprietors and the growth of the white-collar working class; more people now rely on the sale of their labor-power as their main source of income. The apparent rise in the share of labor income has a dampening effect on tendencies toward increased income inequality over time.

Thus far we have proceeded with the simplifying assumption that all income could be attributed directly to the ownership of factors of production. But the growth of an economy derives not only from the accumulation of factors of production but also through technological changes in the productive process that arise out of the development of new products and new methods of production. Such changes generate income that is received ultimately in the form of higher capital or labor incomes by the individuals involved, but the income really represents a return to technological innovation or entrepreneurial initiative.

Inequalities arising from and perpetuated by the differential ownership of labor-power and capital tend to be exacerbated by the impact of technological changes in a capitalist economy. It is generally those who own capital and/or control the work process who are best able to introduce new technologies and new products and thereby to reap the initial and very important monetary gains associated with their introduction. Likewise, it is the highly educated groups in society who are best able to adapt themselves to the new requirements of technical change and to seek out the most remunerative outlets for their labor. And, conversely, it is the least educated who are the least mobile geographically and occupationally, and therefore the least able to protect themselves by adapting to rapid technical and economic change.

CONCLUSION

In summary, there are important dynamic forces at work in the process of capitalist growth that tend to accentuate the degree of overall income inequality over time. There are also forces working in the opposite direction, whose strength will vary with the historical context. One cannot therefore predict that a capitalist society will necessarily always tend towards greater income inequality over time. One can say, however, that there are very serious constraints on the reduction of existing income inequality in a capitalist society.

Some of the constraints which inhibit the reduction of income inequality under capitalism act as formidable barriers to intergenerational income mobility. The inheritance of capital ownership and of labor-power precludes equality of income-earning opportunity and assures that the hierarchy of income inequality will be transmitted to a significant degree from one generation to the next. Intergenerational income immobility remains an inherent characteristic of a capitalist society no matter what the precise trend in the degree of income inequality over time.

Although equality of income and equality of opportunity to earn income (income mobility) cannot be achieved in a capitalist society, some of the pressures for further inequality and further immobility might in principle be countered by deliberate state interference with the natural processes involved. For example, the state could redistribute income by taxing the rich much more than the poor; it could redistribute capital by levying high inheritance taxes; it could redistribute labor-power by providing for compensatory education, etc. Whether such actions are in fact undertaken depends upon the forces that act upon the state—the direct influence of the most powerful groups in the society, the indirect influence of the prevailing ideology, and the pressures exerted by the poor and the weak. In most capitalist societies, the evidence suggests that relatively little redistribution has in fact been achieved by state action. And it remains fundamentally true that a significant degree of inequality and immobility is functionally essential to the institutions of a capitalist society. No amount of political intervention short of a complete transformation of these institutions—i.e., a change in the mode of production—could eradicate such inequalities under capitalism.

21 Approaches to the reduction of poverty*

ROBERT J. LAMPMAN

The greatest accomplishment of modern economies has been the raising of living standards of the common man and the reduction of the share of the population in poverty. Contrary to the gloomy predictions of Malthus, production has increased faster than population and, unlike the expectations of Marx, inequality of income has not steadily increased. The growth in value of product per person is generally understood to arise out of more capital, economies of scale and specialization, better management and organization, innovation with regard both to end products and techniques of production, greater mobility of factors, and improved quality of labor. All of these in turn yield additional income which, in a benign spiral, makes possible more and higher quality inputs for further growth.

The process of growth has not meant simply higher property incomes. As a matter of fact, income from property has fallen as a share of national income. Neither has growth meant a widening of differential for skill in labor incomes. Rates of pay for the most menial of tasks have tended to rise with average productivity. Social policies in fields such as labor and education aimed at assuring opportunities for all have narrowed initial advantages of the more fortunate. Such policies, along with taxation, social insurance, and public assistance measures which redistribute income toward the poor have tended to stabilize if not reduce the degree of the income inequality.

A growth in productivity of 2 percent per person per year and a relatively fixed pattern of income inequality probably have combined to yield a net reduction in poverty in most decades of American history. However, the rate of reduction has undoubtedly varied with changes in the growth

* From "Approaches to the Reduction of Poverty," *American Economic Review*, 55 (May 1963), pp. 521–29. Copyright American Economic Association, 1963. Reprinted with permission of publisher and author. Robert J. Lampman is Professor of Economics at the University of Wisconsin, Madison, Wis.

rate, shifts from prosperity to depression, changes in immigration, in age composition, and in differential family size by income level.

The poverty rate and the poverty income gap.   Using a present-day standard for poverty and even without recognizing the relativity of poverty over long periods, we would estimate that poverty had become a condition that afflicted only a minority of Americans by the second decade of this century. This situation was upset by the Great Depression of the 1930s but later restored by the booming economy of World War II. The postwar period has yielded a somewhat above average rate of growth in productivity and a reduction in poverty which probably is at least average for recent decades. The number of families in poverty (as marked off from non-poverty by a $3,000 income at 1962 prices) fell from 12 million in 1947 to 9 million in 1963. This was a drop from 32 percent to 19 percent of families.

The rate of reduction one records or predicts will vary somewhat with the definition of poverty which he adopts. The Council of Economic Advisers adopted an income cut-off of $3,000 of total money income for families and $1,500 for unrelated individuals. It is not inconsistent with those guidelines to make further modification for family size, using $3,000 as the mark for an urban family of four persons with variations of $500 per person and to set a lower mark for rural families. Such a procedure yields a slightly lower rate of reduction in the percentage of all persons in poverty than is suggested by the 32- to 19-percent drop shown above. This discrepancy is due to a shift in family size and the rural to urban migration during the postwar years.

It is possible that consideration of personal income as opposed to total money income, of average rather than one year's income, of assets and extraordinary needs as well as income, and of related matters would alter our understanding of how poverty has been reduced. It is clear that some of these considerations affect the number and the composition of the population counted as poor; and it is obvious that the rate of reduction would vary if we varied the poverty line over time.

These matters of definition are important to a refinement of the generalized goal of elimination of poverty to which President Johnson has called us. Economists can assist in reaching a national consensus on the specific nature of the goal, of ways to measure the distance from and rate of movement toward the goal.

At this point in time, poverty is clearly a condition which afflicts only a minority—a dwindling minority—of Americans. The recent average rate of change, namely, a fall in the percentage of families in poverty by one percentage point per year, suggests that the poverty problem is about twenty years from solution. This rate of reduction may be difficult to maintain as we get down to a hard core of poverty and a situation in which further growth will not contribute to the reduction of the poverty rate.

My own view is that this rate is still highly responsive to changes in the growth rate and that it will continue to be so for some time ahead. The relationship between the two rates is a complex one and is influenced by such things as demographic change, changes in labor force participation, occupational shifts in demands for labor, and derived changes in property incomes and social security benefits. Some groups—notably the aged, the disabled, and the broken families—have poverty rates that appear to be relatively immune to growth in average income. One powerful drag on the responsiveness of the poverty rate to growth, which has now about run its course and will shortly reverse, is the aging and reduction in labor force participation of family heads.

While the size of the poverty population is dwindling, the size of what can be called the "poverty income gap" is diminishing. This gap—the aggregate amount by which the present poor population's income falls short of $3,000 per family or $1,500 per unrelated individual—is now about $12 billion, or 2 percent of GNP. As time goes on this gap will assuredly be less, both because of economic growth and because of scheduled increases in social insurance benefits. (Transfers now make up about $10 billion of the $25 billion income of the poor.) Projecting recent rates of change suggests that by 1975 the poor will be no more than 12 percent of the population and the poverty income gap will be as little as 1 percent of that year's GNP.

As I see it, the goal of eliminating poverty needs to have a time dimension and intermediate targets. I assume we want a rate of progress at least as fast as that of recent years. Further, it helps to think of the goal in two parts: the reduction of the poverty rate and the reduction of the poverty income gap. This means we want to work from the top down and from the bottom up, so to speak. The aim of policy should be to do each type of reduction without slowing the other and to do both with the least possible sacrifice of and the greatest possible contribution to other important goals.

Why poverty persists.   As background to such strategic decisions, it is useful to categorize the causes of poverty in today's economy. But perhaps it is necessary first to brush aside the idea that there has to be some given amount of poverty. Most economists have long since given up the idea that a progressive society needs the threat of poverty to induce work and sobriety in the lower classes. Similarly, one can consign to folklore the ideas that some are rich only because others are poor and exploited, that if none were poor then necessary but unpleasant jobs would go undone, that the middle class has a psychological need to exclude a minority from above-poverty living standards, and that poverty is a necessary concomitant of the unemployment which necessarily accompanies economic growth.

Why, then, is it that there remains a minority of persons who are involuntarily poor in this affluent society? How does our system select the particular members for this minority? To the latter question we offer a three-part answer: (1) Events external to individuals select a number to be poor. (2) Social barriers of caste, class, and custom denominate persons with certain characteristics to run a high risk of being poor. (3) The market assigns a high risk of being poor to those with limited ability or motivations.

One cannot look at the data on who are the poor without sensing that many are poor because of events beyond their control. Over a third of the 35 million poor are children whose misfortune arises out of the chance assignment to poor parents. In some cases this poverty comes out of being members of unusually large families. Among the poor adults, about a third have either suffered a disability, premature death of the family breadwinner, or family dissolution. A considerable number have confronted a declining demand for services in their chosen occupation, industry, or place of residence. Some have outlived their savings or have lost them due to inflation or bank failure. For many persons who are otherwise "normal" poverty may be said to arise out of one or a combination of such happenings.

A second factor that operates in the selection of persons to be poor is the maintenance of social barriers in the form of caste, class, and custom. The clearest example of this, of course, is racial discrimination with regard to opportunities to qualify for and to obtain work. (It is perhaps worth emphasizing here that only a fifth of the present poor are nonwhite, and that only a minority of the nonwhites are presently poor.) Similar types of arbitrary barriers or market imperfections are observable in the case of sex, age, residence, religion, education, and seniority. They are formalized in employer hiring procedures, in the rules of unions and professional and trade associations, in governmental regulations concerning housing and welfare and other programs, and are informally expressed in customer preferences. Barriers, once established, tend to be reinforced from the poverty side by the alienated themselves. The poor tend to be cut off from not only opportunity but even from information about opportunity. A poverty subculture develops which sustains attitudes and values that are hostile to escape from poverty. These barriers combine to make events nonrandom; e.g., unemployment is slanted away from those inside the feudalistic walls of collective bargaining, disability more commonly occurs in jobs reserved for those outside the barriers, the subculture of poverty invites or is prone to self-realizing forecasts of disaster.

The third factor involved in selecting persons out of the affluent society to be poor is limited ability or motivation of persons to earn and to protect themselves against events and to fight their way over the barriers. To the extent that the market is perfect one can rationalize the selection for poverty (insofar as earnings alone are considered) on the basis of the abilities and skills needed by the market and the distribution of those abilities and skills in the population. But we note that ability is to some extent acquired or environmentally determined and that poverty tends to create personalities who will be de-selected by the market as inadequate on the basis of ability or motivation.

Countering "events." Approaches to the reduction of poverty can be seen as parallel to the causes or bases for selection recounted above. The first approach, then, is to prevent or counter the events or happenings which select some persons for poverty status. The poverty rate could be lessened by any reduction in early death, disability, family desertion, what John Kenneth Galbraith referred to as excessive procreation by the poor, or by containment of inflation and other hazards to financial security. Among the important events in this context the one most relevant to public policy consideration at this time is excessive unemployment. It would appear that if the recent level of over 5 percent unemployment could be reduced to 4 percent, the poverty rate would drop by about one percentage point. Further fall in the poverty rate would follow if—by retaining and relocation of some workers—long-term unemployment could be cut or if unemployment could be more widely shared with the nonpoor.

To the extent that events are beyond prevention, some, e.g., disability, can be countered by remedial measures. Where neither the preventive nor the remedial approach is suitable, only the alleviative measures of social insurance and public assistance remain. And the sufficiency of these measures will help determine the poverty rate and the size of the poverty income gap. It is interesting to note that our system of public income maintenance, which now pays out $35 billion in benefits per year, is aimed more at the problem of income insecurity of the middle class and at blocking returns to poverty than in facilitating exits from poverty for those who have never been out of poverty. The nonpoor have the major claim to social insurance benefits, the levels of which in most cases are not adequate in themselves to keep a family out of poverty. Assistance payments of $4 billion now go to 8 million persons, all of whom are in the ranks of the poor, but about half of the 35 million poor receive neither assistance nor social insurance payments. One important step in the campaign against poverty would be to reexamine our insurance and assistance programs to discover ways in which they could be more effective in helping people to get out of poverty. Among the ideas to be considered along this line are easier eligibility for benefits, higher minimum benefits, incentives to earn while receiving benefits, ways to combine work-relief, retraining, rehabilitation, and relocation with receipt of benefits.

Among the several events that select people for poverty, the ones about which we have done the least by social policy are family breakup by other than death and the event of being born poor. Both of these could be alleviated by a family allowance system, which the United States, almost alone among Western nations, lacks. We do, of course, have arrangements in the Federal individual income tax for personal deductions and exemptions whereby families of different size and composition are ranked for the imposition of progressive rates. However, it is a major irony of this system that it does not extend the full force of its allowances for children to the really poor. In order to do so, the tax system could be converted to have negative as well as positive rates, paying out grants as well as forgiving taxes on the basis of already adopted exemptions and rates. At present there are almost $20 billion of unused exemptions and deductions, most of which relate to families with children. Restricting the plan to such families and applying a negative tax rate of, say, 20 percent, to this amount would "yield" an allowance total of almost $4 billion. This would not in itself take many people out of poverty, but it would go a considerable distance toward closing the poverty income gap, which now aggregates about $12 billion.

It would, of course, be possible to go considerably further by this device without significantly impairing incentives to work and save. First, however, let me reject as unworkable any simple plan to assure a minimum income of $3,000. To make such an assurance would induce many now earning less than and even some earning slightly more than $3,000 to forego earnings opportunities and to accept the grant. Hence the poverty income gap of $12 billion would far understate the cost of such a minimum income plan. However, it would be practicable to enact a system of progressive rates articulated with the present income tax schedule. The present rates fall from 70 percent at the top to 14 percent at income just above $3,700 for a family of five, to zero percent for income below $3,700. The average negative tax rates could move, then, from zero percent to minus 14 percent for, say, the unused exemptions that total $500, to 20 percent for those that total $1,000 and 40 percent for those that total $3,700. This would amount to a minimum income of $1,480 for a family of five; it would retain positive incentives through a set of grants that would gradually diminish as earned income rose.

The total amount to be paid out (interestingly, this would be shown in the federal budget as a net reduction in tax collections) under such a program would obviously depend upon the particular rates selected, the definition of income used, the types of income-receiving units declared eligible, and the offsets made in public assistance payments. But it clearly could be more than the $4 billion mentioned in connection with the more limited plan of a standard 20 percent negative tax rate. At the outset it might involve half the poverty income gap and total about $6 billion. This amount is approximately equal to the total federal, state, and local taxes now paid by the poor. Hence it would amount to a remission of taxes paid. As the number in poverty fell, the amount paid out under this plan would in turn diminish.

Breaking down barriers.   The approaches discussed thus far are consistent with the view that poverty is the result of events which happen to people. But there are other approaches, including those aimed at removing barriers which keep people in poverty. Legislation and private, volunteer efforts to assure equal educational and employment opportunities can make a contribution in this direction. Efforts to randomize unemployment by area redevelopment and relocation can in some cases work to break down "islands of poverty." Public policy can prevent or modify the forming of a poverty subculture by city zoning laws, by public housing and by regulations of private housing, by school redistricting, by recreational, cultural, and public health programs. It is curious that medieval cities built walls to keep poverty outside. Present arrangements often work to bottle it up inside cities or parts of cities and thereby encourage poverty to function as its own cause.

Improving abilities and motivations. The third broad approach to accelerated reduction of poverty relates to the basis for selection referred to above as limited ability or motivation. The process of economic growth works the poverty line progressively deeper into the ranks of people who are below average in ability or motivation, but meantime it should be possible to raise the ability and motivation levels of the lowest. It is interesting that few children, even those of below average ability, who are not born and raised in poverty, actually end up in poverty as adults. This suggests that poverty is to some extent an inherited disease. But it also suggests that if poor children had the same opportunities, including preschool training and remedial health care, as the nonpoor (even assuming no great breakthroughs of scientific understanding), the rate of escape from poverty would be higher. Even more fundamentally, we know that mental retardation as well as infant mortality and morbidity have an important causal connection with inadequate prenatal care, which in turn relates to low income of parents.

A belief in the economic responsiveness of poor youngsters to improved educational opportunities underlies policies advocated by many educational theorists from Jeremy Bentham to James B. Conant. And this widely shared belief no doubt explains the emphasis which the Economic Opportunity Act places upon education and training. The appropriation under that Act, while it seems small relative to the poverty income gap, is large relative to present outlays for education of the poor. I would estimate that the half-billion dollars or so thereby added increases the national expenditure for this purpose by about one-seventh. To raise the level of educational expenditure for poor children—who are one-fifth of the nation's children but who consume about a tenth of educational outlay—to equal that of the average would cost in the neighborhood of $3 billion. Such an emphasis upon education and training is justified by the fact that families headed by young adults will tend, in a few years, to be the most rapidly increasing group of poor families.

22 The rich, the poor, and the taxes they pay*

JOSEPH A. PECHMAN

The distribution of income has always been a hotly debated subject. What-ever has happened or is happening to the distribution of income, some people will always assert that the rich are getting a bigger share of the pie than is "fair," while others will seek to show that this is not the case. Few people, however, bother to find out the facts and fewer still understand what they mean.

The same applies to the tax system. Everybody knows that there are loopholes in the federal tax laws, but few realize that there are loopholes for persons at all income levels. Even fewer have a clear idea about the effects on the distribution of income of closing the more controversial loop-holes. And only the experts know the state-local tax structure is in more urgent need of reform than the federal structure.

This article is intended to put these matters in perspective by sum-marizing the available information. What has happened to the distribution of income before taxes in recent years, and how has the tax system modified it? What's wrong with the national tax system? What reforms are needed to make it a fairer system? What are the chances of getting these reforms? And, beyond such reforms, what would be the shape of a tax distribution that most Americans today might agree to be "fair"?

I. THE DISTRIBUTION OF INCOME

Despite the proliferation of sophisticated economic data in this country, the United States government does *not* publish official estimates of the distribution of income. Such estimates were prepared by the Office of Busi-

* From "The Rich, the Poor, and the Taxes They Pay," *The Public Interest,* 17 (Fall 1969), pp. 21–43. Copyright © National Affairs Inc., 1969. Reprinted with permission of publisher and author. Joseph A. Pechman is Director of Economic Studies, Brook-ings Institution, Washington, D.C.

ness Economics for a period of years in the 1950s and early 1960s, but were discontinued because the sources on which they were based were acknowledged to be inadequate. We have data from annual field surveys of some 30,000 households conducted by the Bureau of the Census, as well as from the annual *Statistics of Income* prepared by the Internal Revenue Service from federal individual income tax returns. But both sources have their weaknesses: the Census Bureau surveys systematically understate income, particularly in the top brackets; tax returns, on the other hand, understate the share received by low income recipients who are not required to file. Nevertheless, if used with care, the two sources provide some interesting insights.

Before turning to the most recent period, it should be pointed out that a significant change in the distribution of pre-tax income occurred during the Great Depression and World War II. All experts who have examined the data agree that the distribution became more equal as a result of (a) the tremendous reductions in business and property incomes during the depression and (b) the narrowing of earnings differentials between low-paid workers and higher-paid skilled workers and salaried employees when full employment was reestablished during the war. The most authoritative estimates, prepared by the late Selma Goldsmith and her associates, suggest that the share of personal income received by the top 5 percent of the nation's consumer units (including families and unrelated individuals) declined from 30 percent in 1929 to 26.5 percent in 1935–36; the share of the top 20 percent declined from 54.4 percent to 51.7 percent in the same period. The movement toward greater equality appears to have continued during the war up to about 1944. By that year, the share of the top 5 percent had dropped another notch to 20.7 percent, and of the top 20 percent to 45.8 percent.

The income concept used by these researchers did not include undistributed corporate profits, which are a source of future dividends or of capital gains for shareholders; if they had been included, the movement of the income distribution toward equality from 1929 to 1944 would have been substantially moderated, but by no means eliminated.[1]

The movement toward equality seems to have ended during World War II, at least on the basis of the available statistics. In 1952, for example, the share of the top 5 percent was 20.5 percent and of the top 20 percent, 44.7 percent. (The differences from the 1944 figures are well within the margin of error of these data, and can hardly be called significant.)

To trace what happened since 1952, we shift to the census data that

---

[1] The year 1929 must have been the high point of inequality during the 1920s, so that the distribution of income in the more recent period may not have been very different from what it was in the early 1920s if account is taken of undistributed profits. Unfortunately, the available data for those years are simply not good enough to say much more.

provide the longest continuous and comparable income distribution series available to us. The best way to appreciate the trend is to look at the figures for income shares at five-year intervals:

TABLE 22–1. Before-tax income shares, census data (percent)

Year	Top 5 percent of families	Top 20 percent of families
1952	18	42
1957	16	40
1962	16	42
1967	15	41

Source: Bureau of the Census. Income includes transfer payments (e.g., social security benefits, unemployment compensation, welfare payments, etc.), but excludes capital gains.

The figures indicate that the share of the top 5 percent declined slightly between 1952 and 1957, and has remained virtually unchanged since 1957; the share of the top 20 percent changed very little. Correspondingly, the shares of the groups at the bottom of the income scale (not shown in the table) also changed very little throughout the period.

Tax data are needed to push the analysis further. These data are better than the census data for our purposes, because they show the amount of realized capital gains and also permit us to calculate income shares *after* the federal income tax. But the great disadvantage of the tax data is that the bottom part of the income distribution is underrepresented because of an unknown number of nonfilers. Furthermore, the taxpayer unit is not exactly a family unit, because children and other members of the family file their own income tax returns if they have income, and a few married couples continue to file separate returns despite the privilege of income splitting, which removed the advantage of separate returns with rare exceptions.

There is really no way to get around these problems, but the tax data are too interesting to be abandoned because of these technicalities. So, we make an assumption that permits us to use at least the upper tail of the income distribution. The assumption is that the top 10 or 15 percent of the nation's tax units are for the most part similar *to* the census family units and the cases that differ represent roughly the same percentage of the total number of units each year. Because we have official Department of Commerce estimates of income (as defined in the tax code) for the country as a whole, the assumption enables us to compute income shares before and after tax for the top 1, 2, 5, 10, and 15 percent of units annually for the entire postwar period.[2]

---

[2] People with money always feel poorer than they are, and it might be useful to indicate what kinds of income we are talking about for these various categories. For the

The tax series confirms much of what we learned from the census series, and adds a few additional bits of information besides. Here are the data for selected years chosen to represent the three sets of federal income tax rates levied, beginning with the Korean War:

TABLE 22–2. Before-tax income shares, tax data, (percent)

Year	Top 1 percent of tax units	Top 2 percent of tax units	Top 5 percent of tax units	Top 10 percent of tax units	Top 15 percent of tax units
1952	9	12	19	27	33
1963	8	12	19	28	35
1967	9	13	20	29	36

Source: *Statistics of Income.* Income excludes transfer payments, but includes realized capital gains in full.

According to tax returns, the share of total income, including all realized capital gains, going to the top 1 percent of the tax units was about the same for the entire period from 1952 through 1967. But the shares of the top 2, 5, 10, and 15 percent—which, of course, include the top 1 percent—all rose somewhat. These trends differ from the census figures which show that the entire income distribution was stable. By contrast, the tax data show that the 14 percent of income recipients just below the top 1 percent —this group reported incomes between $12,000 and $43,000 in 1967— *increased* their share of total income from 24 percent to 27 percent.

If the figures are anywhere near being right, they suggest two significant conclusions:

First, in recent years the very rich in our society have not enjoyed larger increases in incomes, as defined in the tax code, than the average income recipient. Although realized capital gains are included in our figures, they do not include nonreported sources, such as tax-exempt interest and excess depletion; correction for these omissions would probably not alter the results very much, because the amounts involved are small relative to the total of reported incomes. Even a correction for the undistributed profits of corporations wouldn't change the result very much because undistributed gross corporation profits have remained between 10 and 13 percent of total reported income since 1950.

Second, a change in the income distribution may have occurred in what are sometimes called the "middle income" classes. These classes consist of most of the professional people in this country (doctors, lawyers, engineers,

year 1967, a taxpayer was in the top 1 percent if his income (including realized capital gains) was over $43,000, the top 2 percent if his income was over $28,000, the top 5 percent if his income was over $18,000, the top 10 percent if his income was over $14,000, the top 15 percent if his income was over $12,000.

I would assume that most of the readers of this article, and of this magazine, are included among the rich and super-rich. I also assume they will find this hard to believe.

accountants, college professors, etc.) as well as the highest paid members of the skilled labor force and white collar workers. The increase in their share of total income from 24 percent to 27 percent, if it actually occurred, represents a not insignificant improvement in their relative income status.

Clearly, this improvement in the income shares of the middle classes could come only at the expense of the lower 85 percent of the income distribution. But this is not the whole story. These figures contain only incomes that are generated in the private economy; they do not include transfer payments (e.g., social security benefits, unemployment compensation, welfare payments, etc.) which are, of course, concentrated in the lower income classes. Correction of the figures for transfer payments might be just enough to offset the increased share of the middle income classes. If this is the case, the constancy of the shares of pre-tax income shown by the census data is fully consistent with the growth in shares of the middle incomes shown by the tax data. And, if this is the explanation of the constancy of the income shares in the census distribution, it means that the lower classes have not been able to hold their own in the private economy; large increases in government transfer payments were needed to prevent a gradual erosion of their income shares.

II. THE EFFECT OF TAXES

Since one of the major objectives of taxation is to moderate income inequality, it is appropriate to ask how the tax system actually affects the distribution of income and whether it has become more or less equalizing. We examine first the impact of the federal individual income tax, which is the most progressive element in the nation's tax system and for which data by income classes are readily available, and then we speculate about the effect of the other taxes in the system.[3]

The federal income tax

While everybody grumbles about the federal income tax, few people realize that tax rates have been *going down* for about two decades. Even with the 10 percent surtax, the rates are lower today than they were from 1951 through 1963. Briefly, the history of the tax is as follows: tax rates reached their peak, and exemptions their low point, during World War II. They were reduced in 1946 and again in 1948, when income splitting and the $600 per capita exemption were also enacted. Rates were pushed up

---

[3] Since the terms are often used loosely, it might be a good idea explicitly to define what *regressive, proportional,* and *progressive* taxation mean. A tax is *regressive* when it takes a larger proportion of a poor person's income than of a rich man's, *proportional* when it takes equal proportions of such incomes, and *progressive* when it takes a larger proportion of a rich man's income than of a poor man's.

close to World War II levels during the Korean War, but were reduced in 1954 and again in 1964. The surtax that became effective for individuals on April I, 1968 moved the rates only half way back to the 1954–63 levels.

The structure of the tax has been remarkably stable during this entire period, despite all the talk about closing loopholes. The preferential rate on long-term capital gains was enacted in 1942; income splitting became effective in 1948; interest on state and local government bonds has never been taxed by the federal government; percentage depletion dates back to the 1920s; and the deductions allowed for interest charges, taxes, charitable contributions, medical expenses, and casualty losses date back to 1942 or earlier. The 1954 law introduced a 4 percent dividend credit, but this was repealed in 1964. (As a compromise, the $50 exclusion for dividends, which was enacted along with the credit, was raised to $100.) A few abuses have been eliminated from time to time, but the revenues involved have not been significant.

The single major victory for tax reform occurred in 1964, when the dividend credit and the deductions for state and local taxes other than income, sales, property, and gasoline taxes were eliminated. All told, these revenue-raising reforms amounted to about $750 million, and they were accompanied by revenue-losing reforms of $400 million (mainly the minimum standard deduction which benefitted only those with very low incomes).

Given this history, it follows that the effective tax rates at specific absolute income levels have been going down since World War II. For example, from 1947 to 1967, the effective rate of tax paid by taxpayers with adjusted gross income of $5,000–10,000 declined from 13.8 percent to 9.5 percent; for those in the $15,000–20,000 class, the decline was from 24.6 percent to 14.0 percent; and above $100,000, the decline was from 57.4 percent to 39.5 percent. (These figures understate actual declines because adjusted gross income excludes half of long-term capital gains that were much larger relative to total income in 1967 than in 1947.)

Although such figures are of considerable interest, they are not directly useful for an analysis of the effect of the tax on the income distribution. For it must be remembered that most people moved up the income scale almost continuously throughout this period; under a progressive tax, they would be taxed more heavily as a result of this upward movement. There is a case for the argument that, as incomes rise, it is only "fair" that progressive tax rates—established on the basis of an earlier income distribution that was considered "fair"—ought to go down somewhat. The key question is: how much? Specifically, has the progressive taxation of increased incomes been offset by the reduction in tax rates, or has there been a "surplus" on the side of either income or taxation?

To answer this question, the effective tax rates were computed for the top 1, 2, 5, 10, and 15 percent of the income tax units, but in this case the full amount of realized long-term capital gains, and also other exclusions, were included to arrive at a total income concept. The data show that, on this basis, average effective tax rates were substantially lower in 1967 than in 1952 for the top 1 percent, slightly lower for the next 1 percent, and roughly constant for the next 13 percent. Note also that the effective rate of tax paid in 1967 by the top 1 percent, whose before-tax income was $43,000 and over, was only 26 percent of their total reported income, including all their realized capital gains.

TABLE 22–3. **Effective federal tax rates on total income (percent)**

Year	Top 1 percent of tax units	Next 1 percent of tax units	Next 3 percent of tax units	Next 5 percent of tax units	Next 5 percent of tax units
1952	33	20	16	14	12
1963	27	20	16	14	13
1967	26	18	15	13	12

Source: *Statistics of Income.* Total income is the sum of adjusted gross income and excluded capital gains, dividends, and sick pay.

It is a fairly simple matter to deduct the tax paid by each of these groups from their total income to obtain their disposable income. The results modify the conclusions we drew on the basis of the before-tax incomes in only minor respects. The shares of disposable income of the top 1 percent remain stable, and the shares of the top 2, 5, 10, and 15 percent go up from 1952 to 1967. Furthermore, the shares of the "middle income classes"—the 14 percent between the top 1 and top 15 percent—rise from 23 to 27 percent on a disposable income basis, or about as much as on a before-tax basis, (Table 22–4).

We may conclude that the federal individual income tax has moderated the before-tax income distribution by roughly the same proportions since 1952. Thus, while tax rates at any given absolute income level have declined, the effect of progression has just about offset the decline, leaving the relative tax bite about the same in the top 15 percent of the income distribution. Furthermore, similar calculations suggest that the post-World War II income tax is just about as equalizing as it was in 1941. The tremendous movement upward in the income distribution pushed much more taxable income into higher rate brackets, but this has been offset by the adoption of income splitting and the increase in itemized deductions.[4]

---

4 But the income tax is surely more equalizing now than it was in 1929, when the top bracket rates were cut to a maximum of 25 percent. This means that the equalization of the distribution of income between the 1920s and the post-World War II period is even more pronounced on a disposable income basis than it is on a before-tax basis.

TABLE 22–4. Shares of total disposable (i.e., after-tax) income (percent)

Year	Top 1 percent of tax units	Top 2 percent of tax units	Top 5 percent of tax units	Top 10 percent of tax units	Top 15 percent of tax units
1952	7	10	16	24	30
1963	7	10	17	26	33
1967	7	11	17	26	34

Source: *Statistics of Income*. Disposable income is total income less federal income tax paid.

It should be emphasized that the foregoing data omit large chunks of income that are received primarily by high-paid employees of large business firms. Tax-exempt interest and percentage depletion have already been mentioned. In addition, beginning with the imposition of the very high indivdual income tax rates and the excess profits tax during World War II, methods of compensation were devised to funnel income to business executives in nontaxable forms. The devices used are well known: deferred compensation and pension plans, stock option arrangements, and direct payment of personal consumption expenditures through expense accounts. There is no question that these devices are used widely throughout the corporate sector. But little is known about the amounts involved, and even less is known about the impact on the distribution of income.

A recent study by Wilbur G. Lewellen for the National Bureau of Economic Research concluded that, even after allowance is made for the new compensation methods, the after-tax compensation (in dollars of constant purchasing power) of top executives in industrial corporations was no higher in the early 1960s than in 1940. The more important finding from the income distribution standpoint is that stock options, pensions, deferred compensation, and profit-sharing benefits rose rapidly as a percentage of the executives' compensation package from 1940 to 1955, and then stabilized. The study did not attempt to measure the value of expense accounts, and omitted firms in industries other than manufacturing. Nevertheless, the results of the study suggest that extreme statements about the possible effects of these devices on the distribution of income in recent years are not warranted.

The corporation income tax

The corporation income tax was enacted four years before the individual income tax and it has been a mainstay of the federal tax system ever since. It produced more revenue than the individual income tax in 17 out of 28 years prior to 1941; today, it is the second largest source of federal revenue. The general corporation tax was reduced to 38 percent after World War II. It was raised to 52 percent during the Korean War and remained there until 1964, when it was reduced to 48 percent.

Public finance experts have argued the merits and demerits of a corporation tax for a long time, but the issues have not been resolved. Its major purpose in our tax system is to safeguard the individual income tax. If corporate incomes were not subject to tax, individuals could avoid the individual income tax by arranging to have their income accumulate in corporations, and later on selling their stock at the low capital gains rate, or holding on until death at which time the capital gains pass to their heirs completely tax free. Short of taxing shareholders on their share of corporation incomes (a method which is attractive to economists, but is anathema to businessmen and most tax lawyers) and taxing capital gains in full, the most practical way to protect the individual income tax is to impose a separate tax on corporation incomes.

Some people have argued that a large part or all of the corporation income tax is shifted forward to the consumer in the form of higher prices. On this assumption, the corporation income tax is a sales tax—a very peculiar one, to be sure—and is therefore regressive. But the majority view among tax experts is that the corporation income tax comes out of corporate profits, as was intended, so that the tax is borne by shareholders. Despite the large post-World War II increases in the number of shareholders, stock ownership is still concentrated in the highest income classes. This means that the corporation income tax is, to some extent at least, a progressive tax.

The major change in the corporation tax in the last two decades has been the enactment of more generous depreciation deductions in 1954 and 1962 and of the investment credit in 1962. As a result, despite relatively constant rates, the corporation tax has declined as a ratio to gross corporate profits (i.e., profits before deduction of depreciation) from 33 percent in 1954 to about 27 percent in 1967. It rose in 1968 to 30 percent as a result of the imposition of the 10 percent surtax. The impending expiration of the surtax and repeal of the investment tax credit will just about offset one another, so that the post-surtax ratio will continue at 30 percent until the continuously growing depreciation allowances will tilt it downward once again. Thus, although the contribution of the corporation tax to the progressivity of the national tax system has declined somewhat (for economic reasons that most economists regard as persuasive), the contribution continues to be on the progressive side.

Estate and gift taxes

In theory, estate and gift taxes are excellent taxes because they have little effect on incentives to earn income and, if effective, would reduce the inequality of the distribution of wealth that in turn accounts for much of the inequity in the distribution of income. In practice, the yield of these taxes is disappointing. Tax rates are high, but there are numerous ways to escape them. The result is that the federal government receives little of its revenue from these tax sources—about 1.7 percent in the current fiscal year. The effective rate of estate taxes on wealth passed each year from one generation to the next must be less than 10 percent; and the gift tax is even less effective. While these taxes are progressive, they have little effect on the distribution of wealth.

The social security payroll tax

We now turn to the features of the national tax system that, in combination, more than offset the progressivity of the federal income and estate and gift taxes. The social security payroll tax, which is levied at a flat rate on earnings up to a maximum of $7,800 under present law, was enacted in 1935 as the basic method of financing social security on the principle that the workers were buying their own insurance. This idea is doubtless responsible for the widespread acceptance of social security as a permanent government institution in this country; but the insurance analogy is no longer applicable to the system as it has developed. Present beneficiaries receive far larger benefits than the taxes they paid would entitle them to—a situation that will continue indefinitely as long as Congress raises benefits as prices and wages continue to rise. The trust funds have not grown significantly since the mid-1950s; the payroll taxes paid by the workers have not been stored up or invested, but have been paid out currently as benefits. When benefits promised to people now working come due, the funds for their payment will be provided out of tax revenues as of that future date.

Nevertheless, the insurance analogy has a strong hold on the thinking of the administrators of social security and the Congressional tax-writing committees. Every time a benefit increase is enacted, the payroll tax rates (or the maximum earnings subject to the tax) are raised, in order to balance out the revenues and expenditures for the next 75 years on an actuarial basis. In a relatively short time, the trust funds begin running large surpluses, which then become the justification for another round of benefit increases by Congress. This requires a further increase in rates for actuarial reasons, payroll taxes are again raised, and so on.

As a result of this process, payroll taxes have been raised seven times since the beginning of 1960. The combined employer-employee tax was 6 percent on earnings up to $4,800 on January 1, 1960; this year the tax is 9.6 percent on earnings up to $7,800. Most economists believe that the burden of the employer tax, as well as the employee tax, falls eventually on the workers (either by substituting for larger wage increases or inflating prices). Thus, the federal government has been placing more and more weight on this regressive element of the federal tax system.

State and local taxes

Although the federal tax system is progressive on balance, the state and local tax system is highly regressive. The states rely heavily on sales taxes, while the local governments rely on property taxes. Personal and corporation income taxes account for only about 11 percent of state-local revenues from their own sources. This situation is disturbing because the state-local tax system is the growing element of the national system. Whereas the federal government has been able to reduce income tax rates several times beginning in 1954, and has eliminated virtually all of its excise taxes, state governments continue to enact new taxes and to raise the rates of old taxes to keep up with their increasing and urgent revenue needs; meanwhile, local governments keep raising the already excessively burdened property tax.

Federal tax receipts have moved within the narrow range of 19 to 21 percent of the Gross National Product since 1951. By contrast, state-local receipts rose from 7.1 percent of the GNP in 1951 to 11.9 percent in 1968. Assuming that state-local taxes respond more or less proportionately to the rise in the national product (a reasonable assumption), the states and local governments must have increased rates by 68 percent in these 17 years to push up their tax yields to current levels. The net result is, of course, that a greater degree of regression is being built into the national tax system by the states and local governments as they continue to seek for more revenues.

Parenthetically, it might be observed that the "tax revolt" which has been so much in the news of late must have been a reflection of the increasing burden of state and local taxes. The revolt is allegedly concentrated in the "middle income" classes living in the suburbs. In this, there is a paradox: this group probably pays a smaller proportion of its income in taxes than the poor and near poor (see below), but the taxes they have been paying, or recently began to pay, are highly visible. Their incomes have risen sharply in recent years, so that their federal income taxes are higher in dollar amounts despite the 1964 rate reduction. Six states have enacted new income taxes in the past eight years and ten states have enacted new sales taxes; many others have raised the rates of both taxes substantially. Most of the new suburbanites are now paying property taxes directly as home owners, rather than indirectly as tenants, and property taxes have also been rising everywhere. Tax morale was, therefore, generally at a low ebb when the federal government requested more taxes to finance a budget containing $30 billion to fight an unpopular war. Since the request was in the form of a surcharge on those already paying taxes, and did nothing about those who escaped, the existing inequities in the federal income tax at last became evident to large masses of taxpayers who have no difficulty in communicating their unhappiness to their Congressmen.

Summary of the national tax system

It is not easy to arrive at an accurate estimate of the impact of the whole tax system at various income levels. Taxes are reported to different federal, state, and local government agencies. No single agency has the responsibility to compel reporting of taxes on a meaningful and consistent basis. A number of isolated attempts have been made by students of public finance to piece together from the inadequate data estimates of the distribution of all taxes by income classes. These studies were for different years, make different assumptions for the incidence of the various taxes, and use different statistical sources and methodologies to correct for the inconsistencies in the data. Nevertheless, they all arrive at similar conclusions regarding the relative tax loads at different income levels.

The most recent estimates were prepared by the Council of Economic Advisers for the year 1965. They show the distribution of taxes by the income classes of families and unattached individuals, income being defined exclusive of transfer payments. The estimates for taxes and transfers separately, and in combination, are summarized in Table 22–5.

TABLE 22–5. Taxes and transfers as percent of income, 1965

	Taxes				
Income classes	*Federal*	*State and local*	*Total*	*Transfer payments*	*Taxes less transfers*
Under $2,000	19	25	44	126	—83*
$ 2,000– 4,000	16	11	27	11	16
4,000– 6,000	17	10	27	5	21
6,000– 8,000	17	9	26	3	23
8,000–10,000	18	9	27	2	25
10,000–15,000	19	9	27	2	25
15,000 and over	32	7	38	1	37
Total	22	9	31	14	24

* The minus sign indicates that the families and individuals in this class received more from federal, state, and local governments than they, as a group, paid to these governments in taxes.

Source: *Economic Report of the President*, 1969. Income excludes transfer payments, but includes realized capital gains in full and undistributed corporate profits.

The following are the major conclusions that can be drawn from these and previously published estimates:

1. Since at least the mid-1930s, the federal tax system has been roughly proportional in the lower and middle income classes, and clearly progressive for the highest classes. Federal income tax data suggest that the preferential rate on capital gains, and the exclusion of interest on state and local bonds and other items from the tax base, have produced some regressivity for the very small group at the top of the income pyramid, say, beginning with incomes of $100,000 or more.

2. State and local taxes are regressive throughout the income scale.

3. The combined federal, state, and local tax burden is heaviest in the very bottom and top brackets, and lowest in the middle brackets. This statement is, of course, based on averages for each group and there are wide variations around these averages for specific individuals, depending on the sources of their incomes, the kind of property they own, and where they live.

4. The poor receive numerous transfer payments (e.g., social security, unemployment compensation, public assistance, etc.) that are financed by this tax system. The net effect of transfers as against taxes is distinctly progressive, because transfer payments make up such a large proportion of total income at the bottom of the income distribution—56 percent for those with incomes of less than $2,000 in 1965. (To some extent, this progressivity is overstated because the transfers do not always go to the same people who pay taxes, the best example being social security retirement benefits that are received only by retirees—many of whom are not poor—while $1.5 billion of the payroll tax levied to pay for these benefits are paid by the poor.) There is no reason in the abstract, why a nation should not levy taxes on and pay transfers to the same groups; but while the nation wages a war on poverty, it is surely appropriate to consider the possibility of providing additional financial assistance to the poor by *tax reduction* as well as through transfer payments.

III. REFORMING THE NATIONAL TAX SYSTEM

The preceding discussion indicates that the agenda for reforming this country's tax system to correct its regressive features is lengthy and complicated. It involves reconstruction of the tax systems at all levels of government, and the development of new forms of intergovernmental fiscal relations. State and local governments need to rely more heavily on income taxes, relieve the poor of paying sales taxes, and deemphasize the property tax. At the federal level, the most important items on the agenda are to alleviate the payroll tax on the poor, to deliver—at last—on promises made by both political parties to close loopholes in the income taxes, and make the estate and gift taxes more effective.

State and local taxes

There are no easy solutions to the state-local problems, given the political constraints under which our federal system operates. At the state level, the trend is for moderate income and sales taxes—34 states already have both, and the number increases every year. Six states have adopted simple per capita credits against income taxes for sales taxes paid (with refunds for those who do not pay income taxes) to alleviate the sales tax burden on the poor. This device eliminates the regressive feature of the sales tax and makes it more acceptable on grounds of equity. Progress on the adoption of state income taxes has been slow, but there has been a new surge of adoptions by the states in the past couple of years as governors and legislators have realized that they cannot get along without the growth-responsive revenues from an income tax.

The states are also beginning to take a more responsible attitude toward their local governments, although the situation is admittedly bad in many parts of the country. More of the states' own revenues should be allocated to local governments through grants-in-aid to prevent the development of city income and sales taxes that tend to drive wealthy taxpayers and businesses to the suburbs. An ideal arrangement, that is already in operation in Maryland for income tax purposes, would be to have statewide income and sales taxes along with modest "piggyback" local taxes—all collected by the state government and subject to state control so that individual communities will not get too far out of line with their neighbors. (As a long-run goal, the federal government should collect state-local, as well as federal, income taxes on the basis of a single return.)

The local governments need to improve local property tax administration to remove the haphazard way in which the tax applies to properties of equal values. The states can help by providing technical assistance and also by forcing the communities to meet minimum standards of administration. Consideration should also be given to the development of new local revenue sources to take some of the pressure off the general property tax. The best alternatives are the "piggyback" income and sales taxes already mentioned, always with the credit or refund for sales taxes paid by the poor.

In addition, it is time to tap the high and rising land values for some of the urgently needed local revenues. The National Commission on Urban Problems, which was chaired by former Senator Paul Douglas, has estimated that land values rose from $269 billion in 1956 to $523 billion in 1966, or about $25 billion a year. This tremendous increase in wealth was not created by the landowners but by society as a whole. This is, of course, the basis of the old "single tax" idea that was oversold by the zealots as a complete and final solution to the nation's tax problems, although correct in principle. The revenue potential of special taxes on land values or on increases in land values is modest, but the approach has merit even if it will not solve the financial problems of our cities and suburbs by itself. It would also discourage the hoarding of land for speculative purposes and thereby encourage more efficient use of land in and around the nation's cities.

But there is no hope for the states and local governments, whatever they do on their own initiative, unless the federal government cuts them in on its superior tax resources. It is true that federal grants to states and local governments have increased rapidly in recent years—from $5 billion in fiscal year 1958 to an estimated $25 billion this year—but the need is even greater than that. To satisfy this need, more money will have to be allocated to the categorical grants already authorized for such programs as education, health, welfare, and housing. Also, a federal-state-local income tax revenue-sharing system should be established to moderate the huge disparities in fiscal capacities of the fifty states and to give governors and local officials unrestricted funds that can be used to help solve their own particular problems. The Nixon administration's proposal, based on a plan devised by a Johnson task force, is a good—though modest—beginning.

Mayors and county managers are suspicious of revenue sharing because they have little faith that the states will distribute the funds fairly. To answer this criticism, various formulas have been devised to require the states to "pass through" at least a minimum percentage of the revenue-sharing grants. Disagreement over the details of the "pass through" should not be allowed to delay the adoption of an idea that will relieve some of the fiscal pressure at the state and local levels and, at the same time, provide revenues from a progressive tax that otherwise would be raised mainly on a regressive basis. Ultimately, the federal government should allocate 2 percent of the federal individual income tax base to revenue sharing, which would amount to $8 billion at current income levels and as much as $12 billion in 1975.

The payroll tax

Much has been said about the need for removing the poor from the income tax rolls, and Congress seems to be prepared to remedy this anachronism. But the more urgent problem is to remove the much heavier payroll tax burden of the poor. The federal income tax bill of the families and individuals who are officially classified as poor is only $200 million a year, as compared with the $1.5 billion they pay in payroll taxes. In addition, the regressive feature of the payroll tax at the higher income levels should be moderated immediately and ultimately eliminated entirely.

Several different approaches might be taken to achieve these objectives. First, part or all of the payroll tax could be converted into a withholding tax for income tax purposes. No formal change in the payroll tax need be involved; at the end of the year, individuals would receive credit against their income taxes (or a refund if they are not income tax payers) for the amount of payroll taxes paid.

Second, contributions from general revenues might be made, on the basis of a fixed formula, to the social security and other trust funds. Such a possibility was foreseen in the earlier days of social security.

Third, the social security system might be combined with a liberalized and modernized public assistance system or some variant of a negative income tax. The negative income tax payments to the aged in such a system would be financed out of general revenues.

But whatever is ultimately done about the payroll tax as the basic revenue source for social security financing, the poor should be relieved of paying this tax as soon as possible. The principle of a minimum taxable level under the income tax—soon to be raised to the poverty levels—should be carried over into the payroll tax. The Internal Revenue Service is already proficient at handling tens of millions of refunds per year under the income tax; the additional payroll tax refunds would not be an excessive burden.

Federal tax reform

As this was being written, Congress was working hard to complete a tax reform bill. The details of the final legislation are still unclear, but it might be useful to list the most important issues that must be settled, now or later.

1. Revision of the treatment of capital gains is the highest priority item. Profits from sale of assets held more than six months are taxed at only half the regular rates up to a maximum of 25 percent, but even this tax may be avoided indefinitely if the assets are transferred from one generation to another through bequests. In the case of gifts, capital gains are taxed only if the assets are later sold by the recipient. As a result, billions of dollars of capital gains are subject to low rates or are never taxed.

Capital gains receive favored treatment for two reasons: first, full taxation in a single year of a large realized gain accumulated over many years would be unfair, unless the impact of the graduated income tax rates were moderated; second, too high a rate on capital gains might "lock" most security holders into their present portfolios. The first of these problems could be solved by averaging capital gains over the period they were held. The "lock-in" effect would be moderated by such an averaging provision, and also by taxing capital gains when assets are transferred, either by gift or at death. Both changes would reduce the advantages of holding on to assets whose values had risen.

A complete reform of the capital gains tax would raise perhaps $8 billion in additional revenues annually, mainly from the top 15 percent of the income population. But the more likely package—including a lengthening of the holding period from six months to a year and elimination of the maximum 25 percent tax rate (but not the exclusion of half of long-term capital gains)—would yield only about $700 million a year.

2. The toughest issue involves percentage depletion for oil, gas, and other minerals industries. These allowances are similar in many respects to ordinary depreciation. The difference is that the amounts written off as depreciation are limited to the cost of the asset, but percentage depletion can—and does—substantially exceed the amount invested. In addition, an immediate write-off is permitted for certain capital costs incurred in exploration and development, thus providing a double deduction for capital invested in these industries. Most economists who have studied the matter have concluded that present allowances are much too generous.

If the preferential treatment for all the minerals industries were entirely eliminated, revenues would be increased by $1.6 billion a year. If the oil depletion allowance is reduced from 27 percent to 20 percent and the other allowances are scaled down proportionately, as seems possible at this moment, additional revenues would amount to about $400 million a year.

3. The tax exemption of interest on state and local government securities is unfair because it benefits only the wealthy. It is also inefficient because the wealthy benefit from the full amount of the interest differential for the tax exemption, which is set by the market at the point where the marginal (and lower income) investor is encouraged to buy tax-exempts. According to one study, the federal government loses $2 of revenue for every $1 of interest subsidy received by the states and local governments. If state-local bond interest were taxed, the revenue could be used directly to help the states and local governments. The estimated revenue gain would be small initially because any legislation that might be enacted would apply only to future issues and a considerable part of the new revenue would be returned to the states in the form of a "sweetener" over and above what the present tax exemption is worth to them.

4. The most irrational and expensive provisions are the deductions for charitable contributions, interest payments, medical expenses, state and local taxes, and other personal expenditures that cut out billions of dollars from the tax base. These deductions are designed to improve the definition of income on which taxes are to be based; in fact, many of the deductions are merely subsidies for particular types of personal expenditures that hardly merit government encouragement.

Deductions for state income taxes do protect taxpayers against excessive rates. There is also some justification for continuing the deduction for sales and income taxes as a device to encourage further state use of these taxes to raise the revenues they desperately need. But the same rationale does not apply to property taxes;[5] and there is certainly no excuse for deducting gasoline taxes, which are levied to pay for benefits received by highway users. The present method of computing the deduction for charitable contributions is also questionable. Limiting the deduction to contributions in excess of, say, 3 percent of income would encourage larger-than-average gifts to charity and save $1.5 billion of revenue each year. In addition, Congress should repeal the unlimited charitable deduction for those whose taxes and contributions together exceed 80 percent of their income for eight out of ten consecutive years. This provision has permitted many wealthy people to escape tax entirely by donating appreciated assets on which capital gains tax has not been paid but which are deductible at their full value (including the gain) against other income.

A series of reforms along these lines might bring in revenues in the neighborhood of $5 billion a year. But Congress will probably do very little in this area—except perhaps to eliminate the unlimited charitable deduction which will bring in $50 million annually and to raise the standard deduction (which will add to the erosion of the tax base—at a cost of $1.4 billion—and do nothing to refine the taxable income concept in a manner that would improve interpersonal equity).

5. The federal income tax has been particularly solicitous of the aged. Taxpayers over 65 years of age have an additional exemption of $600, pay no tax on their social security or railroad retirement pensions, and receive a tax credit on other retirement income if their earnings are below $1,524. These benefits are worth more than $3 billion a year. There is every reason to help the aged through public programs, but the tax system is a bad way to do this because it gives the largest amount of relief to those who need it least. It would be better to eliminate these deductions and use the revenue to increase social security benefits for all aged persons. The Kennedy and Johnson administrations recommended a more modest approach that would limit the income tax relief to low-income aged, but not raise any additional revenue.

6. Income splitting was enacted in 1948 to equalize the tax burdens of married persons living in community and noncommunity property states. (The former had already been able to split their incomes for tax purposes.)

---

5 I have omitted the favored tax treatment of homeowners from this list of major tax issues for obvious practical reasons. An individual who rents a house and invests, say, $20,000 in securities yielding 5 percent is taxable on the $1,000 of interest and dividends he receives. Another who invests the $20,000 in an identical home is not taxable on its rental value (which is income to him, even though he does not actually receive any cash) and deducts his property taxes and mortgage interest. These benefits are worth $8 billion annually to homeowners, but they are sacrosanct. I know of no Congressman who would publicly support elimination of the deductions for property taxes and mortgage interest, let alone the inclusion of the rental values of owner-occupied homes in taxable income. Encouragement of individual home ownership—and, increasingly, apartment ownership—is deeply imbedded in the American political grain, even though its rationale is not nearly as cogent as it used to be.

But the provision introduced an unfair discrimination against single people, and reduced taxes by an estimated $10 billion a year. There are ways to eliminate this discrimination without introducing the old community property problems, but the large revenue loss—which goes almost entirely to married couples with incomes above $10,000—is probably irretrievable. This year, Congress seems to be in a mood to extend half the advantages of income splitting to single people aged 35 years or older and this will cost $650 million a year.

7. A few years ago, the Senate refused to accept a relatively simple House plan to withhold income tax on interest and dividends. Instead, they required information returns by corporations and financial institutions, a copy of which would go to the taxpayer. There was some improvement in the reporting of interest, but not nearly enough (dividends were never underreported very much). The introduction of withholding is the only practical method of recovering the estimated $1 billion of tax that is now lost annually through the carelessness, inadvertence, and dishonesty of taxpayers (mainly in the lower and middle income classes).

8. Although some income tax avoidance will be eliminated by the new legislation, the final bill will not close all the loopholes. As a safeguard to prevent a few wealthy people from taking advantage of the special provisions that would remain, two reforms are now being seriously considered by the Congress. The first would require the allocation of personal deductions allowed to individuals between taxable and nontaxable income sources. Thus, if only half of a taxpayer's income is subject to tax, he would be entitled to only half his deductions. The second would introduce a minimum income tax at half the ordinary rates on an individual's total income (including all nontaxable sources) or require an individual to pay tax at the full rates on at least half his total income. These revisions would add $800 million of tax revenue a year if the income definition included all sources of income. But they are not a substitute for comprehensive reform, but they will be needed until all the income tax loopholes have been plugged—and that is not likely to happen very soon.

9. The corporation income tax would not be in bad shape if the depletion allowances were modified, but a few technical reforms are also needed. Corporations should not be allowed to reduce their taxes by splitting up into a large number of smaller corporations. (Each corporation has a $25,000 exemption against the corporation normal tax, which is worth $6,500 for each corporation.) Banks and other financial institutions have overly generous allowances for additions to reserves for losses on their loans; these should be made more realistic. Real estate operators should not be allowed to deduct depreciation at accelerated rates and then, when the property is sold, taxed at the capital gains rates on their profits (which is partly the result of the excessive depreciations). These revisions, which

are incorporated in this year's reform bill (except that the real estate loop-hole was kept open for residential construction), would add close to $2 billion a year to the corporation income tax yield. In addition, the $100 deduction for dividends under the individual income tax—worth about $200 million a year in lost revenue—is silly and should be repealed.

10. Taxes on property transferred from one generation to the next are avoided in two ways. First, wealthy people put money in trust funds for their wives, children, and grandchildren that are taxed when they are set up but not when the income passes between generations or when the trusts terminate. It is possible to escape estate taxes for two or three generations in this way. Second, since gift tax rates are much lower than estate tax rates, wealthy individuals can reduce the taxes on their wealth or eliminate them entirely by systematically distributing the assets over a period of years through gifts.

Avoidance through gifts can be reduced by combining the estate and gift taxes into one tax. (An integrated tax would reduce the avoidance through gifts, but not eliminate it entirely, because an individual could earn interest on any tax he postponed.) The trust loophole is more diffi-cult to close, but methods have been devised to tax trust assets once every generation. Another improvement in the estate and gift taxes that would lower rather than raise revenues, would be to permit husbands and wives to transfer wealth freely between them without tax; under present law, half of these transfers are taxable.

The prospects

The long list of needed revisions in our federal, state, and local tax system should convince anyone that the reforms now being contemplated will not make a significant change in the progressivity of the system. Con-gress could, if it wishes, increase the yield of the present tax system by $25 billion a year, an amount that would be sufficient substantially to relieve the tax burdens of the poor and low-income nonpoor and to lower tax rates clear across the board. Instead, the revenue to be gained from this year's tax reform bill—a Herculean effort by past standards—may be in the neighborhood of $3 billion a year and much of this will be used to reduce the taxes of the "middle" income classes by what amounts to little more than a pittance, while the poor continue to bear much heavier tax burdens.

According to the Council of Economic Advisers, total taxes of those with incomes below $2,000 amounted to $7.3 billion in 1965, of which $4.2 billion were state and local taxes and $3.1 billion were federal. Those with incomes between $2,000 and $4,000 paid another $11.5 billion con-sisting of $6.8 billion federal and $4.7 billion state-local taxes. The total tax bill of $18.8 billion of those with incomes below $4,000[6] suggests what regressivity really means in a country collecting taxes amounting to about 31 percent of its GNP.

The classic objection against an attack on tax regressivity has been that there is simply not enough income in the higher classes to do the job. Would a substantial reduction in regressivity require confiscatory rates? To appreciate one of the significant magnitudes involved, suppose the federal government decided to refund all general sales, payroll, and property taxes on housing paid by those who are officially classified as poor. (The remaining taxes are selective excise taxes levied for sumptuary purposes or in lieu of user charges, which could not be refunded in any practical way. After this year, the poor will not pay any federal income taxes.) These refunds would amount to about $4 billion—perhaps three-quarters of the total tax burden of the poor and one-sixth of the burden of those with incomes below $4,000—less than what this year's tax reform bill may give away in higher standard deductions and rate reductions.

WHAT A PROGRESSIVE TAX SYSTEM WOULD LOOK LIKE

It might be thought that such a proposal—to lift three-quarters of the tax burden of the poor—is too timid. Why not go further? That indeed could be done, but only as part of a larger redistribution of the tax burden. After all, it is both inequitable and politically impossible to create a noticeable "tax divide" between the poor (a fluid concept, in any case) and the rest of society. To make the tax system progressive, it would not be enough drastically to reduce the tax burden of the poor; the burdens of the near poor and others at the lower end of the income scale would have to be cut simultaneously. Indeed—again on principles of equity and political feasibility—the relief should be diffused upwards until it benefits, say, the lower half of the income distribution (or, more technically, those receiving less than the median income, which is now in excess of $9,000).

There are a number of ways of modifying the tax system to redistribute the tax burden in this way. The most straightforward—and perhaps even the most practical, given the federal system of government in this country—would be to give taxpayers credits against the federal income tax for a declining percentage of the major taxes they now pay to federal, state, and local governments, except for income taxes. Suppose we make refunds to the poor for the general sales, payroll, and property taxes they pay and permit others to claim credits against their federal income taxes for 75 percent of these same taxes if they are in the $2,000–4,000 class, 50 percent in

---

[6] It will be recalled that the income definition we are using for 1965 excludes transfer payments. Hence, this $18.8 billion of tax is paid both by poor and nonpoor families and individuals. The poor alone pay about 30 percent of this amount.

the $4,000–6,000 class, and 25 percent in the $6,000–8,000 class. (Obviously, refunds would be paid to those with credits larger than their federal income taxes.)

Let us further assume that the taxes paid by those with incomes between $8,000 and $10,000 remain the same, and that the revenues needed to pay for the relief below $8,000 would come from those with incomes above $10,000 in proportion to the taxes they now pay. Again, we need not be concerned with the details of how this can be done. It would certainly be more equitable to close the major federal income tax loopholes first and then raise whatever additional revenue is needed by an increase in the rates above $10,000. Either way, the ratio of total taxes to income for any specific income class could be set at the same figure, although the burden *within* each class would be distributed much more equitably if the loopholes were closed first.

It turns out that, in 1965, the credits (and refunds) would have reduced taxes for those with incomes of less than $8,000 by $19 billion, and this would have required an increase in the taxes paid by those in the $10,000–15,000 class from an average of 27 percent to 32 percent and by those above $15,000 from 38 percent to 46 percent, or an average tax increase of about a fifth. The resulting effective rates of tax in this system compare with the rates as they were in 1965 as follows:

TABLE 22–6. Taxes as percent of income, 1965

Income classes	Present tax system	Alternative tax system
Under $2,000	44	13
$ 2,000– 4,000	27	14
4,000– 6,000	27	19
6,000– 8,000	26	23
8,000–10,000	27	27
10,000–15,000	27	32
15,000 and over	38	46
Total	31	31

Income includes capital gains, but excludes transfer payments.

A glance should convince anyone that this tax system would by no means eradicate taxes at the lower end of the income scale. Most people would regard tax burdens of as much as 13–14 percent for those with incomes below $4,000 and 23 percent for those between $6,000 and $8,000 as much too high. Yet, the idea of relieving tax burdens for the lower half of the income distribution even in this relatively modest way is clearly impractical; Congress would face a revolt if it tried to raise taxes on incomes above $10,000 by an average of 20 percent.

Perhaps we exaggerate the difficulties by using 1965 figures? Incomes have risen substantially so that there is much more income to be taxed above $15,000. But state and local taxes have also risen and the degree of regressivity in the tax system has been aggravated. On balance, the rise in incomes has probably been more powerful, but not enough to alter very much the general conclusions that we have reached from the 1965 data.

The prospects for making the tax system progressive are more discouraging when one notes the way Congress usually behaves when it reduces taxes. On the basis of past performance, one can predict with certainty that Congress will not limit income tax reduction to the lowest income classes. In 1964, when federal income taxes were reduced by an average of 20 percent, incomes above $15,000 were given a tax cut of 14 percent. This year, much more than the revenue to be gained from closing the loopholes and repealing the investment credit may be given away in tax rate reductions. Of course, these actions reflect the pressures on the Congressmen. The influence of the groups arrayed against a significant redistribution of the tax burden is enormous, and there is no effective lobby for the poor and the near poor.

It may be that, at some distant future date, the well-to-do and the rich will have enough income to satisfy not only their own needs, but also to help relieve the tax burdens of those who are less fortunate. In the meantime, the tax system will continue to disgrace the most affluent nation in the world.

E. Economics of black capitalism

Is black capitalism a rational solution for America's ghetto unrest and the glaring inequality of incomes between blacks and whites? In the rhetoric which one hears from America's corporate leaders and from both the political left and right of the white community, the answer appears to be an enthusiastic yes! Numerous legislative proposals have recently been publicized and some corporate dollars have been invested. However, many economists and black leaders have raised serious questions about both its efficacy and propriety. Thus black capitalism has been called everything from the "integrationist's solution within the establishment" to unworkable, neocolonial, or black separatism.

In the following reading, William Tabb appraises the likelihood of success for such efforts. He evaluates both the strengths and nature of resistance to black capitalism in its three variations: attempts to help individual black small businesses, white corporate involvement in the ghetto, and proposals for community development corporations. He concludes with recommendations for greater "black cooperativism."

23 Black power—Green power*

WILLIAM K. TABB

If the ghetto is viewed as an internal colony, it becomes easier to see why white political and corporate leaders are working so hard to convince ghetto dwellers that what they really want is "black capitalism." However, the idea of black capitalism runs counter to an important anti-capitalist strand in the black power ideology.

Black power demands black control over black institutions. This can be achieved in two ways. Individual blacks may own the important resources of the ghetto, or the black community may, in common, own and run its economy. Increasingly blacks are choosing the second course. The "white power structure," on the other hand, prefers individual ownership by blacks, which of necessity will have to be in cooperation with outside white interests. The reason for this choice is apparent. Such an arrangement is amenable to neo-colonial rule, since it guarantees the indirect control of the ghetto economy through a local native class essentially dependent on larger white businesses. The aim is twofold: to win loyalty of an important group of potentially influential local leaders, and to channel protest into less threatening, and incidentally, less useful goals. In this light, increasing the number of ghetto blacks in ownership positions appears to be an important prerequisite for ending ghetto unrest. If blacks are upset because they lack control over the institutions of the ghetto, because they are charged high prices for inferior merchandise, victimized by credit racketeers, and exploited by employers, then perhaps—some would argue—greater black ownership will help end these conditions (or at least lessen anti-white feelings because the local merchants would be black). If the ghetto lacks leadership and a stable middle class, then enlarging the number of black entrepreneurs may provide such leadership and foster stability.

* From "Black Power—Green Power," *The Political Economy of the Black Ghetto*, New York: W. W. Norton & Company, Inc., 1970, pp. 35–59. Abridged and reprinted with permission of the publisher. The footnotes from the original article have been deleted except for the citation of lengthy direct quotations. William K. Tabb is Associate Professor of Economics at Queens College of City University of New York, Flushing, N.Y.

If the problem is lack of racial confidence, the success of black capitalists would build pride. If riots are caused by people who have tenuous allegiance to our system, ownership is the best way to build a commitment to working for change within the system. Increasing the ownership class, in short, is a way to add stability, increase local leadership, lessen the visibility of white domination of the ghetto economy, and funnel ghetto discontent into acceptable channels.

Interest in black capitalism also strikes a responsive chord in the corporate sector. Proposals for black capitalism involve minimal direct government intervention. They provide for subsidies to cooperating private firms. Even though black hostility toward white businesses is increasing, the "Negro market, a market expected to reach $52 billion in 1975," cannot be ignored by even the largest firms. Market penetration is possible through joint corporations partly owned or managed by blacks. Franchising local blacks to distribute products in the ghetto and setting up independently owned but captive suppliers may also be in the corporation's interest. Banks limited by law to city boundaries find that as the black population grows they need to make more loans to minority-group businessmen to maintain their profit position. Labor shortages in a period of rapid growth have sent many firms out to recruit in the ghetto, spurred on by Manpower Development and Training Act (MDTA) funds and a desire to get on better with the increasingly large number of blacks living in the inner city where their plants are located. Thus pushed by the demands of the black community and pulled by societal and corporate interest, government, industry, and black organizations are moving to promote black capitalism.

The purpose of this chapter is to assess the likely success of such efforts and to evaluate the strength and the nature of resistance to black capitalism. Three variations on the theme will be considered: attempts to help individual black small businesses, white corporate involvement in the ghetto, and proposals for community development corporations. Finally, different patterns of ghetto development and their impact on the economic structure of the ghetto will be considered. But it is first necessary to describe the ghetto marketplace itself.

THE GHETTO MERCHANT AND THE CONSUMER

Some economists draw a contrast between how markets work in the ghetto and how they operate elsewhere. There are differences, to be sure, but they should not be allowed to obscure the essential fact that the market mechanism works in the ghetto pretty much in the way traditional theory would lead us to expect. Low-income people, lacking purchasing power and information concerning the quality of available merchandise, and restricted to shopping in ghetto markets, end up with inferior merchandise at higher prices. Seeking to maximize profit, the ghetto merchants adjust their sales practices to the nature of their customers, who are characterized as having low incomes and comparatively limited education.

. . . . .

As in the case of the slum landlord, the typical ghetto merchant does not appear to be making high profits. The market, with a large number of buyers and sellers and ease of entry and exit, assures that only normal profits are earned in the long run. In addition, the major studies in this area all show that marketing goods to low-income consumers is costly. Insurance premiums are high, pilfering and robbery are major problems, and the use of salesmen who canvass on a house-to-house basis, make home demonstrations, and collect debts are expensive. Summarizing a study of durable goods merchants, the FTC reports: "Practically all of the substantially higher gross margin of the low-income market retailers were offset by higher expenses and did not result in markedly higher net profits as a percentage of sales."

It seems doubtful that exchanging black merchants for white in ghetto stores would make much of a difference, given the realities of doing business in the ghetto. The discussion of black capitalism which follows must be seen in the light of these economic realities.

BLACK CAPITALISTS

The small size of the black business class has generally been explained in two ways. First, there are barriers to an individual's advancement in business because he is black. Second, the nature of segregation and the economic relations between the black ghetto and the white society preclude, for the most part, the possibility of successful black businesses. Stressing one of these approaches over the other has major policy consequences; if blacks have not been successful because of discrimination, then classic civil rights strategies of groups like the Urban League and the NAACP should be followed. If the ghetto is viewed as an internal colony requiring collective liberation, then other strategies are called for.

Many scholars have pointed out the conspicuous absence of blacks in managerial and proprietary positions. It has been argued that this situation exists because blacks are arriving in the cities at a time when opportunities for the establishment of small businesses are on the decline. This may well be true, but the black man's failure to achieve success as a businessman must certainly be attributed more centrally to racism. As Eugene Foley has written, "The culture has simultaneously unduly emphasized achievement in business as the primary symbol of success and has blindly developed or imposed on all-pervading racism that denied the Negro the necessary opportunities for achieving this success."

The only area in which black businessmen were able to gain entry was within their own segregated communities. In this regard the closing off of the ghetto may have helped black businessmen as a group. But even in the ghetto other groups often have the most prosperous businesses. In many cities Jews are more heavily represented in retail businesses than other groups as a result of past European restrictions on Jews which forced a disproportionate number to become traders and merchants because other professions were closed to them. Of the immigrant groups to come to America the Jews were as a result the group whose members went heavily into trade. In many ghettos anti-white feeling against merchants has taken on strong anti-semitic tones. However, a study of New Orleans, where the black ghetto businesses are heavily owned by Italians, showed the presence of strong anti-Italian feeling. In all cases hatred is aimed at the group which economically dominates the ghetto.

In getting started in business the European immigrants had three major advantages over the blacks. First, the immigrants usually had a sense of clannishness. Glazer and Moynihan point out that because of such group solidarity, funds were more readily available. "Those who had advanced themselves created little pools for ethnic businessmen and professionals to tap." This has not been as true of blacks, until the present decade, when a sense of identity and group pride has developed among a sizable number of blacks. Second, there is the legacy of slavery. Blacks have not only the "badge of color but also the ingrained burden of generations of cultural and economic deprivation."

The plantation system offered the Negro no experience with money, no incentive to save, no conception of time or progress—none of the basic experience to prepare him for the urban money economy. Instead, it indoctrinated him to believe in his own inferiority, to be resigned, while it held him in a folk culture dominated by a spiritual, other-worldly, escapist outlook. . . .[1]

This is a limited view of the effects of slavery. It ignores the "calculated cruelty . . . designed to crush the spirit," the malice and the hatred which blacks endured under slavery. Nor does such a view speak to the continuing record.

"When slavery ended and large scale physical abuse was discontinued, it was supplanted by different but equally damaging abuse. The cruelty continued unabated in thoughts, feelings, intimidation and occasional lynching. Black people were consigned to a place outside the human family and the whip of the plantation was replaced by the boundaries of the ghetto."

Whether one blames the dominance of folk culture or at a more fundamental level the limits slavery placed on black development, it may be

---

[1] Jeanne R. Lowe, *Cities in a Race with Time* (New York: Random House, Inc., 1967), p. 283.

concluded that blacks do lack "managerial skills and attitudes. Negroes as a race have been little exposed to business operations and lack technical experience and entrepreneurial values that are necessary for succeeding in business."

In the 1920s and 1930s West Indian-born blacks coming to this country did very well as a group, going into business and proving quite successful. They had drive and determination to succeed, and did so in surprisingly large numbers. Sociologists have attributed their success to the Jamaican social structure, where in spite of British colonial administration rule, there was upward mobility for blacks. Coming to this country, West Indians had separate customs and accents and an identity distinct from the masses of black descendants of American slaves. The Jamaicans showed the same self-confidence and motivation as did other immigrant groups. While this experience is not conclusive evidence, certainly enough has been written about the debilitating effect of the slavery experience that it must be counted high as a cause of the lack of black entrepreneurship. It is also of interest to note that the race pride and self-help ethic preached by the Black Muslims may well be responsible for their success in numerous ghetto-based business operations.

A third and last factor, also difficult to assess, is the importance of an economic base in some occupation or trade in which the group has a special advantage—a phenomenon not found among the black population.

Thus the Chinese in America, a small group who never dreamed until World War II of getting jobs in the general American community, had an economic base in laundries and restaurants—a peculiar base, but one that gave economic security and the wherewithal to send children to college. It has been estimated that the income of Chinese from Chinese-owned business is, in proportion to their numbers, *forty-five* times as great as the income of Negroes from Negro-owned business.[2]

The lack of business tradition may in and of itself be a handicap of some significance. The businessman is an important customer for other businessmen, and Italian bakeries are more likely to hire Italian truckers, suppliers, and so on. Such ties are both natural and important. This is why black groups use their buying power to force white-owned businesses to hire black sales personnel. Black ownership could lead to the informal formation of "black" forward and backward linkages in procurement and sales patterns.

Another disadvantage the black businessman has is that he is limited to the ghetto as a place of business. This means that his customers have lower incomes than those of businessmen located elsewhere; his insurance rates, if indeed he can get insurance at all, tend to be much higher than elsewhere; his customers are worse credit risks; loss rates from theft are

---

2 Nathan Glazer and Daniel Patrick Moynihan, *Beyond the Melting Pot* (Cambridge, Mass.: The M.I.T. Press and Harvard University Press, 1963).

higher; and so on. Further, when the black businessman goes to get bank loans, all of these disadvantages are thrown back at him. A commercial loan is "based on the proven management ability of the borrower in a stable industry and a stable locality." Black businesses are for the most part marginal, unstable, and very poor credit risks. They also tend to be almost exclusively in retail and service trades. If "there exists, among Negroes, a rather low image of the significance and possibilities of business endeavors," this feeling seems justified. The evidence available suggests a low rate of return for black entrepreneurs.

There are black businessmen who have grown quite wealthy and others who are modestly well-to-do who have built up sizable businesses in the black communities of Atlanta, Durham, Chicago, and New York, but they have done so by overcoming extensive obstacles. The argument here is twofold. First, black business is much smaller and less profitable than white business. Further, small business—white or black—will not do well and is not what the ghetto needs.

In a 1964 study of the Philadelphia black ghetto it was found that "[p]ersonal services were the most numerous, hairdressing and barbering comprising 24 percent and 11 percent, respectively, of the total number of Negroes in business. Luncheonettes and restaurants comprised 11.5 percent of the total. Many of the businesses would be submarginal if free family labor were not available. For example, median sales for a sample of Negro-owned beauty shops were $2,500, for Negro-owned luncheonettes, $6,800, and for barber shops, $4,400."[3] It seems safe to say that the 1970s will not be the decade of the small businessman. The number of black-owned businesses decreased by more than a fifth between 1950 and 1960, faster than the also declining rate for white-owned small businesses. In spite of the relatively unimportant and declining role of small businesses in the economy, blacks are being encouraged to open such businesses.

Restraining potential violence seems to be the major reason for the push for black ownership. One reporter making the ghetto tour in the spring of 1969 found:

Despite the ruins and other physical deterioration, black leaders say there is a new spirit of restraint, and perhaps a little more hope, among the people. "A community that sees itself coming into ownership of businesses and other property," said Thomas I. Atkins, Negro member of the Boston City Council, "is not anxious to destroy that which it will own."[4]

A great effort is therefore being made to give more blacks "a piece of the action."

---

[3] Eugene P. Foley "The Negro Businessman: In Search of a Tradition," in Parsons and Clark, *The Negro American* (Boston, Mass.: Houghton Mifflin Co., 1966), p. 561.

[4] John Herbers, "Mood of the Cities: New Stakes for Blacks May Cool Things Off," *The New York Times,* April 27, 1969. © 1969 by The New York Times Company. Reprinted by permission.

HELPING INDIVIDUAL BLACK BUSINESSMEN

One of the major differences in the ways white middle-class communities and black ghettos are organized is in the nature of formal and informal communication and decision-making. In white communities one of the most important groups on school boards, in charity fund raising, and in other commercial undertakings is the business community. The lack of black businessmen in the ghetto deprives the community of the important contribution such groups make elsewhere. A second disadvantage in this regard is absentee ownership. As James Q. Wilson has pointed out, "Communal social controls tend to break down when persons with an interest in, and the competence for, maintaining a community no longer live in the area. . . ." Resident businessmen, it is believed, add stability to their community.

The desirability of fostering the growth of small businesses has been recognized and accepted by the federal government for a long time. The Small Business Administration (SBA) makes loans to aid struggling businessmen. The extent of such aid going to blacks before the middle 1960s was minimal. A study of the ten and a half years of operation of the Philadelphia office of the SBA showed that out of 432 loans made through the fall of 1964 only 7 had been to black businessmen. Attempting to remedy this situation, the SBA set up a program on an experimental basis in Philadelphia to reach the "very" small businessmen, especially Negro businessmen, who operate a large segment of the very small business sector. The program involved loans up to $6,000 for 6 years (hence the name "6 × 6" Pilot Loan and Management Program). The SBA also offered individual training and counseling. The program was judged successful in overcoming traditional barriers faced by black businessmen, and, to the surprise of some old-time SBA people, the delinquency rate was very low.

In the late 1960s the SBA accelerated its search for qualified black borrowers, instituting special outreach programs, lowering equity requirements (which in 1968 could be less than 15 percent), guaranteeing up to 90 percent of bank loans, and developing counseling programs in cooperation with volunteer groups such as the Service Corps of Retired Executives (SCORE) and Minority Advisors for Minority Entrepreneurs (MAME). In fiscal 1968 the SBA aided 2,300 minority-owned businesses with various services and promised to increase this number in years to come. One thousand six hundred seventy-six minority loans were approved in fiscal 1968, about 13 percent of total SBA loans, and 5 percent of the total value of loans made.

Unfortunately, the rapid increase in the number of loans made to minority businesses was dramatically matched with climbing loss and default rates. In fiscal 1966 the loss rate was 3.6 percent. The next year it was 8.9 percent, and in fiscal 1968 the loss rate was nearly 12 percent of loan disbursement. It was hinted in the spring of 1969 that the climbing rate of losses on loans might lead to cutbacks in the SBA program. Once the best prospects were helped, the economies of the more typical ghetto business had become evident. Merchants with limited capital and markets purchase on a small scale and so must charge higher prices, creating customer resentment.

One way to minimize the failure rate of new businesses is through franchising, which utilizes a "proven" product, service, and marketing technique. The franchisor usually provides location analysis, helps negotiate a lease, obtains a loan, initiates training for the personnel, helps design and equip the store, and offers economies of centralized purchasing and advertising. Franchising is also a safe way for white firms to enter the ghetto market. Franchising and the SBA programs are subject to the same criticism: small retail businesses are on the decline, and certainly to rely on small business as a way to promote black advancement in competition with which capitalism "is little more than a hoax." An equally important criticism of attempts to create a greater number of black businessmen is that the economics of the ghetto may itself force the black capitalist to shortchange his "brothers," selling inferior merchandise at high prices just as other ghetto merchants do. For these reasons two other strategies seem more relevant to the economic development of the ghetto—the involvement of big business in partnership with the local community and local development corporations owned and operated by neighborhood residents.

THE WHITE CORPORATION IN THE BLACK GHETTO

The latter part of the 1960s witnessed the growing awareness on the part of the business community that it should become more "involved" in urban problems. Writing as a mayor of a large city with a background in business, Alfonso Cervantes stated in the fall of 1967 in the *Harvard Business Review* that before Watts he believed "businessmen should commit themselves to making money, politicians to saving the cities, do-gooders to saving the disadvantaged, and preachers to saving souls. . . . Observing the riots of Watts (and now Newark, Detroit, and other Harlems throughout the country) has converted me to an updated social orthodoxy. As a public administrator I have discovered that the economic credos of a few years ago no longer suffice; I now believe the profit motive is compatible with social rehabilitation."[5]

·   ·   ·   ·   ·

While involvement would unquestionably be of benefit to corporations as a whole, unless there is a profitable return to individual firms they will

5 Alfonso J. Cervantes, "To Prevent A Chain of Super Watts," *Harvard Business Review,* September–October 1967, pp. 55–56.

not participate. The problem for government is to insure profitability through subsidies and tax incentives without allowing unearned windfall gains. As the Nixon Administration found out when it tried to make good on campaign promises, this is a difficult balance to achieve.

The pattern of support that has emerged in the late Johnson and early Nixon years is that an independent corporation with a name like "Opportunity Unlimited" or "Economic Resources Corporation" is set up with a predominantly black board of directors, funded by Economic Development Administration grants and loans, Labor Department training funds, and perhaps an Office of Economic Opportunity grant and Department of Housing and Urban Development assistance. The key ingredient is an ongoing relation between the newly established corporation and a large established firm which supplies know-how and a long-term contract for the independent firm's output. Thus, in one well-publicized case a black group, FIGHT, in Rochester, New York, was assisted by Xerox in getting started. The extent of dependency in such a relationship has been described as follows:

> FIGHT's venture would have been a pipedream without the unstinting support of Xerox Corporation—from planning to production. Xerox helped to define FIGHT's product-line—metal stampings and electrical transformers. The office-copier giant will lend FIGHT two key management advisors, conduct technical training, and open the doors to bank financing. Even more important, Xerox has guaranteed to buy $1.2 million of the firm's output over a two year period.[6]

In discussing the role of Xerox in getting the Rochester firm started, another writer stated:

> Here lies one of the principal strengths of the program: a corporation often initiates a company, guarantees it a market, helps set up the business, furnishes the training, and helps iron out any start-up problems. Indeed, all the manufacturing enterprises have been established so far at the instigation of potential corporate customers.[7]

The encouragement of black entrepreneurship not only raises the income of blacks who manage the new businesses, but changes or reinforces their attitudes towards the proper methods of achieving social change. One counselor who evidently learned "a good deal from his experience" in helping a black man enter the business world, describes in the following terms the enlightened attitude of his pupil toward Negro development:

> As a leading Negro, Howard has not been fully able to accept the rebellious nature of the present civil rights movement. Certainly, he resents the forces that

---

[6] Martin Skala, "More blacks own and run U.S. concerns." Quoted by permission from *The Christian Science Monitor*, July 26, 1968. © The Christian Science Publishing Society. All rights reserved.

[7] Robert B. McKersie, "Vitalize Black Enterprise," *Harvard Business Review*, September–October 1968, p. 98.

have limited the Negroes' development, but in many ways he rises above this. He sees himself not only as a Negro but as a member of the society of man. As the movement advances and Negroes become more educated, Howard's values may be accepted. As he says, "Education without civilization is a disaster." He expresses his indebtedness to society when he says, "Let me be recognized, let me contribute."[8]

"Howard" would be described by some militants as an Oreo (black on the outside, white on the inside) or simply as a Tom. The achievement of such black men only reinforces the idea that blacks must struggle as individuals to escape their poverty. What is needed is not the salvation of a few but the redemption of all. This, militants argue, can be done only if all ghetto dwellers cooperatively own the economic resources of the ghetto and use these resources for the common good.

THE COMMUNITY DEVELOPMENT CORPORATION

The contrast between those who favor aiding individual blacks or encouraging white corporations to become involved in the ghetto and those who want independent black development is not always very distinct. Current proposals being put forward in the Congress have in fact adopted the rhetoric of militancy and the trappings of the radicals' own analysis. For example, Senator Jacob Javits, addressing the U.S. Chamber of Commerce in late 1968, compared the ghetto to an emerging nation which rejects foreign domination of its economy. He suggested:

American business has found that it must develop host country management and new forms of joint ownership in establishing plants in the fiercely nationalistic less-developed countries, [and so too] this same kind of enlightened partnership will produce the best results in the slums of our own country.[9]

In 1968 Javits along with others (including conservative Senator John Tower) proposed a bill which would establish community self-determination corporations to aid the people of urban (and rural) communities in, among other goals, "achieving the ownership and control of the resources of their community, expanding opportunity, stability, and self-determination." The proposed "Community Self-Determination Act" had the support of some militant Black Power groups such as the Congress on Racial Equality (CORE) because it promised self-respect and independence through ownership by blacks and community control of its own development. The bill set as an important aim the restoration to the residents of local communities of the power to participate directly and meaningfully in the making of public policy decisions on issues which affect their everyday lives. "Such programs should," the bill stated, "aim to free local com-

---

8 Ibid., p. 96.

9 Jacob Javits, "Remarks to the 56th Annual Meeting of the U.S. Chamber of Commerce," in *U.S. Congressional Record*, 90th Cong., 2nd Sess., May 7, 1968, p. 5053.

munities from excessive interference and control by centralized governments in which they have little or no effective voice." While the proposal was not enacted into law, it gives some indication of the type of thinking being done by influential groups and individuals. It has also directed attention to the community development concept.

Most schemes for community development corporations (CDCs) propose (1) expanding economic and educational opportunities through the purchase and management of properties and businesses; (2) improving the health, safety, and living conditions through CDC-sponsored health centers, housing projects, and so on; (3) enhancing personal dignity and independence through the expansion of opportunities for meaningful decision-making and self-determination; and (4) at the discretion of the corporation, using its profits to pay a "community dividend" rather than a return to stockholders. The relation between CDC-sponsored businesses and privately owned ones is hard to delineate satisfactorily.

Some proposals suggest that the CDC should also be a development bank to make loans and grants to local businesses in order to encourage ownership. Others suggest CDCs should bond black contractors and act as a broker between ghetto residents and outside groups for government grants, franchising, and subcontracting. Such an organization would be something on the order of a central planning agency, making cost-benefit studies of business potential in different lines, keeping track of vacancies, and conducting inventories of locally available skills. One study in Harlem has made (feasibility analyses," detailed cost-benefit "profiles," for different industries which might be developed in the ghetto. These involve a consideration of employment and income-generating potential as well as any externalities not reflected in private profit calculations. After detailing the best development plan (developed by technical analysis, subject to community approval under some suitable organizational form), a development planning group would make two final measures. First, an estimate would be made of the *efficiency gaps* (the expected differences in unit operating costs between Harlem projects' activities and similar businesses already operating outside the ghetto). "These gaps will suggest the magnitude of the public subsidies necessary to complement private capital in the implementation of the plan." Second, estimates would be made of needed infra-structural requirements which would "permit the Project businesses to function efficiently. This bill of requirements will then be presented to local government officials," or funded by a well-financed CDC. Under such a plan the CDC would provide social infra-structure and funds but eschew an ownership role.

Such a development bank and planning agency approach would encourage black entrepreneurship through low-cost loans and technical help. It downplays mechanisms for community control while stressing neighborhood involvement in an individual entrepreneurial role, rather than community cooperation.

The CDC schemes are expected to be financed either through stocks and bonds sold in the local community or through funding by federal agencies. Some suggest that in addition to the Neighborhood CDCs there should be a national Urban Development Corporation (UDC). The UDC, it is suggested, would not engage in development projects but could give financial and technical advice to the CDCs. The UDC would sponsor experiments and demonstration projects. A UDC could "be a source of knowledge, as well as assistance, generating new ideas for community ventures. It would develop, test, and disseminate knowledge of new means for organizing and implementing projects for creating housing, nurturing new businesses, training the unskilled, and so forth." By selective distribution of resources, based on performance measures, the UDC could increase the scale of operations of the more "effective" CDCs. In this view, the CDC would be limited for funding to what it could earn and what the UDC allocated to it as a "reward for social effectiveness." Profit in the usual sense would not be the measure of efficiency.

The power relations here are subject to much debate. The idea behind the CDC is to give an organizational tool for ghetto development. The extent of control by any group outside the ghetto would in all likelihood be fought by the local leadership. Rosenbloom argues that a UDC would be needed as a "surrogate" for the market, since many CDC undertakings (day care centers, a community newspaper, health services, and so on) might not be run as profit-making ventures but are important programs worthy of financing. Through financial rewards, the UDC would recognize enterprises which improve community conditions. The danger that such controls might lead to covert or overt "manipulation" and the charges of "same old paternalism" have been recognized, but it is also pointed out that there must be an overseeing of public funds through audits and some sort of supervision.

Conflicts might also arise between CDC and powerful local interests. CDC housing rehabilitation programs might not get very much cooperation from local slumowners; buyers' cooperative stores might find local merchants using their influence to fight them; the community-run schools might have trouble reaching agreements with the city-wide board of education, the teachers' union, and so on. On the other hand, the inclusion of (white) businessmen in advisory capacities to take advantage of local expertise might be rejected by the community. The demand by the mayor and city council that they be given veto power over projects or that all money should be channeled through them would also be resisted vigorously. If poverty program experiences are indicative, militant local CDC's would find their funds cut off as political pressures of the vested interests

made their power felt. The Model Cities Program has been carefully channeled through the local governments, and the ghetto has usually lost the
battle for community control. Some of the problems involved, from the
city council point of view, are shown in the vigorous resistance to giving
neighborhood boards real power under Model Cities legislation. This occurs partly because mayors and councilors do not like to "play second fid-
dle" to locally elected boards. There is a feeling that special consideration
is unfair and that all parts of the city should be treated equally, and the
argument that "fairness" requires restitution for past misallocation are
rarely accepted by residents of the wealthier white neighborhoods. The
narrow-mindedness of most local white electorates indicates that clashes
between local autonomy and federal priorities may prove to be one of the
more important conflicts in intergovernmental relations in the coming
years. Distinguishing among proposals which will encourage local control
by black communities while not allowing racist policies in white neighborhoods which democratically vote to be racist is a problem that can be overcome through the application of the U.S. Constitution. It is not as difficult
a task as some suggest; in fact, the suggestion that local control strengthens
white bigotry, while real enough, is often stressed by those who do not want
to see black communities gain real power. The inner-city blacks are asking
only for the same degree of autonomy as is already enjoyed by the suburban
whites who do run their police, school boards, etc. Each small town in
suburbia duplicates facilities, some of which might on economic grounds
be run on an area-wide basis. They do so to retain local control, even at
the expense of the added financial burden.

BLACK COOPERATION

Corporations have been criticized by some for not going far enough
in terms of ghetto autonomy. Others suggest that such proposals, by going
too far towards ghetto autonomy, encourage black separatism.

The limits of black capitalism have been well stated by James Sundquist:

Federal credit and technical assistance should be extended, and discrimination
against Negro enterprises in such matters as surety bonds and other forms of insurance should be dealt with—if necessary, through federal legislation. Much can
be said for a federal program to support and assist ghetto-based community development corporations that will have power to operate or finance commercial
and industrial enterprises. But even with all these kinds of encouragement, to
suggest that Negro entrepreneurship can produce much more than a token number
of new jobs for the hard-core unemployed, at least for a long time to come, is pure
romanticism. Ghetto anarchy is impossible. Even if the ghetto markets could be
walled off, in effect, through appeals to Negroes to "buy black," the market is not
big enough to support significant manufacturing, and the number of white em-

ployees who could be replaced by black workers in retail and service establishments is limited.[10]

For the ghetto to develop a strong "export" sector would take a great deal of expertise and capital. Both would have to be imported from outside, and for this to happen, long-standing flow patterns would have to be reversed. There are three ways this could happen.

First, private funds could be guaranteed against "expropriation" and special tax treatment given to assure profitability. The difficulty here would be that given foreign ownership, decisions would be made externally and profits could be repatriated.

Second are the proposals usually offered to help any underdeveloped nation badly in need of capital: better terms of trade and technical assistance. Foreign aid could be used to build up social overhead capital, to make investment in human capital, and to give loans to local entrepreneurs. The ghetto's one major export, unskilled labor, could be aided through a continuing national commitment to full employment. Technical assistance would include economic consultants, the establishment of research facilities to study potentially profitable lines of ghetto development, and a financial commitment to pursue such avenues.

Third, if the problem is viewed as one of underdevelopment, efforts could be made to retain profits and wages of ghetto-based enterprises by demanding that those who work in the area live there. Those who hold jobs as policemen, teachers, postal employees, clerks, or small businessmen would have a greater interest in "their" community if they lived in it. Cooperative forms of ownership would also lead to greater community control and to a greater retention of capital in the ghetto.

The timing and the substance of the gains blacks make will be determined by whether they rely primarily on aid from the corporate sector and the government or instead organize locally to control their own economy. Self-development implies organizational strength, a will and an ability to fight for political power. Thus Barry Bluestone has argued that:

while the creation of a black economy in the ghetto may not lead inexorably to a viable economic base—competitive with the staunchest of white enterprise—the act of striving toward an inner city economy yields a powerful tool for organizing the black community into a coherent political force capable of extracting concessions on jobs, housing, income, and dignity from the government and from the corporate establishment. While black socialism alone may not be capable of rooting out poverty, it may root out powerlessness and thus gain for the black community the indirect means to freedom from poverty and the manifestations of racism. In

---

[10] James L. Sundquist, "Jobs, Training, and Welfare for the Underclass," in *Agenda for the Nation,* ed. Kermit Gordon (Washington, D.C.: The Brookings Institution, 1968), p. 58.

the striving for economic independence, not only is dependence on the white power structure for jobs and poverty incomes reduced, but the economic incentive to coalesce within the black community increases as well. Jobs and income are created within the community and it is from such a base that political and social power are born.[11]

There is evidence that important sections of the black community hold views similar to those of Bluestone.

In the spring of 1969 when the Thirty-fifth American Assembly decided to devote its attention to "Black Capitalism," a sounding of the invited black participants persuaded sponsors to change the conference name to "Black Economic Development." "We do not want parity in the present system," one of the young black participants explained; "our goal is not simply to get a greater share in what already exists. . . . We want a new concept of American economic organization." Black business, participants stressed, should function to serve blacks. This principle was illustrated by the example of a Harlem investment group which "weighed the relative merits of a computer type industry and an all night drugstore and decided on the all night drug store because of the community need for one." Another conference participant spoke of the need for opportunity for blacks like that given to the farmer, the oil industry, and the railroads—i.e., subsidies.

Dick Gregory has expressed similar views:

What is needed is a concept of black cooperativism. Black capitalism as it is currently understood means a few individuals establishing a business to make a profit. The development of cooperative businesses allows many black people to work for profit and survival. It is cooperativism, rather than capitalism, which stands a chance of ending the current paternalistic overtones of federal programs.[12]

The argument for community control stems from two lines of analysis. First, white society may be scared by riots into making some concessions, but this is a costly strategy both in terms of loss of black lives and liberties and because of the strengthening of anti-black feelings among large numbers of whites. Second, there is the view that development by outsiders takes out of the hands of the community the control over extent and speed of development. In this light the purpose of black capitalism schemes seems to be to prevent future urban guerrilla warfare. In spite of the large amount of publicity so far, very few blacks have benefited. It appears that the programs are meant to do little more than "cool things" by making promises and calling for more patience.

---

[11] Barry Bluestone, "Black Capitalism: The Path to Black Liberation?" *The Review of Radical Economics* (Ann Arbor, Mich.: Union for Radical Political Economics, May 1969), p. 53.

[12] Dick Gregory, "Black Capitalism or Black Cooperativism," *Connecticut Daily Campus*, February 5, 1969.

There is also the fear that if black capitalism works, the ghetto will turn inward, in attempts to build a corner-store capitalism, rather than outward in attempts at restructuring economic goals and societal allocation of resources. The success of black businessmen in the ghetto could remove one source of tension without significantly altering the conditions of most blacks.

A more demanding stance would call for massive federal funds to make investments in deteriorated public facilities, community control of the economic base through cooperative forms of ownership, neighborhood control of local public institutions, and, finally, the demand for production for use. Demands for such changes could have a major impact on the larger society's future development. Community control or black cooperativism is, in itself, not a complete statement of this demand, much less a strategy for its attainment. But, as an alternative to individual black capitalism, it is a proposal which points away from neo-colonial control over the ghetto.

Part III
THE PUBLIC ECONOMY

A. The public/private mix of goods: Is there a social imbalance?

Does the United States currently have serious imbalances in its provision of public and private goods and services? Many critics of contemporary society think we do. Galbraith in his best seller, *The Affluent Society,* makes the argument that consumption is conditioned by social forces which lead to an unfortunate and unnecessary stress upon the production of superfluous private goods while public needs are neglected. He points out that such social forces as our truce on income inequality, the "dependence effect," and our propensity for inflation are all inherent tendencies which cause public services to fall behind private production. Consequently, this failure to keep public goods and services in minimal relation to private production and use is a cause of our social disorder and impairs our economic performance.

In response to Galbraith, Wallich contends that, even though one may be irritated by certain manifestations of our contemporary civilization, it does not follow that more public spending is the only or best alternative. "Better private spending is just as much a possibility." According to Wallich, "the choice between public and private money is primarily a choice of means." Many of our "new needs"—provision for old age, education, and health care—can be accommodated by the private sector; providing for many of these needs and wants through the public sector can lead to inefficiencies through the political process.

Siding with Galbraith on the "social imbalances" question, Ritter goes beyond the argumentative stage and poses the hard questions for action. "What are the dimensions of reordered priorities (in our national policies)? What are our most urgent domestic needs? What dollar amounts are involved? Who will foot the bill?" In attempting to answer some of these questions, Ritter examines the potential for a post-Vietnam "peace dividend," a "growth dividend" and a reordered national budget. His conclusion is that a large share of any reordered priorities in the 1970s will have to be financed by higher taxes. Do you agree?

24 The theory of social balance*

JOHN KENNETH GALBRAITH

It is not till it is discovered that high individual incomes will not purchase the mass of mankind immunity from cholera, typhus, and ignorance, still less secure them the positive advantages of educational opportunity and economic security, that slowly and reluctantly, amid prophecies of moral degeneration and economic disaster, society begins to make collective provision for needs which no ordinary individual, even if he works overtime all his life, can provide himself.

—R. H. TAWNEY[1]

The final problem of the productive society is what it produces. This manifests itself in an implacable tendency to provide an opulent supply of some things and a niggardly yield of others. This disparity carries to the point where it is a cause of social discomfort and social unhealth. The line which divides our area of wealth from our area of poverty is roughly that which divides privately produced and marketed goods and services from publicly rendered services. Our wealth in the first is not only in startling contrast with the meagerness of the latter, but our wealth in privately produced goods is, to a marked degree, the cause of crisis in the supply of public services. For we have failed to see the importance, indeed the urgent need, of maintaining a balance between the two.

This disparity between our flow of private and public goods and services is no matter of subjective judgment. On the contrary, it is the source of the most extensive comment which only stops short of the direct contrast being made here. In the years following World War II, the papers of any major city—those of New York were an excellent example—told daily of the shortages and shortcomings in the elementary municipal and metropolitan services. The schools were old and overcrowded. The police force was under strength and underpaid. The parks and playgrounds were insufficient.

* "The Theory of Social Balance" from *The Affluent Society*, 2d ed., Revised. Copyright © 1958, 1969, by John Kenneth Galbraith. Reprinted by permission of the publisher, Houghton Mifflin Company. John Kenneth Galbraith is Professor of Economics at Harvard University, Cambridge, Mass.

1 *Equality* (4th revised ed.; London: Allen & Unwin, 1952), pp. 134–35.

Streets and empty lots were filthy, and the sanitation staff was under-equipped and in need of men. Access to the city by those who work there was uncertain and painful and becoming more so. Internal transportation was overcrowded, unhealthful and dirty. So was the air. Parking on the streets should have been prohibited, but there was no space elsewhere. These deficiencies were not in new and novel services but in old and established ones. Cities have long swept their streets, helped their people move around, educated them, kept order, and provided horse rails for equipages which sought to pause. That their residents should have a nontoxic supply of air suggests no revolutionary dalliance with socialism.

The discussion of this public poverty competed, on the whole successfully, with the stories of ever-increasing opulence in privately produced goods. The Gross National Product was rising. So were retail sales. So was personal income. Labor productivity had also advanced. The automobiles that could not be parked were being produced at an expanded rate. The children, though without schools, subject in the playgrounds to the affectionate interest of adults with odd tastes, and disposed to increasingly imaginative forms of delinquency, were admirably equipped with television sets. We had difficulty finding storage space for the great surpluses of food despite a national disposition to obesity. Food was grown and packaged under private auspices. The care and refreshment of the mind, in contrast with the stomach, was principally in the public domain. Our colleges and universities were often severely overcrowded and underprovided, and the same was even more often true of the mental hospitals.

The contrast was and remains evident not alone to those who read The family which takes its mauve and cerise, air-conditioned, power-steered and power-braked automobile out for a tour passes through cities that are badly paved, made hideous by litter, blighted buildings, billboards and posts for wires that should long since have been put underground. They pass on into a countryside that has been rendered largely invisible by commercial art. (The goods which the latter advertise have an absolute priority in our value system. Such aesthetic considerations as a view of the countryside accordingly come second. On such matters, we are consistent.) They picnic on exquisitely packaged food from a portable icebox by a polluted stream and go on to spend the night at a park which is a menace to public health and morals. Just before dozing off on an air mattress, beneath a nylon tent, amid the stench of decaying refuse, they may reflect vaguely on the curious unevenness of their blessings. Is this, indeed, the American genius?

II

In the production of goods within the private economy, it has long been recognized that a tolerably close relationship must be maintained between the production of various kinds of products. The output of steel and oil and machine tools is related to the production of automobiles. Investment in transportation must keep abreast of the output of goods to be transported. The supply of power must be abreast of the growth of industries requiring it. The existence of these relationships—coefficients to the economist— has made possible the construction of the input-output table which shows how changes in the production in one industry will increase or diminish the demands on other industries. To this table, and more especially to its ingenious author, Professor Wassily Leontief, the world is indebted for one of its most important of modern insights into economic relationships. If expansion in one part of the economy were not matched by the requisite expansion in other parts—were the need for balance not respected—then bottlenecks and shortages, speculative hoarding of scarce supplies and sharply increasing costs would ensue. Fortunately in peacetime the market system combined with considerable planning serves to maintain this balance, and this together with the existence of stocks and some flexibility in the coefficients as a result of substitution, insures that no serious difficulties will arise. We are reminded of the problem only by noticing how serious it is for those countries which seek to solve it by a more inflexible planning and with a much smaller supply of resources.

Just as there must be balance in what a community produces, so there must also be balance in what the community consumes. An increase in the use of one product creates, ineluctably, a requirement for others. If we are to consume more automobiles, we must have more gasoline. There must be more insurance as well as more space on which to operate them. Beyond a certain point, more and better food appears to mean increased need for medical services. This is the certain result of the increased consumption of tobacco and alcohol. More vacations require more hotels and more fishing rods. And so forth. With rare exceptions—shortages of doctors and some kinds of private transportation facilities are exceptions which suggest the rule—this balance is also maintained quite effortlessly so far as goods for private sale and consumption are concerned.

However, the relationships we are here discussing are not confined to the private economy. They operate comprehensively over the whole span of private and public services. As surely as an increase in the output of automobiles puts new demands on the steel industry so, also, it places new demands on public services. Similarly, every increase in the consumption of private goods will normally mean some facilitating or protective step by the state. In all cases if these services are not forthcoming, the consequences will be in some degree ill. It will be convenient to have a term which suggests a satisfactory relationship between the supply of privately produced goods and services and those of the state, and we may call it social balance.

The problem of social balance is ubiquitous, and frequently it is obtrusive. As noted, an increase in the consumption of automobiles requires a facilitating supply of streets, highways, traffic control and parking space. The protective services of the police and the highway patrols must also be available, as must those of the hospitals. Although the need for balance here is extraordinarily clear, our use of privately produced vehicles has, on occasion, got far out of line with the supply of the related public services. The result has been hideous road congestion, an annual massacre of impressive proportions and chronic colitis in the cities. As on the ground, so also in the air. Planes are endlessly delayed or collide in the air with disquieting consequences for passengers when the public provision for air traffic control fails to keep pace with private use of the airways.

But the auto and the airplane, versus the space to use them, are merely an exceptionally visible example of a requirement that is pervasive. The more goods people procure, the more packages they discard and the more trash that must be carried away. If the appropriate sanitation services are not provided, the counterpart of increasing opulence will be deepening filth. The greater the wealth, the thicker will be the dirt. This indubitably describes a tendency of our time. As more goods are produced and owned, the greater are the opportunities for fraud and the more property that must be protected. If the provision of public law enforcement services does not keep pace, the counterpart of increased well-being will, we may be certain, be increased crime.

The city of Los Angeles, in modern times, is a near-classic study in the problem of social balance. Magnificently efficient factories and oil refineries, a lavish supply of automobiles, a vast consumption of handsomely packaged products, coupled for many years with the absence of a municipal trash collection service which forced the use of home incinerators, made the air nearly unbreathable for an appreciable part of each year. Air pollution could be controlled only by a complex and highly developed set of public services—by better knowledge of causes stemming from more public research, public requirement of pollution control devices on cars, a municipal trash collection service and possibly the assertion of the priority of clean air over the production of goods. These were long in coming. The agony of a city without usable air was the result.

The issue of social balance can be identified in many other current problems. Thus, an aspect of increasing private production is the appearance of an extraordinary number of things which lay claim to the interest of the young. Motion pictures, television, automobiles and the vast opportunities which go with the mobility, together with such less enchanting merchandise as narcotics, comic books and pornographia, are all included in an advancing Gross National Product. The child of a less opulent as well as a technologically more primitive age had far fewer such diversions. The red schoolhouse is remembered mainly because it had a paramount position in the lives of those who attended it that no modern school can hope to attain.

In a well-run and well-regulated community, with a sound school system, good recreational opportunities and a good police force—in short, a community where public services have kept pace with private production—the diversionary forces operating on the modern juvenile may do no great damage. Television and the violent mores of Hollywood and Madison Avenue must contend with the intellectual discipline of the school. The social, athletic, dramatic and like attractions of the school also claim the attention of the child. These, together with the other recreational opportunities of the community, minimize the tendency to delinquency. Experiments with violence and immorality are checked by an effective law enforcement system before they become epidemic.

In a community where public services have failed to keep abreast of private consumption, things are very different. Here, in an atmosphere of private opulence and public squalor, the private goods have full sway. Schools do not compete with television and the movies. The dubious heroes of the latter, not Miss Jones, become the idols of the young. The hot rod and the wild ride take the place of more sedentary sports for which there are inadequate facilities or provision. Comic books, alcohol, narcotics and switchblade knives are, as noted, part of the increased flow of goods, and there is nothing to dispute their enjoyment. There is an ample supply of private wealth to be appropriated and not much to be feared from the police. An austere community is free from temptation. It can be austere in its public services. Not so a rich one.

Moreover, in a society which sets large store by production, and which has highly effective machinery for synthesizing private wants, there are strong pressures to have as many wage earners in the family as possible. As always, all social behavior is part of a piece. If both parents are engaged in private production, the burden on the public services is further increased. Children, in effect, become the charge of the community for an appreciable part of the time. If the services of the community do not keep pace, this will be another source of disorder.

Residential housing also illustrates the problem of the social balance, although in a somewhat complex form. Few would wish to contend that, in the lower or even the middle income brackets, Americans are munificently supplied with housing. A great many families would like better located or merely more houseroom, and no advertising is necessary to persuade them of their wish. And the provision of housing is in the private domain. At first glance at least, the line we draw between private and public seems not to be preventing a satisfactory allocation of resources to housing.

On closer examination, however, the problem turns out to be not greatly different from that of education. It is improbable that the housing industry is greatly more incompetent or inefficient in the United States than in those countries—Scandinavia, Holland, or (for the most part) England—where slums have been largely eliminated and where *minimum* standards of cleanliness and comfort are well above our own. As the experience of these countries shows, and as we have also been learning, the housing industry functions well only in combination with a large, complex and costly array of public services. These include land purchase and clearance for redevelopment; good neighborhood and city planning, and effective and well-enforced zoning; a variety of financing and other aids to the house-builder and owner; publicly supported research and architectural services for an industry which, by its nature, is equipped to do little on its own; and a considerable amount of direct or assisted public construction for families in the lowest income brackets. The quality of the housing depends not on the industry, which is given, but on what is invested in these supplements and supports.

III

The case for social balance has, so far, been put negatively. Failure to keep public services in minimal relation to private production and use of goods is a cause of social disorder or impairs economic performance. The matter may now be put affirmatively. By failing to exploit the opportunity to expand public production, we are missing opportunities for enjoyment which otherwise we might have had. Presumably a community can be as well rewarded by buying better schools or better parks as by buying bigger automobiles. By concentrating on the latter rather than the former, it is failing to maximize its satisfactions. As with schools in the community, so with public services over the country at large. It is scarcely sensible that we should satisfy our wants in private goods with reckless abundance, while in the case of public goods, on the evidence of the eye, we practice extreme self-denial. So, far from systematically exploiting the opportunities to derive use and pleasure from these services, we do not supply what would keep us out of trouble.

The conventional wisdom holds that the community, large or small, makes a decision as to how much it will devote to its public services. This decision is arrived at by democratic process. Subject to the imperfections and uncertainties of democracy, people decide how much of their private income and goods they will surrender in order to have public services of which they are in greater need. Thus there is a balance, however rough, in the enjoyments to be had from private goods and services and those rendered by public authority.

It will be obvious, however, that this view depends on the notion of independently determined consumer wants. In such a world, one could with some reason defend the doctrine that the consumer, as a voter, makes an independent choice between public and private goods. But given the dependence effect—given that consumer wants are created by the process by which they are satisfied—the consumer makes no such choice. He is subject to the forces of advertising and emulation by which production creates its own demand. Advertising operates exclusively, and emulation mainly, on behalf of privately produced goods and services.[2] Since management and emulative effects operate on behalf of private production, public services will have an inherent tendency to lag behind. Automobile demand which is expensively synthesized will inevitably have a much larger claim on income than parks or public health or even roads where no such influence operates. The engines of mass communication, in their highest state of development, assail the eyes and ears of the community on behalf of more beer but not of more schools. Even in the conventional wisdom it will scarcely be contended that this leads to an equal choice between the two.

The competition is especially unequal for new products and services. Every corner of the public psyche is canvassed by some of the nation's most talented citizens to see if the desire for some merchantable product can be cultivated. No similar process operates on behalf of the nonmerchantable services of the state. Indeed, while we take the cultivation of new private wants for granted, we would be measurably shocked to see it applied to public services. The scientist or engineer or advertising man who devotes himself to developing a new carburetor, cleanser or depilatory for which the public recognizes no need and will feel none until an advertising campaign arouses it, is one of the valued members of our society. A politician or a public servant who dreams up a new public service is a wastrel. Few public offenses are more reprehensible.

So much for the influences which operate on the decision between public and private production. The calm decision between public and private consumption pictured by the conventional wisdom is, in fact, a remarkable example of the error which arises from viewing social behavior out of context. The inherent tendency will always be for public services to fall behind private production. We have here the first of the causes of social imbalance.

IV

Social balance is also the victim of two further features of our society—the truce on inequality and the tendency to inflation. Since these are now part of our context, their effect comes quickly into view.

With rare exceptions such as the postal service, public services do not carry a price ticket to be paid for by the individual user. By their nature, they must, ordinarily, be available to all. As a result, when they are improved or new services are initiated, there is the ancient and troublesome

---

2 Emulation does operate between communities. A new school in one community does exert pressure on others to remain abreast. However, as compared with the pervasive effects of emulation in extending the demand for privately produced consumer's goods, there will be agreement, I think, that this intercommunity effect is probably small.

question of who is to pay. This, in turn, provokes to life the collateral but irrelevant debate over inequality. As with the use of taxation as an instrument of fiscal policy, the truce on inequality is broken. Liberals are obliged to argue that the services be paid for by progressive taxation which will reduce inequality. Committed as they are to the urgency of goods (and also, as we shall see in a later chapter, to a somewhat mechanical view of the way in which the level of output can be kept most secure), they must oppose sales and excise taxes. Conservatives rally to the defense of inequality— although without ever quite committing themselves in such uncouth terms —and oppose the use of income taxes. They, in effect, oppose the expenditure not on the merits of the service but on the demerits of the tax system. Since the debate over inequality cannot be resolved, the money is frequently not appropriated and the service not performed. It is a casualty of the economic goals of both liberals and conservatives for both of whom the questions of social balance are subordinate to those of production and, when it is evoked, of inequality.

In practice, matters are better as well as worse than this description of the basic forces suggests. Given the tax structure, the revenues of all levels of government grow with the growth of the economy. Services can be maintained and sometimes even improved out of this automatic accretion.

However, this effect is highly unequal. The revenues of the federal government, because of its heavy reliance on income taxes, increase more than proportionately with private economic growth. In addition, although the conventional wisdom greatly deplores the fact, federal appropriations have only an indirect bearing on taxation. Public services are considered and voted on in accordance with their seeming urgency. Initiation or improvement of a particular service is rarely, except for purposes of oratory, set against the specific effect on taxes. Tax policy, in turn, is decided on the basis of the level of economic activity, the resulting revenues, expediency and other considerations. Among these, the total of the thousands of individually considered appropriations is but one factor. In this process, the ultimate tax consequence of any individual appropriation is *de minimus,* and the tendency to ignore it reflects the simple mathematics of the situation. Thus it is possible for the Congress to make decisions affecting the social balance without invoking the question of inequality.

Things are made worse, however, by the fact that a large proportion of the federal revenues are preempted by defense. The increase in defense costs has also tended to absorb a large share of the normal increase in tax revenues. The position of the federal government for improving the social balance has also been weakened since World War II by the strong, although receding, conviction that its taxes were at artificial wartime levels and that a tacit commitment exists to reduce taxes at the earliest opportunity.

In the states and localities, the problem of social balance is much more severe. Here tax revenues—this is especially true of the General Property Tax—increase less than proportionately with increased private production. Budgeting too is far more closely circumscribed than in the case of the federal government—only the monetary authority enjoys the pleasant privilege of underwriting its own loans. Because of this, increased services for states and localities regularly pose the question of more revenues and more taxes. And here, with great regularity, the question of social balance is lost in the debate over equality and social equity.

Thus we currently find by far the most serious social imbalance in the services performed by local governments. The F.B.I. comes much more easily by funds than the city police force. The Department of Agriculture can more easily keep its pest control abreast of expanding agricultural output than the average city health service can keep up with the needs of an expanding industrial population. One consequence is that the federal government remains under constant and highly desirable pressure to use its superior revenue position to help redress the balance at the lower levels of government.

V

Finally, social imbalance is the natural offspring of persistent inflation. Inflation by its nature strikes different individuals and groups with highly discriminatory effect. The most nearly unrelieved victims, apart from those living on pensions or other fixed provision for personal security, are those who work for the state. In the private economy, the firm which sells goods has, in general, an immediate accommodation to the inflationary movement. Its price increases are the inflation. The incomes of its owners and proprietors are automatically accommodated to the upward movement. To the extent that wage increases are part of the inflationary process, this is also true of organized industrial workers. Even unorganized white collar workers are in a milieu where prices and incomes are moving up. The adaption of their incomes, if less rapid than that of the industrial workers, is often reasonably prompt.

The position of the public employee is at the other extreme. His pay scales are highly formalized, and traditionally they have been subject to revision only at lengthy intervals. In states and localities, inflation does not automatically bring added revenues to pay higher salaries and incomes. Pay revision for all public workers is subject to the temptation to wait and see if the inflation isn't coming to an end. There will be some fear—this seems to have been more of a factor in England than in the United States—that advances in public wages will set a bad example for private employers and unions.

Inflation means that employment is pressing on the labor supply and that private wage and salary incomes are rising. Thus the opportunities for moving from public to private employment are especially favorable. Public employment, moreover, once had as a principal attraction a high measure of social security. Industrial workers were subject to the formidable threat of unemployment during depression. Public employees were comparatively secure, and this security was worth an adverse salary differential. But with improving economic security in general, this advantage has diminished. Private employment thus has come to provide better protection against inflation and little worse protection against other hazards. Though the dedicated may stay in public posts, the alert go.

The deterioration of the public services in the years of inflation has not gone unremarked. However, there has been a strong tendency to regard it as an adventitious misfortune—something which, like a nasty shower at a picnic, happened to blight a generally good time. Salaries were allowed to lag, more or less by neglect. This is a very inadequate view. Discrimination against the public services is an organic feature of inflation. Nothing so weakens government as persistent inflation. The public administrations of France for many years, of Italy until recent times, and of other European and numerous South American countries were deeply sapped and eroded by the effects of long-continued inflation. Social imbalance reflects itself in inability to enforce laws, including significantly those which protect and advance basic social justice, and in failure to maintain and improve essential services. One outgrowth of the resulting imbalance has been frustration and pervasive discontent. Over much of the world, there is a rough and not accidental correlation between the strength of indigenous communist parties or the frequency of revolutions and the persistence of inflation.

VI

A feature of the years immediately following World War II was a remarkable attack on the notion of expanding and improving public services. During the depression years, such services had been elaborated and improved partly in order to fill some small part of the vacuum left by the shrinkage of private production. During the war years, the role of government was vastly expanded. After that came the reaction. Much of it, unquestionably, was motivated by a desire to rehabilitate the prestige of private production and therewith of producers. No doubt some who joined the attack hoped, at least tacitly, that it might be possible to sidestep the truce on taxation vis-á-vis equality by having less taxation of all kinds. For a time, the notion that our public services had somehow become inflated and excessive was all but axiomatic. Even liberal politicians did not seriously protest. They found it necessary to aver that they were in favor of public economy too.

In this discussion, a certain mystique was attributed to the satisfaction of privately supplied wants. A community decision to have a new school means that the individual surrenders the necessary amount, willy-nilly, in his taxes. But if he is left with that income, he is a free man. He can decide between a better car or a television set. This was advanced with some solemnity as an argument for the TV set. The difficulty is that this argument leaves the community with no way of preferring the school. All private wants, where the individual can choose, are inherently superior to all public desires which must be paid for by taxation and with an inevitable component of compulsion.

The cost of public services was also held to be a desolating burden on private production, although this was at a time when the private production was burgeoning. Urgent warnings were issued of the unfavorable effects of taxation on investment—"I don't know of a surer way of killing off the incentive to investment than by imposing taxes which are regarded by people as punitive."[3] This was at a time when the inflationary effect of a very high level of investment was causing concern. The same individuals who were warning about the inimical effects of taxes were strongly advocating a monetary policy designed to reduce investment. However, an understanding of our economic discourse requires an appreciation of one of its basic rules: men of high position are allowed, by a special act of grace, to accommodate their reasoning to the answer they need. Logic is only required in those of lesser rank.

Finally, it was argued, with no little vigor, that expanding government posed a grave threat to individual liberties. "Where distinction and rank is achieved almost exclusively by becoming a civil servant of the state . . . it is too much to expect that many will long prefer freedom to security."[4]

With time, this attack on public services has subsided. The disorder associated with social imbalance has become visible even if the need for balance between private and public services is still imperfectly appreciated.

Freedom also seemed to be surviving. Perhaps it was realized that all organized activity requires concessions by the individual to the group. This is true of the policeman who joins the police force, the teacher who gets a job at the high school and the executive who makes his way up in the hierarchy of General Motors. If there are differences between public and private organization, they are of kind rather than of degree. As this is written, the pendulum has in fact swung back. Our liberties are now menaced by the conformity exacted by the large corporation and its impulse to create, for its own purposes, the organization man.

Nonetheless, the postwar onslaught on the public services left a lasting imprint. To suggest that we canvass our public wants to see where happiness can be improved by more and better services has a sharply radical tone. Even public services to avoid disorder must be defended. By contrast, the man who devises a nostrum for a nonexistent need and then successfully promotes both remains one of nature's noblemen.

---

3 Arthur F. Burns, Chairman of the President's Council of Economic Advisers, *U.S. News and World Report,* May 6, 1955.

4 F. A. von Hayek, *The Road to Serfdom* (London: George Routledge & Sons, 1944), p. 98.

25 Could Galbraith be wrong?*

HENRY C. WALLICH

Public needs are underfinanced while private tastes are overindulged—that is the proposition.

The two parts of the proposition seem neatly to complement each other —too much of one, therefore too little of the other. In fact they don't. It is one thing to be irritated by certain manifestations of our contemporary civilization—the gadgets, the chrome, the tailfins, and the activities that go with them. It is quite another—and something of a *non sequitur*—to conclude from this that the only alternative to foolish private spending is public spending. Better private spending is just as much a possibility. My contention here will be that to talk in terms of "public vs. private" is to confuse the issue. More than that, it is to confuse means and ends. The choice between public and private money is primarily a choice of means. The sensible approach for those who are dissatisfied with some of the ends to which private money is being spent, is to specify first what other ends are important and why. Having determined the ends, the next step is to look to the means. That is the order in which I propose to proceed here.

WHAT IS WRONG WITH PRIVATE SPENDING?

One may share the irritation of the new social critics as they look upon some of the fluff and the floss on our standard of living. My personal feelings can be characterized by noting that I have a 1951 car and no TV. The critics may want to bear in mind, however, that not all the money in this country is spent by people for whom life begins at $25,000. The median family income is $5600. Would these critics of the affluent society want to try living on much less than that? When Galbraith inveighs eloquently against switchblades, narcotics, and other phases of juvenile delinquency, he deserves the support of all right-thinking representatives of what he calls

* From " 'Private vs. Public'; Could Kenneth Galbraith be Wrong?" Copyright © 1961, by Minneapolis Star and Tribune Co., Inc. Reprinted from the October 1961 issue of *Harper's Magazine* by permission of the author and publisher, pp. 12, 14, 16, 22, 25. Henry C. Wallich is Professor of Economics at Yale University, New Haven, Conn.

the "conventional wisdom." But are the sources of these aberrations more intimately tied to affluence or to poverty? The exponents of the new social criticism may also want to remember the outcome of that "noble experiment," Prohibition. It should have taught us that it is futile to become our brother's dietitian. I hope that it has also imbued us with wholesome doubt about the moral right of some members of the community to regulate the lives of the rest.

Irritation with the poor judgment of other people who fail to appreciate one's own more advanced tastes is not new. It was a familiar situation during the 1920s. The critics then quoted T. S. Eliot's *The Waste Land*, and some went off to Paris in search of greener cultural pastures. The feeling behind the new social criticism is not dissimilar. Hence one might suppose that the reaction would likewise turn in a cultural direction. One might expect the critics of contemporary materialism to plead for more intensive preoccupation with things of the mind. Some fits and starts in that direction there have been, to be sure. But they have not been in the main stream of the movement. The principal alternative to private materialism that has been offered to us has been public materialism.

SIGNS OF QUALITY

Obviously, the quality of our culture could be greatly improved by public expenditures for education and support of the arts. The sales of good paperbacks and LPs are encouraging signs. But if contemporary materialism is to be leavened by such pursuits, it will be principally because large number of individuals make private decisions to that end. Social criticism is constructive if it helps precipitate these decisions. It obstructs a desirable evolution if it suggests that public creature comforts are the only alternative to private.

But while emphasis on nonmaterial ends seems sadly lacking in the new social criticism, the critics are right in pointing out that new material needs also have been carried to the fore by social and economic evolution—even though they mislabel them as public needs. In the good old days, when this was still a nation of farmers, most people had no serious retirement worries, there was no industrial unemployment problem, good jobs could be had without a college degree, most diseases were still incurable—in short, social security, education, and health care found primitive and natural solutions within the family and among the resources of the neighborhood. Today, these solutions are neither adequate nor usually even possible.

Meanwhile mounting wealth and advancing technology have brought within reach the means of meeting these needs. We can afford to live better in every way—more creature comforts, more leisure, more attention to matters of the mind and the spirit. At the same time we can take better care of retirement, of unemployment, of illness, of education, of the possibilities opened by research, than ever before.

There are indeed new needs. The citizen-taxpayer has his choice of meeting them, as well as all his other goods or services he wants privately, for cash or credit. Or he can buy them from the government, for taxes.

The nation as a whole pays taxes to buy public services as it pays grocery bills to buy groceries. The tax burden may be heavier for some individuals than for others. But the nation as a whole has no more reason to complain about the "burden" of taxes than about the "burden" of grocery bills—and no more reason to hope for relief.

Of the two stores, the private store today still is much the bigger. The public store is smaller, but it is growing faster.

Each store has some exclusive items. The private store sells most of the necessities and all of the luxuries of life, and in most of these has no competition from the government side. The public store has some specialities of its own: defense, public order and justice, and numerous local services that the private organization has not found profitable. But there is a wide range of items featured by both stores: provision for old age, health services, education, housing, development of natural resources.

THE NEW NEEDS

The bulk of the new needs are in this competitive area. The fashionable notion is to claim them all for the public store and to label them public needs. The statistics say otherwise. They say in fact two things. First, the supply of this group of goods and services has expanded very rapidly in recent years; and second, they are being offered, in varying degrees, both by the private and the public suppliers. Let us run down the list.

Provision for old age is predominantly private. The average American family, realizing that while old age may be a burden it is the only known way to achieve a long life, takes care of the matter in three ways: (1) by private individual savings—home ownership, savings deposits, securities; (2) by private collective savings—life insurance, corporate pension funds; and (3) by public collective savings through social security. Statisticians report that the two collective forms are advancing faster than the individual. The increases far exceed the rise in the Gross National Product of almost 80 percent (in current prices) over the past ten years; they do not indicate either that these needs are neglected or that they are necessarily public in character.

Education: the bulk of it is public; but a good part, particularly of higher education, is private. Total expenditures for all education have advanced in the last ten years from $9.3 billion to $24.6 billion ($19.3 billion of it public). Education's share in the national income has advanced from 3.8 percent to 5.8 percent. The silly story that we spend more on advertising than on education is a canard, though with its gross of over $10 billion, advertising does take a lot of money.

Health expenditures are still mainly private. At considerable expense, it is now possible to live longer and be sick less frequently or at least less dangerously. In the past, most people paid their own doctors' bills, although health care for the indigent has always been provided by public action or private philanthropy. Since the war, the proliferation of health insurance has given some form of collective but private insurance to three-quarters of our 182 million people. This has greatly reduced pressure for a national health service along British lines. For the aging, whose health-care needs stand in inverse proportion to their capacity to pay or insure, public insurance has finally been initiated and needs to be expanded. The total annual expenditure on health is estimated at over $25 billion, a little more than on education. Of this, about $6 billion is public.

So much for the allegation that the "new needs" are all public needs. Now for some further statistics on the public store, which is said to have been neglected. Some of them could make an investor in private growth stocks envious. Research expenditures (mainly for defense and atomic energy) have gone from about $1 billion to over $8 billion in the last ten years. Federal grants to the states have advanced from $2.2 billion to $7 billion during the same period. Social security benefits rose from $1 billion to over $10 billion. All in all, public cash outlays (federal and state) advanced from $61 billion to $134 billion over ten years, 57 percent faster than the GNP.

For those who feel about public spending the way Mark Twain felt about whiskey, these figures may still look slim. (Mark Twain thought that while too much of anything was bad, too much whiskey was barely enough.) To others, the data may suggest that the advocates of more public spending have already had their way. Could their present discontent be the result of not keeping their statistics up-to-date? In one of his recent pamphlets Arthur M. Schlesinger, Jr. claims that the sum of the many neglects he observes (including defense) could be mended by raising public expenditures by $10 billion to $12 billion. That is well below the increase in public cash outlays that actually did take place in one single fiscal year, from $118.2 billon in 1958 to $132.7 billion in 1959. In the three fiscal years 1957–59, these outlays went up more than $31 billion, though the advance slowed down in 1960. More facts and less indignation might help to attain better perspective.

Some parts of federal, state, and local budgets have expanded less rapidly than those cited—in many cases fortunately. The massive build-up in defense expenditures from the late 'forties to the 'fifties has squeezed other programs. Unfortunately, on the other hand, some programs that both political parties have favored—including aid to education, to depressed areas, for urban renewal—have been delayed unduly by the vicissitudes of politics. But the figures as a whole lend little support to the thesis that politicians don't spend enough, and that the government store is not expanding fast enough.

THE CITIZEN IN THE STORES

The two stores—private and public—work very hard these days to capture the business of the citizen-taxpayer. Here is what he hears as he walks into the private store:

"The principal advantage of this store," the private businessman says, "is that you can shop around and buy exactly what you want. If I don't have it, I'll order it. You, the consumer, are the boss here. To be sure, I'm not in business for charity but for profit. But my profit comes from giving you what you want. And with competition as fierce as it is, you can be sure the profit won't be excessive."

If the proprietor has been to Harvard Business School, he will perhaps remember to add something about the invisible hand which in a free economy causes the self-seeking of competitors to work for the common good. He will also, even without benefit of business school, remember to drop a word about the danger of letting the public store across the street get too big. It might endanger freedom.

As the citizen turns this sales talk over in his mind, several points occur to him. Without denying the broad validity of the argument, he will note that quite often he has been induced to buy things he did not really need, and possibly to neglect other, more serious needs. Snob appeal and built-in obsolescence promoted by expensive advertising don't seem to him to fit in with the notion that the consumer is king. Looking at the brand names and patents and trademarks, he wonders whether most products are produced and priced competitively instead of under monopoly conditions. The invisible hand at times seems to be invisible mainly because it is so deep in his pocket.

Bothered by these doubts, the citizen walks across the street and enters the public store.

"Let me explain to you," says the politician who runs it—with the aid of a horde of hard-working bureaucrats doing the chores. "The principles on which this store is run are known as the political process, and if you happen to be familiar with private merchandising they may seem unusual, but I assure you they work. First of all, almost everything in this store is free. We simply assess our customers a lump sum in the form of taxes. These, however, are based largely on each customer's ability to pay, rather than on what he gets from the store. We have a show of hands from the customers once a year, and the majority decides what merchandise the store is to have in stock. The majority, incidentally, also decides how much everybody, including particularly the minority, is to be assessed for taxes.

"You will observe," the politician continues, "that this store is not run for profit. It is like a co-operative, run for the welfare of the members. I myself, to be sure, am not in politics for charity, but for re-election. But that means that I must be interested in your needs, or you would not vote for me. Moreover, there are some useful things that only I can do, with the help of the political process, and in which you and every citizen have an interest. For instance, everybody ought to go to school. I can make them go. Everybody ought to have old-age insurance. I can make that compulsory too. And because I don't charge the full cost of the service, I can help even up a little the inequalities of life.

"By the way," the politician concludes, "if there is any special little thing you want, I may be able to get it for you, and of course it won't cost you a nickel."

The citizen has some fault to find with the political process too. He notes that there is not even a theoretical claim to the benefits of an invisible hand. Majority rule may produce benefits for the majority, but how about the other 49 percent? Nor is there the discipline of competition, or the need for profits, to test economy of operation. There is no way, in the public store, of adjusting individual costs and benefits. And the promise to get him some small favor, while tempting, worries him, because he wonders what the politician may have promised to others. The political process, he is led to suspect, may be a little haphazard.

He asks himself how political decisions get to be made. Sometimes, obviously, it is not the majority that really makes a decision, but a small pressure group that is getting away with something. He will remember that—after payments for major national security and public debt interest—the largest single expenditure in the federal budget is for agriculture, and the next for veterans.

THE EXPANDING BELT

Next, the citizen might consider the paralyzing "balance-of-forces" effect that often blocks a desirable reshuffling of expenditures. The allocation of public funds reflects the bargaining power of their sponsors, inside or outside of the government. A classical example was the division of funds that prevailed in the Defense Department during the late 'forties. Army, Navy, and Air Force were to share in total resources in a way that would maximize military potential. By some strange coincidence, maximum potential was always achieved by giving each service the same amount of money. It took the Korean War to break this stalemate.

What is the consequence of the balance-of-forces effect? If the proponents of one kind of expenditure want to get more money for their projects, they must concede an increase also to the advocates of others. More education means more highways, instead of less; more air power means more ground forcees. To increase a budget in one direction only is as difficult as letting out one's belt only on one side. The expansion tends to go all around. What this comes down to is that politicians are not very good at setting priorities. Increases in good expenditures are burdened with a political surcharge of less good ones.

The last-ditch survival power of federal programs is a specially illuminating instance of the balance of forces. If a monument were built in Washington in memory of each major federal program that has been discontinued, the appearance of the city would not be greatly altered. In contrast, when the Edsel doesn't sell well, production stops. But the government is still reclaiming land to raise more farm surpluses and training fishermen to enter an occupation that needs subsidies to keep alive. Old federal programs never die, they don't even fade away—they just go on.

The citizen will remember also the ancient and honorable practice of logrolling. The unhappy fate of the Area Development bill illustrates this admirably. As originally proposed, the bill sought to aid a limited number of industrial areas where new jobs were badly needed. It got nowhere in the Congress. Only when it was extended to a large number of areas with less urgent or quite different problems, were enough legislators brought aboard to pass it. Because of the heavy political surcharge with which it had become loaded, the President vetoed the bill. A bill was finally enacted early this year, long after aid should have been brought to the areas that needed it.

Finally, the citizen might discover in some dark corner of his mind a nagging thought: Any particular government program may be a blessing, but could their cumulative effect be a threat to freedom? He has heard businessmen say this so often that he has almost ceased to pay attention to it. He rather resents businessmen acting the dog in the manger, trying to stop useful things from being done unless they can do them. He is irritated when he hears a man talk about freedom who obviously is thinking about profit. And yet—is there any conclusive rebuttal?

THE CITIZEN'S FAILURES

The citizen would be quite wrong, however, if he blamed the politician for the defects of the political process. The fault lies with the process, or better with the way in which the process, the politician, and the citizen interact. The citizen therefore would do well to examine some of his own reactions and attitudes.

First, when he thinks about taxes, he tends to think of them as a burden instead of as a price he pays for a service. As a body, the nation's taxpayers are like a group of neighbors who decide to establish a fire department. Because none is quite sure how much good it will do him, and because each hopes to benefit from the contribution of the rest, all are prudent in their contributions. In the end they are likely to wind up with a bucket brigade.

But when it comes to accepting benefits, the citizen-taxpayers act like a group of men who sit down at a restaurant table knowing that they will split the checks evenly. In this situation everybody orders generously; it adds little to one's own share of the bill, and for the extravagance of his friends he will have to pay anyhow. What happens at the restaurant table explains—though it does not excuse—what happens at the public trough.

Finally, in his reaction to public or free services, the citizen takes a great deal for granted, and seldom thinks of the cost. Public beaches mistreated, unmetered parking space permanently occupied, veterans' adjustment benefits continued without need—as well as abuses of unemployment compensation and public assistance—are some examples. This applies also, of course, to privately offered benefits, under health insurance, for instance. The kindly nurse in the hospital—"Why don't you stay another day, dearie, it won't cost you anything, it's all paid for by Blue Cross" —makes the point.

By removing the link between costs and benefits, the political process also reduces the citizen's interest in earning money. The citizen works to live. If some of his living comes to him without working, he would be less than rational if he did not respond with a demand for shorter hours. If these public benefits increase his tax burden so that his over-all standard of living remains unchanged, the higher taxes will reduce his work incentive. Why work hard, if much of it is for the government?

THE POLITICAL DOLLAR AT A DISCOUNT

These various defects of the political process add up to an obvious conclusion: the dollar spent by even the most honest and scrupulous of politicians is not always a full-bodied dollar. It often is subject to a discount. It buys less than it should because of the attrition it suffers as it goes through the process, and so may be worth only 90 cents or 80 cents and sometimes perhaps less. The private dollar, in too many cases, may also be worth less than 100 percent. But here each man can form his own judgment, can pick and choose or refuse altogether. In the political process, all he can do is say Yes or No once a year in November.

The discount on the public dollar may be compensated by the other advantages of the government—its ability to compel, to subsidize, to do things on a big scale and at a low interest cost. Whether that is the case needs to be studied in each instance. Where these advantages do not apply, the private market will give better service than the political process. For many services, there is at least some leeway for choice between the private and public store—health and retirement, housing, research, higher education, natural-resource development. Defense, on the other hand, as well as public administration, public works of all kinds, and the great bulk of education—while perhaps made rather expensive by the political process —leave no realistic alternative to public action.

The argument I have offered is no plea to spend more or less on any particular function. It is a plea for doing whatever we do in the most effective way.

26 Reordering national priorities: A day of reckoning*

LAWRENCE S. RITTER

One cannot help suspecting that a large part of the reason for virtual unanimity on the desirability of "reordered national priorities"—but almost no action whatsoever toward their attainment—is that the phrase itself has become little more than a platitude. Devoid of solid content, it floats serenely above the political arena, comforting but meaningless.

What are the dimensions of reordered priorities? What dollar amounts are involved? Who will foot the bill? Priorities are relative—if some are ranked higher, then others must be dropped lower; but which ones and how much lower?

To many advocates of reordered priorities, these are irrelevant or even hostile questions. They seem to think that such issues will be resolved painlessly, with a post-Vietnam "peace dividend" or a "growth dividend," or both, spontaneously providing sufficient resources to satisfy all needs. And no one, least of all those running for public office, appears willing to acknowledge the reality that, if there is to be any substance to reordered priorities, they will have to be accompanied by higher, not lower, taxes. There will be costs, and they will not be negligible.

We blundered into Vietnam without knowing where we were going; it would be tragic indeed if we were to do the same thing all over again on the domestic front. A day of reckoning before the fact is surely preferable to a body count afterward.

THE POST-VIETNAM PEACE DIVIDEND

The size of the post-Vietnam peace dividend, for example, is sure to prove a severe disappointment to those who have been counting on it so

* From "Reordering National Priorities: A Day of Reckoning," an original paper adapted from articles that appeared in the Morgan Guaranty Survey (July 1971) and the Saturday Review (October 1971). Reprinted with permission of the author. Lawrence S. Ritter is Professor of Finance at New York University, New York, N.Y.

heavily. Such a dividend can be defined as the resources that would be released by a fallback in defense spending to 1965 levels, prior to the massive buildup in Southeast Asia. In 1965 defense expenditures were $50 billion. Last year (1970) they were $77 billion. On the basis of those figures, one would expect $27 billion a year to become available for alternative uses once the fighting ends.

However, such calculations are oversimplified. They fail to consider the inflation that has taken place since 1965. If the government today were to try to buy the same defense package it paid $50 billion for in 1965, pre-Vietnam, the price tag now would be approximately $64 billion. Relative to last year's $77 billion, this would release only $13 billion a year for alternative uses. That is the maximum that a post-Vietnam dividend, per se, can be expected to provide. This is small potatoes when set against the sums needed to make a meaningful dent in our domestic problems.

QUANTIFYING REORDERED PRIORITIES

What are our most urgent domestic needs? Aside from the direct reduction of poverty, which we will return to later, there appears to be general agreement that more intensive effort should be devoted in the 1970s to (1) improving mass transit in urban and suburban areas; (2) curbing environmental pollution; (3) improving police protection, law enforcement, and the judicial and penal systems generally; (4) upgrading the quality of education, especially in the larger cities; (5) improving health care and medical research; and (6) alleviating a growing nationwide housing shortage.

None of these problem areas can be improved by purely financial measures any more than purely military means succeeded in resolving the Vietnam situation. "Spend more money" is a first cousin to "send more troops." No additional expenditure will be effective unless it is part of thoroughgoing social and institutional reform—without such reform, a disproportionate share of additional monies spent on education, law enforcement, and prison reform, to name but three, will simply line the pockets of incompetent teachers, corrupt police, and sadistic prison guards. In the current jargon of sociologists, in other words, public service "delivery systems" have to be restructured if an additional dollar of spending is in fact to yield an additional dollar of benefit where intended.

It is equally true, however, that improvements cannot be expected unless more money is indeed spent. There may not be progress with more spending, but there surely will be none without it. At present, estimates of the dollar amounts needed to make significant headway toward these goals in the 1970s are little more than guesswork, and even less thought has been given to least-cost methods of realizing objectives within the context of this country's social, political, and economic institutions. Nevertheless, such crude calculations as have been made can give a rough idea of the magnitudes involved.

For example, it has been estimated that, in terms of 1970 prices, an average of $4 billion a year over and above the 1970 level will be required during the coming decade to make a meaningful contribution to mass transit; $10 billion a year more for pollution control; $12 billion a year more for law enforcement and reform of the judicial and penal systems; $20 billion a year more for nationwide school reform at all levels; another $20 billion a year for better health and medical care and research; and $30 billion a year more to reach our announced national housing goal of 2.6 million units constructed annually. This package adds up to $96 billion a year more than 1970 expenditures.[1]

Generally speaking, these estimates are on the conservative side. The additional $10 billion a year for pollution control, for instance, compares with a recent approximation of $10 to $14 billion by Joseph Scherer, a Federal Reserve economist. The $20 billion for health and medical care contrasts with the estimated $65 billion a year figure attached to Senator Edward Kennedy's "cradle to the grave" health insurance plan; even Medicredit, the proposed system supported by the American Medical Association, has been estimated to cost the government about $15 billion annually. As for housing, the $30 billion spent on home construction in 1970 resulted in fewer than 1.5 million housing starts, well below publicized national goals. To make up for the homebuilding decline of recent years and attain stated national objectives during the coming decade would require an annual expenditure of at least twice the $30 billion spent in 1970.

These needs must be weighed against the background of existing priorities. Table 26–1 shows existing priorities, as represented by the actual composition of goods and services produced in this country in 1970.

Table 26–2 adds the $96 billion more needed to satisfy reordered priorities to the appropriate spending categories listed in Table 26–1. This

TABLE 26–1. The allocation of resources, 1970 ($ in billions)

Spending on goods and services by category:	Dollars	Percent
Consumer spending	$617	63
State and local government	121	12½
Business plant and equipment	109	11
Federal defense	77	8
Residential construction	30	3
Federal nondefense	23	2½
Total (= Gross National Product)	$977	100

---

1 These estimates were derived primarily but not exclusively from *An Agenda for the Nation*, Kermit Gordon, editor (Brookings Institution, 1968); *Setting National Priorities*, Charles L. Schultze, et al. (Brookings Institution, 1970 and 1971); and the National Urban Coalition's *Counterbudget* (New York: Praeger, 1971).

326   *Current issues of economic policy*

means, first of all, adding $30 billion annually to residential construction. Most of the remaining $66 billion will have to be in the form of additional government spending—federal, state, or local—because most of the problem areas either encompass traditional governmental operations (education and law enforcement) or involve functions that private enterprise has failed to perform satisfactorily (mass transit, pollution control, and health care). If we arbitrarily allocate roughly three quarters of the $66 billion (or $49 billion) to state and local governments and one quarter (or $17 billion) to the federal government, we emerge with the conclusions summarized in Table 26–2: To realize reordered priorities

TABLE 26–2. The implications of reordered priorities in the 70s (in billions of $)

	1970	+	Additional needed	=	Average annual target for the 1970s
Spending category:					
State and local government . .	$121		$49		$170
Residential construction . . .	30		30		60
Federal nondefense	23		17		40
Total	$174	+	$96	=	$270

over the 1970s, state and local government spending will have to average $170 billion a year, residential construction $60 billion a year, and federal nondefense spending $40 billion a year, all reckoned in terms of 1970 prices.

A GROWTH DIVIDEND

What about the possible contribution of economic growth toward the needed $96 billion—the ability of industry to generate output in ever-increasing volume? A dozen years ago, our Gross National Product was $450 billion. Last year (1970) it was $977 billion. Fully 48 percent of this growth is illusory, the result of marking higher prices on the same quantity of goods and services. But the remaining 52 percent is real enough: Not including price changes, the amount of goods and services this country turned out grew at the rate of about 4 percent a year from 1958 through 1970.

The most optimistic forecasts for the 70s anticipate a growth rate, excluding price changes, of 4.5 percent a year at best. In 1971 that figure will be lucky to reach 3.5 percent, and a more realistic guess for the decade as a whole is probably closer to 4 percent a year. Nevertheless, for the sake of argument let us assume a 4.5 percent annual growth rate from 1970 through 1979. At that rate, the country's productive capacity, measured in terms of 1970 prices, would gradually rise from $977 billion in 1970 to $1,220 billion by 1975, and then continue higher over the remaining years of the decade. The 1975 figure of $1,220 billion is conveniently representative of the decade as a whole, standing as it does at the midpoint. (If one assumes straight-line growth, shortfalls below $1,220 billion in the years 1971–74 would be counterbalanced by overruns above $1,220 billion in the years 1976–79, so that 1975's Gross National Product can be used as representative of *average* annual figures for the entire time span 1971–79.)

One way of reckoning the contribution of economic growth—a growth dividend, so to speak—would be to take the entire $243-billion potential increase in national productive capacity, from $977 billion in 1970 to $1,220 billion in 1975, and consider all of it as being available for the desired purposes. This would be more than enough to satisfy the additional $96 billion needed—so what is all the worrying about? Unfortunately, not *all* of this increase will be devoted, in the normal course of events to these areas. Many other claimants are also lined up awaiting *their* share of the growth increment: consumers, many of whom are not so impressed by the minimum-consumption life-style of their offspring; and business firms, for whom growth and profits remain goals worth pursuing.

The process of growth, by itself, does no more than generate resources, which then are up for grabs. A growth dividend, strictly defined, refers to the potential increase in resources available for the desired purposes *given* the existing relative ranking of priorities. If state and local government spending, residential construction, and federal nondefense spending continue to receive the same share of the pie as they did in 1970—18 percent—then in 1975, with a projected output of $1,220 billion, such outlays would add up to $219 billion. This would be $45 billion more for these purposes than in 1970, but it would still fall far short of the additional $96 billion needed. This figure of $45 billion represents the most that growth, per se, can be expected to contribute. *Anything additional will have to be diverted away from other potential claimants by deliberate and purposeful public policy.*

At best, then, no more than $58 billion of the requisite $96 billion can reasonably be expected to arise from the combination of peace in Southeast Asia and growth in the economy—$13 billion accruing from peace and $45 billion from growth.

The remaining $38 billion will have to come from the considerably more painful process of using governmental authority—through taxation, for instance—to deliberately rechannel resources away from "undesirable" uses and into "desirable" ones. In addition, similar public policy will also have to make up for any deficiency in either the peace or growth dividends —as would be the case, for example, if military spending fails to shrink by $13 billion after Vietnam or if economic growth does not average a brisk 4.5 percent a year during the 1970s.

DELIBERATE RESIDUAL RESOURCE REALLOCATION

Table 26–3 illustrates the extent to which spending may have to be deliberately redirected by public policy. The two left-hand columns show how a Gross National Product of $1,220 billion in 1975 would be divided, if each spending category received the same percentage share of the total as it did in 1970. Under such circumstances, the three spending categories at the top of the table—which is where priorities should be revised upward—would, at 18 percent of the total, add up to only $219 billion in 1975, well below their $270 billion target.

By way of contrast, the two right-hand columns show that reaching the target figure would absorb 22 percent of total output. In other words, the reordering of priorities requires that the three top sectors receive 4 percentage points more of the pie than at present.

But an upward revision of some priorities necessarily implies a downward revision of others: A corresponding 4 percent of total output has to give way somewhere, somehow. The three spending categories at the bottom of Table 26–3 are all that remain, so that retrenchment must occur

TABLE 26-3. Resource allocation in 1975 under "old" vs. "new" priorities ($ in billions)

	1975 allocation with same priorities as 1970		1975 allocation with priorities reordered to reach social targets	
	Dollars	Percent	Dollars	Percent
State and local government. . .	$ 152	12½%	$ 170	14% ⎫
Residential construction. . . .	37	3	60	5 ⎬ Target
Federal nondefense	30	2½	40	3 ⎭
Business plant and equipment .	134	11	134	11
Federal defense	98	8	64	5
Consumer spending.	769	63	752	62
Total (= Gross National Product)	$1,220	100%	$1,220	100%

among them. On the basis of 1970 priorities, they would take 82 percent of total output. But if the sectors at the top are to obtain 22 percent of the total, those at the bottom can have no more than 78 percent. The question is what to cut and by how much. It is precisely here that the strength of the American public's desire for reordered priorities will meet its severest test.

A favorite starting point for radical surgery is business plant and equipment spending. Let the giant corporations pull in their belts—are they not already too big? But this approach is likely to be self-defeating. Unless business firms continue to build and improve their plant and equipment, at least at current rates, productivity will falter and there will be little chance of maintaining the postulated 4.5 percent growth rate. A smaller expansion in the economy's productive capabilities will then erode the $45 billion growth dividend, thereby compounding the difficulties.

This leaves federal defense and consumer spending as the only candidates left for contraction. It is here that something must give. These two sectors absorbed 71 percent of annual output in 1970. Cutting them back by 4 percentage points, to 67 percent of the total, would make room for expenditures by the top three sectors to expand as targeted. The basic choice thus becomes not *whether* to contract defense spending and/or consumer spending, but *how* and in what proportions.

In the right-handed columns of Table 26–3, defense spending is arbitrarily decreased to the pre-Vietnam level of $64 billion, which would amount to 5 percent of average annual output over the 1970s. This permits 62 percent of output to take the form of consumer goods and services. Views will differ on the wisdom of this 5 percent/62 percent split between defense and consumer spending. It may be that national security will require larger outlays than this; if so, then consumer spending will have to be squeezed even further. Or it may be that defense can get by with less; if so, consumer spending need not be restricted. The essential point is that in the 1970s, given reordered priorities and high levels of employment, every additional dollar spent on guns will literally mean a dollar less for butter. The great danger is that we will choose the *guns* and the butter and thereby abandon reordered priorities.

In summary, the additional $96 billion annually, on average, that is needed to reorder priorities in the 1970s can be obtained as follows: $13 billion from a Vietnam peace dividend; $45 billion through a normal growth dividend; $21 billion by diverting that much normal growth away from federal defense outlays over to the desired target areas; and $17 billion by a similar reallocation away from consumer spending.

PRIORITIES AND TAXES

Targeting reordered priorities is, of course, easier than realizing them. In an economy in which most spending is undertaken by the private sector, there can be no guarantee that any particular distribution of national output will emerge from the countless individual decisions that eventually make up the totality of spending. Nevertheless, targets have policymaking value even in a predominantly private enterprise economy. A wide variety of governmental measures can be employed to nudge spending in particular sectors up or down, including various forms of taxation and governmental lending and loan guarantee programs as well as direct government spending where necessary.

Pushing consumer spending down to 62 percent of Gross National Product in the 1970s would mean eliminating $17 billion of annual spending that would normally flow into retail markets. Achieving this reduction will require higher taxes—not the lower taxes that many public officials appear to be promising once the war in Vietnam has ended. Indeed, since the purpose of the higher taxes will be not so much to raise money to finance government outlays as to restrain the spending of consumers, net taxes[2] will have to rise by *more* than $17 billion—say, by close to $20 billion—to bring about the needed cutback in consumer spending. This is because many households are likely to pay part of the higher taxes by reducing their saving rather than their spending.

A question might be raised as to whether business investment spending would stay up if consumer spending is held down. Why would corporations expand to produce more when consumers are buying less? The answer is that business concerns never have been particular about who their customers are, and increased spending by state and local governments, by homebuilders, and for federal nondefense purposes would replace what would have been spent by consumers.

Such a sizable diversion away from consumption must come mainly from restraint on middle-income families. As a practical matter, it cannot be accomplished solely by increasing taxes on business or the rich. Business investment in new plant and equipment, as noted above, is a necessary precondition for the attainment of an adequate growth rate; despite recent questioning of some of the byproducts of economic growth, the fact remains that it is still the most important single producer of usable resources. "Soaking the rich" is no answer, either. This approach would not come close to freeing sufficient productive capacity, particularly since the rich would be the most likely to react to higher taxes by contracting their saving rather than their spending. Nor, of course, can any help be expected to come from reducing the consumption of those already at or close to the subsistence level. The conclusion is inescapable that a large share of the cost, in terms of less-than-desired consumption, will have to be borne (in taxes) by middle-income people, simply because they comprise the bulk of the population and do most of the consumer spending.

The alternative to achieving reordered priorities without explicit taxation is an *implicit* tax imposed through inflation. Aggregate spending in excess of the economy's productive capacity will reduce people's purchasing power by driving prices higher. The result generally is to penalize most those who are least able to protect themselves, such as the elderly and fringe workers in nonunionized employment.

---

2 Net taxes are defined as total tax receipts of all types—income taxes, corporate taxes, sales taxes, Social Security contributions, estate taxes, etc., state and local as well as federal—minus all governmental transfer payments. In 1970, total tax receipts amounted to $303 billion, a gross tax rate of 31 percent of the $977 billion GNP. But governmental transfer payments of $92 billion (in the form of veterans' benefits, Social Security payments, unemployment compensation, welfare payments, etc.) reduced net tax withdrawals to $211 billion or 22 percent of GNP.

POVERTY: THE NUMBER ONE PRIORITY

Finally, there is the direct attack on poverty per se. This is somewhat different from the kind of steps that have been mentioned above (although many of those would in fact be of substantial benefit to the poor). Improving mass transit, upgrading the quality of education, and so forth, involve the shifting of resources from one category of spending to another. The objective of income maintenance programs, on the other hand, is not to direct spending to particular uses but to direct income to particular people: the main effect would be a redistribution within the total of consumer spending, from higher income groups toward lower.

It has been estimated by the Census Bureau that direct action to bring all Americans up to the subsistence level, via some plan of family allowances or negative income taxes, would cost approximately $10 to $11 billion a year. Again, this would have to be financed in substantial part by taxes on middle-income families. The addition of this $10 to $11 billion would bring the total tax bill for the entire package to about $30 billion a year—*roughly 10 percent or $300 a year more in taxes for the average tax-paying family* than it would have to pay under existing tax rates (that reflect present priorities). In the final analysis, our willingness, or lack of it, to impose this 10 percent burden on ourselves—and our ability to do it both equitably and without destroying incentives—is likely to go a long way toward determining the future of the United States.

In the mid-1960s, Lyndon Johnson decided to play games with the American people. Once he became involved in Vietnam, he compounded the tragedy by hoodwinking the public as to its cost. We are still paying the price in terms of inflation. Unlike Southeast Asia, the reordering priorities is something we *should* get involved in. There is, nevertheless, a right way and a wrong way to go about it. The wrong way—acting again as though there are no costs involved—is likely to kindle an inflationary explosion even greater than Vietnam.

B. Economics of war and peace

President Eisenhower's warning in his farewell address about a "military-industrial complex" and the increasingly unpopular Indo-China war have aroused serious questioning about the impact of the military upon American political-economy. Is the military a wasteful bureaucracy, an inefficient "enclave" in the midst of a competitive market economy? Or has the whole economy become dependent on and structured to fit the military-industrial firms? Does war and military spending bring the stimulus of full employment, new technology and growth, or the frustration of inflation and forfeited priorities? Does world peace and disarmament mean economic opportunity or disaster? The following two readings only begin to explore these large and important questions.

Reich and Finkelhor show that the major defense contracting corporations are among the nation's largest and most powerful firms, and that the earnings from military spending extend from these large prime contractors into nearly every industry. The cost-overruns, planned technological obsolescence, and other "mistakes" which have angered liberal politicians and economists (and taxpayers) are here viewed as essential structural features of monopoly capitalism. More important, they argue that United States capitalism needs war and wasteful military spending as "a cushion to ward off stagnation and economic crisis." World War II rescued the economy from the prolonged depression of the 1930s (after New Deal spending efforts failed), and military spending since 1945 has sustained further growth. The liberals cannot replace military spending with large social welfare spending programs because such programs are not sufficiently wasteful; they might eliminate the pool of unemployed workers who "discipline" the labor market (to accept low wages and unpleasant jobs), and they threaten private enterprise, consumerism, profits, and capitalist dominance of the class structure. The military-industrial complex is thus politically and economically entrenched, and there is no way of diminishing it short of socialist revolution.

Eisner also emphasizes the damaging economic impact of military spending, or at least of Indo-China spending in particular—the gigantic $200 billion of direct military spending, plus the hidden costs of conscripted labor and the permanent loss of the dead and wounded. The real costs of the war are revealed in inflation and high taxes, declining real wages, profits, and stock market values, and in shortages of housing, education, and other needed government services.

Although radicals and liberals agree in their hostility to current military spending, their long-run policy conclusions are in sharp conflict. Eisner admits that military spending can bring a depression economy to full employment (as in the 1940s), but he does not share the radicals' fear of chronic depression or stagnation. The economy was essentially at full employment in 1965, and the Vietnam war therefore diverted and wasted resources which otherwise would have been productively employed to meet civilian needs. Eisner clearly believes that the liberal's Keynesian macroeconomic policies can sustain full employment growth and prevent stagnation. Such policies would include not only government spending on social welfare (which Reich and Finkelhor think politically impossible), but also tax cuts and monetary expansion to stimulate private spending (which they do not effectively rule out). The reader must judge for himself whether political decision-makers and taxpayer-voters are prepared to undertake new social programs (or the other Keynesian policy options) to replace Indo-China war spending. And if that seems feasible, consider the much larger reduction of military spending which would accompany disarmament. Can the American political-economy afford "a generation of peace"? Would it bring stagnation, or an opportunity to meet new national priorities (see Reading 26) in a growing economy?

27 The military-industrial complex*

MICHAEL REICH AND DAVID FINKELHOR

THE IMPACT OF MILITARY SPENDING ON THE ECONOMY

Before World War II, military spending never exceeded 1 percent of the Gross National Product. Over a trillion dollars have been spent on the military since 1951, consuming on the average about 10 percent of the GNP. In 1967, 4.08 million civilian employees worked on defense-related jobs, add to this the 3.5 million soldiers in uniform, and we have well over 10 percent of the entire labor force engaged in military-related employment.

The military sector of the economy is huge. Yet the image of the weapons industry often projected by liberals is of a small, albeit powerful, coterie of contractors, many of whom owe their existence solely to defense work. Producing exotic military hardware, these corporations form an economic *enclave* somehow separated from the remainder of the economy.

According to the enclave view, most corporations in the country are not affected one way or another by the military budget (except, of course, insofar as aggregate incomes and demands are stimulated). There is some superficial evidence for this image. After all, only one hundred corporations receive over two-thirds of all prime contract awards each year and fifty corporations receive 60 percent, and the list of the top one hundred contractors has exhibited very little turnover in the last twenty years. Prime contract awards are concentrated among just four industries: aircraft (43 percent), electronics and telecommunications (19.3 percent), shipbuilding and repairing (10.3 percent), and ammunition (5 percent). Moreover, subcontracts appear to be just as concentrated among the big firms.

---

* From "The Military Industrial Complex: No Way Out" by Michael Reich and David Finkelhor. From *Up Against the American Myth,* edited by Tom Christoffel, David Finkelhor, and Dan Gilbarg, Holt, Rinehart and Winston, Inc. Copyright © 1970 by Michael Reich and David Finkelhor. Reprinted by permission of the authors. Michael Reich is Assistant Professor of Economics at Boston University, Cambridge, Mass.

But this enclave image is highly misleading. First, a list of the top military contractors is virtually a list of all the largest and most powerful industrial corporations in America. Nathanson estimates that of the 500 largest manufacturing corporations in 1964, *at least* 205 were significantly involved in military contracts, either in production or in research and development. Among the top 100 firms, 65 are significantly involved in the military market. All but 5 of the largest 25 industrial corporations in 1968 were among the 100 largest contractors for the Defense Department. Of these 5, one—Union Carbide—is the largest Atomic Energy Commission contractor, two are oil companies indirectly involved in military sales, and one is a steel company also indirectly involved. It is difficult to think of these top corporations as constituting an "enclave."

Second, there are no self-contained enclaves in the American economy. As the study of input-output economics has revealed, the structure of American industry is highly interdependent. Focusing only on the prime contractors is like looking at only the visible part of an iceberg. This is only the direct impact of the military budget; the indirect impact on subcontractors, on producers of intermediate goods and parts, and on suppliers of raw materials ties military spending into the heart of the economy. For evidence, look at the wide range of industries over which direct and indirect effects of military spending were distributed in 1967. With the exception of the aircraft and electrical equipment industries, no one industry accounted for more than 7 percent of total private military-related employment. Aircraft and parts accounted for 15 percent, and electrical equipment and supplies accounted for 13 percent. This industrial profile shows that despite the enclave image, a broad spectrum of the domestic corporate economy is involved in military production.

Third, corporations in the civilian market have been racing to get a piece of the military action. Between 1959 and 1962, years for which a study was done, "manufacturing firms outside the defense sector purchased 137 companies in the defense sector (i.e., aircraft and parts, ships and boats, ordnance, electrical machinery, scientific instruments and computers)." By 1966, ninety-three of the top five hundred manufacturing firms had diversified into the defense sector from a traditional nondefense base.

Military spending is very important for a large number of industries within manufacturing. About 11.5 percent of all manufacturing output as early as 1958 is attributable to military-related expenditures; the corresponding figure is 20 percent for the metal-working production sector, comprised of metals and metal products, nonelectrical machinery, electrical equipment and supplies, transportation equipment, ordnance, and instruments. The percentage of profits attributable to military spending are probably even higher, given that profits rates are higher on military contracts—as is shown below.

HOW GREAT A STAKE IN THE MILITARY

Having seen that the military sector comprises the very heart of Capitalist America, we can now ask what stake the economy has in the existence of this Leviathan.

First, we shall point out the stake of the most privileged and powerful segments of the economy. Military spending is in large part responsible for the increasing concentration of economic power in the hands of a small group. It plays a role in the perpetuation of substantial inequality among the population as a whole. And it is a key factor behind the profitability of many of America's largest corporations.

But we shall go further and argue that the entire capitalist economy has a stake in militarism. For military spending is responsible for much of the economic growth the country has experienced in the postwar period. Without militarism, the whole economy would return to the state of collapse from which it was rescued by the Second World War.

Military spending has been a key force behind the trend toward increasing concentration of economic power. We have already observed that prime contract awards are concentrated among a small number of corporations; fifty firms in an average year get 60 percent of the procurement contract dollar, about 94 percent of the research, development and testing contract dollar. This makes the war industry much more concentrated than the economy as a whole, where the top one hundred firms usually account for only 35 percent of the manufacturing sales. The business of the war industry goes to the biggest firms and is used by them as a base from which to expand their area of control. So it is not surprising that between 1947 and 1963 the top two hundred industrial corporations, boosted by defense business, increased their share of total value added in the economy from 30 percent to 41 percent.

Let's look at the increasing concentration produced by military spending on an industry level. Almost all of military spending goes to the most concentrated industries in the economy. The standard measure of concentration in an industry is the percentage of sales accounted for by the top four firms. Industries in which four firms monopolized over 50 percent of the sales accounted for about one-quarter of all sales by manufacturing industries in 1958. But 90 percent of all military contracts go to these most concentrated industries. The most powerful elements in the economy have a large stake in the military production because of the opportunities it provides them to increase the concentration of their economic control. Military expenditures have a political base far stronger than the magnitudes involved would suggest.

Military spending has also created privileged interest groups within the occupational structure; it is an important factor tying many professionals, universities, and labor union leaders to government policy. A large number of the most highly trained people in the economy owe their jobs to defense spending. For example, nearly half of all engineers and scientists employed in private industry are at work on military or space-related projects. Many of the scientists and engineers pursuing research in the universities receive money from the Pentagon.

The military industries generally employ a highly skilled work force. A 1962 Department of Labor study of the electronics industry showed that at military- and space-oriented plants 59.2 percent of employees were highly paid engineers, executives, or skilled blue-collar craftsmen. In the consumer-oriented plants of the same electronics industry, in contrast, 70.2 percent of the employees were semiskilled and unskilled blue- and white-collar workers. Professional and managerial workers comprise 22 percent of all private defense-related employment, but only 15 percent of all U.S. manufacturing employment. Thus, a large proportion of the people in the most educated strata, many still university-based, are tied by military spending to a vested interest in existing national priorities. A large number of blue-collar workers are engaged in military-related work. The carrot the government can dangle in front of major union leaders has been a factor in their growing conservatism and endorsement of Cold War policies.

Military spending has a regressive impact on the distribution of income within the U.S., that is, benefits the rich and hurts the poor. This is suggested by the higher proportion of professional and skilled workers in defense-related work. Computations by economist Wassily Leontief show that one dollar of military spending generates half as many jobs, but 20 percent more in salaries, then does one dollar of civilian spending. This means that tax money extracted from the whole population is paid out in such a way as to benefit high earners much more than low earners. Perhaps by accident, or perhaps by design, military spending is one of the mechanisms by which higher income groups use the government to prevent redistribution of income from taking place.

Last, but not least, the military sector is a source of enormous profits for the corporate elite. It is an organized system of governmental subsidy for corporate coffers, or as C. Wright Mills called it, "socialism for the rich." We can see how deeply wedded the corporate giants are to this arrangement by examining the opportunities the military sector presents to them.

ATTRACTIVENESS OF THE MILITARY MARKET

The attractiveness of the military market to big corporations—the opportunities for growth and fantastic profits—has been described by a number of journalists and muckrakers. In recent years, the hearings conducted by the Senate Subcommittee on Economy in Government (chaired by Senator William Proxmire) have provided further glimpses into the shadowy world of the military contractor. The mass media have reported horror stories from these hearings and tales of corporate greediness and bureaucratic favoritism gleaned from the Proxmire investigations have been retold in excellent analyses by Henry Nieburg, Walter Adams, Richard Kaufman, and by the Proxmire Committee itself (in its pamphlet, *The Economics of Military Procurement*). The reader is strongly urged to examine one or more of these documentations of the waste and profiteering endemic to the military sector of the economy. These studies reveal that the excesses and horror stories presented in the mass media about the military contracting business are far from isolated or atypical examples. Where these studies fall short, however, is in failing to emphasize that the waste and profiteering have a systematic basis in the structure of the military "market." This market differs in several important respects from markets in the civilian economy.

Unlike other industries, military contract work is not determined in a "market" at all, in any usually understood sense of the word. Contracts are arrived at through negotiations between a company and Pentagon contracting officers. The arrangement is rife with opportunities for the companies. Government as purchaser is alleged to have the same interest as a private consumer in cutting costs and buying only what is needed. In fact, this is not the case. First of all, procurement officers—who represent the government in these affairs—have an interest as military men in expanding the arsenal of weapons and thus the power and prestige of their branch of service. And so long as there is slack in the economy, higher-ups don't pressure them to hold down costs. Second, if they are on the lookout for their future in the business world, and they are, they have the most appealing reasons for currying the favor of the corporations with whom they are supposed to "bargain." When they retire, many military men involved in procurement regulation go directly to jobs in one of the defense companies. In 1967, 2,072 retired regular military officers were employed by the ninety-five top contractors. The top ten contractors had an average of 106 former officers apiece on their payrolls.

Contracting is supposed to take place competitively. In fact, it almost never does. Any one of a catalogue full of excuses can be reason for bypassing the competitive bidding procedure, for example, if the item is critical, if delivery is urgent, if security considerations preclude it, etc.; 90 percent of the Pentagon's contract dollars are negotiated under such "exceptions."

The exotic technologies involved in weapons provide a perfect opportunity for boondoggles. Only specialists understand what is a superfluous and what is a necessary expenditure. This allows for enormous padding and excessive costs, as a number of Senate investigations have charged. A contractor may sell the Pentagon a two billion dollar missile when a one billion dollar one would have worked equally well. Subcontracting creates the opportunity for pyramiding profits on multiple tiers of subcontracts. Moreover, once a contractor has done some work on a weapons system— whether in another contract or in a research and development study—he obtains a virtual monopoly over the area. Since he is the only one with relevant experts and the relevant experience, the government is stuck with giving him the business. It is practically impossible to oversee and account for the operations in these areas. Both the complex technology and security considerations bar most outsiders.

So there is no bad blood created when costs of production far overrun those that were written into the contract. Final costs average 320 percent of the original cost estimates. That is, the average contractor ends up charging the government over three times the cost estimate he initially submitted to "win" the contract. Since most contracts are on a cost-plus basis, his profits go up three times also.

Companies do not lose their privileged status if their weapons do not meet up to specifications or perform properly. A recent study of thirteen major aircraft and missile programs since 1955, which cost in total forty billion, revealed that only four of these (costing five billion) performed at as much as 75 percent of the design specifications. Yet the companies with the poorest performance records reported the highest profits.

What this all amounts to, of course, is that profits for defense work are higher than those in every industry except pharmaceuticals. This is obscured by the Defense Department, which sometimes releases profits computed as a percentage of sales or costs. But, in the normal business world, profits are figured as a percentage of *investment*. Defense contractors invest very little of their own money because in most cases the government provides most of the investment and working capital needed by contractors to set up plants and machinery and to buy the necessary materials and parts. The profits when measured against investment are often huge.

A study by Murray Weidenbaum, formerly an economist for the Boeing Company and now Assistant Secretary of the Treasury, of a sample of large defense contractors showed that between 1962 and 1965 they earned 17.5 percent on investment, compared to average civilian market earnings of 10.6 percent. And this probably understates the case. Many military contractors also sell in the civilian market. The machinery provided free by the Pentagon, the allocation of all overhead costs to military contracts, and the technological edge gained in cost-plus military contracts can be of enormous importance in increasing profits on *civilian* sales for firms doing some business with the Pentagon. In one of the most outrageous cases that has come to light, a tax count showed in 1962 that North American Aviation Company had realized profits of 612 percent and 802 percent on its investment on "military" contracts in two successive years.

Everyone—except the Pentagon, of course—agrees that laxity and profiteering are part and parcel of military procurement. Liberals take this to be indicative of the way in which the military complex has escaped the normal checks and balances of the political process. To radicals, this seems a gross understatement of reality. Politicians, bureaucrats, and businessmen all know that these "excesses" exist. These "excesses" are not a subversion of normal government procedure—they are the normal government procedure.

The waste and profiteering—the enormous amount of military spending—are not aberrations or mistakes. Waste is winked at because the entire economy has a stake in it.

Of course, military men dabble in corrupt practices. Of course, large corporations use strong-arm pressures to obtain favors. But waste of this magnitude is neither simple profiteering nor economic gangsterism. Massive, wasteful military spending is allowed to exist because it fulfills a need of the system as a whole. The waste is what helps military spending fulfill its function: providing a cushion to ward off stagnation and economic crisis.

MILITARY SPENDING AND STAGNATION

Among liberal optimists, one used to be able to find those who argued that government spending of any kind could be cut with no ill effects on long-run economic growth. The money freed from spending could be returned to taxpayers and corporations in the form of tax cuts. This would quickly be ploughed back into the economy in the form of increased consumption and increased investment—no slowdown necessary. There are few proponents of this view left.

Most everybody understands today that high levels of government spending are necessary for economic stability and growth. The depression of the 1930s illustrated the incredible levels of unemployment and business lethargy the system would generate if left alone. Only World War II showed how to cope with the problem. Massive levels of government spending in defense were necessary to create demand and alleviate unemployment. In the post-war period too, military spending has been responsible for a large part of the economic growth that has taken place. The fluctuation of military spending has virtually determined the cyclical pattern of the economy. Declines in military spending have been followed by declines in overall economic growth.

Not all advanced capitalist countries have leaned on military spending to the extent the United States has. In part this is because the United States, as the most industrialized country in the world, has the greatest problem of inadequate aggregate demand. But there is more to American militarism than this. After World War II, the United States emerged as by far the dominant leader of the worldwide capitalist system. It took on the task of defending the "Free World." This required a large military establishment, and the United States, the only country with its industrial economy intact after World War II, was the only country capable of taking on this role. Furthermore, the necessity of rebuilding in Western Europe and Japan postponed aggregate demand problems in these countries for almost two decades—the destruction of antiquated machinery also removed some of the fetters on production. Hence, the United States was far more in need of a stimulus for demand than other advanced capitalist countries. Finally, the tradition of "étatisme" is much stronger in Western Europe, where most governmental functions are highly centralized. The decentralized and multilevel nature of government in the United States provides an additional fetter on civilian government spending.

Liberals do not deny that arms spending has served the necessary function of averting stagnation. But they argue that other forms of public sector spending are equally feasible. Instead of weapons, the Federal government could sponsor vast projects to improve health, education, housing, transportation, etc., etc.—some even envisage a "domestic Marshall plan."

But in order to provide an equivalent aggregate economic stimulus, social welfare spending like that called for by liberals would have to be roughly the same magnitude as the present level of military spending. It would have to be just as expandable to keep pace with the growth of the economy. Can social welfare spending do this? The historical answer seems to be no.

Massive civilian government spending was tried as a stimulus in the 1930s and failed. In the depths of the depression, one of the impulses of the New Deal had been to increase social spending to stimulate the economy back to life. Between 1929 and 1939 government expenditures on nondefense purchases and transfer payments nearly doubled from 9.1 billion dollars in 1929 to 17.8 billion dollars in 1939. But this stimulus was not enough—the economy hardly budged. The GNP in the same period slumped from 104.4 billion to 91.1 billion and unemployment rose from 3.2 to 17.2 percent. Enough stimulus was just not generated by social spending. But government spending on arms, once the war mobilization had begun, was enough—exactly what the disease called for. Between 1939 and 1944, military spending increased from 1 billion to 77 billion; GNP shot up in the same years to 211.4 billion.

Spending on arms succeeded where social services spending had failed, because only government spending on arms can be enormous and expandable almost without limit. Why is this so? For one, only military spending is so amenable to waste that can be made publicly and politically acceptable. Second, only military spending can expand so freely without damaging the basic framework of the economy. Massive social spending would compete with the private sector; it would damage the labor market; it would clash head on with hundreds of powerful vested interests at every level of the economy. Given such opposition, social spending could never expand adequately to fill the economic gap. Consider the factors that allow the enormous size, rapid expandability, and wastefulness of the military budget.

First, a convenient rationalization of the need for massive armaments expenditures exists. The ideology of anticommunism and the Cold War has been drummed into politicians and public alike for over twenty years. This is a powerful force behind defense spending as well as a general legitimizer of capitalism.

Second, armaments are rapidly consumed or become obsolete very quickly. Bombers get shot down over Vietnam, ammunition gets used up or captured, and so on. More important, the technology of advanced weapons systems becomes obsolete as fast as defense experts can think of "improvements" over existing weapons systems (or as soon as Soviet experts do). Thus, many weapons systems have proved obsolete even before production on them was completed. The demand for weaponry is a bottomless pit.

Third, the kind of machinery required for armament production is highly specific to particular armaments. So each time a new weapon is needed or a new process created, all existing production machinery must be scrapped. Extensive retooling at very great new outlays is required.

Fourth, there is no generally agreed upon yardstick for measuring how much defense we have. How do we know when an adequate level of military security is achieved? National Security Managers can always claim that by some criteria what we have is not enough. Terms like nuclear parity and superiority are easily juggled. Military men always have access to new "secret intelligence reports" not available to the general public. Since few people are willing to gamble with national defense, the expertise of the managers is readily accepted. Politicians and the general public have little way of adequately questioning their judgment.

These factors combine so that defense expenditures can be enormous and expandable probably without limit. But the same is not the case for social services spending. The above factors are all highly specific to the military sector.

No readily available rationalization yet exists behind massive social service spending. Of course, everyone has to admit health care, hospitals, and schools are good, but that does not mean they are prepared to see masses of federal tax dollars funneled into these areas.

Investments in social facilities are usually durable—they do not become obsolete very quickly and are not rapidly consumed. Right now, of course, there are plenty of unmet needs in these areas. But once everyone is provided with a decent house, once there are new schools and health clinics stocked with materials, then what? They cannot be immediately torn down and built all over again.

The technology of social welfare facilities is not particularly exotic. Very conventional standards exist to tell us how much a house should cost and how much a hospital should cost. There is no possibility for enormous padding here to absorb funds.

Furthermore, there are generally accessible yardsticks to ascertain how well social needs have been met. The public knows when adequate and convenient public transportation is available. No one would want to extend it out to a suburb that did not exist.

In general, social spending beyond a certain point cannot be rapidly and wastefully expanded. The difference here is that investment in social services deals with people, not objects like weapons. People are much more resistant to allowing their lives to be dominated by the priorities of waste —even if it does help to keep the economy running.

For example, what would happen if a housing project were built in the same way as a new missile? If a missile doesn't work, the company is excused and the planners go back to their drawing boards armed with another huge contract. Since it already has the expertise, the same company is more than likely to get a new missile contract. Imagine the political repercussions of a lousy, but expensive, housing project? The tenants complain, a public scandal is declared, and all contracts are canceled. The housing bill has a rough going the next time it comes up in the legislature.

So social spending can never provide the opportunities for waste that are provided by military spending. But this is not the most important reason why social spending is impossible. For massive social spending inevitably interferes with the basic operations of a capitalist system. How does this occur?

First, many kinds of social spending put the government in direct competition with particular industries and with the private sector as a whole. This is taboo in a capitalist economy. For example, if the government built low-cost housing in large amounts, it would cut heavily into profits of private builders and landlords who own the existing housing stock. It would add to the supply of housing and take land away from private developers who want to use it for commercial purposes. Similarly, building *effective* public transportation would compete with the automobile interests.

Any one of these interests taken by itself might not be sufficient to put insurmountable obstacles in the way of social spending. Most social service programs affect only one particular set of interests in the private economy. But there are so many forms of potential interference. Each of the vested interests are aware of this and so work to help one another out. They fuel a general ideology that says that too much social spending is dangerous. They refer to creeping socialism, the dangers of bureaucracy, the faith in individualism and self-help, and the unpleasant image of giving handouts to those who don't deserve it. The spectre of interference haunts all those in the private sector. So they engage in the practice of "log-rolling." You oppose interference with me, and I'll oppose interference with you. Massive political opposition to rather minor increases in social spending is thus forged. Furthermore, the capitalist system as a whole is threatened by massive governmental social spending because the very necessity of private ownership and control over production is thereby called into question. The basic assumption in any capitalist society that goods and services should be produced by private enterprise according to criteria of market profitability also fuels the general ideology limiting social spending.

Second, social spending upsets the labor market, one of the essential institutions of a capitalist economy. Public expenditures on an adequate welfare program would make it difficult for employers to get workers. If the government provided adequate nonwage income without social stigma to recipients, many workers would drop out of the labor force rather than take low paying and unpleasant jobs. Those who stayed at jobs would be less likely to put up with demeaning working conditions. The whole basis of the capitalist labor market is that workers have no income source other than the sale of their labor power. Capitalist ideology has long made a cardinal rule that government must not interfere with this incentive to work. Powerful political forces thus operate to insure that direct income subsidization at adequate levels can never come into being.

Third, social service spending is opposed because it threatens the class structure. Education, for example, is a crucial stratification mechanism that determines who gets to the top and legitimizing their position there. Good universal education, extending through college, would put the whole system of inequality into question. Moreover, having the possibility to get an advanced education would undermine the labor market as well. Few workers would settle so willingly for the miserable, low paying jobs they now do.

Finally, good social services, since they give people security, comfort, and satisfaction, that is, fulfill real needs, interfere with the market in consumer goods. Corporations can only sell people goods in an economy of abundance by playing on their unsatisfied needs and yearnings. In an era when most basic necessities have been provided, these new needs are mostly artificially created; the need for status, sex appeal, etc. They are based on fears and anxieties and dissatisfactions that people have and that are continually pandered to by the commercial world. But if people's needs were being fulfilled by the public sector, that is, if they had access to adequate housing, effective transportation, good schools, and good health care, they would be much less prey to the appeals of the commercial hucksters. These forms of collective consumption would have interfered with the demand for consumer products in the private market.

In addition, massive social services spending runs up against the obstacles of the existing vested interests in the social services sector itself. The AMA opposes the extension of federal aid to medical education and is thereby able—in part with corporate assistance from the drug companies

—to limit the supply of doctors produced each year. Entrenched civil service bureaucracies find grave threats in extensive Federal intervention in local programs. The list could be prolonged indefinitely.

The opposition of vested interests, the constraints of capitalist institutions and a much lower potential for expandability—these are the most important factors distinguishing the social service sector from the military weapons sector. Military spending is acceptable to all corporate interests. It does not compete with already existing industries, it does not undermine the labor market, it does not challenge the class structure. Social spending does all these things and, thus, faces insurmountable obstacles for its own expansion. Liberals have not been able to overcome these obstacles to obtain even small increases in social services. How can they expect to overcome these obstacles on the massive scale that would be needed if the defense outlet were cut off?

The facile liberal response to this argument—one that views the problem in an abstract fashion—is that "anything can be made appealing" to corporations just by making the incentive sufficiently large. With enough promised profit, defense corporations can be lured away from defense to just about anything. Even assuming that a total giveaway to corporations could be somehow made politically palatable—a dubious assumption—this view lacks plausibility.

Corporations do not make large scale investment decisions just in terms of short-term profit from a particular project. Their minimum horizon is much greater, and a substantial element of inertia operates. First, what is to convince corporations that there are long-term growth opportunities in the social services sector? Corporate executives are well aware that social service spending has in the past been very capricious. Since the impetus behind a conversion program might well dry up after a few years, corporations are reluctant to make large long-term commitments for fear of becoming shipwrecked. The risk of navigating uncharted waters is large. No convincing proof will ever be offered that conversion is profitable like defense has been profitable.

There have been attempts by major defense contractors in the last twenty-five years to initiate large-scale conversion. But almost without exception, these have been failures. Murray Weidenbaum, the expert on military economics cited earlier, has reviewed the history of these efforts from the end of World War II to the late 1960s.[1] He concludes his survey of early diversification efforts as follows:

Most of the diversification activities by the major, specialized defense contractors which were begun at the end of World War II were abandoned as unsuccessful or marginal or sold to firms traditionally oriented to industrial or consumer markets.

---

1 Murray Weidenbaum, excerpts from Chapter 3, *The Modern Public Sector*, © 1969 by Basic Books Inc., Publishers, New York, N.Y.

The expansion of the military budget brought on by the Korean War soon turned the primary attention of these firms back to the military market. When faced with the alternative, few aircraft companies preferred to manufacture powered wheelbarrows or busses rather than bomber or fighter airplanes.

Efforts at diversification after the Korean War were equally unsuccessful:

Most of these industrial diversification efforts outside of aerospace fields have since been abandoned. The surviving diversification programs continue generally at marginal levels—either actually losing money, barely breaking even, or at best showing profit results below typical military business returns.

The explanation of these failures is offered by Weidenbaum; many top corporate executives were convinced that military spending would continue to expand, perhaps a self-fulfilling prophecy:

. . . the belief of the top managements (is) that there are adequate sales opportunities in government work and that the profit rates are, if anything, higher than on risky commercial ventures. Interviews with chief executives of the defense industry repeatedly brought out their firm belief in the long-term nature and rising trend of the military market. Also, their many prior unsuccessful diversification attempts have engendered a strong conviction that inadequate commercial opportunities exist for companies which have become oriented primarily to government work.

The corporate elite is not going to sponsor a move away from military expenditures on its own. If they continue to oppose conversion, and we have every reason to believe they will, there is little reason to believe their opposition can be overcome within the existing political and economic framework. The conclusion which emerges: the military sector is just too crucial to capitalist stability and to capitalist profits.

28 The war and the economy*

ROBERT EISNER

1. THE MYTH

A stubborn myth haunts the nation: that the American economy in some sense "needs" the war in Indochina. Widespread among its opponents, and a prop to proponents of our Southeast Asian venture, is the notion that prosperity depends upon war, and that peace will mean depression. Critics see economic interest in prolonging the war as a major obstacle to their efforts to end it. Supporters, particularly some trade union leaders, have even stressed publicly that millions of jobs are dependent upon our defense program.

The simple fact is that the war with all its ramifications is rapidly turning into a relative disaster for the American economy.

The basis for the myth that the war sustains prosperity and that peace will bring depression is not hard to find. It goes back to many decades of experience with frequent if not chronic unemployment, culminating in the collapse of the 1930s. We were indeed finally pulled from the Great Depression by the outbreak of World War II.

It is true that if a burst of military or war spending is superimposed upon an economy with underemployment, the immediate effect is to give jobs to the unemployed. What is more, those previously unemployed spend their newly received income, as do their employers. These additional expenditures mean new income and jobs for the sellers and producers of the goods and services purchased; the "multiplier" makes its rounds.

By way of numerical illustration, imagine an economy with idle capacity in men and machines that could produce $90 billion per year in addition to current production. If the government suddenly begins to demand and order $30 billion of goods and services for war, these can be produced by drawing on one-third of the idle capacity. Then, as the $30 billion of

* From "The War and the Economy," *Changing National Priorities,* hearings before the Joint Economic Committee, 91st Congress, Second Session, 1970, pp. 671–76. Abridged and reprinted with permission of the author. Robert Eisner is Professor of Economics at Northwestern University, Evanston, Ill.

additional income are spent and respent, something in the order of the other $60 billion of idle capacity might eventually be put to use for production of the nonwar goods which can be purchased out of increasing incomes.

2. THE REALITY

So much for the rationale of the myth. For that numerical illustration does not describe this war. Major escalation of our military role in Southeast Asia, beginning in 1965, took place against the backdrop of an economy near full employment. Resources for war mainly had to come not from idle capacity, but at the expense of nonwar production. That expense had to come out of somebody's real, after-tax income. In fact, the cost came out of the real income of almost everybody: workers and businessmen, young and old, students and servicemen. Let none be fooled. The American economy as a whole is worse off by at least the more than $100 billion estimated to have been spent thus far in connection with our operations in Indo-China. That some individuals have enjoyed "war profits," whether as investors, defense contractors, workers producing war material, or black market operators in Saigon, cannot obscure the total picture. If the economy as a whole has lost $100 billion, the arithmetic requirement that the whole equal the sum of its parts means that if some have gained, say, $50 billion, others must have lost $150 billion: $-100 = +50 - 150$.

This loss has been felt in a variety of ways, some the direct consequences of the war, some the less immediate results of governmental measures designed to cope with these consequences. The list of war costs reads like a catalog of evils and suffering in the American economy.

The war has caused inflation. The war has caused high taxes. The war has contributed to housing shortages. The war has drained resources in the areas of education, transportation, housing and all the services of government, from police protection to postal delivery. And the war and consequent inflation and government efforts to combat that inflation have now brought on the greatest stock market crash since the thirties, the highest rates since the Civil War, falling production and rising unemployment!

Increases in prices and in taxes are easy to document. The consumer price index rose from 109.9 in 1965, when major military escalation began, to 134.4 in May 1970, an increase of 22.3 percent. Individual income tax payments have risen by almost $45 billion, from $48.8 billion in the fiscal year 1965 to an estimated $92.2 billion in fiscal 1970, an increase of 89 percent, far more than the 50 percent increase in personal income over this period. The consequences of these sets of facts for real, after-tax incomes are not hard to grasp.

Looking at average weekly earnings for production workers in manufacturing, for example, we see in Table 28–1 that these rose substantially in current prices, from $107.53 in 1965 to $132.40 in March 1970. But earnings in *real* terms, *after taxes,* showed no improvement over this five year period. Indeed, converting to March 1970 prices, and taking account of the effects of inflation and taxes, the figures for average real *"spendable earnings"* of a worker with three dependents go from $117.30 in 1965 to $114.85 in 1970, a drop of some 2 percent. The same measure for workers in all private non-agricultural industries shows a drop of 1.2 percent.

TABLE 28–1. Average gross and spendable weekly earnings

Year and month	Manufacturing industries			All private nonagricultural industries		
	Current prices		Constant, March 1970 prices[1] spendable	Current prices		Constant, March 1970 prices[1] spendable
	Gross	Spendable		Gross	Spendable	
1965	$107.53	$ 96.78	$117.30	$ 96.06	$ 86.30	$104.60
1969	$129.51	$111.44	$116.24	$114.61	$ 99.99	$104.30
March 1970	$132.40	$114.85	$114.85	$117.92	$103.39	$103.39
Percent change, 1965 to March 1970 .	+23.1	+18.7	−2.1	+24.0	+19.8	−1.2

[1] Earnings in current prices multiplied by ratio of the March 1970 to current consumer price indexes.

Sources: U.S. Department of Labor, Bureau of Labor Statistics, *Employment and Earnings* and *Economic Report of the President.*

If a drop in real, after-tax earnings of 1 or 2 percent does not seem large, one had better reflect on how sharply it contrasts with the long term trend of rising income in this most prosperous of nations. In the five-year period, 1960–65 prior to major war escalation, the average weekly spendable earnings of a worker with three dependents had increased 13.3 percent in manufacturing and just under 11 percent in all private nonagricultural industries. One might well have expected workers' real earnings to rise by another 10 or 11 percent in the five year period 1965–70. The fact that there was actually a drop of 1 or 2 percent suggests a deficit of 11 or 12 percent against the rising expectations to which workers had become accustomed.

Many American workers are tense and angry at the frustrations of a society which seems to be drifting more and more into chaos. They have hardly been brought over in large numbers to the antiwar camp, let alone to the ranks of protesters. But though relatively few may see the basic cause, this palpable loss in real, after-tax income must be a major factor in working class malaise and tension.

Let none nourish the illusion that while wage-earners have suffered, corporate profits have soared. Rather, as noted by Louis B. Lundborg, Chairman of the Board of the Bank of America, the largest bank in the world, "During the four years prior to the escalation of the conflict in Vietnam, corporate profits after taxes rose 71.0 percent. From 1966 through 1969 corporate profits after taxes rose only 9.2 percent." The calculations in Table 28–2 are more than confirming. From 1965 to the first quarter of 1970, corporate profits have declined by 11 percent. Accounting for inflation by putting these figures in first quarter, 1970 dollars, we see that after a rise of 61.2 percent from 1961 to 1965, real income in the form of profits has declined by 16.8 percent since escalation of the war beginning in 1965. (With population of course increasing, real *per capita* profits have actually declined significantly more.)

TABLE 28–2. Corporate profits

	Corporate profits after taxes	
Period	Billions of current dollars	Billions of constant, 1970–71, dollars[1]
1961	24.2	34.4
1965	46.5	55.4
1969	50.5	52.1
1970–71	46.1	46.1
Percent changes:		
1961–65	+71.0	+61.2
1965–69	+ 8.6	− 6.0
1965–70–71	− 1.1	−16.8

[1] Using GNP implicit price deflator.
Sources: *Economic Report of the President* and *Survey of Current Business*.

Individuals realize their corporate profits mainly in the form of capital gains on the stock that they own. Over many months, at every apparently significant rumor of moves toward peace (and many not so significant) security prices soared. And at every dashing of peace hopes or expansion of the war, the market sagged again. The stock market did indeed enjoy a substantial rise for a while, if one could forget the general inflation which cancelled out most of the stock price increases over the 1966–68 period, as indicated in Table 28–3.

But almost anyone from "middle America" can testify as well as an economist to what has happened as the war in Southeast Asia has dragged on. As this article is written, the financial markets are reeling from the shock of the Cambodian invasion, and stock prices are at their lowest level in more than seven years. After a *real* rise of 48.5 percent from the end of 1960 to the end of 1965, the real value of stocks has, as of May 26, 1970, declined almost $280 billion dollars since the escalation year of 1965, a drop of 36.5 percent in constant dollars. And many additional billions have been lost in the value of bonds and other securities.

It may well be argued that the market suffers not from the war alone but from measures taken to combat inflation brought on by the war. There is certainly a measure of truth to this. As pointed out, costs of the war have

TABLE 28-3. Capital gains and losses (dollar amounts in billions)

Period	Initial value of holdings of corporate stock[1]	Gross capital gain	Net capital gain (adjusted for change in real value of capital stock)[2]	Net capital gain in constant 1970-71 dollars	Net gain as percent of initial value, all in constant 1970-71 dollars
End of 1960 to end of 1965	$398.1	$238.4	$207.6	$244.6	+48.5
End of 1965 to end of 1968	643.7	116.5	42.0	44.4	+ 5.9
End of 1968 to May 26, 1970	764.8	−277.6	−321.2	−321.2	−39.7
End of 1965 to May 26, 1970	643.7	−161.1	−276.6	−276.6	−36.5

[1] Sum of holdings by households, institutions, mutual savings banks, and private pension funds. Changes in the value of holdings, from 1 period to the next, are the sum of net acquisitions, not reported in this table, and gross capital gains, shown in the next column. Since net acquisitions (essentially purchases minus sales) are not generally zero, gross capital gains are not generally equal to the changes in value of holdings.

[2] GNP quarterly implicit price deflators used for adjustment. Stock indexes used in end-of-year calculations are December and January means of daily closing averages.

Source: Michael McElroy, "Capital Gains and the Theory and Measurement of Income," Northwestern University doctoral dissertation, 1970, and special compilations by Mr. McElroy. Original data used in calculations taken from Jean Crockett and Irwin Friend, "Characteristics of Stock Ownership," in "Proceedings of the Business and Economics Section," American Statistical Association, 1963, pp. 146–168; Federal Reserve Board, "Flow of Funds Accounts," 1945–67, pp. 103–104; Federal Reserve Bulletin, May 1969, February 1970; "National Income and Product Accounts of the United States, 1929–65"; Survey of Current Business, April 1970; Standard & Poor's 500 Stock Index, and the New York Stock Exchange Index.

in fact been met by both inflation and higher taxes. The higher taxes, in the form of corporate profits, tax surcharges, and abandonment of the investment tax credit have directly reduced business earnings and the expectation of future business earnings. But further, the extremely high rates of interest, brought on by inflation and resulting tight money policies, mean a greater rate of discount for expected future earnings, whether from bonds or stock, and lower prices for both.

Resources have been drained to finance the war, and almost nowhere has the impact been more sharply felt than in housing. The combination of inflation, tight money and existing financial institutions has priced much of possible new construction out of today's market. Increases in costs of land, labor and materials have been notorious, running to 10 percent, by one estimate, from 1968 to 1969 alone. But the high interest rates, a product of both inflation and the efforts to check inflation with tight money, have themselves paradoxically raised the cost and reduced the availability of housing.

The huge rise in interest rates has brought corresponding increases in monthly payments on mortgage loans. For example, the rise in mortgage rates from approximately 5.5 percent in 1965 to some 8.4 percent in 1970 means that monthly payments on a new 20 year loan have risen 25.4 percent. Over the full life of a 20 years, $20,000 mortgage, the increased rates mean increased payments of $8,491. And even this is only part of the story.

In fact, mortgage loans are difficult to get and many would-be borrowers who might have obtained money under pre-war conditions cannot obtain loans now.

In real terms, housing progress or lack of it may be measured in the number of "starts," that is, the number of housing units on which construction has commenced. In February of 1968, President Johnson called for construction over the next ten years of 26 million new housing units, which have been translated into 2.6 million units per year. Average non-farm housing starts from 1960 to 1966 had been only 1.4 million units per year. In 1967, the figure was down to 1.3 million units. By December 1969 starts were down to an annual rate of 1.245 million units and by April 1970 to 1.18 million. It has been predicted that starts on single family homes will probably decline 14 percent in 1970 and rental apartment construction by 19 percent. In the face of great need, a need recognized as at the core of serious social problems, we have fallen further and further behind in this war economy.

Failure to construct needed housing now is not only a current cost but a cost for the future as well. Indeed, financing a war by deferring investment of any kind is a way of passing the real cost of the war on to a "future generation," which will lack the capital goods—in this case houses—that should have been constructed now. The housing shortages to which we have been contributing during these war years, and to which we are continuing to contribute, will plague us for years and decades to come.

Housing is one of the prime sectors to have suffered from the draining of resources to war. It is certainly not the only one. A whole generation, particularly in ghettos, is growing up without education. Public schools, faced with overcrowding, inadequate facilities, insufficient and relatively inexperienced staffs, and overwhelming neighborhood problems, have in many instances virtually given up educational efforts.

Problems of urban and suburban transport have become critical. We are choked in our own cars and exhaust fumes. Solution of our difficulties would take money and resources. These resources have been devoted, in a profligate fashion, to war but not to the pressing problems of peace.

3. TOTAL DOLLAR COSTS OF THE WAR

Budget costs of the Vietnam War, derived from estimates of the Defense Comptroller, are given in Table 28–4. They total 104.9 billion current dollars and 113.4 billion fiscal year 1970 dollars, reaching a peak annual rate in the neighborhood of $30 billion in fiscal year 1969.

Large as they are, these costs are only the expenditures paid out by the U.S. Treasury. Actual costs to the economy may be and in fact are much more. A first major addition relates to the true cost of those of our armed forces for which we do not pay a market price, but which we rather draft

TABLE 28–4. Budget costs of the Vietnam war, in current and fiscal year 1970 dollars, fiscal years 1966–70[1]

Fiscal year	Billions of current dollars	Billions of fiscal year 1970 dollars
1966	5.8	6.8
1967	20.1	23.1
1968	26.5	29.6
1969	28.8	30.7
1970	23.2	23.2
5-year total	104.9	113.4

[1] Taken from a background paper prepared by Peter T. Knight of the Brookings Institution. Some of the information in this table is also presented in Charles L. Schultze, "Setting National Priorities, the 1971 Budget" (Brookings, 1970), table 2–12, p. 48.

Sources: Statement of Hon. Robert C. Moot, Assistant Secretary of Defense (comptroller) before the Subcommittee on Department of Defense Appropriations of the Senate Committee on Appropriations in connection with the fiscal year 1971 budget estimates of the Department of Defense, released Apr. 13, 1970, table 4. Deflator (or rather inflator) used to obtain fiscal year 1970 prices was the implicit deflator for Federal Government expenditures taken from various issues of the annual report of the Council of Economic advisers on a quarterly basis and computed for fiscal years 1966–69. The link to 1970 prices was made by using the deflator implicit in the statement of total defense expenditures in Robert C. Moot's testimony cited above, table 3.

at remuneration far below even the minimum wages set in civilian work. One very conservative measure of this added cost comes from *The Report of the President's Commission on an All-Volunteer Armed Force*. The Commission estimates that shifting to an all-volunteer force by July 1, 1971, apparently presuming a substantial de-escalation of the Vietnam conflict and reduction of total armed forces by that date, would imply a net cost to the Treasury of $2.7 billion. The larger forces involved in the major military activity in which we have thus far been engaged must clearly cost considerably more.

The true cost of a soldier or a sailor or a marine is not what we pay him when he is drafted or is a "reluctant volunteer" to avoid the draft. It is rather what we would have to pay him if he were not *forced* to serve. This indeed measures not merely a cost of the war in terms of psychological aversion on the part of its participants but an economic cost in terms of incomes they would be earning—the goods and services they would be producing—if they were civilians.

There are other usually unmeasured costs of the war and the means, including the draft, by which it has been prosecuted. How many hundreds of thousands of young men have been wasting years in colleges that they do not wish to attend and wasting educational resources which they do not want and do not use, because they find this the most effective means of avoiding service in a war of which they want little part? How many young men have been forced into idleness or temporary jobs because employers would not hire them in view of the possible imminence of military service? How many indeed have left the economy, in literally hiding from the draft, fleeing the country or going to prison? At least some of these costs of conscription are indicated in Table 28–5. It will be noted that, after the major troop escalation of fiscal 1966, they have run at rates of 14 to 22 billion dollars yearly.

TABLE 28–5. Estimates of added economic costs of conscription

Fiscal year (ending June 30)	Average armed forces (millions of men)	Added costs of conscription[1]
1966	2,870	$ 2.9
1967	3,344	13.9
1968	3,483	19.5
1969	3,534	21.8
1970	[2]3,456	18.3

[1] Billions of fiscal year 1970 dollars.
[2] Estimate.

On a macabre note, one must also measure the lost earnings of our war casualties. There were 50,067 American deaths in the Vietnam theatre as of May 16, 1970. In addition, there were 140,286 injuries requiring hospitalization and 137,720 injuries not requiring hospitalization. Vietnam-era recipients of service-connected disability compensation totaled 145,008. The mean disability rate of these recipients is 35.5 percent.

Fifty thousand Americans who have died in Southeast Asia might have produced $20 billion of goods and services over their lifetimes. It might be argued that some of this would have been used for their own support, but a significant portion certainly would have gone to support wives and children and society as a whole. Several hundred thousand wounded will have their economic productivity impaired for weeks or months or years or all of their lives. Many of them will require costly medical care long after the war is over. Here are uncounted billions of war costs rarely measured in conventional accounting.

The dismal summary of the costs of five years of war is presented in Table 28–6. In dollars of fiscal year 1970 purchasing power, budgetary expenses come to $113.4 billion. The added cost of conscription is another $76.4 billion. Costs of the dead and wounded, calculated by discounting to the present some detailed estimates of the lost incomes they might have earned, are put at $23.1 billion. Total costs come finally to $213 billion.

How can one comprehend such a staggering total? To what is it equivalent in dwelling units for our people, in classrooms for our children, in police protection, in medical research, in foreign aid for peaceful development?

And yet the war and measures to cope with it have had still other in-

TABLE 28–6. Estimates of total costs of war, based on involvement from July 1965 to June 1970 only (in billions of dollars, fiscal year 1970)

Item:	Amount
Budgeted current expenses	113.4
Added economic cost of conscription	76.4
Cost of the dead.	11.6
Cost of the wounded.	11.5
Total costs	212.9

direct costs. At the moment, in the midst of one of the worse inflations in our history we are also suffering a rise in unemployment and decrease in production. The Nation's unemployment rose from 4.4 to 4.8 percent of the civilian labor force in April, the sharpest rise in ten years, and rose further, to 5.0 percent in May. The real rate of Gross National Product has now declined for two successive quarters and personal income in May showed the largest monthly drop ever recorded (from $801.3 billion to $793.5 billion, with special factors contributing, however, to the high April figure). All this is clearly accountable to measures taken to counteract war-induced inflation.

Whatever the vagaries of reflection of costs of war upon the economy in the nation, we face one underlying fact. There is a real loss in the diversion of resources of men and capital, of the capital not constructed because of the production for war, of the lives ruined and destroyed because of the war. The best laid plans of economists in the way of tax policy or monetary policy can merely reduce the magnification of these losses and costs.

In their original magnitude, the costs are real and inescapable. But these costs are just our own. We have said nothing in this discussion about the economic loss and ravished earth and destroyed capital and men, women and children in the land on which we fight.

C. Economics of higher education

With the recent explosion in the number of students attending postsecondary educational institutions in the United States, a number of public policy issues regarding higher education have emerged in unsettled form. What are the real costs and benefits of higher education? Which of these costs and benefits accrue to the individual and which accrue to society? Does this make a difference as to how public higher education should be financed? Is low tuition the only answer? Any resolution concerning most of these issues necessitates an understanding of the economics of higher education.

In the first reading by Bolton, some of the distinctive economic aspects of higher education are discussed. He reviews a number of aspects of the costs and benefits of higher education which, in turn raise some doubts as to whether total reliance on private financing is appropriate. Particular attention is given to differentiating between societal and individual costs and benefits of higher education.

Hanson and Weisbrod address the subject of equity in the provision and financing of higher education—that is, how "thoroughly" are the additional income returns and costs of public higher education shared? With regard to both efficiency and equity, doubts are raised as to whether conventional reliance on low tuition is appropriate as a device for subsidizing higher education.

Reflective questions while reading: (1) What is the total real cost of a college education to you as an individual (to society)? (2) Based on the studies and data reviewed by Bolton, what are your expected future earnings 20 years from today? (3) Is it "fair" that you may be receiving public subsidy in your college education while others are not? (4) Should all college age youth be assured of low tuition public education? (5) Which form of subsidy would you recommend for higher education in your state?

29 The costs and benefits of higher education*

ROGER E. BOLTON

In this section I shall discuss some of the distinctive economic aspects of higher education. These are aspects which the economist *qua* economist focuses on in assessing whether the economic system functions properly with respect to higher education. What special steps, if any, must be taken to make sure enough higher education is produced, to make sure that it is produced in the right way, and to make sure that the distribution of its benefits among society's members is according to the society's fundamental goals?

An examination of these aspects offers insights into just how higher education is similar to the other goods and services the economic system produces, and how it is different. There are important ways in which it is different, but it must not be forgotten that it is also similar in certain ways to other goods. Higher education is an output of the economy, albeit an intangible one, and it uses up resources which might have been used to produce other things. It is theoretically possible to have too much of it. This point is not always well enough appreciated, and policies are sometimes advocated which would produce only a very small amount of additional higher education at a very great expense in resources, or at the cost of achieving other important goals, such as an equitable distribution of income.

The discussion here is not extensive, and centers only on the most important principles. Its conclusions are actually rather familiar, and my purpose is merely to introduce widely accepted notions about higher education in a way which best leads into the later chapters.

---

* From "The Costs and Benefits of Higher Education," *The Economics and Financing of Higher Education in the United States.* Submitted to the Joint Economic Committee, 91st Congress, First Session, 1969, pp. 22–38. Abridged and reprinted with permission of the author. Roger E. Bolton is Associate Professor at Williams College, Williamstown, Mass.

In this section I shall first review briefly three important aspects of the costs and benefits of higher education which raise doubts as to whether reliance on private financing is appropriate. Then I shall go into more specific details about costs and benefits in turn, which are also relevant for the details of any subsidy arrangements the public may want to make.

THREE SPECIAL ASPECTS

The public interest

A traditional distinction in the economic literature on higher education is the distinction between private benefits and external benefits. Private benefits refer to benefits which a person investing in higher education receives himself; external benefits refer to the ones which accrue only to society in general, without directly increasing the satisfaction of the individual who possesses the education.

The benefits to the individual, which show up in his monetary income or his non-monetary advantages, are very large. This explains why individuals and families finance a great deal of investment in higher education out of their own time and funds. But it has always been assumed that some of the benefits of all levels of education accrue only to society as a whole. These benefits are external to the individual, in that they result from his own education, but cannot be turned by him into his own satisfaction directly. The education benefits his neighbors as well, and the realm of the "neighborhood" is very large indeed in the modern world, because of migration, because the economy depends heavily on the diffusion of new knowledge for growth, and because all men must work and live closely with others. Taxpayers have long accepted that such external benefits are legitimate grounds for their support of higher education. The extensive development of state and city colleges and universities demonstrates this. The reasoning behind this traditional public decision to subsidize higher education does not focus on equity; it is not that since some of the benefits accrue to society at large, society at large *ought* to pay some of the educated person's costs, as a matter of fairness. Rather, it focuses on the fear that if the public does not commit itself in advance to pay part of the costs, it will not be able to get the benefits. In short, without some sort of subsidy, it is feared, individuals will underinvest in education—too little of it will be produced, meaning that additional investment in it would have a value to society greater than the subsidy which would be necessary to make the additional investment. The subsidy, then, is an effort to induce the production of more higher education than individuals would want otherwise. For higher education (and even high school, beyond the age up to which persons are compelled to attend), the traditional subsidy is best seen as a bribe.

Investment in human capital

A crucial feature of higher education is that it is a capital good. Creating it is investment. Education has a long life over which it provides its benefits, both the ones which the individual does enjoy and the ones which spread over all of his neighbors in society. Like other long-lived durable goods, higher education is expensive; since it is something which can pay off its cost only over a very long period, its cost looms large compared to the annual income of the average family. It is not surprising that a good which lasts so long is expensive to build. Training the mind in general habits of thought and in the knowledge of specific facts to equip it for a lifetime of work takes a lot of the student's own time and other costly resources. The costs of higher education, in the broader social sense of the resources which are absorbed, must be paid for—while the capital good is being created. Since the costs loom so large compared to annual income, financing the purchase is a major proposition for a family. The sacrifices of the young person's time and of the goods and services which must be given up to free income for the purchase of schooling are very great indeed. The largest part of the goods sacrificed by the person or his family are the ones they could have bought if his time had been spent earning a cash income instead of studying. Without subsidies, there would be enormous obstacles to the purchase of higher education by poorer families. Since the present subsidies do not restore much of the earnings lost by not working instead of studying, they still leave significant obstacles to poorer families. These obstacles are not really different from the ones which prevent poor families from buying new Cadillacs or summer homes or vacations in Europe, but the public may be less willing to let them remain as barriers to education.

Difficulties of loan finance

Another feature of higher education makes it hard to resort to what would seem a natural solution, financing investment by borrowing. Because education is investment in human capital, it is notably less amenable to loan finance than physical investment in buildings, machines, or inventories. There is a lack of security for the lender; he cannot take out a mortgage on the educated person's ability. Then, too, so much of whether education succeeds or not depends on things other than the education, like motivation, which create risk the loan cannot be repaid. Education is a different kind of capital from machines or buildings, because it is not embodied in a concrete form, the productivity of which is largely independent of who owns it. The productivity of education depends heavily on personal characteristics of the borrower which are beyond the control of the lender and about which he may have little knowledge. If the owner of physical capital defaults on a loan he used to finance it, the lender can repossess the capital and resell it to someone else; no such option exists if the loan had financed education. By its very nature, education is an investment with some risk even to the person getting the education, merely because of the lack of knowledge of whether it can be put to good use long enough to pay off. The risk may inhibit even a rich person able to finance all costs himself. The situation is worse for a poorer person, for he will find it difficult to borrow in the normal capital market because he can offer no physical security to lenders. Thus, *either* low self-confidence *or* low income will prevent people from investing in themselves unless the public intervenes. Unfortunately, self-confidence may be lowest in the groups whose income is lowest.

THE COSTS OF HIGHER EDUCATION

The costs of higher education are properly measured by the value of opportunity uses elsewhere of the real resources used in the production of the education. In economics, the cost of a good is measured by the value of the other goods which must be given up in order to employ resources in the production of the good in question. For higher education, it is important to distinguish "direct" and "indirect" costs. Most direct costs are the costs of the resources, including labor, used by the educational institution for instructional purposes. If the market prices of these resources measure their opportunity values (because their prices reflect how much producers of other goods would be willing to pay for them), direct costs are the wages and salaries paid to faculty and other employees, expenditures on routine operating and maintenance supplies and services, and capital costs. Annual capital costs are usually considered to include depreciation and imputed interest on buildings and long-lived equipment, and imputed rent on land. As noted in the previous chapter, these capital costs are not accurately reflected in the usual budget statements of colleges and universities. In the statements, capital expenditures refers to the total expenditure for the purchase of buildings and equipment during a year. Not all this amount is true capital costs in any one year, because the property lasts much longer. The cost of using capital resources in any one year is better measured by the depreciation during the year, plus an estimate of the return the capital would earn in the best opportunity use. This opportunity return can be measured only imperfectly, but a reasonably good estimate can be made by multiplying some market interest rate, such as the rate of return on similar capital used in competitive industry, times the net (depreciated) value of the capital used. The imputed interest on buildings and equipment and the imputed rent on land are genuine costs of using these resources, whether the educational institution actually makes such payments to landowners and bondholders or not.

The "indirect" costs of higher education are the labor earnings which a student must forego in order to devote himself to study. The student's own time and effort are resources with opportunity uses which must be given up if they are used in the educational process. In valuing them at the opportunity earnings they could command in some other use, we are merely being consistent with the use of market wages and salaries to value the other labor inputs included as direct costs. Studying can be regarded as one form of employment, with the compensation for the trouble of studying coming not in the form of money wages, but in the receipt of a capital good—the education. From the student's point of view, not working in the labor force means that he must sacrifice the consumer goods he could buy with the earnings, or someone else, like his family, or taxpayers, must sacrifice consumer goods if he does not. From the whole economy's point of view, the student's not working in the labor force means that what he could have produced there is lost; instead of those other things, what the economy produces with his time and effort is the education the student gets. Considering the annual wage which even young unskilled labor can earn in today's economy, it is apparent that foregone earnings cost is a very large part of total costs and can easily be more than half of it.

So far, nothing has been said of the living costs at college. Students living away from home must pay room and board costs. But those are not properly called costs of education if they would have to be borne regardless of what the young person is doing. Only the costs which are incurred *because the student attends college* are truly costs of higher education. If the living costs would have been incurred no matter what the student did —and this may cover most of the ordinary living costs—they are costs of the student existing, not of his getting an education. They would not be saved by the student doing something else, and so are not opportunity costs of education. However, some living costs are really higher because of attending college and are appropriately included in direct costs.

This should make it clear that the true costs of education cannot be identified by any particular total of money expenditures by students and colleges. Some real costs are not reflected in money outlays, and not all money outlays represent real costs. In practice, of course, it is exceedingly difficult to determine just what expenditures qualify as real costs. The determination depends on just how "education" is defined. If living away from home costs students more than commuting between home and college, but if living away from home is an important part of one's education, then the extra costs are properly considered costs of education. Other problems are raised by recreational and entertainment costs and research costs. To what extent are dramatic and athletic events considered a part of college education? Although such events are attended by some people not in college, the nature of the events and their setting may make them integral parts of college education. In research, there is temptation to distinguish it from education, but this requires making a distinction between discovering knowledge and imparting existing knowledge, which may not be a meaningful distinction. Even if they are distinguished, research needs public support as well as education, and it may be desirable to subsidize the same institutions to do both. Then the merit in distinguishing the two is that clear labeling of things aids intelligent decisions. At any rate, the questions which arise in defining education are difficult ones to which no firm answers can be given. However, they assume considerable importance when it comes actually to flushing out a practical public subsidy plan.

The total costs of higher education are direct plus indirect costs. They are thus all costs incurred by institutions for educational purposes, plus the part of costs incurred by institutions for housing and feeding students which exceed the costs the students or their families would have to pay anyway (including imputed rent, interest, and property tax on dormitories and dining halls), plus the food and lodging expenditures by students who live and eat off campus which exceed the living costs they would have to pay anyway.

One important difference between direct and indirect costs is that the direct costs vary greatly from institution to institution, while indirect costs do not. Indirect costs are the earnings which the student could make by not going to college; they are the wages he could command, given his ability, experience and previous education. These potential earnings foregone are probably not much affected by which college he goes to. Employers are not likely to be influenced by those decisions so the wage he is offered for participation in the labor force are little affected. On the other hand, the direct costs are much higher in some institutions than in others. This would be true even without subsidies, although the variation in the share of institutional costs recovered from the student is an additional factor. Ignoring the subsidies, the variation partly reflects the variation in the quality of education offered. Institutions of approximately the same size, thus equally able to achieve economies of scale, may incur widely different costs per student, because the resources they employ per student differ widely in quantity and quality. Some institutions employ high quality faculty, paying them the salaries and fringe benefits necessary to keep them, and also operate with a high faculty-student ratio; other institutions employ lower quality faculty at lower salaries and also employ fewer faculty per student.

In addition to the quality variation, the living costs which are marginal to higher education may vary with the institution attended, because whether the student lives at school or at home makes a difference.

Another important distinction is between social costs and private costs.

Social costs are the opportunity value to the society as a whole of the resources used in higher education. If market prices equal opportunity costs, the costs talked about above will be the social costs. Private costs are less than social costs for two main reasons. Direct costs are less to the student than they are to the economy because of the extensive subsidies given by governments and by private donors to colleges and universities. These allow the educational institution to incur more costs than are reimbursed by students and their families. Private indirect costs are also less than social ones. Social indirect costs are the value of the student's potential earnings measured before income taxes are deducted. The value of a worker's social productivity in the labor force is measured by earnings before tax, because taxation represents merely a particular use of the economy's product, not a diminution of product. However, if he did work the student would have to pay income tax, and all he would have available for consumption is his earnings after tax. It is earnings after tax which the individual must sacrifice. Subsidies therefore reduce private direct costs, and income taxation reduces private indirect cost, below the social counterparts.

PRIVATE BENEFITS OF HIGHER EDUCATION

In the case of benefits, there is a crucial distinction between private benefits and social benefits. This distinction explains much of traditional economic policy in education.

Earnings

A major private benefit of higher education is the extra earning power it gives the individual. Human capital brings financial returns. It is partly in their additional earnings, over the earnings of persons similar in other respects but having less education, that the education pays off for the educated people. Table 29–1 shows some evidence of the private returns to education. In the first of the two we see a strong positive relationship between the income of a family and the education of the person who heads it (the data in Table 29–1 are based on a sample of 52,500 households). The correlation is unmistakable, even when color and age are held constant. On every single line of the table, the median income rises as the number of years of education completed rises.

Naturally, it is socially significant that better educated families are better-off families. But the data have shortcomings for determining the pay-off to college attendance as an investment decision. A family's income includes not just the head's, so some of the variation in income may be due to varying participation of wives and other family members in the labor force. The figures include monetary income of working wives but not non-monetary benefits families receive from having educated women

TABLE 29–1. Median money incomes of families, 1967, by education of head

			Years of school completed by head		
				College	*All*
Category	*8*	*12*	*1 to 3 years*	*4 or more*	*families*
All families, head 25 years old or more	.$6,470	$ 8,822	$10,176	$12,672	$8,168
White	6,608	8,962	10,277	12,770	8,471
Nonwhite	4,397	6,665	8,189	10,485	5,232
All families, head 25 years old or more	6,470	8,822	10,176	12,672	8,168
Head aged 25 to 34 years.	6,049	8,090	8,976	10,708	8,095
Head aged 35 to 44 years.	7,599	9,281	10,628	13,631	9,239
Head aged 45 to 54 years.	8,103	10,238	12,072	14,916	9,676
Head aged 55 to 64 years.	7,091	9,272	10,917	15,163	8,042
Head aged 65 years or more	3,835	5,156	6,024	7,710	3,928

Source: U.S. Bureau of the Census, *Current Population Reports, Series P–60, No. 59, Income in 1967 of Families and Persons in the United States*, U.S. Government Printing Office, Washington, Apr. 18, 1969, pp. 42–44.

as homemakers. It is true that similar data for individual persons, as opposed to families, also show a strong correlation between income and number of years of school completed. But even that evidence does not meet another problem of interpretation of the data in Table 29–1, which is that the figures there include not just earnings—wages, salaries, and professional earnings—but all money income. Total income includes property income, relief payments, pensions, and the like. Therefore, it is not the relevant figure for assessing how well education pays off; it is earnings which really represent the returns to educational capital. Data on earnings are shown in Table 29–2. They come from a survey of 5 percent of the population taken as part of the 1960 Census. Because the returns to a woman's education often do not show up in monetary earnings, but rather in the improvements in the life of the family, Table 29–2 covers only males. Again, education and earnings are correlated even when age and race are held constant.

However, no data on earnings differentials can present the whole picture. One problem is that while education pays off handsomely on the average, there is great variability in earnings. This variability may make many persons less than fully confident that education will pay off for them. I shall return to this point at length in this chapter, after dealing with other problems.

Estimates of rate of return

There are two other major problems in interpreting the data. One is that added earnings alone cannot make education an attractive investment; the added earnings expected in the future must be discounted and then compared to the costs of education. The crucial question is how the rate

TABLE 29-2. Median earnings for males in the experienced civilian labor force with earnings, 1959

Category of worker	Elemen-tary 8	High school 12	College 1 to 3 yrs	College 4 yrs	College 5 yrs or more	All males[1]
All experienced males in civilian labor force aged 25 to 64 . .	$4,474	$5,541	$6,119	$7,428	$7,968	$5,083
Aged 25 to 34	4,097	5,174	5,478	6,309	6,232	4,906
Aged 35 to 44	4,559	5,826	6,664	8,497	8,907	5,461
Aged 45 to 54	4,633	5,757	6,657	8,686	9,523	5,112
Aged 55 to 64	4,455	5,471	6,211	8,183	9,097	4,619
All white males aged 25 to 64 .	4,578	5,624	6,236	7,792		5,278
Aged 25 to 34	4,263	5,268	5,564	6,356		5,102
Aged 35 to 44	4,685	5,906	6,779	8,797		5,651
Aged 45 to 54	4,722	5,829	6,765	9,233		5,317
Aged 55 to 64	4,516	5,545	6,322	8,691		4,802
All nonwhite males aged 25 to 64	3,205	3,925	4,280	5,023		3,037
Aged 25 to 34	2,844	3,657	4,078	4,439		3,004
Aged 35 to 44	3,362	4,266	4,623	5,479		3,322
Aged 45 to 54	3,396	4,017	4,312	5,482		2,966
Aged 55 to 64	3,211	3,780	3,998	5,108		2,678

[1] Includes males who completed less than 8 years, not shown separately.

Source: U.S. Bureau of the Census *U.S. Census of Population: 1960. Subject reports.* "*Occupation by Earnings and Education.*" *Final Report PC(2)-7B.* U.S. Government Printing Office, Washington, D.C., 1963, pp. 2–3.

of return on education compares to that for other investments. If a college graduate had added earnings of $500 per year for 40 years because he graduated from college, he might still regard the experience as unprofitable if it had cost him more than $20,000, including the earnings he had sacrificed; he would have earned a negative rate of return, in fact. Even if he earned $1,000 more a year for 40 years, his $20,000 would be earning less than 4 percent (based on standard financial tables).

The other problem is that correlation is not necessarily causation: do the data show that educated people earn more because of their education, or only that they possess certain natural abilities and motivation which explain *both* greater educational attainment and higher earnings? Does the education really make that much difference?

Some economic studies have tackled these problems. Some of the conclusions from them will be summarized here, especially those from the best known of them, Gary Becker's *Human Capital.*[1] Becker estimated the rate of return to education beyond high school for various population groups

[1] Becker, Gary, *Human Capital,* National Bureau of Economic Research, New York, 1964. The following several pages summarize parts of Chapters IV and V of this work.

in 1939 and 1949, years for which census data on earnings were available. Data did not permit separating college education from graduate education. Becker's rate of return is meant to be the rate for private pecuniary returns, so he based it on money earnings after tax and did not attempt to quantify external benefits. The costs of education on which the estimates are based are also the private costs to students, not the full costs of institutions of higher education.

Because the data covered both college and graduate education, Becker calculated costs for four and one-half years of attendance. Direct costs for tuition, books, and the added living expenses at college for the average student were estimated. The indirect costs for a year were estimated at alternative earnings for nine months. Indirect costs were 74 percent of the total costs.

Becker's calculation of returns required estimates of the future earnings history of the 1939 graduates over their own lifetime. He assumed the earnings of different age groups of college graduates in 1939, after some adjustments, were reasonable estimates of how the 1939 graduates' earnings would rise as they themselves aged over time. The adjustments included one to reflect higher tax rates after 1939, and one to reduce the average earnings in each age group by the probability of not surviving to that age. He also assumed the earnings of both high school and college graduates would rise over time because of increasing productivity of labor in general; the earnings of both were increased by the same annual rate of growth, which meant the differences between them were increased.

Having estimated the future stream of earnings and the costs of investing in education, Becker calculated the rate of return. The result would be the return to a college education if the higher earnings were explained only by the education and nothing else. The result depends on which assumptions about future productivity growth, tax rates, and so forth are used, but Becker reports 14.5 percent as probably the best single estimate of the annual return to the 1939 urban white male college graduates, and 13 percent for the same group in 1949.

There remained the task of adjusting these rates for the contribution of native ability, motivation, and other characteristics. Let us subsume all these under the word "ability." The typical college graduate has more ability than the typical high school graduate, so that the 14.5 percent is more than would be earned by the average high school graduate if he went on to college. The essential problem is to estimate how much more a person with the ability to graduate from college would earn if he did graduate than if he did not.

Becker examined studies of the earnings of men in various samples taken as part of efforts to isolate the effects of college graduation from the effects of ability. These samples included one of college graduates employed in the Bell Telephone System; one of about 2,800 men who had graduated from high school 15 to 20 years before, collected by Wolfle and Smith for the Commission on Human Resources; one of men taken by the Survey Research Center, for whom information on earnings, rank in school, and other social characteristics was available; and a sample of pairs of brothers who shared many characteristics but had different levels of education. Rank in high school was often used to indicate the ability of these persons.

From all these bits of evidence, Becker concluded that although the average college graduate is more able than the average of all high school graduates, college education is an extremely important element in transforming the ability into higher earning power. Men who had the ability to graduate from college, but did not do so, earned little more than the average high school graduate. In groups of men none of whom graduated from college, differences in ability seemed to make little difference for earnings, but in groups in which all graduated from college earnings were associated with ability. The greater ability of college graduates seemed to permit them to benefit more from college experience than the average high school graduate would have, but the college education was still crucial.

Becker therefore concluded that if a man did have the ability to graduate from college, he would have to go to college to earn more. The college education itself essentially explained almost all the extra earnings. For such men, he felt the correct adjustment for ability would reduce the rate of return hardly at all: the rates of 14.5 percent and 13 percent remained good estimates of the returns to education. The typical high school graduate, of course, has less ability to be transformed into earning power, and so his return from college would be less than this; Becker estimated it as about 12 percent in 1939 and 11 percent in 1949.

The conclusion that the educational experience itself, rather than other factors like ability and background, is the predominant explanation for higher earnings is supported by a more recent analysis by Weisbrod and Karpoff. They analyzed a later sample of Bell System employees, about 7,000 male college graduates as of 1956. For each employee, earnings, rank in college graduation class, and years of service with company were known, and also a rough assessment of the quality of his college. By intuitive judgment of what his rank and quality of college revealed about a graduate's ability, Weisbrod and Karpoff concluded that only about one-fourth of the differences in earnings between high school and college men are attributable to differences in variables other than education (non-schooling variables). For example, the authors thought it reasonable to assume that men who graduated in the bottom third of their classes from average quality colleges have the same level of non-schooling variables as the average high school graduate. In the Bell sample, the earnings differential (over high school graduates) for such men was about 75 percent as large as the earnings differentials for college graduates in general in the same occupations. Standardizing for other variables reduces the differentials by 25 percent, therefore, leaving 75 percent due to educational differences.

Alternatively, one could assume that men who graduated from the middle third of below average colleges had ability equal to the average high school graduate; their earnings differentials were 82 percent as great as for college graduates in general. Or, if one assumes the lowest third of graduates from below average colleges is the appropriate comparison group, one finds their earnings differentials over high school graduates were 69 percent as large as the differentials for all college graduates. In view of these fractions, the authors suggest that 75 percent is a reasonable estimate of the fraction of the differences in earnings which are due to education.

To return to Becker's study, he also estimated the rate of return to college drop-outs. The results of 9.5 percent and 8 percent for the 1939 students and the 1949 students, respectively, are important evidence on adjustment for ability differences. This is because drop-outs did not seem to have much higher I.Q.'s or high school ranks than high school graduates who did not enter college. Therefore, the returns to them are simply returns to a partial college education per se and do not need any adjustment. Becker also estimated the (unadjusted for ability) rates of return for non-white men; he found them to be 12.3 percent and 8.3 percent for the 1939 and 1949 groups, respectively, of typical college graduates.

Nonpecuniary private benefits

Precise empirical analysis must be confined to monetary earnings, but it is clear that for many people education pays off in nonpecuniary terms as well as—or instead of—pecuniary terms. We know this because many people choose lifetime occupation like teaching and the ministry, which pay relatively little in monetary returns, but for which they must get a great deal of higher education. These non-pecuniary returns may be subsumed under the concept of earnings.

While the major emphasis in the economic literature on education and in this study is one the earnings benefits broadly defined, it is also generally agreed there are other benefits, although they are hard to measure. For one thing, there is the consumption benefit while attending college. A college education, in other words, is not entirely an investment which sacrifices the present to the future. As many college songs and alumni reunions suggest, it is also sometimes fun.

The relative size of consumption benefits is of some importance in the framing of public policy to subsidize higher education. How important they are depends on the aims of public policy. There may be a question of whether there are any immediate external benefits from college attendance, and in this troubled time many persons will strongly argue there are *harmful* external effects! Others regard the present system of protected dissent as an extremely desirable feature. The relative extent of private consumption benefits is also important. A major task of policy is to induce more higher education than the market would otherwise provide. Private earnings make many families willing to finance higher education on their own, and private consumption benefits merely increase this tendency. Subsidies to such families merely give a windfall, rather than being necessary to coax them to buy more higher education. This is all the stronger point if the consumption benefits, and thus the windfall gains, so largely to higher income families, because public opinion regards giveaways to the rich with more than the usual animosity if the giveaways finance consumption rather than investment. However, it is not clear just how much private investment in education is augmented merely because of the consumption benefits. One suspects it is rather limited if for no other reason than the enormous cost of the consumer goods involved.

Many people feel another aim of higher education subsidies is perhaps more important than the one of raising the aggregate real income of society by increasing the allocation of resources to education. They feel that aid to education is a particularly good way of altering the *distribution* of income in the long run, which can be accomplished by concentrating aiding investment by aid on lower income groups. To these people the existence of consumption benefits is of less concern, since the aims of increasing the consumption of lower income groups is a welcome byproduct of increasing the amount of educational capital they possess.

It is likely that a major part of the consumption value is derived from college experiences associated with the educational process, but not an integral part of it. Much of the "fun" comes from associating with other young people in various activities outside the classroom. If the public worries about the danger of subsidizing pure consumption, it can partially protect itself by limiting the kinds of costs it will defray.

Another non-earnings benefit which some might claim is that the educated person "enjoys life more." What this really means is that the educated person enjoys the life of the typical educated person more than a non-educated person would. The statement that being educated permits one to enjoy life more is empty of empirically verifiable content, since we cannot measure enjoyment very well. Casual empiricism suggests that the educated person certainly lives differently, and allocates his consumption expenditures differently, but that he may not really enjoy life any more.

EXTERNAL BENEFITS OF HIGHER EDUCATION

As used here, the term "social benefits" encompasses the private benefits plus the "external benefits" of higher education. The external benefits of higher education are ones which increase the satisfaction of other members of society, but for which, as a practical matter, the educated person cannot be compensated. His education increases the welfare of all of society, but his own income does not reflect this. References to such benefits of education are common, but many writers do not feel that they can be attributed in significant amounts to *higher* education, but rather that they are much more a function of primary and secondary education.

For example, Friedman, using the term "neighborhood effects" for external benefits, writes:

> A stable and democratic society is impossible without widespread acceptance of some common set of values and without a minimum degree of literacy and knowledge on the part of most citizens. Education contributes to both. In consequence, the gain from the education of a child accrues not only to the child or to his parents but to other members of the society; the education of my child contributes to other people's welfare by promoting a stable and democratic society. Yet it is not feasible to identify the particular individuals (or families) benefited or the money value of the benefit and so to charge for the services rendered. There is therefore a signifiant "neighborhood effect."[2]

Friedman goes on to say that this refers primarily to primary and secondary education, and that the neighborhood effects of higher education are not strong. What external benefits higher education has come from its "training youngsters for citizenship and for community leadership . . . [but] the large fraction of current expenditure that goes for strictly vocational training cannot be justified in this way . . ."[3]

Kaysen distinguishes the various "outputs" of colleges and universities, noting that what is called higher education is not a single product, but a complex bundle of them: liberal education, preprofessional and professional education, applied research, fundamental research, and the preservation of knowledge and culture. The first and last of these are the ones with external benefits:

> Liberal education alone, stripped of elements of specific preprofessional training, is both an important individual consumer good and a social good as well. Many of the arguments that justify public provision of primary and secondary education can easily be extended to training in arts and sciences at the college level . . . [in the case of] basic scientific research and the preservation of knowledge and culture . . . no particular group of users short of society as a whole can be said to get the benefits of these activities, and therefore society as a whole should support them.[4]

---

2 Friedman, M., "The Role of Government in Education," in Robert A. Solo, ed., *Economics and the Public Interest,* (New Brunswick, N.J.: Rutgers University Press, 1955), pp. 124–5. A very similar statement is in his *Capitalism and Freedom,* p. 86.

3 Ibid., p. 134. Recently, Friedman has come to doubt even more that higher education has external benefits. See the article cited in chapter IV, note 10.

4 Kaysen, Carl, "Some General Observations on the Pricing of Higher Education," *Review of Economics and Statistics,* Vol. 42, No. 3, Part 2 (Supplement: August 1960), pp. 56–57.

Weisbrod notes that wider education appears to develop a greater interest in political participation, for example in voting and discussion of political issues with an aim to influence the votes of others. This is a socially commendable result of education. He also notes that education permits the saving of certain social costs; general literacy and competence with arithmetic operations permits, for example, the substantial role of checking accounts and taxpayer-prepared tax returns, which permit the saving of real resources. But again, it is doubtful whether higher education adds much to secondary education as far as these go.

However, in recent years, an external benefit which has attracted a great deal of attention is the favorable effect of education on economic growth, and this effect does seem to depend on college and university education. The key to the argument is the claim that the contributions of educated scientists, engineers, managerial personnel, etc., are not fully reflected in their monetary compensation. As Rivlin put it:

> . . . it is clear that highly educated people may make positive contributions to economic growth from which society reaps much of the benefits. They have ideas, do research, make discoveries, invent new products and processes and procedures. Usually, anyone can use these basic ideas and discoveries. It is because their origi-nator may get little or none of the increase in income which they create that not enough people may be induced to invest in the expensive education which this kind of creative activity requires. . . . Unfortunately—although it is easy to point to highly educated people who have made important contributions to national income for which they have received little personal remuneration—no one has developed a method of estimating the total return that society is getting, or might get, on its investments in higher education.[5]

Thus the importance of higher education for discovery and diffusion of new knowledge has been emphasized as a reason for crediting it with external benefits. One reason the benefits are external to the educated people responsible is that scientific discoveries of the most basic kind are not patentable, so that private profit cannot be protected by a legal patent monopoly.

The discovery of new knowledge and its rapid diffusion increase the productivity of all workers and capital in the economy, and thus the in-comes of workers and capital-owners. Even a worker who does not possess a college education will find his productivity and income higher because some other people do have a college education, and have used their train-ing to discover new knowledge. Some of the knowledge necessary for eco-nomic growth is so complex it requires training well beyond high school for its discovery and for its efficient incorporation into production methods.

---

5 Rivlin, Alice. *The Role of the Federal Government in Financing Higher Education,* The Brookings Institution, Washington, D.C., © 1961, pp. 135, 137.

It is also possible that educational attainment increases the acceptance of new technology by lower levels of management.

That these external benefits have been important has been suggested by authors of recent studies of modern economic growth in advanced countries. The increases in labor and capital, measured in physical units, fall far short of explaining all the growth in income. What has happened is that the productivity of each physical unit—of each labor hour and of each machine—has increased greatly. Some of the increased productivity is due to increased education. Now, naturally, not all the increased productivity is to be considered an external benefit, for much of it has been reflected in higher earnings of educated people. But even after making allowances for the increased earning power of education in the market, there appears to be some additional element of growth, explained by education but not traceable to the education of specific people. This element is part of the general effect of the "advance of knowledge," to use Denison's phrase. How big a part remains unknown:

> The proportion of the economic gain from new knowledge that the individuals or firms responsible for the advance can secure varies greatly. It is far larger for the sorts of knowledge that may be loosely described as patentable than for advances in either science or managerial technique. The scientists whose discoveries provided the basis for modern technology and the engineers who devised time and motion studies generally benefited, in a monetary way, only insofar as an accretion to prestige enabled them to place a higher price on their personal services than could others who quickly adopted their ideas. . . . More and better education would presumably contribute something to a more rapid advance of knowledge even without diversion of additional resources to research. In my classification of the sources of growth, this is a byproduct of education that affects the contribution of the advance of knowledge. How much of growth allocated to the advance of knowledge is an indirect consequence of improving education cannot be calculated, nor can the extent to which it could be influenced by accelerating the improvement of education.[6]

Rivlin has pointed out that if the external benefits of higher education in promoting the discovery and spread of new knowledge are realized by the economy through *organized research* by educated people, the proper public policy may be not to subsidize higher education, but to subsidize research. Although scientists cannot sell the fruits of basic research for high returns, they can sell their research activity in the market. If the government subsidized basic research, the salaries paid to scientists would be sufficiently high eventually to attract enough of them to become educated to the required degree and enter the field. These salaries would offer suf-

---

6 Denison, Edward F., *The Sources of Economic Growth in the United States*, Committee for Economic Development, New York, N.Y., 1962, pp. 251, 253. Denison points out that much of the knowledge which augments productivity in the United States originates in other countries. There are thus international external benefits of education.

ficient inducement, without direct support of the education of scientists. However, subsidies to science education might be a quicker way of subsidizing research, if potential students could more easily be made aware of the availability of financial aid than they could be made aware of their future salaries as scientists. On the other hand subsidizing the education of scientists as a substitute for subsidizing research directly has some dangers. It may tend to bias the use of inputs in research, leading to the overuse of scientific labor and underuse of equipment and nonscientific labor in research.

Space remains for only a few more observations on external benefits. In a recent article, Schultz made the penetrating observation that the three main functions of higher education are instruction, research, and *discovering talent*. The last of these is little talked about, although it is complementary in production with the other two functions and is traditionally carried on in the same institutions as they are.

It is "a process which provides students with opportunities to discover whether they have the particular capabilities that are required for the type and level of education at which they are working."

This activity has important social benefits. In attempting instruction, groups of faculty and students together discover talents, but there is no practical way of compensating the students, especially the ones which turned out to have no talent, for their services in the endeavor. Subsidies are thus necessary to induce students to "try out" college so that society can uncover the talent of the ones who would not otherwise go to college. It may be that many of the discovered students will earn enough later in life to pay the full cost of their education, and enough that society feels they *should* pay the full cost, but they would not have come to that situation if they had not been induced to try college in the first place. This has implications for a subsidy plan. Perhaps the freshman year should be more highly subsidized than later years. The problem may be viewed as one of reducing the risk to prospective students of spending money and time at college, which view suggests that in addition to any general subsidy extended the fees charged for the freshman year should be retroactively lowered for those who *fail*. This no doubt is paradoxical to those who feel higher education should reward the intelligent and motivated students who succeed. But it is consistent with the view that the *market* will reward those who succeed, and that the problem is to overcome the inhibitions many young persons have about investing time and money in discovering more about their own abilities. Society may well gain more in uncovering hidden talent than it loses in wasting resources on those who had no talent to be uncovered.

In the end education's external benefits cannot be exactly calculated, neither the benefits of a "better society," nor the economic benefits of more rapid growth. Some would undoubtedly consider some of the actions of typical educated people as imposing harmful external effects on other people. But there seeems to be general agreement that the net external effects are favorable, so that sole reliance on private decisions based on private benefits and private costs will cause the loss to society of investment which is worthwhile to it, but not worthwhile to the individual. It is clear, however, that a large part of education's benefits *are* private, and that society can reasonably expect individuals to finance a significant part of the costs, because they get a significant part of the returns. This is a reasonable requirement even for some low-income families, who could often at least sacrifice foregone earnings, although the exact fraction they should contribute from their own resources will depend on income distribution goals.

There is one final point, one of terminology. Some writers include in external benefits something like social justice or the equality of opportunity which is achieved by assisting the attainment of education by youngsters who are qualified but prevented by circumstances from getting it. While equality of opportunity may be one of the main goals of educational policy, I do not include it as an external benefit. I use the term "external benefits" to cover the productivity and welfare effects just discussed, but not to include favorable changes in the distribution of income. The definition of external benefits is partly a matter of taste, but I keep the two goals of correcting for external benefits and improving the distribution separate, because I think the latter requires stronger value judgments than the former. The role of value judgments ought to be kept explicit, even though in this case they are accepted by many. However, chronic violation of equality of opportunity may engender social unrest which reduces productivity. If so, insuring equality of opportunity will have some external benefits even in the sense I use the phrase.

30 The search for equity in the provision and finance of higher education*

W. LEE HANSEN and BURTON A. WEISBROD

Who should be eligible for public higher education? Should those young people who are not eligible—or if eligible, are unable or unwilling to go to college—should they be deprived of the public subsidies obtained by the college goers? What can be said about the actual distribution of public subsidies for higher education—that is, who actually receives them? And who pays for them? These and related questions are explored in this paper, which is addressed to the subject of equity in the provision and financing of higher education. . . .

EQUITY AND EFFICIENCY: CONCEPTUAL ISSUES

How should public higher education be financed? There are actually two separatable questions: one, *who* should bear the costs of public higher education; and two, *how* the portion of costs that is borne by students should be paid. More precisely, the question of *who* should pay involves determining the share of costs to be paid by students versus taxpayers. The question of *how* students should pay relates directly to the tuition issue, but "the tuition" is not a simple concept. Should tuition be the same for all students? Whatever the level or levels of tuition, should it be paid at the time the education is received, or later? Should the level of tuition be determined at the time the education is received, or should the amount be contingent on future benefits?

The nature of these choices will be described more fully below. While

* From "The Search for Equity in the Provision and Finance of Higher Education," *The Economics and Financing of Higher Education in the United States.* Submitted to the Joint Economic Committee, 91st Congress, First Session, 1969, pp. 107–13. Abridged and reprinted with permission of the authors. Both W. Lee Hansen and Burton A. Weisbrod are Professors of Economics at the University of Wisconsin, Madison, Wis.

our primary concern in this paper is with equity, we recognize that sound public policy should also strive for efficiency in the use of resources. Thus, we begin with a discussion of what we mean by "efficient" and "equitable" solutions to educational finance questions.

By "economic efficiency" we mean the degree of success of higher education in producing outputs (trained students, for example) that are more valuable than the resources used up in the process of production.

In the economy at large, the value of output is generally measured by what people are willing to pay for it; and, so, as a first approximation, the value of college education may be measured by the increased salaries that employers are willing to pay for workers who are college educated rather than only high school educated. Efficiency, in the present context, can thus be thought of in terms of the amount by which National Income (or Gross National Product) is raised by higher education.

But which people receive this increased income? And which pay the costs of the resources—teachers, classrooms, laboratories, etc.—that are required to produce the increased income? In other words, how "fairly" are the additional income and costs of public higher education shared? This is the issue of equity.

The distinction between efficiency and equity is essential if we are to come to grips intelligently with difficult issues of public policy. Higher education may be found to be efficient in raising incomes, but the method of financing higher education might be regarded as inequitable. By contrast, it may be felt that higher education is being financed equitably, but that it is really not an efficient way to use resources—there being better ways to increase people's real incomes (such as by devoting more resources to improving technology). Of course, there are intermediate positions, in which various degrees of inefficiency and inequity are adjudged to exist.

Debate over issues in higher-education-finance can only be fruitful if there is a recognition of when, and to what extent, the dispute centers on factual matters of efficiency, and when it centers on value judgments regarding the fairness of the distribution of benefits and costs. This is not to deny, however, that both classes of issues are difficult to resolve, for the factual data relevant to assessment of efficiency are difficult to find, as is consensus on what should be regarded as equitable.

The social objectives of efficiency and equity are in fact quite likely to conflict, thereby complicating the issue. Consideration of efficiency might suggest that higher education should be provided to some young people but not to all; implicit is the widely held assumption that not everyone can benefit significantly from higher education. But there is still the equity question: is it "fair" for some youngsters to receive public subsidies while others do not? An efficient allocation of resources can be inequitable.

And an equitable allocation of resources can be inefficient. If, for example, *every* youngster were not only offered the opportunity to go to college for four years, but were required to go, then all college age people would receive a similar public subsidy. But if this is more equitable it is doubtless less efficient, for not everyone is likely to benefit enough to cover the costs of resources required to educate them. The conflict between equity and economic efficiency in higher education planning appears to be a genuine one; we do not attempt to resolve it here, but rather focus on the issue of equity itself.

Throughout this paper our attention is directed primarily to decision-making in the *public* sector. This orientation is somewhat artificial; the fact that there exists a private as well as a public sector in higher education means that success in devising an efficient and equitable finance system for public higher education does not assure either efficiency or equity for the higher education system as a whole. Our analysis of efficiency and equity issues in the financing of public higher education is applicable, though, to private as well as public higher education. The question of what separate and distinct roles ought to be fulfilled by the public and private sectors in higher education is an important one, but scant attention has been given to it. To have considered carefully the role of the private colleges, however, would have further complicated an already knotty matter.

Efficient pricing

Before embarking on our detailed investigation of equity, we turn to a brief analysis of some implications of seeking efficient pricing of higher education. As already noted, both kinds of considerations are relevant to the evaluation of alternative methods of financing public higher education.

The cost of a college education to a student and his family—apart from the income foregone—can be analyzed in two parts. One is what can be termed the "price" of the education—the tuition charge, the books and supplies, and so forth. The second is the "ease of financing" that price—that is, the availability and terms of loan funds and scholarships.

The level of the price of college education, and the ease of financing it are jointly relevant to individuals' decisions. An apparently high tuition rate may be quite manageable if grants or scholarships are widely available or if loans can be obtained at sufficiently low interest rates. Similarly, even a total failure of scholarship programs and capital markets to provide financing assistance can turn out to be inconsequential if the total price of education (including foregone income) is sufficiently low. Thus, there would seem to be trade-off possibilities between the price of education and the means of financing it—combinations among which any particular individual would be indifferent.

But considerations of public policy dictate that we go beyond an analysis of any individual's preferences to take account of all the resources used up in the process of satisfying those preferences. Thus, we are led to consider the questions of what is a socially efficient price of education, as well as what is a socially efficient set of finance terms, including an interest rate.

Economic efficiency may be said to exist in a market when the price of the good or service is equated with the marginal opportunity cost (value of the best alternative use) of the resources used to produce it, and both are equated with the benefits from an additional unit of the good. Thus, given the distribution of income, the preference of all individuals in society, and the technological production possibilities, the efficient price for any given unit of production (e.g., man-year) of higher education is the price which is equal to the marginal *net* social cost of providing that education and the marginal benefit received by *the* student. By net cost we mean the marginal cost of production *minus* any marginal "external" benefits—that is benefits that are not captured by the individuals whose education produced them. To the extent that such external benefits occur, the efficient price to charge students would be below the marginal cost of producing the education services.

This view of pricing clearly implies that society (taxpayers in general) should subsidize higher education as a matter of efficiency. Since some external benefits may be realized within local areas while others may be distributed more broadly, all levels of government—federal, state and local—would presumably share in the costs. Insofar as the bulk of externalities accrue at the national level—in part because of population migration—this would argue for a reallocation of public financing of higher education away from state and local governments and to the federal government.

Public subsidies can take a variety of forms. In addition to "low" tuition rates, there are low-cost loans, income tax credits or deductions to parents, and outright cash grants to students—all of which can be equivalent to a tuition reduction. Any of these forms, and no doubt others as well, could be used to produce the desired public subsidy and, in turn, result in an efficient "price." The choice among them rests largely on an equity consideration—that is, the extent to which persons not in "need" would benefit.

There are some individuals who may be "qualified" for college but who will not attend college because the combinations of available price and interest charges are "excessive" relative to their financial situation and to the strength of their desire to attend. The willingness to incur these costs is conditioned by factors including family income and wealth, family size, and parental health. Yet there appears to be a social concensus that these factors ought not to bar college attendance, so that "needy" individuals with the ability and motivation to benefit from college should go.

If compulsion is to be avoided, these barriers to college attendance could be offset in three general ways: (1) incomes of such students and their families might be supplemented; and/or (2) the price of college education for them could be reduced; and/or (3) the interest rate applicable to their borrowing for college could be reduced.

One might argue that the judgment that a student "should" go to college, even though family circumstances would lead him not to go, represents an implicit social decision that his family's income is "too low." Thus, an increase in family income would seem called for. If the objective, however, is to make it possible for this student to attend college *at a minimum cost to others,* then the approach of giving to needy students cash transfers that are not restricted as to use, is likely to be inefficient; very substantial transfers might be required before any of the additional money would be used for the student's higher education. A possible variant is to restrict the use of cash grants to higher education. But this alternative may be difficult to implement, since as a practical matter there is no means for preventing some of the grant money from going to families—even some of them with very low incomes—whose children would have gone to college anyway, and who now, having received the grant, will be able to increase their expenditures on other goods and services. Grants to such families are not necessarily undesirable, but the point is that grants may not be required to achieve *educational* objectives, however justified they may be from the point of view of a more general anti-poverty effort.

Consider now the alternatives of reducing the price and/or interest rate for the "needy." If, to begin with, the price and interest rate were set at levels that were economically efficient—in terms of the costs involved, as discussed in the preceding section—then further reducations would sacrifice some allocative efficiency in order to bring about effects that were deemed more equitable. Such a trade-off of efficiency for equity is by no means unique to higher education, nor is it necessarily undesirable.

In practice, each of the alternatives is bound to fall short of fully realizing equity objectives. Subsidies, whether in the form of cash, tuition rate reductions, or reductions in interest rates, are certain to go to some persons other than those whom "society" specifically wishes to assist, since the "needy" and "deserving" are frequently difficult to identify. Thus, subsidies go, at least to some extent, to the "wrong" people—with taxpayers, some of whom are themselves worthy of help, paying the cost.

Some perspectives on the dimensions of need can be obtained by a theoretical disaggregation of the population into several different groups. Group I includes those students (and their families) who are willing and able to pay at least the full long-run marginal cost (which we suggested above might be approximated by average instructional plus capital cost) net of estimated external benefits, and the full market interest rate. A portion of this group, while willing to pay these costs, can do so only by incurring some "hardship." Group II includes those who are willing and able to pay some lower, positive price and interest rate, and some fraction of this group could pay these amounts only with some hardship. Finally, Group III includes those people who would need bribes to cause them to attend college, being unwilling to attend at any combination of a positive price and positive interest rate. All three groups are defined to include only those deemed "eligible"—in terms of aptitude and motivation—to attend college.

One of the implications of the structuring of these three groups is that the amount of subsidy required to cause an individual to attend college is a continuous variable with a wide range of values. Some students will require very substantial subsidies and others none at all in order to provide full equality of opportunity in higher education.

Identifying those who are deserving of additional subsidies to enable them to go to college or to go without undue hardship is a most difficult task. Assume, however, that the "need" for higher-education subsidies can be estimated in a satisfactory, if rough, manner, perhaps applying the standards used in student financial aid analyses. The perplexing question then is who should pay for these equity-based subsidies? Utilizing taxpayers-in-general as a source of revenue, while having merit, does imply that any sum of money that students and their families "cannot afford" to pay, *can* be paid by, and *should* be paid by taxpayers. But when it is borne in mind that "taxpayers-in-general" include many quite low income taxpayers, it becomes clear that a shifting of the financial burden from students and their families to taxpayers involves to some extent, a shift of the burden to families whose incomes and ability to pay may be less than the ability to pay on the part of students and their parents.

This raises a more fundamental issue of the meaning of "ability to pay." Just as standards have been established for determining how much a family can "afford" to pay for *higher education,* so might standards be established to determine how much a family could "afford" to pay in *taxes.* If such a study were done, it might well conclude that families of given size, given needs, and with incomes below some specified amount, could not afford to pay any taxes at all; nevertheless, we suspect that many such families are, in fact, actually paying taxes—and would be required to pay even more taxes if state support for higher education were increased.

Another possible source of subsidy funds for the needy is other college students and their parents. We noted above that there are some families, particularly in Group I, who are able and willing to pay more than the efficient price of education. If they were charged a higher price, the subsidies required for needy students could be obtained outside the tax system. This would amount to the use of classic price discrimination, to charge what the traffic will bear. One might think of the resulting schedule of charges as reflecting a sliding-scale college payment plan, with the possibility of negative charges for the most needy.

On the assumption that a choice can be made regarding the most appropriate subsidy device for achieving greater equity, there is still a larger issue concerning the propriety of limiting subsidies to those who choose college rather than some other means for enhancing individual and social well-being. For the many young people not deemed qualified for college or not interested in attending college under any reasonable pricing conditions, there is a variety of other methods by which they can enhance their incomes and future satisfaction, and otherwise become effective citizens. Job-training and investments in small businesses are only two substitutes to college-going. Whether from the standpoint of achieving equity or efficiency in resource allocation, it would be highly desirable to make these and perhaps other alternatives available to those young people who do not opt for college. A broadened subsidy program might well be more costly. But it would at the same time do much to provide greater equality of opportunity for *all* young people, not merely for college students.

D. Economics of urban problems

The citizens and political leaders of America's largest cities increasingly portray their daily lives as a losing battle against a decaying social environment. The cost of living rises and the quality of life declines. Traffic has become more congested, the streets more unsafe, housing more deteriorated, health care more inaccessible, and the environment more polluted. Meanwhile city governments fear virtual bankruptcy as their revenue sources cannot keep up with the rising costs and demands for service. (For one proposed solution to this fiscal crisis, see Readings 34 and 35 on revenue sharing).

Many aspects of the urban crisis (problems such as health, poverty, and education, are shared by small town and rural America; in fact the reciprocal dynamics of rural depopulation and urban congestion indicate the need for a synthesizing national prospective. Nor is this complex and many-sided social crisis exclusively or predominantly an economic problem. But the following three readings on specific urban problems—crime, transportation, and health—illustrate how economic analysis can be applied to understand the causes of the problem and to devise policy remedies.

The economist's most basic tools of supply and demand can help to explain the extent and direction of criminal activity. The "demand" for crime depends on the popular desire for forbidden goods or services—drugs, gambling, prostitution, stolen merchandise, usurious loans—and on the anticipated income which the criminal could earn by meeting these desires. The "supply" of criminal labor depends on the availability and the income level of alternative employment. The amount and type of "output" supplied by this criminal labor force will depend on the cost of capital equipment (guns, roulette wheels, drugs, counterfeit plates), and particularly on the risks and penalities assigned to various times, locations, or types of criminal activity. Katzman reminds us that these costs and risks are influenced not only by police efforts at deterrence, detection, and apprehension, but also by private efforts such as buying alarms or hiring guards. Where the "spillover" (external) effects of such private efforts benefit one's neighbors (at no cost to them), and where there are economies of scale in fighting crime, the demands for government intervention are greatest. Katzman emphasizes that police budgets and police program efforts should be shaped by an awareness of "trade-offs." Society has many goals and limited resources, so it must make choices between "police" and other government or private priorities, as well as among alternative police programs which deter or punish different crimes and criminals, and protect different neighborhoods and social groups. We must quantify and compare the marginal social benefits and costs of these alternative programs, and then select the blend of police inputs (foot patrolmen, patrol cars, communications gear, etc.) which will provide the optimum services at minimum cost.

The public discussion of the urban transportation crisis has often polarized into a battle between the defenders of the automobile and the advocates of new systems of fixed-rail mass transit. The automobile has provided convenient individualistic transportation, but its federally subsidized freeways and polluting exhausts are choking the cities. Rail transit systems promise glamorous technology, speed, and comfort, but the existing commuter railroads grow older and more unpleasant while the projected costs of new systems rise astronomically. Stepping into the no-man's-land between auto defenders and rail transit advocates, Kain offers a proposal for bus rapid transit. He argues that for very little added cost we could control the rush-hour traffic on our existing freeways so as to greatly increase its passenger carrying capacity. Express buses with priority access and right-of-way could then compete favorably in time, cost, and comfort with automobiles, while operating with far lower capital costs and greater route flexibility than rail transit.

In their discussion of the current problems in delivery and financing of medical care, Lave and Lave sharply criticize the present forms of legal restrictions and government subsidies, and urge more use of economic calculation and individual incentives. They reveal (as Katzman does for the crime problem) a popular failure to weigh the benefits of further improvements in the quality of medical care against the added costs. Prepaid group practice and medical insurance rules (covering only hospital treatment), as well as government-subsidized care for the poor and aged, encourage doctor and patient to ignore or distort costs. They believe that added dollars to attack poverty and pollution might actually provide greater health benefits than added dollars of medical care, and they suggest that a more efficient use and equitable distribution of present medical technology and resources could provide Americans with all the medical services that they really need.

31 The economics of defense against crime in the streets*

MARTIN T. KATZMAN

Economists have had relatively little to say about the deterrence of crime. In other problem areas, such as the business cycle, economic thinking has been a generation ahead of the public in visualizing solutions. Public concern about crime, on the other hand, highlighted by the report of the (1967) President's Commission on Law Enforcement, catches the economist either unconcerned or unprepared to contribute to the discussion. Detachment on the part of economists is unfortunate and untimely because the federal government is preparing to spend considerable sums on local police forces. This essay is an attempt to clarify some of the important trade-offs and economic choices which confront a society in deterring crime. In this essay, we shall first sketch the systematic relationships among the activities of the public, the criminals, and the police. We shall then focus on the behavior of the police as an economic activity. Hopefully, the discussion compensates for its relative lack of elegance by its relevance.

CRIMINAL BEHAVIOR AND THE PUBLIC

Typology of criminals

We distinguish among three types of criminals, who differ by type of crime, responsiveness to punitive threats, and by rationality. The first, the "organized criminal," is a member of a business engaged in providing illegal services (such as gambling), often using illegal means (such as violence and extortion). The organized criminal is fairly well acquainted with

* From "The Economics of Defense Against Crime in the Streets," *Land Economics,* 44 (November 1968), pp. 431–40. Copyright in the name of The Regents of the University of Wisconsin Systems. Reprinted by permission of Land Economics and the author. Martin T. Katzman is Associate Professor of City Planning at Harvard University, Cambridge, Mass.

the law relevant to his own enterprise, and may engage in profitable bargains with the police to encourage the enforcement of the law in his favor. Of all types of criminals, he is probably most affected by changes in police methods of detection because his crimes often have no victims—e.g., gambling and prostitution. The "unorganized professional," the second criminal type, tends to commit crimes against property—e.g., larceny, forgery, or counterfeiting. While not necessarily adverse to committing violence, the professional sees the end of his criminal activity as mostly economic. Furthermore, this activity is a full-time vocation, which requires considerable rational calculation for survival. By far the largest number of crimes are committed by the third criminal type, the "amateur." The amateurs comprise the would-be professionals who lack the skill of avoiding arrest and also individuals who commit criminal acts in moments of passion or irrationality. The murderer, the rapist, and the joyrider are involved in crimes whose ends are not basically economic or whose costs and benefits have not been carefully evaluated. It is the amateur, responsible for most of the crime in the streets, upon whom this essay focuses.

The supply of criminals

Perhaps the major explanation for differences in the rate and type of crime in the various neighborhoods of a metropolis is the supply of criminals. The supply of criminals in a neighborhood is related to the sex, age, class, and ethnic composition of its residents, and those who have easy access to it. For example, neighborhoods with large numbers of lower-class teenagers tend to have high crime rates. Despite journalistic tales of increasing middle class crime, most crime is committed *by* lower-class people, *against* other lower class people, *in* lower class areas. Especially in crimes of violence, such as murder, assault, and rape, the victim and offender are not only of similar lower class background, but they are often acquaintances.

The opportunities for crime

The opportunities for criminal activity are affected by three factors. First are the alternative costs to the potential offender for criminal activity. In times of heavy unemployment, when the most crime-prone class and age groups are also the least likely to hold a job, legitimate economic activity does not compete with criminal activity. Similarly during the evenings and summers, the peaks of crime cycles may result from increased opportunities for leisure. Second are the perceived costs and benefits of engaging in criminal activity. The land use pattern of a metropolis delimits the areas in which crimes of different types are likely to occur. In commercial areas, where the wares of an affluent society are alluringly displayed, the opportunities for as well as the benefits from larceny are at their peak. In residential areas, where people have the leisure to commit violence on one another, murders and rapes attain their peaks. Third are factors which affect the probability of successfully consummating a crime. These are the private crime detecting and deterring mechanisms. Jane Jacobs cites as an inadvertent crime deterrent: the "eyes on the street" of her "slum" neighbors when chatting from their windows or doorways.

Perhaps a considerable amount of crime might be deterred by action on the part of the victim. For example, more than 40 percent of all stolen cars had keys left in the ignition; an even larger percentage of such cars were left unlocked. Theft victims on the whole act as if the nuisance of locking one's car outweighed the value of the increased security. Even if they were fully informed of the probable losses associated with locked versus unlocked cars, theft victims might in their private calculus rationally prefer negligence. Private calculus, however, does not consider the social costs of recovering the stolen vehicle, the costs to the usually youthful offender who was led into a criminal career by a misperception of easy gains, and costs to others who may become more prone to victimization, and a process discussed below. Business can similarly affect its chances of being victimized. Omitting the tellers' cages in new suburban banks and providing self-service retailing increases the probability of being robbed. Bankers and retailers may rationally choose to suffer pilferage when more than offset by increases in business. Clearly, individuals and firms do expend considerable sums on private police forces, common to factories, department stores, and universities. Although an individual may perceive benefits from his private crime deterrence activities, the very existence of housebreaking or shoplifting attests to the fact that at a point with a positive crime rate, the private costs of crime deterrence are greater than the private benefits. The private cost-benefit calculations may have serious spill-overs. An amateur auto thief might be deterred from attempting to rob a particular car, whether or not it had an alarm, if from his past experience most other cars had burglar alarms. One might argue that all car owners would be better off if unlocked cars were ticketed, with especially heavy fines for those with keys left in the ignition.

While there is some evidence that individuals avoid victimization by foregoing certain desired activities, this is a costly though somewhat effective means of deterrence. For example, not walking at night or avoiding the subways or parks, may effectively reduce the chances of being mugged, but the inconvenience of these private activities is what prompts the public demand for protection against "crime in the streets."

POLICE AND THE PUBLIC

One popular image of the police is of their prevention of crime by vigilance against evildoers. Actually, the relationship between the police and crime is extremely complex, involving the populace and the courts. At best, the police have a very indirect role in deterring crime—a role mediated through the public. . . .

Police activities: Detection

Far from being omnipresent or omniscient, police rarely catch a criminal in a violent act. More often, police detection of crime depends upon a report by the victim, the public, or even the criminal. Because he may be vulnerable to prosecution himself (e.g., for carrying a weapon, for suspicion of some other crime), a victim often will not report a crime. Similarly, the public may not wish to get involved by reporting a crime, and may accept crime as one of the risks one must take in life, or settle accounts themselves. Quite often a criminal himself will report a crime although his motives may not be those of crime deterrence.

Another influence on the detectability of a crime by the police is the public's evaluation of the gravity of the crime. Organized crime such as prostitution or drug addiction lacks an outraged victim to report the crime. Either because the public is disinterested or unaware, there is rarely a third party to report the offense.

Often the victim does not perceive his misfortune as resulting from a criminal act. For example, if two men engage in a barroom brawl, at least one of them has technically committed assault and battery. Were the brawlers lower class, they are unlikely to consider their behavior criminal. If the combatants were middle class, the loser would undoubtedly report a case of assault. A final influence on the detectability of crime by the police is the probability of restitution to the victim. The robbery of small, uninsured items is less likely to be reported than the loss of a valuable, identifiable insured item.

The one set of "crimes" which the police detect themselves, the attitudes of the victim notwithstanding, are traffic violations. These violations are generally visible outdoors and little information is needed for their detection except for that given on the instruments of the police. The detectability of various crimes can be summarized by comparing official rates of the uniform crime reports to the rates determined by surveys. In general, less than half of all property crimes and about half of all crimes of violence are reported, as shown in Table 31–1. These estimates of reported crimes are conservative in using the victim's rather than the police's judgment as to whether an event was a crime. Most auto thefts were reported, because loss is insurable and the auto is recoverable. If crimes without victims—e.g., traffic offenses and vice—were enumerable, they would prove to be the least detectable.

Investigation and apprehension

If a crime has been detected, say if a victim reports a robbery, the next

function the police may attempt to perform is to discover and to appre-
hend the criminal. How long and hard the police will search for an offender
depends upon the chances of finding him and the gravity of the crime.
The probability of apprehension increases with the speed with which the
police arrive at the scene of the crime or with the degree to which the vic-

TABLE 31–1. Comparison of actual versus reported crime, 1965–
1966 (per 100,000 population)

Crime	Actual	Reported	Percent reported
Traffic offenses	N.A.	N.A.	N.A.
Abortion	N.A.	N.A.	N.A.
Vice	N.A.	N.A.	N.A.
Forcible Rape	42.5	11.6	27
Burglary	949.1	299.6	32
Larceny ($50+)	606.5	267.4	44
Aggravated Assault	218.3	106.6	49
Robbery	94.0	61.4	65
Auto Theft	206.2	226.0	110
		Total Traffic	N.A.
		Total Vice	N.A.
		Total Property	45
		Total Violence	52

Source: President's Commission on Law Enforcement, p. 22.

tim can identify the offender. The willingness of the public to provide the
police with information, hence the ability to investigate, may increase with
the seriousness of the crime. Aside from crimes without victims, there is a
remarkable consensus among the public of all classes, the police, and judges
as to the seriousness of various crimes. For example, most people agree that
murder is more serious than assault, which is more serious than auto theft.
There may be some disagreement, however, among the public of different
classes and between the police and the public as to whether as assault
against a lower class Negro woman is as serious as an assault against a
middle class white woman.

Recovery

If the police were able to recover the criminal's benefit from the crime
and provide restitution to the victim, the police might deter criminals and
compensate victims. Even if the police "get their men," restitution is often
impossible, as in cases of personal violence. For some property crimes, the
stolen goods may have been consumed or damaged. Since the benefit to the
auto thief is generally the joy of riding in a stolen car, the auto is returned
to its rightful owner in about 80 percent of thefts.

Retribution

Although the police are not officially society's arm of retribution, police contact may be the only punishment a criminal may experience since only a small percentage of those arrested ever serve in jail. Apprehension *per se* may be punishing if it leads to time consuming and costly incarceration and litigation, even if one is declared innocent. The costs of litigation may be so high that, in cases where the punishment is minor such as traffic offenses, individuals may pay a fine in lieu of a trial. The direct administration of "curbstone justice" by the police, however, seems to be declining as a form of retribution.

Deterrence

While retribution may be of benefit to some members of society, most people view deterrence as the most important output of the institutions of law enforcement and the administration of justice. In other words, the public believes that the police can and ought to decrease "crime in the streets." Before discussing the deterrence of crime by police protection, we discuss the kinds of economic trade-offs the police can make in combatting crime.

Allocation of police resources

Police administrators have developed rules of thumb for the deployment of their resources. Framed in terms of "desirable" patrolmen/street mile, or patrolmen/population ratios, they provide no insight into the kinds of trade-offs the police face in their internal allocation of resources nor provide a method of evaluating the productive efficiency of a particular allocation.

Budget constraint

The first economic choice involving the police is the level of their budget. Given the method of operations of the police, what is the marginal output of the force in terms of crimes deterred or criminals apprehended for an additional $X of expenditures? How are given police resources disbursed among neighborhoods, program, and items of expenditures?

Choices among neighborhoods

Because policemen in one neighborhood cannot quickly respond to a reported crime in another neighborhood, there may be trade-offs in deterring crimes among different neighborhoods. Allocative choices among neighborhoods are simultaneously distributive; that is, *who is protected* is determined.

Choices among crimes

Which crimes the police try to detect and investigate are a matter of discretion. While a patrolman may produce the joint products of simultaneous vigilance against murder, arson, robbery, traffic violations, etc., the investigator has to choose which offenders at large are worth pursuing. Often the choice among crimes is quite explicit. A patrolman may deliberately not detect a petty criminal—e.g., a drunk or vagrant, who in exchange might provide information about more serious crimes in the future. The existence of many people vulnerable to arrest in a neighborhood can be a valuable resource to the policemen who can stock up on "potential arrest." The effect of mutual exchanges in police-community relations is discussed below.

Choices among programs

There are trade-offs between detective and apprehensive programs. Total commitment of resources to detection leaves little manpower for apprehending criminals not caught in the act. Total commitment to investigation leaves many crimes undetected. Just as there cannot be consumption without some investment, there cannot be apprehension with detection, and there are trade-offs to consider in trying to maximize the number of criminals detected *and* apprehended.

Choices among items of expenditure

The police budget is expended on several classes of inputs in pursuit of crime-fighting programs among the several neighborhoods of a big city. The major items are manpower (patrolmen, investigators, administrators); vehicles (automobiles, motorcycles, scooters, and often helicopters and horses); and the communication network (alarm boxes, two-way radios, telephone lines).

Besides cost trade-offs, there are output trade-offs in choosing among items of expenditure. For example, a patrolman on foot is less mobile than one in an auto but he may have greater contacts with the public on his beat. His closer contact with the public may facilitate their cooperation in crime detection and investigation or, on the other hand, provide more opportunities for "brutality." From the point of view of police administration the foot patrolman is less communicative with headquarters, hence less controllable than an auto patrolman with constant access to a two-way radio.

Other types of trade-offs among inputs are not hard to understand: a one-man patrol car with a finer spread of manpower and higher capital costs versus a two-man car with doubled manpower for any emergency and perhaps higher morale; widespread public alarm boxes facilitating both the reporting of crimes and false alarms, etc.

Normative constraints

An important exogenous influence on police allocation decisions is the normative proscription on police technology and behavior. As articulated by the courts, these norms proscribe, among other actions, wire-tapping, random searches of citizens, arrests without warrant, and the extraction of confessions through torture, all of which may possibly increase the ability of the police to detect and investigate criminal behavior. While such constraints may facilitate detection and investigation, it is not clear that they affect the police's ability to *deter* crimes by amateurs, or even more rational professionals. Most likely these constraints proscribe the ability to deter organized crime without victims. Although it is not clear how the criminal behavior of amateurs, who commit most crimes on the street, would be affected by a less constrained police force, it is quite clear that inconvenience to the public would be increased. Just as there is the cost of tasting bitter pills in fighting disease, there is the cost of police inconvenience to third parties in fighting crime.

Choices between criminal and noncriminal activities

Although police view themselves as "protectors of law and order," they often perform functions usually associated with social work in the public mind. The range of noncriminal services performed depends upon both the socio-economic composition of the population and the willingness of the police to engage in such "nonprofessional" services. In Boston the police locate missing persons, get raccoons out of cellars, provide information about parking regulations and baseball scores, converse with lonely people, and mediate domestic disputes. While the Boston police routinely offer first aid and drive people to hospitals, the Los Angeles police generally refuse involvement with medical problems.

Clearly all types of service demands do not emerge randomly from the population. Middle-class people are less likely to request all kinds of services than do lower-class people. Older, less nimble and mobile individuals often require medical assistance or emergency household repairs. Females heading households often request assistance in disciplining children. Solitary people are most likely to call the police just to talk.

Although these services may seem unprofessional to some police administrators, they provide considerable benefit to the public *per se* and enhance the police image among the groups whose cooperation may be extremely important in detecting and investigating crime. Rather than being a pure drain on police resources "community relations" activities may serve as an intermediate input to the crime deterrence process by increasing the public's willingness to cooperate with the police.

In an economic sense the provision of many social services is nearly cost-less. Because criminal activity tends to be cyclical the police have considerable periods of slackened "demand." For men in the communications department, giving information and advice is nearly a free good, both helping the public and freeing the policemen from demoralizing inactivity. Service work by men on patrol is economically cheap, too. While it may reduce their vigilance on the beat, the patrolmen, like radiomen, learn to judge when the slack periods on their beats will occur. During peaks of criminal activity, not only do the police hesitate to answer social service calls, but the public often hesitates to ask. For other social services, such as police athletic leagues, there are real manpower costs to improving community relations.

THE DETERRENCE OF CRIME IN THE STREETS

Interactions of public, criminals, and policemen

In Figure 31–1 we summarize the systematic interrelationships in the behavior of the public, the criminals, and the police. We identify the final outputs (circles) and policy variables (triangles) of the system. Where relevant, the direction of the effects are indicated by pluses (direct variation) and minuses (inverse variation).

Two outputs of the system are negatively correlated. Specifically, policies which deter crime better also inconvenience the public more. Ideally, one would want to know the costs of changing any policy variable on the deterrence of crime, retribution, and inconvenience, all of which have their prices. In fact, pitifully little is known of the precise effects of any of these policy changes on any one output, e.g., deterrence. Rather than masking ignorance with mathematical rigor, we present below the kinds of economic trade-offs in crime deterrence.

1. Criminal activity increases with cyclical unemployment, which lowers the alternative costs to the criminal. What are the marginal costs in crime if the unemployment rate increases by X percent? What are the costs, if any, of providing employment for the potentially criminal subgroups in society?

2. What are the trade-offs between public and private resources in the detection of crime? Considering the by-products of both private and public expenditures on crime fighting, what is the best mix of private and public protection?

FIGURE 31-1. Interrelations among the police, the public, and criminals

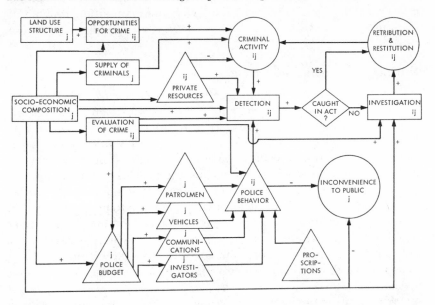

i = Type of crime
j = Type of neighborhood
Output encircled
Policy variable in triangle

3. What are the technological trade-offs between patrolmen and vehicles in detecting a given crime? Given the budget constraint, what combination(s) of patrolmen and vehicles detect the most crime, weighted by its gravity?

4. What are the technological trade-offs between patrol and investigative manpower in detecting a crime *and* apprehending a criminal? Given the budget constraint, what is the best combination(s) of patrol and investigative resources for apprehending the most criminals, weighted by the gravity of their crimes?

5. What effects do the detection of crime and the apprehension of criminals have on the rate of different crimes? Given the public evaluation of each type of crime, what is the deterrent value of police activity for different neighborhoods?

6. What are the shadow prices of policemen, investigators, and vehicles? In terms of crimes deterred, what are the benefits of easing the budget constraint on the police?

7. What are the effects of the normative constraints on police behavior? Do the courts really "handcuff" the police in their fight against crime? If the public were willing to tolerate the inconvenience of a less restrained police force, how much additional crime would be deterred?

8. What are the costs of providing social services to the public? What

are the trade-offs in terms of crimes deterred between resources devoted to professional, direct anti-criminal activity, and maintaining community relations?

Distribution of police protection

Even if we were able to methodically trace out the effects of police protection on inconvenience to the public, recovery of stolen goods, retribution against criminals, and deterrence of future crimes, we are faced with the more difficult question of *who benefits from it?* While costs of inconvenience may be traced to those experiencing police contact and benefits of recovery may be traced to the victim, the benefits of retribution and deterrence are not so easily traced. All individuals do not evaluate retribution against a convicted offender similarly. At one extreme some may view him as an unfortunate creature of circumstance who may hopefully be rehabilitated. At the other extreme, others may view him as deserving to pay "an eye for an eye." For criminals who have no victims (gamblers, dope pushers, abortionists, bootleggers), there may even be remorse on the part of the clientele.

Aside from the obvious case of crimes without victims, all individuals do not benefit equally from the deterrence of a given crime. The simple reason is that we are not equally likely to be victimized. The probability of coming to violence, as mentioned before, depends upon one's socio-economic status. The losses from property crimes are perhaps most sharply felt by owners of property, for example.

While the upper-middle classes are unlikely to be victims of any crime, much less organized crime, they tend to be outraged by vice and gangland killing. For this class, crime deterrence, regardless of the potential victim, is perceived as a public good and the police as the enforcers of their civic morality.

CONCLUSION

The main points of this essay are quite simple. First, society faces trade-offs in allocating resources to crime deterrence and other goals. In private decisions individuals trade off the expected losses from crime against the costs of taking safety precautions, self-service firms trade off the costs of salesmen against the losses due to crime, and banks trade security for attractiveness to customers. In public decisions, there are trade-offs between resources spent on police protection and those expended on other goals. Second, there are trade-offs in the internal economy of a police department among items of expenditures, programs, crimes to be deterred, and neighborhoods to be protected. The internal economic choices are somewhat constrained by public opinion and court edicts. Third, painfully little quantitative knowledge of the several trade-offs described is available. In the absence of such hard knowledge, it is difficult to evaluate alternative crime deterrent policies or efficiency of police operations.

In principle, the analysis of crime deterrence should be easier than that of nuclear deterrence, mainly because the output of police protection, a drop in the crime rate, is more palpable than the output of the Defense Department, a drop in the probability of war with Russia. One must be intellectually prepared to accept a finding that the police have negligible effects on the crime rate, as some anthropologists argue. If this were true, then millions poured into local police departments might be better spent on improving the economic conditions of potential criminals or on other social goals. Although frustrating to the political activist, one might find changing the criminal behavior of the lower class as difficult as changing their educational behavior.

32 How to improve urban transportation at practically no cost*

JOHN F. KAIN

A revolutionary improvement in the quality and quantity of urban transportation services could be obtained in virtually every U.S. metropolitan area in a relatively short period of time. Moreover, it would require expenditures no larger, and possibly smaller, than those presently programmed. These gains could be achieved by converting existing urban expressways to rapid transit facilities through the addition of electronic surveillance, monitoring, and control devices and the provision of priority access for public transit vehicles.

Comparative cost analyses prepared by John R. Meyer, Martin Wohl, and me indicate that bus rapid transit systems on either their own rights-of-way or on congestion-free, general-use expressways have a commanding cost advantage over rail under most circumstances and can provide higher levels of service. The cost of grade-separated rail transit systems becomes competitive with new bus rapid transit systems only when urban density is extremely high or when rail transit investments have already been made.

Moreover, there are no technical reasons why freeway rapid transit systems should not have peak-hour speeds equal to or well in excess of those anticipated from any proposed rail rapid transit system, such as the BARTD [Bay Area Rapid Transit District] system currently under construction in the San Francisco Bay area or those proposed for Seattle and Atlanta. Express buses are inherently faster than rail transit because their smaller unit size reduces the number of stops they must make to obtain a full load. In addition to having higher potential line-haul speeds, freeway express buses have the ability to act as their own residential collectors,

* From "How to Improve Urban Transportation at Practically No Cost," hearings before the Joint Economic Committee, Subcommittee on Economy in Government, 91st Congress, Second Session, 1970, pp. 1141–45. Reprinted with permission of the author. John F. Kain is Professor of Economics at Harvard University, Cambridge, Mass.

saving the time and inconvenience of transferring from feeder buses to the rapid transit line.

Still, these higher potential speeds are less important than the markedly lower capital costs of freeway rapid transit. Because they are able to share costly right-of-way facilities with other users, such systems can be provided at a fraction of the cost of fixed-rail systems. There are no major unsolved technical obstacles. We are prevented from obtaining such systems only by our lack of imagination and unwillingness to overcome existing political and organization rigidities. Development of these systems requires a complete integration of highway and transit planning and a willingness to impose certain rational restrictions on the use of high-performance urban highway facilities, particularly during peak hours.

Modern limited-access highways move huge numbers of vehicles at high speed and with great safety for 20 hours a day. However, for 4 hours they are allowed to become so badly congested that vehicle capacity, speed, and safety are seriously reduced. This is inexcusable. The design of these facilities makes it relatively simple to meter vehicles onto the expressway and thereby maintain high performance and high speeds even during peak hours.

If transit vehicles were simply given priority access to these uncongested high-performance highways, they could achieve higher average speeds than private automobiles during peak hours in congested areas. Current peak-hour commuters must choose between a relatively slow and unreliable private automobile system and an even slower and undependable public transit system. If the proposed system were implemented, the commuter would have the choice of an automobile system that provides service no worse than that presently available and a transit system with vastly improved service. Since the new high-performance transit system would be substantially faster and more reliable than existing transit service and would also be considerably cheaper than private automobile commutation for many workers, significant numbers of automobile commuters might shift from private transportation to the transit system. If this occurred, automobile commuters who, because of their origins and destinations, are poorly served by rapid transit or who prefer to drive for other reasons might reduce their travel times.

Even more optimistically, this new high-performance alternative might reduce the demand for expensive highway facilities serving central areas and release large amounts of highway funds for use in rapidly growing suburban areas and less urbanized areas or for other purposes entirely. Similarly, if fewer highways were needed in central areas, the dislocations that have caused so much unrest in recent years would be that much reduced. These system effects are a major part of the justification for the BARTD system in San Francisco and for similar rail transit proposals in other cities. However, these rail rapid transit systems are orders of magnitude more costly and provide far less coverage (fewer route-miles) than the highway rapid transit systems proposed here.

In addition to having much lower initial cost, express bus systems can be closely tailored to changes in the location, composition, and level of demand. Metropolitan areas are experiencing increases in incomes, changes in job locations, and suburbanization of the population. All of these forces are causing rapid and significant changes in commuting patterns. Fixed-rail systems are almost incapable of responding to these shifts. However, an express bus system, of the kind described here, can adjust rapidly to these changes since it can operate in a variety of ways over any part of the existing or expanded regional highway network. Each new expressway link enriches the rapid transit system and provides penetration of new areas. In addition, such systems can be easily scaled up or down to meet changes in demand levels. If demand declines, there is almost no loss since there is no unique fixed investment. If employment and population dispersal proceeds far enough or if consumers demand more flexible, costly, and personalized forms of transportation, the proportion of the common right-of-way devoted to public transit during peak hours can be relinquished to automobiles, trucks, and other vehicles.

A number of metropolitan areas already possess extensive expressway networks linking the downtown area with the entire metropolitan area. Fortunately, the rapid development of these expressway systems has been matched by a steady buildup in the know-how and hardware needed to make an expressway rapid transit system operational. Thus, all that is currently needed to create extensive metropolitan rapid transit systems in a number of metropolitan areas is a limited outlay for instrumentation, some modification of ramp arrangement and design, and most importantly a policy decision to keep congestion at very low levels during peak hours and to provide priority access for public transit vehicles.

Instrumentation of the type required is already being evaluated by a number of state highway departments. This is not, as far as I know, because any of them are seriously contemplating the development of highway rapid transit systems. Rather, it is because installation of such electronics on urban expressways is probably justified under any circumstances. Increases in highway capacity and reliability alone will probably pay for such instrumental highways—without even considering the very large benefits that would accrue from using such facilities for rapid transit. Still if these electronic highways are to be used for both rapid transit and private vehicles during peak hours, it would probably be desirable to maintain higher speeds and levels of service than if the facility were to be used for general traffic only. The result of such operating policies would probably be to reduce peak-hour vehicular volumes by some small amount and greatly increase passenger volumes.

In 1966 when I was employed as a consultant to the Department of

Housing and Urban Development, Thomas Floyd, director of the demonstration grant program, and I designed a feasibility study of the freeway rapid transit concept and persuaded Vergil G. Stover of the Texas A. & M. Research Foundation to submit a proposal. We asked the Texas A. & M. group to undertake the work because of its substantial experience with expressway monitoring and control systems.

The contract required that preliminary designs and detailed cost analysis be carried out for four existing freeway corridors. The facilities serving these corridors were selected so as to pose a variety of engineering and control problems. The expressways analyzed in the study were:

    (1) The Lodge Freeway in Detroit;

    (2) The Gulf Freeway in Houston;

    (3) I-35W in Minneapolis, and

    (4) The Penn-Lincoln Freeway in Pittsburgh.

From analysis of these four test sites, Stover, and his associates determined that: "only minor construction modifications plus the installation of a surveillance and control system would be needed to implement service on existing freeways."

Both the capital costs of these modifications and their variation among sites are surprisingly small, ranging from $26,000 to $34,000 per mile for the four facilities despite the wide range of topography and freeway design at the four locations. The annual operating costs for surveillance and control varied between $15,000 and $20,000 per mile for the four facilities.

The additional capital outlays required for such a system would differ from one metropolitan area to another, depending principally on the size and complexity of its freeway system. Although obtaining precise cost estimates for individual metropolitan areas would require detailed engineering studies for each, ball-park estimates can easily be made from the cost data developed by Stover and Glennon. For example, it appears that a freeway rapid transit system for Detroit would have an incremental capital cost of about $5.5 million and a yearly operating cost of about $3.2 million. For this investment the Detroit metropolitan area would obtain 162 route-miles of rapid transit. A smaller metropolitan area, such as Atlanta, could install a system of this kind for an additional capital outlay of about $4.2 million and a yearly operating cost of approximately $2.5 million.

A large-scale demonstration project in one or two medium-sized metropolitan areas would provide an opportunity to work out some of the remaining technical problems, provide a test for consumer acceptance, and simplify the problem of getting decisionmakers to agree to the highway operations policies that are central to the proposal. The Departments of Transportation and Housing and Urban Development might pay all or a major portion of the cost of a demonstration project for the first state or metropolitan area agreeing to implement such a plan on a 5-year trial basis, if state or city officials would agree to limit peak-hour expressway usage. To provide a meaningful test of the proposal, it would be desirable to select a metropolitan area that has a significant downtown development, a well-developed highway system serving downtown, and fairly high levels of congestion.

The needed electronics could be installed and the surveillance and control system operated for a 5-year demonstration period for between $15 and $30 million. However, to fully test the demand for high-performance transit systems, it might be desirable to provide operating subsidies for saturation transit services throughout the entire region during all or part of the demonstration.

The public's response to fast and frequent service would provide much needed information about the demand for high-performance transit services. It is essential that these high levels of service be provided long enough for potential users to regard them as more or less permanent. Five years should be a sufficiently long period to evaluate the longrun impacts of these service improvements on such matters as choice of residence and decisions whether to buy either a first or second car.

It is difficult to estimate the dollar cost of these operating subsidies prior to choosing a particular city and deciding on the level and duration of subsidized service. However, I would guess that a very significant experiment could be carried out for less than $50 million. This is by no means a trivial amount of money, but it still compares favorably with the $1½ billion capital cost of the "BARTD experiment." The comparison is still more favorable since this $50 million buys a system with two to three times as many rapid transit route-miles as the BARTD system.

In the nearly 10 years since John Meyer, Martin Wohl, and I proposed the concept of freeway rapid transit in a report for the White House panel on civilian technology, there has been a growing interest in the idea. Indeed, the Department of Transportation has recently awarded a contract to study the feasibility of a closely related system which would reserve a freeway lane for car pools and buses. However, neither this proposal nor any of the others I have examined is daring enough or begins to exploit the possibilities of the concept. The interdependence of the urban transportation system requires a far more ambitious attack than any of these proposals contemplates.

33 Medical care and its delivery*

JUDITH R. LAVE and LESTER B. LAVE

GOURMAND AND FOOD—A FABLE

The people of Gourmand loved good food. They ate in good restaurants, donated money for cooking research, and instructed their government to safeguard all matters having to do with food. Long ago, the food industry had been in total chaos. There were many restaurants, some very small. Anyone could call himself a chef or open a restaurant. In choosing a restaurant, one could never be sure that the meal would be good. A commission of distinguished chefs studied the situation and recommended that no one be allowed to touch food except for qualified chefs. "Food is too important to be left to amateurs," they said. Qualified chefs were licensed by the state with severe penalties for anyone else who engaged in cooking. Certain exceptions were made for food preparation in the home, but a person could serve only his own family. Furthermore, to become a qualified chef, a man had to complete at least twenty-one years of training (including four years of college, four years of cooking school, and one year of apprenticeship). All cooking schools had to be first class.

These reforms did succeed in raising the quality of cooking. But a restaurant meal became substantially more expensive. A second commission observed that not everyone could afford to eat out. "No one," they said, "should be denied a good meal because of his income." Furthermore, they argued that chefs should work toward the goal of giving everyone "complete physical and psychological satisfaction." For those people who could not afford to eat out, the government declared that they should be allowed to do so as often as they liked and the government would pay. For others, it was recommended that they organize themselves in groups and

* From "Medical Care and Its Delivery: An Economic Appraisal." Reprinted with permission of authors and publisher, from a symposium "Health Care: Part I" appearing in *Law and Contemporary Problems*, 35 (Spring 1970), published by the Duke University School of Law, Durham, N.C. Copyright 1970, by Duke University. Judith R. Lave is Associate Professor of Economics and Urban Processes at Carnegie-Mellon University; and Lester B. Lave is Professor of Economics at Carnegie-Mellon University, Pittsburgh, Penn.

pay part of their income into a pool that would undertake to pay the costs incurred by members in dining out. To insure the greatest satisfaction, the groups were set up so that a member could eat out anywhere and as often as he liked, could have as elaborate a meal as he desired, and would have to pay nothing or only a small percentage of the cost. The cost of joining such prepaid dining clubs rose sharply.

Long ago, most restaurants would have one chef to prepare the food. A few restaurants were more elaborate, with chefs specializing in roasting, fish, salads, sauces, and many other things. People rarely went to these elaborate restaurants since they were so expensive. With the establishment of prepaid dining clubs, everyone wanted to eat at these fancy restaurants. At the same time, young chefs in school disdained going to cook in a small restaurant where they would have to cook everything. The pay was higher and it was much more prestigious to specialize and cook at a really fancy restaurant. Soon there were not enough chefs to keep the small restaurants open.

With prepaid clubs and free meals for the poor, many people started eating their three-course meals at the elaborate restaurants. Then they began to increase the number of courses, directing the chef to "serve the best with no thought for the bill." (Recently a 317-course meal was served.)

The costs of eating out rose faster and faster. A new government commission reported as follows: (1) Noting that licensed chefs were being used to peel potatoes and wash lettuce, the commission recommended that these tasks be handed over to licensed dishwashers (whose three years of dishwashing training included cooking courses) or to some new category of personnel. (2) Concluding that many licensed chefs were overworked, the commission recommended that cooking schools be expanded, that the length of training be shortened, and that applicants with lesser qualifications be admitted. (3) The commission also observed that chefs were unhappy because people seemed to be more concerned about the decor and service than about the food. (In a recent taste test, not only could one patron not tell the difference between a 1930 and a 1970 vintage but he also could not distinguish between white and red wines. He explained that he always ordered the 1930 vintage because he knew that only a really good restaurant would stock such an expensive wine.)

The commission agreed that weighty problems faced the nation. They recommended that a national prepayment group be established which everyone must join. They recommended that chefs continue to be paid on the basis of the number of dishes they prepared. They recommended that every Gourmandese be given the right to eat anywhere he chose and as elaborately as he chose and pay nothing.

These recommendations were adopted. Large numbers of people spent all of their time ordering incredibly elaborate meals. Kitchens became marvels of new, expensive equipment. All those who were not consuming restaurant food were in the kitchen preparing it. Since no one in Gourmand did anything except prepare or eat meals, the country collapsed.

I. INTRODUCTION

There is a pervasive feeling of imminent crisis with respect to the delivery of medical services in the United States. Expenditures on medical care are rising without any offsetting decline in our mortality rates—which compare poorly with those of many other countries. The costs of medical care are increasing at an accelerating rate. Many big-city hospitals, which service the poor, are in a state of financial distress. Medicare and Medicaid, the programs developed to enable the disadvantaged to obtain medical care, set off the current price spiral by creating a rapid increase in the demand for medical services while the supply of those services could be increased only slowly. The middle class now finds it difficult to obtain the kind of medical care it has come to expect, namely that of an interested, warm physician who is familiar with the family history. There is a perceived over-all shortage of nurses and physicians. Moreover, many concerned individuals believe that the existing physicians are not distributed well. They argue that there are relatively too few primary physicians and too many specialists, too few physicians in the inner cities and in rural areas, and too many in the affluent suburbs.

As a response to these and many other problems, government involvement in the delivery of medical services has increased. The share of personal expenditures on medical services financed by public funds rose from twenty-two percent in fiscal 1966 to thirty-six percent in fiscal 1969. These funds have been expended on demonstration projects to experiment with alternative ways of delivering medical care and on innovative training programs, as well as on more traditional services. The trend is clear, and few people believe that government participation will decrease in the future.

The purpose of this paper is to discuss some aspects of the structure of the medical care industry, with special emphasis on some of the interrelationships that we believe are important and should be considered in formulating policy. Since medical services are desired not for their own sake but because they are an important input into the acquisition of health, we begin with a discussion of the nature of this relationship.

II. THE RELATIONSHIP BETWEEN MEDICAL CARE EXPENDITURES AND HEALTH

Medical services are but one of the many inputs contributing to improved health. Health, itself an amorphous concept, has been defined by the World Health Organization as "a state of complete physical, mental and social well-being and not merely the absence of disease or infirmity."

The relationship between medical care expenditures and "complete physical, mental and social well-being" is weak, and, even when we move from the very abstract concept of health to more conventional ones, the association between medical care expenditures and health remains tenuous. Few of the occasions when medical care is sought are matters of life and death. Some medical care expenditures are necessary to sustain life, to deter incapacitation, or to rehabilitate members of society, but, as the majority of illnesses are self-limiting, most medical services provide support, reassurance, and palliation without affecting the length of the illness. Some medical expenditures, such as nose restructuring, facial uplifts, and bosom expansions, are purely luxury expenditures of the rich or vain.

Since one's basic state of health is affected partly by one's socioeconomic status and physical environment, it may be more efficient to attack the cause of bad health rather than the symptom of it. Let us elaborate further.

Many "diseases" are more prevalent among the poor; the poor experience more days of complete or partial disability. The low-income morbidity is caused not only by a relatively low use of medical services but by the poverty itself. Poverty is usually accompanied by bad nutrition, substandard housing, and inadequate sanitation. The interrelationships are complicated: poverty contributes to poor health, poor health to poverty. Peter de Vise has presented a grim picture of the health status of the residents of the Chicago ghetto. One could well argue that what he describes is a prime symptom of poverty; while better medical care may temporarily alleviate the symptoms, the root causes will remain. This argument has been succinctly put by Geiger: "To treat symptoms, and then to send the patients back, unchanged in knowledge, attitude or behavior to the same physical and social environment—also unchanged—that overwhelmingly helped to produce that illness and will do so again is to provide antibiotics for cholera and then send the patients back to drink again from the Broad Street pump."[1] For poorer families, we would contend that resources devoted to the alleviation of poverty and health education would have greater impact on improving family health than would resources devoted to medical services.

An individual's general health status depends not only on his socioeconomic status but also on his life style and environment. His drinking, sleeping, eating, and exercising habits all influence his health, as does the environment in which he works and lives. It has been shown that air pollution leads to increases in the incidence of bronchitis, lung cancer, other respiratory diseases, and many other diseases. A recent study concluded that a fifty percent abatement in the level of air pollution would lower

---

[1] H. Geiger, "Poor and Professional, Who Takes the Handle of the Broad Street Pump?", paper presented at the 94th annual meeting of the American Public Health Association, San Francisco, Nov. 1, 1966.

the economic cost of morbidity and mortality almost as much as finding an immediate and complete cure for cancer. For middle class families in large cities, air pollution is probably the single most important factor adversely affecting family health. Relatively small expenditures on abating pollution would do more to improve the general health of the family than much larger expenditures on medical care that the family currently undertakes. We must shift our attention from medical care as an end in itself to medical care as only one of many inputs into improved health.

III. THE AMORPHOUS CONCEPT OF QUALITY

Since higher medical costs are often attributed to higher quality medical care, we must discuss the quality problem. We consider two dimensions of quality: (1) the subjective perception of the patient of the care he is receiving, and (2) objective medical efficacy (accuracy of the diagnosis and effectiveness of the treatment). These two dimensions are not totally separable since the patient's perception of his treatment is likely to affect both his response to and his acquiescence in the treatment program.

The Gourmandese found that the setting and service of their dinner was of primary importance. As long as the cost is zero, the customer will demand more attendants and a more attractive setting; if it costs no more, why not get the best? The Gourmandese also found that they wanted their sauces prepared by specialists, rather than general cooks, since it cost no more. After all, the better the training of the chef, the more likely that the product is better, even if one is not capable of tasting the difference. The better the training of the chef, the more prestige accrues to the customer who is knowledgeable enough to choose him.

As with the Gourmandese, the patient often focuses on the setting in which he receives care. This is certainly true with institutionalized care. But, as is true with restaurants, better service, higher quality foods, and more pleasant surroundings usually cost more to provide. Perhaps more important, few patients know enough about medicine to have any way of judging a physician other than by his credentials, his attitude toward them, and the warmth and respect offered by those working with him. There is little reason to believe that the patient's perception of the quality of the medical care he received would correlate highly with the judgment of other physicians who might serve as consultants.

There are two aspects of the objective measure of quality that we wish to discuss: first, the costs associated with reducing the probability of error or mishap (defined as a deviation from the desired outcome) and, second, the impossibility of giving everybody the "best possible medicine."

Nothing is sure in medicine. There is some small probability that a child will go into shock and die when administered a routine injection. No one can undergo even minor surgery with complete assurance that he will live through the operation, much less that the operation will be a success. Everyone would agree that reducing the probabilities of error or mishap would enhance quality, but one unfortunate property that medicine shares with almost all other human activity is that it is increasingly costly to continue to lower such risks. For example, in perhaps one appendectomy in a thousand a situation will arise where a gastrointestinal surgeon could do a better job than a general surgeon. On the other hand, it is both costly and time consuming to give general surgeons the extra training required to become gastrointestinal surgeons. Is it worthwhile to spend such extra time and money so that all appendectomies can be done by gastrointestinal surgeons or so that all broken bones can be set by orthopedic surgeons? If the reader's answer to these questions is affirmative, we could cite even more extreme instances where minute increases in quality are achieved only at astronomical costs.

A second and much misconceived aspect of quality is reflected in the ubiquitous assertion that every American is entitled to the best medicine. Just as there are only a few really superb chefs but a large number of good ones, there are only a few really superb physicians but many who are quite competent. It is conceptually impossible for everyone to be served by the few top physicians, and some people will always be served by the few worst physicians.

The contradiction is not quite so obvious when we think about the scope of treatment rather than the skill of the physician. For example, the American Academy of Pediatrics has published a set of standards which delineate what is deemed adequate care for a child under the age of eighteen. These standards specify the number and timing of physical examinations and innoculations. Without regard to the geographical maldistribution of pediatricians, one study estimates that if only the recommended care were provided, all pediatricians could treat only one-third of the children in the United States. This would mean "good" medical care for one-third of the children; no medical care for the rest.

The response to this analysis has been twofold. The first is to study which of the pediatricians' tasks could be performed as well by people with much less training. The basic conclusion of these studies is that about eighty percent of the average pediatrician's practice could be done by people who have much less training. The second is to ask whether all the items recommended by the American Academy of Pediatrics are really efficacious. Why should a newborn be seen eight to twelve times during his first year of life? Why should he have four complete physical examinations? Could not four to six visits be arranged so that the child received just as good medical care? (Note that the validity of immunization is not at issue.)

At the end of this paper we will return to the issue of quality in discussing whether we really want "the best possible medical care for everyone," even if it could be produced. We now turn to describing some aspects of the medical care service industry itself. In particular we focus on the following issues: (*a*) factors affecting the individual's decision to seek medical care, (*b*) the extent of substitution that can be obtained in treating a patient, (*c*) the concept of the paramedic, (*d*) the mode of delivering medical care, and (*e*) the interrelationships between financing and costs.

IV. THE DEMAND FOR MEDICAL SERVICES

The demand for medical care originates with the individual. His decision to seek care—which usually begins with a visit to a physician—will depend in part on the following interrelated factors: (1) his underlying state of health, (2) his perception of when he needs medical care, and (3) the cost to him of obtaining care. We have already discussed the first factor. The perception of when medical care is needed has changed a great deal over time. At one point, medical care was sought only if an individual could no longer function adequately, and even then only if it appeared that the problem would not correct itself. Much of the demand for medical care of course still revolves around acute remedial situations, such as accidents or severe illnesses. One quite different perception of the need for medical care that has emerged involves the seeking of "preventive maintenance" in the form of routine physical examinations or, more currently, "multiphasic health screening." Finally, some people seek medical care whenever they are not in a "state of complete physical, mental and social well-being." The perception of when medical care should be sought depends on the age, sex, marital status, income, and education of a person.

The cost to a person of obtaining care seldom has much connection with the price charged by the physician or hospital. In many cases, care is costless because of medical insurance or group-practice prepayment. In other cases, the cost of a simple visit may be extraordinarily high because of the difficulty and expense of giving up work and traveling to the physician. While the evidence on relationships is not as conclusive as one might desire, cost to the consumer is an important factor influencing the demand for care. When the cost of a visit is zero, as under group-practice prepayment plans, people demand more visits than when they must pay for each visit. When hospitalization is free because of comprehensive insurance coverage, people are apt to be hospitalized more than when they must pay the full costs themselves.

Once the decision has been made to seek care, the consumer cedes his decision-making power to the physician. It is the physician who determines the inputs of goods and services and what risks to take. As Arrow has pointed out, the consumer has the dual characteristics of being ignorant about medicine and loathing to take risks concerning his health. Thus, he is likely to ask the physician to make all the decisions and to instruct him to spare no expense. This arrangement is an unusual one in our economy, unusual even for the circumstances. Few people would think of giving their auto repairman or plumber the same instructions, in spite of their ignorance and concern.

V. THE TECHNOLOGY

In treating a given illness, the various medical inputs—the nurse, the aide, the physician, the surgeon, the drugs, and the hospital bed—can be combined in different ways. In fact, it is an important economic insight that there are many ways of delivering medical care. A routine physical examination, for example, can be performed solely by a physician, or by a nurse-physician combination where the medical history, weight, height, and temperature are taken by the nurse, or by a nurse-technician-physician combination where technicians perform a vast number of tests and the role of the physician is limited to the interpretation of the tests (as in multiphasic screening). These different ways of delivering the same service can be designed to provide medical care of a similar quality but with vastly different implications for cost and utilization of scarce resources, such as physician time. These substitutions are not only limited to routine care or to ambulatory care. At one time, many of the tasks (such as the drawing of blood and the giving of intravenous injections or anesthesia) which are now handled competently by paramedics and allied health manpower could be legally performed only by physicians.

There are many limitations on the extent to which these possible substitutions are actually used. The physician, who usually manages the case, has been trained to give "the best possible care" and may not consider alternatives. Quality may be defined (by the patient especially) in terms of the inputs rather than the outcome. The method used to finance care may distort the cost relationships so that the cheapest treatment program for the patient is not the cheapest to society. Professional prerogatives may set arbitrary limits on who can do what. Fear of malpractice suits leads doctors to conformity in their actions and inhibits anything that might be construed as corner-cutting. Legal limitations on some substitutions are set. These legal limitations are always advocated as ways to protect the patient from bad quality medical care, but they often work to serve the self-interest of professional groups and to raise costs. Consider, for example, the fact that most states prohibit nurse-midwives from delivering babies. While these laws might once have protected women from untrained amateurs, an RN with special training in obstetrics can handle a normal delivery and can recognize more complicated cases which warrant the obstetrician's special skill. It takes twelve years to train an obstetrician and four years to train a nurse-midwife. The cost differences are much greater than three to one since medical school and residency are more expensive per year than nursing school. Nor is this a new, untried idea dreamed by well-meaning but ignorant economists. In European countries, where the infant and maternal mortality rates are low (the contrast with the United States is embarrassing), most obstetrical care is provided by the midwife.

The current interest in developing paramedics (personnel being trained to assume some of the tasks usually performed by the physician) may be interpreted as an attempt to increase the substitution possibilities in the production of health. Task analyses have indicated that physicians perform many tasks which could easily be delegated to paramedics, and there have been a number of demonstration projects in which nurses with some additional training have adequately performed tasks usually undertaken by the physician. There have been a number of training programs—some of which give nurses additional training, others of which train new personnel—in which individuals are specifically trained to supplant the physician in the performance of certain tasks. The full implications of these programs will be unknown for some time. Analyses of existing programs indicate that paramedics can perform their tasks well and that the paramedics are generally well accepted by the patient. General physician acceptance is unclear, but physicians who have worked with them report satisfaction. Acceptance by other health professionals, who may feel threatened, has been slow. Legal issues having to do with licensure have not been solved. Long-run effects on the redistribution of income within the health services industry are unknown.

VI. PHYSICIAN CHOICE OF PRACTICE SETTING

The institutional settings in which medical care is delivered probably have some effect on costs. A physician may decide to practice by himself, in partnership with a small number of colleagues (such as a group of obstetricians or pediatricians), or in a larger institutional setting, such as a clinic or formal group practice. Some years ago, group practice, especially prepaid group practice, was heralded as the solution to many cost (and quality) problems. Investigators liked what they saw in the Kaiser groups and attempted to persuade physicians to replicate this situation and to encourage the government to promote group practice. More recently, questions have been raised as to whether group practice itself really does result in a more efficient utilization of physicians and facilities. One may wonder whether the original investigators were guilty of trying to generalize from the experience of a prepaid group that had considerable constraints on its access to hospital beds.

As economists we would predict that physicians would decide to locate their practice in a place which they find both pleasant and challenging. Certainly one aspect of the locational decision will be the amount of service they can render, but other aspects will include the income earned, number of hours worked, associations with colleagues, and the availability of amenities of life. It is not hard to understand why physicians are becoming more concentrated in urban business areas and in the suburbs, leaving rural areas and inner city ghettos with little or no medical care.

We make the above observations because they imply that many current policies will be ineffective. Increasing the number of physicians is unlikely to increase the number who settle in rural areas. It would probably take a massive increase in the supply before physicians would give up the amenities of urban or suburban life for the higher incomes associated with rural practice. (This judgment may be incorrect if the social awareness of current medical students is as strong as reported.) Directly increasing the income of rural physicians is also not likely to have much of an effect in attracting physicians. There are currently rural communities that offer higher incomes than many urban physicians are earning but are still unable to secure physicians. Indeed, the policy of increasing the supply of physicians may have some bad implications for resource allocation, as suggested by Ginzsberg.

Should the government intervene directly and tell physicians where to practice? The cost of such a policy in a democratic society would be great. Instead, we should design mechanisms to encourage physicians to practice in rural areas for a part of their career. For example, the military draft for physicians could be used to supply physicians to rural areas for two or three years. Probably a better mechanism would involve offering to pay tuition, or some part of the expenses, of medical students in return for two or three years of practice in specified areas (as does Canada's province of Newfoundland). Other suggestions to improve medical services in these areas include the development of paramedics. If paramedics could be made available to work with rural physicians or to function in field stations without a physician present, some of the unattractive features of rural practice, such as excessively long hours, might diminish, perhaps increasing the flow of physicians to rural areas.

VII. THE RELATIONSHIP BETWEEN FINANCING METHODS AND THE COST OF MEDICAL CARE

If the resources needed to treat a particular medical case were fixed in proportion, if the prices of medical inputs never changed (the supply of inputs being perfectly elastic), and if the price of medical care never affected how much was demanded, then there is no way that the method of financing medical care and of reimbursing the providers of medical care could affect costs. In fact, however, an individual's decision to seek medical care often depends on its price to him, medical inputs can be combined in many different ways, and prices often reflect the patient's ability to pay. Consequently we believe that the methods of financing and reimbursement are a crucial element. Let us explore these relationships in four aspects.

(1) *Impact of more spending.* Increasing expenditures on medical services do not necessarily give rise to proportionately more of such services. This statement has been supported by our experience in the period immediately following the implementation of Medicare and Medicaid. The effect of increasing purchasing power of some consumers was to redistribute existing resources—perhaps in a socially more optimal way, to draw some more medical services into the industry, and to cause an increase in prices. Cooper has estimated that, of the total dollar increase in expenditures for health services since 1966, approximately fifty percent can be attributed to price increases alone.

(2) *Distortions created by insurance coverage.* Medical insurance which covers the costs of some medical inputs and not of others will probably influence the treatment pattern of a specific disease as the patient, or the doctor acting in his interest, attempts to minimize the patient's expense; this process may result in higher over-all costs. Thus, it is common for insurance to cover the costs of certain diagnostic tests only if they are performed while the insured is in a hospital; a patient might therefore be hospitalized, say, for two days at a cost of $200, of which he pays nothing, in order to avoid his having to pay $40 for these tests as an outpatient. This kind of selective insurance provides built-in incentives to substitute more expensive inputs for the cheaper inputs with no improvement in the quality of care. While evidence of the existence or extent of misallocative effects from these perverse incentives is not strong, in the short run, any increase in the demand for inputs which are in relatively fixed supply could be expected to contribute to an increase in their prices; in the long run, pressure would develop for expanding the more expensive resource. The consequence of the tendencies adverted to in the foregoing example would be that hospitals would be enlarged so that most testing could be done on an inpatient basis to accommodate those with insurance.

(3) *Physician self-interest in decision making.* The way in which a physician is reimbursed may affect his decision on how to manage a particular case. While we have no desire to impugn any individual physician or his selected treatment pattern, we do argue that decisions will be colored by personal gain. When the patient presents himself to the physician, the physician chooses the course of treatment and the various inputs that will be used. One of these inputs is his own skill and time. Models of physician behavior are incomplete, but Mosma has suggested that, since the physician also has a financial interest in the treatment of the patient, the patient's interest may not be the only factor affecting the physician's advice. He argues that one of the factors influencing a physician's behavior may be the marginal revenue to him for performing the services. The ethical problem may seem less substantial to the physician where a third-party insurer or the government, rather than the patient, is paying the bill.

Mosma develops a number of hypotheses which stem from the above argument. He tests them by examining physician behavior under fee-for-service practice and in salary settings. He focuses primarily on the extent of surgery, since it is here that major effects should occur. His results show clearly that the rates of surgery are much higher for groups in which the individuals are treated by physicians under fee-for-service than those treated by salaried physicians. The prime effect shows up in those procedures the efficacy of which is often subject to some doubt, such as tonsillectomies, appendectomies, and hysterectomies. He concludes that the differences in rates of recourse to surgery seem to represent overutilization in the fee-for-service situation rather than underutilization in the salaried group situation.

Proponents of salaried group medical practice also believe that a fee for service may create incentives for physicians to recommend additional visits. There has been no good empirical work undertaken to test this hypothesis. The argument does, however, suggest that alternative ways of financing medical care should be encouraged.

(4) *Inefficiences encouraged by cost reimbursement.* The costs of hospital care are likely to be affected by the method of reimbursement. Economic models of the interaction between the methods chosen to reimburse hospitals and hospital costs have not been fully developed and tested. There is some consensus that hospital costs are rising rapidly since most reimbursement is done on the basis of cost. Concern about this possibility has prompted legislative proposals looking toward "prospective reimbursement" and more sophisticated cost limitations under Medicare.

VIII. HOW MUCH MEDICAL CARE?

The last question we would like to raise is this: How much medical care do we really want? Stated otherwise, what level of medical intervention with the disease process is socially optimal?

The question is generated by the many miracles of modern medicine, by the unbelievable techniques that can postpone death for a short period of time, by transplant techniques and the technology of artificial organs, and by the entire genre of medical care exemplified by that given President Eisenhower in the last year of his life. Decisions about the amount of care to be rendered in a particular case are often made by physicians; but, since costs are being increasingly borne by society, the question must be regarded as one of public policy. If an individual completely finances his own medical care, the decision is of course solely his, and he should not be denied what he is able and willing to pay for. But if the individual's care is being financed either through groups (by means of insurance or a prepaid group plan) or by the government, then the decision is no longer an individual one.

Group insurance is much less expensive than individual contracts. This means that the individual is not motivated to learn the range of choices of contract possible and the costs of adding various kinds of coverage. Thus, group contracts seem to have a way of providing greater and greater coverage over time. But it is not true that all would agree greater coverage is a good thing. For example, psychiatric care (unlimited visits to a psychiatrist's office), renal dialysis, and organ transplants may be benefits most people want to have available, but, given the potential cost of such treatments and the small probability of success of some of them, many people would prefer to take their chances with reduced coverage and lower premiums.

There are really two aspects of the problem. The first aspect concerns the allocation of resources within the medical care industry itself. The crucial nature of the problem is brought out by John Knowles:[2]

When I was recently ["]the visit["] on the medical service, the first five patients presented to me all happened, by a curious coincidence, to have the same problem. And it serves to point up the incongruity of what we're doing here. All five were elderly, chronic alcoholics with massive GI bleeding and end-stage liver disease. All five were in coma and we were treating them vigorously, with everything medicine has to offer. They had intravenous lines, and central venous pressure catheters, and tracheostomies, and positive pressure respirators, and suction and Seng stocking tubes, and all the rest. They had house staff and students and nurses working on them around the clock. They had consultants of every shape and sort. They were running up bills of five hundred dollars a day, week after week. . . . Certainly I think they should be treated, just as I think that a large hospital like this is the place where this brand of complex medicine ought to be carried out. But you can't help reflecting, as you look at all this stainless steel and tubing and sophisticated equipment, that right outside your door there are people with TB who aren't getting antibiotics, and kids who aren't getting vaccinations, and women who aren't getting prenatal care.

As economists, we would point out that the truest measure of the social cost of treating the five patients described is not just the dollars spent in providing the care. Rather it is the value of the best alternative use—Dr. Knowles suggests some poignant possibilities—to which those health dollars *might* have been put. Evaluated in terms of such "opportunity costs," the social losses from the misallocation of medical resources might be staggering indeed.

The second aspect of the resource allocation problem is of course how much of society's total resources we really want to allocate to providing medical care. How can we choose? If we all had the best possible medical care and could avail ourselves of the modern medical technology, we could easily devote one-third of our resources to medical services, without feeling very much healthier! At present, there are recreational facilities to be en-

---

2 Quoted in M. Chrichton, *Five Patients: The Hospital Explained 200,* © Alfred A. Knopf, Inc., (1970).

joyed, books to be read, houses to be built, good food to be eaten, and children to be educated. Do we really want to go the way of the Gourmandese?

SUMMARY AND CONCLUSION

There is a growing crisis in the delivery of medical care. We have argued that some economic insights could have been used to foresee the current crisis and to identify which proposed solutions would prove helpful and which would not. We have stressed that medical care is only one way of improving health and aired our suspicion that in 1970-America we are probably spending too much on medical care and too little on other means of achieving better health. We have noted that there are many possibilities for substituting inputs in the production of medical care and that much of the current crisis could be relieved if some of the artificial traditional, institutional, and legal barriers were removed so that patients could get needed (and only needed) treatment at the least cost. Immediate progress could be expected from changes in the direction of economic incentives and expansion of utilization of paramedical personnel.

As a nation, we have been pumping many extra dollars into the medical care sector without realizing that the sector had little capability of giving additional service. Either we must relax some demands on the sector or engage in policies to expand the production of services radically. But up to now we have concentrated unwisely on removing those incentives needed to discourage the patient from seeking the best possible care, when something less would serve about as well, and from demanding other amenities without regard to the cost.

Much of the over-all problem seems to us to stem from illusions about the value of medical care that tend seriously to distort the outcomes of political processes in dealing with health issues. Regrettably, we have not analyzed here what we believe good quality to be in medicine, but we have said enough to reveal our doubt that more care is always necessarily better from a social standpoint or that quality questions can be divorced from cost. It is time for illusions on these points to be reexamined, for expectations to be modified, and for policy makers to attempt to solve some of the real problems. As a nation, we have come to expect too much from medicine and to regard physicians, or at least their services, as the best chance for earthly salvation. Unfortunately, medicine is not going to secure for us, at any price, "a state of complete physical, mental and social well-being."

E. Revenue sharing

State and local governments have dramatically expanded their services in recent decades, particularly in education, welfare, and highway construction. The social crises of the 1960s and 1970s—such as urban riots and rural decay, increasing crime, traffic congestion, and pollution—have generated increased demand for government services. All these expanded programs cost money, yet many state and local governments have already come to the brink of bankruptcy or taxpayer rebellions. One proposal to bridge this financial gap is "revenue sharing"—distribution of federal income tax revenues to state and local governments, according to a per capita or other fixed formula, for expenditure at their virtually complete discretion. Both Presidents Johnson and Nixon have backed revenue sharing plans, and Congress has conducted extensive hearings and debates on various proposals.

Heller, one of the leading advocates of revenue sharing, argues that it will help equalize America's income distribution, by relying more on the progressive federal income tax and less on the regressive state and local sales and property taxes. By including in the distribution formula some additional allocation to the poorest states, we could also upgrade their most inadequate programs of education, welfare, and other services. Heller also foresees a "renaissance" in our decentralized federal system of government, as new political talents are attracted to use the augmented resources of state and local governments.

Revenue sharing has been attacked from both right and left political flanks. Conservatives anticipate more power and bureaucratic waste in Washington, and fear that such "manna from Washington" will induce reckless spending by state and local politicians who no longer must raise local taxes to finance their programs. They hope that more localized tax burdens will keep government decentralized and smaller, leaving more of our economic activity, and social problem solving, to the free market economy.

Ulmer raises most of the liberal criticisms of revenue sharing. He doubts the political competence or social conscience of many local politicians. He anticipates that they would use the federal revenues to cut local taxes (as conservatives would hope) rather than to finance local programs. He questions whether revenue sharing will really aid the poor, or our largest cities. He proposes an alternative package of federal tax credits and centralized federal financing and supervision of welfare and other social programs.

Questions: How will revenue sharing affect the size and efficiency of different levels of government? How will it affect income distribution between states, between individuals? What political assumptions and value preferences underlie the different viewpoints on revenue sharing?

34 Should the government share its tax take?*

WALTER W. HELLER

Washington *must* find a way to put a generous share of the huge federal fiscal dividend (the automatic increase in tax revenue associated with income growth) at the disposal of the states and cities. If it fails to do so, federalism will suffer, services will suffer, and the state-local taxpayer will suffer.

Economic growth creates a glaring fiscal gap; it bestows its revenue bounties on the federal government, whose progressive income tax is particularly responsive to growth, and imposes the major part of its burdens on state and local governments. Closing that gap must take priority over any federal tax cuts other than the removal of the 10 percent surcharge. And even this exception may not be valid. For, as New York Governor Nelson A. Rockefeller has proposed, the revenue generated by the surcharge can easily be segregated from other federal revenue and earmarked for sharing with the states. So perhaps even the taxpayer's "divine right" to get rid of the surcharge may have to give way to the human rights of the poor, the ignorant, the ill, and the black.

For when the state-local taxpayer is beset with—and, indeed, rebelling against—a rising tide of regressive and repressive property, sales, and excise taxes, what sense would it make to weaken or dismantle the progressive and growth-responsive federal income tax? Whether our concern is for justice and efficiency in taxation, or for better balance in our federalism or, most important, for a more rational system of financing our aching social needs, there is no escape from the logic of putting the power of the federal income tax at the disposal of beleaguered state and local governments.

Calling for redress of the fiscal grievances of our federalism is, of course, far from saying that state-local government has reached the end of its fiscal

* From "Should the Government Share Its Tax Take?", *Saturday Review* (March 1969), pp. 26–29. Copyright *Saturday Review*, 1969. Reprinted with permission of author and publisher. Walter W. Heller is Regents Professor of Economics of the University of Minnesota, Minneapolis, Minn.

rope. The taxpayer's will to pay taxes may be exhausted, but his capacity is not:

Our overall tax burden—roughly 28 percent of the GNP—falls far short of the 35 to 40 percent levels in Germany, France, the Netherlands, and Scandinavia. Small solace, perhaps, but a strong suggestion that the U.S. taxpayer has not been squeezed dry.

Untapped and underutilized tax sources still abound in state and local finance. For example, 15 states still have no income tax, and six still have no sales tax. If all 50 states had levied income taxes as high as those of the top ten, state income tax collections in 1966 would have been $11 billion instead of $5 billion. The same type of computation for state and local sales taxes shows a $5-billion add-on. As for that sick giant of our tax system the property tax, the aforementioned top-ten standard adds $9.3 billion to the existing collection of $24.5 billion.

It is only fair to point out, however, that states and localities have not been exactly reticent about tapping these revenue sources. In spite of taxpayer resistance and the frequent political penalties that go with it, the 50 states have been doing a land-office business in new and used taxes. In the past ten years, the six major state taxes (sales, personal and corporate income, gasoline, cigarette, and liquor) were the subject of 309 rate increases and 26 new adoptions. Instead of slowing down, the pace has speeded up; in 1967 to 1968, the states raised major taxes on 80 occasions and enacted seven new levies. Meanwhile, property tax burdens have risen faster than anyone thought possible ten years ago.

Yet, this effort has all the earmarks of a losing battle. Economic growth generates demands for new and better services while leaving a massive problem of water, air, land, and sound pollution in its wake. Population growth, especially the rapid rise of taxeaters relative to taxpayers (the number of Americans in the school-age and over-65 groups is increasing more than twice as rapidly as those in-between), is straining state-local budgets. And inflation—which increases the prices of goods and services bought by state-local governments about twice as fast as the average rate of price increase in the economy—also works against state-local budgets.

In trying to meet these spending pressures, state and local governments are inhibited by fears of interstate competition, by limited jurisdiction, by reliance on taxes that respond sluggishly to economic growth, and by fears of taxpayer reprisals at the polls. But it would be a mistake to assume that the case for federal support rests wholly, or even mainly, on these relentless fiscal pressures and handicaps. Far from being just a fiscal problem—a question of meeting fiscal demands from a limited taxable capacity—the issue touches on the very essence of federalism, both in a political and in a socioeconomic sense.

Indeed, it is from the realm of political philosophy—the renewed interest in making state-local government a vital, effective, and reasonably equal partner in a workable federalism—that much of the impetus for

FIGURE 34-1. Federal, state, and local tax receipts* (selected fiscal years 1927–1968) in billions of dollars

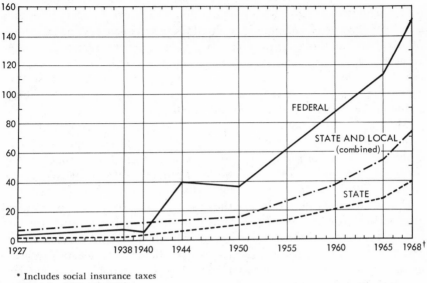

* Includes social insurance taxes
† Data for 1968 estimated
Source: Department of Commerce, Bureau of the Census.

more generous levels and new forms of federal assistance has come. The financial plight of state-local government cannot alone explain the introduction of some 100 bills in Congress for various forms of revenue sharing or unconditional block grants since 1954, when my proposal for apportioning taxes was first made public and converted into a detailed plan by the presidential task force headed by Joseph A. Pechman.

In this connection, I have been amused by how often the following sen-

TABLE 34-1. Federal aid to state and local governments (selected fiscal years of 1949–1969) in millions of dollars

	1949	1959	1967	1968ª	1969ª
Agriculture	86.6	322.5	448.0	599.4	644.0
Commerce and transportation	433.6	100.6	226.3	431.7	618.6
Education	36.9	291.3	2,298.7	2,461.9	2,398.2
Health, labor, welfare	1,231.5	2,789.7	6,438.0	8,207.1	9,135.0
Housing, community development	8.6	188.4	768.3	1,185.2	1,812.5
Highway and unemployment trust funds	—	2,801.2	4,501.7	4,773.1	4,796.7
Other	5.5	319.7	1,120.2	1,239.9	1,418.0
Total	1,802.7	6,813.4	15,801.2	18,898.3	20,823.0

ª Data estimated
Source: Bureau of the Budget

tences from my *New Dimensions of Political Economy,* published in 1966, have been quoted, especially by surprised conservatives: "The good life will not come, ready made, from some federal assembly line. It has to be custom-built, engaging the effort and imagination and resourcefulness of the community. Whatever fiscal plan is adopted must recognize this need." In expressing similar thoughts publicly for a quarter-century, I have not been alone among liberals. Yet, the statement is now greeted as if the power and the glory of decentralization has just been revealed to us for the first time. May I add that when we are embraced by those "who stand on their states' rights so they can sit on them," we may be forgiven for wincing.

Moving from the political to the economic, one finds strong additional rationale for new and expanded federal support in the economic—or socioeconomic—theory of public expenditures. It is in this theory that our vast programs of federal aid to state and local governments—projected to run at $25 billion in fiscal 1970 (triple the amount in 1960)—are firmly anchored. All too often, they are thought of simply as a piece of political pragmatism growing out of two central fiscal facts: that Washington collects more than two-thirds of the total federal, state, and local tax take; and that nearly two-thirds of government public services (leaving aside defense and social security programs) are provided by state-local government. Throw in the objective of stimulating state-local efforts through matching provisions, and, for many people, the theory of federal grants is complete.

In fact, it is only the beginning. Consider the compelling problems of poverty and race and the related problems of ignorance, disease, squalor, and hard-core unemployment. The roots of these problems are nationwide. And the efforts to overcome them by better education, training, health, welfare, and housing have nationwide effects. Yet, it is precisely these services that we entrust primarily to our circumscribed state and local units.

Clearly, then, many of the problems that the states and localities tackle are not of their own making. And their success or failure in coping with such problems will have huge spillover effects far transcending state and local lines in our mobile and interdependent society. The increasing controversy over the alleged migration of the poor from state to state in search of higher welfare benefits is only one aspect of this. So, quite apart from any fiscal need to run hat in hand to the national government, states and cities have a dignified and reasonable claim on federal funds with which to carry out national responsibilities. Only the federal government can represent the totality of benefits and strike an efficient balance between benefits and costs. Therein lies the compelling economic case for the existing system of earmarked, conditional grants-in-aid. Such grants will, indeed must, continue to be our major mechanism for transferring funds to the states and localities.

But the interests of a healthy and balanced federalism call for support of the general state-local enterprise as well as specific services. It is hard to argue that the benefits of sanitation, green space, recreation, police, and fire protection, street maintenance and lighting in one community have large spillover effects on other communities. Yet, in more or less humdrum services such as these lies much of the difference between a decent environment and a squalid one, between the snug suburb and the grinding ghetto.

Given the limits and inhibitions of state-local taxation and the sharp inequalities in revenue-raising capacity—compounded by the matching requirement in most categorical grants, which pulls funds away from non-grant activities—too many of the states and the cities are forced to strike their fiscal balances at levels of services well below the needs and desires of their citizens. The absence of a system of federal transfers to serve the broad purpose of upgrading the general level of public services, especially in the poorer states, is a serious gap—both economic and political—in the fiscal structure of our federalism. Tax sharing could fill it.

The core of a tax-sharing plan is the earmarking of a specified share of the federal individual income tax take for distribution to states and localities, on the basis of population, with next to no strings attached. The so-called Heller-Pechman plan has the following main elements:

The federal government would regularly route into a special trust fund 2 percent of the federal individual income tax base (the amount reported as net taxable income by all individuals). In 1969, for example, this would come to about $7 billion, roughly 10 percent of federal individual income tax revenues. This amount would be channeled to the states at fixed intervals, free from the uncertainties of the annual federal appropriation process.

The basic distribution would be on a straight population formula, so much per capita. Perhaps 10 percent of the proceeds should be set aside each year as an equalization measure—to boost the share of the 17 poorer states (which have 20 percent of the nation's population).

To insure that the fiscal claims of the localities are met, a minimum pass-through—perhaps 50 percent—to local units would be required. In this intrastate allocation, the financial plight of urban areas should be given special emphasis.

The widest possible discretion should be left to the state and local governments in the use of the funds, subject only to the usual accounting and auditing requirements, compliance with the Civil Rights Act, and perhaps a ban on the use of such funds for highways (for which there already is a special federal trust fund).

How well does the tax-sharing plan (also called revenue sharing, unconditional grants, and general assistance grants) measure up to the economic and sociopolitical criteria implicit in the foregoing discussion? Let me rate it briefly, and sympathetically, on six counts.

First, it would significantly relieve the immediate pressures on state-local treasuries and, more important, would make state-local revenues grow more rapidly, in response to economic growth. For example, a 2-percentage-point distribution on a straight per capita basis would provide, in 1969,

$650 million each for California and New York, $420 million for Pennsylvania, $375 million for Illinois, $140 million each for Mississippi and Wisconsin, $125 million each for Louisiana and Minnesota, and about $65 million each for Arkansas and Colorado.

The striking growth potential of this source of revenue is evident in two facts: (1) had the plan been in effect in 1955, the distribution of 2 percent of the $125-billion income-tax base in that year would have yielded a state-local tax share of about $2.5 billion; and (2) by 1972, the base should be about $450 billion, yielding a $9-billion annual share.

Second, tax sharing would serve our federalist interest in state-local vitality and independence by providing new financial elbow room, free of political penalty, for creative state and local officials. Unlike the present grants-in-aid, the tax-shared revenue would yield a dependable flow of federal funds in a form that would enlarge, not restrict, their options.

Third, tax sharing would reverse the present regressive trend in our federal-state-local tax system. It seems politically realistic to assume that the slice of federal income tax revenue put aside for the states and cities would absorb funds otherwise destined to go mainly into federal tax cuts and only partly into spending increases. Given the enormous pressures on state-local budgets, on the other hand, tax shares would go primarily into higher state-local expenditures and only in small part into a slowdown of state-local tax increases. Thus, the combination would produce a more progressive overall fiscal system.

Fourth, tax sharing—especially with the 10 percent equalization feature —would enable the economically weaker states to upgrade the scope and quality of their services without putting crushingly heavier burdens on their citizens. Per capita sharing itself would have a considerable equalizing effect, distributing $35 per person to all of the states, having drawn $47 per person from the ten richest and $24 per person from the ten poorest states. Setting aside an extra 10 percent for equalization would boost the allotments of the 17 poorest states by one-third to one-half. Thus, the national interest in reducing interstate disparities in the level of services would be well served.

Fifth, the plan could readily incorporate a direct stimulus to state and local tax efforts. Indeed, the Douglas Commission (the National Commission on Urban Problems), like many other advocates of tax-sharing plans, would adjust the allotments to take account of relative state-local tax efforts. In addition, they propose a bonus for heavy reliance on individual income taxation.

A more direct stimulant to state and local efforts in the income tax field would be to enact credits against the federal income tax for state income taxes paid. For example, if the taxpayer could credit one-third or two-fifths of his state and local income tax payments directly against his federal tax liability (rather than just treat such taxes as a deduction from taxable income, as at present), it would lead to a far greater use of this fairest and most growth-oriented of all tax sources.

Ideally, income tax credits should be coupled with income tax sharing and federal aid in a balanced program of federal support. But if relentless fiscal facts require a choice, the nod must go to tax sharing because (1) credits provide no interstate income-level equalization; (2) at the outset, at least, much of the federal revenue loss becomes a taxpayer gain rather than state-local gain; and (3) since one-third of the states still lack broad-based income taxes, the credit would touch off cries of "coercion." Nevertheless, it is a splendid device that ought to have clearcut priority over further tax cuts.

Sixth, and finally, per capita revenue sharing would miss its mark if it did not relieve some of the intense fiscal pressures on local, and particularly urban, governments. The principle is easy to state. The formula to carry it out is more difficult to devise. But it can be done. The Douglas Commission has already developed an attractive formula that it describes as "deliberately 'loaded' to favor general purpose governments that are sufficiently large in population to give some prospect of viability as urban units." I would agree with the Commission that it is important not to let "no-strings" federal aid sustain and entrench thousands of small governmental units that ought to wither away—though I still prefer to see the tax-sharing funds routed through the 50 state capitals, rather than short-circuiting them by direct distribution to urban units.

Supported by the foregoing logic, espoused by both Democratic and Republican platforms and candidates in 1968, and incorporated into bills by dozens of prestigious Senators and Congressmen, one would think that tax sharing will have clear sailing as soon as our fiscal dividends permit. Not so. The way is strewn with obstacles and objections.

For example, tax sharing poses threats, or seeming threats, to special interest groups including all the way from top federal bureaucrats who see tax sharing's gain as their agencies' and programs' loss; through the powerful lobbyists for special programs such as housing, medical care, and pollution control programs, who recoil from the prospect of going back from the federal gusher to 50 state spigots; to the Senators and Congressmen who see more political mileage in tax cuts or program boosts than in getting governors and mayors out of their fiscal jam.

But, of course, opposition goes far beyond crass self-interest. It also grows out of philosophic differences and concern over the alleged shortcomings of tax sharing. There is the obvious issue of federalism versus centralism. A strong contingent in this country feels that the federal government knows best, and that state and local governments cannot be trusted. Others fear that revenue sharing or unrestricted grants will make state-local government more dependent on the federal government—a fear for which I see little or no justification.

On the issues, some would argue that it is better to relieve state-local budgets by taking over certain burdens through income-maintenance programs like the negative income tax; while others feel that too much of the revenue-sharing proceeds would go down the drain in waste and corruption. Here, one must answer in terms of a willingness to take the risks that go with an investment in the renaissance of the states and the cities. Some costs in wasted and diverted funds will undoubtedly be incurred. My assumption is that these costs will be far outweighed by the benefits of greater social stability and a more viable federalism that will flow from the higher and better levels of government services and the stimulus to state-local initiative and responsibility.

In sum, I view tax sharing as an instrument that (1) will fill a major gap in our fiscal federalism; (2) will strengthen the fabric of federalism by infusing funds *and* strength into the state-local enterprise; and (3) will increase our total governmental capacity to cope with the social crisis that confronts us. The sooner Congress gets on with the job of enacting a system of tax sharing, even if it means postponing the end of the 10 percent surcharge, the better off we shall be.

35 The limitations of revenue sharing*

MELVILLE J. ULMER

No benevolent and omniscient dictator, starting from scratch, would establish boundaries for the fifty states as they now exist in the United States,
nor would he carefully delineate the 81,000 local jurisdictions, often overlapping, which share governmental responsibilities within those states. In
social, economic, and financial terms there is little justification for the particular components that comprise the present federal "system," and hence
no grounds for expecting an impeccably logical pattern of legal and functional relationships among them. The division of labor linking the various
jurisdictions is sealed in large measure by tradition, and revised from time
to time, sometimes quite abruptly, by pragmatic adaptations to changing
circumstances. It is no wonder that the financial relationships among the
states, cities, and federal government should also require occasional and
sometimes urgent re-examination, as they have during the past decade. In
this paper I shall focus on these financial problems with particular emphasis on revenue sharing as one of the significant, but I believe least meri-
torious, proposals advanced for their amelioration or solution.

PRESENT INTERGOVERNMENTAL FISCAL RELATIONS

One dominant belief about intergovernmental financial relationships
in the United States that remains virtually unchallenged is that the federal
government is the most important, efficient, and fairest raiser of revenues
among all the governmental bodies that presently levy taxes of various
kinds. In 1970, the total national tax burden came to $274 billion dollars,
about 30 percent of the total Gross National Product, or exactly $1,348
for every man, woman, and child in the country. More than two out of
every three tax dollars was levied and collected by the federal government.

* From "The Limitations of Revenue Sharing," *Annals of the American Academy of
Political and Social Science*, 397 (September 1971), pp. 48–59. Copyright American Academy of Political and Social Science, 1971. Reprinted with permission of author and
publisher. Melville J. Ulmer is Professor of Economics at the University of Maryland,
College Park, Md., and contributing editor to *The New Republic*.

The remaining dollar, or a bit less, was collected in roughly equal proportions by the state governments on the one hand and the localities on the other. That the federal government is the largest tax collector, therefore, is indisputable. The contention that it is the most efficient rests mainly on considerations of economies of scale; thus, the federal government, in contrast with states and cities, requires only one set of income tax forms and one centrally directed collection agency for the entire nation.

The contention that the federal government's tax system is the most equitable rests on analysis of the sources of revenue by level of government. The progressive income tax is commonly judged the fairest of all levies because it distributes its burden among individuals, more closely than any of the others, in proportion to their ability to pay .The federal government obtains merely 60 percent of its total tax revenue through the income tax, against only 12 percent for all state and local governments together. The sales and property taxes, which yield three fourths of the revenue for states and cities, are largely regressive in that they take larger *proportionate* amounts from the incomes of the poor. In addition, the income tax schedules in those states and cities that use them are much less progressive than that of the federal government.

The dominant position of the central government as tax collector is in great measure the result of its growing functional activities. Progressively more of the nation's social and economic problems have become its business. In 1970, the federal government collected 68 percent of the nation's total tax revenue, but before World War I, when the central government was relatively inactive, that proportion was only 29 percent. The great revenue collectors then were the local governments, accounting for 58 percent of the aggregate tax take. However, the collection of taxes, by branch of government, is not a perfectly accurate indicator of their relative activity as spenders of the public funds. In 1970, the federal government turned over $17 billion directly to the states and more than $2 billion directly to the cities, primarily in the form of grants-in-aid on a variety of projects ranging from education and highway construction to urban renewal and environmental care. In virtually all instances, the projects toward which these funds were directed were those in which there was considered to be a clear national interest.

THE ASSUMPTIONS OF REVENUE SHARING

Revenue sharing, were it enacted, would constitute an entirely new and unprecedented addition to the federal fiscal structure. In its purest and most popular form, it calls for taking some fixed proportion of federal income tax receipts and distributing it among the states with no restrictions on its use whatsoever. The allocation formulas differ somewhat from plan to plan, but generally they provide relatively more of the revenue sharing fund to states with lower per capita personal incomes, which are primarily rural, and correspondingly less to the "richer" and more highly urbanized states. This characteristic was notably present in the two most important and widely considered revenue sharing plans offered thus far: that of Walter Heller, who developed his proposal in the mid-sixties as chief economic adviser to President Johnson, and that of President Nixon, which was initially presented in his Budget Message to Congress in 1971.

The assumptions underlying the Heller plan were: (1) that the states were in a financial crisis because they had virtually exhausted their financial resources and could not be expected to raise taxes further to meet rapidly rising outlays; (2) that the federal government's efficient tax system would generate surplus funds which could more or less painlessly be diverted to the states; and (3) that the plan would put money where it was needed most. The assumptions underlying President Nixon's plan were similar, as was the plan itself, except with two qualifications. Nixon's proposal came five or six years after Heller's and conditions had changed. Since the federal government's fiscal program was generating huge deficits, which averaged about $11 billion per annum from 1967 through 1971, it was no longer possible to speak of federal surpluses, or "fiscal dividends," as Heller had called them. Also because of altered circumstances, President Nixon exhibited somewhat more concern for city problems, and his plan required the states to turn over part of their revenue shares to the localities. But both placed great emphasis on what in an earlier era had been called "states' rights." Heller wrote of the need for "revitalizing the states." President Nixon spoke of "giving government back to the people," by which he meant, as he made perfectly clear, transferring some of the federal government's functions to the states and cities. The same bias was exhibited by the father of revenue sharing, the present Defense Secretary, Melvin R. Laird, who as a congressman from Wisconsin introduced the first bill of this kind in 1958, labeling it the "Great Republican Alternative to the Great Planned Society."

THE ALLEGED FINANCIAL CRISIS OF THE STATES

Without doubt, some states—and even more, many cities—have encountered financial difficulties during the past decade, nearly all of which are attributable to specific causes, such as the unprecedented rise in welfare costs in some areas or the evolving fiscal conflict between cities and suburbs. But such conditions differ completely from the kind of general crisis postulated by revenue sharing. A general crisis, ineluctably engulfing all or most states and localities, could conceivably be relieved with at least some minimum degree of efficiency and equity by a general distribution of funds such as revenue sharing contemplates. But it is easy to show that that kind of crisis neither exists nor is likely to develop in the foreseeable future.

One important fact that has misled some observers is that during much of the 1960s, state and local expenditures rose at an unprecedented rate because of burgeoning requirements in the three great areas of their financial concern: education, public welfare, and highway construction. Indeed, it was this brisk rise, of somewhat more than 100 percent between 1959 and 1969, that led the unwary to suspect a crisis. As we shall see a bit later, this surge has already begun to subside, and because of altered demographic and legislative conditions is virtually certain to slow down further in the years just ahead. But an even more significant error of the revenue sharers is contained in their associated allegation about the potential revenue of state and local governments. Their contention is that the states, including their cities, have exhausted present financial resources, so that they cannot possibly raise tax rates to levels sufficient to meet prospective obligations. The allegation implies a generalization about the states that would, were it true, constitute a necessary (though not sufficient!) justification for a broadside distribution of federal funds as proposed under revenue sharing. And yet it conflicts clearly and sharply with the facts.

Indeed, the financial situations of the states (including the local governments, as is done throughout the following discussion) vary so enormously that very few generalizations about them are possible. Take the matter of the income tax, a tool that revenue sharers claim has been "pre-empted" by the federal government. The fact is that five states—Wisconsin, New York, Oregon, Hawaii, and Delaware—make excellent use of the income tax, raising a substantial proportion of their total revenue by this means and imposing marginal rates up to 10 percent or more at middle or upper income brackets. Yet thirteen states have no personal income tax at all, while in the majority of others the effective rates are almost negligibly small. If all fifty states had levied income taxes as high as those of the five named above, their total revenue would be raised by $7 or $8 billion, considerably more than the $6 billion of new money promised in President Nixon's revenue sharing plan.

Similar diversity characterizes the degree in which other revenue sources are exploited. Six states levy no tax on the income of their corporations. Five states have no sales taxes, although for many others this is the major source of revenue. In general, taking all sources of revenue into account, the aggregate "tax efforts" made by the states—the proportion of their personal incomes paid out in taxes—also vary widely. Only a very small part of the variation is due to differences in their income levels. A rich state, it is true, can afford to allocate a larger part of its income to public services. But much the greater part of the variation in tax effort seems to be due to differences in what we may term their levels of social consciousness or morality—or, in any event, their willingness to meet their respective social obligations. To assess quantitatively the significance of this variation, I arrayed the states in the order of their per capita personal incomes and then divided them into five groups, in each of which the income levels were approximately the same. In each group I then selected the state with the highest tax effort and computed a hypothetical tax revenue for the other nine states in the group on the assumption that they duplicated the effort of the leader. On that assumption, I found, total state and local revenue would have been raised by $18 billion. The most generous estimate of the states' additional revenue needs in 1971 was that of Governor Nelson Rockefeller of New York, who in behalf of the 50 states asked President Nixon for $10 billion in revenue sharing. What our simple experiment shows is that the states, including the cities, are fully capable of raising nearly double that amount on their own and from their own resources. The only requirement would be for the majority of states to ask as much from their citizens, in taxes, as a few conscientious states are now asking of theirs.

Before closing this section a few observations are in order on the subject of probable state and local financial requirements in the years ahead. In particular, is it likely that their expenditures will need to grow in the next decade by as much, relatively, as they did from 1959 to 1969? The most important reason for the tremendous expansion of the past decade is attributable to the birth rate explosion following World War II. The yield was an unprecedented flow of children into the schools during the 1960s, requiring a gigantic construction program together with swiftly mounting operating charges for teachers, administrators, and all the rest. The rise in the number of children and youth aged five to nineteen between 1960 and 1970 was more than 50 percent; this, however, is a rate of expansion that is not likely to be duplicated during the lifetime of the present generation. Indeed, the dramatically different prospect portrayed by the Census Bureau for the next decade is for a decline of about 3 percent in the number of school-age children, owing to a downturn in birth rates that began in the late 1950s. Hence, there is practically no likelihood of a substantial increase in educational expenditures in the years ahead, much less a repetition of the spectacular jump of the 1960s. Education alone accounted for nearly one-half of all the spending by state and local governments in 1970.

The other two major branches of state/local expenditures, public welfare and highway construction, also promise to slow down, if not actually contract in the near future, although both have grown vigorously in the past. At present writing, it appears almost certain that most or all of the nation's welfare programs will be "federalized"; bills recently presented by the Administration and by the Democratically controlled House Ways and Means Committee both provide federal financing for the bulk of the welfare system. Instead of swift growth as in the past, therefore, the likelihood is for a substantial decline in state/local financial requirements for such purposes.

A somewhat similar prospect is in view for highway construction. No plans now in the offing are comparable to the interstate and defense highway programs that resulted in doubling street and highway expenditures between 1955 and 1965. A flattening-out of such expenditures has already begun and seems due to continue. No doubt, other branches of state/local spending, such as mass transportation, sanitation, crime prevention, and medical care will increase in the years ahead, and perhaps accelerate. But education, public welfare, and highway construction now account for more than two-thirds of all expenditures of state and local governments. If they slow down dramatically, as appears virtually certain, the growth of the total is bound to be retarded. A contributing element in the prospective slowdown is the probability that federal assistance, through grants-in-aid and similar devices, will continue to grow, as it already has, in areas such as medical care, crime prevention, mass transportation, and urban renewal.

THE POTENTIAL USES OF REVENUE SHARES

An integral characteristic of a revenue-sharing plan is that the shares be distributed among the states "with no strings attached." Insofar as restrictions were added, the transfer would resemble grants-in-aid. The chief distinguishing characteristic and presumed advantage of revenue sharing, in support of the states' rights bias mentioned earlier, is that such restrictions are avoided. Their absence, however, raises a question concerning how the revenue shares might be used. The assumption of Walter Heller, Joseph A. Pechman, and other revenue sharing advocates is that the plan would help to reduce the huge disparity that now prevails in the level of social services provided by the states. This would be accomplished by allocating relatively more funds to the poorer states, relatively less to the richer ones. And underlying the assumption about leveling disparities is the further one that the revenue shares in general would be used conscientiously to satisfy the most pressing social needs.

The question raised now is, what grounds do we have for supposing that the funds would be so used? The answer would seem to be, no assurance at all. Coming as a bonanza to governors, mayors, and their legislative bodies, revenue shares do not by their nature encourage the same degree of responsibility in use as do the normal flows of revenue. And of course, since no restrictions are applied, states may use their federal money for meeting ordinary expenses of government, for road-building, monuments, elevating the living standards of deserving politicians, or even for reducing their own taxes. It is true that a frivolous employment of the funds is unlikely in the more progressive states, but not necessarily in the others. A survey by the *Washington Post* revealed that some states and cities have openly expressed their intention to use the revenue shares, if they get them, for reducing their own taxes. Such an objective would be entirely within the law, though obviously not among those contemplated by the advocates of revenue sharing. Were a tax reduction the intention, it would be far simpler and fairer to skip revenue sharing and reduce the federal income tax directly.

Recent experience with so-called "special purpose" revenue sharing suggests even more depressing possibilities. For example, under the Law Enforcement Act, funds were distributed to the states with no restriction except that they be used to support police activities. In Alabama, the grant made it possible for certain state officials to send their sons to college, not only tuition-free but with salaries of $6,000, on the grounds that they might consider joining the police department on graduation. It is true that such horror stories do not prove a rule, but a more general and cogent warning is provided by the tremendous diversity in the ways in which states and cities now use the ordinary funds at their disposal.

Reference here is to the great disparity in state practices related to the most important social services. A favorite contention of revenue sharers is that education is substandard in certain states because, they are poor and can't afford any better, that the tax efforts of some states are small and ineffective because they are poor and can't do any better, or that welfare benefits are negligible, even brutally low, because such poor states can't afford any more. Now, differences among states in income levels do obviously account for a certain part of the differences we observe in expenditures for education, welfare, and in their tax efforts—but only in smaller part. The greater part of these differences, as we shall see, is apparently due to variations in their willingness, their social conscienceness, or their political, administrative, and moral maturity.

The point is easily illustrated by specific example. Florida and Wisconsin have almost exactly equal per capita personal incomes. But Wisconsin has one of the highest and most effective income taxes of all the states. Florida has no income tax. Wisconsin pays an average benefit of $185 monthly to its welfare families. Florida pays only half as much—$95. Wisconsin spends almost $900 per pupil on its primary and secondary school education. Florida spends only $700, or about 25 percent less. Something other than income levels must obviously account for these differences. The same idea may be reinforced by more general and systematic analysis. Thus, in multiple correlation tests, I found that income differences among the fifty states account for only one third of observed variations in the amounts they spend on education per pupil. I found no correlation at all between the tax efforts made by states and their income levels. Given this diversity in political morality, as suggested by these findings, what grounds remain for faith that the states in general will put to responsible use funds which they have had no responsibility for raising?

THE ALLOCATION OF REVENUE SHARES

One feature of both the Nixon and Heller revenue-sharing plans that has won the commendation of some liberals is the formula by which rebate funds are shared among the fifty states. The distribution is made primarily on the basis of population, with a modest weight for relative tax efforts.

Another possibility, of course, would be to return to each state the same fixed proportion of the amount it had contributed, via income taxes, to the federal revenue. The Nixon approach has the apparent advantage, from an equity standpoint, of giving much more to the poorer states, relative to their contributions. The actual results of the formula, however, may look less attractive when examined more closely, for the main effect is to redistribute money away from the highly urbanized and "wealthy" states, where problems of poverty and crowded ghettos are most pressing, to the more rural states where needs may be less.

Thus, for every dollar that New York contributes through the income taxes of its citizens to the revenue-sharing kitty, it would receive from the federal government only 87 cents in the Nixon plan. In contrast, Mississippi would receive $2.50 for every dollar paid out. Similarly, Pennsylvania would receive 79 cents and Illinois 60 cents for every dollar contributed, but Alabama would get $1.56. Other prominent losers in the plan would be Connecticut, Delaware, the District of Columbia, New Jersey, Ohio, Missouri, New Hampshire, Massachusetts, Rhode Island, Maryland, Indiana, and Michigan—in other words, the states that have been most urgently calling for assistance. They are also the areas in which middle-income groups are now pressed most severely by relatively high state and local taxes. The largest gainers, aside from Mississippi and Alabama, would be North Dakota, New Mexico, Louisiana, South Dakota, Arkansas, Idaho, Arizona, South Carolina, Wyoming, Kentucky, Utah, Hawaii, and Alaska. As Congressman Wilbur Mills, chairman of the House Ways and Means Committee, declared, "It seems to me that this [revenue sharing plan] actually is the reverse of facing up to the urban problem that we have been hearing about."

Mills's observation gathers greater force when one speculates on the chance that the funds going to Mississippi, Alabama, and similar states will actually filter down in significant volume to the poor people. It is true that the average monthly welfare payments to families in Mississippi in 1969 was less than $50 as against $250 in New York, but it is much less than certain that this frightful disparity would be narrowed by revenue sharing. A more reliable approach is to federalize welfare, or at least set federal standards for its dispensation. The best way to help the poor, in other words, may be to help poor people rather than states.

The fact is, moreover, that serious fault could probably be found with any formula that might be devised for a revenue sharing plan. For it isn't possible to develop an objectively fair or accurate formula when there is no clear indication of how the funds are to be used and when, in addition, the needs, resources, and tax efforts of the various states differ so widely. Indeed, to the writer's knowledge, no revenue sharer has ever indicated what the specific objectives of a distribution formula might be. Should it reward the virtuous and the generous, or the selfish and the miserly? those with low public service standards and great present needs, or those with high standards and low present needs? those with low taxes, or high taxes? the rural states, or the urban? And, without knowing the objectives and being able to agree on them, arguments in support of a particular formula's effectiveness or accuracy inevitably degenerate into mere expressions of arbitrary opinion.

THE PROBLEM OF RESPONSIBILITY

Congressman Wilbur Mills has properly emphasized the fact that revenue sharing divorces the joyful privilege of spending public revenue from the burdensome responsibility for raising it. It thereby violates one of the fundamental principles of good government, with consequences, necessary or likely, that are predictably unpleasant. The first of these has already been mentioned. Revenue sharing proffers an invitation to the frivolous or even dishonest use of funds that is not present, in the same degree, in ordinary revenue flows. Aside from this, revenue sharing inhibits the rational decision-making of taxpayers and also discriminates against taxpayers on the basis of their geographical location. Both points require explanation.

A conference sponsored a few years ago by a private organization in Washington directed itself to the question, "How large should government be?" The two leading speakers, former Senator Paul Douglas and Chicago University economist Milton Friedman, represented opposing points of view. Yet neither speaker answered the central question posed, nor did he try—quite naturally. For the question of how big government should be must, in fact, be answered by a process rather than by an arithmetical estimate or a fixed formula.

The proper size of the government must be, or ought to be, determined from year to year by an enlightened electorate making reasoned decisions. Even rough approximations to such reasoned decisions are possible, of course, only if the public is aware of the relevant alternatives, or of what economists call the "opportunity costs" of particular public projects proposed. More simply, the public must be aware of the purposes for which its tax money is used, and enabled to have a voice in deciding which services are worth the cost and which ones are not. This is the only way in which we can hope to make a rational democratic choice between private goods and public services in the aggregate; in other words, it is the only way to determine how big government should be.

We are a long way, I think all would agree, from having the careful determination of priorities in public spending, and the intimate communication between government and the people, that such reasoned choices would require. And yet it is obviously a worthy objective, to try to move as much as possible in that direction. It is so obvious, it seems to me, that it barely warrants mention, and I refer to it now only because revenue sharing would move us in just the opposite direction. For revenue sharing transfers funds from one governmental body (federal) to others (state and local) with no restrictions. In so doing, it relieves the taxpayer of any chance of knowing, or controlling, how his money is spent, and therefore of judging whether more or less, or any at all, ought to be devoted to the purposes for which the money is actually used.

The final point in this section relates to the uneven impact of revenue sharing on taxpayers in different parts of the country. Because I have dealt with this matter at some length elsewhere, I shall confine myself here to stating that, in effect, through revenue sharing, a federal tax is converted into a state levy. Notoriously, people in the same income brackets are treated very differently from state to state, as indicated in our discussion of their income tax rates. Hence, the new state taxes, implicit in the diversion of funds through revenue sharing, enter with very different weights into the burdens of taxpayers, depending on where the taxpayers live. A fundamental principle in public finance states that people equally situated, financially, ought to be treated equally. It is this principle that revenue sharing violates.

THE ALTERNATIVES TO REVENUE SHARING

In a previous section of this paper, I made some effort to demonstrate that the idea of a general financial crisis for all or most states and cities is a myth or an illusion. I am not denying that there are serious social and economic problems, especially in the cities, for this is obvious to all—or that there is in general a need for more and better public services of numerous kinds. But the specific needs and problems, of which every newspaper reader is aware, must be met head on with specific correctives, thoughtfully and purposefully, not sloughed off with the broadside distribution of funds called revenue sharing. It is in this spirit that I offer the following three proposals:

Federalization of welfare

Ample reference has already been made to the tremendous variation in the way the poor are treated in different sections of the country, and to the demonstrable fact that differences in the willingness to help, more than financial limitation, account for these disparities among states. The situation calls for federal leadership, not simply money. Specifically, the proposal is that the federal government set national minimum standards for welfare benefits and also assume full responsibility for their costs. Not only would the poor be helped directly, but state and local treasuries would be benefited through this measure by several billion dollars more than the amount provided in President Nixon's welfare bill. As already indicated, legislation moving toward federalization of welfare is under consideration in Congress at present writing.

Tax credits

Earlier reference was made to the possibility that most states may be capable of helping themselves, despite all the lachrymose visits of governors to Washington during the spring of 1971. Fortunately, there is a simple method available by which all the states can be both enabled and induced to help themselves—a practice that could do more for their "revitalization" than the most generous handouts from the federal treasury. The method involves permitting taxpayers to charge some substantial part of their state and local income tax payments against their federal income tax liability. As a sample of what could be done, and what it would accomplish, consider the following:

Present regulations allow the citizen to deduct from his own income all the state and local taxes he paid, before computing the income tax he owes the federal government. For a taxpayer in the 20 or 25 percent tax rate bracket, this "itemized deduction" permits a saving of 20 or 25 cents for every dollar paid to the states, cities, or counties. Now, suppose an additional credit is allowed, amounting to 50 percent of the state and/or local income tax, and permit this credit to be charged directly against his federal tax liability after all itemized deductions had been figured. A citizen who paid $200 to his state in income tax could reduce his net federal liability by $100. For the average taxpayer, the saving derived from the state or local income tax, taking account of the itemized deduction and also the special credit, would be about 70 cents on the dollar.

Just one limitation to this allowance would be necessary so that the central government could maintain a reasonable control over the size of its own revenue. The credit allowed would have to be limited to some proportion of the federal income tax owed, perhaps 10 percent. Then, if the citizen paid $200 in state income tax and owed $1200 to the federal government, he could deduct a full 50 percent or $100 from his federal liability. But if his state income tax were raised to $300 while his federal liability remained the same, he could deduct just $120 rather than $150, because of the 10 percent limitation.

The result of first interest for state and local governments is that the proposed credit, on top of the itemized deduction already allowed, would enable them to raise an additional dollar of income tax receipts at a net cost to the average taxpayer of less than 30 cents. If they made full use of their opportunities, up to the maximum credit allowed against income tax, as I think they would, state and local revenue could be increased by about $12 billion annually in the year or two ahead. If the federal government assumed full financial responsibility for welfare, as proposed above, an additional $7 billion of uncommitted revenue would be made available for state and local governments. This grand total of nearly $20 billion of additional revenue is more than three times the amount of new funds provided in the President's revenue-sharing plan, and about twice the amount the governors have publicly dreamed about in their most immodest entreaties to Washington.

The tax credit has some additional advantages over the revenue-sharing plan. It would not divorce the taxing responsibility from the spending responsibility in the states, cities, and counties. It would not discriminate against the more urbanized states in favor of the others. It would not preserve the tremendous disparity in taxes which now exists for citizens in the same income bracket in different parts of the country, as revenue sharing does. Instead, the tax credit motivates reform. It encourages authorities that now make little or no use of the income tax to exploit this measure in preference to their other, more regressive levies. (Note that the special credit is allowed only for state and local income taxes.) It stimulates lagging states to raise the additional revenue required for neglected public services. At the same time, the tax credit plan preserves a desirable degree of fiscal flexibility for state and local authorities. Instead of receiving some lump sum from the federal government, always in some degree unpredictable, as in revenue sharing, they would remain in full command of their own budgets. By the same token, taxpayers would retain a greater interest in, and control over, what was done with their money. A bill proposing a tax credit of the kind described here was recently introduced in Congress by Senator Vance Hartke of Indiana.

More federal leadership and grants-in-aid

In promoting higher social and economic standards, history suggests, the states not only have been led by the federal government, but they must be so led. The instances are virtually numberless, from the Civil War itself to the enactment of federal legislation in 1938 protecting women and children in industry. Of course, it is true that some states have on occasion pioneered in social legislation. Three states had enacted laws to limit the hours of work of women and children nearly 100 years before the more comprehensive Federal Fair Labor Standards Act. But at the same time, the vast majority of states had lagged.

There is a basic reason why many states will always lag in adopting progressive legislation, and this is aside from differences in moral standards, educational levels, and such. This reason has to do with the competition among the states for industry. Some aspects of this competition are socially unhealthy and economically self-defeating. The competition may be so classified when it results in luring industry to one state rather than another by sacrificing values related to the welfare of the state's own people, or of people elsewhere. For example, one state by itself may fear imposing regulations on its industry by limiting air or water pollution. Its hand is strengthened, and in fact this aspect of competition is eliminated, by federal legislation imposing a general standard.

If anything, such federal prerogatives have been underemployed rather than overused. Federal standards for education—in the form of uniform, nationwide examinations to insure minimum accomplishments for primary and secondary school graduates—would probably do more for raising educational levels, where this is needed most, than further federal grants at this stage, although more money is undoubtedly needed, too. Such standards should indeed be tied to federal aid. The example cited illustrates the constructive use to which grants-in-aid may be put in problem areas such as welfare, environmental care, housing, and transportation, as well as in education; and, of course, in considerable measure are so used today. The fact that numerous federal programs of this kind presently in operation, some 500 or so, urgently require simplification and coordination, is no argument against them, but simply a reminder that there is ample room for improvement in the way they are conducted.

One important factor that helps to account for the enormous expansion of the federal government's role in the social and economic life of the nation over the past half century is the historical trend toward greater economic interdependence. In modern America, people throughout the nation buy the same general brands of goods produced by the same giant corporations. The people of one state breathe the air and traverse the rivers polluted by those of another. The population is so mobile that the very phrase, people of a state, may be called into question. The roads as well as the education provided by any one state affect, and intimately so, all its neighbors. Population mobility, industrialization, and the spectacular advances in transportation and communication have, in short, bound the nation into a cohesive whole. So much so, that barely any of the important economic or social problems of the day—be they automobile safety or business recession—can be solved by one state alone. They promise that the federal government will grow stronger rather than weaker. Viewed in this setting, revenue sharing is an anachronistic gesture running counter to the major trend of modern economic history.

Part IV
THE INTERNATIONAL ECONOMY

A. United States trade policies in the 1970s

Economists have traditionally advocated "free competitive trade among the nations of the world" because the efficient specialization of production which trade permits will offer larger total output at lower cost to the world's consumers. The doctrine of "comparative advantage" shows that each nation, whatever its size, technology, or prevailing wage level, may share in these gains of "free trade." Specific firms or workers may gain from protective tariffs or import quotas, but consumers pay higher prices and real national income is lower.

Many American business and labor leaders have echoed these "free trade" arguments in the past, at least to support negotiated, *reciprocal* reductions of trade barriers (not unilateral tariff disarmament!). But recent declines in America's balance of trade have aroused stronger demands from both business and labor for more protective policies to stimulate exports and reduce imports.

Meany argues that "free trade" slogans, based on hypothetical competition between independent producers of different nations, are unrealistic. First, consumers do not benefit because many American markets are imperfectly competitive, and "imports are sold at the American price, with substantially widened profit margins." More important, the American multinational corporation supercedes national competition by moving its capital and technology freely among nations, often exploiting cheap foreign labor while marketing at home under an American brand name.

Rose questions the extent and severity of foreign tariffs or quota restrictions against American exports. Our declining trade balance is not due to our losing a nationalistic "trade war" but to other factors: American inflation and European recessions in the 1960s, and the overvalued dollar exchange rate (since devalued—see Reading 39). Rose denies Meany's assertion of massive job losses due to a "flood" of imports, and emphasizes offsetting new jobs in domestic or export industries.

Rose does not comment directly on Meany's references to multinational corporations exporting American capital, technology, and jobs. But he does happily anticipate our emergence as a "mature creditor" economy in which income from cumulated foreign investments finances a trade deficit (imports exceeding exports). Since this implies large profits to American capital but reduced labor income, Meany naturally rejects this vision and favors restrictions on foreign investment. These issues of the division of income between labor and capital, as well as between multinational corporations and other businesses, lie at the center of the political infighting over trade policy. (The consumer's interest in more efficient worldwide production and lower prices has usually been politically underrepresented.)

To counter the protectionist lobbying, Rose and other "free traders" support liberal "adjustment allowances" to assist the displaced firms or workers in finding alternative sources of incomes. Whether such government compensation will convert protectionists to a more expansive trade policy remains to be seen.

36   A trade policy for America*

GEORGE MEANY

The AFL-CIO welcomes these hearings because world trade and international investment are of direct importance to American workers.

Specifically, the current deterioration of the United States' position in world trade is having a major adverse impact on America's steelworkers, machinists, electrical workers, on clothing, garment, textile and shoe workers, on glass and pottery workers, on shipyard and maritime workers and many others. Almost no segment of America's work force has escaped some adverse effect. The American worker is today the major victim of the fall-off in exports or the flood of imports or both.

The American workers have come to their unions for help. And their unions, in concert, seek redress and remedies to this very great threat. Tens of thousands of American workers are suffering loss of jobs, underemployment, a lowered standard of living, and loss of their dignity and their role in our work-oriented society. These workers' grievances are with the government of the United States because it is the government's foreign trade and investment policies that have been responsible in most part for this situation.

The AFL-CIO intends to pursue this issue and intends to fight for international trade and investment policies that will end these hardships.

The AFL-CIO seeks a national policy of healthy expansion of international trade on a reciprocal basis. We seek a trade policy that enhances the well-being of the American people in place of one that enhances private greed.

This is not a problem of the unions alone. It is a problem of all Americans because the loss of our productive base and the loss of our industrial employment will most certainly be followed by job losses in all segments of the economy. And with those losses will go much of the American standard of living.

* From "A Trade Policy for America," hearings before the Subcommittee on International Trade, Senate Finance Committee, 92nd Congress, First Session, 1971. Reprinted with permission of the author. George Meany is President, American Federation of Labor and Congress of Industrial Organizations, Washington, D.C.

Since 1934, the trade union movement has provided consistent support to government policies for the expansion of world trade. We have based our support on the trade union goal of increasing employment and improving living standards both at home and abroad. We are not interested in trade for trade's sake alone.

For many years, as world trade expanded, the majority of Americans and, for that matter, the majority of the people of the world benefited. But during the 1950s, changes in world economic conditions occurred and they accelerated in the 1960s. The benefits to Americans of expanded world trade decreased. The problems grew. And the American workers suffered.

By the late 1960s, imports were taking over large and growing portions of U.S. domestic markets of manufactured goods and components.

The U.S. has become a net importer of steel, autos, trucks and parts, as well as such products as clothing, footwear and glass. In consumer electrical goods, imports have taken over major parts of the U.S. domestic market. Even in electrical and non-electrical machinery, during the 1960s, imports increased more rapidly than exports—posing serious potential problems for the days ahead.

These events are the result of changes in world economic conditions. They require that changes be made in the United States' trade policies. The hard facts of life dictate that the government's foreign trade policies be swiftly modernized in light of these rapidly-moving events.

Our insistence on change is not a new concept for us. Since 1965, the AFL-CIO has sought a shift in government policy. To date, our proposals have not been met and the situation has grown more urgent.

The causes are rooted in the many changes in the world economic scene.

MANAGED ECONOMIES

Since World War II, most countries have moved to manage their economies. As part of such national economic management, governments have established direct and indirect subsidies for exports and barriers to imports.

All countries, including the United States, have every right to protect and advance their interests as they see them. But certainly subsidies for exports and barriers to imports are not free trade.

These policies are one reason for the flood of imports into the United States—the market that is most open to imports of all major industrial nations. At the same time, expansion of U.S. exports is held down by direct and indirect barriers erected against American-made goods by other governments.

FOREIGN INVESTMENT

Another major change, which gained momentum in the sixties, is the soaring rate of investment by American companies in foreign operations. These investments—combined with patent and license agreements with foreign companies—have transferred American technology to plants throughout the world. Many of these plants, operating with American machinery and American know-how, pay workers as little as 15 cents an hour.

In 1960, for example, United States firms invested about $3.8 billion in plants and machinery in foreign subsidiaries. In 1971, the Commerce Department says U.S. firms plan to invest over $15 billion. These estimates for 1971 show that more than $8 billion will be invested abroad in manufacturing. This is about one-fourth of the $32 billion planned investment in manufacturing, in the United States this year.

This large investment of United States corporate funds abroad has now changed the meaning of trade, investment and production worldwide. For example, in 1969, Ford was reported to be England's biggest exporter and IBM was the leading French exporter of computer equipment.

In the past 25 years, according to estimates by Harvard Professor Raymond Vernon, about 8,000 subsidiaries of U.S. companies have been established abroad, mostly in manufacturing. Their impact on the U.S. market and U.S. exports to other nations is obvious. It is estimated that the annual sales of foreign branches of U.S. firms are approximately $200 billion —about five times U.S. exports.

Let me cite an example of what all this means in terms of U.S. foreign investment, U.S. technology and U.S. jobs. During last year's trade hearings before the House Ways and Means Committee, William Sheskey told how he purchased a modern U.S. shoe plant and immediately shut it down.

He told the committee: "I shipped the lasts, dies, and patterns and the management and much of the leather to Europe, and I am making the same shoes under the same brand name, selling them to the same customers, with the same management, with the same equipment, for one reason. The labor where I am now making the shoes is 50 cents an hour as compared to the $3 that I was paying. Here is a perfect example of where I took everything American except the labor and that is exactly why I bought it."

Another example is an advertisement in the *Wall Street Journal* of July 15, 1970, which said, "If you have a patented product or a product that has a market in the U.S., we can help you find a responsible licensor in Mexico."

Mexico, incidentally, is a managed economy. It won't let imports into Mexico unless it wants them in. But the advertisement seeks U.S. firms to produce their ideas behind the Mexican trade barrier to sell in the U.S. market at U.S. prices—while taking advantage of low Mexican wages.

In March 1970, the *Wall Street Journal* reported that Zenith Radio Corporation, in the process of completing a large plant in Taiwan, had said it would "reduce its work force by about 3,000 jobs this year, and more than one-third of those laid off would be blacks." The chairman, Joseph S. Wright, said that in addition to the 3,000 layoffs in 1970, probably another 4,000 layoffs will occur in 1971.

Such operations by American companies obviously displace U.S. produced goods in both American markets and in world markets. These companies export American technology—some of it developed through the expenditure of government funds paid by American taxpayers. Their biggest export, of course, is U.S. jobs.

EXPORT OF U.S. TECHNOLOGY

As an example of the export of U.S. technology, let me cite one particular company, General Electric.

This firm is divided into five international GE-spheres of influence. Area Division-Europe, Area Division-Far East, Area Division-Latin America, IGE Export Division and International Business Support Division. In all of these areas U.S. technology has been exported, but for the sake of example here, I shall cite only examples of U.S. technology that have been licensed by GE to Japan alone. All of these examples—from a list of 84 separate licensing agreements—were, with little doubt, developed at the expense of the U.S. taxpayer.

The licenses to Japan for production include: Carrier System Microwave device; torpedo; a new type of radar; an M-61 Vulcan type of 20 mm machine cannon for defense aircraft; gun sight for F-4E jet fighter; technologies pertaining to the hull of space ships, communications systems of space ships and other controlling mechanisms for space ships; nuclear fuel energy; aircraft gyro compass system, and boilers for nuclear power reactors.

As you can see, none of this is outmoded technology, but the latest, most sophisticated type of manufacture upon which our industrial society is based. This is the technology upon which Americans depend for their jobs and upon which our national defense must rely.

MULTINATIONAL FIRMS

An additional major change since World War II, and particularly in the last decade—is the emergence of a new kind of business, the multinational firm. These are often American-based companies with plants, sales agencies and other facilities in as many as 40 or more countries around the world. Some are conglomerates, such as ITT and Genesco. Some are big auto firms, such as Ford and General Motors. Some are big names in computers, such as IBM.

These multinational firms can juggle the production of parts and finished products from one subsidiary in one country to another. A multinational corporation can produce components in widely separated plants in Korea, Taiwan and the United States, assemble the product in Mexico and sell the product in the United States at a U.S. price tag and frequently with a U.S.-brand name. Or the goods produced in the multinational's plants in a foreign country are sold in foreign markets, thus taking away the markets of U.S. made goods.

The multinational firms can juggle their bookkeeping and their prices and their taxes. Their export and import transactions are within the corporation, determined by the executives of the corporation—all for the benefit and the profit of the corporation. This is not foreign trade. Surely it is not foreign competition.

The complex operations of multinationals—with the aid of Madison Avenue advertising—have utterly confused the picture of the national origin of products. For example, Ford's Pinto has been heralded as the U.S. answer to imported small cars. But the engines are imported from England and Germany, and the standard transmissions are imported from Europe.

This phenomenon is far different from the development of corporations here in America during the last 100 years. The multinational is not simply an American company moving to a new locality where the same laws apply and where it is still within the jurisdiction of Congress and the government of the United States. This is a runaway corporation, going far beyond our borders. This is a runaway to a country, with different laws, different institutions and different labor and social standards. In most instances, even the name changes.

To demonstrate how far-reaching are the tentacles of American industry in foreign lands, we are making available to the committee a list of some major U.S. multinational corporations and the names by which they are known in other lands.

Ironically these are the same multinational corporations who have sought to influence U.S. trade legislation in the name of "free trade."

Meanwhile, back in the United States, expansion of large national corporations has been tempered to a degree by government regulations, standards, and controls. And, in the past few decades, large U.S. corporations have had to meet responsibilities to their employees through labor unions. Moreover, the multinationals' global operations are beyond the reach of present U.S. law or the laws of any single nation.

IMPACT ON U.S.

All of these developments—the multinational corporations, the managed economies, the foreign investments, the export of technology—have had a serious impact on U.S. international economic relationships and have displaced large portions of U.S. production.

A Congressional estimate—and this is conservative—is that auto imports are now 20 percent of the U.S. market, TV receivers 30 percent, glassware over 40 percent, sewing machines and calculating machines nearly 60 percent. As far as we have been able to determine, 100 percent of all cassettes are imported. Nearly all radios sold in the U.S. are imported. Similarly, large proportions of U.S. production of shirts, work clothes, shoes, and knitgoods are being displaced by imports. And many of the parts and components of products assembled in the U.S. are imported—including defense items.

IMPACT ON JOBS

The impact on America's production is, of course, most adversely felt by the American worker. Unlike capital, the worker cannot move about with ease.

While capital and machinery can be moved from one part of the country to another—or to other countries—workers do not have full mobility. Workers have great stakes in their jobs and their communities. They have skills that are related to the job or industry. They have seniority and seniority-based benefits, such as pensions, vacations and supplemental unemployment benefits. Workers have investments in their homes, a stake in the neighborhood, schools and churches.

This lack of mobility is not a fault. It is a virtue. It is an important factor in giving stability to a community and to society.

Moreover, a worker's skill is among his most valuable assets. It cannot, however, be transferred to another industry or occupation with ease, if at all.

Labor is not an interchangeable part, as some economists believe. A job-less shoe worker in Maine does not automatically become a clerical worker in New York or even in Portland. More likely, a displaced worker will be unemployed for many weeks and may wind up with a job at lesser skill and lower pay.

Unfortunately, there is a marked indifference to these trade-caused workers' problems. There are those who recommend, airily, that a worker must "adjust"—equating a worker with the re-tooling of a machine. This attitude is not only shocking in terms of social ethics, it also reflects an ignorance of workers' problems.

Further illustration of this indifference is the lack of data and information on the impact that international trade has on U.S. workers. There is a great void of information bearing on the employment impact and other effects on workers. This shortcoming can only be attributed to a lack of interest by foreign trade experts in government and business. We note that there is a great abundance of information and data available from the U.S. government to businessmen who wish to relocate their business abroad.

One scrap of data is available, however. The U.S. Department of Labor estimates that there was a loss of about 700,000 job opportunities in the

1966–1969 period because of imports. This does not include an estimate of the job loss caused by foreign trade barriers or the markets lost to U.S. multinational companies abroad. For the same period, the Bureau of Labor Statistics estimated that the number of jobs attributable to exports increased by only 200,000. Thus, in that three-year period we suffered a loss of 500,000 job opportunities. These figures are undoubtedly conservative, but they do make clear a heavy net loss of jobs to imports.

More recently, the Department of Commerce disclosed that employment in the electronic industries declined by an estimated 107,000 last year. For years, government statisticians have told the unions that jobs were not being lost and there were no problems in that industry. The Commerce Department statement pointed out that imports now represent more than 30 percent of domestic consumption of consumer electrical goods and rougher times are ahead. It warned that a new area of electronics—the domestic telephone equipment industry—would be the next to suffer rapidly rising imports.

It must also be pointed out that imports and exports do not of themselves necessarily create an industry and jobs of Americans. We are the world's largest trading nation—with ports on two oceans and the Gulf of Mexico—yet the merchant marine sector of our economy has nearly gone down the drain.

We carry about 5 percent of this nation's trade in ships flying the U.S. flag. We have suffered staggering job losses among seamen, ship builders and ship repairmen. Yet, at the same time, runaway shipping operations of U.S.-owned firms, including multinational firms, are flying the tax-haven flags of Panama, Liberia and Honduras. Needless to say, the wages paid to the foreign seamen on these vessels are a fraction of the American wage standard.

But the impact on U.S. workers is not solely the loss of jobs. We are told that imports serve to "discipline" prices. Often, however, the American consumer receives no benefit at all. The imports are sold at the American price, with substantially widened profit margins.

Frequently, the process results in the loss of workers' jobs, while the consumer receives little, if any, benefit.

The actual "discipline" is often more directly on the workers' wages and fringe benefits and his union's negotiating strength. For example, copper imports by major U.S. corporations in 1967 and 1968, contributed to prolonging the copper strike.

It is also false to claim that increasing imports to compete with U.S. products will benefit consumers through lower prices.

There is little, if any, genuine price competition in many areas that are dominated by powerful corporations. For example, the auto companies raised prices on their 1971 models despite a surge of auto imports. And shoe prices rose 38 percent between 1960 and 1970—faster than the 31 percent increase in the overall Consumer Price Index. During this period shoe imports skyrocketed, thousands of American shoe workers lost their jobs, yet the consumer benefited very little.

INTERNATIONAL BANKS

In the 1960s we have seen an important related phenomenon—the expansion of United States-based international banks, which service and help to finance foreign subsidiaries of U.S. companies. At present, there is a vast global network of branches of U.S. banks which moves funds easily from one country to another, beyond the direct reach of the monetary policies of any government, including our own.

In 1969, when the government's squeeze on the American money market threw homebuilding into a recession and hit other groups in the American economy, the U.S. international banks increased their borrowings from their foreign branches by an amazing $7 billion.

This $7 billion was for the aid and comfort of the American central offices of those international banks and their prime customers—the big corporations. The rates to the special customers were considerably less than those paid by small businessmen or home-buyers.

When the money squeeze eased here, and the interest rates declined, this same "hot money" was transferred back abroad, and was partly responsible for the recent dollar crisis in the European money markets. Financial reporters attributed much of the manipulation in the money market to the treasurers of multinational corporations who were busy selling their dollars for stronger currencies.

In view of these developments by the banks, the multinational firms and the radically changed concepts of international relationships, the question must be asked: How long can the United States government and the American people permit such operations of private companies and banks to continue without regulation?

The worldwide operations of United States-owned multinational companies do not represent free, competitive trade among the nations of the world. What they do represent is a closed system of trade, within the corporation, among its various subsidiaries in numerous countries. They represent the export of American technology and the export of American jobs.

These issues of foreign trade and investment require United States government attention. They need government action. Government controls over the investment outflows of United States companies to foreign subsidiaries are essential. In addition, the government must develop machinery to regulate the United States-based multinational companies and banks.

We in the AFL-CIO are not isolationists and have no intention of becoming isolationists.

We support the orderly expansion of world trade. We oppose the promotion of private greed at public expense or the undercutting of United States wage and labor standards. We want expanded trade that expands employment at home and abroad and that improves living standards and working conditions, here and abroad. We want the U.S. government to protect the interests of American workers against the export of American jobs.

AFL-CIO PROGRAM

Because of our great concern with this problem, the AFL-CIO Executive Council has adopted a program calling for new international trade and investment legislation.

In these statements we offered specific steps for the protection of American workers and for the preservation of our industrial society. These proposals include:

1. The U.S. government must stop helping and subsidizing U.S. companies in setting up and operating foreign subsidiaries. Sections 806:30 and 807 of the Tariff Schedules should be repealed; these sections of the Tariff Code provide especially low tariffs on imported goods, assembled abroad from U.S.-made parts. Moreover, the U.S. tax deferral on profits from foreign subsidies should be eliminated, so that the profits of these subsidiaries will be subject to the U.S. corporate income tax for the year they are earned.

2. The government should regulate, supervise and curb the substantial outflows of American capital for the investments of U.S. companies in foreign operations.

3. The government should regulate, supervise and curb the export of American technology—by regulating the foreign license and patent arrangements of American companies.

4. The government should press, in appropriate international agencies, for the establishment of international fair labor standards in world trade.

5. In the face of growing unresolved problems, an orderly marketing mechanism is needed immediately—to regulate the flow of imports into the U.S. of those goods and product-lines, in which sharply rising imports are displacing significant percentages of U.S. production and employment. Such quotas that bar the rapid displacement of U.S. production and employment by flood tides of imports, could slow down the disruptive impacts on American society and help to provide an orderly expansion of trade.

37 U.S. foreign trade: There's no need to panic*

SANFORD ROSE

Listening to U.S. businessmen talk about foreign competition these days, it seems almost impossible to believe that only a decade ago most business-men were enthusiastic free traders. America's great flagship industries, beginning with steel and autos, appeared to be firmly committed to free trade. Henry Ford II was fond of quoting a statement that his illustrious grandfather had made some years earlier: "Comfortably tucked away behind a tariff wall which shuts out competition and gives industry an undue profit which it has not earned, the business of our country would grow soft and neglectful. We need competition the world over to keep us on our toes and sharpen our wits."

Scarcely any businessmen talk that way nowadays—certainly not any in steel or autos. Both industries had trade surpluses in the early 1960s. But by 1970 the trade balance on iron and steel products was over $750 million in the red, while the automotive deficit approached $2 billion. Ford himself told his shareholders last May: "I frankly don't see how we're going to meet foreign competition. We've only seen the beginning. We may become a service nation someday because our manufacturers could not compete with foreigners."

To be sure, many of the companies threatened by stiff competition from imports are divided about how to react. They want protection at home but are concerned that foreign retaliation against U.S. protectionist measures may imperil their global earnings. C. Peter McColough, president of Xerox, is for imposing some trade restrictions, but admits, "Joe Wilson, my chairman, and I don't agree on this. I think I represent more people in my company than he does."

The textile companies, reputed to be bastions of protectionist thinking,

* From "U.S. Foreign Trade: There's No Need to Panic," *Fortune,* 84 (August 1971), pp. 109–111 and 186–89. Copyright *Fortune,* 1971. Abridged and reprinted with permission of the publisher. Sanford Rose is Associate Editor of *Fortune.*

are also somewhat less than monolithic. Says Tilford Gaines, a vice president at Manufacturers Hanover Trust, who is a director of United Merchants, a large textile company: "As a company, United Merchants stands shoulder to shoulder with the textile industry in asking for quotas on imports. But in actual fact it doesn't give a damn. For one thing, a substantial part of the company's earnings comes from overseas investments. For another, the company is highly innovative and believes that it can 'outcompete' any Japanese producer."

THE CHANGE IN GEORGE MEANY

Still, there are a lot of new protectionists in American business, and they have an important ally: the American labor movement. The old-line industrial and craft unions that speak for labor—with the possible and increasingly equivocal exception of the United Auto Workers—are determined to restrict imports and prevent multinational corporations from "exporting U.S. jobs," as they put it, by producing overseas.

This position, too, represents a major change. In March, 1962, President George Meany of the AFL-CIO said: "We need the things we import. To get what we need, we have to open up our own markets to such products as British woolens, German cars, and Japanese toys." In May, 1971, Meany was calling for "an orderly marketing mechanism . . . to regulate the flow of imports into the U.S. in industries where these imports are displacing significant percentages of U.S. production and employment."

The current campaign for trade restrictions is being waged with an almost apocalyptic intensity, with a shrillness that often drowns out sober voices in the business community. Either you are for trade restrictions, say many businessmen, or else you are against America and its future. Ely Callaway, the president of Burlington Industries, strikes a particularly martial pose: "I say that a trade war is *here*—we are in it, and we are losing it." Callaway is particularly incensed at those companies that have established plants overseas to export inexpensive goods back to the U.S. He says flatly: "Kayser-Roth is a company that is bad for America. And so is Bell & Howell."

WHO'S CHEATING WHOM?

The new protectionists, then, have a lot of zeal and a lot of support. It is not so clear that they have a good case. And to anyone who has followed the history of free-trade debates over the years, their arguments will seem less original—and less compelling—than the protectionists suppose them to be.

One of the most insistent themes of current protectionist rhetoric involves an assertion that the U.S. is being victimized by the unfair trading practices of foreign competitors. Actually, the protectionists repeat almost ceremonially, they would themselves be all in favor of free trade—except that no one else practices it. Most other countries are run by conscious economic nationalists. They artificially restrain their imports and stimulate their exports. The U.S. has far lower tariff barriers and far fewer quotas on imports than other industrialized countries, especially those in the European Economic Community and Japan, and these countries habitually sell to the U.S. at lower prices than prevail in their own domestic markets— i.e., they "dump" goods.

These constantly reiterated assertions are gospel to protectionists nowadays, and they are seldom challenged. Yet their main point—that other countries are taking advantage of the U.S. commitment to free trade—is debatable. An unpublished analysis by John Renner, head of the international-trade section of the State Department, shows that when the Kennedy Round reductions are completed at the end of his year the U.S. will have an average nominal tariff rate of 8.3 percent on industrial products. The rate will be 8.4 percent for the Common Market, 10.9 percent for Japan, and 11 percent for Canada. In other words, less than three points separate the lowest from the highest aggregate rate.

. . . . .

In addition, Renner's data show an increased use of quotas by the U.S. We now have so-called universal quotas, i.e., those working to limit imports from nearly all major countries, on sixty-seven industrial-product categories; the products range from essential industrial commodities like steel and oil to minor consumer items like brooms. The Europeans have sixty-five universal quotas and the Japanese sixty-one. (The Europeans also have a number of quotas aimed exclusively at Japanese goods.) Since 1963 the Japanese have eliminated seventy-one quotas and they plan to drop another twenty by October. The E.E.C. has eliminated eleven quotas since 1963. The U.S. has *added* sixty of them during the same period. Moreover, U.S. quotas cover close to 17 percent of total industrial imports. The Japanese barriers cover nearly 12 percent of their imports, while E.E.C. restrictions cover approximately 4 percent of imports.

Admittedly, as Renner points out, these percentages cannot just be taken at face value. A lot depends on the *kinds* of quotas a country has. Very generous quotas, for example, permit substantial imports, which raise the percentages. Renner nevertheless concludes that, when all is said and done, the E.E.C.'s quantitative restrictions affect a comparatively small amount of industrial trade, Japan's quotas affect a considerable amount of this trade, and U.S. restrictions affect the *largest* volume of trade.

A number of U.S. businessmen point out, however, that Japan and the E.E.C. practice forms of trade restriction that are not in their laws—what might be called restriction by administrative nonfeasance. Walter Wriston, chairman of First National City Bank, quips that whenever the Europeans or Japanese want to exclude a particular U.S. product without imposing a formal quota, "the customs inspector simply goes out for lunch when the ship docks." Renner acknowledges that he heard numerous complaints of this type from businessmen when he was our economic counselor to the E.E.C. in Brussels. But, he adds, "whenever I asked for documentation so I could complain to the appropriate foreign authorities, businessmen were never able to come up with any. When specifics are not forthcoming, I usually conclude that the problem does not exist."

THEY DON'T GET THE EVIDENCE

There is also a remarkable lack of documentation of the rather widely held belief that other countries—in particular, Japan—have in recent years intensified their dumping in the U.S. market. Many businessmen complain endlessly about Japanese dumping; but few of them, oddly enough, have managed to persuade the government. If the Bureau of Customs in the Treasury Department decides that a sale has been made at less than "fair market value," it sends the case to the Tariff Commission to determine whether the complainant has been injured by the sale. If the commission agrees that there has been some injury, antidumping duties are imposed on the foreign product.

In recent years the staff that handles dumping complaints at the Treasury has been increased from five to thirty-five. Nevertheless, the Treasury has sent very few cases to the Tariff Commission—only fifteen in the period from the beginning of 1970 to mid-1971, and only seven involving Japanese goods. Says Peter Flanigan, an assistant to the President who specializes in economic affairs: "I keep telling businessmen who think they have evidence of foreign dumping to give us the facts. But they don't." Renner adds: "I know the people who handle dumping matters at the Treasury. They would be *delighted* to find more cases, but they don't get the evidence."

If foreign companies were dumping a lot of goods in the U.S., that would certainly be a problem for American companies operating in the same markets. Whether it would be bad for the U.S. as a whole is quite another question. It is a fundamental question but one that, in the somewhat hysterical atmosphere that now envelops much discussion of free trade, is seldom asked. As Leland Yeager, a professor of economics at the University of Virginia, puts it: "How is the American economy hurt if foreign sellers set prices that discriminate *in favor of* Americans? The circumstances that permit the foreign sellers to discriminate against their own countrymen may be regrettable from some points of view, but to Americans, bargains are bargains."

According to economists like Yeager, persistent dumping means, in effect, that foreign producers have successfully conned their fellow citizens into working cheaply for the U.S. by trading many of their goods for a few of our own. If foreigners want to make us a gift of their resources, this just increases our welfare at their expense. Moreover, if they dump goods whose prices, even under so-called competitive conditions, seriously understate their social cost (because the cost of pollution is not included), they're doing even more for our welfare. This point is made by Milton Friedman, perhaps the best-known apostle of free trade in the U.S. economics profession (which is overwhelmingly committed to free trade). Says Friedman: "If Japan exports steel at artificially low prices, it is also exporting clean air. Why shouldn't we take it?"

. . . . .

A second major theme developed at length by the new protectionists concerns the U.S. trade balance. Our trade surplus has declined sharply in recent years, from $7.1 billion in 1964 to $2.7 billion last year, and possibly to even less this year. A sizable number of businessmen now argue that this slippage results from our commitment to free trade.

In fact, it is most unlikely that our export surplus has deteriorated because of any difference between our trade practices and those of our competitors. U.S. trade difficulties can more plausibly be explained by differences in the rate of inflation and in the level of economic activity among the major industrial countries. Until last year's recession the U.S. maintained an excessively high level of economic activity and also experienced a rapid rise in prices. On the other hand, a number of our major trading partners had a considerable amount of slack in their economies during parts of this period—notably Germany in 1966–67, Japan in 1965–66, France and Belgium from 1966 to early 1968, and Italy for much of the period since 1964. At the same time, prices in these countries increased more slowly than in the U.S.

F. Gerard Adams, a professor of economics at the University of Pennsylvania, and Helen Junz, an economist with the Federal Reserve Board, have made a serious effort to discover how trade flows would have been affected if the major industrial countries had kept their economies fully employed during 1965–69 while the U.S. and Canada had grown at noninflationary rates. Using an econometric model of world trade, the two analysts concluded that the U.S. trade balance in the first half of 1969 would have been improved by an annual rate of more than $5 billion.

. . . . .

A LITTLE REVALUATION GOES A LONG WAY

The trade balance would be in even better shape if certain changes were made in exchange rates. Changes are in fact quite likely. Hendrik

Houthakker, until recently a member of the Council of Economic Advisers (he is now back at Harvard), confidently expects the Japanese to revalue their currency upward some time in the next two years.

.   .   .   .   .

A revaluation of the yen would enormously stimulate U.S. exports to Japan; there is abundant evidence that Japanese demand for U.S. goods is extremely sensitive to price changes. Stephen Magee, who is a professor of international business at the University of California at Berkeley, and who has done considerable research on trade for the C.E.A., estimates that for every 1 percent drop in U.S. export prices the volume of U.S. exports to Japan would rise by about 3 percent. To be sure, revaluation would eventually work to hold down Japanese incomes and Japanese prices, and this would moderate the increase in U.S. exports. On the other hand, Japanese sales to the U.S. and other countries would obviously fall off somewhat because the dollar price of those exports would rise. After weighing all these considerations, Magee concluded that if the Japanese had revalued by 10 percent at the beginning of 1971, the U.S. trade balance for the year would have improved by as much as $2.4 billion. A revaluation of 5 percent—the figure commonly suggested by Japanese economists— would have produced half the improvement, or $1.2 billion. Evidently, small changes in the price of the yen will generate rather large changes in the total U.S. foreign-trade position.

THE PAYOFF ON FOREIGN INVESTMENTS

But the trade balance after 1975 is admittedly a quite different matter. In the late 1970s the trade balance may well turn negative—and stay negative for many years thereafter. The reason is that U.S. business will probably be earning so much on its overseas investments that other countries may have to export more than they import from us in order to obtain enough dollars to pay us our dividends.

According to tentative projections made by the Council of Economic Advisers, by 1975 other countries will be paying us $17 billion a year in dividends, fees, and royalties on our foreign investments, while we pay them only about $6.5 billion on their U.S. investments. Houthakker says that this projection of our investment income is actually somewhat conservative since it is based on the low rates of return on U.S. overseas assets that prevailed for most of the 1960s.

The council did not estimate the size of the investment-income balance after 1975, but Lawrence Krause, an economist at the Brookings Institution, has continued the exercise for the years through 1980. Krause concludes that the net balance on investment income and fees could rise to $16 billion by that year. He believes the U.S. is fast becoming a "mature creditor" country, something like Great Britain during much of the nineteenth and twentieth centuries. Britain had no difficulty balancing its international accounts even though it routinely bought more goods than it sold in foreign markets. The country simply lived off the income from its foreign assets. Krause suggests that the U.S. can and should play the same role during the late twentieth century.

Not all students of trade agree that this arrangement would work. Harold van B. Cleveland, an economist at the First National City Bank, is uneasy over Krause's projections and their implications. Notes Cleveland: "I don't think Europe can get the dollars it will need by selling us more goods than it buys. It is politically difficult for the U.S. to maintain a liberal import policy unless we also run a trade surplus."

An alternative trade scenario for the late 1970s has the U.S. balancing its accounts by exporting more to the less-developed world than it imports, while importing more from the industrial world than it exports. The trade deficit with Europe would be financed by dividend remittances, while the trade surplus with the less-developed world might be financed by an increase in U.S. investment and by foreign aid. The details of all such scenarios are arguable, of course; but it seems clear that neither our trade balance nor our over-all payments position is in the sorry state described by the protectionists.

REAL GAINS AND HYPOTHETICAL LOSSES

Even if the country's trade and other international accounts were in balance or in surplus, some industries would always be losing their advantage in international trade (and thus encountering stiffer competition from imports). These industries might be able to point to declining employment. Not surprisingly, unemployment is another major theme of the new protectionists today.

In the opinion of George Meany, American labor has been one of the casualties of trade. He cites a Department of Labor finding that in 1966 it would have taken about 1,800,000 workers to produce domestically those imported goods that are most competitive with U.S. products. By 1969 it would have required 2,500,000 workers—i.e., the number of jobs lost to imports rose by 700,000. During this period the number of "export jobs" increased by 200,000. Therefore, argues Meany, from 1966 to 1969 we had a net loss of 500,000 jobs because of trade.

The trouble with this analysis is that the export jobs created during this period were real, whereas the jobs lost because we imported what could have been produced domestically are hypothetical. From 1966 to 1969 the U.S. had full employment; much of the time there were severe labor shortages. We probably couldn't have found those extra 500,000 people even if we had tried. And if we had somehow managed to create that many more jobs, the result would have been an enormous increase in inflationary pressures. The fact is that under full-employment conditions imports help most people, including most workers, because they enable us to acquire goods that we cannot produce domestically without overstraining our resources.

Viewed from the perspective of a 6 percent rather than a 4 percent unemployment figure, the case is admittedly quite different. But can we eliminate our unemployment through trade restrictions? The answer is that we almost certainly cannot. If we attempted to "export our recession" by cutting down our imports, other countries would obviously export it right back by cutting off our overseas sales.

Many businessmen and labor leaders believe that import restrictions would help low-paid southern textile workers or New England shoemakers. But if we placed restrictions on imports of textiles and shoes, Europe and Japan would obviously retaliate. And retaliation would surely reduce the income of, for example, Mississippi soybean farmers, who are big exporters to Europe and Asia. It would also seriously hurt the Appalachian coal miners; U.S. exports of coal to Japan have risen from $77 million in 1965 to $412 million in 1970. And it would produce considerable distress among the farmers of the state of Washington, about 75 percent of whose wheat output is exported to Asia, principally to Japan. As union leaders had considerable opportunity to learn in the 1930s, trade wars don't cure unemployment; they worsen it.

It is true, however, that unemployment may be a real problem in particular industries that are having trouble competing with imports. In an unpublished paper, the Department of Labor has been trying to shed some light on the "industry-specific" (i.e., as opposed to aggregate) employment effects of rising imports. The department's economists have been matching up employment changes with changes in imports in 190 industries; the industries cover most of U.S. manufacturing employment.

The department found that in 1965–69, the period of greatest import penetration, only thirty-seven of the 190 industries suffered any net employment decline at all. In eleven of the thirty-seven there were no imports to speak of; only twenty-six had both employment declines and a rising level of imports. The total number of jobs lost in these twenty-six industries from 1965 to 1969 was 117,000—about 0.5 percent of total manufacturing employment in 1969. (And during 1965–69 about two million *new* manufacturing jobs were being created.)

Moreover, even though employment in a particular industry is declining while imports are increasing, it does not necessarily follow that the imports are causing the decline. In a number of these twenty-six industries, employment fell, not because imports rose but because domestic demand dropped or productivity increased. Indeed, according to Jerome Mark of the U.S. Labor Department, normal productivity increases alone are probably pushing out more workers in these twenty-six industries than are imports.

Just about everyone in the Labor Department who has worked on the problem of import-related joblessness is persuaded that it is not especially widespread. Figures on labor turnover rates tend to reinforce this belief. If imports have in fact caused companies to shut down plants and throw workers out of jobs in substantial numbers, this fact should be reflected in high layoff rates in the industries affected. Yet over the last five years the number of people laid off in these industries has consistently been less than the number who voluntarily leave their jobs.

. . . . .

In general, those who argue for import quotas to protect the South from economic disaster seriously underestimate the mobility of the average southern worker. Most southern states have actually been growing at faster rates than the U.S. as a whole. Indeed, the textile industry in the South has grown, not contracted, in the last decade. The same is true of the chemical and electronics industries in the South. Moreover, the region is now building up its lumber and furniture industry to help satisfy the prospective surge in nationwide housing demand. The average southern worker, it would appear, can choose from a growing number of employment opportunities should competition from imports eventually force him out of the textile mill.

Textile executives nevertheless continue to talk as though their displaced workers had practically no place to go. In a recent panel discussion on trade, Donald McCullough, president of Collins & Aikman, a medium-sized textile company, argued that other industries that might absorb these workers had import problems of their own. "We have heard a great deal about shifting people from low- to high-technology industries," he said. "What is a high-technology industry? We used to call that electronics. Well, in fact, the electronics industry has a greater import penetration than many parts of the textile industry." McCullough is factually correct, but it is also a fact that electronics *exports* have been rising. Indeed, in 1970 the net trade balance of electronics (the excess of exports over imports) was $700 million greater than in 1966. And employment in the industry had actually risen by 90,000.

Moreover, if the textile or apparel worker displaced by imports really had no place to go, this fact would be reflected in the statistics on hardcore unemployment. The proportion of the total work force that has been jobless for long periods naturally rises during recession periods; but otherwise it has stayed remarkably stable over the past decade.

SOME DON'T WANT ASSISTANCE

It would be foolish to suggest that rising imports have no adverse employment effects at all. Obviously, some workers and businesses have been hurt by imports. And even if the total unemployment rate is held down to levels of about 4 percent, some of the displaced workers will have to be assisted to enter new lines of work. The government has recognized its responsibility to provide assistance, but existing laws have made the assistance too difficult to get.

Workers and companies can qualify for retraining and relocation allowances, tax incentives, or supplemental compensation only if the imports threatening their jobs have entered the country as a result of tariff concessions made by the U.S. Government. If imports that displace workers cannot be related to concessions, the workers are out of luck. In addition, companies can qualify for assistance only when the entire firm is injured. If a particular plant is affected but the company as a whole is not, assistance is denied. As a result of these provisions, very few companies or individuals have been able to obtain help. The Tariff Commission, the agency responsible for hearing adjustment-assistance cases, has recently begun interpreting its legislative mandate somewhat more liberally. But it would obviously be helpful if Congress passed new legislation that made assistance easier to get.

When many businessmen hear the phrase "adjustment assistance," they reach for their proverbial guns. Burlington's Callaway comments acidly: "Who wants to be paid to go out of business? When people like Professor Houthakker talk about adjustment assistance, they usually throw out a figure of between $200 million and $250 million a year. Burlington's annual payroll is twice that amount."

Fortunately, it isn't likely that entire companies will go out of business because of imports—least of all Burlington—and adjustment assistance might prove useful to a lot of them. But the assistance must be used in conjunction with research. We need many more in-depth Labor Department studies to dissociate the effect of imports from other sources of business or employment decline—for example, bad management, shifts in domestic demand, or increased automation. After such studies have been made, it may indeed be found that the cost is more than $250 million a year. Whatever figure is arrived at, it will probably be a bargain. The gains to society from increasing imports would appear to exceed by a great deal the costs of providing assistance.

DISTURBING THE "QUIET LIFE"

Last year Andrew Brimmer, a governor of the Federal Reserve Board, made an analysis of the gains from trade in two industries, apparel and shoes, that are asking for protection from imports. He estimated that consumer spending on apparel would probably reach $52.7 billion by 1975. But, Brimmer argued, if there were quotas on apparel imports (they were then being advocated by Representative Wilbur Mills), consumers would have to pay $54.5 billion for the same amount of clothing. In other words, those increased imports would save the consumer about $1.8 billion. Similarly, without a quota, the public would pay about $5.9 billion for shoes. With a quota the cost would be about $7.8 billion.

The cost of import restrictions was also developed at some length a year ago by a Cabinet Task Force on Oil Import Controls. Its study found that "in 1969 consumers paid $5 billion more for oil products than they would have paid in the absence of import restrictions. And by 1980 the annual cost to consumers would approximate $8.4 billion."

Studies like these do not even attempt to take into account the indirect benefits of increased imports. Countries that supply imports to the U.S. market acquire the wherewithal to buy U.S. goods, and this stimulates employment in our export industries. Also, as imports drive prices down, consumers change their spending patterns: they may decide to buy more apparel, shoes, and oil products than they had originally intended. Part of the increased demand will be satisfied by foreign suppliers, but another part will be met by domestic companies. As a result, some of the workers initially displaced by imports may be rehired.

Many of the gains from increased imports are almost impossible to estimate—even though these gains may be more sizable than those that can be measured. In many areas of the economy, for example, price competition is particularly weak. If companies in these industries had to worry only about domestic competition, they could relax and enjoy a business life with no undue strains. Foreign competition may force the inherently inefficient out of business, but it also forces the potentially efficient to work a little harder at staying competitive. The ultimate beneficiary is the consumer. And he gets so many tangible benefits that he ought to be willing to pay to assist those who must be retrained for jobs.

Protectionists are in effect rejecting long-term social gains in order to avoid much smaller short-term costs. Since policy makers and legislators are inevitably preoccupied with the short term, they tend to pay far too much attention to the protectionist din. The case for protection is a little like the case against technological progress. Clearly, if we bottled up progress, some people would be spared the necessity of finding new jobs. But we would also be undercutting the dynamism of the economy, and eventually we would all end up a little poorer.

B. International monetary system

The world of international trade and finance has been troubled in recent years by two interacting problems—a chronic deficit in the American balance of payments, and periodic crises in the system of fixed exchange rates and international monetary reserves. The link between these two problems is simple: The dollar is a key "reserve" currency for many nations, and America's balance of payments deficits have been financed by flooding other countries with an excess of dollar reserves.

To eliminate both problems Friedman proposes the adoption of worldwide floating exchange rates, where the relative value of each nation's money is determined by its supply (from imports and foreign lending) and demand (for exports and borrowing) in the currency marketplace. The balance of payments accounts are automatically balanced by the shifting exchange rate, leaving each country free to pursue its domestic macroeconomic goals, and leaving the whole world free to negotiate lower tariffs and trade barriers. Gaines and other critics reply that floating exchange rates increase the risk and uncertainty for trade and finance. In any case political leaders will never permit the dollar or their own currencies to float without manipulation, because of the political risks of devaluation (higher cost of living, lost monetary "prestige") or revaluation (lost jobs and profits in export industries).

The fixed exchange rate system which has operated under International Monetary Fund auspices since 1945 has offered day-to-day exchange stability, but also periodic disruptive crises in the pattern of exchange rates, due to chronic balance of payments deficits (Britain, United States, France, and many poor countries) or surpluses (Germany, Japan, and a few other nations). Attempting to reduce its deficit, the United States has restricted and inefficiently distorted its trade and finance through export subsidies (to agriculture and shipping), import tariffs and quotas, taxes and controls on foreign investment, and "buy American" campaigns on tourism and military spending. Finally in August 1971 President Nixon was forced to "float" the dollar exchange rate temporarily, while negotiating the December dollar devaluation (relative to gold, the Japanese yen, the German mark, and several other currencies). As Gaines indicates, subsequent speculation against the dollar raises the possibility of another devaluation.

463

Meanwhile the dollar's instability has intensified negotiations for a broader reform of the entire world monetary system. As Friedman would wish, a greater degree of exchange rate flexibility has been introduced through "wider bands" (the float limits permitted around the official rate) and "transitional float" when a country is exploring a change in its fixed rate. Despite the recognized need for greater flexibility and quicker adjustment, the world's financial leaders (the elite "group of 10" nations on whom Gaines would rest the decisions) still adhere to the fixed exchange rate system. The most intriguing (and highly political) issue which must still be faced is the relative importance of gold, dollars, and IMF credits (including the SDRs, Special Drawing Rights) as components of world monetary reserves.

38 Exchange rates—How flexible should they be?*

MILTON FRIEDMAN

OVERCOMING A BALANCE-OF-PAYMENTS DEFICIT

Many people concerned with our payments deficits hope that since we are operating further from full capacity than Europe, we could supply a substantial increase in exports whereas they could not. Implicitly, this assumes that European countries are prepared to see their surplus turned into a deficit, thereby contributing to the reduction of the deficits we have recently been experiencing in our balance of payments. Perhaps this would be the initial effect of tariff changes. But if the achievement of such a result is to be sine qua non of tariff agreement, we cannot hope for any significant reduction in barriers. We could be confident that exports would expand more than imports only if the tariff changes were one sided indeed, with our trading partners making much greater reductions in tariffs than we make. Our major means of inducing other countries to reduce tariffs is to offer corresponding reductions in our tariff. More generally, there is little hope of continued and sizable liberalization of trade if liberalization is to be viewed simply as a device for correcting balance-of-payments difficulties. That way lies only backing and filling.

Suppose then that the initial effect is to increase our expenditures on imports more than our receipts from exports. How could we adjust to this outcome?

One method of adjustment is to draw on reserves or borrow from abroad to finance the excess increase in imports. The obvious objection to this method is that it is only a temporary device, and hence can be relied on only when the disturbance is temporary. But that is not the major objection. Even if we had very large reserves or could borrow large amounts

* From "Exchange Rates—How Flexible Should They Be?" *The United States Balance of Payments, Exchange Rates—How Flexible Should They Be?* Hearings before the Joint Economic Committee, 88th Congress, First Session, 1963, pp. 451–56. Abridged and reprinted with permission of the author. Milton Friedman is Professor of Economics at the University of Chicago, Chicago, Ill.

from abroad, so that we could continue this expedient for many years, it is a most undesirable one. We can see why if we look at physical rather than financial magnitudes.

The physical counterpart to the financial deficit is a reduction of employment in industries competing with imports that is larger than the concurrent expansion of employment in export industries. So long as the financial deficit continues, the assumed tariff reductions create employment problems. But it is no part of the aim of tariff reductions to create unemployment at home or to promote employment abroad. The aim is a balanced expansion of trade, with exports rising along with imports and thereby providing employment opportunities to offset any reduction in employment resulting from increased imports.

Hence, simply drawing on reserves or borrowing abroad is a most unsatisfactory method of adjustment.

Another method of adjustment is to lower U.S. prices relative to foreign prices, since this would stimulate exports and discourage imports. If foreign countries are accommodating enough to engage in inflation, such a change in relative prices might require merely that the United States keep prices stable or even, that it simply keep them from rising as fast as foreign prices. But there is no necessity for foreign countries to be so accommodating, and we could hardly count on their being so accommodating. The use of this technique therefore involves a willingness to produce a decline in U.S. prices by tight monetary policy or tight fiscal policy or both. Given time, this method of adjustment would work. But in the interim, it would exact a heavy toll. It would be difficult or impossible to force down prices appreciably without producing a recession and considerable unemployment. To eliminate in the long run the unemployment resulting from the tariff changes, we should in the short run be creating cyclical unemployment. The cure might for a time be far worse than the disease.

This second method is therefore also most unsatisfactory. Yet these two methods—drawing on reserves and forcing down prices—are the only two methods available to us under our present international payment arrangements, which involve fixed exchange rates between the U.S. dollar and other currencies. Little wonder that we have so far made such disappointing progress toward the reduction of trade barriers, that our practice has differed so much from our preaching.

There is one other way and only one other way to adjust and that is by allowing (or forcing) the price of the U.S. dollar to fall in terms of other currencies. To a foreigner, U.S. goods can become cheaper in either of two ways—either because their prices in the United States fall in terms of dollars or because the foreigner has to give up fewer units of his own currency to acquire a dollar, which is to say, the price of the dollar falls. For example, suppose a particular U.S. car sells for $2,800 when a dollar costs 7 shillings, tuppence in British money (i.e., roughly £1 = $2.80). The price of the car is then £1,000 in British money. It is all the same to an English-man—or even a Scotsman—whether the price of the car falls to $2,500 while the price of a dollar remains 7 shillings, tuppence, or, alternatively, the price of the car remains $2,800, while the price of a dollar falls to 6 shillings, 5 pence (i.e., roughly £1 = $3.11). In either case, the car costs the Englishman £900 rather than £1,000, which is what matters to him. Similarly, foreign goods can become more expensive to an American in either of two ways—either because the price in terms of foreign currency rises or because he has to give up more dollars to acquire a given amount of foreign currency.

Changes in exchange rates can therefore alter the relative price of U.S. and foreign goods in precisely the same way as can changes in internal prices in the United States and in foreign countries. And they can do so without requiring anything like the same internal adjustments. If the initial effect of the tariff reductions would be to create a deficit at the former exchange rate (or enlarge an existing deficit or reduce an existing surplus) and thereby increase unemployment, this effect can be entirely avoided by a change in exchange rates which will produce a balanced ex-pansion in imports and exports without interfering with domestic employ-ment, domestic prices, or domestic monetary and fiscal policy. The pig can be roasted without burning down the house.

The situation is, of course, entirely symmetrical if the tariff changes should initially happen to expand our exports more than our imports. Under present circumstances, we would welcome such a result, and con-ceivably, if the matching deficit were experienced by countries currently running a surplus, they might permit it to occur without seeking to offset it. In that case, they and we would be using the first method of adjustment —changes in reserves or borrowing. But again, if we had started off from an even keel, this would be an undesirable method of adjustment. On our side, we should be sending out useful goods and receiving only foreign currencies in return. On the side of our partners, they would be using up reserves and tolerating the creation of unemployment.

The second method of adjusting to a surplus is to permit or force domestic prices to rise—which is of course what we did in part in the early postwar years when we were running large surpluses. Again, we should be forcing maladjustments on the whole economy to solve a problem arising from a small part of it—the 5 percent accounted for by foreign trade.

Again, these two methods are the only ones available under our present international payments arrangements, and neither is satisfactory.

The final method is to permit or force exchange rates to change—in this case, a rise in the price of the dollar in terms of foreign currencies. This solution is again specifically adapted to the specific problem of the balance of payments.

Changes in exchange rates can be produced in either of two general ways. One way is by a change in an official exchange rate; an official devaluation or appreciation from one fixed level which the Government is committed to support to another fixed level. This is the method used by Britain in its postwar devaluation and by Germany in 1961 when the mark was appreciated. This is also the main method contemplated by the IMF which permits member nations to change their exchange rates by 10 percent without approval by the Fund and by a larger amount after approval by the Fund. But this method has serious disadvantages. It makes a change in rates a matter of major moment, and hence there is a tendency to postpone any change as long as possible. Difficulties cumulate and a larger change is finally needed than would have been required if it could have been made promptly. By the time the change is made, everyone is aware that a change is pending and is certain about the direction of change. The result is to encourage flight from a currency, if it is going to be devalued, or to a currency, if it is going to be appreciated.

There is in any event little basis for determining precisely what the new rate should be. Speculative movements increase the difficulty of judging what the new rate should be, and introduce a systematic bias, making the change needed appear larger than it actually is. The result, particularly when devaluation occurs, is generally to lead officials to "play safe" by making an even larger change than the large change needed. The country is then left after the devaluation with a maladjustment precisely the opposite of that with which it started, and is thereby encouraged to follow policies it cannot sustain in the long run.

Even if all these difficulties could be avoided, this method of changing from one fixed rate to another has the disadvantage that it is necessarily discontinuous. Even if the new exchange rates are precisely correct when first established, they will not long remain correct.

A second and much better way in which changes in exchange rates can be produced is by permitting exchange rates to float, by allowing them to be determined from day to day in the market. This is the method which the United States used from 1862 to 1879, and again, in effect, from 1917 or so to about 1925, and again from 1933 to 1934. It is the method which Britain used from 1918 to 1925 and again from 1931 to 1939, and which Canada used for most of the interwar period and again from 1950 to May 1962. Under this method, exchange rates adjust themselves continuously, and market forces determine the magnitude of each change. There is no need for any official to decide by how much the rate should rise or fall. This is the method of the free market, the method that we adopt unquestioningly in a private enterprise economy for the bulk of goods and services. It is no less available for the price of one money in terms of another.

With a floating exchange rate, it is possible for Governments to intervene and try to affect the rate by buying or selling, as the British exchange equalization fund did rather successfully in the 1930s, or by combining buying and selling with public announcements of intentions, as Canada did so disastrously in early 1962. On the whole, it seems to me undesirable to have government intervene, because there is a strong tendency for government agencies to try to peg the rate rather than to stabilize it, because they have no special advantage over private speculators in stabilizing it, because they can make far bigger mistakes than private speculators risking their own money, and because there is a tendency for them to cover up their mistakes by changing the rules—as the Canadian case so strikingly illustrates—rather than by reversing course. But this is an issue on which there is much difference of opinion among economists who agree in favoring floating rates. Clearly, it is possible to have a successful floating rate along with governmental speculation.

The great objective of tearing down trade barriers, of promoting a worldwide expansion of trade, of giving citizens of all countries, and especially the underdeveloped countries, every opportunity to sell their products in open markets under equal terms and thereby every incentive to use their resources efficiently, of giving countries an alternative through free world trade to autarchy and central planning—this great objective can, I believe, be achieved best under a regime of floating rates. All countries, and not just the United States, can proceed to liberalize boldly and confidently only if they can have reasonable assurance that the resulting trade expansion will be balanced and will not interfere with major domestic objectives. Floating exchange rates, and so far as I can see, only floating exchange rates, provide this assurance. They do so because they are an automatic mechanism for protecting the domestic economy from the possibility that liberalization will produce a serious imbalance in international payments.

WHY AREN'T FLOATING EXCHANGE RATES MORE POPULAR?

Despite their advantages, floating exchange rates have a bad press. Why is this so?

One reason is because a consequence of our present system that I have been citing as a serious disadvantage is often regarded as an advantage, namely, the extent to which the small foreign trade sector dominates national policy. Those who regard this as an advantage refer to it as the discipline of the gold standard. I would have much sympathy for this view if we had a real gold standard, so the discipline was imposed by impersonal forces which in turn reflected the realities of resources, tastes, and technology. But in fact we have today only a pseudo gold standard and the so-called discipline is imposed by governmental officials of other countries who are determining their own internal monetary policies and are either being forced to dance to our tune or calling the tune for us, depending primarily on accidental political developments. This is a discipline we can well do without. See my article entitled "Real and Pseudo Gold Standards."

A possibly more important reason why floating exchange rates have a bad press, I believe, is a mistaken interpretation of experience with floating rates, arising out of a statistical fallacy that can be seen easily in a standard example. Arizona is clearly the worst place in the United States for a person with tuberculosis to go because the death rate from tuberculosis is higher in Arizona than in any other state. The fallacy in this case is obvious. It is less obvious in connection with exchange rates. Countries that have gotten into severe financial difficulties, for whatever reason, have had ultimately to change their exchange rates or let them change. No amount of exchange control and other restrictions on trade have enabled them to peg an exchange rate that was far out of line with economic realities. In consequence, floating rates have frequently been associated with financial and economic instability. It is easy to conclude, as many have, that floating exchange rates produce such instability.

This misreading of experience is reinforced by the general prejudice against speculation; which has led to the frequent assertion, typically on the basis of no evidence whatsoever, that speculation in exchange can be expected to be destabilizing and thereby to increase the instability in rates. Few who make this assertion even recognize that it is equivalent to asserting that speculators generally lose money.

Floating exchange rates need not be unstable exchange rates—any more than the prices of automobiles or of Government bonds, of coffee or of meals need gyrate wildly just because they are free to change from day to day. The Canadian exchange rate was free to change during more than a decade, yet it varied within narrow limits. The ultimate objective is a world in which exchange rates, while free to vary, are in fact highly stable because basic economic policies and conditions are stable. Instability of exchange rates is a symptom of instability in the underlying economic structure. Elimination of this symptom by administrative pegging of exchange rates cures none of the underlying difficulties and only makes adjustment to them more painful.

The confusion between stable exchange rates and pegged exchange rates helps to explain the frequent comment that floating exchange rates would introduce an additional element of uncertainty into foreign trade and thereby discourage its expansion. They introduce no additional element of uncertainty. If a floating rate would, for example, decline, then a pegged rate would be subject to pressure that the authorities would have to meet by internal deflation or exchange control in some form. The uncertainty about the rate would simply be replaced by uncertainty about internal prices or about the availability of exchange; and the latter uncertainties, being subject to administrative rather than market control, are likely to be the more erratic and unpredictable. Moreover, the trader can far more readily and cheaply protect himself against the danger of changes in exchange rates, through hedging operations in a forward market, than he can against the danger of changes in internal prices or exchange availability. Floating rates are therefore more favorable to private international trade than pegged rates.

THE CONSEQUENCES OF MAINTAINING FIXED EXCHANGE RATES

Though I have discussed the problem of international payments in the context of trade liberalization, the discussion is directly applicable to the more general problem of adapting to any forces that make for balance-of-payments difficulties. Consider our present problem, of a deficit in the balance of trade plus long-term capital movements. How can we adjust to it? By one of the three methods outlined: first, drawing on reserves or borrowing; second, keeping U.S. prices from rising as rapidly as foreign prices or forcing them down; third, permitting or forcing exchange rates to alter. And, this time, by one more method: by imposing additional trade barriers or their equivalent, whether in the form of higher tariffs, or smaller import quotas, or extracting from other countries tighter "voluntary" quotas on their exports, or "tieing" foreign aid, or buying higher priced domestic goods or services to meet military needs, or imposing taxes on foreign borrowing, or imposing direct controls on investments by U.S. citizens abroad, or any one of the host of other devices for interfering with the private business of private individuals that have become so familiar to us since Hjalmar Schacht perfected the modern techniques of exchange control in 1934 to strengthen the Nazis for war and to despoil a large class of his fellow citizens.

Fortunately or unfortunately, even Congress cannot repeal the laws of arithmetic. Books must balance. We must use one of these four methods. Because we have been unwilling to select the only one that is currently fully consistent with both economic and political needs—namely, floating exchange rates—we have been driven, as if by an invisible hand, to employ all the others, and even then may not escape the need for explicit changes in exchange rates.

We affirm in loud and clear voices that we will not and must not erect trade barriers—yet is there any doubt about how far we have gone down the fourth route? After the host of measures already taken, the Secretary of the Treasury has openly stated to the Senate Finance Committee that if the so-called interest equalization tax—itself a concealed exchange control and concealed devaluation—is not passed, we shall have to resort to direct controls over foreign investment.

We affirm that we cannot drain our reserves further, yet short-term liabilities mount and our gold stock continues to decline.

We affirm that we cannot let balance-of-payments problems interfere with domestic prosperity, yet for at least some 4 years now we have followed a less expansive monetary policy than would have been healthy for our economy.

Chairman Douglas. We thank you for that, Professor Friedman.

Mr. Friedman. Even all together, these measures may only serve to postpone but not prevent open devaluation—if the experience of other countries is any guide. Whether they do, depends not on us but on others. For our best hope of escaping our present difficulties is that foreign countires will inflate.

In the meantime, we adopt one expedient after another, borrowing here, making swap arrangements there, changing the form of loans to make the figures look good. Entirely aside from the ineffectiveness of most of these measures, they are politically degrading and demeaning. We are a great and wealthy Nation. We should be directing our own course, setting an example to the world, living up to our destiny. Instead, we send our officials hat in hand to make the rounds of foreign governments and central banks; we put foreign central banks in a position to determine whether or not we can meet our obligations and thus enable them to exert great influence on our policies; we are driven to niggling negotiations with Hong Kong and with Japan and for all I know, Monaco, to get them to limit voluntarily their exports. Is this posture suitable for the leader of the free world?

Chairman Douglas. I do not wish to interrupt you, but I would like to say that I think many visits to Monaco are for a different purpose. [Laughter.]

Go ahead.

Mr. Friedman. It is not the least of the virtues of floating exchange rates that we would again become masters in our own house. We could decide important issues on the proper ground. The military could concentrate on military effectiveness and not on saving foreign exchange; recipients of foreign aid could concentrate on how to get the most out of what we give them and not on how to spend it all in the United States; Congress could decide how much to spend on foreign aid on the basis of what we get for our money and what else we could use it for and not how it will affect the gold stock; the monetary authorities could concentrate on domestic prices and employment, not on how to induce foreigners to hold dollar balances in this country; the Treasury and the tax committees of Congress could devote their attention to the equity of the tax system and its effects on our efficiency, rather than on how to use tax gimmicks to discourage imports, subsidize exports, and discriminate against outflows of capital.

A system of floating exchange rates would render the problem of making outflows equal inflows into the market where it belongs and not leave it to the clumsy and heavy hand of Government. It would leave Government free to concentrate on its proper functions.

In conclusion, a word about gold. Our commitment to buy and sell gold for monetary use at a fixed price of $35 an ounce is, in practice, the mechanism whereby we maintain fixed rates of exchange between the dollar and other currencies—or, more precisely, whereby we leave all initiative for changes in such rates to other countries. This commitment should be terminated. The price of gold should be determined in the free market, with the U.S. Government committed neither to buying gold nor to selling gold at any fixed price. This is the appropriate counterpart of a policy of floating exchange rates. With respect to our existing stock of gold, we could simply keep it fixed, neither adding to it nor reducing it; alternatively, we could sell it off gradually at the market price or add to it gradually, thereby reducing or increasing our governmental stockpiles of this particular metal. In any event, we should simultaneously remove all present limitations on the ownership of gold and the trading in gold by American citizens. There is no reason why gold, like other commodities, should not be freely traded on a free market.

39 International monetary arrangements*

TILFORD GAINES

The agreement to realign their currency values reached in mid-December among the ministers of the Group of Ten countries was a most encouraging example of international cooperation for the common good. A potential for international monetary disruption had existed for at least a decade, and the most recent four years had been a period of intermittent crises. But when the "crunch" finally came, when a sweeping readjustment of currencies became essential if the system were to continue to function, all the principal countries cooperated to resolve the problem.

As this was written at the middle of January, the dollar was again under pressure in relation to a few other currencies, partly because of uncertainty as to whether the Congress would in fact vote to devalue the dollar against gold, but more importantly because of some "professional" judgments that the realignment of these currencies upward against the dollar had not been large enough. The answer to the first reason for uncertainty will soon be known. Congress appears to be receptive to a devaluation request from the President, and there is no apparent reason to expect problems. But no political issue with as much emotional history as this can be predicted with absolute certainty.

Resolution of the second matter—that certain currencies are still undervalued against the dollar—is impossible in the short run. There is no scientific way to judge, within broad bounds, how much realignment is too much, how much is not enough. Only the shifts in trade and investment flow patterns over two years or more can resolve the issue, and by the time these shifts have occurred changes in underlying economic and political circumstances may have made the answer irrelevant to the original question. What is important in this matter is not the validity of the judgments

* From "International Monetary Arrangements," *Economic Report* (January 1972). Reprinted by permission of Manufacturers Hanover Trust Company, New York, N.Y. Tilford Gaines is Senior Vice President and Economist with the Manufacturers Hanover Trust.

that currencies are still out of line but the fact that the sensitive market into which these "judgments" drop can move vast amounts of money from one currency to another and thus create currency "crises," whether in fact there is any justification. More on this later.

U.S. BALANCE OF PAYMENTS

From the point of view of the United States, the outcome was both more and less satisfactory than might have been anticipated—an inevitable result in any bargaining process. On the one hand, the extent of overall upward realignment of other principal currencies against the dollar—averaging 10 percent to 12 percent, depending upon the method of calculation—was somewhat larger than most people had expected, although less than the bargaining target set by the United States. On the other hand, the liberalization of trade practices by other countries that the United States had set as a prime objective was not immediately realized, although there is reason for hope that steady progress in this direction might be achieved over the months—and years—ahead.

The most important short-term consequence of the agreements in Washington last month will be some improvement in the United States trade balance and, therefore, in the United States balance of payments. Since the reflection in product prices of the higher values of other currencies will make U.S.-produced goods more competitive both in foreign markets and at home, our exports should be encouraged and imports to this country should be restrained. However, the precise estimates of the amount of improvement in the trade balance that have been circulating should be taken with a grain of salt. One must be a bit awed by those who profess to know enough about the price and income elasticities of demand for the dozens of countries and thousands of products involved, particularly in view of the non-price barriers to trade, to be able to derive precise estimates of the impacts on trade.

As a rough guess—not scientific—the overall improvement in the United States trade balance for 1972 may be in the neighborhood of $3 billion, leading to a trade surplus of $1½ to $2 billion after 1971s trade deficit (the first in nearly 80 years). The improvement could be greater, particularly in view of the various circumstances such as the dock strikes, the labor negotiations in the metals industries, advance buying in anticipation of currency realignments, etc., that adversely affected U.S. trade last year. However, the relatively slow economic growth rates expected for most other developed countries and the rapid growth rate expected for this country will have the effect of stimulating imports more than exports and, therefore, of deferring until later years the full beneficial impact of the new currency relationships.

Another plus for the U.S. balance of payments in 1972 and subsequent years should be in the capital accounts. It is broadly expected, for example, that the reduced price of U.S. common stocks because of the changes in currency values plus the better profit performance expected for U.S. companies versus foreign companies could lead to a record $3 billion or more of net foreign investments in U.S. equity shares. This total would compare with the previous $2 billion record in 1968 and only $0.3 billion (estimated) in 1971. The shift in the relative attractiveness of investment in producing facilities in this country vs. the rest of the world, as a result of the lower value of the dollar, should also over time tend to reduce our direct capital investments abroad and attract direct investments by foreign companies.

Pulling the pieces together, the "basic" U.S. balance of payments in 1972 could improve by at least $6 billion, and perhaps by as much as $8 billion. (The "basic" balance of payments does not include short-term capital movements.) As a result, the U.S. basic balance of payments deficit should be reduced to a range of $1 to $4 billion, a level which, if achieved, should lead to a considerably stronger dollar.

RESTRUCTURING THE MONETARY SYSTEM

The prospect of a stronger dollar resulting from a strengthened U.S. balance of payments is critically important for the orderly functioning of the international payments system over the next few years. Whatever the ultimate restructuring of international monetary arrangements might encompass, the dollar will remain the key currency during the transition. If the deliberations on the ways in which the systems should be amended are to be conducted in an atmosphere conducive to statesmanlike compromise of national interests, the existing system must be functioning smoothly. It can not function smoothly unless the dollar is strong.

Recognizing this, however, it must also be recognized that the December 1971 agreements that brought monetary "peace in our time" did not solve any of the underlying problems in existing arrangements that have led to the disturbances of the past several years. For the time being, the broader band for currency fluctuations around parity (2¼ percent vs. 1 percent) is helping to limit speculative money flows, but it should not be expected that the greater speculative risk in this broader band would by itself, in the absence of other adjustments in the system, preserve monetary harmony.

No doubt the most important part of the December agreements was not anything in the agreements themselves but the evidence of willingness on the part of the Group of Ten countries to compromise their differences when the chips were down.

It would be presumptuous to attempt to draw a blueprint for the ways in which the international monetary system should be redesigned so as to function most smoothly in the future. No one person writing from a single point of view could comprehend in his analysis all of the conflicting interests that will have to be compromised in negotiation. But the importance of the issue does invite comment on at least the broad outline of those things that might be considered.

THE QUESTION OF FLEXIBILITY

At the root of the problems plaguing international monetary relations in recent years has been the fact that the so-called "adjustment process" has not worked as it was supposed to. In the theory of fixed exchange rates for currencies, it is assumed that individual countries will take the appropriate domestic policy actions—restrictive or expansive—to maintain the value of their currencies in relation to each other, and that such policies will be effective. In actual fact, the world-wide drive in recent decades for rapid growth and low unemployment has often made the necessary policies politically unacceptable. And the varying propensities toward inflation among countries has made given policies more effective toward their end in one country than another. The consequence has been general recognition of the need for more frequent *adjustment of parities* to compensate for the failure of the *adjustment process.*

One approach toward more flexible adjustment of currency values that has been favored by many people, particularly academic economists, has been a system in which currency values would fluctuate freely against one another. Logically, if the values of individual currencies were to be permitted to find their own levels in a free market, it would not be necessary for a country's economic policies to be dictated by balance of payments considerations. Since, in the modern world, domestic full-employment and growth objectives are almost certain to take precedence over the balance of payments in any advanced country, acceptance of a floating currency system is no more than acceptance of the inevitable.

Flaws in floating system

The experience with a system of floating exchange rates between August 15 and December 20 last year exposed, conclusively, the fatal weakness of such a system. While almost all the principal currencies were nominally floating, their values were in fact regulated by intervention of the various central banks in the foreign exchange market. The intervention was intermittent and unpredictable as to the levels at which it might occur. The resulting uncertainty was demoralizing to the normal flow of trade and financial funds. Free float advocates argue that the system *would* have worked if the finance ministers and central banks had not intervened, i.e., if they had not felt a political obligation to take an interest in the value of their currencies. But if ever there were to be that ideal situation in which there was no such compulsion upon financial officials, the problem of obtaining prompt adjustments of currency values would disappear, whatever the "system." It is precisely because changing a currency's value, particularly upward, has important political implications that neither the present nor any foreseeable generation of financial officials will find it possible to absolve itself of responsibility for the process.

The same fatal flaw characterizes the "crawling peg" and any other automatic approach to currency relationships that would attempt to eliminate the element of political decision. As a general proposition, it may be asserted that national governments usually will not permit free market forces to determine automatically the values of their currencies. If this proposition is valid, it follows that while a period of nominal or "controlled float" might be a useful device for getting from one set of currency values to another, a truly floating system is not at this time a workable arrangement for maintaining currency values in proper relationship.

If reliance may not be placed upon a system of floating currency values to maintain equilibrium among currencies in the way that a free market maintains proper balance among the prices of competitive products, what arrangements might be devised to assure that currency parities will be changed promptly in the future so as to avoid the wrenching speculative disturbances of recent years? The simple answer is that, under present circumstances, nothing can be done to *assure* that parity adjustments will be prompt. Such assurance would require a supranational authority with power to force sovereign nations to change their currency values. The world would seem still to be far from a willingness to delegate such power to the International Monetary Fund or any international body.

Granting that the need for more prompt currency adjustments will not for the foreseeable future be met through some "automatic" device such as floating exchange rates or through a rewriting of the Articles of Agreement to give vastly greater power to the IMF, there still is reason for optimism that currency parities will be adjusted more quickly in the future and that the disruptive currency flows of recent years will be avoided. It is in the nature of international problems that involve national political interests that simple, neat solutions are not available. But having recognized the problem as one of general concern, it is likely that "untidy" solutions will be evolved as needed.

Specifically, the regular meetings of the Group of Ten countries, working in harmony with the IMF, provide the forum in which the principal free world countries may discuss and decide the marginal realignments among their currencies that may be needed from time to time. Cooperation among the Group of Ten is all that is likely to be needed for some while in the way of a formal mechanism to maintain broad equilibrium among the leading currencies.

THE PROBLEM OF CURRENCY FLOWS

The two underlying circumstances that made it impossible for the central banks and the finance ministries to maintain their currency parities once those parities had gotten badly out of line with one another were, first, the huge volume of world trade that had developed since the Second World War and, second, the growth of the international money market as a medium through which unprecedented amounts of money could be transferred from one currency to another. It was the amount of trade that generated the demand for stronger currencies to hedge future commitments denominated in weaker currencies. At the same time, the existence of a foreign exchange market big enough to service the vast growth in international trade and an international credit market big enough to provide credit funds for hedging purposes have been essential components in the growth of trade itself. Therefore, despite the problems that the huge international movements of money have created in recent years, there is no tendency on the part of financial officials in the principal currencies to take action that would cripple the market's capacity since, to do so, could endanger the future of trade itself.

This is not to say that certain actions might not or should not be taken to bring the Eurodollar market under closer supervision. If such actions were to be taken, however, it is likely that they would be motivated more by worries about credit problems in the market itself than by the market's capacity to generate flows from one currency to another. There is a good deal of interest in securing better reports from the participants in the Eurodollar market, in order that financial officials of the principal countries might better understand that market and, thereby, might be in a better position to regulate its activity. It is a safe guess, however, that any such regulation will stop short of impediments that might hamper the very useful functioning of the Eurodollar market as the credit medium to support continued growth in world trade.

The inescapable fact is that if there is to be the capacity for hedging of forward commitments that steadily growing world trade demands, and if simultaneously the international monetary system is to be orderly, then the values of the principal currencies must not be permitted to get as badly out of line as they have been in recent years. It should be expected that evidence of large misalignments of currencies will unavoidably lead to large movements of funds. With trade among nations at the levels to which it has risen, particularly among the developed countries of Europe, North America, and Asia, the potential for movements of money from one currency into another when currency parities become obviously out of line is far greater than any realistic level of international reserves could be expected to cope with. Therefore, the problem that large currency flows has created in the past few years relates primarily to the fact that the various principal countries permitted their currencies to get badly out of line rather than to the fact that a market for financing such flows existed. It follows that a first step to guard against disruptive currency flows in the future is to prevent currencies from getting seriously out of line.

Wider currency band?

A consensus had developed recently that the first and simplest action that might be taken to discourage disruptive currency flows among nations would be to broaden the band of permissible currency fluctuation around parities. The Group of Ten at their meeting last month adopted such a wider band, 2¼ percent either side of parity versus the former 1 percent. The question should be asked, however, whether a wider currency band is either at all times desirable or in any way part of a realistic solution. The greater the degree of currency fluctuations around nominal parities, the greater is the risk for the foreign exchange traders who make spot and forward markets in currencies, and the greater is the premium they must charge for accepting this risk. Also, of course, the greater the amount of fluctuation the greater is the potential direct cost to an importer or exporter. It would seem to follow that this added cost would impose some amount of restraint upon international trade. There has been evidence of this recently. Particularly in the case of smaller or less sophisticated importers and exporters, the cost of hedging or buying the currencies they need for settlements has appeared to be exerting a rather significant burden.

The solution

The problem is to structure a system that would hold currency fluctuations most of the time in the narrowest possible band around par, while at the same time preventing disruptive currency flows. The first and most obvious part of the solution is to realign currency parities promptly, as needed, and by small amounts, so as to avoid the very large misalignments of currencies that have been seen recently. If the exchange market recognizes that the maximum disequilibrium that will be permitted among currency values is a very small one, there should be an automatic tendency for speculative money flows to be smaller than they have been recently. But there's the rub. Even a small expected change in the values of two currencies relative to one another is worth speculating against in the very short run. And the influence that rumors from various sources are able to have upon expectations and movements of funds, as clearly evidenced for the past while, suggests that such speculative money flows will continue to be a problem for the future.

The object then becomes to find an arrangement whereby the day-to-day fluctuation of currencies around their par values will be held to a minimum, so as to promote trade, but whereby the influence of rumors upon large flows of funds will be discouraged. The solution that suggests itself is to increase appreciably the risk to those who choose to move money on the basis of unsubstantiated and often ridiculous rumors. A way in which risks could be increased for such people, and for the "professionals" who feed them their rumors, would be for the central banks to set out consciously to punish such speculation. For example, the rule might be that convertible currencies should be maintained within something less than one point of parity at all times, except when sizable movements of funds are set in motion. At such times, individual countries would be authorized to widen the band of fluctuation to some larger amount such as two or three percent. Currencies then would be permitted to move outside their ordinary bands, with the demand for the stronger currency satisfied by the central banks. At their option, the central banks could then step in to drive the affected currencies back to their former parities. Operating in this way, it should not take too long to get the message across that changes in official parities will be made only as and when the authorities judge they should be made and will not, under any circumstances, be forced by speculative flows of funds generated by unfounded rumors.

There is no reason why order should not be maintained in the foreign exchange markets, while at the same time holding currencies close to their par values. But for this to be accomplished it will be necessary that the present influence of those "professionals" who can move the market by generating unfounded rumors be broken. This objective should be a priority in moving toward a more orderly international monetary mechanism.

THE DOLLAR IN THE SYSTEM

A subject that has been much discussed as the negotiations on international monetary arrangements have gone forward has been the future role of the dollar in the system. The position of this country is understandably somewhat ambivalent. There have been real advantages to the U.S. in being the reserve currency country, and in having the dollar the medium in which most trade and financial flows have been denominated. At the same time, a reserve currency country has certain responsibilities in the conduct of its affairs that are not borne to the same degree by other countries. And it has certain constraints upon its ability to change the value of its currency as circumstances warrant. For these reasons, there has been a temptation for U.S. authorities to wish the dollar were "only another currency."

Decisions upon the role of the dollar are likely to be among the most difficult confronting the ministers of the Group of Ten and the Directors of the International Monetary Fund. At the end of 1971, foreign official accounts held approximately $53 billion in their international reserves, an increase of more than $30 billion in the preceding two years. Even if one were to estimate that as much as $20 billion or so of these official dollar holdings are temporary in the sense that they will gradually flow back into private hands after a stable set of currency parities has been assured, there would still remain some $35 billion in official reserves, or about 45 percent of total international reserves of other countries. With the best will in the world, these dollars will not disappear. Moreover, the dollar as the vehicle currency in which so much of trade and other international transactions are denominated is a situation that will not easily be changed if, for the foreseeable future, it is changed at all. Finally, even if the U.S. were prepared to repay the official dollar holdings that foreign officials consider excessive, the only way in which this could be done would be for the United States over a period of years to run balance of payments surpluses sufficiently large to generate the exchange earnings necessary to make repayments possible. U.S. surpluses of this order would constitute deficits for other countries, which they would surely be unwilling to incur.

Prerequisite

The problem is even more complicated than indicated above. As remarked earlier, a prerequisite for orderly negotiations leading to sustainable revisions in international monetary arrangements is that the dollar be strong. This is, of course, the reason for the recent agreements on currency parities. But if these efforts succeed, if the dollar does become strong and remain strong for a period of years, it will again become a desirable reserve currency asset. In that event, particularly since official holdings of dollars are invested in income earning assets, the dollar might again become the preferred currency as against any other national currency or, for that matter, as against Special Drawing Rights. Moreover, the reemergence of the dollar as a strong currency would not only fortify it as a reserve asset but would also strengthen it as the international vehicle currency which, in turn, would require over time an increased supply of dollars both to meet private market needs and to add to official dollar holdings for intervention purposes in the markets.

Therefore, the need for the dollar to be strong if the system is to be examined and reformed in an orderly setting automatically makes it less likely that there will be any fundamental alteration in the role of the dollar, either as an international reserve asset or as the primary currency used in private market settlements. On the other hand, failure to re-establish the dollar as a strong currency would be unthinkable not just because of the barrier it would put in the way to orderly reform of the monetary system but also because it would imply that other countries would be willing indefinitely to continue accumulating surplus dollars in their international reserves. Since this would not be an acceptable outcome, it must follow that the necessary actions will be taken in domestic U.S. economic policies, in setting currency parities, in sharing the burden of defense and aid costs, and in reducing barriers to trade that will make the dollar strong.

Gold vs. monetary system

Still another knotty issue facing the monetary authorities is the question of the relationship between dollars and gold and, more broadly, the future relationship of gold to the monetary system. There has been some pressure upon the U.S. to offer assurance that the dollar will once again be automatically convertible into gold when the U.S. balance of payments has been brought into approximate equilibrium. It would not seem too likely that the U.S. will be prepared to offer such assurance. At the same time, the U.S. probably should not expect other countries to accumulate dollars without limit and with no opportunity to exchange those dollars for other assets, a situation that has prevailed for some years. In other words, the U.S. must be prepared in the future to take action as necessary to maintain a balance of payments position that will supply no more dollars to the rest of the world than private and official holders are freely willing to accept. Assuming our ability to achieve this objective, the U.S. would then be in a position to make the dollar fully convertible into other international assets in the same way that the currencies of the other leading countries are convertible. That is to say, dollars presented to the U.S. by any other country would be redeemed with SDRs, gold, or the currency of the country presenting dollars, at the option of the U.S. Our existing credit rights with the International Monetary Fund plus the swap agreements that have been negotiated in the past decade, along with steady growth in the total of Special Drawing Rights outstanding, should provide adequate reserve resources to handle any occasional and temporary deficits in the balance of payments.

The broader question of the role of gold in the international monetary system is one that probably will be discussed and debated indefinitely until, at last, the issue finally fades away. In view of the affection for gold still held by much of the rest of the world, it is not realistic to talk about demonetizing gold or consciously phasing it out. The resolution of recent problems and the restoration of orderly currency arrangements should, in time, put to rest the myth that only a gold exchange system can be an orderly system. Growing acceptance of Special Drawing Rights, accompanied by proof through their use that they are "as good as gold," should also contribute toward the debility—not demise—of gold. Meanwhile, the immediate outcome is likely to be that official gold reserves will remain at about present levels as new gold production is sold into the free market, that all principal currencies will continue to be defined in terms of their gold content, and that Special Drawing Rights also will retain their present gold definition although they will not be freely convertible into gold.

IN CONCLUSION

It seems to this observer that there are two important considerations that monetary officials should keep in mind as they attempt to rebuild the international monetary mechanism. First, they should not be lulled by the thought that the realignment of currency values achieved last month, along with the broader band for currency fluctuation, is in any sense a solution to the problems that have plagued the system. Second, they should not accept the ambitious notion that sweeping changes should or could be made in the basic Bretton Woods structure that the world has lived with for more than twenty-five years. The immediate objective, of course, should be adoption of those cooperative efforts that will reestablish an acceptable U.S. balance of payments. Assuming success in this endeavor, and it must succeed if an orderly system is to be maintained, the longer objective should be to develop a system for *managing* the international monetary system, from month-to-month and year-to-year. This proposal would no doubt imply somewhat greater responsibilities for effective action by the International Monetary Fund. But the IMF is too unwieldly an organization to be given full responsibility, at this point in history, for effective monetary management. Such management probably will be effected primarily through the Group of Ten, where discussions on the need for changing currency parities, and other matters, can be conducted continuously.

So, where it all comes out, is that the structure of international monetary arrangements for the foreseeable future will be substantially unchanged from what it has been in the recent past. Now that some of the rhetorical fog has blown away, it becomes even clearer than before that the delegates at Bretton Woods did, indeed, build a fine structure.

C. Problems and strategies of economic development

While the United States and other rich nations struggle with the mysteries of international trade or finance, the majority of the world's people struggle for survival, and look for ways to accelerate the development of their nation's economies. The poor nations have in common their low per capita incomes, but they vary remarkably in density of settlement, literacy and educational levels, natural resource endowments, reliance on agriculture or foreign trade, and other economically relevant characteristics. When we add political and cultural diversity to these economic differences, small wonder that they have followed different development strategies.

Yet, as the following readings suggest, there are certain economic problems which all countries must face in order to accelerate development. Raising per capita incomes requires raising the productivity of labor. This involves augmenting the quantity and quality of capital per worker (including his own skill or "human capital"), as well as drawing idle or under-employed labor into new uses (which also usually requires more capital). More rapid accumulation of capital requires a larger share of current output directed to investment rather than to consumption. This larger investment may be financed by increased voluntary saving, by taxation (forced saving), or perhaps by loans or aid from abroad. The developmental payoff from the additional capital depends on how efficiently it is allocated among agriculture, manufacturing, and other sectors, and on how much of it is "capital deepening" (more capital per worker) rather than "capital widening" (duplicate capital to supply an expanded population).

Coale demonstrates that rapid population growth is a major deterrent to economic development. Low mortality rates will soon be almost universally achieved in the poor countries, so a planned reduction of fertility is the only means remaining to defuse the "population bomb." For the first 25 years, such a low-fertility policy would not significantly affect the adult labor force, but it would greatly reduce the number of dependent children. With the same total output the country could reduce its consumption and raise its investment level. Less of the new capital would go to housing, education, or additional tools for the growing population; more could go

485

to raising the capital per worker and labor productivity. Even in frontier economies (Brazil), slower population growth (and hence more capital per worker) would accelerate growth. Capital deepening and industrialization is also the solution for underemployed agricultural labor in the "over-crowded" countries.

Letwin implicitly attacks the centrally planned, "big push" development strategy which gives top priority to heavy industry and government-sponsored "social overhead" projects. He favors instead a less forced, more decentralized, and market-oriented path to development. This approach would use labor-intensive technology in a labor-surplus economy, and allocate investment resources to the socially most profitable uses, whether in agriculture or manufacturing, in government or the private sector. Foreign trade also permits the poor country to specialize in its most productive sectors, agricultural or industrial, and may also help attract foreign capital investments.

Weisskopf blames international capitalist political, social, and economic structures for much of the worsening poverty and inequality in the "third world" nations. The poor nations remain subordinate and powerless, their ruling elites caught up in the capitalist job and status structures. Dependent on exports of raw materials, imported finance, and costly capital-intensive technology, they find foreign trade no channel for industrial development. "Demonstration effect" imitation of the rich nations' consumption levels saps their saving or tax potential and misallocates their restricted investment resources into consumer goods industries or unproductive government projects. Weisskopf clearly believes that Letwin's market-oriented approach may enrich a small elite and the foreign capitalists, but it cannot produce real economic development for the masses; this would require a revolutionary socialist development strategy.

40 Population and economic development*

ANSLEY J. COALE

Most underdeveloped areas of the world have birth rates of forty per 1000 or higher and an average number of children born at the end of the fertile period—at age of forty-five or fifty—of at least 5. This fertility contrasts with experience in Europe, where birth rates are, with only two or three exceptions, below twenty per 1,000, and total fertility is two to three children. The fertility of Japan is at the low end of the European scale. Other highly industrialized areas outside of Europe—the United States, the Soviet Union, Australia, New Zealand and Canada—have birth rates between twenty and twenty-eight per 1,000 and a total fertility of three to four children.

As a consequence of the invention and application of low-cost techniques of public health, underdeveloped areas have recently experienced a fall in mortality more rapid than ever seen before. They have not had to wait while the gradual process of developing medical science took place; nor have they had to depend on the possibly more rapid but still difficult process of constructing major sanitary engineering works and building up of a large inventory of expensive hospitals, public health services and highly trained doctors. Instead, the underdeveloped areas have been able to import low-cost measures of controlling disease, measures developed for the most part in the highly industrialized countries. The use of residual insecticides to provide effective protection against malaria at no more than twenty-five cents per capita per year is an outstanding example. Other innovations include antibiotics and chemotherapy, and extend to the discovery of relatively low-cost ways of providing a safe water supply and

* From "Population and Economic Development" in Philip M. Hauser, Editor, *The Population Dilemma*, 2nd Edition, © 1969 by The American Assembly, Columbia University, pp. 59–84. Reprinted with permission of Prentice-Hall, Inc., Englewood Cliffs, N.J. Ansley J. Coale is Professor of Economics and Public Affairs at Princeton University, Princeton, N.J.

adequate environmental sanitation in villages that in other ways remain little touched by modernization.

The result of a precipitous decline in mortality while the birth rate remains essentially unchanged is, of course, a rapid acceleration in population growth, reaching in some instances rates of three to three and one-half percent per year. The underdeveloped areas with more moderate growth rates of one and one-half to two and one-half percent per year are typically in the midst of a rapid decline in death rates, and are experiencing steep increases in the rate of growth of their populations.

The high fertility of low-income countries produces a large proportion of children and a small proportion, in consequence, of adults in the economically most productive ages. The underdeveloped countries have forty to forty-five percent of their population under age fifteen, in contrast with a maximum of twenty-five to thirty percent in the highly industrialized countries. Differences in mortality among countries, whether industrialized or not, have only slight effect on the distribution of the population by age, and specifically on the proportion of the population that children constitute. Indeed, the effect of a lower death rate on the proportion of children is in a surprising direction. Mortality is typically reduced the most in infancy and early childhood; and if fertility remains unchanged, a reduction in mortality of the sort usually occurring increases the proportion of children and reduces rather than increases the average age.

There are great variations in population density from one low-income area to another, with fewer than ten persons per square mile in Bolivia, and more than 600 in Korea.

In this chapter we shall consider how these characteristics of the population affect the process of industrialization or modernization to which the low-income areas aspire. Their populations at present suffer from inadequate diets, enjoy at best primitive and overcrowded housing, have a modest education or no formal education at all (if adult) and rarely attend school (if children), and are often productively employed for only a fraction of the year. These populations suffer all of the misery and degradation associated with poverty. They naturally wish to enjoy the universal education, adequate diet, housing equipped with modern amenities, the long and generally healthy life, the opportunity for productive work and extensive voluntary leisure that the highly industrialized countries have shown to be possible. To do so the underdeveloped countries must modernize their economics.

The changes in social and economic structure that make up the process of modernization or industrialization are many and profound. More productive techniques must displace traditional methods of manufacturing, agriculture, trade, transport and communications. Economic activity must become more diversified and more specialized. The emphasis in production must shift from extractive industries, especially agriculture, to manufacturing, trade and communications. The interchange of goods through a monetary medium or widespread markets must replace local consumption of goods produced on the farm or exchanged only in small village markets. The labor force must be transformed from illiteracy to literacy. A sufficient supply must be found and trained of what has become to be known as "high talent manpower"—doctors, lawyers, engineers, entrepreneurs and managers. Production must shift from small, family-oriented enterprises into large, impersonal, professionally supervised organizations. However, many of these essential changes are related only indirectly to demographic characteristics such as growth and age distribution.

Here two important aspects of industrialization or modernization will be considered. One aspect is increasing income per person as a consequence (and an index) of industrialization, and the other is the attainment or maintenance of productive employment for the labor force.

POPULATION AND INCOME PER HEAD

Examining the implications of population change for the growth of real income we shall consider nations rather than areas within nations. The selection of the nation as the unit for analysis implies that gains or losses of population through migration can generally be considered of negligible importance. There are a few exceptions (perhaps four or five small countries that can expect gains or losses from migration of important magnitude compared to natural increase), but for the majority of underdeveloped countries and certainly for the larger ones there is no such realistic likelihood.

For somewhat different reasons, the possibility of alternative courses of mortality can also be ignored, at least for a generation or two. The basis for paying little attention to different possible courses of mortality is that the technical feasibility of reducing mortality to lower levels—of increasing expectation of life at birth at least to some fifty or sixty years—has been widely demonstrated in the underdeveloped areas themselves. Unless the effort to start and continue the process of modernization fails completely, or unless there is a breakdown in world order, the attainment and maintenance, at least for a short time, of low mortality rates seems potentially within the reach of most low-income countries. It does not appear that widespread famine or even severe increases in malnutrition are a necessary consequence in the next few decades, even if the low-income countries experience population growth rates of two to three and one-half percent.

The agricultural and industrial technology that can be introduced into low-income countries is, in a sense, parallel to the medical technology that can be imported to achieve a rapid reduction in mortality rates. Rates of increase in agricultural output of at least three or four percent a year appear technically feasible, even in such a densely settled, highly agricultural country as India. If the birth rate in India is not reduced, the population will probably double in the next generation from about 450 million to about 900 million persons. Agricultural experts consider it feasible within the next twenty or twenty-five years. In the short run, then, it can be assumed, provisionally at least, that mortality reduction can be achieved and maintained.

Finally, if sickness can be reduced and death postponed within the resources available to the health authorities in the underdeveloped countries, assisted by the World Health Organization, UNICEF, and directly by the industrialized countries, it is scarcely imaginable that by deliberate policy these opportunities would be foregone. In other words, the only factor that can be realistically considered as variable in causing population change by deliberate policy is fertility. We shall be concerned here with the implications, for the growth in per capita income and for the provision of productive employment, of alternative possible future courses of fertility. The specific alternatives to be considered are the maintenance of fertility at its current level (which would involve in almost all underdeveloped countries the continuation of an essentially horizontal trend that has already continued for generations) and, as the contrasting alternative, a rapid reduction in fertility, amounting to fifty percent of the initial level and occupying a transitional period of about twenty-five years.

Economic development and demographic variables

We shall consider primarily the implications of our demographic variables for the capacity of the economy to divert effort and resources from producing for current consumption to producing for the enhancement of future productivity. In other words, it will be assumed that to accelerate the process of modernization an economy must increase its level of net investment. Net investment here means additions to factories, roads, irrigation networks, fertilizer plants and other productive facilities. It also can include in a broad definition resources and effort devoted to education and training. It is not an intended implication that merely stepping up the rate of new investment automatically insures a major speed-up in industrialization, or assures the attainment of the fastest possible pace of modernization. Resources mobilized for productive purposes must be wisely allocated. Adequate leadership must be found for the new forms of productive organization that an industrialized society requires. Long-standing customs and traditions must be altered if new and more effective techniques of production are to be employed. In other words, a high level of net investment is a *necessary* but not a *sufficient* condition for a rapid pace of industrialization. In the ensuing analysis it will be assumed that the other crucial elements in modernization are present.

Age distribution and investment

At the end of twenty-five years there is only a four percent difference in the size of the labor force or, more precisely, a four percent difference in the number of persons fifteen to sixty-four. Let us suppose that productive employment can be found for all males of labor force age seeking employment and for all females who are not bound to housekeeping duties by lack of education, tradition, and the necessity to care for small children and who also are in search of productive employment. Let us assume further that twenty-five years from now the progress toward modernization has included the establishment of virtually universal primary education, so that the effective age of entry in the labor force is not before age fifteen. Let us also make the provisional assumption, which we shall reexamine shortly, that national income is, in the twenty-fifth year, the same for the two projected populations. If the reader objects that this provisional assumption seems unrealistic because the high fertility population would have some four percent more persons of labor force age, let him consider the offsetting fact that the low fertility population would contain only about half as many young infants and half as many pregnant women. If allowance is made for the greater number of women free to work outside the home, the number of persons actually available for productive employment would not really be four percent less in the low fertility population but might actually be slightly greater. It is certainly reasonable to disregard the small difference in size of population over age fifteen.

If there were the same total national income to be utilized by the two projected populations, the pressure toward utilizing nearly all of it for consumption would be substantially greater in the high fertility population, as a direct result of the greater burden of dependency that must be borne by the labor force. In the high fertility population after twenty-five years, there would be ninety-six persons in the dependent ages for every one hundred persons in the productive ages, while in the low fertility population there would be only sixty-five dependents for every one hundred persons fifteen to sixty-four.

The pressure to spend a higher fraction of national income on consumption can take many forms in different kinds of economies. In a capitalist economy, where investment is financed out of private savings, the fact that families with a large number of children find it more difficult to save reduces the volume of savings and hence the level of investment. When low-income families are not an important source of savings, higher fertility creates social pressure to increase the share of national income received by the poorest earners (the non-savers) in order to maintain minimum standards of consumption.

High fertility can depress private savings in two ways: (1) by reducing the volume of savings by individual families when such savings are an important component of the national total; (2) by increasing the proportion of national income that must accrue to non-savers if standards of consumption play any part in determining the earnings of low-income families.

When it is the government rather than individual entrepreneurs that provides a large proportion of national investment, fertility affects the level of investment through its effect on the capacity of the government to raise money through taxation. Suppose the government attempts to maximize the fund it mobilizes for net investment. For any given level of deprivation that it is prepared to impose, it can raise more taxes from a low fertility population than from a high fertility population with the same national income and the same number of adults in each. Even if the government does not calculate the maximum revenue it can assess, the existence of such factors as exemptions for children would automatically reduce income tax revenues.

After this lengthy review we reach a simple conclusion. Given the same labor force and the same total national income, a low fertility population will achieve a higher level of net investment than a high fertility population. It will therefore be able to make larger additions to the productive capacity of the country and achieve a higher national product in the next year. In addition, the population with a higher burden of child dependency feels a constant pressure to divert investment funds to less productive or at least to less immediately productive uses. To meet given target dates for achieving universal literacy or universal primary education, more funds must be spent on education. In a population of large families rather than small, more construction must be diverted to housing rather than to factories or hydroelectric plants.

During a short-run period of twenty-five to thirty years, the age distribution effect of declining fertility enhances the capacity of the economy to increase its net investment, and to utilize investment in more immediately productive ways. The labor force available for productive employment during the short-run period is the same, or perhaps a little larger during the first fifteen years because persons over fifteen would be the same in number and more women could participate in productive employment. Actual numbers available for employment probably become equal in the two projections some time between twenty-five and thirty years after the decline of fertility starts. The resources available would presumably be identical. In consequence, there emerges a conclusion that may seem paradoxical. During a period of twenty-five or thirty years, at least, after fertility reduction begins, the population reducing its fertility would produce a more rapidly growing national product than a population which kept its fertility unchanged. This more rapid growth would cumulate into a consequentially higher total product at the end of the thirty-year period. In other words, in the short run not only does a population with reduced fertility enjoy the benefit of dividing the national product among a smaller number of consumers, it enjoys the additional benefit of having a larger national product to divide.

Effects of labor force growth

After twenty-five or thirty years declining fertility begins to cause major differences in the growth rate, and later on major differences in the size of the adult population. The difference in dependency burden reaches a maximum by about forty years, thereafter remaining unchanged. The high fertility labor force must continue, as in the short run, to share what it produces with a distinctly greater number of dependents, and this necessity continues to impair the capacity of the economy to attain a high level of investment. But after the short run a new element, the different rate of growth of the labor force itself, assumes important dimensions.

The significance of the growth of the labor force for income per head is that higher rates of growth imply a higher level of needed investment to achieve a given per capita output, although there is nothing about faster growth that generates a greater supply in investible resources. A larger labor force requires a larger stock of productive facilities in order to have the same productivity per head. The percent of national income that must be invested merely to keep productivity from declining is some three times the annual percent rate of increase of the labor force. In other words, if the labor force were growing by three percent a year, a level of net investment of nine percent of national income would be required to prevent declining productivity, while if the rate of growth of the labor force were one percent a year, the needed level of investment for this purpose would be only three percent of national income.

This rule of thumb assumes that the stock of capital must increase as much as the labor force to prevent a decline of productivity, and assumes further that the stock of capital is roughly three times as large as the current level of national income. Yet the faster growing labor force has no intrinsic advantages in achieving a high level of savings to finance the needed higher level of investment. It needs more investment but has no inherent advantages in achieving more.

Another way of presenting the difference between a rapidly growing and a slowly growing labor force is to consider the effect of net investment at the respectable rate of fifteen percent of national income. A population with a rate of growth of three percent in its labor force can with such a level of net investment add about two percent per year to the endowment of capital per worker. If the labor force were growing at one percent, the annual increase in the stock of capital per worker would be four percent.

An economy where additional members of the labor force settle on empty land, a "frontier society," is a partial exception to the above line of reasoning. If frontier settlement provides an outlet for the growth in the labor force, it is possible that new members provide most of their own capital—by clearing land, constructing roads, building log houses, etc. Under these hypothetical circumstances the rate of capital formation might be automatically higher with a more rapidly growing labor force. However, it is uncertain whether there are genuine instances of this kind of frontier settlement in the world today. Indonesia has attempted to resettle families from densely populated and rapidly growing Java to the relatively empty land in Borneo. However, the Indonesian government has felt impelled to make a generous capital investment in the form of tools and equipment for each family, the numbers involved have been at most a trivial fraction of the annual increase in Java's population, and many of the pioneers have returned to Java after a short period.

Most underdeveloped countries find it difficult to invest as much as fifteen percent of their national incomes, and hence will find it necessary for the next generation to utilize more than half of their investment merely to provide capital for the growing labor force. In the short run a reduction of fertility would not affect this necessity. However, even in the short run the age distribution advantages of reduced fertility would increase the level of net investment that would be attained. During the intermediate period, when reduced fertility results in a substantially slower growth of the labor force, the age distribution advantage would continue. A greater capacity to allocate output to investment would be combined with a less imperative necessity to invest merely to keep up with the growth of the labor force.

Effect of density

The question of population density tends to be the dominant concept in most casual thought about the population problems of underdeveloped areas. The notion of excessive density is certainly implicit in the term "overpopulation." The underlying idea is that when there are too many workers relative to the available resources, per capita output is smaller than it would be with a smaller number of workers. Given gross enough differences in the numbers of workers being compared, it is certainly possible in principle to establish that overpopulation in this sense exists. For example, in 150 years the high fertility population that we projected would be eighteen times as large as the population that would result from fifty percent reduction in fertility. Even the labor force with reduced fertility would imply a density more than twelve times greater than at present, while the population with sustained fertility would involve a density more than 200 times greater than at present. There is little doubt that in most countries a density 200 times greater would have a depressing effect upon per capita output compared to a density twelve times greater.

There are, however, two reasons for doubting the immediate usefulness of the concept of densilty in considering population problems of under-developed areas. The first is that in this period of human history few countries have any genuine freedom of choice of policy that would have an important effect on population density (or, more specifically, on the density of the labor force) in the short run. There are few areas where realistic alternatives of promoting or retarding international migration would have an important effect upon density. It is unlikely, and I would argue strongly undesirable, that an underdeveloped country should contemplate a deliberate restraint on its public health programs in order to retard the decline of mortality and thus prevent an increase of population density. . . . A reduction in fertility does not have an important effect on density for a long time in the future. The difference in the size of the labor force is less than ten percent thirty years after a rapid and extensive decline in fertility begins. After thirty years, however, the difference in density between sustained and reduced fertility rapidly mounts, reaching a factor of two in about sixty years, a factor of three in seventy-five years, and a factor of eighteen after 150 years. In other words, so far as acceptable and attainable policies are concerned, only in the relatively distant future can the density of the labor force relative to resources be affected. In the meantime the policy that would have a long-run effect on density, namely one that reduces fertility, would through changes in dependency and differences in the annual rate of growth of the labor force have produced major economic effects.

A second reservation about the relevance of density is that it is of clear-cut importance only in a closed economy—i.e., one that does not trade extensively—or in an economy where the principal industry is extractive. Only in extractive industries—mining, agriculture, and forestry—are resources as related to numbers of workers a dominant element in productivity. For example, if India were compelled to continue to employ seventy percent of its labor force in agriculture, increasing density would inevitably mean smaller average holdings. The average holding today is only about two acres per person aged fifteen to sixty-four dependent on agriculture, and the possibility of bringing new areas under cultivation is limited.

In non-extractive industries international trade can greatly reduce the effect of limited resources. In all industries, extractive or otherwise, productivity is determined to a large degree by the stock of capital per worker. The underdeveloped areas have in common a small endowment of productive equipment per worker relative to the industrialized countries; in other words, the underdeveloped countries all have a "high density" of workers relative to capital, whether the country appears to be sparsely or densely settled relative to land and other resources.

In the normal course of industrialization the proportion of the population engaged in agriculture and other extractive industries steadily declines. In the history of every highly industrialized area a period was reached during which the number of persons dependent on agriculture was stabilized so that all increases in population of labor force age caused increases only in non-agricultural employment. The period of unchanging numbers engaged in agriculture has typically been followed by a shrinkage in the absolute number. This sequence has been typical both in countries where the initial density of agricultural settlement was very high, such as Japan, or where it was relatively low, as in the United States or New Zealand. The implications of this sequence for employment in industrializing countries will be considered later. Here its relevance is that for countries in the earlier stages of economic development some of the increases in the labor force must seek employment in extractive industries. If the agricultural population is already densely settled (as in India), this necessity undoubtedly constitutes a greater hardship or barrier to rapidly increasing incomes than in a less densely settled country.

As was noted earlier, the underdeveloped countries all suffer from what might be called a high density of population relative to *capital*. Therefore the effects not only of the age distribution but also of the rate of growth of the labor force (with their respective implicaions for the ease with which capital formation can proceed and for the rate at which it must proceed to attain given objectives in per capita output) operate in sparsely settled as well as in densely settled countries. In very sparsely settled countries the adverse effect upon the possible reduction of density relative to capital of rapid growth of the labor force may be partially offset by an increasingly advantageous relationship between numbers and land area and other resources. A larger population may, when original density is unusually low, permit the use of more efficient large-scale operations. This possibility does not imply, however, that the more rapid the rate of growth the better. Additional capital for the additional labor force is still essential, and rapid growth prevents an increase in the capital/worker rates. Moreover, from a strictly economic point of view the most advantageous way to attain a larger labor force is through immigration, because it is possible by this means to obtain additional labor without incurring the expense of childhood dependency.

Declining fertility and per capita income

A reduction in fertility has the immediate effect (during the first generation after the decline begins) of reducing the burden of child dependency without any major effect on the size of the labor force. After twenty or twenty-five years the decline in fertility begins to effect a major reduction in the rate of growth of the labor force. In the more remote future, beginning after forty or fifty years and with increasing importance with the further passage of time, reduced fertility produces a population of lower density—with a smaller labor force relative to the available resources. The age distribution effect of reduced fertility operates to produce during the first generation a larger total national product than would result if fertility had not been reduced. The greater rise in total output results from the fact that the same number of producers—the same number of persons eligible for participation in the labor force—is accompanied by a smaller number of consumers. The smaller number of consumers decreases the fraction of national output that must be allocated to current consumption, and thus promotes the mobilization of resources for economic growth. Both private savings and the ability of the government to raise funds for development are increased.

In addition, a smaller number of consumers (especially children) permits the expenditure of savings and tax receipts in ways that raise national output more (or more immediately) than other uses. Less must be spent for primary education, housing and "social overhead" purposes generally.

Another indirect effect of reduced fertility is that, as a result of larger per capita consumption, the labor force is perhaps more productive because of better nutrition, and because of the effects of rising consumption in combatting apathy, and in providing better work incentives. These effects of a reduced number of consumers relative to the producers in the population caused in the short run by a decline in fertility continue into the future so long as fertility remains below its former level. Starting after twenty-five or thirty years is the additional effect of reduced fertility in slowing down the growth of the labor force. A reduced rate of growth of the labor force means that a given level of net investment can be used to add more to the per capita endowment of the labor force in productive equipment than if the labor force were growing more rapidly.

In the long run the slower rate of growth that reduced fertility brings would result in much lower density of population than with the continuation of high fertility. Even with a fifty percent reduction in fertility, the population in most underdeveloped areas would grow very substantially during the next two or three generations. For example, in the projection presented earlier showing typical prospects for Latin American countries, with fertility falling by one half, density would be multiplied by 2.46 in thirty years and by 1.71 in the ensuing thirty years, a total increase of 4.2 times in sixty years. In spite of greatly reduced fertility, the density of workers relative to resources would increase by a factor of something like four in the next two generations.

Brazil is often cited as a country that might derive economic benefits from more dense settlement. Even with a fifty percent reduction in fertility, the population of Brazil aged fifteen to sixty-four will have increased from 38 million to 161 million in the next sixty years. This would give Brazil a population at these ages sixty years from now forty-two percent larger than that of the United States today. It is hard to argue that this density would be too small to achieve an efficient exploitation of Brazil's resources, especially since much of Brazil's vast area is of uncertain economic value. Not all underdeveloped areas have as high a current growth potential as Latin America. Current fertility is in many instances below that found in Mexico or Brazil, and in other instances success in reducing mortality is somewhat behind the achievements of the more advanced Latin American countries. . . .

The population density that would result from a fifty percent reduction in fertility in the next twenty-five years would in almost every underdeveloped area be at least adequate for the efficient exploitation of the resources available. The much *higher* density that would result from sustained fertility, a margin of higher density that would increase with ever greater rapidity the further into the future one looks, might in the most favorable circumstances cause no insuperable difficulties for a few decades. It might be possible, for example, to offset a high density of population in some areas, as Hong Kong has done, by engaging in trade, provided there remain areas of the world prepared to supply agricultural products and raw materials in exchange for finished goods and services. But in all areas, a prolonged continuation of rapid growth would lead to intolerable overcrowding.

Delaying reduction in fertility

There is a persuasive *laissez-faire* position on population policy in the pre-industrial countries, based on the following argument. Every country that has become highly industrialized has experienced a decline in fertility amounting to at least fifty percent of the pre-industrial level. Therefore, the argument runs, public policy should be concentrated on achieving the maximum pace of industrialization. The decline in fertility will take care of itself.

The generalization upon which this argument rests is well founded. All countries that have become predominantly urban, that have shifted away from agriculture as the source of employment for as much as half of the labor force, and that now have adult populations that are at least eighty-five percent literate have experienced at least a fifty percent decline in fertility. Included among these countries are: all of Europe (except for Albania); the overseas industrialized countries with predominantly European populations—Australia, New Zealand, Canada and the United States; Japan and the Soviet Union. However, it is far from clear precisely what aspects of industrialization have been instrumental in causing the decline in fertility in these countries. In some instances industrialization had preceded for a long time and had effected major changes in the economy and society before any tangible reduction in fertility occurred. For example, a marked decline did not begin in England and Wales until the 1880s, nor in Japan until about 1925. For countries that are as yet in the early stages of modernization, having very low current per capita incomes, it might take at least thirty to sixty years to attain a state of industrialization that would in itself cause a rapid decline in fertility. In fact the adverse effects of continued high fertility in the interim might in itself postpone the attainment of the needed state of advanced industrialization.

POPULATION AND THE LABOR FORCE

It is of course a drastic oversimplification to treat industrialization and modernization wholly in terms of increases in income per head. Such increases are surely a valid and necessary objective of economic development, but there are other goals widely shared in the underdeveloped areas, including better health and improved and more widespread education, rightly viewed as values in themselves, as well as means of achieving larger incomes. A nearly universal goal is that of providing productive employment for male adults and for a proportion of adult women that steadily increases as modernization proceeds. This goal, like those of better health and education, is considered as valuable in its own right, because of the degrading effect of unemployment or of unproductive employment.

The problems of "unemployment" and "underemployment," which are the subject of so much comment in the underdeveloped areas, are essentially reflections of the poverty and low productivity to which these areas are subject. Underemployment is sometimes defined as a situation in which a reduction in the number of persons engaged in a given activity would not cause an important reduction in total output from the activity in question. Examples are the presence of more porters in a railway station than are needed to carry the normal load of luggage, farming operations where a traditional set of tasks are divided among whatever family members have the responsibility for operating the farm, or a cluster of small retail shops carrying essentially identical merchandise in which the clerks or proprietors are idle most of the day because of the scarcity of customers. In most underdeveloped areas such examples are common. The existence of essentially redundant manpower that these examples indicate is called "underemployment" rather than "unemployment" because the redundancy does not show itself in the form of large numbers actively looking for work. The measurement of unemployment (and the technical definition of unemployment) has become increasingly a matter of determining the number of persons actively seeking jobs.

In most underdeveloped areas a major increase in the number of productive jobs would be needed to make serious inroads into current underemployment and unemployment. The prospective rapid growth in the labor force that such countries face adds greatly to the difficulties of achieving satisfactory employment goals. During the first generation the number of additional productive jobs that must be provided is scarcely affected by the course of fertility. The labor force thirty years following the start of a fifty percent reduction in fertility spread evenly over a twenty-five year period is less than ten percent smaller than the labor force resulting from a continuation of unchanged fertility. In a typical Latin American population the labor force would increase in thirty years by a factor of 2.44 should fertility be reduced, and 2.67 should fertility remain unchanged. In either case the provision of adequate employment opportunities is a job of frightening proportions. An annual increase of about three percent or more in the number of jobs is required if unemployment and underemployment are not to increase.

In underdeveloped areas the barrier to more adequate employment opportunity is not primarily that lack of sufficient effective demand which many economists see as the source of the apparently chronic problem of attaining full employment in the United States. The simultaneous existence of unemployed persons and idle capital equipment in the United States (a conspicuous example is the steel industry) is not the situation typical of the underdeveloped countries. The absence of opportunities for productive employment is primarily the result of insufficient productive equipment and resources for labor to work with, compounded by the lack of education and training on the part of the labor force itself.

In the earlier discussion it was seen that a population with reduced fertility has important advantages in its capacity to accumulate capital. It also can more readily provide a rapid attainment of specified educational standards. Consequently, even during the first twenty-five or thirty years following the start of fertility decline, when the number of new jobs needed each year is not much affected by reduced fertility, the advantages in reduced dependency that lower fertility brings would, by enabling higher levels of investment, permit the more rapid expansion of employment opportunity. In the longer run the reduced rate of growth of the labor force resulting from lower fertility would make the achievement of adequate employment opportunities much easier. After sixty years, for example, the rate of increase in the labor force in our model projection for a Latin American country would be 3.7 percent if fertility were sustained, and only 1.3 percent if fertility were reduced. By that time the number of persons sixteen to sixty-four in the lower fertility projection would be nearly 4.2 times as great as today, and with sustained fertility it would be eight times as great.

The magnitude of the problem of providing future jobs in the underdeveloped countries can be better appreciated when one considers the typical change in the composition of employment that accompanies the process of industrialization. In general terms the change in patterns of employment is one of increasing diversity, with reduced proportions in the traditional occupations, especially in agriculture. If the employment history in the industrialized countries is examined, the universal trend during the process of industrialization is found to be a steadily decreasing proportion in agriculture. In fact all of the more highly industrialized countries have reached or passed through a phase in which the *number* in agriculture remains constant, so that all of the increases in the population of labor force age are absorbed in the non-agricultural sectors of the economy. This phase has then typically been followed by a decline in the absolute number of persons dependent on agriculture. It is not surprising that such a decline has been experienced in countries such as England and Wales, known for their emphasis on manufacturing and for their exports of manufactured products and imports of agricultural products. It is somewhat unexpected that a decline should have occurred in Denmark, a major exporter of agricultural produce. Decreases in the absolute number in agriculture have also been recorded in countries of very different densities, ranging from England and Japan on the one hand to the United States, the Soviet Union, and New Zealand on the other.

At some stage, then, an industrializing country must, if it follows the sequence common to the history of the now industrialized countries, look to the non-agricultural sector of the economy for the provision of employment opportunities sufficient for the whole increase in the labor force. . . . In most underdeveloped countries it will be impossible to achieve these rates of increase in non-agricultural employment. They will be forced to continue to increase the number of persons engaged in agriculture. Such continued increases are at best a necessary evil. In fact these unavoidable increases in agricultural employment show the cost of an initial high level of density in a country that has a high proportion of its labor force engaged in agriculture. Such countries cannot provide non-agricultural employment opportunities for the whole of the increase in their labor forces, and because of the small land holdings that high density implies, additions to the labor force in agriculture add mostly to underemployment in this sector.

It is a reasonable, almost an essential objective that within a generation most countries should plan to provide non-agricultural employment for the whole of their additions to the labor force. . . .

This sketchy analysis is sufficient to show that the reduction of fertility would play an even more crucial role in attaining the goal of adequate employment opportunities than in the closely related but not identical goal of insuring a more rapid increase in income per consumer.

41 Four fallacies about economic development*

WILLIAM LETWIN

By fallacy I mean a truism that has been misunderstood. It is a statement which, if hedged in by enough qualifications, would be correct, but which, as commonly understood, is false.

It cannot be demonstrated that the human mind is especially given to fallacies when exercising itself on problems of economic development. But the idea of economic development is so vague that it invites confusion. Development is generally understood as the going from an underdeveloped economy to a developed economy, and an underdeveloped economy is generally supposed to be less developed than a developed economy. This circularity in the definition leads to quite unnecessary paradoxes. For instance, the national income of Nepal (the most underdeveloped economy presently on record) has been growing recently; despite that, Nepal must now be considered more underdeveloped than ever before—because the highly developed economy of the United States has been growing faster. Nobody would be satisfied to have it said that a growing boy was becoming less developed because a bigger boy was growing faster. Such a paradox is not essential to the subject.

Economic development can be spoken of simply as the process by which a nation grows richer. An underdeveloped economy, then, is an economy that is poor in a special sense—by comparison with its own economic potential in the foreseeable future. A nation founded on a tiny island in the Antarctic wastes, its land consisting of naked volcanic rock, snow-bound, ice-locked, and wind-swept eleven months of the year; peopled by a race that is unskilled, untaught and unteachable, possessing no capital—that nation would be poor but not underdeveloped, for it might have reached

* From "Four Fallacies about Economic Development." Reprinted by permission of *Daedalus*, Journal of the American Academy of Arts and Sciences, Boston, Mass. (Summer 1963), *Themes in Transition*, pp. 396–414. William Letwin is Senior Lecturer at the London School of Economics, London, Eng.

the limits of its economic capacity. Most poor nations are not poor in quite so ultimate and hopeless a sense.

The practical problem of economic development is how to make poor countries richer absolutely. To make them as rich or nearly as rich as the United States or any other rich country is irrelevant and meaningless: are they to be made as rich as the United States is now, was some time ago, or will be hence? We can hope to help the underdeveloped nations eradicate hunger; it is fatuous to hope that the citizens of all nations will some day eat the same amount of food; it is utopian to hope that all men will some day have the same incomes. In any event, to eliminate hunger and misery is a far more commendable and humane goal than to aim for mathematical equality.

The question then is how nations have become richer in the past and how others can become richer in the future. Much is known about this and much more surmised. The four fallacies cover only a small part of the ground, although all alike are fundamental and popular.

The first fallacy. Manufacturing is more productive than agriculture.

This fallacy underlies the widespread belief that the prime or exclusive cure for national poverty lies in industrialization.

Folklore has it that human beings, when they first appeared on the earth, earned their living by hunting. Later, understanding how efficient it would be to keep their prey in easy reach, men supposedly turned to grazing. As communities formed, peace and order were established, and with them the likelihood that a man could reap without hindrance where he sowed; thus cultivation began. And finally—so the legend goes—when farmers had become so proficient that they could raise more food than they needed themselves, the surplus was used to sustain urban workers who earned their claim to food by exchanging for it fabricated things, or manufactures, as they are still called.

Some such broad historical scheme—sketching a development from husbandry to industry—has been borrowed from folklore by social philosophers and social scientists, who by endorsing it and systematizing it have reinforced the public faith. This picture underlies the schematic views on economic history of men as diverse as Adam Smith, Thomas Jefferson and Thorstein Veblen, to mention only a few. It underlies also, for instance, the classification of goods that is part of an economist's everyday vocabulary: "primary" goods being those produced by agriculture and extractive industries; "secondary" goods, manufactures; and "tertiary" goods, those commodities and services generated by "service industries."

Although the notion of the historical priority of agriculture is embedded in folklore, it is not false. On the contrary, the fundamental assertion—leaving aside the details of the story—is more nearly correct than its opposite: it is certain that industry did not predate the extractive occupations, including agriculture. But the historical doctrine in its ordinary form is nevertheless fallacious, for the truth is that agriculture and industry have always coexisted; extraction and fabrication both have gone on together ever since the beginning.

Endless evidence exists for the early practice of manufacturing. Stone-Age arrowheads show that the act of capture was preceded by handicrafts; Stone-Age scrapers and knives show that the act of capture was immediately succeeded by acts of fabrication. Man is, among other things, a tool-making animal; and tools are essential because men are neither strong nor agile enough to capture many animals without tools, and also because Nature does not provide many raw materials that human beings can use, without first transforming them, for food, shelter, or especially clothing. Even the life of men as primitive as can be, is cluttered with spears, knives, pots, bags, huts, ropes and cloths—all fabricated things. Taking things from the earth and molding those things to human ends are equally essential parts of human activity.

History cannot clearly distinguish between agriculture and manufacture according to the order of their appearance; theory cannot more sharply distinguish between their natures. Both activities use land, labor, and capital in the production of commodities. The way each uses them and the character of the commodities that each produces do not fall into the neat and expected categories.

Does manufacture use more capital relative to labor than agriculture? Quite the contrary; it turns out that now, at least, and in many places, agriculture is more capital-intensive than manufacturing. Does manufacure use more power than agriculture? Some forms of it probably do; but on the other hand, the highly mechanized branches of agriculture use more power than an industry as advanced and complex as electronic-components manufacturing. Is the planning period for agricultural production longer than for manufactures? Possibly; but whereas it takes about four or five years from the time a particular automobile model begins to be planned until it comes off the assembly lines, agricultural processes such as mushroom culture take only a few weeks from seed to fruit. Does agriculture produce food, and manufacture other sorts of things? Obviously not, since manufacture produces bread, whereas agriculture produces jute, indigo, and beeswax. Does agriculture produce necessities, and manufacture luxuries? No; manufacture produces boots and brooms, but agriculture produces silk, strawberries, and orchids.

Everyone knows the difference between a farmer and a mill hand, but for the purposes of economic policy too much is usually made of that difference.

These caveats having been entered, it should be pointed out that all underdeveloped economies depend heavily on agriculture, whereas all highly developed economies generate very little of their income by agriculture. Only 5 percent of the income of the United States arises in agriculture, forestry and fishery; and only 8 percent of the American labor force is engaged in those activities. In Nepal, by contrast, 93 percent of the labor force is engaged in agriculture. In India, about half of the national income derives from agriculture, forestry and fishery. But in New Zealand, whose citizens enjoy the third highest average income in the world, only one-sixth of the labor force is engaged in agriculture, and they produce only one-fifth of the national income. The other countries of the world arrange themselves more or less neatly on this scale, neatly enough so that one would be warranted in betting that a country which specializes in agriculture is a poor country and that a country which does not is relatively rich.

That this is not a mere happenstance, but an outcome of the general process of enrichment can be seen by examining the long history of the American economy. In 1840 probably more than half of American output was being produced in the agricultural sector; by the end of the Civil War the contribution of agriculture had shrunk to one-fifth; by the end of World War I to about one-tenth, and by now to less than one-twentieth. The same pattern could be exhibited in the history of the United Kingdom or of any other industrialized society. An inevitable concomitant of national enrichment is that agriculture ceases to be the single greatest contributor to national income and in time becomes, instead, one of the lesser contributors.

But the evidence should not be misread. Agriculture ultimately becomes less important when a nation has become fairly rich; although its agricultural output may continue to rise absolutely, the *fraction* of the national income produced by agriculture steadily declines because other forms of production take on greater significance. But this does not mean that agriculture is a crutch that can be abandoned. Although agriculture is superseded in rich nations, there is good reason to think that during the period of its primacy it was agriculture, above all, in nations such as the United States or New Zealand or Great Britain, which established the base for enrichment. At some points in the development of any economy, agriculture rather than manufacture *may* be the best means of enrichment.

Agriculture, then, though neither historically prior nor analytically distinguishable, tends to be superseded by manufacture in the course of enrichment. And it should be added, manufacture in turn tends to be displaced somewhat by service industries. For what reason?

The fundamental cause of this sequence is a fairly universal human taste for refinement. In the history of the Western world, for instance, white wheaten bread has always been preferred to wholegrain wheaten bread. But white bread is inevitably more expensive than dark—all else being equal—because the former uses up more wheat per ounce of bread; in consequence, the bread of the rich was always whiter than that of the poor. For similar reasons the linens of the rich have always been finer and whiter, their furnishings more delicate, their manners more elaborate. To refine nature's products to the standards which the human imagination invents requires much transformation, that is, much manufacture, which is costly. Hence, as men's incomes rise, they spend an increasing fraction of their incomes on the manufacturing processes that turn the immediate products of nature into the goods and services that fancy requires.

A poor savage, for want of better, sits in the sand eating meat of the bear that he has himself slain, quartered, and roasted over fire. The wealthy aesthete eats the meat of a duckling that has been reared in domestic tranquility, which has been pressed and cooked with the aid of ingenious machinery and talented labor and in the presence of artfully contrived wines, and which is served to him in a setting far from natural. The former, whose income is small, eats a meal the main ingredient of whose cost is an agricultural or extractive effort. The latter, in paying for his meal, pays mainly for the labor and capital that went into setting the dish before him, the refined dish in its refined setting; only a miniscule part of the cost is accounted for by the effort of producing the duckling, that is, by specifically agricultural costs.

The technical terms describing this behavior are that the income elasticity of demand for agricultural products is low. It is not, of course, as low as all that. "Food" is not a homogeneous stuff. As their incomes rise, men choose to consume foods of the more tender and delectable sorts: spareribs and lamb forequarters are replaced by tenderloin, in the American version; in France, ordinary wine gives way to Burgundy; among Indian peasants, millet is abandoned in favor of rice. Nevertheless, in all places, the *fraction* of income devoted to the raw—that is, purely agricultural—ingredients of the diet falls as income rises. That is the chief reason why the fraction of income generated by agriculture—as "income" and "agriculture" are defined in national income statistics—is lower in rich countries than in poor countries.

This indisputable fact has been widely misinterpreted after the *post hoc ergo propter hoc* fashion. If rich countries do much manufacturing, does it not follow that a country wishing to be rich should expand its manufactures? Such reasoning is part of the doctrine, albeit only part, which suggests to impoverished nations throughout the world that to erect a steel mill is to make the first step toward national opulence.

It is easy enough to specify circumstances in which it would be anything but reasonable to set up a steel mill, or any other manufacturing enterprise. Imagine a very poor nation, very sparsely settled, absolutely closed off from the rest of the world; and suppose that each inhabitant had the same income, an income hardly sufficient to keep his family alive. In those circumstances agriculture and other extractive occupations would be the only ones; everyone would farm and fish and hunt, and in his spare hours everyone would be busy making clothing and housing, preparing meals, and fashioning implements. In such a setting, were incomes miraculously to rise a bit, nobody would think of spending the increase on anything but extra food. Nobody would think of buying any manufactured goods whatsoever, unless his income were to rise vastly beyond its existing range. Even if a foreign expert could demonstrate that the same effort required to increase the output of rice by one pound could produce instead one hundred pounds of steel, the demonstration would fall on deaf ears—for the inhabitants would want rice so badly that no amount of steel, or gold, would be an acceptable substitute. In a very poor and utterly closed economy, manufacture would be an inimical luxury.

Underdeveloped nations are neither so poor nor so closed as that hypothetical one. Since at least some of their inhabitants are not on the verge of starvation, the nation is already consuming a certain amount of manufactured goods, which may be made inside the country or imported from abroad. At that point it becomes plausible to ask whether the most efficient way to raise the average incomes of inhabitants is by investing capital— supposing there be some to invest—in agriculture or in manufacturing. The manufactured goods might, of course, find no buyers within the country; but that would be immaterial as long as the goods could be exchanged elsewhere in the world for additional food, if additional food were wanted. On the other hand, the manufactured goods might be of such a sort that they could find no buyers abroad; but that would be no fatal objection if they could be sold domestically to persons who until then had been buying similar goods imported from abroad. Whether the manufactured goods increased the nation's exports or decreased its imports, either way the foreign exchange acquired in the process could be used to buy extra food, if extra food were wanted.

In an open economy, in short, manufacturing may be a better way of getting food than the practice of agriculture. Similarly, agriculture may be a more efficient way of getting manufactured goods. The rational rule, then, is to pursue that activity which is most efficient. A nation that wants steel should not produce steel unless producing it is the cheapest way to get it; the possibility of international trade means that the cheapest way for some nations to get their steel is by producing butter or by catching fish.

Whether manufacturing is more productive than agriculture is therefore a question that cannot be answered in general, but only when one knows which branches of either group are being considered, and where, and when, and at what prices and costs. If an underdeveloped nation can produce radio circuits at a price far below world prices, but cannot produce its staple breadstuff as cheaply as others can, it will enrich itself more quickly by making the former and buying the latter. But which of these two, or of any other form of production it can carry on most efficiently, depends on the intricate relations, at each given moment, between such variables as the levels of income and rates of change of incomes throughout the world; of wage rates, interest rates, and rents at home and everywhere; of private tastes and diplomatic relations at home and abroad; and many more considerations of that sort.

All such qualifications being made, and in view of the fact that incomes have been rising throughout the world—despite the fears of neo-Malthusians who warn that the world's population will soon outrun the world's capacity to grow food—it is a safe general rule that *eventually* it will pay every nation to devote an increasing fraction of its productive efforts to manufacturing. But this is not all. The day may come when incomes have risen so high everywhere that manufactured goods too, like agricultural goods now, despite being more plentiful become insignificant in the budgets of consumers, who will begin to satisfy increasingly their desire for services.

The second fallacy.   More capital is better than less capital.

This fallacy underlies the supposition that the problems of underdeveloped countries can be overcome merely by providing them with more capital.

A simple example will demonstrate the nature of the fallacy. Consider a small farm cultivated by farmer and ox. The man follows the plow from morning until night, under a hot sun; his life is hard. Imagine that the farmer acquires a tractor. The tractor chugs merrily through the day's work in an hour, the farmer driving it comfortably under an awning; his life has become easy and leisurely. The picture rightly comforts all humanitarian observers. The only difficulty is that the farmer is now starving. True, he has more leisure, but his crop is no larger than before, and the cost of keeping up the tractor (including as its main ingredient the interest charges on the loan with which he bought the tractor) is eating up a great deal of the food he previously had. The handy, efficient piece of machinery is impoverishing him.

The case of the farmer and his tractor, translated into technical terms, shows that the use of more rather than less capital is economically rational only if the labor saved by introducing an additional capital good is worth more than the costs added by using the capital good. As underdeveloped economics typically suffer from considerable unemployment, overt or disguised, the labor saved by introducing *certain* capital goods into *certain* occupations has a proper economic value of zero. That is to say that the real economic cost of using an hour's labor in any given enterprise is measured by its "opportunity cost," the additional output which that hour's labor would have produced in alternative employment. If Robinson Crusoe can gather a pound of brambleberries in an hour or catch half a pound of fish, then what the pound of fish really costs him is the two pounds of brambleberries he must forego for it. To return to the peasant and the tractor, the opportunity cost to the peasant of the hours of labor that the tractor saves him may be zero because he cannot use the saved time productively. In that case, the use of labor-saving capital goods is sheer waste.

The more general rule under which the peasant's case falls is that the most efficient combination of resources—efficiency being measured by costs —in the production of any goods is that which uses but little of the most costly resources and much of the cheaper resources. In an economy where wages are high and the use of machinery is cheap, goods that technically could be produced either by hand work or by machine work, will tend to be produced by machine. The converse would naturally hold in an economy where wages are low relative to the price of machinery.

The application of this rule explains, for instance, why Americans buy so many new cars. The American motorists' buying habits are generally thought to be a manifestation of lightheadedness, a proof that the consumer is enslaved by advertisers, and an illustration of conformism. By contrast, the tendency of motorists elsewhere to keep their cars for much longer stretches is supposed to result from a higher sobriety or more elevated taste. All that may be; yet the contrast can be explained simply in terms of economic rationality. In countries where labor is plentiful in comparison with producers' goods, the cheapest way to repair a car is by hand labor, that is, labor equipped with a minimal supply of simple tools. In a country like the United States, where labor is more expensive relative to capital goods, the cheapest way to keep a car up to a certain standard of performance is regularly to buy a new one from an automobile factory, where relatively little labor is combined with a vast supply of highly mechanized tools. The most efficient way to repair a car in the United States is to build a new car; the most efficient way to build a new car in most other places is to repair an old one.

In the same way it is equally sensible to build roads in the United States with bulldozers and diesel earthmovers and to build roads in China by using large gangs of laborers shifting gravel with no equipment other than picks, shovels and buckets. From the purely economic standpoint, to save much of that labor in China by using many bulldozers would be a sheer waste.

It is a fallacy, therefore, to believe that using more capital in any given enterprise is economically more efficient than using less. Capital goods, like other productive factors, are efficient only when they are properly allocated among all of the various uses to which they can be put.

The decision as to how much capital should be invested in any particular enterprise cannot be divorced from another decision, how much total capital a nation should accumulate, create or use.

At any given moment, to be sure, the amount of capital at a nation's disposal is not a matter of choice but of fact. Over any stretch of time, however, the amount can be expanded or contracted. Capital goods are produced, like all other goods, by the use of land, labor and capital. The only way a nation can by its own efforts expand its stock of capital goods, therefore, is by using resources that could otherwise have been devoted to making additional consumption goods. This interchangeability, in the production process, of capital goods and consumption goods is illustrated in a farmer's choice between eating his harvest and planting it as seed; the more he eats, the less he can plant; the more he uses for current consumption, the less he can use as capital. The monetary counterpart of this choice is that income can be spent on consumption goods, or set aside as savings; and in an economy that is working smoothly, the relative outputs of consumption goods and capital goods will match the ratio of consumption expenditures to savings. All that the people of an underdeveloped economy need do to expand the national stock of capital is to consume less than they produce. Leaving aside economic perturbations and peculiarities, the less they consume relative to current output, the faster their supply of capital will grow.

A slight defect in this prescription is that underdeveloped nations are so poor that they cannot generate much capital. The income of a very poor man hardly suffices for the ordinary needs of life; he cannot be expected to restrict his consumption in favor of future benefits; his needs press too urgently to allow much concern for the future. A man who is twenty and starving would be whimsical to invest in an annuity payable at sixty. A nation full of such men would not rationally do much saving, hence would not generate much capital. It would not, that is, if the voluntary individual choices of its citizens were allowed to prevail.

But the rate of capital formation in an underdeveloped economy can be speeded up by its government. Suppose the citizens are on the average currently saving 5 percent of their incomes. If the government increases the tax rate and spends the added revenue on capital goods it can push the *national* savings rate, and the national rate of capital formation, up to any level it chooses short of the limit imposed by the size of national income. Programs of forced savings have been instituted by the governments of many underdeveloped nations. Insofar as the tax burden falls on the relatively wealthy citizens of those nations, the policy of forced savings is in effect a program of redistribution, open to approval or disapproval on the grounds generally applicable to schemes for equalizing income and wealth. Unfortunately, however, in very poor economies the national rate of capital formation cannot be raised much by any level of taxation applied to the wealthy few. Where that is the case, and it is probably a fairly typical case, the regime of forced savings may be extended to citizens who are poor absolutely, with the result that those who were already underfed are required to reduce their consumption further. The offer held out to them is that by making this coerced sacrifice now, by foregoing current consumption in order that extra capital may be created, they are guaranteeing themselves a higher income at some future time. But if it would be whimsical or mad for a very poor man voluntarily to save too much, it is surely whimsical or inhumane for a government to force him to save too much. One reads with shock of the aged bachelor brothers discovered lying dead of starvation on mattresses stuffed with money; the spectacle would be hardly more edifying had they died so because the state commandeered their income to build, for the national good, a splendid atomic power station.

There is still another way in which a nation can increase the supply of capital at its disposal, which is to borrow it from foreigners. This method, which has been used by underdeveloped nations for many centuries, is especially suitable since it can put at their disposal, quickly, capital far in excess of the amounts they could generate at home. Moreover, it is made feasible not only by the benevolence of foreign governments; the self-interest of foreign capitalists moves them, too, to invest in underdeveloped countries, for the rate of return in countries that as yet possess little capital is apt to be much higher than the rate capital can earn in richer economies. Unfortunately capital borrowed from private lenders is seldom or never received so warmly by the underdeveloped nation as when it is proffered to the government by other governments or international agencies. The reason is not only that public lenders are more likely to offer bargain rates. More often reluctance is dictated by the feeling that when foreigners invest in and own a country's facilities, especially its public services, they acquire too great a power in its political affairs. Whether this fear is realistic, and if realistic, so compelling that a nation should forego possibilities of more rapid enrichment in order to exclude the threat, is a question fruitless to consider in the abstract. It can be usefully answered, in concrete instances, only by the exercise of fine political prudence. As to the purely economic issue, there is no doubt that foreign financing is the quickest way for underdeveloped nations to expand their supply of capital. It is convenient, also, that transfers of capital conceived as loans, sometimes end life as gifts.

To accumulate capital, no matter how a nation comes by it, means necessarily to defer current consumption. As men can be short-sighted, so too can they be excessively long-sighted; they can cheat the present as easily as they can cheat the future, and in that sense more capital is no better than less.

The third fallacy. More roads are better than fewer roads.

In this fallacy, "roads" stands as a symbol for all installations having to do with transportation and communications, or more broadly, all those commonly called public works. The fallacy urges that economic development is peculiarly dependent on a dense network of avenues and wires.

As all public works are capital goods, the general arguments given earlier as to getting and spending capital apply to them also. It is urged in extenuation, however, that public works have a special character, indicated by the technical titles commonly assigned them, Infrastructure or Social Overhead Capital.

Roads are called "Social" capital not only because they are generally owned by and used by the public, but mainly because a road bestows benefits on persons who have never seen it, much less travelled it. The person in farthest Utah, as he drinks his morning's orange juice, drinks it cheaper because of a little road in Florida that enables the oranges to reach their market with less effort. It can be said, of course, that though he has not travelled that road in the flesh, he has travelled it vicariously by the motion of those oranges he consumes. Yet similar benefits will be realized also by persons who are utter strangers to the public improvement, such as the driver of a car who finds his journey to work eased because so many other commuters have taken to travel by subway, or the village gossip who sparing the expense of a telephone nevertheless feasts on the news it carries. Every public facility does social good far outside the circle of its users.

A road is "Overhead" capital because the cost of the road does not vary with the services it provides. Its cost is overhead in the same way that the cost of maintaining a facory building is no less or greater when the factory is working overtime than when it is standing idle. It is overhead cost by contrast with variable costs, such as the cost of the wood or labor that goes into table making, the total amount of it varying with the number of tables the factory constructs.

Because a road is overhead capital, and the amount of it required cannot be meted out in accordance with how intensely it is used, the investment required for it is said to be "lumpy." Some considerable investment is needed to build a length of road, whether one man or a hundred were expected to walk on it during any day. Moreover, the investment may take a long time to yield fruit. From the first moment capital begins to be sunk in the building of the road until the road is bearing enough traffic to justify its cost, years may elapse.

Now because of these three characteristics imputed to roads and other such facilities—the large investment, the long time elapsing before the investment yields commensurate benefits, and the enjoyment of benefits by people who do not in any direct or ordinary sense "use" the facility—some experts argue that social overhead capital must necessarily be provided or subsidized by the state. They argue that private investors cannot or will not make such big investments, that they cannot or will not wait so long to start earning a return on their investment, and that in any event they cannot get a sufficient return on their investment because so many of the beneficiaries are unknown, or even if known, could not be required to pay for their benefits.

Let us consider the arguments in order. A road needs a big investment, but private investors do not make big investments. But surely a big investment is only required for big roads. A short and narrow path does not need much capital. A long superhighway needs very much capital. But is it not surprising, then, that many of the biggest and longest superhighways in the United States, built by huge investments of capital, were financed by private capital, accumulated by the sale of turnpike-authority bonds in the open, competitive, private bond market? If it is said that in no under-developed economy could private citizens provide the capital to finance such a project, it might be answered that no underdeveloped country needs such roads at this point in its development—its scarce stocks of capital can be put to much more efficient uses.

The second argument is that private individuals will not wait as long as is required to realize returns on such investments. There is much evidence to the contrary. A young man freshly awarded his Ph.D. can be thought of as a capital good into which investment has been poured for a quarter of a century before it even begins to yield any monetary return. Shortly there-after, the young man will begin investing about 5 percent of his income in life-insurance, an investment guaranteed, on the average, to pay no return until half a century later. Orchards bear no fruit for five to fifteen years after planting; yet many private men invest in orchards. Private lumber companies plant seedlings that will not be harvested for thirty years. It is not clear that the state has a monopoly of patience.

The third argument is that the benefits of roads leak off, as it were, to many people who do not use them; hence the private investor could not capture an adequate return from investment in roads. The premise that leakage of benefits takes place is undeniable; but in the context it is fallacious because it implies that this is a special characteristic of roads as contrasted with other capital goods or other commodities. It is not special at all. A small boy who buys a chocolate for a penny may feel that he has been favored by a gift from the gods; he would gladly have given three cents or seven, had it been demanded. Every bargain in the eye of the buyer represents a leakage of benefits in the eye of the seller; the seller is prevented from charging a price exactly equal to the benefit only by force of the competition that presses prices down toward the cost of production. Moreover, in private production it also regularly happens that benefits leak off to persons that were not privy to the transaction. When the lady of fashion walks out in her latest creation, the boulevardier glories at the sight, but Mme. Chanel knows no way to levy a charge on him for the pleasure that her creation is occasioning. Neither can my neighbor who plants a beautiful garden.

If leakage of benefits were a fatal objection to private industry, there could not be any private industry at all. But private investors do not base their calculations on whether they can charge for *all* the utility their efforts give rise to, but only whether they can charge for enough to yield a suitable rate of return for the investment. It is true that were the leakage exceptionally severe, private investors would be dissuaded from investing, *even though* the total of all benefits realized by the whole community might amply justify the investment. In such cases, where the social benefit of an undertaking vastly exceeds the rate of return that the private investor could make it yield to him, there is occasion for the state to invest in the facility. A prime instance is a lighthouse.

Yet the abstract case that can be made for state investment in such projects encounters one great difficulty in practical application. The value of leaked benefits—or non-pecuniary social income—is difficult or impossible to assess: they are spread widely and nobody knows what precise value, in dollars, to attach to any one of them. To make investments in such cases is risky because the poverty of information subjects government officials to error, but safe because the critics of government investment cannot conclusively demonstrate that the investment was wasteful. For both reasons, the presumption ought to run against government investment in roads and other social facilities. The existence of privately financed railroads, turnpikes, airlines, canals, telegraph companies, newspapers, radio and the like demonstrates that private investors have not refused to construct social overhead capital.

Although, if the building of all public facilities were left to private enterprise, there would almost certainly be somewhat too few of them; if government builds and operates them on a subsidy basis—that is, in such a way that the charges to direct users do not completely cover the costs—there will almost certainly be too many of them. This tendency will result inevitably from the fact that every individual has a private incentive to be subsidized by government, that is to have benefits conferred on him at the expense of other citizens. This incentive operates all the more forcibly to the extent that the citizens have been taught to make a sharp distinction between subsidies from government and subsidies from their fellow citizens; the former can be claimed proudly as of right; taking the latter could not fail to have an ethically dubious tone when the grantee knows that his fellow citizens are giving the gift under compulsion. It would be too much to say that every man looks forward with delight and an ardent sense of righteousness to receiving public subsidies; yet many do. Does the man living on top of a remote mountain doubt that his letters have an immutable right to be transported to the other end of the country for 5 cents, if that is the fee required of all other Americans, for instance of a New Yorker mailing an announcement to his next-door neighbor?

The private citizen demands that his government build better roads, better schools, better facilities of all sorts. There are many private citizens; taken together, they issue commands for facilities far beyond the resources available to satisfy them. Each, after all, is asking for something that would in fact benefit him considerably but that would cost him little or nothing. Would not the total demand for foodstuffs, housing, or automobiles be exorbitant if the price to the individual demanding it were a negligible part of its cost?

Faced with such demands, may not the government provide too much road? It is possible; to answer whether it is true would require a most exquisite calculation to determine whether the benefits to be realized by the community from an additional dollar invested in roads are at any moment greater or less than the benefits from that dollar's investment in any other capital good. The question cannot be answered.

But, since every one who talks about roads says that there are not enough roads, it is important to notice that there *can* be too many roads and that a democratic government may systematically err in favor of too many roads.

The fourth fallacy. Rapid economic development is better than slow economic development.

The need for rapidity is emphasized by those who point out that the impoverished masses in underdeveloped areas are impatient and that public impatience must lead to political disorder and perhaps to communism, unless it is soothed by quick and dramatic improvements in the standard of living.

Leaving aside important doubts as to whether the citizenry of the underdeveloped nations really are as impatient as all that, and whether the inevitable outcome of impatience is more likely to be political chaos than increased economic effort, one should nevertheless point out that the remedy proposed is impossible to achieve. It is impossible to accomplish simultaneously the *greatest* possible increase in the standard of living and the *speediest* increase.

The most feasible means—though neither a certain nor a unique means —to improve the standard of living is to build up one's stock of capital. But every addition to capital is necessarily made at the expense of current consumption; it is therefore impossible simultaneously to consume as much as possible in the present and to make the best possible arrangements for increasing future income. If a man wants to maximize consumption *this year,* he should consume all his current income and more: that behavior would reflect the extreme of impatience. If another one wants to maximize his consumption next year, ten years hence, or at any future date, he should consume nothing this year, next year, or any year up to the final one, but invest, invest, and invest; in the year when he finally turns to consumption, the income available to him will be the highest possible, a proper reward for uncommon patience. If one compares the standard of living of the two, it is clear that the first one is better off for each of the years while the other is biding his time and building his fortune, and after that the second is able to live much better. In short the *level* of consumption that can be achieved and the *speed* with which it is achieved stand in direct opposition to one another.

Economic policy, to be meaningful, must be based on a choice as to *when* the maximum level of consumption that the system is capable of producing should be achieved. To decide *when* is also to decide on *how high* the attainable level will be. These two variables are linked; they are the pans of a scale, and to raise one is necessarily to lower the other.

The choice of how much economic growth a nation should aim for and when it should start enjoying the fruits of that growth in increased consumption is not a single choice but a never-ending succession of choices. In order to make those choices rationally, a great array of tastes must be consulted. Each individual knows more or less well his own tastes about how much of his income he prefers to use now and how much he prefers to set aside for the future. It is not essential that this matter of individual choice be turned into a political question, to be decided by majority vote or the judgment of experts.

If rapidity of economic growth were not costly in terms of other human objectives, everyone should endorse it without qualification; as it is, no reasonable man can prefer it to the exclusion of all other goals. It is one of many objectives, and must be weighed against the rest.

However difficult and complex the whole problem of economic development is, one of its most confusing aspects is the difficulty of ascertaining exactly how poor the poor nations are.

There is no doubt that the standard methods of national-income accounting exaggerate their poverty. In rural and simple economies, people make for themselves many of the things that the inhabitants of complex industrialized economies do not make for themselves but buy from others. National income statistics usually and necessarily differentiate between goods exchanged in markets and identical goods that do not enter the market; the value of the former appearing in the total, the latter not. The textbook instance is that national income falls when a man marries his housekeeper, and rises when instead of shaving himself he goes to a barber. But in African villages, householders build their own huts; and throughout the underdeveloped world, neighbors sing and dance for each others' entertainment instead of going to concert halls to buy the services of paid performers. National income statistics cannot easily register the value of unbought services since those do not leave tangible traces in accounting records. The standard of living in non-industrial nations is much understated by ordinary statistics.

This is all the more true because national income statistics cannot and do not take into account the value of leisure. Imagine two identical farms, each producing one thousand bushels of wheat in a year, the only difference being that one farmer works fourteen hours each day and the other somehow manages to do the work in six; from the standpoint of national income statistics, the two farmers would be enjoying identical incomes even though it is obvious that the true income of the second is very much greater if he attaches any positive value to leisure. Time free from labor is not necessarily leisure, as it may yield nothing but boredom or frustration; but it should be remembered that men who live in industrialized societies have very assiduously trained themselves to attach a lower value to leisure than men have at other times and places. To the extent that people in underdeveloped nations do attach a high value to leisure, the statistics badly understate their total incomes by leaving out of account the psychic, non-pecuniary components of their incomes.

A further consideration suggesting that the poverty of underdeveloped nations is different in character than we suppose, arises from the reflection that the poorest nations are almost all tropical and tropical nations are poor. Not much is made of this beyond the platitude that men do not thrive in extreme heat, but insects and bacteria do. It seems a more plausible generalization, however, that a perpetually warm climate is highly favorable to human life; it reduces man's need for food, clothing and shelter; and at the same time it puts in his hands throughout the year—and not only in one short season—a plentiful supply of plants and animals.

From this standpoint the economic civilization that northern peoples have developed is a colossal exercise in irony. Having deliberately planted themselves in inhospitable regions, they have been forced to overcome the hazards of nature by donning heavy clothing, erecting bulky housing, and forcing crops from a reluctant earth. Then, having made all those things, the need for which was imposed only by the unsuitable setting in which they perversely decided to live, they have weighed all those goods, and finding them many, they call themselves rich.

But, if by contrast the inhabitants of perpetually warm places have Nature as an ally, why are they in fact so poor? The answer, perhaps, is that only in warm places can people as poor as they continue to live.

It cannot be denied that in the underdeveloped nations, however high a value the inhabitants may assign to leisure and the other pleasures of a simple life, many of them are too poor to enjoy anything at all. The entirely laudable desire to help relieve them will not have been very effective if, in the rush for a remedy, it urges cures that eradicate old miseries only to install new miseries in their place. A physician carried away by the pain of the victim and the impatience of the victim's friends does not work at his best.

42 Capitalism and underdevelopment in the modern world*

THOMAS E. WEISSKOPF

I shall argue in this paper that capitalism in the poor countries of the modern world is likely to *perpetuate* underdevelopment in several important respects. First, the increasing integration of the world capitalist system will tend to heighten the economic, political, and cultural subordination of the poor countries to the rich. Second, capitalist institutions within the poor countries will tend to aggravate rather than to diminish inequalities in the distribution of income and power. And third, capitalism will be unable to promote in most poor countries a long-run rate of economic growth sufficiently rapid to provide benefits to the whole population or to reduce the income gap between the poor and the rich countries.

THE PRESENT SITUATION

To analyze the role of capitalism in the poor countries, it is useful first to consider some economic characteristics of contemporary underdevelopment. These characteristics are to a significant degree the result of the colonial history of the poor countries—a long history of subjugation that has transformed their social, political, and economic structure.

First of all, and most obviously, there is an enormous gap between standards of living in the poor and the rich countries. The average per capita income of the poor countries of Asia, Africa, and Latin America is less than one-tenth of its value for the rich capitalist countries. Second, the distribution of income and wealth tends to be even more unequal in the poor than in the rich countries. The available evidence suggests that the top 5 percent of the population receive on the average about 30 percent

* From "Capitalism, Underdevelopment and the Future of the Poor Countries." Abridged and reprinted with permission of the Macmillan Company from *Economics and World Order* by Jagdish Bhagwati. Copyright © 1972 by the Macmillan Company. Thomas E. Weisskopf is Associate Professor of Economics at the University of Michigan, Ann Arbor, Mich.

of the income in the nonsocialist poor countries and about 20 percent in the nonsocialist rich countries.

Third, the poor countries today are in various respects economically dependent upon the rich. Exports from the poor countries consist chiefly of primary products (agricultural produce and raw materials) and flow mainly to markets in the rich countries, whereas the imports of the poor countries consist chiefly of manufactures that are obtained mainly from the rich countries. Export earnings in most poor countries are highly concentrated in a few commodities: on the average, the principal export commodity accounts for almost one-half, and the top three commodities almost three-quarters, of total earnings from merchandise exports. This concentration makes the poor countries extremely vulnerable to changes in a few commodity prices and results in periodic balance of payments crises for which external assistance is required. Most areas of the underdeveloped world show a marked deficit in their balance of trade that must be met by an inflow of foreign capital. Furthermore, there remains in most poor countries a substantial degree of foreign ownership and/or control of domestic resources.

Finally, most of the poor countries are characterized by a pronounced economic dualism. A modern, foreign-oriented, largely capitalist sector can be found in a few major urban centers and around important sources of raw materials, while the rest of the country remains dominated by a more traditional, wholly indigenous, largely precapitalist sector. The significance of the modern sector varies greatly among poor countries, depending upon their colonial history and the more recent impact of the postwar expansion of world capitalism.

Related to these economic characteristics are several important socio-political features of contemporary poor countries that affect the growth and operation of capitalist institutions. First of all, the poor countries are typically characterized by a class structure in which power is highly concentrated among a small set of elites. These include on the one hand classes whose power is associated with the traditional sector and who constitute an aristocracy of long standing: large holders of land, wealthy traders, and other precapitalist elites whose dominance in the countryside was accepted and often strengthened by colonial rule. The elites also include several newer classes whose prominence is associated with the growth of the modern sector and the achievement of political independence: the big bourgeoisie, including established foreigners and emerging nationals, and the highly educated and westernized national professionals, bureaucrats, and military officers who have displaced their colonial predecessors. While the relative strength of these elite classes varies from country to country, depending on the local conditions and the extent of social and economic change, their combined membership is almost everywhere very small in comparison to the mass of small cultivators, landless agricultural laborers, unskilled workers, and unemployed or underemployed persons of all kinds who make up the bulk of the population. Between the elite classes at the top and the masses at the bottom here is usually only a very small middle class of pety businessmen, semiskilled blue- and white-collar workers and small property owners.

Such a class structure in turn results in a state apparatus that is largely controlled by and responsive to the interests of the elites—no matter what the formal nature of the political system. Because of their overwhelming power and prestige, the elites form a relatively cohesive ruling class: internal conflicts are minimized by a strong common interest in maintaining overall ruling class hegemony. Thus there are rarely decisive struggles between older and newer elites; the society remains in some degree both pre-capitalist and capitalist, and the nonruling classees are rarely able to turn ruling class divisions to their own advantage.

A final important characteristic of contemporary poor countries is their dependent relationship with the centers of capitalist enterprise. This dependence arises partly out of the colonial legacy. Many economic activities in the modern capitalist sector depend either directly on foreign ownership and control or indirectly on foreign technological or managerial aid. Under such circumstances, it is only natural that a considerable fraction of the emerging domestic capitalist class finds itself in a subordinate and dependent position vis-à-vis the foreign capitalist class. For similar reasons, many governments in the poor countries are dependent upon the advanced capitalist powers for political and military support. Thus, capitalism in the poor countries today is not the relatively independent capitalism of old which stimulated the economic growth of England, the United States, Japan, and other rich capitalist countries. Rather, the capitalism which is spreading in today's poor countries is far better described as a dependent form of capitalism, embedded within the world capitalist system as a whole.

INCREASING SUBORDINATION

There are several factors at work within the world capitalist system to reinforce the subordination of the poor to the rich countries. These can briefly be described as the demonstration effect, the monopoly effect, the brain-drain effect, and the technology effect. Each of these effects serves to intensify the demand of the poor countries for resources and skills available mainly in the rich, thereby contributing directly to economic dependence and indirectly also to political and cultural subordination.

First of all the increasingly close ties between the poor and the rich countries that accompany the integration of world capitalism give rise to a "demonstration effect" whereby the consumption patterns of the rich countries are to some extent emulated by those citizens in the poor countries who are in a position to afford it. Of course, the majority of the population of a poor country cannot afford to consume like the majority of the population in a rich country; however, the elite classes in the poor countries (and, to some extent, the middle classes) can orient their consumption patterns toward those of their counterparts in the rich countries. To the extent that they do so, their consumption tends to rise and to be oriented toward characteristically foreign types of goods. This in turn leads to a relatively high demand for foreign exchange, either because the goods must be directly imported from a foreign country, or because their production in the underdeveloped countries requires the import of foreign raw materials, technology, or expertise.

The second important factor that tends to perpetuate the economic dependence of the poor on the rich countries—the "monopoly effect"—arises from the relationship between domestic and foreign private enterprise. Foreign enterprise has a distinct advantage over domestic enterprise in the poor countries with respect to technology, know-how, markets, finance, etc.; often their monopolistic control of some or all of these factors accounts for their interest in investing in the poor countries. Even when the poor country does not rely directly on foreign enterprise to produce goods and services, it is often the case that it must rely on collaboration with foreign firms or on some kind of indirect affiliation with foreign private enterprise. While such collaboration and affiliation may serve to increase the productive capacity of the economy, at the same time it carries with it an unavoidable relationship of dependence.

Furthermore, it is typically within the interest of foreign private enterprise to maintain the conditions in which its activities or its aid are essential, for considerable monetary rewards accrue to its monopoly of productive techniques and expertise. Thus the incentives are structured in such a way that it is usually not in the interest of a foreign firm to impart to a domestic counterpart the knowledge or the skills or the advantages upon which its commercial success is based. Under such circumstances, domestic enterprise remains in a subordinate position and an important part of the indigenous capitalist class remain dependent upon foreign capitalists. The interest of this part of the indigenous capitalist class becomes associated with that of their foreign collaborators or benefactors, and the impetus as well as the means for them to develop into an autonomous national bourgeoisie is dulled.

The technical and managerial dependence of poor on rich countries is often exacerbated by a substantial "brain drain": the emigration of scientists, engineers, business managers, and other highly educated professionals from the poor to the rich countries where they can expect better-paying jobs and a more stimulating work environment. This outward flow of skilled labor, small in absolute size but very great in potential value because of its scarcity in the poor countries, is both facilitated and promoted by the increasing integration of world capitalism. Where people are encouraged to respond to individual monetary rewards, rather than collective social goals, and where strong forces are operating to attract valuable resources from backward to advanced areas, disparities tend to become cumulatively greater over time.

The last general factor that tends to reinforce the economic dependence of the poor on the rich countries within the world capitalist system results from the choice of production techniques adopted in the poor countries. The technology that is used both by foreign and domestic firms in the modern sectors of the economy is typically very much influenced by production techniques that are used in the rich countries. Such techniques, arising as they do from an economic environment in which labor is scarce and capital is relatively abundant, tend to use more capital and less labor than would be desirable in poor countries. Since the required capital goods—and often also the patents and other rights associated with the production and marketing of the output—must usually be imported from abroad, these techniques tend also to generate a relatively high demand for foreign exchange. This effect is most pronounced when a foreign firm establishes itself directly in a poor country because that enterprise will have an interest in using equipment and services from its own country. But the same effect comes about indirectly when domestic firms collaborate with foreign firms or even if they simply borrow technology from a rich country.

Continued economic dependence implies also continued political subordination. So long as governments of poor countries must seek short- and long-term economic aid from the advanced capitalist countries and the international organizations that are primarily funded by those same countries (the International Bank for Reconstruction and Development, the International Monetary Fund, etc.), their political autonomy will be severely restricted. Furthermore, it follows from the nature of the links between domestic and foreign capital described above that a significant part of the domestic capitalist class is likely to be relatively uninterested in national autonomy insofar as it conflicts with the interests of its foreign capitalist partners or benefactors. Thus the state is likely to be under considerable domestic pressure to curtail whatever nationalist instincts it might otherwise have.

Finally, the continuation of economic and political dependence is likely to limit the development of cultural autonomy as well. The more dependent the country is on foreign help of one kind or another, the greater will be the foreign presence in the country, and the greater the impact on indigenous social and cultural life. International capitalism is especially threatening to the cultural autonomy of poor countries because of the strong interest that capitalist firms have in transmitting the kind of consumerist mentality that stimulates the market for their products. The same kind of demonstration effect that biases demand in the poor countries in favor of foreign goods and services also serves to favor the import of foreign styles and fashions at the expense of domestic cultural autonomy. Just as a concentration of purchasing power in the hands of the elite classes accentuates the demand bias, so the dominance by the foreign-oriented elite—and often foreigners themselves—of educational institutions, communications media, and cultural resources tends to amplify the threat to indigenous cultural development.

INCREASING INEQUALITY

The nonsocialist poor countries are already characterized by great inequality in income, wealth, and power—greater even than in most of the nonsocialist rich countries. Yet there are forces at work in the poor countries that are likely to increase further the degree of inequality over time. Some of these forces are common to all capitalist societies; others are operative only in poor countries within the contemporary world capitalist system. The tendency toward increasing inequality in the poor countries means that the benefits of any economic growth will accrue primarily—if not wholly—to a privileged minority, and very little will trickle down to the masses.

In analyzing the distribution of income in the poor countries, it is useful to distinguish not only between the two basic factors of production—labor power and capital—but also between "pure" labor power and labor "skills." Pure labor power represents the natural productive ability that every able-bodied person has; it is by definition very equally distributed in any society. Labor skills represent additional productive attributes that can be acquired by an individual through a process of formal or informal education and training. Like capital, labor skills can be very unequally distributed.

The vast majority of the people in the poor countries depend wholly or primarily on their own pure labor power for their sustenance. The ownership of most of the capital and labor skills is confined to a small minority of the population, including often foreigners as well as domestic elite groups. In a society in which income is distributed roughly according to the market value of the factors of production owned by each individual such equal factor ownership necessarily results in a very unequal distribution of income. In order for income inequality to be reduced in the nonsocialist poor countries, there would have to be either: (a) a more equitable distribution of ownership of capital and labor skills; or (b) an increase in the share of national income representing the returns to the most equally distributed factor—pure labor power.

A redistribution of existing claims to capital is not likely to get very far. In the first place, the respect for private property that is fundamental to capitalism precludes any large-scale dispossession of the rich in favor of the poor. The requirement of compensation and the political strength of the rich vis-à-vis the poor will work to limit the comprehensiveness and the effectiveness of any measures of redistribution. And the labor skills acquired by the educated elites cannot by definition be redistributed among the population.

Increases in the supply of capital and labor skills are unlikely to be any more equitably distributed. Capitalist growth has always been characterized by a tendency toward increasing concentration of capital. Even the distribution of new skills through the expansion of the educational system tends to provide disproportionately great benefits to those classes already most favored. To expect intervention by the state to counter effectively these tendencies is to attribute to the lower classes a degree of political power and influence that could only result from a fundamental transformation of the social structure of the society.

The prospects for any improvement in the distribution of income thus appear to hinge on the possibility of an increase in the share of national income due to pure labor power. The amount of income due to pure labor power is equal to the product of the number of fully employed workers (or their equivalent) and the basic annual wage paid for pure labor. In order for this amount to increase as a share of national income, either the level of employment or the basic wage rate (or some combination of the two) would have to rise more rapidly than the total income of the economy.

In most of the poor countries in recent times the rate of growth of population has not been as rapid as the rate of growth of total income, and we can infer that the growth of the labor force has also lagged behind the growth of income. Under such circumstances, it would take a continuous and substantial reduction in the rate of unemployment merely to enable the level of employment to keep pace with the growth of income. A long-run increase in the share of total income due to pure labor power would most likely depend upon a rise in the basic wage rate more rapid than the growth of income. In fact, however, there are several forces which restrain the growth of demand for pure labor in a nonsocialist poor country and thereby limit reduction of unemployment and increases of the basic wage rate. As a result, the share of total income due to pure labor power is unlikely to increase over time.

First of all the adoption of techniques of production in both industry and agriculture that have been developed in the rich countries tends to limit the demand for pure labor power. This is because the technology developed in the rich countries, where capital and labor skills are relatively less expensive, is designed to economize on the use of the relatively more expensive pure labor power. But foreign firms naturally tend to import techniques of production from their home country. And domestic firms that collaborate or enter into licensing agreements with foreign concerns are also likely to be influenced by foreign technology. In general, the more closely the poor country is integrated into the world capitalist system, the stronger will be the tendency to adopt excessively labor-saving techniques of production.

A second factor influencing the choice of techniques by capitalist enterprise in the poor countries relates to the problem of labor discipline. Because of the difficulty of organizing large numbers of untrained workers, the individual capitalist employer often has an incentive to keep down the size of his work force and to pay a small number of more skilled workers relatively high wages rather than pay a large number of untrained workers low wages. And the capitalist class as a whole has an interest in cultivating a labor aristocracy whose interests will be tied to those of the ruling elites rather than to the masses; this serves to fragment the labor force and thus to inhibit the development of a revolutionary working class consciousness. To the extent that such forces operate, the benefits of employment are limited to only a part of the working classes, and labor skills are substituted for pure labor power.

The tendency to underutilize pure labor power is further reinforced by the distorted prices that often characterize markets in the nonsocialist poor countries. Money wage rates in urban areas of poor countries are usually higher than the rate at which employers would be willing to hire all the available labor. This results *inter alia* from concessions made by the state to organized labor in response to union pressures; it favors the minority of organized workers at the expense of the majority who are unorganized. At the same time, the price of capital to private enterprise is often understated because of the various types of government programs, subsidies, and other benefits which aid the investor. The result is that firms tend to use more capital and less labor than would be desirable from the point of view either of greater efficiency or of a more equitable distribution of income.

All these effects serve to restrain the growth of demand for pure labor power in the poor nonsocialist countries. As a result, the share of pure labor power in national income is likely to decrease over time, and growing inequalities in the ownership of the other factors—capital and labor skills—will contribute to growing inequality in the overall distribution of income. Corresponding to this increasing economic inequality—and continually reinforcing it—will be an increasing inequality in the distribution of political power as well.

INADEQUATE GROWTH

Increasing subordination and increasing inequality are not necessarily inconsistent with a positive rate of economic growth. Yet capitalist institutions—both domestic and international—impose serious constraints upon the ability of poor countries to sustain a long-run rate of growth adequate to provide material gains for everyone. Economic growth depends in large measure upon the accumulation of physical capital, the spread of labor skills and education, and the adoption of improved methods of economic organization and production. These, in turn, require that the economic resources of a society be mobilized on a substantial scale and channeled into productive investment and other growth-oriented activities. In the following pages, the constraints imposed by capitalism on resource mobilization and resource utilization in the poor countries will be discussed in turn.

Resources can be mobilized either from internal sources, principally in the form of domestic savings, or from external sources, in the form of foreign aid or private capital inflow. The highly unequal distribution of income that characterizes the nonsocialist poor countries would at first appear to favor relatively high rates of domestic saving, for it restrains the consumption of the majority of the population while placing very high incomes in the hands of the few. These high income recipients might be expected to save a larger share of their excess income than would be saved by the poor if the income were redistributed to them.

Yet there are also important forces working in the other direction. The demonstration effect of consumption patterns of the rich countries on the upper and even middle classes in the poor countries tends to stimulate luxury consumption rather than saving. This effect is likely to increase with the increasing integration of the world capitalist system and, therefore, to constitute an increasingly serious obstacle to private domestic saving in the poor countries. As for public domestic saving, the high concentration of political power that follows from the inequality of income distribution in nonsocialist poor countries seriously limits the ability—if not the desire —of governmental authorities to raise revenues from the excess income of the upper classes. Furthermore, the demonstration effect often operates just as strongly on government officials to increase public consumption as it does on private individuals to increase private consumption.

Even where a substantial amount of domestic savings can potentially be mobilized in a poor country, these savings may not in fact be transformed into productive investment because of a shortage of critical imported materials required for investment. It has been noted earlier that world capitalist integration tends to generate an excessive demand for imported products in the poor countries. The result is often serious balance of payments difficulties which limit the availability of foreign exchange for investment projects.

Finally, one potentially very important source of domestic resource mobilization in the poor countries is largely ruled out by a capitalist system of social organization. In many poor countries—especially in densely populated areas—there is much labor power that remains idle because of widespread unemployment or underemployment. In principle, this labor power could be usefully applied to public development projects. Yet it has proven very difficult in the nonsocialist poor countries to mobilize this labor for productive purposes, because the workers potentially involved have little reason to believe that the benefits of their endeavors would be distributed any more equally than income is generally distributed in their society. Furthermore, an important element in mobilizing a large and previously idle labor force to useful activity is a psychological sense of solidarity and commitment to a common, worthwhile cause. With its emphasis on individual achievement and competition, capitalism fails to provide an ideological basis for rallying large numbers of inexperienced and previously idle laborers to a constructive, collective effort.

Because of the difficulties of domestic resource mobilization, many of the governments of poor countries have looked to the richer countries for much needed resources. Unfortunately, for those countries that are inclined to rely on foreign help, the prospects for increasing net inflows of foreign capital from the rich countries to the poor do not appear very bright. As far as foreign aid is concerned, the overall level of net aid provided by the rich capitalist countries to the poor fluctuated between six and seven billion dollars in the 1960s and now shows every sign of decreasing rather than increasing. At its peak, the flow of net aid was only equal to approximately 15 percent of gross investment in the nonsocialist poor countries.

Even though the prospects for high levels of foreign aid appear rather bleak, it remains conceivable that the flow of private capital could take up the slack. Such is in fact the exhortation often made in the rich capitalist countries. Yet foreign private capital does not flow to the poor countries out of a sense of service; it flows in the expectation of generating profits which will ultimately be remitted at home. Whether these profits are repatriated directly in the form of investment income or indirectly in the form of artificially high prices of inputs exported from the home base, they constitute a return flow of capital that sooner or later offsets the original flow to the poor country. In every year since World War II, the reported income repatriated from U.S. foreign private investment has in fact exceeded the outward flow of private investment funds. Unless foreign investment rises continuously and rapidly in a poor country, it is unlikely to make a net contribution to the mobilization of resources.

In sum, only these countries whose small size makes it possible for limited amounts of foreign capital to go a long way can expect to rely largely on external sources of funds. The only nonsocialist poor countries that are likely to escape any problems of resource mobilization are those which are fortunate enough to be well-endowed with scarce natural resources (such as oil) that yield both high profits to the firms exploiting them and high tax revenues to the state. In such countries, the question is simply whether the available resources will in fact be utilized productively by the existing government authorities.

There are several forces at work in nonsocialist poor countries which tend to limit the effectiveness of resource utilization. In the first place, a substantial amount of private investment resources is drawn into activities which are relatively unproductive from the point of view of long-run growth. Such fields as trade, commerce, and real estate are attractive to private investors because they often promise quicker and surer returns than agricultural or industrial investment. For similar reasons, private—and especially foreign—investors typically prefer to invest in consumer goods industries rather than in capital goods industries. Consumer goods cater to well-established markets and involve limited risks, while capital goods often require a larger and longer commitment of resources and generally face less predictable demand conditions. This preference for consumer goods on the supply side serves to reinforce the consumption-oriented structure of demand that limits the mobilization of resources for growth. The failure to develop domestic capital goods industries in a poor country also hinders long-run growth because it confines the available technological options to productive techniques associated with the use of foreign capital equipment.

Just as capitalist market institutions in poor countries tend to turn the sectoral allocation of investment against growth-oriented activities, they also have an unfavorable impact on the choice of techniques within any given activity. For reasons described above, there tends to be insufficient employment of unskilled labor and excessive use of skilled labor, capital, and foreign exchange in nonsocialist poor countries. Quite apart from its impact on subordination and inequality, this represents a form of resource utilization that is inefficient from the point of view of increasing output and growth. Skilled labor, capital, and foreign exchange are scarce resources in the poor countries and should be carefully economized rather than lavished on a limited number of activities. And unskilled labor is an abundant resource that could make a much greater contribution to output if given adequate employment opportunity.

The inefficiencies inherent in the use of the free market criterion of private profit maximization to allocate resources have been widely recognized and much discussed in the literature on economic development. There are many good theoretical and institutional reasons to expect that the unconstrained operation of the free market would not maximize economic growth, much less any more broadly defined social goal. For these reasons, the state is usually called upon to intervene directly or indirectly into the operation of a capitalist economy in order to steer it toward desired objectives. In many nonsocialist poor countries, the government does in fact affect significantly the allocation of resources. However, the critical question is not *whether* the state intervenes, but *how* it affects the operation of the economy.

To answer this question, one must recognize that the capitalist state does not function in a political vacuum; it responds to the dominant political forces in the society. Thus the government of a nonsocialist poor country will intervene to promote economic growth only insofar as this does not significantly conflict with the interests of the more privileged and influential classes. Unless the interests of the latter coincide with a growth-maximizing strategy, government policy can not be expected to lead to maximum growth.

In fact, in many important respects a growth-oriented policy does conflict with powerful class interests. The disinclination or inability of government authorities to raise substantial revenues by direct taxation of upper-class incomes has already been cited as an obstacle to resource mobilization in nonsocialist poor countries. As far as resource utilization is concerned, government policy can and does in many ways serve limited interests at the expense of overall economic growth. High import tariffs to protect domestic industries often permit indigenous and foreign firms to make lavish profits while producing in a costly and inefficient manner. Government rationing of capital and foreign exchange often allows the most influential firms to obtain these factors at a relatively low price and thereby permits high profits while encouraging low priority use of scarce factors. As noted above, minimum wage legislation can serve the interests of organized labor at the cost of overpricing and hence under-utilizing unskilled labor.

The allocation of government expenditure is also subject to many points of conflict between a growth-maximizing strategy and the interests of elite minorities. For example, the power of the urban upper classes operates to influence the educational expenditures of the state in favor of urban and higher education at the expense of rural and lower education. Yet there is evidence that the economic returns to primary education are much greater than to higher education in most poor countries. Government expenditures on public sector activities that might compete with private enterprise—domestic or foreign—tend to be discouraged in favor of investment in infrastructural facilities that lower the cost of essential inputs to private firms. All this is not to deny that—within the limits imposed by its ability to raise resources—the state in a nonsocialist poor country can and does undertake programs to stimulate growth. The essential point, however, is that the extent and the effectiveness of these programs are invariably compromised by the class interests that constrain the functioning of the state apparatus.

In sum, capitalist institutions in the poor countries—linked to and strengthened by the expanding world capitalist system—place important constraints upon the mobilization and the utilization of resources for economic growth. As a result, it would appear likely that only a few of the most favored nonsocialist poor countries could achieve a satisfactory long-run rate of growth.

D. Market pricing in different economic systems

Market capitalism and central-planning socialism have traditionally been considered the opposing extremes or "ideal types," of political-economy. Ideological conflict between American capitalism and Soviet Communism has sharpened this apparent polarity. The "third world" of less developed nations supposedly stands apart and between the two dominant systems, uneasily choosing one of the dominant models for economic development, or sometimes seeking a compromise "neutral" position.

In place of this traditional "cold war" dualism, Galbraith and others have predicted the "convergence" of the capitalist and socialist systems. The expanding capitalist state has penetrated and diminished the laissez-faire market sphere, in order to plan growth, maintain Keynesian stability, redistribute income, and pursue other social goals. Meanwhile Soviet central planners, seeking the allocative efficiency and productivity gains required for sustained economic growth, have increasingly relied on market prices and profit incentives.

Going beyond the traditional capitalist-socialist dichotomy, and its "convergence" corollary, Lindblom proposes a more pluralistic interpretation of diverse political economies, combined with a nonideological conception of prices and markets as economic mechanisms which may function under any of the systems. He demonstrates that prices can serve as "signals" for decisions on what goods to produce or what mix of capital and labor inputs to employ, whether these decisions are made by sovereign consumers, Soviet central planners, Indian investment planners, or American Congressmen. Usually these price signals are transmitted and become influential through some sort of market exchange process between buyers and sellers (including the government in either role), but "shadow prices" even arise in nonmarket decision making by Soviet planners. He might have added that these same computerized "shadow prices" guide nonmarket planning within General Motors and other multidivisional capitalist corporations!

Lindblom surveys the historical evolution of the price-market mechanism in various capitalist, socialist, and "third world" countries. He emphasizes a trend toward increased and more sophisticated use of the mechanism, and argues that further use would especially benefit the less developed economies, where "selective intervention" by central planners in an expanded market system might compensate for scarce administrative skills and investment resources and enlist mass participation in growth-oriented decisions and behavior. Imagine Adam Smith as a central planner, or Karl Marx with a computer at Macy's!

43 The rediscovery of the market*

CHARLES E. LINDBLOM

What is the significance of the great debate, already several years old, on the appropriate role of profits in the planned economies of Communist Europe?

One interpretation of this sea change in Communist thinking is that Communism is turning capitalist. Since imitation is the sincerest form of flattery, many Americans are delighted to accept this interpretation. But the Communists do not see their reforms in this light; and Professor Liberman, whose name is foremost in the Soviet debate over the profit motive, has explicitly denied that Communist use of the profit motive is capitalistic. On his side of the argument there is some weighty evidence: namely, the existence of profit-oriented *socialist* enterprises all over the world—e.g., municipally-owned public utilities in the U.S., the nationalized industries of Britain and Western Europe, and the socialized enterprises of many developing nations (like Hindustan Machine Tools of India).

Indeed, the significance of the reforms has little to do with the antithesis capitalism-socialism. The new and growing use of profitability criteria in Communist enterprises can better be understood as a phase in *a worldwide rediscovery of the market mechanism.*

Now, capitalism and the market mechanism are not the same thing. Understandably, they are often confused with each other, because it was under capitalist auspices that the market mechanism first became, on a vast scale, the organizer of economic life. But the market mechanism is a device that can be employed for planned as well as unplanned economies, and for socialism and communism as well as capitalism. Today the market mechanism is a device both for the organization of the relatively unplanned sectors of the American economy and for such central planning as is practiced· in the United States. In Britain and Scandinavia, it organizes both

* From "The Rediscovery of the Market," *The Public Interest*, 4 (Summer 1966), pp. 89–101. Copyright © National Affairs Inc., 1966. Reprinted with permission of author and publisher. Charles E. Lindblom is Professor of Economics and Political Science at Yale University, New Haven, Conn.

the private and the socialized sectors of the economy. In Yugoslavia it serves as an overall coordinator for an economy of publicly-owned enterprises. In many underdeveloped countries it is a powerful tool of development planning. It is this market mechanism rather than capitalism that the U.S.S.R. and its satellites are trying to employ—precisely to improve their planning.

Except for a convulsive attempt between 1918 and 1921, Soviet policy has never questioned the practical usefulness of money and prices. This does not mean, however, that the Soviet Union has heretofore made much use of the market mechanism. By the market mechanism, we mean the use of money and prices in a very particular way: prices and price movements are employed—instead of targets, quotas, and administrative instructions—to give signals to producers with respect to what and how much they should produce; and prices on labor and materials consumed are set to reflect the relative value of these inputs in alternative uses to which they might be put.

It is the possibility of using a pricing process to evaluate alternative possibilities and to cue producers accordingly—whether to suit the preferences of individual consumers in the market or the preferences of central planners, whether to administer the resources of an advanced economy or to guide the developmental choices of an underdeveloped economy—that has struck a new note in Communist economic policy, in the economic reorganization of Western Europe, and in the economic development of the nations still in early stages of growth. The significance of the development, of which Communist reforms are only a part, can be appreciated in the light of its own history.

II

Adam Smith and laissez faire. Most people who know anything at all about the market mechanism seem not to have advanced beyond Adam Smith's view of it. He saw it as *an alternative* to government control of economic life. He was concerned about inefficiency and other defects of mercantilism; and, to speak anachronistically, he thought he had found in the market mechanism a substitute for incompetent planners. His specific insights were profound. He saw the possibility that resources could be systematically allocated in response to human needs as a by-product of "selfish" individual decisions simply to buy or to sell. He saw that prices established by consumers in their trading with producers could establish a set of signals that could direct the productive processes of the whole economy. He saw that competitive bidding for inputs would establish a market value for them that would make possible a comparison of their productivities in alternative uses. He saw that a comparison of input prices and output prices, that is, of the money cost of production with money receipts, could control the flow of resources into each of their alternative possible uses. Finally, he saw that the market mechanism was for all these reasons an extraordinarily powerful device for decentralizing economic decisions. In all this, however, his vision was limited: the market mechanism was always a private enterprise market and always an alternative to planning.

Market socialism. It was not until the development, over a century and a half later, of the theory of market socialism that any significant number of people perceived the possibilities of using the market mechanism in a completely socialized economy. Even today the idea of market socialism remains esoteric. In 1920, Ludwig von Mises published his now famous challenge to the socialists to indicate whether they had any system in mind for the actual administration of economic affairs in a socialist order. It was a challenge that many socialists brushed aside, believing that they could cross that bridge when they came to it. But a few socialists, conspicuous among them the late Oskar Lange, turned back to the 1908 work of the Italian economist Barone, to construct a model of a socialist economy that would practice a systematic and decentralized evaluation and allocation of its resources. They showed that prices could be manipulated by government in such a way as to reflect the values that consumers put on consumer goods and services, and also to reflect the values of inputs in alternative uses. Their discussion of the pricing process under socialism clarified the useful functions that prices can perform. If, for goods and services in short supply, prices are systematically raised by government pricing authorities, the high prices can be taken as signals for increased production, while being at the same time at least temporary deterrents to consumption. Similarly, if prices are systematically lowered for goods in overabundant supply, the low prices can be taken as signals by producers to curtail supply, and by consumers to increase consumption.

Lange's 1936 exposition of these possibilities made it clear that prices could be systematically regulated to perform the signalling and evaluating functions even in the absence of those competing private sellers whose rivalry sets prices in a private enterprise economy. Moreover, his exposition demonstrated that prices so set permit a systematic comparison of alternative patterns of allocation, a comparison that would not be possible without prices of this kind.

If the development of the theory of market socialism made it clear that the market mechanism could serve socialism as well as capitalism, it neverthless did not much interest the socialists of Western Europe or the planners of Communist Europe. For the market socialist had developed a model of a socialist economy that left very little room for central planning. Their socialist market mechanism was designed, as was the market mechanism of classical economics, to serve the preferences of individual consumers rather than the priorities of central planners. As in a capitalist economy, in this kind of market socialism the consumer remained sovereign—at a time when most socialists, planners, and Communists were looking for ways to effect collective purposes and national goals, rather than individual preferences. Although socialist theory considered harnessing the market mechanism to centrally determined priorities, it did not construct a persuasive case as to how it could be done.

In the Communist countries, the possibilities of market socialism were underrated for still other reasons. Communist ideology was antagonistic to the very idea of the market, hence inevitably to market socialism. Academic and professional Soviet economics was also antagonistic to the orthodox tradition in economic theory out of which the theory of market socialism sprang. Finally, with respect to formal planning and resource allocation, the overwhelming concern of Soviet policy was "balance" rather than what economists call optimality. Optimality involves a careful evaluation of returns to production in alternative lines. To Soviet planners, however, the need for big allocations to steel, electric power production, and national defense seemed obvious. Speaking very roughly, all that remained to be done was to insure that allocations for the rest of the economy were roughly consistent with, or in balance with, the crudely calculated but obviously necessary allocations to these high priority sectors. And even this formal interest in balance was secondary to their interest in the crude growth of physical output.

The market mechanism for centrally determined objectives. If the market mechanism was ever to be of any use for central planning, it had to be shown that prices could be set to reflect centrally determined values, and not merely individual consumer values. In the economics of the West, it has in fact long been clear that they can do so. For example, a subsidy to maritime shipping lines or to airmail carriers is a way of raising the price received by those who provide these transport services, thus signalling them to increase their production of the services. Similarly, a tax on liquor is a way of depressing the price received by manufacturers and distributors, hence a way of signalling them to restrict output. The result of these interventions—either subsidies or taxes—is to achieve a price that reflects both individual consumer preference *and* the preferences of governmental authorities.

A government can go even further—and in wartime often does. It can completely eliminate the effect on price of individual consumer demands so that producers respond to a price set entirely by government. This can be done either through the imposition of a legal price or by exclusive government purchase of commodities and services, after which government agencies either consume the purchased goods and services themselves or, in the case of consumer goods, redistribute them in some way to consumers.

Using the market mechanism in this way is an alternative to direct administrative control—to targets, quotas, physical allocations, specific instructions, etc. It is not always a good alternative, but it often is, since it is a way of manipulating incentives powerfully while leaving the actual decision—to produce or consume more or less—in the hands of the agency or enterprise whose price has been altered. Hence, a general virtue of the market mechanism as an instrument of central direction is that it permits extraordinary decentralization of detailed decision making.

To understand the possibility of subordinating the market mechanism to governmental rather than to individual choice, it is essential to distinguish between actions in which governments signal their production targets through prices, and actions in which they intervene in the market mechanism to alter the results without, however, actually using prices systematically as such a signalling device. To raise agricultural prices, for example, in order to stimulate agricultural production is a way of employing the market mechanism for the achievement of a centrally-determined goal of high agricultural production. On the other hand, to raise agricultural prices as part of a complex process of restricting farm output (as in the U.S.) is an entirely different kind of operation, in which direct administrative controls (such as acreage quotas) replace the market mechanism. Or again: depressing the price received by a manufacturer by imposing a tax on his output is a way of implementing a central decision to discourage consumption of the commodity, whereas the general imposition of legal maximum prices to control inflation has the effect of interfering with the market's ability to reflect either collective or individual choices and will ordinarily give rise to rationing, or to some other administrative device for the allocation of goods and services.

Perhaps it is the easy confusion of miscellaneous intervention in the pricing process (which the Communist economics have always practiced) with the skillful use of pricing to implement central planning of production that has contributed to Communist indifference to the latter. In any case, the Western demonstration that the market mechanism could be used to implement central priorities did not significantly affect Communist policy until certain other developments occurred. Even as late as 1950, the model of market socialism seemed to be consigned to a limbo of interesting irrelevancies. Ideological barriers were still strong; so also was the obstacle of fundamental ignorance in Soviet economics about the pricing process.

Yugoslavia. The Yugoslav economy was the one sensational exception to Communist indifference to the market mechanism. Yugoslav Communism was indigenous, not imposed by the U.S.S.R. as in the satellites generally. Political relations with the Soviet Union were such that in Yugoslavia independence in economic policy came to be valued rather than feared. Moreover, Yugoslav intellectuals and politicos had closer ties with their counterparts in the West than did any of the other Communist countries. Whatever the reasons, in 1952, recoiling from the inefficiencies of detailed administrative control over the economy, Yugoslavia brought into being a greatly decentralized market socialism. The change of direction, taken together with the rapid growth that ensued, excited much interest in the Communist world. The significance for Communism of the Yugoslav venture was greatly diminished on one score, however. For when the Yugoslavs abandoned detailed administrative control over the market mechanism they also went a long way toward consumer sovereignty as a replacement for the central direction of the economy. Hence, in the eyes of Communists elsewhere the Yugoslavs had largely abandoned central planning itself.

New freedom for economic inquiry. New possibilities for economics were opened up by Stalin's death in 1953. Soviet economists, engineers, and administrators could finally look with some freedom at the lessons to be learned from foreign experience with the market mechanism. One especially noteworthy gain for economic analysis was the lifting of Stalin's capricious ban on mathematical economics (input-output analysis, and linear programming, etc.).

Soviet mathematical economics, reaching back to work originating in the 1930s but not then pursued further, demonstrated independently of Western economics that pricing can be made useful to the planning of resource allocation even in the absence of any actual exchange between a buyer and seller. If we consider all the alternative combinations of end products that an economy can choose from, and all the alternative combinations of inputs that might be used to produce any given output, we see that there are vast possibilities of substitution—of one end product for another, and of one input for another. These possibilities of substitution can be represented by "substitution ratios"—and these substitution ratios can be expressed as a system of prices. (In the absence of any actual transaction in which a real price would be set, they are often called "shadow prices.") *Pricing turns out, therefore, to be implicit in the very logic of rational choice among alternative uses of resources.*

This discovery clearly removes certain traditional ideological objections to market pricing, for it makes clear that pricing is not a capitalist invention but a logical aid to rational calculation even in circumstances far removed from capitalist buying and selling. Whether in fact the discovery has yet achieved this consequence for Soviet thought is not certain, however; for Soviet mathematical economists have, on the whole, drawn the inference, not that the market mechanism might now be more openly examined, but that such pricing as might be achieved through the market mechanism can in principle now better be achieved through further mathematical analysis and electronic computation.

The "in principle" is crucial, since a prodigious amount of information needs to be gathered and processed in order to substitute computers for actual markets; and so far the accomplishment is beyond the capacity of economists, Soviet or Western. Nor can it be said with confidence that there is any way to gather and test the required information except by putting consumers or planners in the position of actual choice in a real market. Still, the exploration of the practical mathematics of resource allocation is far from its maturity.

The rising concern for allocative efficiency.   In any case, the discovery of "shadow pricing" did not of itself overcome Communist disinclination to exploit the market mechanism. A final consideration was the growing complexity of the Soviet economy, with complexity outstripping admittedly growing Soviet competence in planning. The economy became more complex for at least two reasons: with the rising standard in living, the demand of consumers for varied and higher-quality consumer goods came to be more pressing; and with technological advance, alternative production possibilities became more numerous and complex. Soviet policy makers could no longer be satisfied with the simple mobilization of large quantities of capital, and the attendant mobilization of agricultural labor, for industry. As one student of the Soviet economy has written:

The Soviet economy again appears to be at a turning point. It is clear, as the debate shows, that it is becoming more and more difficult to plan *everything* centrally. The Soviet economy has grown not only in size, but in sophistication in concern for the consumer. As a result, campaigns and storming can no longer solve all the problems that arise. There are simply too many sectors which need attention. They can not all be manipulated from the center. It has been estimated that, if the economy continues its present growth, by 1980 the planning force will have to be thirty-six times its present size.

It is especially noteworthy that the older Communist concern for "balance" is, in the face of this new complexity, no longer thought sufficient. It is increasingly difficult to find some clear superiority of one pattern for a few key industries over another alternative pattern. And that being so, Communist countries can no longer be satisfied with merely balancing the outputs and inputs of all other industries to satisfy a prior commitment to a few key programs. In short, consistency in an economic plan is no longer enough; optimality in a plan is now becoming a pressing objective. Hence, finally, the new interest in the market mechanism.

In their forthcoming study, *The Soviet Capital Stock 1928–1962,* Raymond P. Powell and Richard Moorsteen will document still another hypothesis to explain the new Soviet interest in improved resource allocation ("optimality"). The Soviet Union, they suggest, has been exhausting the possibilities for rapid growth through indefinitely larger and larger capital investment; it must now either find an alternative source of growth—i.e. a better allocation of resources—or resign itself to a lower growth rate.

Paradox of planning.   How far the Communist economics will go in employing the market mechanism of course remains to be seen. An ideological and traditional resistance to the market mechanism does not quickly evaporate and presumably will never wholly evaporate. Moreover, a market mechanism is not always and universally a serviceable instrument for economic organization. Even in an economy like that of the U.S., in which ideology is all on the side of the market mechanism, its use has to be constrained by the recognition of its limitations.

In the Communist case, there remains one conspicuous obstacle to extending the employment of the market mechanism, sometimes referred to as the "paradox of planning." The problem can be posed this way: if the planners intend to use prices to signal production goals for the economy, they cannot set appropriate prices for end products until they first decide what quantities of various end products they desire. But they cannot intelligently decide on appropriate quantities of end products unless they know their costs, i.e., the resources used up in their production. Now, in a market mechanism, these costs are represented by prices; and this is to say they cannot determine desired quantities of end products until they know prices. But we have just said that they cannot determine prices until they know what quantities of end products they desire!

This problem does not arise when the price mechanism is used to implement any single collective choice, as in a Western economy, because a decision, say, to expand the production of maritime transport services can take as given the relevant prices already prevailing on the market. Planning an increase in the production of no more than a few commodities or services does not so alter price relationships and production patterns for the entire economy as to invalidate prevailing prices as guide lines for the planners. But to plan through pricing, a production pattern *for an entire economy* promises readjustments of prices that will invalidate the very set of prices that the planners depend upon for making their plans.

It follows that the fullest use of a market mechanism as an instrument for central planning would require that central planners actually operate, not directly through a master plan in which all major lines of production for the economy are simultaneously established, but through a large number of (and a series of) specific choices for each of all outputs or industries to be planned. When a choice is made for any output or industry, the outputs and prices for other industries need to be regarded—for planning purposes—as unchanged. To make the fullest use of the market mechanis, central planners need to work out a strategy for goal-setting and pricing (against a background of the overall general plan) that proceeds through many specific *and sequential* price and production decisions.

Such a procedure, it may be the case, is already in embryo in the Communist economies—even though, for lack of understanding of its utility, it is more often hidden than openly displayed. Given the complexity of the task of comprehensive, synoptic national economic planning, and given also the inevitable limits on man's intellectual capacities, even where these capacities are extended by electronic computation, planning all over the world tends to break down into clusters and sequences of specific decisions. The mere construction of detailed five-year plans does not prove that anyone or any organization has achieved an integrated synopsis of the elements of the plan; instead these plans are typically a collection of targets and policies from many sources.

III

The rediscovery of the market in the West. Outside the Communist orbit, an appreciation of the usefulness of the market mechanism has been most conspicuously on the rise since World War II. With good reason, the market was under great attack in the depression of the '30s, the severity of disillusionment with its usefulness nowhere more vivid than in the American NRA, an attempt at partial displacement of the market in favor of private and public administrative controls. But in the late '30s, Keynesian economics began to hold out the promise of ending depressions by improving rather than eliminating the market mechanism; and Western governments, learning the lesson, have in recent years sustained higher levels of employment than used to be thought possible. Similarly, taxation and transfer payments, as well as provision of subsidized public goods like education, have attacked problems of inequality in income distribution— such problems can therefore no longer motivate proposals to disestablish the market mechanism. The result is that, in the West, the market mechanism is in better repute than ever before, as is indicated in the decline of socialist opposition to the market mechanism both on the continent and in Britain, where after World War II socialists deliberately subjected their newly nationalized enterprises to market controls rather than to the battery of administrative controls they had once contemplated. And the great event in Western European development in recent decades has been a substantial move toward unification, not through common government, flag, army, or language, but through the Common *Market*.

The developing nations. As a group, the underdeveloped nations of the world are lagging in their understanding of the usefulness of the market mechanism. Abstractly, they should be eager to exploit every possibility for economic advance; in fact, they stand in a kind of backwater.

One reason is that their leaders and intellectuals are often prisoners of a once exciting but now stifling orthodoxy. Some of them are prisoners of early Marxian doctrine on planning, the very orthodoxy from which European Communism is escaping. Others are prisoners of English socialism of the style and date of Harold Laski, or even of earlier versions of English socialism—in either case antagonistic to the market mechanism. But times change: although Nehru was a prisoner of both, his daughter may turn out to be a prisoner of neither.

Another reason is, oddly enough, the insistence of the United States, the World Bank, and other lenders that underdeveloped countries formulate national economic plans in order to qualify for aid. They mean by a plan a balanced and consistent set of investment outlays. The effect is to divert some of the best brains in these countries away from high priority questions of growth strategy to the construction of reconciled investment programs reminiscent of those the Communist countries are trying to leave behind as inadequate. In India, for example, the question of the size and internal consistency of the five-year plans overshadows in public discussion, and in the attention it receives from experts in Indian government, many more rewarding questions of growth strategy, including such questions as how the market mechanism might be employed to hold out incentives to farmers to raise food production or how it might ration scarce foreign exchange in such a way as to substantially raise the level of economic achievement.

To be sure, just how much the underdeveloped economies should count on the market mechanism is subject to much dispute. The point being made here is only that the underdeveloped countries themselves do not well understand the issues, and have often not tumbled to the fact that, for many of the specific developmental problems they face, they can employ the market mechanism in tandem with other methods of controlling and planning economic development.

The prospect that the underdeveloped countries may take a new view of the market mechanism as an instrument of development planning is, of course, greatly enlarged by what they now see developing in Communist Europe. For even if they do not intend to follow the Communist path to development, the evidence that Western and Communist economies alike are finding the market mechanism useful is certain to impress them.

How they can best employ the market mechanism depends upon the particulars of their circumstances. But on a few counts a general usefulness of the market mechanism for these economies can be predicted. First, they all suffer desperately from a shortage of administrative skills and organization: they are not very competent in executing *any* kind of plan, economic or otherwise. Even the best of their civil services have developed procedures and traditions more suitable to keeping the peace than to stimulating economic development. Hence, on this score alone, they need the market mechanism more than do the advanced countries of the world.

Secondly, most of them have accumulated a mixed bag of administrative interventions in the market mechanism, such as price controls and exchange allocations, which have undercut the serviceability of the market mechanism without putting any positive administrative program in its place. To impose, for example, maximum prices on food grains in order to hold down the price of food in towns and cities saps the farmer's incentive to produce more. It takes away the monetary incentive and puts nothing in its place—it destroys one mechanism of development without substituting another.

Thirdly, while the development of an economy through administrative techniques furiously engages the energies of a planning elite, participation in development through the market mechanism is open to everyone and, indeed, typically engages most of the adult population. Cueing, signalling, rewarding, and penalizing through the market mechanism are methods of drawing on the largest possible number of responses—and, in addition, a method of extricating a traditional peasantry from older institutions and habits of life that retard development.

Fourthly—and here is a consideration of enormous importance to most underdeveloped countries—they need the market mechanism because they cannot take the route to rapid development that the Soviet Union took from the 1920s to the '60s. Foreswearing in that period any hope for skillful allocation of their resources, the Soviets instead counted on achieving growth through restricted consumption and massive investment. Their strategy worked because the restriction of consumption was in fact possible. It was possible for two reasons: the standard of living was high enough to permit forced savings, and the Soviet government was willing and able to use compulsion. In many underdeveloped countries, neither of these conditions holds; in some, only one does. In many cases, the surplus over and above what is essential to consumption is much smaller than in the Soviet case, where development proceeded from an already advanced stage of early industrialization and food availability. And in ever more cases neither effective systems for tax administration nor other instruments of compulsion are sufficient to gather the savings that are hypothetically available. Hence, except to the extent that capital assistance from abroad can take the place of forced savings and investment, these underdeveloped countries cannot successfully imitate the older Soviet pattern. They need to understand, as even the Soviet Union in its new condition is coming to understand, the indispensibility of a judicious use of the market mechanism for efficient use of the limited resources they can command.

No paradox for planning. That the non-Communist underdeveloped nations can use the market mechanism to satisfy the individual needs of consumers is of course clear. But what of the usefulness of the market mechanism for implementing centrally-determined social priorities—to strengthen the industrial sector, for example, or to give a special push to agriculture, or to establish a steel-producing capacity? It follows from what was said above, about the paradox of planning, that it is just this kind of precise intervention for which the market mechanism is a demonstrably effective instrument of central planning. For this kind of *planning through selective intervention,* the paradox of planning does not arise; and no special techniques need to be devised to overcome it, as do need to be devised in the Communist countries of Europe. Hence, it turns out that the kind of "central planning" to which these underdeveloped economies are committed is the very kind for which the market mechanism is best suited.

IV

That the market mechanism can be serviceable to planned and un-planned economies alike, to public and private enterprise alike, to collective and individual choice alike, is a discovery the significance of which may soon dwarf what we have seen of its consequences so far. To say this is not to take sides in the many disputes in many countries in which, for particular purposes at hand, the question has to be settled as to how far and under what circumstances market organization ought to be pushed. It is only to take note of the fact that, although these disputes will remain, and although different countries will choose different combinations of the market and other forms of organization of economic life, the market mechanism is now everywhere coming to be recognized as a fundamental method of economic organization which no nation can ignore and which every nation can well afford to examine freshly. Even China, bent on its own course, may come to be caught up in the movement toward the market. For lack of experience with, and personnel for, direct administration, China has perhaps gone less far in disestablishing the market under Communism than its ideological claims would suggest. If so, we may be witnessing a race in China between an old-fashioned Marxian determination to undermine the market as soon as administrative competence permits and a growing sophistication about the market's usefulness—with the result unpredictable, if momentous.